HENRY ADAMS

Henry Adams

ERNEST SAMUELS

THE BELKNAP PRESS OF HARVARD UNIVERSITY PRESS

Cambridge, Massachusetts, and London, England

First Harvard University Press paperback edition, 1995

Designed by Marianne Perlak; typeset in Sabon.

Library of Congress Cataloging-in-Publication Data

Samuels, Ernest, 1903–
Henry Adams / Ernest Samuels.
p.   cm
Bibliography: p.
Includes index.
ISBN 0-674-38735-X (cloth)
ISBN 0-674-38736-8 (pbk.)
1. Adams, Henry, 1838-1918.   2. Historians—United States—Biography.   I. Title.
E175.A2S26   1989   88-35087
973'.072024—dc19   CIP
[B]

To
Amanda

Preface

Henry Adams is an abridgment of the three volumes of my biographical and critical study of Henry Adams and his writings, published over a period of sixteen years ending in 1964: *The Young Henry Adams; Henry Adams: The Middle Years;* and *Henry Adams: The Major Phase.* In recent years I have served as one of the editors of *The Letters of Henry Adams,* published in six volumes by Harvard University Press. That edition has greatly enlarged the corpus of Adams's known letters and has purged previously published letters of the reticences, errors, and deletions of earlier editions. It has led to significant corrections, and revisions of style and emphasis, in the present narrative. My aim in this abridgment has been to bring Adams's personality and career into sharper focus than the detailed treatment of the earlier volumes permitted.

Adams, himself a biographer and an insatiable reader of biographies, had equivocal feelings about the art and feared its scrutiny. "All memoirs lower the man in estimation," he warned Elizabeth Cameron, overlooking for the moment his own generous biography of Albert Gallatin. In 1908, when he sent a copy of his autobiographical *Education* to Henry James, he insisted that it was "a mere shield of protection in the grave." He added, "I advise you to take your own life in the same way, in order to prevent biographers from taking it in theirs." Twenty years earlier, on reading Trollope's autobiography, he had urged the same precaution upon John Hay. "I mean to do mine," he had written. "After seeing how coolly and neatly a man like Trollope can destroy the last vestige of heroism in his own life, I object to allowing mine to be murdered by anyone except myself."

Adams must have been aware, however, that his cautionary recommendations were rather disingenuous. Although he professed to fear the biographer, he readied a welcome for him in his voluminous correspondence. He always knew that his vivid and often provocative letters were carefully preserved by their recipients. Late in life he did not hesitate to urge Elizabeth Cameron to publish the letters of their intimate circle; he felt that they had a valid claim upon posterity. Moreover, posterity had rights of its own, as he indicated to Ambassador Whitelaw Reid when collecting the letters of John Hay for publication. "I feel no great hesitation in ignoring the order to 'burn when read,' because I believe it meant only as a safe-guard during his life-time . . . As editor I have always strained liberality of assent. No editor ever spared any one of my family that I know of, and, in return, we have commonly printed all that concerned other people."

Thanks to his scruples as a historian, Adams has collaborated with his biographers by providing the documentary evidence to challenge the accuracy and emphasis of his "shield of protection." That *The Education of Henry Adams* is a literary masterpiece of the first order is undeniable, but it is also true that its philosophical theme obscures the man and his achievement as a writer. My biography has grown out of my desire to exhibit the man behind the "shield."

Northwestern University
January 1989

Acknowledgments

I wish to express my thanks to Thomas Boylston Adams, who long ago gave me unrestricted access to the Adams Family Papers at the Massachusetts Historical Society and thus made possible the completion of the second and third volumes of my critical biography of Henry Adams. I also owe a special debt to Stephen T. Riley, the former director of the Society, for his advice, encouragement, and many courtesies during his tenure there. My many debts to librarians, institutions, and individuals are gratefully recorded in the earlier volumes.

It is a particular pleasure to thank my associates in the preparation of *The Letters of Henry Adams* for their editorial scholarship and cooperative spirit. They are J. C. Levenson, Edgar Allan Poe Professor of English, who directed the project, and Charles Vandersee, Associate Professor of English, both of the University of Virginia; Viola Hopkins Winner; Eleanor Pearre Abbot; and Jayne N. Samuels. The authoritative transcripts in that edition provided most of the texts used in the present biography.

I am grateful to Maud Wilcox, editor-in-chief of Harvard University Press, whose friendly oversight has been an inspiration to me for many years. I am indebted to Ann Hawthorne for her painstaking and perceptive editing of the manuscript.

My greatest debt is owed to my wife, Jayne Newcomer Samuels, who has given me her wise and learned counsel on everything I have written since the making of *The Young Henry Adams* more than forty years ago.

Contents

Illustrations

HENRY ADAMS

Brahmin Pattern

ONE DAY IN 1843 when Henry Adams was five, his grandfather John Quincy Adams, the former President of the
United States, took him, his mother, and two of his brothers on an
excursion to the Quincy seashore. There was a need for him to teach
a painful lesson. In three days the anniversary of the battle of Bunker
Hill was to be celebrated in Boston with the dedication of the recently
completed Bunker Hill Monument. Across the bay the impressive
shaft stood visible in the clear air all the way from its base to the
pyramidal top two hundred feet above. Every granite block of it had
been hauled from the quarries of Quincy, the town which had been
the home of the Adamses for two hundred years. As a lad of eight in
the family farmhouse there, he and his mother had heard "the thundering cannon" of that "awful day" in 1775 and had seen the smoke
of burning Charlestown.

There was no pleasure now in the distant view across the bay, for
the impending ceremony by the Boston committee would affront the
moral principles of the Adamses, as the State Street Federalists had in
an earlier time. At the shrine of liberty the guest of honor was to be
President John Tyler, a Virginia slaveholder. John Quincy Adams,
who for more than a dozen years had vehemently challenged the
"Slave Power" in Congress, had nevertheless been asked to sit with
the dignitaries and to dine afterwards at a grand banquet in Faneuil
Hall. Outraged at the proposed sacrilege, he wrote in his diary that
he had had to struggle to find language sufficiently polite in which to
decline the invitation. The presence of the "Slave Monger" Tyler and
his cabinet of "Slave Drivers," he felt, would "desecrate the solem-
nity" of the occasion. To his wife in Washington he wrote scornfully
of the "tournament" to be held for "Captain Tyler and his rabble

rout." The lesson that State Street and its business leaders were always opposed to Adams family ideas was one that Henry Adams
would never forget.

A few weeks later grandfather Adams taught little Henry a different sort of lesson about rebellion. The whole family of Charles Francis Adams, Henry's father, were quartered at the President's Mansion
while their summer residence on the hill was being readied for them.
Henry's elder brothers had been sent off for schooling with a family
in Hingham. Their father was out of the way, being much preoccupied preparing his Independence Day oration, the "fourth descendant
in a mighty line" to be so honored, as his mother reminded him. One
morning, when the time arrived for Henry to set out for Mrs. Gay's
school in Quincy, he defied his mother with childish fury. Grandfather
Adams came down the stairs, silently took his hand, marched him
down the road on that hot July day, and didn't let go until Henry was
seated in the classroom. By August the little rebel had completely reformed. A letter from his mother informed him, "Papa says you have
been a good boy and been at the head of your class." When this en-
comium was read out to him, his eyes glistened with pleasure.

During almost every Quincy summer Congressman John Quincy
Adams returned from Washington to the healing quiet of the Mansion, where he busied himself with experiments in his much-prized
orchard. There would also come opportunities to teach his grandchildren their special responsibility as members of the Adams family. On
a birthday of Henry's eldest brother, John Quincy, he expressed the
hope that the youngster would "live to bear and carry down the name
to after generations brightening as it descends." At the time that Andrew Jackson displaced the discomfited John Quincy Adams as President of the United States, Charles Francis reflected in his diary, "Family pride does strongly enter in him. It has become an absorbing
passion."

When Charles Francis became the husband of Abigail Brooks and
the parent of a growing family he had to face up to his duty as his
father's sole surviving son. The suicide of his wayward brother
George in 1829 had been soon followed by the death of his remaining
brother, John, at the age of thirty-one. "The continuation of the respectability of our name," he wrote, "depends much upon me and its
distinction entirely." When, however, he reflected upon the "last sixty
years" of the family he asked himself "if the distinction had not been

too dearly purchased." The thought afterwards became a grievance against "the species of hatred which runs below the surface against which my father for forty years contended, and his father for fifty years before him. This will press me down."

John Quincy Adams had reason to be urgent on the subject of their posterity to his son and his grandchildren. The family had achieved great distinction only in the two most recent generations, and that in the face of stubborn hostility which had cost him and his father re-election to the Presidency. Those two generations had been preceded in America by four undistinguished ones. His critics already sneered at the pretensions of the Adams "dynasty."

The first American Adams was a certain Henry Adams who came from Somersetshire to the Massachusetts Bay Colony in the 1630s. A maker of brewer's malt, he disembarked at Boston with eight of his nine children and took up a grant of forty acres at Mount Wollaston, near the rugged seashore south of Boston, the Merry Mount of the "licentious" Thomas Morton. After Henry's death his son Joseph stayed on in what came to be called Braintree and modestly increased his patrimony. (In 1792 the town of Quincy was detached from Braintree.) Joseph fathered another Joseph, who prospered and begot among his offspring a particularly pious Puritan, John, who added to his patrimony and rose to become deacon of the First Church and selectman of the town. In his cottage at the foot of Penn's Hill his son John, the future second President of the United States, was born in 1735. To him his father bequeathed in 1761 a cottage and twenty-nine acres. John graduated from Harvard College, studied law, and entered practice in the village of Braintree. Ambitious to succeed, he asked himself in the diary he had begun to keep, "Shall I look out for a cause to speak and exert all the soul and body I own, to cut a flash, strike amazement, to catch the vulgar . . . Shall I creep or fly?"

By great good fortune he married Abigail Smith in 1764. Abigail was the daughter of a parson who had married into the important Quincy family. Her letters, still popular, reveal a perceptive, cultivated, and witty observer who did much to give a resolute cast to her husband's character. With him the family first rose to prominence when he became a leader in the movement toward independence. From the time of the first Continental Congress in 1774 he kept his contentious place at the center of national affairs. He helped negotiate the treaty of 1783 ending the Revolutionary War, served thereafter as minister to England, became Vice-President under Washington, and succeeded Washington for a single term which was marked by bitter dissension. Not until his old age did he make his peace as a fellow philosopher with Thomas Jefferson, to whom he had angrily relinquished the White House in 1801.

John Adams's scholarly son John Quincy inherited a passion for disinterested public service that during his diplomatic career under Jefferson permanently alienated the prominent Federalists of Boston's commercial class. Ralph Waldo Emerson was to characterize him as a "bruiser" who "loves the mêlée" and "must have sulphuric acid in his tea." He served as minister to Russia and helped negotiate the Treaty of Ghent, which ended the War of 1812. Like his father before him he was appointed minister to the Court of St. James's. As Secretary of State under President Monroe, he drafted the famous Monroe Doctrine. He served as the sixth President of the United States for a single much-harried term. Defeated for reelection in a campaign marred by the most scurrilous abuse, he swallowed his chagrin and in 1831 entered Congress.

The marriage of his son Charles Francis to the youngest daughter of Peter Chardon Brooks in September 1829 significantly altered Charles's worldly prospects. Brooks was reputed to be the richest man in Boston. He bought the "little house" on Hancock Avenue a short way below the Boston State House for the use of the newlyweds. The twenty-one-year-old husband had just been admitted to the bar, and the couple would for the time being have to live on the allowances from their fathers.

Henry Brooks Adams was born on February 16, 1838, and named after his mother's youngest brother, who had died in 1833. In spite of Abigail's "gloomy fancies" the ten-pound infant caused her "less suffering than on former occasions." Henry's father, who had had to dash out in the middle of a snowstorm at three in the morning to summon Dr. Bigelow, passed the day reading in Greek Sophocles' *Oedipus* and Aristotle's *Politics* and, in the evening, Walter Scott's *The Pirate*, piously thankful for "the favorable results of this day." Henry was the fourth of the five children to be born in the Hancock Avenue house. He had been preceded by Louisa in 1831, John Quincy II in 1833, and Charles Francis, Jr., in 1835. With the birth of Arthur in 1841 Peter Chardon Brooks commissioned his son-in-law to find a larger house for the family. Charles Francis felt it "a disagreeable business to be dependent upon another," and when he finally fixed upon the nearby house at 57 Mount Vernon Street, he feared his wife would not think it "good and handsome enough" and that Brooks would not think it cheap enough. Both objections were overcome, and the house was bought for $14,000. Brooks thriftily kept the title in his name and paid the taxes.

The removal to the new house on Mount Vernon Street had to be postponed until the providentially mild day of January 12, 1842, for late in 1841 Henry had become ill with the much-dreaded scarlet fever. Word had come to Charles Francis while he was attending his father in Washington. Knowing Abigail's inveterate imagination of disaster, he kept the news from her until the following day. They hurried back to Boston and found Henry worse than they had feared. Dr. Jackson was called in to consult with Dr. Bigelow. Hearing their conventional expedients, Henry's father confided to his diary, "Oh! how my heart was at my throat in all this, and how utterly did I feel the vanity of trusting to medical help in this moment of agonizing trial." Henry's recovery was painfully slow, and his father watched long nights at his bedside.

Charles Francis, though outwardly reserved in manner and often preoccupied with his political articles and speeches, was deeply attached to his family. He thought his children a much more agreeable study "than any of which he had read in a sermon." Every Sunday he had them read out passages in the Bible or gave them hymns to memorize. He worried much over their schooling and their illnesses. When the children grew older he took them with him to "divine service" at the First Church in Quincy, where the earnest exhortations of the Unitarian ministers went on "all day," as he recorded in his diary, in which he regularly wrote a précis of the sermon. He often took walks with them in the Quincy woodlands, helped them fish from the wharves in the long summers, or took the boys to the beach to teach them swimming. In the intervals before the summer sessions, he felt it important to keep school each morning, but he discovered that his children were "on the whole not very willing scholars." There was indeed a good deal of the pedagogue in his nature, and, like his father, he was given a great deal to conscientious moralizing. He approved the credentials of local school teachers, gave entrance examinations to applicants to the Quincy high school, and regularly examined Harvard College students on their proficiency in Greek.

Abigail, who had been accustomed to the luxury of her father's splendid home and retinue of servants, had little genius for running her household. Her spells of illness and nervous prostration were a recurring cause of worry to her husband. "Her children," Charles Francis observed, when there were but three little ones, "are almost too much for her." When the brood had grown to five, a visitor found the children "very disorderly and noisy" and the mother a willing slave to them. The household was still to be increased by two more children, Mary in 1846 and Brooks in 1848. Abigail was no taskmaster, and in the family discipline was relaxed. The result was an unusual frankness and vehemence among all the individualists, a frankness that stayed with all of them to the end of their lives and filled their letters to each other with lively and uninhibited opinion.

In the unruly atmosphere of the household the shy Henry tended to be a quiet onlooker. His winning ways as a child made him a favorite in the family, especially with his older sister, Louisa. She talked so much about him at her boarding school in Lenox that the girls asked her to bring the marvel to the school. When their request was conveyed to him, Henry "looked very red and smiled in his peculiar way" in embarrassment. The boy Henry early showed a zest for social experience. He was "delighted with his dancing" when at nine he was enrolled in Lorenzo Papanti's famous dancing academy, and he so thoroughly mastered the art that afterwards as a young man in Washington he was reputed to be one of the best ballroom dancers in town.

A new epoch opened for the family with dramatic suddenness in February 1848. John Quincy Adams collapsed on the floor of the House on the twenty-first and died two days later. His grieving son exclaimed, "The Glory of the family is departed." The outpouring of veneration that accompanied the coffin from city to city for more than two weeks on its passage to Boston overwhelmed Charles Francis. "A funeral pomp of 500 miles is a new thing under the sun," he said, and "not one that rejoices the domestic heart." Henry Adams, then ten, never forgot the impressive ceremony in the First Church of Quincy on March 11 "over the body of one President and the ashes of another." Henry was one of the four older children who attended the great memorial service with their parents a month later in Faneuil Hall. There Edward Everett, president of Harvard College and one of Abigail's famous brothers-in-law, delivered the funeral oration to the members of the Massachusetts legislature. Charles Francis recorded that the eloquent eulogy went on for nearly two hours.

The death of John Quincy Adams freed Henry's father for an independent political career at the age of forty-one. The press reported that "Mr. Adams has left a large amount of property, certainly not less than half a million dollars." Whatever the actual figure, Charles Francis was sure of "a tolerably ample fortune." Henry and his brothers and sisters received small legacies. Then a year later Peter Chardon Brooks died, leaving an estate of $2.5 million. Henry's mother was named a beneficiary of a trust amounting to $250,000, and the title of the house on Mount Vernon Street at last passed to her. In 1850 the *Boston Atlas,* which bitterly opposed the political activities of Charles Francis on the side of the "Conscience Whigs," scornfully described him as one who "rolls in wealth" but is not given to philanthropy. Henry, like each of Brooks's sixteen grandchildren, received a legacy of $5,000. How to invest his legacies would become a subject of keen discussion with his elder brothers for many years after he reached the age of twenty-one.

When he was twelve Henry went into Boston in July to take the entrance examination for the Latin School. He passed "with approbation," as his father recorded, but was told by Master Dixwell that he could not be admitted because of a new and "absurd exclusive rule" which required that the child's father be a tax-paying resident of Boston. Charles Francis Adams's house in Quincy was his legal residence, and it was as a resident of Quincy he subsequently ran for office. He did not have title to the Mount Vernon Street house, and the taxes were presumably paid by the trust for Henry's mother.

Epes Sergeant Dixwell, who had been a mainstay of the school for fifteen years, suffered in the same general proscription. He resolutely established a private Latin School at 20 Boylston Street, and there Henry's father promptly sent him. Benevolent and spectacled Master Dixwell was a lawyer who had turned to less worldly pursuits and had prospered in them. Few men were better representatives of what John Quincy Adams admired as "the Boston standard of thought and the mental scale of Harvard." In his school young men prepared with single-minded diligence for the Harvard entrance examinations, studying Latin, Greek, mathematics, history, geography, English composition, and, of course, declamation.

The influence of his early schoolmasters upon Henry's intellectual growth was doubtless considerable; but in those impressionable boyhood years his father's influence outweighed all else. The elder Charles Francis Adams exemplified the Boston standard of thought even more thoroughly than Master Dixwell. In his universe the paths of duty and of right were drawn like meridians of the celestial sphere, and he charted his course in life and politics as if with a sextant to his eye. His high-minded detachment often made him an unsparing critic of his sons' vagaries. But to Henry his remarkable balance of mind finally became an object of veneration.

In the Mount Vernon Street household the moral and intellectual influence of Charles Francis Adams visibly centered in the second-floor library. This accumulation of eighteen thousand volumes, by far the largest private collection in Boston, preempted the finest room in the house, a sunlit oasis in an otherwise somber dwelling. Here Henry's father read his hundred lines in the Greek classics each morning for pleasure and, like his father before him, drove his quill pen with ink-stained fingers across countless pages of political articles and speeches. Here Henry made endless forays upon the long ranks of well-entrenched authors, ancient and modern. Here also he first beheld the labor of the file when he held copy for his father's ten-volume edition of the works of his great-grandfather. With what double emphasis must the world of John Adams have entered his mind as he sat beside his father, the sounding rhetoric reviving old controversy and recalling to father and son the legacy of political responsibility which was theirs. No classroom could have made so deep an impression upon a sensitive boy as the room where the editorials for the *Boston Daily Whig* took shape and a boy might hear the winged words of Charles Sumner, Richard Henry Dana, and John Gorham Palfrey as they debated the path of conscience with his father in that era of Manifest Destiny. Here in the "front ranks" of the Conscience Whigs his father carried on the fight against "the powerful monied interests" of Boston's State Street who were willing to tolerate chattel slavery in the South. Thoroughly imbued with lofty principles, Henry Adams went across the river to Cambridge in July 1854 to take the entrance examinations.

ATTENDANCE AT HARVARD COLLEGE was a long-established tradition in the Adams family. Henry's father, his grandfather, and his great-grandfather were only the more distinguished members of a lineage which had made the mental scale of Harvard its own. One lost count of cousins and uncles and connections by marriage, unless they were as distinguished as Edward Everett and Nathaniel Frothingham or as munificent as Peter Chardon Brooks. It was Brooks, for example, who, when his son-in-law Edward Everett was president of Harvard in 1846, provided the funds for a new President's House. In the direct line, John Quincy Adams commanded veneration for his service as Boylston Professor of Rhetoric and Oratory from 1806 to 1809. There were few years in which an Adams was not serving as a member of the Board of Overseers or on a committee promoting reform of the curriculum.

All of these associations were strengthened by nearer ones. Henry's eldest brother, John Quincy, who was graduated in 1853, was a marked man from the beginning. John's first declamation in Harvard Hall, as he stood beneath the portraits of great-grandfather John Adams and grandfather John Quincy, moved one of his classmates to record that singularly impressive sight in his diary. Henry's second brother, Charles, now a junior, took him in as a roommate and ensured the continuity of family admonition.

The most characteristic sound in the Yard was the tolling of the bell atop Harvard Hall which called the students to morning prayers at seven (six, after the first Monday in April) and to evening prayers. Evening prayers, which had been used to keep the students from mischief, were discontinued in Henry's sophomore year when gas lighting was installed, because they could now be given class work for an additional hour and a half. Sunday services continued unabated, with attendance mandatory both morning and afternoon.

Attendance at classes and most lectures was also compulsory, and absences were penalized by deductions from a student's academic score. Each student's score constituted a kind of savings account, the deposits calculated according to the system of academic price fixing called the Scale of Merit. Every recitation and every college exercise had its numerical price. The scores accumulated from month to month, term to term, and year to year, slowly rising like an alluvial deposit and serving at last to fix a graduate's standing among his fellows. Violations of discipline or public order had a special array of deductions enforced by the detested Parietal Committee, whose members served as detectives, prosecutors, and judges; and as this committee included almost half of the college faculty, the effect upon faculty-student relations was not a happy one.

Even during the first three years of his course, when his conduct was most exemplary, Henry occasionally fell afoul of the Orders and Regulations. One episode particularly outraged classmate Nicholas Anderson. He wrote to his mother: "I am completely disgusted. Adams had been studying hard for the purpose of pulling up; he is one of the smartest men in the class . . . A few nights since he sat up late to write a theme. The consequence was he did not get up the next morning until it was too late to dress himself completely for the 7 o'clock recitation. Accordingly he went without his collar and rec'd therefor a 'private.' *This private has counteracted the study of a whole term and he now stands 34* . . . Is college justice human justice?"

Thereafter Adams crossed swords again and again with the Parietal Committee; and his "somewhat noisy" ebullience which his French instructor, Luigi Monti, had noted on the class record became open defiance. The faculty minutes implacably record the rebel's progress. One private admonition followed another for smoking in the Yard, lounging in the Chapel, "calling up to a college window under aggravating circumstances," repeatedly cutting class in history and philosophy, and, most heinous of all, persistently absenting himself from prayers. After twenty-two more absences, he was summoned up for a public admonition, and a suitably disapproving letter was sent to his father.

His achievement in individual courses exhibited considerable variation. He averaged well within the highest third of his class in Latin and Greek. His French profited from the early instruction which his father had given him, and he stood within the highest quarter of the class. In German he fared less happily, falling from the highest to the lowest third in one year. He excelled in botany and achieved the rank list in astronomy, but fell short of the mark in chemistry and physics. In mathematics, he averaged only a little above the middle of the class. His strongest subjects were literary composition and elocution. Professor Francis Child recognized the excellence of his compositions by ranking him the fifth scholar among ninety-four in one course and the second scholar in another.

Looking backward on Adams's development as a thinker across the half-century which separates *The Education of Henry Adams* from the course of study at Harvard College, one is struck by the persistence of certain fundamental ideas. Studied in detail, the intellectual climate of 1854–1858 assumes a significance in the genealogy of his thought quite different from that depreciated by him in the *Educa-*

tion. "Beyond two or three Greek plays," reads the indictment in the *Education,* "the student got nothing from the ancient languages. Beyond some incoherent theories of free-trade and protection, he got little from Political Economy." The course in chemistry "taught him a number of theories that befogged his mind for a lifetime. The only teaching that appealed to his imagination was a course of lectures by Louis Agassiz on the Glacial Period and Paleontology, which had more influence on his curiosity than the rest of the college instruction altogether."

Agassiz did indeed stimulate his curiosity, but toward geology and, unfortunately for the validity of his future study of scientific thought, away from the experimental and biological sciences. Agassiz maintained toward science the antirationalist point of view of a devout Christian. He impatiently rejected the views of the evolutionists as contrary to manifest religious truth: "The resources of the Deity cannot be so meager that, in order to create a human being endowed with reason, he must change a monkey into a man." Professedly a scientist, he nevertheless grasped at the acknowledged imperfections in the geological record and magnified their importance in order to discomfit the evolutionists, a device adopted by Adams when he later reviewed the work of the Darwinist Sir Charles Lyell.

Agassiz's intellectual dictatorship did not go entirely unchallenged, although no one was Agassiz's equal in dogmatic argument. Professor Josiah Cook, whose instruction in chemistry "befogged" Henry's mind, was himself a scientist of considerable reputation, as was also Professor Joseph Lovering, in physics. A meeting of the Academy of Arts and Sciences, of which Henry's father was a member, marked the beginning of the violent controversy between Agassiz and the Harvard botanist Asa Gray over the question of the origin and distribution of species. Henry Adams, who was then a senior at Harvard, must have been allowed an inconspicuous chair at the meeting. His sympathies undoubtedly were with Agassiz, whose brilliant lecture on the coral reefs of Florida he had heard that morning. Gray had recently received from Charles Darwin an outline of his theory of the evolution of species from a common center. Agassiz, on the other hand, rigorously supported the theory of the simultaneous creation of identical species. Though colleagues like Jeffries Wyman were sympathetic with Gray, they kept silent and avoided the anathema of Agassiz and the religious majority. Gray shrewdly appraised Agassiz's

limitations as those of "an idealizing philosopher." The weakness, he
said, of men of Agassiz's temperament was that they "refuse to hold
questions in abeyance, however incompetent they may be to decide
them. And curiously enough, the more difficult, recondite, and per-
plexing the questions are or hypotheses are . . . the more impatient
they are of suspense."

By a strange trick of memory Adams came to think of himself as a
"Darwinist before the letter: a predestined follower of the tide," yet
the name of the one American to whom he should have been drawn
in such case, Asa Gray, he let slip away into oblivion. As for Darwinists Tyndall and Huxley, these survived in recollection as mere "triflers." Agassiz remained the hero of the piece.

Professor Bowen's course in philosophy radiated equally theologi-
cal and antiscientific influences. It frankly aimed to combat "the licentious and infidel speculations which are pouring in upon us like a
flood." On the side of ethics, President Walker used Théodore Jouffroy's *Introduction to Ethics* to instruct the seniors in "the facts of
man's moral nature" and to warn them against "the philosophical
systems which, in their principles, are destructive of ethical science."
He placed under the ban of his disapproval the systems of Hobbes,
Spinoza, Hume, Bentham, Smith, and others, a disapproval which
Adams remembered a few years later when he began to study those
philosophers.

If Adams required a rationale for the school of morals in which he
was bred, the school that he always believed was native to New England and Massachusetts, Jouffroy provided it. Certainly Adams
never doubted that he belonged to that élite for whom Jouffroy wrote,
"those who live in the future, and who are seeking, from government
and the laws . . . a new system of faith on the grand questions which
must forever interest man." But in speaking of revolutionary movements Jouffroy cautioned, "When we once comprehend what is really
to be accomplished, we see that it cannot be done in a moment . . .
revolution must be gradual."

In political economy, which was taught by the versatile Bowen as
"one of the Moral sciences," the doctrine was conservative and na-
tionalistic. Bowen's text, *Principles of Political Economy Applied to
the Condition, the Resources, and the Institutions of the American
People,* published in 1856, proclaimed that the causes of the admirable increase of capital in the United States were "moral rather than

physical," the moral excellence of the American consisting in his "disposition to toil, to dare, and to save." As proof of this proposition, Bowen cited the current prosperity of Massachusetts. Unfortunately for the force of his evidence, the Panic of 1857 broke just before Adams and his classmates began the study of this text.

For his authority on currency matters Bowen relied chiefly on Horne Tooke, "the able advocate in England of what is called 'the banking principle' of circulation." This exposition of sound money principles supplied a theoretical basis for what Adams had long been learning in the household of his father, who was then president of the Mount Wollaston Bank and an ardent advocate of a currency redeemable in gold on demand. Bowen's text also presented the official position on socialism of the Harvard hierarchy and its conservative graduates. Henry, like his father, would have seen no reason to question the explanation of the revolutions of 1848 as "the disastrous consequences of the insane attempts" of socialism and communism to reorganize society. It was the object of "the great truths" of political economy to show the fallacies of egalitarianism or economic democracy. The final import was that economic law was the highest law of the land, immutable and eternal, like the human nature on which it was founded.

Adams's complaint in the *Education* that as a student at Harvard he heard neither the name Karl Marx nor the title *Capital* illustrates how his memory sometimes played fast and loose with the facts. It was true that Marx and Engels had issued their *Manifest der Kommunisten* at the end of 1847, but knowledge of the contents of that pamphlet was confined to a few obscure German émigrés and their labor union associates. Not even the first volume of *Das Kapital* was put into print until 1867, and it was not published in an English translation until 1877.

Adams's twin complaint that he did not hear mention of the French positivist Auguste Comte was equally unjustified. In the summer of 1854 when Henry was preparing to enter Harvard, Professor Bowen wrote a sarcastic review of Harriet Martineau's translation of Comte's *Cours de philosophie positive*. The article appeared in the *North American Review,* the most carefully read periodical in the Adams household. A different opinion of Comte was available to young Adams among his own books, for in October 1857 he bought a copy of George Henry Lewes's *Biographical History of Philosophy,* and the underscorings indicate that he read at least the preface, in which Lewes urged "everyone who takes an interest in philosophy" to read Comte's book, the "opus magnum of our age."

In Professor Torrey's history course the most influential text was probably François Guizot's *History of the Origin of Representative Government in Europe*. Guizot's great generalizations were of a sort to delight the philosophical statesmen of the Adams school. He analyzed the rise of representative government not as a series of isolated phenomena, but as part of a great organic and progressive movement, a movement demonstrating that "unity and consecutiveness are not lacking in the moral world, as they are not in the physical." In Guizot Adams encountered the first intimation of the nature of that Tannhäuser quest upon which the prospective historian must embark. He must establish the continuity of history. Facts as such could not engage the interest of the true historian; their drift was all. Like Jouffroy, Guizot recognized the need of a political élite. "There will always arise and exist," he said, "a certain number of great individual superiorities who will seek an analogous place in government to that which they occupy in society." Henry Adams's family had helped to meet that need, and the members of the fourth generation were prepared to play their proper roles.

In the realm of first principles, in science, theology, philosophy, economics, and history, these then were some of the winds of doctrine that eddied across Harvard Yard and made its intellectual atmosphere. And there is every reason to believe that young Adams willingly sailed before the wind. If in science there were appreciable countercurrents, the prevailing pressure was, so to speak, from the northeast, sternly conservative in all the "moral sciences," deeply Christian in its ethics, idealist in the drift of its philosophy, and contemptuous of alien philosophies. Adams may have later felt that Harvard imposed no bias upon the minds of its students. In a sense it did not need to: it had only to provide an adequate rationale for that already there. Only on rare occasions did Adams ruefully glimpse the truth, that he never truly escaped from either Harvard or Boston.

One more professor who deeply influenced Henry Adams was James Russell Lowell. To his admiring students the pithy opinions of Hosea Biglow already had the force of proverbs. His *Fable for Critics* displayed an impeccably Cantabrigian taste, as his *Vision of Sir Launfal* asserted an equally irreproachable idealism. Moreover, his sentimental resentment against the erosive action of the new science upon religious belief chimed in perfectly with the opinions of his colleague Bowen. Fresh from a year of hard study in Europe, Lowell communicated his humanistic enthusiasms to Adams in the literary seminars that met in his study, and he stimulated in his protégé a desire to go to the fount of German scholarship.

The brilliantly discursive criticism which Lowell heaped to the brim with allusion and satire must have shown Adams the interesting possibilities of sheer opinionativeness. Here was a critic who took few intellectual risks among the little-known writers, but on familiar ground asserted himself like an urbane sea rover, making the law on his own quarterdeck. It was criticism that relied on the sharp and colorful epithet and solicited the quick rewards of iconoclasm. The example captivated Adams.

The college education which the *Education* would have scornfully crammed into four months embraced in fact a Baconian breadth of interest. Greek and Latin were an important part of the curriculum for the three years in which they were required. Henry's father's facility in both languages set a salutary example. In Professor "Corny" Felton's class in Greek young Adams read Homer's *Odyssey,* the *Alcestis* of Euripides, the *Panegyrics* of Isocrates, and the *Ajax* and *Oedipus Tyrannus* of Sophocles. Tutor Chase took him through Livy, Cicero's *Tusculan Disputations,* and the *Odes* of Horace. Professor Lane helped Adams explore the legacy of Rome in Cicero's *Brutus,* the *Satires* of Horace, the *Annals* of Tacitus, and the *Institutio Oratoria* of Quintilian. The Department of History placed these texts in perspective with the study of works like Sir William Smith's recently published *History of Greece.* In mathematics, tutor James Peirce drilled him in plane and solid geometry, trigonometry, and algebra. Not being proficient in mathematics, Adams was obliged to study analytical geometry with the "Jackson guards" while the more proficient upper third of his class, scornfully known as "Peirce's Reliques," were admitted to the mysteries of "Curves and Functions." In the Department of Rhetoric Professor Child devoted six semesters to such works as Edward Vernon's *Anglo-Saxon Guide,* Robert Gordon Latham's *English Grammar,* James Murdoch and William Russell's *Orthophony,* William Russell's *American Elocutionist,* and Bishop Richard Whately's great treatises on rhetoric and logic, all supplemented of course by a generous program of declamations, themes, and written forensics. In the field of constitutional history, Professor Henry W. Torrey relied chiefly upon Furman Sheppard's elementary *Constitutional Textbook* and Bishop Whately's *Easy Lessons on the British Constitution*. Among the modern languages, Henry studied French, German, and Italian.

Adams's later scorn for the meager residue of the "ancient languages" obscures the resource of allusions which he delighted to use like Attic salt to season his writings. It also overlooked his early pleasure in Latin poetry. Later, in the dark days of the Civil War, he sent his treasured pocket Horace to his brother to drive away the tedium of the camp. His tribute to the value of his study appeared in his Class Day oration of 1858. He declared that "ten years after graduating a great part of every class . . . recollect no more of Horace and Livy and Cicero than they do of Descartes and Spinoza, and care as little for the grace of the first as for the logic of the last . . . [but] contact with those old pagan writers has tinged our minds with the richness of their mental dyes."

The track of Adams's general reading during these years is lost in an immense maze of literary acquaintances. He accumulated a small library of his own, numbering something over a hundred titles. These he meticulously catalogued during the lazy August days in Quincy while marking time before his departure for Europe in the fall of 1858. Many passages in the books were neatly marked for future reference. Indications of his literary taste appear in his *Harvard Magazine* article "Reading in College." In it he deplored the shallow reading habits of the students. As a remedy he proposed the following list of books not "commonly read here": Scott, Bulwer-Lytton, Cooper, Dickens, G. P. R. James, Thackeray's *Vanity Fair, Pendennis,* and *Book of Snobs,* Dumas, Eugène Sue, George Sand, Paul de Kock, Carlyle's *Sartor Resartus,* Emerson, Humboldt, Ruskin, Macaulay, Prescott, Niebuhr, Grote, Theodore Parker's sermons, De Quincey, Irving, Gibbon, Shakespeare, *The Spectator, Paradise Lost, The Divine Comedy,* Homer, Euripides, Aeschylus, Demosthenes, and Cicero.

OUTSIDE THE CLASSROOM and the lecture-hall Harvard bustled with life and camaraderie, unlike the "very retired and quiet" life of Quincy, which had burdened Adams as a boy with "care and ambition and the fretting of monotony," as he wrote in his Class Life. In

1855 he became a member of the Institute of 1770, described by his friend Nicholas Anderson as "a chartered literary society of great renown." His maiden contribution of "three pieces, one in prose, one poetical and one editorial," induced the secretary to record for posterity: "These productions were excellent of their kind and were received by the Society in a manner which must have been highly gratifying" to the author. Adams's lectures impressed the secretary as "manly and forcible." Aware of his reputation as a contributor to the newly founded *Harvard Magazine,* the Institute elected him its editor, charged with the duty of overseeing the compositions submitted by the members.

Henry Adams was initiated into the Hasty Pudding Club in 1856, and in a few months he took the part of Captain Phobbs in the Pudding's production of John Madison Morton's farce *Lend Me Five Shillings.* The playlet succeeded so well that Henry and his fellow actors repeated the performance at one of Dr. Johnston's private theatricals in Cambridge. Much luster was added to the occasion by the novelty of assigning the women's parts to Cambridge girls. In the following winter Adams shone as "the argument-loving Sir Robert" in George Colman's *Poor Gentleman;* but the role he longest remembered and which most delighted him, as one of the shortest members of the cast, was that of the overbearing Captain Absolute in Sheridan's *The Rivals.* He appeared in at least one other play, *In for a Day,* his lack of brawn (he weighed only 125 pounds) qualifying him for the part of Mrs. Comfit. The actors were "incited to strenuous exertions," especially when Professor James Russell Lowell was seen applauding enthusiastically.

Adams's bookish inclinations were early recognized. By the end of his second year he was elected librarian of the Hasty Pudding Club. There devolved upon him and his friend Anderson the "Herculean job" of revising the catalogue of some six thousand books. Adams's part of the task was "to re-arrange the books, re-fit and repair those which were dilapidated, and renovate the whole system." Anderson, impressed by his friend's knowledge of books, praised Adams as a "Modern Magliabechi," learnedly recalling the seventeenth-century bibliophile. A further honor paid tribute to the librarian's satiric wit. He was elected to the office of "Alligator" or "Krokodeilos" of Hasty Pudding, and he paid the customary forfeit with a piece of smutty doggerel, still treasured among the arcana of the club. Next followed his election as club orator. His chief performance in this office took place at the semiannual celebration of the club, January 15, 1858. His oration "The Fool's Cap and Bells" exhorted his hearers to avoid such follies as pedantry, literary pretentiousness, and cynicism toward men's secret motives. But worst of all follies, perhaps—and here he may have glanced toward Concord—was the folly of impractical idealism which sought "to regenerate the world and call it back from the hard, selfish juggernaut track upon which it has trodden for these three thousand years." Seventeen of the company adjourned to Fontarives's French House for supper and achieved "a general and exceedingly jolly and fiendishly noisy drunk." On their homeward journey they were lectured on their behavior by three watchmen.

From the far side of the Charles River, other energies than alcoholic commonly exerted their attraction upon the mind of Henry Adams, for Boston was still the literary and cultural capital of America. Plays, operas, concerts, orations, and even raree-shows competed for the patronage of Harvard students. In the journals and letters of Adams's friends we momentarily cross his path a hundred times going to and from Boston. Perhaps he is in the company of Crowninshield, puffing a cigar on his way to hear Bendalari at the Melodeon. It may be there are tickets to be bought for a concert of the Swiss pianist Sigismond Thalberg or the German basso Karl Formes. Now he is at the Boston Theatre, where the drama glows "in its full splendor and purity." We hear his cry of admiration at Booth's performance of *Richard the Third,* "That man is acting as no man ever did before; it is magnificent, magnificent!" There were other great occasions: Charlotte Cushman as Lady Macbeth or as Walter Scott's Meg Merrilies; Fanny Kemble reading *Twelfth Night.* More often, of course, when time hung heavy one had to be content with plays like *Who Stole the Pocketbook?* and *Retribution* or the minstrel antics of Perham's Ethiopians and the cavortings of the *Wild Man of Ceylon.*

Visiting lecturers and orators provided models of the grand style. In December 1855, Thackeray, at the peak of fame, lectured on "The Four Georges." Horace Mann, another of Adams's heroes, gave his satire on "Man." Far more impressive to college orators was Edward Everett's eulogy of Washington in June 1857. They "thrilled with delight at the superb eloquence of the modern Cicero," whose "every sentence was a jewel in itself." When Thomas Hart Benton, greatest of the western statesmen, lectured on the Union, the laconic Crowninshield needed more than his usual one word for his comment:

"There was a great deal of truth in his remarks." Rufus Choate thrilled his hearers with an oration on Hamilton and Burr. Among the dignitaries on the platform behind Choate sat Henry Adams's father and "other wealthy men of Boston," who seemed "highly pleased" by the attack on troublemaking "republican politicians."

Harvard did not weaken Henry's interest in public affairs, once again the *Education* to the contrary notwithstanding. Study assignments may often have crowded politics to the back of his mind, but he was not isolated from the great world. Harvard was closer to the maelstrom than Quincy. In his freshman year the aftermath of the sensational failed "rescue" in June of Anthony Burns, an escaped Negro slave, violently excited the student body. The conservative law students voted to censure the Board of Overseers because it had removed Judge Edward G. Loring as a lecturer on law for having complied with the Fugitive Slave Law by ordering the return of the slave to his owner. Adams, like his frustrated fellow Free-Soilers, backed the antislavery Board of Overseers.

The political volcano began rumbling during the election year of 1856 and erupted late in May. Senator Charles Sumner of Massachusetts rose to speak on "The Crime of Kansas." His insulting invective against Senator Andrew Butler of South Carolina was avenged by Butler's kinsman, Preston Brooks, who strode into the Senate chamber where Sumner was at his desk and "beat him senseless with a stout cane." Brooks's attack upon the man whom Henry Adams respected next only to his father gave him an intensely personal interest in the slavery controversy. The agony of another presidential campaign soon came to a climax, and students hurried to Boston to hear the election returns. No sooner was James Buchanan inaugurated than the *Dred Scott* decision by the Supreme Court that slaves had no rights which a white man had to respect furnished new fuel for debate. But such matters grew remote as the Panic of 1857 cast its shadow over Harvard and the young men faced the rigors of hardtimes parties. To Adams the suspension of specie payment in October had much more than a social interest, for his father had to meet the crisis as president of the Mount Wollaston Bank.

The period from 1854 to 1858 made as imperative a claim upon Adams's political consciousness as any other period in his life. As he lectured classmates in 1858, "For four years we have associated together on the common ground of toleration; years during which the bitterest party spirit has excited the whole country, and stretched its influence even over us at times." A few months after graduation, when he took stock of himself he clearly saw two traits at work in himself: "One is a continual tendency toward politics; the other is family pride."

AS AN UNDERGRADUATE, Henry Adams's response to the intellectual challenge of Harvard took characteristic form. Before the first year was out he was contributing to the newly founded *Harvard Magazine*. The necessity for self-expression lived in the blood. From time immemorial, Adamses had worn out their lives at their writing desks, conscientiously transferring their views of a refractory world to the endless pages of their diaries. Grandfather John Quincy Adams had stated the rationale: "A man who commits to paper from day to day the employment of his time, the places he frequents, the persons with whom he converses, the actions with which he is occupied, will have a perpetual guard over himself. His record is a second Conscience." Henry, like his brother Charles, scrupulously entered each day's epitaph for posterity.

Even from the beginning Henry's writing had guidance of a sort, for Charles had an affectionate interest in his progress. At the opening of their correspondence in 1858 we break in upon a long-standing debate in which Charles insistently urges greater literary activity and Henry humbly acknowledges, "I stand in continual need of some one to kick me, and you use cowhides for that purpose." By the middle of the second semester of his freshman year Adams's first article was in print, a fanciful historical sketch called "Holden Chapel," in which that storied piece of Harvard architecture served as a peg on which to hang four reverent vignettes of Revolutionary times. In "My Old Room," his sophomore's farewell to Hollis 5, he said his room was "the coldest, dirtiest, and gloomiest in Cambridge," but, he went on, "to me it will always be haunted by my companions who have been there, by the books that I have read there, and by a laughing group of bright, fresh faces, that have rendered it sunny in my eyes forever." He protested that "dissipation is the exception, and not the rule," and rejected the common imputation of atheism. "If at any time stray professors of infidelity have come among us, their opinions have arisen in another soil, and have found nothing kindred to themselves."

His article "College Politics" touched upon the chief controversy of his college career: the corrupting influence of the Greek letter societies. Its roots went back to the day when his grandfather persuaded the Phi Beta Kappa chapter to abandon its secret rites. Henry's father bequeathed the family horror of secret societies in words like those prefixed to his edition of John Quincy Adams's *Letters and Addresses of Freemasonry:* "An obvious danger attending all associations of men connected by secret obligations, springs from their susceptibility to abuse in being converted into engines for the overthrow or the control of established governments." Like his father, Henry believed that "secret combinations of men, which attempt to exercise a political influence upon others by means of their organization, are bad in theory and practice."

His essay "Retrospect," filled with sententious and sentimental meandering on the subject of vacation and angels "in muslin," has an unintended value because it hints at the frustration that sometimes clouded his boyhood in Quincy. "The time is not slow in coming when we want to be back with our friends again; to be back in the delicious independence of student life . . . Even home becomes irksome . . . It is mortifying to associate with our elders." Evidently there were times when his father's self-righteousness exasperated him. As he confided to Charles, "God Almighty could not get an idea out of his head that had once got in."

A *jeu d'esprit* jibing at a new edition of the *Fairy Mythology* contained a first version of a comforting principle: "If to be consoled by the faults of others makes a man a dunce, we acknowledge the infirmity, and are not afraid of the epithet." In his Class Day oration he put the point more plainly: "But though we acknowledge our own ignorance, we know that every one else is ignorant also." By the time of the *Education* the formula had become a fetish.

Having made his mark in the *Harvard Magazine,* Henry set about in his last year at college to vindicate his reputation as a scholar. He competed for the Bowdoin Prize, an annual literary contest in which his brother Charles had won first prize a few years earlier. He won second place and $30 prize money. Being currently preoccupied with the ethical systems of Bowen and Jouffroy, Henry elected to write on Saint Paul and Seneca. His essay was history in the vein of Plutarch, and history as his grandfather preferred it, a "school of morals."

What was especially notable in the piece was the highly sculptured

character of the prose, filled with rolling Ciceronian periods, an extreme example of what he soon recognized as the "stilts" of his college writing. The stately antitheses were here and there ornamented
with such classical similes as the following: "Like the signal fire that
announced to Clytemnestra the capture of Troy, it flashed from Mt.
Ida and Mt. Athos, and bounded over the plain of Asopus even to the
Saronic gulf and to the roof of the Atridae." In his moralizing conclusion he asked cynics to contemplate history "and say if they can that
the world is not infinitely better and happier than it was."

Of all his college compositions the one that most fully reflected his
romantic idealism and his abiding spiritual hunger was the address
which he read as Class Day orator on June 25, 1858. The day arrived
with a temperature of ninety in the shade and not a breath of air
stirring among the elm trees of the Yard. Shortly before noon, after a
collation of ice cream, the class of 1858, the faculty, and the crowd
of guests marched from the President's House to the First Parish
Church to hear the earnest-looking spokesman of the class who
mounted the platform garbed in the traditional black gown. He was
short in stature, not more than five feet three inches, but the impression faded before the searching glance in his dark eyes with their reminiscence of presidential ancestors.

The main theme of his oration was the dangers of materialism and
the commercial spirit. He scored the low ambitions which so many of
his classmates professed. Unwittingly the study of moral philosophy
had fostered that spirit because it taught "how false the hopes of the
young are." Had not "all philosophy from Solomon to the last number of *The Virginians* been singing that old song, *Vanitas Vanitatum*"?
And yet, their course in political economy, which professed to be a
sister science of ethics, seemed to enjoin upon them that chief vanity,
the duty of amassing wealth. There were a few, however, who still
held their scruples. "Some of us still persist in believing that there are
prizes to be sought for in life which will not disgust us in the event of
success . . . that this nation of ours furnishes the grandest theatre in
the world for the exercise of that refinement of mind and those high
principles which it is a disgrace to us if we have not acquired."

The study of past ages and the classics had also helped to show him
the limitations of modern science. "It is puffed up by its self-conceit
because a certain Francis Bacon, some two centuries ago, happened
to put it upon the right track and it has run along downhill ever

since." (Professor Agassiz must have solemnly nodded agreement.) The study of mathematics, chemistry, and metaphysics had taught him "that though man has reduced the universe to a machine, there is something wanting still; that there are secrets of nature which have puzzled chemist and philosopher even in these days of science, and which still wait for a solution . . . that there are problems in the relations of man to man which political economy has tried to solve again and again and never succeeded; that there are questions in the relation of man to the universe and to the future, which all metaphysicians from Thales downwards have worn away their whole lives in striving to answer, but have failed, always failed."

It was the sermonizing of a troubled young man, Puritan to the core in his contempt for the world as he found it. Harvard had helped him discover the immense chasm separating the moral order from the contradictions of the modern world. Neither man's reason nor his science held out much promise of bridging that chasm. The hope of the world must therefore lie in faith in the supremacy of the moral order.

In an editorial in the *Springfield Republican* eleven years later, his father's friend Sam Bowles recalled that the oration was "distinguished for little except its irony and cynicism." Pessimistic it may have been, but hardly cynical. Two contemporary comments acknowledge its merits. His friend Crowninshield, who had been busy all day with the Class Day arrangements, hastily jotted down, "Very good." His father, Charles Francis Adams, entered in his diary for the day: "Henry has been noted for his faculty as a writer which is the thing that secured him this honor, and he sustained himself both as a speaker and a writer on this occasion."

Among the crowding activities of the last term, there was one final bit of writing that can also be set against the disenchanted mood of the *Education*. This was an autobiographical sketch which tradition required Adams to contribute to the huge "Life Book" of the class of 1858. In it, in accord with college custom, he gave the genealogical credentials of both the Adams and the Brooks families. Of his college years he candidly admitted, "I have had an infinitely pleasanter time than I ever had before . . . I do not believe it would be possible to pass four pleasanter years." As for his plans for the future, he wrote: "Having now come to the end of the Course, and feeling no immediate necessity of making money, it is probable that I shall soon go to

Europe . . . My immediate object is to become a scholar, and master of more languages than I pretend to know now. Ultimately it is most probable that I shall study and practise law but where and to what extent is as yet undecided. My wishes are for a quiet and literary life, as I believe that to be the happiest and in this country not the least useful."

2

The Grand Tour

I N THE LONG SUMMER DAYS in Quincy following the Harvard commencement of July 21 Henry Adams busied himself with plans for two years' study abroad which his father agreed to finance with $1,000 a year. Young Adams fixed on a course of study in which he hoped to master German, attend a course of lectures on civil law at the University of Berlin, and at the same time engage a Latin tutor and learn to translate Latin into German. Afterwards he expected to study in Heidelberg and possibly Paris. Others of his classmates were similarly busy with their plans; for, as Anderson reported, "Quite a deputation will be sent from my class to polish off in the elegant cities of Europe, and obtain that knowledge of the modern languages so necessary to the present age."

Adams's decision to study civil law at the University of Berlin was demonstrably a sound one, however it may have seemed to him in retrospect. There, in 1810, Karl von Savigny had founded the modern study of Roman law, and there his pupil Georg Puchta, whose *Cursus der Institutionen* became Adams's vade mecum in his travels about Europe, introduced the scientific study of the subject in the seminars for which the university was growing famous. As for the value of the subject itself, Henry and his father had every reason to know what they were about, though long afterwards Henry denied it. When the edition of John Adams's *Works* took form between 1848 and 1856, father and son read in the diary of their first President how at the age of twenty-two he began the study of Justinian's *Institutes:* "Few of my contemporary beginners in the study of the law have the resolution to aim at much knowledge in the Civil Law; let me, therefore, distinguish myself from them by the study of the civil law in its native languages, those of Greece and Rome." Courses in civil law had been offered at Harvard as recently as 1850–51. Moreover, Henry and his father may well have considered the role that a knowledge of the Continental codes was likely to play in American legislation. The movement toward the codification of state laws was already under way. There was also the example of their admired friend Senator Charles Sumner. To prepare himself for his career at the bar, Sumner had spent three years in Europe in hard study of Continental government and jurisprudence.

Part of the "deputation" of gilded youths, Adams among them, left Boston on September 28 and sailed from New York harbor on the following day aboard the luxurious sidewheeler, the *Persia*. The party included such congenial classmates as Nicholas Anderson, Benjamin Crowninshield, and Louis Cabot. The eleven-day passage to Liverpool proved rough and tedious. Prone to seasickness, Adams was no doubt wretched much of the time. After a few days in London he crossed to Antwerp with Crowninshield, stopped off at Hannover, where he left his companion, and proceeded alone to Berlin.

Upon reaching Berlin on October 22, Henry was delighted to learn that the "Governor," his father, who had emerged from his long retirement from public life, had won the nomination to Congress on the very first ballot, and the subsequent news of the election made him jubilant. "The old Free Soilers, sir, are just about the winning hosses, I reckon, just now," he wrote to Charles.

His elder brother had recently completed his apprenticeship as a law clerk in the office of Richard Henry Dana, one of the family's oldest intimates, and had been admitted to the bar. While waiting for paying clients, he now turned much of his energies as a counselor toward his younger brother Henry, whose carefully laid plans had gone awry from the beginning.

Henry justified his original plan of study as being "simple enough; useful enough; and comprehensive enough." But he soon realized he would not be ready to join the university until the middle of the term, certainly not before January. Besides, even if it were wise to break "in on a course of lectures," he could scarcely hope to become a student of civil law unless he were "an absolute master of written and ordinary Latin." For a time, therefore, he grasped at straws and gravely floundered among alternative projects while his family back home lavished advice on him. His father cautioned, "Above all . . . the study of ethics is of the greatest value to a man in active life." His mother more practically urged him not to sleep with his "windows too much open." When Henry reported that his expenses steadily outran his budget, his father admitted that he never "believed in the cheapness of living in Europe." He would send an additional $500 after the first of the year, with the understanding that all advances "shall be charged against the capital you will be entitled to from my estate," as there was no other way of equalizing things among the six children. He also informed Henry that on his twenty-first birthday he would receive his legacy from his grandfather's estate, the $5,000 which had doubled to $10,000.

The German language proved intolerably difficult. "I can't once in a dozen times speak a grammatical sentence, and understand what is said only when very slowly spoken," he complained to brother Charles. As a result he was able to endure only a few visits to the University of Berlin, where the lecturers tended to gulp their words, and he turned from a direct assault upon civil law to a more prudent campaign against the language. Putting pride aside he enrolled in the Friedrichs-Wilhelm-Werdesches Gymnasium.

Henry tried to satisfy his brother's doubts about the wisdom of his current studies by outlining his long-term plans. After Europe he proposed to return to Boston to study law for two years and then emigrate to St. Louis. "What I can do there, God knows," he exclaimed. "But I have a theory that an educated and reasonably able man can make his mark if he chooses." Repelled by the humiliations of a political career, he was determined, he said, not to "quit law for politics without irresistible reasons."

With sharp insight Charles thought his younger brother unfitted for the law; besides, "our country does not need lawyers." The alternatives with which he tempted him ranged from newspaper writing to "greater literary works," such as novels and histories. Henry gloomily acknowledged that he felt "as certain that I shall never be a lawyer, as you are that I'm not fit for it"; at the same time he felt himself unprepared to attempt a pretentious literary work.

Thus at twenty he despaired of his own powers. "I am actually becoming afraid to look at the future, and feel only utterly weak about it." His brother, he protested, expected him to combine "the qualities of Seward, Greeley, and Everett." He vehemently disclaimed such qualities: "Mein lieber Gott, what do you take me for? Donnerwetter! . . . You would make me a sort of George Curtis or Ik. Mar-

vel, better or worse; a writer of popular sketches in Magazines; a
lecturer before Lyceums and College societies; a dabbler in metaphysics, poetry and art; than which I would rather die, for if it has come
to that, alas! verily, as you say, mediocrity has fallen on the name of
Adams."

Law would at least supplement his investment income and serve as
a springboard for a public career, as in the case of Everett, Sumner,
Palfrey, and their own father; whereas there were few "literary pursuits that produce money." He insisted, however, that their ideas of
success were not really as far apart as Charles seemed to think; it was
merely that Henry desired to avoid unnecessary hazards. They were
both in approximately the same case, and "beautifully adapted to
work together." Ignoring Henry's morbid anxieties, Charles offered
to find a market for any article that Henry should care to write. Under
pressure Henry admitted that "it would not be impossible to write an
article on the Prussian schools" now that he was enrolled in a German gymnasium.

He faithfully drudged away at the study of languages in the company of his young classmates. These had such "perversely wrong"
notions of American life that he amused himself, as he told his distinguished correspondent Charles Sumner, "by giving them original and
somewhat astounding ideas of my own. Indeed I expect that in a short
time they will really believe that I am an Indian with two squaws and
corresponding papooses and live in a wigwam adorned with scalps."
Adams became the champion of the smaller youngsters against the
bullies of the class. Often they showed their gratitude by cramming
some of their breakfast of black bread into his mouth as they climbed
all over him and rode upon his back. To Sumner, who showed a
friendly interest in his studies, he sent a respectful report of progress:
"I am in school every day from three to six hours, and generally have
to come at eight o'clock in the morning. Yesterday I translated into
German a page of Xenophon, before the class, and today in Caesar."
To his brother, who approved the gymnasium course somewhat too
warmly for Henry's comfort, he adopted a strongly deprecatory tone:
"You estimate the effect of school too highly however. It has enabled
me to give method and concentration to my studies, but I have found
here that it is impossible to go back ten years in one's life."

By early March 1859, the article on the Prussian schools had passed through the research stage in which he explored many works on "das preussische Schulwesen." Not until May did he finally finish recasting the troublesome composition as "Two Letters on a Prussian Gymnasium." It seemed to him "wholly unpublishable." The article was rescued from oblivion by a historian long after Henry's death.

He had been horrified by the squalor of the German classroom, and in the article he recalled his own school days with an entirely new pleasure. When he looked at his pale, badly nourished German classmates, he was swept with homesickness for the sight of his healthy schoolfellows as they used to crowd into the classroom glowing and breathless after wholesome play. Even though he did not believe that his own school days had been the happiest days of his life, he nevertheless now thanked Heaven that he had not been educated under what people unthinkingly called "the most perfect school system in the world."

If Adams was dilatory about "Two Letters on a Prussian Gymnasium," the same thing could not be said of his letter writing. Perhaps mindful of his father's maxim that "there is no species of exercise, in early life, more productive of results useful to the mind, than that of writing letters," he practiced that art with the enthusiasm of a Horace Walpole, and wrote at least one long missive daily. Exposed to a new current of experience, he filled his letters with the full savor of his new life. "I always had an inclination for the Epicurean philosophy," he told Charles, "and here in Europe I might gratify it until I was gorged." Life was not "wildly exciting" in Berlin, burdened as he was by his studies. Yet often enough he yielded to the temptations of the opera, where the "glorious" orchestra, scenery, and ballet carried him more or less safely across the abyss of the language, and to a lesser extent he patronized the theater. Mozart's *Zauberflöte* and Beethoven's *Fidelio* taxed his understanding somewhat, and *Hamlet* in German sounded rather "flat," but Fräulein Taglioni's ballet dancing was an unalloyed pleasure.

For companionship he counted chiefly on James J. Higginson, one of Charles's classmates, in the main avoiding compatriots so that he might establish German connections. In this he was disappointed, as there was little student life, and that was "dirty and fleay." Though a bottle of wine was the "outside" of what he could carry, he made it a point "never to refuse a good glass when it's offered." There were therefore moments when he found himself flushed with wine, the in-evitable cigar in his hand, and "talking very fast." He was wary of young women, however, having for three years, he reminded Charles, "wasted a good deal of superfluous philanthropy" on Carry Bigelow in Boston. He now believed that "all women are fools and playthings until proved the contrary." In any case the women of Berlin were "a damned humbug."

At the close of the first semester of the Friedrichs-Wilhelm-Werdesches Gymnasium, Henry cleared out of Berlin and departed for Dresden in the company of Crowninshield and Higginson. The madcap threesome, having now become four with the arrival of young John Bancroft, the historian's son, started on a walking tour through the Thuringian forest. In the snow-swept mountains Ben Crowninshield's "real ten-horse power" Tom and Jerries "had a mi-raculous effect" on their spirits, but on the third day the four com-panions compromised on a wagon and whiled away the time "in an intellectual and highly instructive series of free fights to keep us warm, which commonly ended in a general state of deshabille all round."

In Dresden Adams did no more than "pretend to read a page of law a day, an effort which unhappily never succeeded." He continued to improve his German by reading the learned Puchta, but deferred more serious study until he should return to Berlin in the following November. For the next several months he and Crowninshield were almost inseparable, and his friend's diary is a record of constant sight-seeing and theatergoing. They attended performances of *Oberon, Rienzi, Don Juan, Tannhäuser, Le Prophète,* and such ephemera as *Berlin, How It Weeps and Laughs.* Dutifully they presented them-selves at the Belvedere concerts, visited the museums and art galleries, and toured the medieval churches of the locale.

Little marred the tourist delights of the two Americans. True, ru-mors of war had filled the papers all winter, and bloody fighting fol-lowed the mobilization of troops in Austria, France, and Piedmont in the early spring; but it had all seemed so remote that Henry could not conceive its affecting his plans for travel. "It isn't probable that any Austrian will shoot me in the valleys of the Tyrol." Professing to be neutral, he yet found it "deuced hard to avoid cheering" when news of the Italian victories at Solferino and Magenta came in. Since he sympathized with the Italians and their French allies in the Italian struggle against Austrian tyranny, he escaped embarrassment with the simple formula "Frankreich und Oesterreich sind mir ganz einerlei [France and Austria are all one to me]."

On the last day of June the young men set out together for an extended tour of Bavaria, Switzerland, and the Rhine country. The sightseeing went on strenuously until early August, when they joined Henry's sister Louisa and her husband, Charles Kuhn, at Thun in Switzerland. Henry found Louisa "hotheaded" and discontented as always and often at odds with her obstinate husband, but gradually being "tamed" by him. Henry went down to Italy with them, the signing of the Treaty of Villafranca having made travel safe. After his return, he resumed the tour with Ben. The travelers pushed on to Louvain, Brussels, and finally Antwerp, omitting no important cathedral or celebrated painting en route. They had now come full circle in their travels, for Antwerp was the first European city they had seen on their arrival a year before. In the distance the tower of the cathedral reminded them agreeably of "the lighthouse to the Port of Boston." Carefully studying their Murray and their Baedeker they went on to Rotterdam, mustered up thirteen gulden to hear the great organ play at Haarlem, and reentered Germany by way of Amsterdam. After the freedom of Belgium and Holland, the "old oppression" of Germany was loathsome to them. As Berlin still seemed depressing, they promptly left for a visit to Hildesheim. Here, after a day of sightseeing with the usual inspection of the local cathedral, the young men explored the wine cellar of the Dom Tavern, and there for the first time in their travels Adams completely forgot Boston. Maraschino followed "the true nectar" of red wine, and "Old Spanish" followed the maraschino, until, as Crowninshield phrased it, "we were, as was natural, a little gay of spirit." Adams wandered off mistily into the night, walked into a strange house, and insisted on making his bed on a convenient trunk, over the protests of a bevy of young women. They finally dissuaded him, and the two friends were safely reunited.

The two revelers returned to Berlin and paid their respects to Minister Wright. Mid-October turned cold and wet, and Adams felt "like a beaten dog with the tail between the hind-legs." Unwilling to face again the cold horror of Berlin in wintertime, he wrote to Dresden, hoping to be taken in by a well-disposed family who might further his German studies. Welcome word came from Frau Reichenbach, wife of the geologist, that she would take him into her family, as earlier she had entertained James Russell Lowell. Gratefully Adams made his way back to Dresden, all thought of study at the University of Berlin extinguished at last.

He settled down again to a regular program, spending three mornings a week with his fencing master and three with his riding master. He taught the daughter of the house to play chess. German continued to be his main object, and he pursued it in books on the "constitutional history of various countries and desultory light reading," a program varied as usual by tourist pursuits, including tours of the geological museum under Herr Hofrath Reichenbach's expert direction. It was a delightful program, but his pleasure was dampened by admonishing letters from home and interminable conversations with Reichenbach's talkative wife. Not for long at a time was he allowed to forget that he was the first of the family to be indulged in the Grand Tour. Ever in his mind was the prospect of the inevitable accounting to his father, who, he was fully prepared to hear, would "lay the fault of every failure and every error in my life to Europe." The tenor of his father's recent letters had not been indulgently understanding. Even Charles refused to be put off easily. Quick to see that Henry's plan to study civil law had come a cropper, he did not hesitate to call him a "humbug" and to reproach him for wasting his opportunities. In his defense, Henry asserted that their father had advised him "against writing magazine articles on the ground that they are ephemeral."

Beneath this contest of purposes there lay the unsettling possibility of their father's "living in the White House some day." Henry feared also that the onset of the "irrepressible conflict," as Seward prophesied, might blow them into the howling darkness of opposition politics. His father, now in Congress, having begun to incline toward Seward and his middle-of-the-road policy on the slavery question, was veering away from the irreconcilable Sumner. Fortune would eventually smile upon them all only if the more conservative Seward could be "quietly elected President of the United States."

More than three years had passed since the brutal attack upon the Senate floor, yet Sumner insisted that he had not yet recovered from its effects. Southerners now accused Sumner of shamming illness "for political effect." His failure to resign his Senate seat lent color to the charge and embarrassed friends like Henry's father who still hoped for compromise. Henry had sent an artfully phrased letter to him at Montpelier, France. "If you can recover in no other way, why not resign your seat and leave public life for two years; five years; ten years, if necessary, and devote your whole time to recovery . . . If you will go and travel in Siberia, I will leave German, Law, Latin, and all, and go with you, and take care of you, and see that you don't speak a word of politics or receive a letter or a newspaper for the next two years." Perhaps alarmed at the evidence of Seward's rising influence upon the Adamses, Sumner quickly reassured his anxious correspondent that his health was much improved and that he expected soon to resume his seat in the Senate.

In February 1860, Henry's father, who had been spending his first term in the House in dignified silence, disconcerted his colleagues in the Massachusetts delegation by announcing that he would not go along with them in approving the routine appointment of a spoilsman House printer. Through two weeks of party pressure and sixteen roll calls he stubbornly stood by his attack on political pork. Thrilled by the "spectacle of an honest man in Congress," Henry praised his father's stand as "the first declaration of the colors we sail under." He had just come upon the story in the first of a series of articles in the *Boston Daily Advertiser* above the signature "Pemberton." The author, he afterwards learned, was his brother Charles, who had written the article as a trial balloon to test public response to his father's stand.

The Pemberton letters "stirred" him up on the eve of an extended tour of Italy. "It has occurred to me," he wrote Charles, "that this trip may perhaps furnish material for a pleasant series of letters . . . If you like the letters and think it would be in my interest to print them, I'm all ready." Charles readily accepted the responsibility. As a result the first of the "pleasant series of letters" appeared in the *Boston Daily Courier* on April 30, 1860. They were uniformly signed "H. B. A.," a disguise that none of Henry's friends could have had difficulty penetrating.

Light as his purpose professed to be, it would have to be carried out against a background of uncommonly serious events, for resurgent nationalism was convulsing Europe. The War of Italian Liberation had come in 1859, but Napoleon III patched up the Treaty of Villafranca just in time to betray the hopes of the Italian patriots for a liberated Venetia. More was lost than Venetia, however, for in 1860 Napoleon III exhorted Savoy and Nice and encouraged Cavour to rescue the Italian monarchy from the socialistic evils of Mazzini's re-

public. Adams had caught a glimpse of the new Italy on his brief
earlier visit in August 1859. Now he was back in northern Italy witnessing the excitement attending the formal annexation of Parma,
Modena, Tuscany, and Romagna. There he heard the news of Garibaldi's landing at Marsala on May 11. Garibaldi and his thousand
went on to Palermo, outwitted the garrison of more than twenty
thousand Bourbon and mercenary troops, and received the capitula-
tion of the city on May 30, 1860.

Since Adams aimed at what is now called "human interest" stories,
he sought out the picturesque and the dramatic. As he said, the assault on Palermo was only "the first act of the melodrama." He therefore deliberately ignored the purely military and political facts reported by such regular correspondents as Henry Raymond of the
New York Times. All manner of persons caught his roving eye, and
each he characterized with engaging and often self-revealing candor.
A fortune-hunting lieutenant aboard the Vienna express diverted him
with foppish "prattle" and started a train of uncomplimentary reflections on the Austrian intellect. When he caught sight of the carriage
of Emperor Francis Joseph he set out in hot pursuit. "So long as I
have good health and am no misanthrope," he told his readers, "I
mean to satisfy as far as I can a healthy and harmless curiosity." King
Victor Emmanuel II disappointed him, for His Majesty "looked like
a very vulgar and coarse fancy man, a prize fighter, or horse jockey."
At the opera he scrutinized the imperturbable Cavour through a pair
of binoculars, "a most quiet, respectable looking, middle-aged gentleman. From his appearance I never could have guessed that he was the
greatest man in Europe."

The most important figure in his gallery of vignettes was, of course,
that of Garibaldi, the dictator of Sicily. Henry's friends having successfully pulled wires for him, he reached Palermo about a week after
its fall. Mounting the grand staircase of the captured palace, where
"one saw everywhere the headquarters of revolution, pure and
simple," he pushed upward through the disorderly crowd until, suddenly, "There we were in the presence of a hero . . . He had his plain
red shirt on, precisely like a fireman, and no mark of authority. His
manner is, as you know of course, very kind and off-hand, without
being vulgar or demagogic . . ." It was the fashion of Europeans, said
Adams, to call Garibaldi "the Washington of Italy, principally because
they know nothing about Washington. Catch Washington invading a

foreign kingdom on his own hook, in a fireman's shirt! You might as well call Tom Jones, Sir Charles Grandison."

Occasionally a note of satire flickered for a moment, casting the chaste image of the Genteel Tradition. In Rome, he discovered that "everyone seems to have a rage after Venuses, from painted ones to fettered ones, and yet it is tolerably safe to say that a statue of Venus, especially a nude, in one's parlor is bad taste, and still more, that, usually, a Venus is the most insipid and meaningless work an artist ever makes." Crudity of another sort was the mark of a certain type of American politician. "One of our gentlemanly Democratic ministers abroad, once crossing a frontier in his normal condition of crazy inebriation, refused to show his passport," at last flinging it into the officer's face. "The principle was correct," commented Adams, "but the manner faultily suave."

These Italian letters highlight the Brahmin cast of Adams's idealism. He tried hard, as he had promised at the beginning of the series, to be "fair and unprejudiced," but when he saw the howling Sicilian mobs he instinctively flinched. "Where is the Sicilian nobility and the gentlemen who ought to take a lead in a movement like this?" he broke out. "One cannot always control his ideas and prejudices. I can never forget, in thinking of Sicily and the Kingdom of Naples, that under the Roman government these countries were the great slave provinces of the empire, and there seems to be a taint of degradation in the people ever since. It is not good stock." He was skeptical of the charges of tyranny leveled against the Grand Duke of Tuscany. "I rather fancy that the government was on the whole an exceptionally good one, and the people among the most happy and honest in all Europe."

If Adams's opinions seem painfully superficial, one needs to remember that they were the complacent insights of a very young man, for Henry Adams had just turned twenty-one. It was inevitable that one of his name should gravitate toward the wellborn and conservative society of Vienna and Rome, a society to which he had almost official entrée. There was no one to remind him, as he strove to be fair to both sides, that the best witnesses against the lay and ecclesiastical rulers could be interviewed only in the prisons and cemeteries of central and southern Europe.

Upon the publication of the last dispatch in the *Boston Daily Courier,* the editor appreciatively commented: "The letter from H. B. C.

[*sic*] is the last we shall have from him on Italian affairs. Our readers, who have been highly entertained, will regret this; for the letters have been much above the average of communications sent home by European travelers . . . What he has gathered abroad he will be sure to turn to advantage at home." Henry's father agreed that the letters were "lively and cheerful," but he recommended that if Henry continued to write for the press he should "give attention to the more solemn changes that are in progress about you."

Adams's private letters vividly counterpointed those in the *Courier.* From Venice he wrote to Charles that he was "delighted with the broken-winded old hole . . . just let me have sunshine, a gondola, and a cigar and I don't care who's king." In Rome he read Gibbon and thought he might "come to anchor like that. Our house needs a historian in this generation and I feel strongly tempted by the quiet and sunny prospect." At sculptor William Wetmore Story's famous studio he talked with Robert Browning and found him "a quiet harmless sort of being."

Three months being yet unexpended of the planned two years of his Grand Tour, Adams left Rome for Paris and settled down to mastery of the French language. He spent all day studying texts and listened almost every night at the theater to catch the idiom. Friends and acquaintances dropped by that summer, and in her husband's absence his sister Loo joined him. Her world of gay and brilliant society was, he said, "poles apart" from his, but she was kind and they got along.

Henry entertained Charles with long and frank letters in French. Their father, he protested, was behind the times about the cost of living. Paris was ruinously expensive. However, at this distance he no longer feared his father's complaints, having discovered that the more money he asked for the less their father grumbled. Henry also confided that young women of easy virtue were a necessity for him "as for everyone else," but he said he was determined not to have a mistress until he should find one more acceptable than any he had so far seen. One evening after a fine dinner and a bottle of Mâcon he felt the need of feminine company. He walked out and, observing the pretty bonnet of a young woman, he accosted her and found the bonnet a snare. They strolled along to the door of his house and he said, "I live here." "So do I," she said, and entered the landlady's apartment. "How nice it would have been if she had been pretty and amiable." Discomfited, he gave up the intrigue, but was afterwards annoyed with himself that he had done so.

Drawing to a close was the two-year holiday agreed to by his father, and yet he had come no closer to the choice of a career. The time had come for Henry Adams to return home whether it was certain or not that he would be able to "turn to advantage" his European experience.

3

Witness to History

WHEN HENRY ADAMS reached Quincy in October of 1860, shortly before the November 6 election, the domestic situation no longer justified any feelings of complacency. North and South once again jockeyed for control of the national government, but a deeper note of urgency now entered the contest. Leading South Carolinians "unanimously resolved that in case of Lincoln's election the state must secede." Other Southern firebrands threatened to prevent Lincoln's inauguration by violence if he should be elected. Even in Quincy the "air" of the young "Wide Awake" Republicans who paraded in disciplined columns through the streets left Adams with an impression that "was not that of innocence."

As war came closer, Charles Sumner's extravagances began to embarrass the Adamses, with whom he was still on the friendliest terms, dining regularly with them each Sunday as he had for nearly a dozen years past. His ranting attack in the Senate chamber on the "Barbarism of Slavery" in June 1860 contrasted disagreeably with the moderation and high-minded dignity of Charles Francis Adams's maiden speech in the House a few days before, in which he described the Republican party as a necessary counterpoise to the "Slave Power." The *Boston Traveler* fatefully commented, "Those who were disaffected by Mr. Sumner's speech cannot fail to admit the power of that of Mr. Adams." It was the first hint of the rivalry that had already begun between the two old friends.

The political orientation of the family had steadily shifted toward center as William Seward of New York rose to leadership in the Republican party. Henry's father chose to follow Seward's footsteps because, as he later said, Seward "alone, of all others, had most marked himself as a disciple of the school in which I had been bred myself."

Charles Francis Adams had gone to the Chicago convention convinced that Seward would be chosen as the Republican nominee for President. To Adams's chagrin, Abraham Lincoln received the nomination. In the interest of party solidarity, Seward swallowed his disappointment, supported Lincoln, and at once began to slough off the radical elements of the party. Recognizing the value of his Massachusetts ally as a counterpoise to the intractable Sumner, Seward visited Quincy and persuaded Charles Francis Adams to join him in a swing through the then Northwest in behalf of Lincoln's candidacy.

Loyal to his party, Henry voted for Abraham Lincoln on November 6. At the same election his father, standing for reelection, won by a very comfortable majority. Election day was also memorable to young Adams as marking his attempt to study law in the office of the influential Judge Horace Gray. But there was to be as little progress in the common law as there had been in civil law. Three weeks later Henry was in Washington as private secretary to his father in time for the opening on December 3 of the tumultuous lame-duck session of the Thirty-sixth Congress. Before leaving Boston he managed to make connections with "the most important" Republican paper in Boston, the *Daily Advertiser,* whose coeditor, Charles Hale, a good friend of the family, appointed him Washington correspondent. Expediency, however, required that the appointment be kept secret.

In the national capital the private secretary and newspaper correspondent immediately displaced the halfhearted law student. The first letter sent to Charles from Washington a week after Henry's arrival indicated where his interest now lay. "It's a great life," the young statesman-in-waiting exulted, "just what I wanted." There was no time for the quiet study of Blackstone's *Commentaries* in the throbbing atmosphere of the capital, where crisis succeeded crisis and treason seemed to lurk behind every window blind. "What with the duties of secretary, of schoolmaster, of reporter for the papers, and of society-man," Henry explained, "I have more than I can do well." For the remainder of the winter law was sunk without a trace, not to reappear again until the following March in Boston, and then only briefly.

From the beginning the young secretary realized that he was an eyewitness to history. He therefore announced to his brother that he would record his testimony for posterity. "I propose to write you this winter a series of private letters to show how things look. I fairly confess that I want to have a record of this winter on file, and though I have no ambition nor hope to become a Horace Walpole, I still would like to think that a century or two hence when everything else about us is forgotten, my letters might still be read and quoted as a memorial of manners and habits at the time of the great secession of 1860."

His work as Washington correspondent of the *Boston Daily Advertiser* once under way, he extended his schoolmastering to fellow members of the press. Even in the cloakrooms of Congress he dispensed "good Republican doctrine and lots of it." His source of information was indeed the fountainhead of such doctrine. Republican leaders like Seward, Sumner, the distinguished apostate Know-Nothing Henry Winter Davis, and a crowd of lesser politicos of all shades of resolution made their rendezvous in the Adams parlor. Usually Henry sat against the wall at these councils, hastily transferring his incisive observations to his "memorial of manners and habits" for Charles's eye. Once he squelched the headstrong Sumner by reading a few lines from Bacon's essay "On Seditions and Troubles" while Sumner was parrying a violent rebuke from Charles Francis Adams, the new "Archbishop of Anti-Slavery" who was beginning to wear the miter of authority.

To Charles, who was as usual unsparing in his criticism, Henry admitted: "Naturally it is hard at first for a beginner as I am, to strike the key note; still I think I can manage it in time." When he feared that his cloak of anonymity might be snatched off, he lectured Charles, "You counsel boldness at the very time when a bold slip might close my mouth permanently. It was but this morning that C. F. A. [Charles Francis Adams] cautioned me against writing too freely."

At the outset, in order to prevent any moves that might upset his father's maneuvers in the Committee of Thirty-three, Henry sedulously played down the bitter wranglings in and out of Congress. He reassured his father's constituents, "It would be an insult to the great leaders of the party to suppose that their ideas on this matter are changed . . . A mere temporary secession is not disunion nor anything approaching it." At all costs the onus of rejecting conciliation would have to be fastened upon the Southern representatives or else the Republican party would be accused of treasonably desiring disunion.

With events moving in kaleidoscopic fashion, and factions North and South clamorously jockeying for position, it was no wonder that Henry Adams had difficulty striking the right keynote in support of his father's cause. What is impressive is the aplomb with which Henry at twenty-three sailed the erratic course plotted by Seward and his father, contriving somehow to tack and run before the wind almost simultaneously. The curious alternations in that policy caused Oliver Wendell Holmes to grumble disgustedly, "If Mr. Seward or Mr. Adams moves in favor of compromise, the whole Republican party sways like a field of grain, before the breath of either of them. If Mr. Lincoln says he shall execute the laws and collect the revenue, though the heavens cave in, the backs of the Republicans stiffen again."

During January the talk of coercion by the radical Republicans brought the country face to face with the possibility of war. The public recoiled in horror, and many New Englanders seemed ready to accept even the most craven compromise. Charles Francis Adams rose in the House on January 31 to define a middle ground. Reviewing the events in the South, he professed to see no evidence of a preconceived plan of disunion except in South Carolina. There the treason was deliberate. He rejected the idea of preventing secession by military means. Another course remained open. "I see no obstacle," he said, "to the regular continuance of the government in not less than twenty states, and perhaps more."

The solemn appeal by the acknowledged spokesman of the Sewardites carried great weight; and it seemed for a while that the nation had turned its dangerous corner. But Sumner's absence on the day of the speech was duly noted. Rumors quickly circulated that the two great rivals had quarreled. Henry, hoping to prevent a disastrous rupture between the two men which might split the party, glossed over the matter in the columns of the *Boston Daily Advertiser* in an effort to flatter Sumner into silence. "By the way," he wrote with studied casualness on February 6, "I see various rumors about a quarrel . . . [the] stories are very unfair to Mr. Sumner indeed, and are only one more example of the evils of 'sensation reports.' There has been no quarrel between these two gentlemen." He was considerably more frank in his report to Charles. "As for Sumner, the utmost that can be expected is to keep him silent. To bring him round is impossible. God Almighty couldn't do it." He suspected the "whole Garrison wing are doing their best to widen the breach."

In truth the breach could not possibly be kept from widening. The antislavery elements in the party were hopelessly divided between conservative and radical, a fateful division that was to plague the whole course of reconstruction after the war. Especially bitter was the tug-of-war over the cabinet appointments, which broke out shortly after Adams's speech. Senator Charles Sumner did not give up hope that Seward might somehow either be kept out of the cabinet or ultimately driven from it. But he was hardly prepared for the indignities which followed. Seward, ignoring Sumner's wishes, urged the appointment of Charles Francis Adams to the Treasury. Lincoln rejected the suggestion. Seward then "begged very hard" for the English mission for Adams, and the President-elect acquiesced because "really, Seward had asked for so little." That "little," however, had been deeply coveted by Sumner. Sumner did not need the comment of the *New York Herald* to know that Seward had advanced Adams in order to get even with him and his radical following for their hostility. Henceforward he would inflexibly oppose the political ambitions of the Adamses.

From the time of his arrival in Washington late in November until mid-February, when he resigned his job as correspondent, being replaced by Charles Hale, Henry Adams found little leisure for anything but the most urgent work. His father's highly literate constituents did not hesitate to make their wishes known. Remonstrances from "Garrisonians or men without weight" might be offset by the flood of letters praising his father's great speech, but acknowledgments had to be written to all. In addition, Henry made transcripts of his father's statements for the use of the printer and members of the press and kept in communication with party leaders in Boston. Long letters went, for instance, to Richard Hildreth, the historian and political journalist, aimed at holding him to his father's course. As Washington correspondent he also was obliged to cultivate his notable acquaintances "to hunt secrets" for himself and his brother Charles.

In the middle of the winter Charles resumed his prodding of Henry, suggesting a substantial essay on the current political situation. Henry's first impulse was to back away, but on second thought he changed his mind, stimulated once more by his brother's example. Charles had begun a series of letters in the *Transcript* to counteract the war talk which had been revived by Lincoln's Indianapolis speech en route to the capital. He was also hard at work on an article for the April *Atlantic Monthly* called "The Reign of King Cotton," in which he predicted that that reign would come to an end simply as a result of internal strain.

Henry decided to write a historical article for the *Atlantic Monthly* entitled "The Great Secession Winter of 1860–61" as a kind of unofficial white paper defending the devious maneuvers of the moderate Republicans. Adopting Charles's attractive hypothesis, he analyzed Seward's strategy as designed "to prevent a separation in order to keep the slave power more effectually under control, until its power for harm should be gradually exhausted, and its whole fabric gently and peacefully sapped away." He traced the current troubles to a source that had plagued the private reflections of his family since 1820, the year of the Missouri Compromise. "By the Constitution a great political, social, and geographical or sectional power within the Government was created; in its nature a monopoly; in its theory contrary to and subversive of the whole spirit of Republican institutions." The election of 1860 had challenged that entrenched power. "For the first time the Slave Power was defeated, and deprived, not of its legitimate power, not of its privileges as originally granted under the Constitution, but of the control of the Government; and suddenly in the fury of its unbridled license, it raised its hand to destroy that Government . . . The great secession winter of 1860–61 was therefore the first crucial test of our political system."

Critically weighing the merits of the article, Henry concluded that he had not adequately solved the problem of form. Toward the end of April 1861 he made a gift of the article to Charles, saying, "Finding that it was not going to be a success, I just finished it and laid it by, thinking that though as a whole it is a failure, there are still parts of it which might be put to use." Charles acquiesced in his judgment, and the article remained unpublished until 1910.

The Adamses attended the inauguration on March 4 and the grand ball that followed. The lack of social breeding of the new President and his wife made an unpleasant impression on Charles Francis Adams. He confided to his diary, "Neither of them is at home in this sphere of civilisation."

Henry returned to Boston shortly before the middle of March for another go at Blackstone in the office of Horace Gray. It lasted only three days. Then, on March 19, came the telegram to Quincy announcing his father's appointment as minister to England. Charles's diary vividly recalls the scene. "It fell on our breakfast-table like a veritable bombshell, scattering confusion and dismay. It had been much discussed in Washington, but Seward had encountered so much difficulty, and the President had seemed so intent on the nomination of Dayton, that the news finally came to us like a thunderbolt. My mother at once fell into tears and deep agitation; foreseeing all sorts of evil consequences, and absolutely refusing to be comforted; while my father looked dismayed." Charles's later comment on his mother's reaction suggests at least one source of Henry's subsequent pessimism. "My mother," Charles wrote, "took a constitutional and sincere pleasure in the forecast of evil." When calm was restored in the household, it was decided that Henry should continue his apprenticeship as private secretary to his father.

Henry's father returned from Washington, having conferred with Secretary of State Seward and President Lincoln. He had not been eager to leave his seat in Congress, for, as he afterwards wrote, it meant a "withdrawal from the great theatre of action at home," after having been triumphantly elected "over determined opposition." What he was able to report of his interview on March 28 confirmed all their fears of the President's incapacity. Lincoln listened "in silent abstraction" while Adams spoke his gratitude. The President said that he should thank Seward for the appointment. "Then, stretching out his legs before him, he said, with an air of great relief as he swung his long arms to his head:—'Well, governor [Seward], I've this morning decided that Chicago post-office appointment.'" The minister, who had hoped to discuss on the level of the highest statesmanship the course of American foreign policy that would need to be pursued during that critical period, "never recovered from his astonishment, nor did the impression then made ever wholly fade from his mind." He reflected in his diary at that time, "For my part I see nothing in the head. The man is not equal to the hour."

Although Charles Francis Adams was commissioned Envoy Extraordinary and Minister Plenipotentiary to England on March 20, he postponed his sailing for six weeks until his eldest son, John Quincy, was married to Fanny Crowninshield of Boston. The Confederate envoys, however, had no equally pressing social obligations and got to London before him in time to inspire Queen Victoria's Proclamation of Neutrality. Happily ignorant of the unpleasant diplomatic surprise that awaited them, the new minister and the private secretary

set sail from Boston harbor on May 1, with no more urgent business
in view than the need of resuming the "gold lace and silk stockings"
of court dress which had been proscribed by the democratic Secretary
of State William Marcy in 1853.

One of the influential persons with whom Henry Adams had become acquainted during the secession winter in Washington was
Henry J. Raymond, editor of the *New York Times*. Raymond had
vigorously supported Seward's candidacy in the Chicago convention
and, like Charles Francis Adams, had thereafter thrown his weight
behind the much-criticized program of conciliation. Before Henry
Adams left for England, he made arrangements with Raymond to act
as London correspondent of the newspaper.

This role required even greater secrecy than the one with the *Boston Daily Advertiser,* for it had to be concealed as well from Henry's
father. As the State Department prohibited "all communications with
the press," the new minister was "very careful to impress upon all the
members of the Legation the importance of obeying the injunctions."
No one knew that Henry was to be a London correspondent except
his brother Charles, who acted as his first agent in collecting the quarterly payments from Raymond. It must have been easy enough to
keep the secret from Raymond's subordinates, but more than ordinary dissimulation would have been needed to keep Henry's father in
the dark, especially as father and son spent whole days together writing opposite each other in the old study of the legation at 5 Mansfield
Street, "as merry as grigs."

Being the full-fledged London correspondent for pay of a leading
New York newspaper did not quite make up for the shortcomings of
Henry's position as private secretary. Impatient to make his influence
felt, he had to content himself at the beginning with countless menial
errands. He was not sure that such might not be his "only duty always," and he gloomily foresaw that his own share "in matters in
general" would be "very small." This fit of depression was the pre-
cursor of many such moments of disillusionment; fortunately, however, the pendulum of his moods swung as often towards elation. As
time went by he entered more and more into his father's confidence,
much to the chagrin of the official assistant secretary of the legation,
Benjamin Moran, who, jealous of his rival, took bitter refuge in his
diary: "The two sit upstairs there exchanging views on all subjects

and as each considers the other very wise, and both think all they do is right they manage to think themselves Solomons and to do some very stupid things."

Though technically outside of the legation, Henry managed at first to get on fairly well with the official staff. Charles Lush Wilson, the former editor of the *Chicago Daily Journal* and a hearty westerner, was the new secretary of the legation. The careerist Moran, whom Charles Francis Adams inherited from his predecessor George Dallas, clung as best he could to his prerogatives as assistant secretary. From time to time the ill-matched threesome went about to official functions at which Henry always demeaned himself, Moran conceded, in a "pleasant and gentlemanly manner." It was a shock to Henry, who had moved with familiar ease in the most exclusive Boston circles, to encounter the exquisite cruelties of British exclusiveness. Keenly aware of his social isolation, he regaled his companion with cynical witticisms. "As Henry Adams says," reads one of the entries in Moran's diary, "after you have bowed to the hostess, made some original remarks to her about the weather, and looked at the family pictures, the stock of amusements is exhausted; unless you find some barbarian present with refinement enough, or, if you please, sufficient confidence in you to present you to a young lady, who will talk, it is a waste of time to remain."

One aspect of British life which simultaneously repelled and yet fascinated Adams was the elaborate mummery of royal levees. He knew that as an American he ought to despise the invidious distinctions and feudal protocol of court society. It seemed to him a society without social existence; yet he could not help wishing to shine in it. The official court dress which his father had diplomatically restored became him "exceedingly well" in Moran's eyes. At his first presentation to Queen Victoria in June of 1861 he made a dashing appearance in the naval blue coat with its richly embroidered stand-up collar and gold eagle buttons, white kerseymere vest and knee breeches, white silk stockings, and a chapeau with gold ornaments. At his side he wore a fine gilt eagle-headed sword. The outfit cost more than $200, but Henry Adams believed he could afford it, as his private income was nearly $2,500 a year.

Part of the malaise that clouded his early months in England was no doubt traceable to his chronic dyspepsia. The seasickness that had "prostrated" him on the ocean voyage had left him easily tired and irritable. At his presentation he was suffering from a cold and was frightened "nearly to death" with fear of a "relapse." Equally trying to his temper was the corroding knowledge that almost alone of his friends he had no part in the military drama back home. Each mail brought news of enlistments and exalted military commissions. More than one-third of his college classmates were marching off to glory and military rank. Those companions of his European *Wanderjahr,* Nicholas Anderson and Benjamin Crowninshield, soon held enviable commissions. Before the year was out his brother Charles was commissioned first lieutenant in a Massachusetts cavalry regiment.

The England to which the young unofficial diplomat came in the spring of 1861 was an England bafflingly changed from the country of his preconceptions. Father and son had expected that British foreign policy would reflect the strong antislavery principles of the ordinary Englishman, who had been bred in the school of William Wilberforce. Neither one was prepared for a foreign policy in which purely economic considerations played so important a part.

The leading English journals had at first sympathetically followed the efforts of the antislavery groups to wrest control of the national government from the South. But as the prospect of armed collision became more and more imminent, idealistic considerations gave way to a growing concern with the probable effect of such a conflict upon British economic interests. Cotton manufacturers were persuaded that the cutting off of the American supply would have a catastrophic effect upon England. The *Times* as a bellwether of the press began to argue that the North should accept secession as an accomplished fact.

For those Englishmen who placed their country's business interests first the developments in Washington were not reassuring. Seward's opinion that the Montgomery government was no government and that secession was a mere rebellion—the view held also by Lincoln—alarmed the realistic British representative in Washington. He carefully transmitted to the Home Government all of Seward's threats about establishing a blockade against British commerce and the even more menacing talk of a "foreign war panacea." To forestall any compromising acts the ministry had promptly drafted the Proclamation of Neutrality and issued it on May 13, the day the Adamses landed at Liverpool. Since the proclamation was a *fait accompli,* Adams could do no more than object that it was precipitately issued and urge its recall. In his effort to analyze the ebb and flow of British opinion,

Henry Adams labored under a serious handicap. He did not have as much knowledge of Secretary Seward's intentions as Lord Russell had. Unknown to young Adams and his father, there had gone on in the American cabinet a struggle for supremacy, one of the most bizarre aspects of which concerned Seward's extraordinary memorandum of April 1. The document outlined an aggressive policy toward the European powers that amounted to an incitement to war. Lincoln quietly shelved this plan; but Seward, still underrating the President's judgment, prepared a fresh piece of provocation, the notorious Dispatch Number 10, demanding that Queen Victoria's government adopt the Northern theory of a rebellion. Fortunately Lincoln required that the dispatch be toned down and directed Henry's father not to deliver it to Russell. The insulting contents of the original version of Number 10 somehow "leaked out," and the terms of the affront were allowed to become public property in England. Even in its emasculated form the dispatch bewildered the American envoy. Henry called the proposed policy "shallow madness" and declared himself "shocked and horrified by supposing Seward, a man I've admired and respected beyond most men, guilty of what seems to me so wicked and criminal a course as this." The minister reduced the heated phrases of his chief to a chill innocuousness. He had saved his mission, but for how long?

HENRY ADAMS TOOK HIS JOB of foreign correspondent with appropriate seriousness, regularly sitting down each Saturday in the privacy of his two-room suite on the top floor of the legation residence to write up his notes on the week's happenings. Before coming to a precipitate close in January 1862 the series of dispatches to the *New York Times* continued steadily for nearly eight months, only one being omitted, that for August 17. Unsigned, they appeared under such captions as "Important from England," "American Topics in England," "American Questions in England," or "Matters at London" and were commonly credited to "Our Own Correspondent." The need for anonymity was imperative, for disclosure would have made his father's mission untenable. He did not dare reveal that he had access to diplomatic secrets. For instance, though he was frantically alarmed by the contents of Dispatch Number 10 he could not let slip knowledge of the offensive details. Henry's efforts were also complicated by the fact that Secretary Seward did not always reveal his diplomatic strategy to Minister Adams. On one occasion "Our Own Correspondent" merrily scoffed at British suspicion that Seward's "amicable proposal" to adhere to the Declaration of Paris was a trap to maneuver England and France into withdrawing their recognition of the South as a bona fide belligerent. That had in fact been Seward's secret intention.

The position which Henry Adams took on Anglo-American affairs continued the conciliatory policy of the *New York Times* correspondent who preceded him. It assumed that the English people were in sympathy with the North. That fact granted, it followed that Americans should do nothing to make for ill will, no matter what provocation might be offered by a few pro-Southern English journals. Discursive and gossipy, his columns ranged at will through the sensations and trivialities of the week, once Anglo-American affairs were disposed of.

His assumption that English public opinion strongly favored the North soon fell victim to the facts. The British public was in fact apathetic. The English people, he wrote, "the bulwark of Liberalism in Europe . . . make it their pride to stand neutral. Neutrality in a struggle like this is a disgrace to their great name." Some weeks later, however, when he read the unexpectedly violent American press attacks on the neutral policy of Great Britain, he tried to lay the tempest that he had helped to raise. "The sympathies of the English people are actively with us because they feel, in their cold and practical way, that their true interests lie with the North, and their common sense tells them that the cause of free institutions, their own cause as much as ours, is bound up on the result of our contest."

Nevertheless, as time went on he reported that "steadily and surely popular opinion is forming here against us" and concluded that "sympathy in England or elsewhere is to be won by the sword alone." So far it was the South that had grasped that weapon by the hilt, as Bull Run and Ball's Bluff proved. What particularly angered him was that the Americans had brought this hostility upon themselves. "How do you suppose we can overcome the effects of the New York press?" he complained to Charles. "How do you suppose we can conciliate men whom our tariff is ruining? How do you suppose we can shut people's eyes to the incompetence of Lincoln or the disgusting behavior of many of our volunteers and officers?"

Among the press his special aversions were the *Times* of London and the *New York Herald*. They were most to blame, he believed, for engendering bad feeling. Almost every dispatch of his contained an attack on the low motives of the *Times*. After Bull Run he wrathfully observed: "The *Times* at once came out in a tone so needlessly insulting and so wantonly malignant that no one could doubt any longer . . . on which side its sympathies lie." When the *New York Herald* published a garbled account of his father's confidential report to Seward of an interview with Lord Russell, Henry denounced the "pretended report" as the work of "the lowest print that has ever disgraced a great nation."

Henry did use his column fairly consistently to discourage attacks upon the English government and upon business and social interests that might be provoked to more active hostility toward the United States. He defended Lord Russell as a friend of America and democracy, and extenuated Russell's issuance of the offending Proclamation of Neutrality as due to the pressure of his colleagues in the cabinet. "So long as Lord Russell is at the head of Foreign Affairs," he affirmed, "I believe America may feel confident that no encouragement will be given to the Slave Power." Palmerston, on the other hand, he portrayed as the evil genius of the ministry, an "old school Machiavellian."

For the most part he vigorously skirmished along the propaganda front, here attacking the causes of grievances, there playing down sources of dissension. Of first importance was the "amelioration" of the Morrill Tariff. When the Confederate raider *Nashville* took refuge in an English port after burning the Union *Harvey Birch,* he pleaded with his countrymen "not to explode until it appears that we are wronged," for, as he attempted to reassure them, England "will not refuse justice now when it is clearly on our side." However, the plea was ill-timed. Captain Wilkes of the USS *Jacinto* had already boarded the royal mail packet *Trent* and arrested the Confederate envoys, James Mason and John Slidell. Adams's embarrassment was heightened by the fact that in an earlier dispatch he had denounced the rumors of a plan to intercept Mason and Slidell as a canard manufactured by Southerners.

The *Trent* affair unnerved him. He admonished his readers that the seizure was "a blunder if not a crime." Desperately, he proposed playing "our last and highest card," the immediate freeing and arming of the slaves in order to bring the war to a quick and successful conclusion and thus take the moral initiative away from the war party in England. Seward frowned upon the suggestion as ill-timed, and the London correspondent retreated to safety. "I am an abolitionist," he reminded his brother, "and so, I think, are you, and so, I think, is Mr. Seward; but if he says the time has not yet come . . . then I say, let us wait. It will come. Let us have order and discipline and firm ranks among the soldiers of the Massachusetts school."

The retreating roar of the *Trent* affair filled Henry's last five dispatches. He pleaded that the British demand for the surrender of the Confederate commissioners should be complied with and complied with "cordially," as was finally done. The right or wrong of the matter was unimportant in the current state of English public opinion; anyway, he comforted his fellow Americans, "We have all eternity to settle our account with England."

After the humiliating defeat of Bull Run, Henry had demanded that his brother obtain a commission for him, "second, third lieutenant or ensign if you can do no better . . . I cannot stay here now to stand the taunts of everyone without being able to say a word in defence." This craven plea was too much for Charles. "Look into the cotton supply question," he urged, "and try to persuade the English that our blockade is their interest . . . Then write to the *Atlantic* of the way fighting America appears in English eyes, of her boasting and bragging, her running and terror . . . Here is your field, right before your nose . . . Don't talk of your connection with the legation to me; cut yourself off if necessary from it and live in London as the avowed *Times* correspondent and force your way into notice of the London press that way . . . Free from the legation you could earn a living by your pen in London and be independent, busy, happy and eminently useful."

Henry resisted being pushed into a new project with such velocity. "My great gun is the Manchester one. Tomorrow evening I start with a pocketful of letters, for Manchester to investigate that good place . . . My present plan is to report with as much accuracy as possible all my conversations and all my observations, and to send them to you. Perhaps it might make a magazine article . . . If I find that I can make it effective in that form, I shall write it out and send it to you for the *Atlantic*." As the report arrived "just too late" for the January *Atlantic*, Charles reluctantly "carried it to the *Courier*" to pay off a debt to that "low-toned and semi-treasonable sheet." Under the head-

ing "A Visit to Manchester—Extracts from a Private Diary" the unsigned two and a half columns of type reported five days of interview-
ing among Manchester industrialists, supported by a study of the
comparative value and availability of non-American cotton.

Henry discovered that both he and his brother had been mistaken
about the reason for the shutdown of factories. Southern propaganda
had successfully persuaded the public that the shortage of raw cotton
was beginning to be felt. Actually, as was explained to Adams, the
shortage could not begin to exert its influence until the following year.
The spinners had so thoroughly anticipated the war that the market
was now glutted with finished goods, and prices were so depreciated
that some mills had found continued operation no longer profitable.
The mills had already experimented with India cotton, and at least
one manufacturer thought the fabrics could replace "all but the finest
Americans, at ordinary prices." In examining the stuffs themselves
Henry could detect no visible differences. If the blockade held,
"spring will find England nearly independent of America for this article, and we shall see the steady advances of a great revolution in the
world's condition."

One incidental comment had a fateful influence upon his career as
a journalist. To enliven the dreary technical aspects for his report, he
interjected a comparison of London and Manchester society, saying
in part: "In Manchester one is usually allowed a dressing room at an
evening party. In London a gentleman has to take his chances of going
into the ball room with his hair on end or his cravat untied. In Manchester it is still the fashion to finish balls with showy suppers, which
form the great test of the evening. In London one is regaled with
thimblefuls of ice cream and hard seed cakes."

The attack upon his London hosts relieved the long-pent accumulation of his social grievances; but it proved an unlucky revenge. The
editor of the *Courier*, pleased to receive a new contribution from the
correspondent whom he had so praised a year and a half earlier, dis-
regarded instructions and blurted out the secret of its authorship.

Here indeed was a morsel for London journalists. To Henry's "immense astonishment and dismay" he found himself "sarsed through
a whole column of the Times" and made the laughingstock of England. The editorial writer denied that Adams's report correctly reflected Manchester opinion and then turned patronizingly to the comment on London society. What Adams needed was a less limited

social experience. "Let him but persevere in frequenting *soirées* and admiring 'family pictures' . . . and we shall not despair of reading some day, a new diary in the *Boston Daily Courier,* wherein the *amende honorable* will be made to the gay world of our metropolis."

On the day following the *Times* editorial the *Examiner* impaled him on its wit, gibing at the "frightful risk" he took "of going into a house with his hair on end and his cravat untied." As for his objections to the "hard seed-cakes and thimblefuls of ice-cream . . . this should be a caution to all persons giving parties . . . to be more careful about their cakes, the softness, and the seeds thereof . . . That hard seed-cake runs through and embitters all the young gentleman's reports of us." Henry's first impulse was to ask his brother to explain to Raymond, "without mentioning names," why his London correspondent had stopped for a time. At all costs their father must not learn of his connection with the *New York Times.* "The Chief bears this vexation very good-naturedly, but another would be my ruin for a long time." Two weeks later he took the matter into his own hands in a "private and confidential" letter to Raymond in which he resigned his post and summarized the critical state of British opinion.

The public attacks so unnerved him that he foreswore further journalism. "I have wholly changed my system," he informed Charles, "and having given up all direct communication with the public, am engaged in stretching my private correspondence as far as possible." The break in what had become an established literary routine touched him more deeply than he at first would acknowledge. Self-mistrust, never far below the surface of his mind, reasserted its claims, and his misgivings overflowed into his letters to Charles. On the deck of the transport lying off Beaufort, South Carolina, the young lieutenant greeted Henry's vaporings with measureless scorn. "Fortune has done nothing but favor you and yet you are 'tired of this life.' You are beaten back everywhere before you are twenty-four, and finally writing philosophical letters you grumble at the strange madness of the times and haven't even faith in God and the spirit of your age. What do you mean by thinking, much less writing such stuff? 'No longer any chance left of settled lives and Christian careers!' "

Completely routed, Henry poured ashes upon his head. "I've disappointed myself, and experience the curious sensation of discovering myself to be a humbug . . . You are so fortunate as to be able to forget self-contemplation in action, I suppose; but with me, my most efficient channels of action are now cut off." Vague plans flitted through his fancy, but his heart was not in them. On the eve of the first anniversary of the war, he wrote *de profundis:* "I feel ashamed and humiliated at leading this miserable life here, and since having been blown up by my own petard in my first effort to do good, I haven't even the hope of being of more use here than I should be in the army." There was nothing for it but to make a new and more philosophical approach to the choice of a career.

‹ 4 ›

A Golden Time

ONCE WHEN REVISITING LONDON in the early 1890s, Henry Adams "lapsed from his usual cynical manner" to give advice to a young companion, Lloyd C. Griscom, who was just beginning a career as a diplomat. Looking back on his own initiation many years before, Adams said, "It was a golden time for me and altered my whole life . . . You're in a remarkable position now. You've every opportunity to make friends that will influence your entire career. Be sure to keep your head and get the most you can out of it." In that moment of musing insight, he evaluated his English experience much more sympathetically than when he again reviewed it in the *Education* a dozen years later. His later judgment was cut from the same mortuary cloth with which he draped his memory of Harvard.

When he reached England in 1861 he was twenty-three years old; he was thirty when he sailed for home in 1868. That interval marked the transformation of the provincial young man who had once been homesick for Quincy and Boston to the cosmopolite "with an English cut to his jib" who gravitated to a capital "by a primary law of nature." He brought ashore with him from the *Niagara* in 1858 a baggage of ideas that bore the labels of Quincy, Boston, and Harvard College, ideas that in a larger world were often indistinguishable from prejudices. His two years on the Continent had scarcely touched these; nor had they shaken his faith in a priori moral and political principles. In the society of congressmen and lobbyists, of politicians, lawyers, and editors, the society in which he had moved in Washington as a journalist, the impending war had displaced all other interests. As a London correspondent his view had widened to include international politics and diplomacy, but he continued to be preoccupied with the parochial concerns of a newspaperman. The abrupt

change caused by the attacks in the London press freed him from
those narrow concerns. As his work as a propagandist became attenuated he no longer had a strong motive to identify himself with his
father's diplomatic and political interests. New influences could now
enter his mind more freely and make their challenge felt—new trains
of thought, new lines of literary interest.

His English associations were prescribed, at least at the beginning,
by an almost iron law of affinity. The highest aristocracy maintained
a stony reserve toward the representatives of the Union cause. Since
his social standing derived from his position as son and private secretary to the minister, Henry Adams fell equally under the ban.
Though themselves members of an American aristocracy, the
Adamses were driven into the arms of the largely unaristocratic English liberals and radical reformers. The names of such enlightened
sympathizers as William E. Forster, economist Nassau Senior, literary
patron and M.P. Richard Monckton Milnes, novelist Thomas
Hughes, M.P. Richard Cobden, and Robert Browning soon began to
appear in Henry Adams's London date book. These men were part of
a brilliant circle which included figures like scientist Charles Lyell,
historian Goldwin Smith, John Stuart Mill, Leslie Stephen, Thomas
Huxley, the positivist Frederic Harrison, and theologian Francis New-
man, all of whom gave aid and comfort to the American legation.
Young Adams struck up a friendly acquaintance with most of the
influential friends of the Union and basked in the sunshine of their
sympathy for his country. But living in the shadow of his father's distinction, he could not yet make his mark in spite of his keen wit and
manifest good breeding.

Thrown into the company of eminent persons generally older than
he, he had to endure the constraint imposed by age upon youth. Usually cast in the role of listener, he was bold enough on one occasion
to debate the subject of free trade with John Stuart Mill, to whom, he
wrote Charles, he "took particular pains to be introduced." At a
"royal evening" at which the company was of "the earth's choicest,"
Robert Browning and novelist Edward Bulwer-Lytton fell into a discussion on fame. "It was curious," Adams reflected, "to see two men
who, of all others, write for fame, or have done so, ridicule the idea
of its real value to them." Another time he was a guest at "a pleasant
dinner" at which Charles Dickens, John Forster, the much-admired
biographer of Oliver Goldsmith, Louis Blanc, the eminent French his-

torian and politician-in-exile, and "other distinguished individuals were present." One of the most memorable experiences was the intimate gathering at Monckton Milnes's Fryston Hall in Yorkshire which brought into his ken one night Algernon Swinburne, whose genius blazed upon him like a comet.

He was soon ready to concede that "society in London certainly has its pleasures," as for instance when he dined at the home of the Duke of Argyll, a Liberal leader in the House of Lords, and there met Charles P. Villiers, a member of Parliament and a prominent free trader; Charles Brown-Sequard, the celebrated neuropathologist; Professor Richard Owen, the paleontologist; and Lord Frederick Cavendish, private secretary to the president of the Privy Council. Again after returning from a breakfast with lawyer-politician William Evarts, Cyrus Field, Richard Cobden, and others, he wrote in a lofty vein: "So we go on, you see, and how much of this sort of thing could one do at Boston!" He continued to insist, however, that these exquisite moments were islands of delight in the "vast nuisance and evil" of fashionable society, and he gave only partial assent to historian Lothrop Motley's dictum that this was "the perfection of human society."

Life in a great world capital was indeed different from the provincial amenities of Boston. The hundreds of entries in his date book, which he kept from 1861 to 1868, tell of an almost endless succession of interviews, calls, breakfasts, dinner engagements, balls, teas, and at homes; and the record glitters with the names of Englishmen and their wives who were helping to make him a man of the great world, anglicizing his speech and manner almost in spite of himself. One of the most memorable social functions was the great reception for Garibaldi which the Duchess of Sutherland gave at Stafford House. Henry told Charles, "I discovered poor Garry in a blue military poncho with a red lining, in the middle of a big room, with the stunning-handsome Duchess gloating on him as it were, in front, while the ponderous figure of the Duchess Dowager with corpulent and condescending smiles, hovered heavily, like a bloated and benevolent harpy, on his shoulder, and your friend the Duchess of Argyll blandly protected his rear."

The legation attracted not only Englishmen of importance but also all visiting Americans great and small. Many of his countrymen whom Adams now met or with whom he renewed acquaintance were

destined to play an important part in his life. American diplomats on
their way to European posts in 1861 almost invariably stopped at the
legation to confer with Henry's father, and Henry was commonly a
party to such conferences. As a result he had the chance to meet Carl
Schurz, the new minister to Spain; John Lothrop Motley, minister to
Austria; James S. Pike, minister to Holland; and poet Bayard Taylor,
chargé d'affaires at St. Petersburg. Charles Hale, his former employer
on the *Advertiser,* likewise paused on his way to Egypt as American
consul. Novelist William Dean Howells, appointed to the consulate
at Venice, came in seeking to be married in the legation, but Secretary
Moran, who thought him a "sleek, insipid sort of a fellow," haughtily
turned him away before he could meet either Henry or his father.
Questions of government finance brought experts like steelmaker
Abram S. Hewitt and Robert J. Walker into the Adams family circle.
William M. Evarts and Thurlow Weed, who came as "roving diplomats," proved the most acceptable of Seward's horde of special
agents. Henry Adams particularly valued Evarts's instruction and dis-
cussed with him "affairs at home and philosophic statesmanship, the
Government and the possibility of effectual reform."

The trickle of American visitors grew to a flood as the Civil War
slowly drew to a close. Among the neatly recorded names of dinner
guests one encounters a number of special significance: Lincoln's secretary Major John Hay, economist David A. Wells, Congressman
James A. Garfield, Congressman James G. Blaine, the legal scholar
Colonel Oliver Wendell Holmes, Senator John Sherman, Phillips
Brooks, Charles Deane, John Gorham Palfrey, and Dr. Robert
Hooper of Boston and his daughter Marian, who was one day to
become Adams's wife. Hay has left a glimpse of one of the parties.
"We tore our friends to pieces a little while. Motley got one or two
slaps that were very unexpected to me. Sumner and his new wife were
brushed up a little." There were of course many others who called at
the legation in the "slum," as Moran disdainfully referred to the
premises at 147 Great Portland Street to which the legation office had
been removed, or who enjoyed the pleasanter hospitality of the residence at 5 Upper Portland, notables like Professor Francis Bowen,
Richard Henry Dana, Jr., Kate Chase Sprague, Henry J. Raymond,
James Gordon Bennett, George Smalley, William Lloyd Garrison,
Henry Ward Beecher, and Julia Ward Howe.

Once for diversion in 1862 Henry decamped to Paris for ten days during the carnival season. He and a Harvard friend took in a masked ball at the Opéra, where they rambled through the theater and "tried to amuse ourselves with swarms of flaming whores and the ridiculous masques." They joined several other college mates, one of whom presented his French mistress for their admiration. Adams lodged with Frank Edmonds and "a young Storrow" and did his best, he said, to "debauch" them, but "it wasn't very gay." He got back to a London much subdued by Queen Victoria's mourning for Prince Albert.

Always in the foreground of attention was the progress of the war. He followed intently the movement of the armies on the official maps of the legation. Charles supplied eyewitness accounts of the activities of his own cavalry squadron and brought the war suddenly close with word of a bloody engagement at Aldie's Gap in Virginia. There were 93 casualties in his force of 151. His men fell all around him as they retreated, but he and his mounts were luckily unscathed. In his long letters to Charles Henry matched his notion of proper strategy with that of the generals, meting out praise and blame. As the intervals of hope rose and fell there came periods of tedium which were relieved by afternoon rides in Rotten Row with his sister Mary. He confessed he was annoyed with her because she had "got the rage for the world, the flesh and the devil as bad as ever her sister [Louisa] Kuhn had it."

The quiet and uncertainty suddenly broke with the tremendous news of the battle of Gettysburg. Deeply moved by the magnitude of the victory and its fearful cost, Henry wrote to Charles, whose squadron had been held in reserve during the battle: "Our generation has been stirred up from its lowest layers and there is that in its history which will stamp every member of it until we are all in our graves." A week later came the news of the fall of Vicksburg to Grant. "I wanted to hug the army of the Potomac," he exclaimed. "I wanted to get the whole of the army of Vicksburg drunk at my own expense."

Slow as Henry's social progress had been at first, the tide had finally begun to turn after the surrender of New Orleans in April 1862. In March 1863 Richard Monckton Milnes (Lord Houghton) had put him up for the St. James's Club, the nomination seconded by Lawrence Oliphant, "a thorough anti-American." In the following month while visiting Cambridge he met Charles Milnes Gaskell, son of James Milnes Gaskell, member of Parliament for Wenlock in Shropshire. Within a short time he was on terms of the greatest intimacy with the young collegian, and the lively sportiveness of his letters to his new friend reflects how deeply grateful he was for the chance of dropping his diplomatic guard. Through Gaskell he soon met the poet Francis Turner Palgrave, Gaskell's brother-in-law, and through him, Thomas Woolner, Palgrave's protégé, and other figures of London's intellectual circles. He also became acquainted with Henry Reeve, the longtime editor of the *Edinburgh Review*. By the end of 1863, alluding to Arthur Clough's poetry, which had just been edited by Palgrave, he was able to write: "Young England, young Europe, of which I am by tastes and education a part; the young world, I believe, in every live country, are reflected in Clough's poems very clearly."

One of the staunchest Northern sympathizers who early allied himself with the legation was Sir Charles Lyell, the foremost geologist in England. In the dark days that followed the defeat at Ball's Bluff and the blunder in the *Trent* affair, Lyell became a frequent visitor and was soon on terms of intimacy with the entire family. He was then busy on the manuscript of his *Antiquity of Man* and moving toward an acceptance of the theory of evolution advanced in 1859 in his friend Darwin's *Origin of Species*. Through Lyell, Henry was inevitably drawn into the passionate struggle over Darwinism.

The clamor over Darwin still echoed in the very month that Adams reached England, for Huxley had just concluded his daring lectures on "The Relation of Man to the Rest of the Animal Kingdom" and was in the midst of his violent controversy with Sir Richard Owen, who fiercely opposed the thesis of the *Origin of Species*. As a subscriber to the *Atlantic Monthly* Henry had already encountered Asa Gray's defense of Darwin against the contemptuous criticisms of Louis Agassiz. Arguing that "Darwin's hypothesis is the natural complement to Lyell's uniformitarian theory in physical geology," Gray concluded that "the rumor that the cautious Lyell himself had adopted the Darwinian hypothesis need not surprise us." Adams found himself obliged to read the work that had touched off the great debate, the *Origin of Species* itself, as well as its lesser companion, the account of the voyage of the *Beagle*. Like many other young intellectuals, he began to dabble in gentlemanly geology, hunting for telltale fossils in the Wenlock Edge district of Shropshire near the estate of Charles Milnes Gaskell. Henry succumbed so completely to Lyell's influence that in February 1863 he confided to Charles, "I have serious thoughts of quitting my old projects of a career, like you. My promised land of occupation, however, my burial place of ambition and law, is geology and science."

The authority with which the new science and its spectacular applications spoke revolutionized Adams's thinking. In April 1862, for example, the British government carried out armor-piercing tests which, according to Henry, showed that "their iron navy, and their costly guns" were "all utterly antiquated and useless." The consequences both dazzled and alarmed him. "You may think all this nonsense," he warned Charles, "but I tell you these are great times. Man has mounted science, and is now run away with. I firmly believe that before many centuries more, science will be the master of man. The engines he will have invented will be beyond his strength to control. Some day science may have the existence of mankind in its power, and the human race commit suicide, by blowing up the world."

As he mastered "the easy and mechanical work" of his official duties, Adams turned to the study of the writers who were seeking to interpret the new movement in science and philosophy. A tremendous new organon was coming into being that was to shape the course of Western thought for at least a half-century, and he was irresistibly drawn into that field of attraction. No realm of knowledge could claim exemption from the scrutiny of the new science. Among the world capitals, the London in which Adams lived constituted a chief center of this renaissance. In the natural sciences Charles Darwin was of course the main figure in the group which included Sir Charles Lyell, Sir Roderick Murchison, Joseph Hooker, Thomas Henry Huxley, John Tyndall, and Hugh Falconer. The revolution in physics stemmed from the researches of such men as Sir William Thomson, Sir Charles Wheatstone, Michael Faraday, James Clerk Maxwell, and their Continental colleagues. Mathematicians like Sir Charles Babbage and George Boole and chemists like Sir William Crookes and Sir Edward Frankland were opening up whole new areas. In this intellectual climate Adams felt he was on the way to satisfying his desire for "a systematic conception of it all."

The triumvirate of writers whose works were best calculated to gratify that wish were Auguste Comte, Herbert Spencer, and Henry Buckle, all of whom expected to reconstruct society according to rational and scientific principles. The meetings of the recently founded Social Science Society in London gave promise that such reconstruction would be the work of the new science of society. When Mill's analytical study *Auguste Comte and Positivism* was published in 1865, Adams was one of the first to read it. The impact of this work upon his questing mind may be surmised from the effect it produced upon his brother Charles, who was then visiting in England. "That essay of Mill's," said Charles, "revolutionized in a single morning my whole mental attitude." The arresting proposals of Comte suggested the possibility of an impersonal social physics freed from the tyranny of "all the great social organizations," as Adams later called the vested interests of society. In the light of his subsequent interest in "scientific history," the most striking passage in the essay reads: "Foresight of phenomena and power over them depend on knowledge of their sequences, and not upon any notion we may have formed respecting their origin or inmost nature." To the young philosophical statesman with a taste for prophecy the prospect of a science of prediction must have been alluring. As he says in the *Education,* "he became a Comteist, within the limits of evolution."

If Comte identified the conditions of such a science, Herbert Spencer first formulated its hypotheses. Spencer, who was one of the philosophers cultivated by Adams's friends at Lord Houghton's Fryston Hall, sought in his *First Principles* to "interpret the detailed phenomena of Life, and Mind, and Society, in terms of Matter, Motion, and Force." He asserted that "the general law of the transformation and equivalences of forces" holds true not only of physical forces, but of vital, mental, and social forces as well. Human society tends to pass through successive states of equilibrium from a homogeneous into a heterogeneous state with a concomitant loss of motion. If we look ahead no farther than the *History of the United States of America during the Administrations of Thomas Jefferson and James Madison,* the great achievement of Adams's middle life, the parallels between Spencer's identification of the social and physical processes and Adams's is more than a coincidence. The adoption in the *History* of the notion that social energy, like an Alpine stream, descended through history to be lost finally in the ocean of democracy would seem certain confirmation.

The generalizations of Comte and Spencer were matched in the field of history by Buckle, who urged that the physical sciences be applied to history because "it is certain that there must be an intimate connexion between human actions and physical laws." The historian must consequently seek to determine the laws of mind and the laws of matter. These daring generalizations, like those of Comte and Spencer, Adams thriftily put aside for future use. They, too, were to leave their mark upon the conception of the *History,* especially of the great opening chapters.

Adams's political thinking was most deeply affected by John Stuart Mill, one of the warmest friends of the North. Mill had applauded Minister Adams's judicious handling of the *Trent* affair, and in his article in *Fraser's Magazine* in February 1862 he echoed the thesis of the legation that the war was becoming more and more a matter involving the abolition of slavery. Even before Henry Adams met Mill, early in 1863, he had come wholly under the sway of his libertarian doctrines, and he passed "the intervals from official work in studying de Tocqueville and Mill, the two high priests of our faith."

Mill's new book, *Representative Government,* systematized for him many ideas which had been household doctrine in the Adams family. In Berlin, for example, he had reminded his brother that, however they approached political philosophy, they both came down to the idea of universal education as the source of New England's moral power. Horace Mann, he said, had lived and died in that conviction. Mill declared that "the most important point of excellence which any form of government can possess is to promote the virtue and intelligence of the people themselves." These were the very words John Adams had used. Liberty, he had said, depends on the "intelligence and virtue of the people," and, as he expounded the matter in his *Essay on the Canon and the Feudal Law,* it is chiefly to be preserved by universal education.

To a member of a family which had been eclipsed by the leveling imperatives of Jacksonian democracy, Mill's precepts brought the shock of recognition. Mill reassured him that the best government is government by the best. "A representative constitution is a means of bringing . . . the individual intellect and virtue of its wisest members, more directly to bear upon the government, and investing them with greater influence in it than they would have under any other mode or organization." Mill warned that the "natural tendency of representative government, as of modern civilization, is toward collective mediocrity, and this tendency is increased by all reductions [restriction of office to local candidates] and extensions [inclusion of the uneducated] of the franchise." The unfortunate consequence in the United

States was that "the highly cultivated members of the community . . .
do not even offer themselves for Congress or the State Legislatures, so
certain it is that they would have no chance of being returned." Mill's
reproach challenged Adams to resist the trend. He agreed with Mill
that "one person with belief is a social power equal to ninety-nine
who have only interests."

The other high priest of his faith, Alexis de Tocqueville, was no
stranger to him. His grandfather John Quincy Adams had once
known that friendly critic of democracy, and his father had long been
familiar with his work. Henry Adams came to *Democracy in America*
because the entire pro-Northern coterie in England drew strength
from Tocqueville's estimate of America's power of survival. The Liberal M.P. Monckton Milnes had championed the high priest in a laudatory article, and Henry Reeve, the influential editor of the *Edinburgh Review,* had made a translation of *De la démocratie en
Amérique*. This translation was now being reissued. The political
economist Nassau Senior, another intimate of the legation, was in the
midst of his nine-volume edition of Tocqueville's works. John Stuart
Mill's endorsement probably carried most weight. "The Montesquieu
of our times," he called him, whose works "contain the first analytical
inquiry into the influence of Democracy." Mill accepted his thesis that
the movement toward democracy was irresistible but that as the individual sank "into greater and greater insignificance" a new political
science needed to be created.

Read at a time when Adams was becoming keenly alive to its implications, *Democracy in America* helped to catch and fix the random
criticisms of America which had been cropping out in his letters—
public and private—into a kind of catalogue of political imperfections. Through Tocqueville's eyes he now saw that the "organization
and the establishment of democracy in Christendom is the great political problem of our times." The cogent analysis of the flaws in the
American system fell in with the old warnings of his grandfather and
father and revived their cankering doubts in him. "I doubt me much,"
he wrote to Charles, "whether the advance of years will increase my
toleration of its faults." Still, Tocqueville's text held open a perilous
route of escape. In Tocqueville's opinion, the true source of democracy in America lived in the New England character; Adams concluded, therefore, that the rescue could be effected by the "New England element."

Here, then, was the mission that could give significance to literary and political action. "I have learned to think De Tocqueville my model," he announced to his brother, "and I study his life and works as the Gospel of my private religion. The great principle of democracy is still capable of rewarding a conscientious servant." A career was possible, if not as "a light to the nations," perhaps as a social and political reformer. In his own metaphor he saw "in the distance a vague and unsteady light in the direction towards which I needs must gravitate, so soon as the present disturbing influences are removed."

For such a role much training would be needed. He indicated to Charles the nature of his self-imposed regimen: "I write and read; read and write. Two years ago I began on history; our own time . . . [I] branched out upon Political Economy and J. S. Mill. Mr. Mill's works, thoroughly studied, led me to the examination of philosophy and the great French thinkers of our own time; they in turn passed me over to others whose very names are now known only as terms of reproach by the vulgar; the monarchist Hobbes, the atheist Spinoza and so on."

The questions of law raised by the *Trent* case had sent him scurrying for enlightenment in still another direction. "I am deep in international law and political economy," he reported to Charles early in 1863, "dodging from the one to other." By May 1 he was once more afield. "So I jump from International Law to our foreign history, and am led by that to study the philosophic standing of our republic, which brings me to reflection over the advance of the democratic principle in European civilization, and so I go on till some new question of law starts me again on the circle."

The "unfinished writing" of these early years in England when he wrote to keep his hand in did not go wholly to waste. Among the salvageable materials were the notes for his article "The Declaration of Paris," which was finally published in his *Historical Essays* in 1891. The article dealt with the negotiation which had puzzled him in 1861 when the British Ministry suspected Seward of baiting a diplomatic trap. Interestingly enough, the final version of "The Declaration of Paris," thirty years after the event, loyally adhered to the debatable view that Seward had acted in perfect good faith.

One composition had an official character. This was a formal report which he made on the great Trades' Union Meeting held on March 27, 1863, at St. James's Hall. Charles Francis Adams sent his son to cover the meeting. The gathering, addressed by a number of Liberal leaders, including Henry's friend John Bright, showed that the laboring classes made "common cause" with the Americans for the restoration of the Union. "They go our whole platform," he wrote his brother, "and are full of the 'rights of man.'" Secretary Seward, to whom the minister sent the report, praised it as "a profound disquisition upon the import of the whole transaction."

Through his association with the friends of Thomas Hughes, Henry Adams became familiar with the political reform counterpart of the revolution in science. To his brother, he wrote of the aspirations of the reform movement. "You have no idea how thoughtful society is in Europe." In England the movement found expression during the closing years of his stay in such symposia as *Essays on Reform, Questions for a Reformed Parliament,* and *The Culture Demanded by Modern Life,* writings which embodied the progressive ideas discussed so often among his friends.

Amidst the uncertainties of his position in London, one thing at least was certain for Henry Adams: he must somehow fit himself for a role in American life. When he passed twenty-five he acknowledged that the pretense of ultimately returning to Boston to study law in the office of Judge Horace Gray was no longer tenable. To the secretary of his college class he still wrote that he should be called "a student of law"; but he was more forthright with his brother. "Can a man of my general appearance pass five years in Europe and remain a candidate for the bar? . . . We are both no longer able to protect ourselves with the convenient fiction of the law. Let us quit that now useless shelter, and steer if possible for whatever it may have been that once lay beyond it."

At first, when it had seemed improbable that he would remain in England more than a few years, he reverted to his old plan to settle in the West, ostensibly to practice law. The real objective, however, would be nothing less than the reformation of American society: "We want a national set of young men like ourselves or better, to start new influences not only in politics, but in literature, in law, in society, and throughout the whole social organism of the country. A national school of our own generation." With his eye on this grandiose scheme Adams was careful to "neglect no opportunities to conciliate" men like Evarts, Seward, and Weed. He would have liked to reach public figures further west, "but," as he put it, "the deuce is that there are so

few distinguished western men." His brother Charles also acknowledged the futility of holding to their youthful plan to use the law as a
stepping-stone to a joint career. More single-minded than Henry, the
young officer declared, "All my natural inclinations tend to a combination of literature and politics and always have. I would be a philosophical statesman if I could, and a literary politician if I must." In
the complexities of London life, Henry, torn between dreams of
power and the fear that those dreams would turn to "dust and ashes,"
found himself gravitating towards precisely the same objectives. One
factor perhaps more than any other delayed the employment of his
literary talents. He could have no plans so long as his course was
"tied to that of the Chief," and at frequent intervals he believed the
termination of the mission to be imminent.

A few days before the election of 1864 he surrendered to his habitual "infirmity" of doubting "at the wrong time" and proceeded to
canvass all the melancholy possibilities. "I am looking about with a
sort of vague curiosity for the current which is to direct my course
after I am blown aside by this one. If McClellan were elected, I do not
know what the deuce I should do . . . But if Lincoln is elected by a
mere majority of electors voting, not by a majority of the whole elec-
toral college; if Grant fails to drive Lee out of Richmond; if the Chief
is called to Washington to enter a cabinet with a species of anarchy in
the North and no probability of an end of the war—then, indeed, I
shall think the devil himself has got hold of us, and shall resign my
soul to the inevitable . . . My present impression is that we are in
considerable danger of all going to Hell together."

Greatly relieved by the reelection of Lincoln, he was ready to believe it the beginning of "a new era of the movement of the world"
and proof of "the capacity of men to develop their faculties in the
mass." Charles Wilson, the secretary of the legation, resigned during
the campaign and returned to America. Seward elevated Moran to
the vacant post and offered the latter's post to Henry Adams. He
promptly declined it: "All that I have seen here in the course of the
past three years has only strengthened my earlier belief that I should
not be acting in the best interests either of the service of the Minister,
or of myself, in accepting any official position in the Legation."

With the war winding down to a victorious close and negotiations
for peace already begun, the minister dispatched Henry to the Continent "as a sort of nurse" to the family. For six months they made a

"slow and stately march across Europe, never sleeping more than three nights in the same house" on the way to Nice. From Nice they journeyed on to Sorrento for a month's stay, then ventured down to Naples and Paestum before settling down in Rome for a month to recapture the delights of his previous visit. Traveling "in one's own carriage" he found "luxury itself." At Story's studio in the Barberini Palace General George McClellan, a "common, carrotty, vulgar-looking hero," was posing for his statue. Henry's mother was not an easy companion; homesick for London, she confessed, "I do not understand at my time of life the pleasures of traveling." News of Lincoln's assassination reached them in Rome. Adams thought Lincoln "rather to be envied in his death . . . I have already buried Mr Lincoln under the ruins of the Capitol, along with Caesar." Henry's father reported his pleasure at learning of his soldier son's engagement to marry and hinted that Henry's would be welcome. "You seem rather hurried to marry me off also," Henry replied, "but I don't find it convenient at present."

In the summer of 1865, the minister hopefully sent his resignation to Seward. Months went by with no sign of action. The likelihood of an early departure evaporated. Henry accepted his fate. "I have much doubt," he confided to Charles, "whether we shall be released next spring, as your papa pretends to expect . . . For my own part, I should not object. I am doing as much for myself here as I should be likely to do anywhere." Henry's long and close association with his father had the curious effect of deepening his sense of alienation. "I find the Chief rather harder, less a creature of our time, than ever," he told Charles. "It pains me absolutely . . . to see him so separate from the human race. I crave for what is new. I hanker after a new idea, in hopes it may solve some old difficulty. He cares nothing for it, and a new discovery in physics or in chemistry, or a new development in geology never seems to touch any chord in him, any more than if the sciences were in as subordinate position now as when the Puritans landed in Plymouth. He bases his world upon moral laws. I rank moral laws with all other laws, as matter for study, development and perhaps change. I am continually puzzled to know how we get along together."

IN NOVEMBER OF 1865 Colonel Charles Francis Adams, Jr., visited London on his wedding trip. What hardheaded advice Charles

gave his brother can easily be surmised. Though already worn thread-
bare by correspondence, their plans for a postwar career needed further working out. The weather-tanned veteran of a half-dozen campaigns, who towered above his younger brother, argued to good
effect. Reviewing the possibility of publishing some of the materials
which Henry had been working over in history and finance, they fixed
upon the two most promising items: a destructive criticism of the
Captain John Smith–Pocahontas legend and a study of British finance
at the close of the Napoleonic wars. For many months Charles had
been preaching that "the management of our finances now seems to
me not only the greatest but the most inviting field of usefulness
which this country affords." Charles proposed to make a simultaneous bid for fame by working up an exposé of American railroads.
When Charles Deane, editor of the recent edition of Captain John
Smith's *A True Relation of Virginia,* came to dine on July 10, 1866,
in the company of Harvard professor Andrew Peabody, Henry had
already begun his assignment.

Adams had first become interested in the question of Captain
Smith's veracity in the spring of 1861, as a result of a conversation
with John Gorham Palfrey, the eminent New England historian. Palfrey had questioned the truth of the Pocahontas story. In October
1861, reporting to Palfrey the results of his preliminary researches at
the British museum, Adams confessed that he was ready to "give it
up." Captain Smith seemed an honest man. Palfrey called upon the
expert knowledge of Charles Deane to set Adams right. Chastened,
the youthful historian went back to work, stimulated by the thought
that the "Virginia aristocracy . . . will be utterly gravelled by it if it is
successful." The "elaborate argument on the old pirate" was finished
late in 1862, but was laid aside as unpublishable by its author. After
the war Palfrey reopened the subject and Adams proposed to rewrite
the whole manuscript and use Deane's recent book as a convenient
"hook" on which to hang it.

An iconoclastic article on the subject might well create a sensation,
as Palfrey had suggested, and get its author talked about as a fearless
champion of truth in history. In the notes to his *A Discourse of Virginia* Deane had suggested that Smith's inaccuracy might be shown
by comparing the various accounts of his captivity, especially as they
referred to Pocahontas. Adams pointed up for his readers the sensational implications of what he had written. "There are powerful social interests, to say nothing of popular prejudices, greatly concerned

in maintaining [Captain John Smith's] credit even at the present day."
Having thus thrown down the gage of battle, he charged full tilt at
the patron saint of Virginia chivalry. With true Brahminic righteous-
ness he charged: "The statements of the *Generall Historie* ... are
falsehoods of an effrontery seldom equalled in modern times." The
article pleased Palfrey, and he undertook to place it in the *North
American Review.*

The exposé of Captain John Smith did create its sensation. Although it was unsigned, as was the practice at the moment, the identity of the author was soon common property. The *Nation* promptly
played up the sectional implications: "The name of Massachusetts
... will henceforth be more bitterly execrated than ever ..." In the
South, aspersion upon saintly Pocahontas was particularly resented.
The editor of the *Southern Review* denounced the "historians who
deal in hints, innuendos, and dark insinuations ... especially when
their oblique methods affect the character of a celebrated woman."
What more could be expected from "two knights of the New England
chivalry" who maliciously perverted history because Captain Smith
had "labored in a different latitude" and because Pocahontas had not
"been born on the barren soil of New England"?

Before dispatching the Captain Smith article to the *North American Review* Adams rewrote the manuscript of an article on British
governmental finance in 1816. It accompanied the Smith article. Editor Charles Norton accepted both manuscripts, printing the first in
the January 1867 issue, one month before Charles's first article on the
railroads, and the second in the April issue.

"British Finance in 1816" reviewed the economic difficulties with
which England had to struggle at the close of the Napoleonic wars.
Adams singled out for special attack the exactions of the protective
tariff, for he had long since been won over to free trade by Mill and
the two leaders of the Manchester school, Cobden and Bright. "Protection coiled like a tangled cord around and over and through every
portion of British finance ... Every petty interest of the country had
its rag of protection,—not merely against the genius or activity or
superior circumstances of a foreign rival, but against allied branches
of industry at home."

Adams then turned to the question of the currency as "another evil
which lay behind them all," but, as there was not space to develop all
the implications for America, he prepared the way for a succeeding

article by asserting that "the history of the process by which Great Britain succeeded at length in restoring its original standard of value . . . requires an entire chapter in itself." For the American reader who might overlook in his account of economic confusion a tract for the times, Adams alluded to the "interest which belongs to it of furnishing instruction to other nations which are placed in circumstances more or less similar." To the thoughtful reader his target was unmistakable: the Morrill Act of 1861, which established protective tariffs as national policy.

By February 1867 the second financial article, "The Bank of England Restriction of 1797," began to take form. It turned out to be "an elaborate and unexpectedly difficult essay," and the task dragged itself out, but by the end of June it was finished. The article made a detailed study, complete with statistical tables, of the British suspension of specie payments in 1797. Adams showed that the troublesome problems involved in the resumption in 1821 were unreal when evaluated in isolation. He argued that "the only effect of the long suspension was to breed a race of economists who attributed an entirely undue degree of power to mere currency." The burden of the article was that no proper comparison could be drawn between the British and the present American experience, because "whatever action may have been caused by the Restriction was upon credit in the first place, and not upon the currency." He could thus reassure the banking interests in the United States that the redemption of the Civil War "greenbacks" in gold might be attempted immediately without precipitating the evil feared by the debtor classes.

Having published three weighty articles in the leading American quarterly, Adams would have been justified in congratulating himself as a coming writer. But the habitual self-depreciation which was the obverse of his desire for fame soon made itself felt. Though he had made an enviable beginning as a publicist, the effort exhausted his nervous energy, and he was swept with a sense of revulsion. Into a bewildering letter to Charles he tumbled all of his dissatisfaction. "The triumph of earning $240 in paper in one year does not satisfy my ambition. John is a political genius; let him follow the family bent. You are a lawyer, and with a few years' patience will be the richest and the most respectable of us all. I claim my right to part company with you both. I never will make a speech, never run for an office, never belong to a party. I am going to plunge under the stream. For

years you will hear nothing of any publication of mine—perhaps
never, who knows. I do not mean to tie myself to anything, but I do
mean to make it impossible for myself to follow the family go-cart."

Still stranger moods took possession of him, as when he suggested
to Charles Milnes Gaskell that they stir up each other's acquaintances
to say ill-natured things about each other. "I would do anything to
experience new sensations, even disagreeable ones, and a good, spite-
ful, vicious attack is such a tonic!" In spite of these vagaries he did
not lose sight of his plan of "practical training" for a career as a
journalist. In April 1867 he asked his brother to subscribe to the
newly founded *Nation* and to send out to him anything that appeared
worth noticing in American literature.

His energetic reconnaissance in the fields of history and finance
completed, Henry was now ready to develop a suggestion made to
him by Sir Charles Lyell. Early in 1867 Lyell had happened to discuss
with him the possibility of getting the recently published tenth edition
of his *Principles of Geology* "properly noticed" in America. Adams
brashly volunteered to do the job himself. Really serious application
had to wait until "The Bank of England Restriction of 1797" was out
of the way. Then in August 1867 he went off with his ailing mother
for two months to the "cure" at Baden-Baden in his recurring role of
"dry nurse" to the family.

He sent a cautiously submissive prospectus to Norton declaring
that, since he was unsure of Norton's and coeditor Lowell's views on
the subject, "I would rather run no risk of offering to you anything
which might seem not conservative enough for your united tastes.
Therefore if you are afraid of Sir Charles and Darwin, and prefer to
adhere frankly to Mr Agassiz, you have but to say so, and I am dumb.
My own leaning, though not strong, is still towards them . . . It is not
likely that I should handle the controversy vigorously . . . but I should
have to touch it." As his father's resignation was at last accepted, the
imminence of departure for America discouraged any further work.
Not until he returned to Quincy did he again take up the formidable
task, finally completing the paper late in August 1868, a year and a
half after he had undertaken the assignment.

The long review appeared in the October *North American Review*
above the signature of "Henry Brooks Adams" and thus avowedly
for "reputation." It had for company articles by Leslie Stephen and

Henry James. Adams's treatment of the antagonists—Lyell and Agassiz—indicates that at heart he was on the conservative side.

He limited himself to a consideration of "some of the most striking changes of view, which make the tenth edition almost a new book." These included, first, Lyell's explanation of the operation of the climatic element in geology; and second, his acceptance, through Darwin, of "the theory of progressive development of species." To explain the variation in climate between "Miocene warmth and glacial frost," Lyell argued that there had occurred an oscillation in the distribution of land masses about the poles and the equator. Adams objected to this explanation with such penetrating insight that the questioned chapters were later recast.

He next examined Darwin's "arguments in regard to the variability of species," which he said had led "Sir Charles Lyell . . . to adopt opinions which many excellent men consider revolting." He went on to say that a "more tangible objection than this repulsiveness" is that Darwin had, "after all, announced only a theory, supported, it is true, by the greatest ingenuity of reasoning and fertility of experiment, but in its nature incapable of proof." Lyell's reluctance to be swept off his feet by Agassiz's glacial theory was for Adams a cause of reproach. "We have already mentioned the unwillingness shown by Lyell to accept the doctrine of great [i.e., catastrophic] climatic changes, when Professor Agassiz, stepping so boldly out of his own strict sphere of science, forced upon geology his celebrated glacial theory." He felt Lyell's "geographical theory does not have quite so large and liberal a character as we might wish." The indulgent Lyell wrote Adams "a very handsome letter" in which he described the article as "the most original he had yet seen on his new edition, and the only one which has called due attention to what is new in it." The *Nation* gave him a reassuring pat on the back, declaring that the author of the review "talks learnedly and, to our mind, sensibly." Norton paid him $100 for it.

With this article Adams's position as a regular contributor to the *North American Review* was assured. He had faithfully followed his father's precept and example and had not wasted his talent in the sort of light literature cultivated by the *Atlantic Monthly*. He had demonstrated a respectable ability in dealing with problems of history, finance, and science. In a sense he had passed his self-imposed examination for the job of "philosophical statesman." But the troubling question remained, Would it pay? There was not much money in such writing, even if it should lead to a New York newspaper.

AS THE END of his father's mission approached and Henry's duties as secretary diminished, he was able to depart for the Continent early in January 1868 for what he hoped would be "a grand, final, drunken blowout." His father did not approve and hated to see him leave: it was "far more depressing to the spirits than anything I have experienced for a long time." The "blowout" came a cropper, since both his intimates, Gaskell and Cunliffe, had to beg off at the last moment. Henry went on alone to amuse himself as a sight-seeing tourist as best he could. He joined Louisa and her husband at their winter residence in Florence and passed some evenings with them at elegant dances.

He got back to the legation in early March to resume taking his father's dictation, in his flawless script, of a continuous stream of official letters. His father's principal chore was to use his influence with Lord Stanley to obtain the release and deportation of the Irish-Americans involved in the Fenian criminal trials in Dublin. Although the mission was to terminate officially on April 1, Charles Francis Adams agreed to stay on until the question of his successor was settled. It was not until May 13 that he was able to present his letter of recall to the Queen. His successor, Reverdy Johnson, was not in fact confirmed until June 13.

The routine business of the legation was turned over to Benjamin Moran, and the minister set off at last on an abbreviated tour of Europe with his family. Henry, left to wind up his own affairs, got over to Paris for a last visit. The theater disappointed him. "Eight years ago the women on the stage here were the freshest young girls in life. And now they are coarse and big." He professed to be passing "my days and nights in my room geologising." Back in London by mid-May, he gave himself up to the bittersweet pleasures of leave-taking. He luxuriated in the "charming rooms" of Sir Robert Cunliffe in Pouncey's Private Hotel in Cavendish Square with free access to Cunliffe's wine cellar. There was also a last comradely call on Gaskell at Wenlock Abbey.

The minister and the rest of the family returned late in June to the monumental task of filling up trunks and packing books. Instead of sailing from Liverpool, where he would have had to give a speech at an "entertainment," he took the family to Chester to enjoy a last visit to the picturesque city, crossed to Dublin, and then proceeded to the port of Queenstown (Cobh) by train, thus also sparing Abigail a day's inevitable seasickness on the open Atlantic. Henry, who had remained behind in London, joined the family at Queenstown. John Lothrop Motley, who had resigned his post as minister to Austria, had already arrived there with his family. On Sunday, June 28, 1868, they all boarded the Cunarder *China* for the westward passage home.

5

A Young Reformer of Thirty

THE ARRIVAL of the two returning dignitaries at New York on July 7 turned out to be a disillusioning anticlimax after the many friendly tributes abroad. A revenue cutter was sent out to take them and their families off the *China* in a driving rainstorm. All got soaked. Having received no word of welcome from ashore, they tried first to find rooms in Jersey City and, failing that, returned to the cutter and proceeded to a New York pier, where Henry and Motley went in search of carriages. Hopefully, they drove to the Brevoort House and were relieved to find that John and Charles, who had not known where to meet them, had reserved sufficient rooms. The Boston delegation which should have welcomed them at the Cunard pier had not yet arrived. After a festive meal at the Brevoort the voyagers gratefully sought rest. In his diary that night Henry's father was moved to exclaim, "What a reception of us after our long term of service abroad!" They all sailed for Boston the following day.

The Adams family came back to confront a changed political situation. The radical Republicans were in full control and were determined to subjugate the South. Only a few weeks earlier John Quincy II, the family's eldest son, who held to the family's moderate principles on Reconstruction, had received the dubious compliment at the Democratic convention of being proposed as a candidate for the Vice-Presidency. Though he declined the honor, his earlier support of President Andrew Johnson's moderate policies was taken as an official act of the family, and the *Boston Daily Advertiser* demanded ostracism. The first blow had fallen early in 1867, when the Senate rejected the appointment of John Quincy II to the Boston Customs House. Senator Sumner's bill to outlaw court dress for American diplomats was an obvious thrust at the unreconstructed minister. The quarrel with

Sumner had not been patched up as Henry had hoped. Sumner did not join in the celebration to honor the return of Minister Adams, and an obliging friend cheered him with a report that "the hall was only half full."

The election that carried Grant to the presidency also saw Sumner returned to the Senate to continue his leadership of the vindictive majority. The Adamses did not believe, however, that the main fight was lost, for they all shared faith in General Grant. Shortly after Grant's election Seward loyally urged that Charles Francis Adams should succeed him as Secretary of State. Secretary of the Navy Gideon Welles jotted in his diary: "Sumner is much disturbed with this rumor." Henry, believing that the "first Cabinet will be a failure," disliked the scheme. The move collapsed, and Henry and Charles Sumner were both greatly relieved, though for quite different reasons. The faithful *New York Times* lamented, "It is among the most prominent infelicities of our practical politics, that Mr. Adams was set aside."

This, then, was the political situation of the family when Henry Adams left Boston for Washington in October 1868, at the age of thirty, to "try his future," his father recorded, "as a writer on public questions of a higher class. He has been to me a most invaluable assistant during my eight years of purgatory in public life. Wisdom, discretion and punctual performance of all details were all that could be desired. While I find no fault with his decision I shall miss him every day and every hour of the rest of my life as a companion and friend. Nobody has known so much of me as he." While in New York, en route to the capital, Henry made arrangements to write for the *Nation* and the New York *Evening Post*. In the midst of his journey he was joined by William Evarts, the new United States attorney general.

Reaching Washington on October 22, he was taken in tow by Evarts, who presented him to Andrew Johnson. The President, "grave and cordial," gave him "a little lecture on Constitutional law." Seward "was also cordial," and before long Adams was in the good graces of Secretary of the Treasury Hugh McCulloch and Secretary of War John Schofield. In November he wrote Gaskell, "The great step is taken and here I am, settled for years, and perhaps for life."

While waiting for the Fortieth Congress to reconvene on December 7, he began to study the subject which he had made his specialty in England—government finance in all of its ramifications. Southern re-

construction still bulked large on the political horizon, but it promised no career for a person of his antiradical views. The Thirteenth
and Fourteenth Amendments had already been ratified. If the recent
impeachment trial of Andrew Johnson taught anything, it taught that
congressional reconstruction must run its course.

For textbooks in finance he used Secretary McCulloch's *Annual
Reports* and the brilliant compilations of David A. Wells, the special
commissioner of the revenue. Wells saw in Adams a chance to train a
fellow schoolmaster. His new report on the revenue delighted Adams.
"I needed it," he wrote Wells. "This report of yours is the first states-
manlike expression of policy I have seen." He had already sounded
out Henry Reeve, editor of the *Edinburgh Review,* on the marketabil-
ity of an article on American finance. His coworker Charles was already well along on his railroad series, having completed his first exposé of the Erie Railroad management. Now he was busy with an
article on railroad inflation.

Not having Charles's Boston leisure or single-mindedness, Henry
proceeded more slowly with his article. The opening of Congress
brought to Washington not only legislators but also a swarm of news-
papermen and lobbyists. From the beginning he attached himself to
militant critics like Charles Nordhoff, the correspondent of the New
York *Evening Post;* Murat Halstead, editor of the *Cincinnati Commercial;* Henry Watterson, editor of the Louisville *Courier-Journal;*
and the unquenchable Sam Bowles, editor of the *Springfield Republican.* He also formed close ties with Wells's able collaborator, Francis
A. Walker, chief of the Bureau of Statistics. This coterie of "working
practical reformers," as the *Nation* called them, made itself felt in
Congress, chiefly through Representatives James A. Garfield and
Thomas Jenckes. When, for example, Representative Benjamin Butler
spoke in favor of greenbacks, Henry informed his brother, "Garfield,
Wells, Walker and I have held his inquest, and Garfield will score him
in the House."

His first contribution to the crusading *Nation,* a report on the Legal Tender Cases, grew out of his friendship with Attorney General
Evarts. In prolonged conversations with Evarts during November
1868, he talked as devil's advocate against the constitutionality of the
wartime greenback bill. The cases came before the Supreme Court for
hearing on December 8, with Evarts and Benjamin Curtis on the government's side in support of the constitutionality of the act. "After

listening for three entire days to the arguments," Adams hurried off his appraisal of the trial to the *Nation*, which published it on December 17. As a hard money man and a strict constructionist, he expressed "a certain feeling of disappointment" at the weakness displayed by the government's opponents. To counter that bad impression he went ahead himself to attack the positions maintained by Evarts and Curtis.

Evarts bore the attack good-naturedly, and his opinionated young friend continued to be a welcome guest at his house. Here, in December 1868, Adams met Moorfield Storey, then twenty-three, who had come to Washington as Sumner's private secretary. Storey afterwards recorded the encounter: "Calling there one evening shortly after I reached Washington, I found a strange young man there who was monopolizing the conversation, as it seemed to me, and laying down the law with a certain assumption. I took quite a prejudice against him during this brief acquaintance, but the next day I met him in the street and he was so charming and his voice was so pleasant that my prejudice vanished, and we formed a friendship which was long lasting." One of the fruits of that friendship seems to have been Henry's resumption of friendly relations with Charles Sumner. At occasional dinners at Sumner's home Henry gave full rein to his passion for argument. Storey, though a half-dozen years his junior, was his match in violence of expression. "He would drop in and get into a fight with me," Storey recalled, "and we two would be so ill-mannered as to monopolize the whole conversation." Adams long afterwards remembered his combative friend as "a dangerous example of frivolity."

The collaboration which Henry and his brother had so often planned now began in earnest. A constant stream of letters passed between Washington and Boston, and Henry's schemes revolved in his head "like rotten maggots." Each week Henry also reported to his father on the state of affairs. As Charles kept "incessantly" after him for "documents, especially about railway matters and nice bits of corruption," Henry besought Congressman Garfield to provide him with "rubbish enough to occupy his too active digestion." Charles had already allied himself with a number of the reform groups, including the American Association of Social Science, of which he was now treasurer, and was becoming widely known in reform circles.

Their letters bubbled with all manner of comment and report, reverent and irreverent, occasionally laced with masculine crudity:

"Take care of the liver," Henry advised the temporarily ailing Charles, "and the balls will take care of themselves." To anticipate Charles's admonitions, Henry teased, "I shall be pleased to have you kick my tail whenever you see the necessity." Henry did not care for the new administration as it was shaping up, but he felt confident he could "get on without it." However, his activities as a lobbyist and anonymous newspaper correspondent did not satisfy his sanguine hopes. "I want to be advertised and the easiest way is to do something obnoxious and to do it well . . . I can work up an article on 'rings' which, if *published in England,* would I think create excitement and react through political feeling on America in such a way as to cover me with odium. Wells says, don't disgrace us abroad. I say: Rot! . . . No home publication will act on America like foreign opinion." A few days' reflection on this project opened up new vistas of sensationalism. "I can't do my 'Rings' in short time. I am going to make it monumental, a piece of history and a blow at democracy."

Henry worked hard at his writing, so that when he wrote to Reeve on February 1 he enclosed the completed manuscript of "American Finance, 1865–1869." The editor ran it in the *Edinburgh Review* for April 1869, declaring, as Henry boasted to Charles, that it was "the best article on American affairs ever printed in an English periodical." Henry added, "I hope it will make me unpopular. Q.E.D."

His panoramic view of American politics gave as grim a view of the subject as a Mathew Brady photograph of a littered battlefield. In his succeeding articles he would do little more than deepen a shadow here and sharpen a highlight there, and each would be developed in the brimstone of his rhetoric. Grant was about to take office. Adams attempted to advise him and the new Congress. In every department of government reform was desperately needed. The leaders of Congress embraced "the wildest financial theories," in defiance of the laws of economics, and Congress betrayed its pledge to the Treasury by failing to order the resumption of specie payments. Bad as the currency system was, he said, the tax system was even worse. "The fact was no longer to be disguised that the whole revenue system was a mass of corruption, intolerable even in America where public opinion tolerates abuses such as would excite in England a revolution." The tariff system, resting as it did on fraud and corruption, was a mass of inequities, the whole tendency of which, as Wells's statistics showed, was to hasten the process by which the rich were getting richer and the poor poorer.

Contrary to Adams's expectations, the article seemed to infuriate no one in America, and in England Charles Milnes Gaskell ran across only one review of it, in a Yorkshire paper. Adams saw the face of his chiefest enemy: apathy; but he was not yet disheartened. Some of the winter's notes overflowed into another article, "The Session," written shortly after Grant's inauguration. He rushed it off to Professor Ephraim Gurney, now chief editor of the *North American Review*, after adding the final touches in a burst of industriousness for "ten hours a day for four days, and politics on top of it."

Its opening sentences dramatically pictured the congressional gauntlet which all legislation had to run: "Within the walls of two rooms are forced together in close contact the jealousies of thirty-five millions of people,—jealousies between individuals, between cliques, between industries, between parties, between branches of the Government, between sections of the country, between the nation and its neighbors. As years pass on, the noise and confusion, the vehemence of this scramble for power or for plunder, the shouting of the reckless adventurers, of wearied partisans, and of red-hot zealots in new issues,—the boiling and bubbling of this witches' caldron, into which we have thrown eye of newt and toe of frog and all the venomous ingredients of corruption, and from which is expected to issue the future and more perfect republic,—in short the conflict and riot of interests, grow more and more overwhelming."

"Reform must come quickly," he wrote. "Perhaps not more than one member in ten of the late Congress ever accepted money," yet this criminal element held the balance of power, and the spoils system fostered this criminality. The lesson to be drawn from the past ten years of "incessant confessions" of ignorance, impotence, and even imbecility was that the administration must adopt a coherent scheme of reform for the entire government.

His friend Sam Bowles wrote in the *Springfield Republican*: "Among the officers of the new 'Reform League' at Boston may be found the names of three Adamses—all sons of the late Minister to England, and great-grandsons of the second president of the United States. Two of these names are well known to the people of the country, both in the present and the past generations,—John Quincy Adams and Charles Francis Adams. But the third—Henry Brooks Adams—designates a young gentleman who has quite as good a chance of becoming prominent in the future politics of the country as either of his brothers, although he is yet but little known . . . He had

the reputation of being one of the three best dancers in the capital . . .
The fruit of his winter's studies in Washington now appears in the
April *North American*—a long and brilliant paper on 'The Session,'
in which, with some conceit and some pedantry, but with more ability
than either, he reviews the doings and omissions of the last session of
the Fortieth Congress."

The delicious taste of fame, fame earned by his own effort, gave
Adams fresh confidence. Enclosing the editorial in a letter to Gaskell,
he exulted, "For once I have smashed things generally and really ex-
ercised a distinct influence on public opinion . . . But you see I am
posed as a sort of American Pelham or Vivian Gray." The sequel, he
said, was a sufficiently curious illustration of journalism. "This leader
was condensed into a single paragraph . . . and copied . . . all over the
country. In this form it came back to New York . . . compressed to
two lines. 'H. B. A. is the author of article etc., etc., etc. He is one of
the three best dancers in W.' "

Advertisement could not confer power overnight, however, and
Adams's influence in the cabinet rapidly deteriorated after the inauguration of Grant. Brilliant David A. Wells was passed over in favor
of unimaginative George S. Boutwell for the Treasury. Adams could
still count on sympathy from Jacob D. Cox in the Interior and from
Attorney General Ebenezer Rockwood Hoar, but these friends of reform had only a precarious hold on Grant's confidence. By March 11
his disillusionment was complete. "It's the old game with fresh cards."

Washington became almost pleasantly deserted when the Fortieth
Congress adjourned. Adams lingered on until the end of June, much
recovered after the recurring fits of wretchedness imposed by his "disordered liver," but spring found him "thin and bearded and very—
very bald."

Henry's loitering displeased the more dynamic Charles, and
Charles read him his customary lecture. Sick of being pushed, Henry
fought back: "I see you are getting back to your old dispute with me
on the purpose of life . . . I will not go down into the rough-and-
tumble, nor mix with the crowd, nor write anonymously, except for
mere literary practice . . . You like the strife of the world. I detest it
and despise it. You work for power. I work for my own satisfaction.
You like roughness and strength; I like taste and dexterity. For God's
sake let us go our ways and not try to be like each other." He knew
that he had committed his forces. Yet he had no clear idea of what he

really wanted; "certainly not office, for except very high office I would take none. What then? I wish someone would tell me." Like his President forebears, Henry hoped to be summoned to a merited destiny and not to be obliged to seek it. He had reminded Charles only a short time earlier, in May 1869, "High appreciation of ourselves was always a strong point in our family, though I protest by Heaven that my conceit is not due to admiration of myself but to contempt for everyone else."

As Wells and Garfield were still in town, he invited them up to Quincy for a council of war, sending word on to Charles, "We will have [Edward] Atkinson too, and Greenough, and cut out our work." Garfield, pleased to make the pilgrimage to Quincy, sent home a glowing account of his hosts, among whom he described Henry, "rapidly rising as a clear and powerful thinker and writer." Though Henry belittled these Quincy conferences as "humbug," they nonetheless fixed the direction of his work. He proceeded to salvage materials left over from his two April "firecrackers." At the end of August, "after near three months of hard labor," he was "accouché of another ponderous article . . . bitter and abusive of the Administration," which upon publication in the October 1869 *North American Review* he planned to distribute as a pamphlet to the members of Congress; its title was "Civil Service Reform."

In essence, the article was an extension of remarks to the April "Session." At the heart of the federal system was the principle of the due separation of powers. Grant's troubles stemmed from the neglect of that principle. Now that the Republicans had "shut the door to reform" by surrendering to the senatorial system of appointments, it would be necessary for the people "to act outside of all party organizations." With "a sympathetic public behind him" ready to discipline the Senate, Grant could himself reform the civil service. Unfortunately for Adams's expectations, the pamphlet expired in a web of silence. No allusion to its prophetic thunders occurred in the course of the long debates on the civil service bills.

Henry stayed on in Quincy until about the end of October, "reading Gibbon and wasting time" while waiting for the Forty-first Congress to convene. Amid the ancestral surroundings he grew more and more restless; he found life to be "on too small a scale for man to sustain it without idiocy." Even though he wrote that "my two brothers and I are up to the ears in politics and public affairs," he still felt the want of "excitement." For the third time his eldest brother was running for the governorship on the Democratic ticket; but the preceding two defeats had engendered a certain degree of stoical resignation in the family.

Relief was in sight, however, for on Black Friday, September 24, 1869, an attempted corner of the gold bullion market had crashed spectacularly about the ears of certain gentlemen of the Erie Railroad, opening up for the Adams brothers the exploitation of a new vein of knavery. Charles had already published two articles on the intricate depredations of the Erie Railroad and could direct his brother to the most savory sources. Henry proceeded to New York and there dined at Samuel Barlow's with William Evarts, now ex–Attorney General. Barlow, who was also counsel for James McHenry, one of the more imaginative railroad financiers, "told some instructive stories about Erie, Atlantic and Great Western, etc." Equally instructive was his remark that Jay Gould and Judge George C. Barnard "had expressed the intention of taking hold" of Charles Adams if he ever came to New York. In New York Henry saw "many editors; some thieves; and many more fools," one of the "thieves" being James Fisk himself.

He reached Washington on November 1 eager to put his hands again on the levers of power, the lurid scenes of "The Gold Conspiracy" already shaping up in his mind. He sketched out the drama in a letter to Reeve of the *Edinburgh Review,* expecting an instant acceptance. Nothing happened. Irritated by several weeks of silence, he damned him as "that animal Reeve" and asked Francis Turner Palgrave to take the offer of the article to the *Quarterly Review.* He promised Gaskell, "I will make my article SUPERB to disgust Reeve." On December 13, shortly after Congress met, Garfield, as chairman of the House Committee on Currency and Banking, was directed to investigate the New York gold panic of September 24, 1869. With an official investigation under way, Henry would now have to possess his soul in patience until the report should be ready, but he could console himself that no other writer was more strategically placed.

There was much to do in Washington. He now threw himself with intense energy into his journalistic work, contributing "about two articles a month to the *Nation.*" His friend General Adam Badeau, with whom he maintained a joint establishment for a time, presented him at the White House, where he found the President and Mrs. Grant so ill at ease that "it was I who showed them how they ought to behave." To economize his energies he never dined with anyone unless there was "something to be gained" and soon felt that he was wound up "in a coil of political intrigue and getting the reputation of a regular conspirator."

The first of the *Nation* series was "Men and Things in Washington." Assuming the guise of a foreign diplomat in Washington, Adams made a devastating survey of Washington society. "There is no art, no music, no park, no drive, no club ... The worst annoyance of all is that society itself exists only in disjointed fragments, and that there is no established centre of intelligence and social activity."

His highly individual style also colors "A Peep into Cabinet Windows." Its opening paragraph gives an early version of his favorite allusion to *Candide*. "The liberal reformer's idea of an administration after his own heart would no doubt at the outset assume, like Voltaire's satire and Presidents' messages, that in this best of all possible worlds this nation is the best of possible nations, and by consequence this Administration the best of all administrations, past or to come." The satire of the administration was squeezed through a labyrinth of subtleties.

The rejection by the Senate of his friend Hoar's nomination to the Supreme Court called forth the mordant contempt of his next dispatch, in which he lashed out at the "cabal" made up of the "dregs of the Senate Chamber," who struck "not so much at the possible judge as at the actual Attorney-General." On January 27 "A Political Nuisance" pounded Sumner and the arrogant senatorial supporters of the harsh "Reconstruction Acts."

Adams's journalistic activities extended also to William Cullen Bryant's New York *Evening Post* and to at least one other New York paper, possibly Manton Marble's *World,* which was especially friendly since John Quincy's conversion to the Democratic party. One of his gadfly attacks provoked a highly visible response. Dennis McCarthy of New York, a "high tariff" member of the Ways and Means Committee, brought up on the floor of the House Adams's unsigned editorial in the *Post* accusing him of corruption. Adams had written, "He had done his work with success. His single vote had saved salt from interference in committee ... Besides protecting his own especial preserve he has found time to watch tenderly over every other monopoly." In an irate speech that occupied a column and a half of the *Congressional Globe,* McCarthy rejected the backhanded compliment as paid "with malicious intent."

In spite of pressure upon him by members of Wells's circle, Adams managed to write one long article for his standby, the *North American Review,* taking the assignment to relieve his friend Francis Walker. In 1869, when Elbridge Spaulding brought out his *History of the Legal Tender Paper Money Issued during the Great Rebellion,* Adams, acting for editor Gurney, got Walker's promise to upset Spaulding's thesis that the act had been necessary. Before Walker could finish his article, the Supreme Court, on February 7, 1870, in the four-to-three decision of *Hepburn vs. Griswold* declared the Legal Tender Act unconstitutional. Walker, who had just been made superintendent of the Census, turned over his notes to Adams. To protect the new Census superintendent from reprisal, Adams signed himself as the sole author of "The Legal Tender Act" when it came out in the April *North American Review.*

The article may have profited from the hand of Walker, but its "impudent political abuse" was unmistakable Adams. Spaulding, who had acquired his financial education by "shaving notes at a country bank," had rejected as discreditable "the simple proposal" made by the New York bankers "that the government should sell its bonds in the open market for what they would bring." This "response," said Adams, "contains the most extraordinary revelation of ignorance and folly that has been offered in a century past by a principal legislator for a great nation." Spaulding "perverted legislation into an instrument of fraud, and is proud of it."

Spaulding circulated a letter to the press denying that he had claimed credit for forcing the Legal Tender Act through Congress. Adams riposted in a long contemptuous letter in the *Nation:* "What the *North American Review* meant to protest against was his notion that a public man may be permitted to receive credit for the authorship of a dishonest measure." The editor of the *Nation* enjoyed the exchange of incivilities, for, he said, Henry's article recalled to him Rufus Choate's allusion to old John Quincy Adams's "peculiar powers as an assailant . . . an instinct for the jugular and carotid artery as unerring as that of any carnivorous animal." Adams's victory was purely rhetorical. In 1871 the Supreme Court, packed by Grant with two more members, reversed itself and held the act constitutional.

GARFIELD BROUGHT OUT his report on the gold panic on March 1, 1870, but most of the findings about the attempted corner of gold bullion were already known to Henry Adams, who had been active "pulling wires." With the mass of testimony before him, he was now ready to begin on "The New York Gold Conspiracy." Knowing that the article would contain "a good deal of libellous language" which he did not dare publish in the United States, he sought English publication.

As usual the writing was incessantly interrupted by his activities as a lobbyist. Early in April, after having helped organize "our forces" as "lieutenant" for Wells, he was pitched into "the middle of a battle over revenue reform, free trade, and what not." In pursuit of the plan to form a new party on these issues, he entertained about a dozen of the leaders in his rooms. They effected "a close alliance" and agreed to "hold a secret but weighty political caucus on the 18th to which our friends—the small number of high panjandrums—from all quarters, are to come." As he dramatically reported to Gaskell, "The world was staked out to each of us and the fulness thereof, and the foundations of Hell were shaken." How he worked his claim is suggested by a letter of May 12 to Congressman Garfield: "Will you see [Carl] Schurz and urge him to introduce your Civil Service Resolution into the Senate as a joint Resolution? Don't let him know that I suggested it, as he might not like my interference."

Completed toward the end of April, the "Gold Conspiracy" was packed off to Francis Palgrave with the expectation it would appear in the *Quarterly Review.* Adams's threat to make the article "superb" succeeded, but the success was again more literary than political. Try as he might, the reformer lost himself in the literary historian as he explored the "curious and melodramatic" aspects of the story. "It is worth while," he explained, "for the public to see how dramatic and artistically admirable a conspiracy in real life may be, when slowly elaborated from the subtle mind of a clever intriguer, and carried into execution by a band of unshrinking scoundrels."

Adams was quite right in surmising that his characterizations of the two chief protagonists were libelous. There "was a reminiscence of the spider" in Jay Gould's nature. He had "not a conception of a moral principle" and "was an uncommonly fine and unscrupulous intriguer." His fellow conspirator "James Fisk was still more original in character. He was not yet forty years of age, and had the instincts of fourteen." His offices adjoined the opera house "and as the opera itself supplied Mr. Fisk's mind with amusement, so the opera troupe supplied him with a permanent harem."

Briefly, the conspiracy which Adams unraveled took the following course. Gould, who was president of the Erie Railroad, conceived the Napoleonic scheme of cornering the market in gold bullion, whose price was regularly quoted in paper greenbacks. Gould, Fisk, and their agents began stealthily to buy gold to create a runaway bull market. They enlisted President Grant's venal brother-in-law Abel Corbin, believing he could influence Grant not to intervene. By the morning of Black Friday the price of gold bullion had gone up to $145 in greenbacks. Fisk flooded the market with buying orders, thinking to wipe out the short interests, and the price rose to $165. Gould, however, had discovered that Corbin was without influence and that Grant was bound to intervene. He secretly unloaded his holdings of gold as the price surged upwards. Before the day was out Grant belatedly ordered the Treasury to sell $4 million in gold. The price of gold plunged to $135 amidst the wildest disorder. The investigating committee concluded that Gould had "determined to betray his own associates," and Adams accepted this interpretation. It was passing strange, however, that the bankruptcy of the Erie's brokers did not touch Fisk. Whether Gould or Fisk actually lost or gained in the complicated venture remains unknown.

As Adams knew that it was Garfield's private opinion that the trail of scandal "led into the parlor of the President," his narrative carried a strong imputation against Grant's probity. Once the author was discovered he must thereafter count on the President's personal hostility. Adams's conclusion paralleled his brother's that the financial manipulators had introduced "Caesarism into corporate life." "The belief is common in America that the day is at hand when corporations far greater than the Erie—swaying power such as has never in the world's history been trusted in the hands of mere private citizens, controlled by single men like Vanderbilt, or by combinations of men like Fisk, Gould, and Lane . . . will ultimately succeed in directing government itself."

With the sulphurous manuscript safely on its way to England, Adams took up his self-imposed chore of writing the epitaph of the first session of the Forty-first Congress for the July *North American*. The "Session" of 1870, like that of 1869, assailed the shortcomings of the political system. The war had abrogated the Constitution, but with Grant the opportunity had come to restore to working order the intricate system of checks and balances. Grant had disappointed the expectations of the people because his "personal notions of civil government were crude" and "his ideas of political economy were those of a feudal monarch a thousand years ago." But most disastrous in Adams's eyes was his packing of the Supreme Court after the February decision in *Hepburn vs. Griswold*.

The mood was that of disenchantment; and the reverberations from Burke and Gibbon and Carlyle rang through the carefully wrought sentences. The *Nation* called it "the most widely attractive article in the *North American Review*," though the tone of some of it was "too unmitigatedly and severely fault-finding and critical." Senator Timothy Howe of Wisconsin considered Adams's effort the first broadside against the Republican party in the campaign of 1870, and with reason, for the article had been released to the Democratic party press in advance of publication as a party pamphlet. Matching gibe for gibe, Howe sneered in his elaborate reply, "The author is proclaimed to be not only a statesman himself but to belong to a family in which statesmanship is preserved by propagation—something as color in the leaf of the Begonia, perpetuating resemblance through perpetual change. The author has a talent for description and a genius for invention. He might succeed as a novelist. He must fail as a historian."

Adams was now more than ready for an English holiday. Amidst the social shortcomings of Washington and Quincy he yearned for his English friends and the amenities of British life. Six months after he had left London he had begun to plan a return visit. He reached England about the first of June for his rendezvous with Gaskell, but in a few weeks his vacation was suddenly cut short by news of his sister Louisa's dangerous illness after a carriage accident at Bagni di Lucca. He hurried off to Italy, reaching his sister's bedside on July 1. At first he felt himself "a wretched coward" when he saw the symptoms of acute tetanus, but Louisa's extraordinary courage and good humor soon communicated themselves to him and he was able to describe to Gaskell with gruesome vividness the mixed horror and gaiety of the sickroom. On July 13, however, he wrote, "It is all over. My poor sister died this morning." The tragedy spoiled his appetite for any kind of merriment, and he made his way back to England in a subdued mood. The impression of Nature's brutal indifference would never leave him.

Passing through Paris late in July a week after the declaration of war against Prussia, he bitterly reflected that the war put "an end everywhere to any chance of carrying out a regular course of politics." Disgusted by Europe's imperviousness to "what we call progress," he wished that both nations could be simultaneously beaten. In England he hunted up some of "the political people still in London" for talk on politics and to determine the fate of his "Gold Conspiracy." The *Quarterly Review* had turned it down. Finally, "as a last experiment" he sent it to the *Westminster Review* just before his departure for America on September 3. It came out in October 1870.

The summer was to be memorable for an even more significant train of events. Henry Adams had had a slight hint of what was afoot in the preceding April when Professor Ephraim Gurney, recently elevated to the post of dean of the faculty at Harvard, offered him the editorship of the *North American*. Not wishing to exile himself from Washington, he had declined the offer, though he stood ready to act as "official editor for politics." A few days after his arrival at Bagni di Lucca he received two letters which had pursued him across Europe. They were from Charles W. Eliot, the new president of Harvard College, and they offered him a post as assistant professor of history. With no family council to urge prudence upon him, he turned down the offer.

When Adams disembarked at Boston he little suspected that his rejection of Eliot's offer had not been taken as final. He wrote Gaskell, "Not only the President of the College and the Dean made a very strong personal appeal to me, but my brothers were earnest about it and my father leaned the same way. I hesitated a week, and then I yielded. Now I am, I believe, assistant professor of History at Harvard College with a salary of £400 [$2,000] a year, and two hundred students, the oldest in the college, to whom I am to teach mediaeval history, of which, as you are aware, I am utterly and grossly ignorant." One of the conditions of the five-year contract was that Henry would relieve Gurney of the *North American Review* and become its "avowed editor." His total income would now amount to about $6,000. At least he would be comfortable while he rode out the storm which Grant had raised in Washington.

In his inaugural address Eliot had demanded that history should be taught "by teachers of active, comprehensive and judicial mind," by "young men and men who never grow old." Gurney, a leader of the reform group and one of Eliot's chief advisers, regarded purely technical qualifications of secondary importance. By such standards Adams was well qualified. Gurney knew him as one of the most frequent and able contributors to the *North American Review.* One of his weightiest studies in financial and political history had also been welcomed by the *Edinburgh Review.* Charles Deane, a leader of the Cambridge historical group, had already praised Adams's ability as a historical writer. In addition, he had the confidence of John Gorham Palfrey, the leader of New England historians, who had encouraged his studies for the past nine years. Finally, his natural dignity, his quick wit in conversation, and his urbanity gained through a half dozen London seasons would have impressed a far worse judge of men than Dean Gurney.

Henry Adams found it hard to give up the life of the capital and the independent career that he had so auspiciously begun. The success of his second annual "Session" had made him the ranking censor of Congress. In the fullness of time he might have become a power in the press, a distinguished peer of such men as Charles Nordhoff, Murat Halstead, Whitelaw Reid, Manton Marble, Charles Dana, and Edwin L. Godkin. Yielding to the family influence was in truth a surrender, and it was done against his strongest inclinations. There was much, however, that his practical-minded brother Charles could argue. His two older brothers were settled in their careers. Charles, as railroad commissioner of Massachusetts, could now turn to matters of practical reform. John had his work as a gentleman farmer and perhaps as perennial Democratic candidate for governor of Massachusetts. Henry was going on thirty-three, and his writings had eliminated whatever likelihood there had been of a political position under President Grant.

Adams bowed his head, consoling himself with the thought that Harvard was a "hospitable shop which kindly offered me a place at its counter." The decision made, he went on to Washington to close up his rooms, and sent a sad little valedictory to Gaskell: "I passed an hour today with Secretary Fish, who was very talkative, but there are few of my political friends left in power now, and these few will soon go out. This reconciles me to going away, though I hate Boston and am very fond of Washington."

6

Harvard College Once More

T HE DUAL JOB which Henry Adams had undertaken turned out to be considerably more than he had gambled on. Nine hours in the lecture room each week, even though he was left "absolutely free" to teach what he pleased "between the dates 800–1649," forced him into a paradoxical situation. To keep abreast of his classes he scrambled through "three or four volumes of an evening," many of them "heavy German books." The first skill which he had to master was the art of improvisation, a task not lacking in perverse entertainment. "There is a pleasing excitement in having to lecture tomorrow on a period of history which I have not even heard of till today." After three months of it, he whimsically reported to Charles Eliot Norton, then sojourning in Italy, "Thus far the only merit of my instruction has been its originality; one hundred youths at any rate have learned facts and theories for which in after life they will hunt the authorities in vain, unless, as I trust, they forget all they have been told."

Old as his historical subjects were, they fostered in Adams no respect for equally old teaching methods. Having been called in to "strengthen the reforming party in the University," he essayed the role with limitless gusto. "The devil is strong in me," he declared in a letter to Jacob Dolson Cox, "and my rage for reform is leading me into an open war with the whole system of teaching." He resented the burdensomely large classes which forced the teacher to take refuge in lectures and professorial vaudeville. Fortunately, he could count on being let alone; he therefore proposed, as he said, to substitute quietly his own notions for those of the college.

He was at his best in the small class in medieval institutions, an undergraduate seminar of some half-dozen students which met in his

well-furnished rooms in Wadsworth House. In order to "give a practical turn" to his young men, he bent the study strongly toward legal
institutions, adopting as his chief text Sir Henry Maine's *Ancient Law*.
His method, as he subsequently explained to Sir Henry, was to encourage his students "to dispute and overthrow, if they could, every
individual proposition in it." He later plunged them into the *Ger-
mania* of Tacitus, Rudolph Sohm's *Lex Salica*, "translating and com-
menting every sentence," Henry Maine's *Village Communities,* John
McLennan, Erwin Nasse, "and everything else they could lay their
hands on, including much Roman law and other stuff."

At the end of the first year he was ready to concede that, "as things
go, and as professors run," he had been fairly successful; "but from
an absolute point of view," he complained, "I am still nowhere." A
strenuous summer roughing it with the Fortieth Parallel Expedition
in the wilds of Wyoming and Colorado, where he first met Clarence
King, refreshed him, and he resumed his work at Harvard in the autumn of 1871 "feeling much more at home" in his medieval chair. He
even "dodged a meeting of politicians at Washington."

The one institution in which the rebel assistant professor attempted
no reform was the Monday evening faculty meeting. The courage
which he displayed in his magazine articles and the unceremonious-
ness that made his classes exciting were no match for "thirty twad-
dlers . . . discussing questions of discipline." As he had no discipline
problems, he regularly relieved his ennui during these three-hour sessions by attending to his correspondence from the safety of a back
seat. So far as the faculty minutes show, he preserved a perfect silence
and after two years quietly withdrew altogether, abandoning the faculty to its solemn thumb twiddling.

He set forth his unconventional views on education in the first long
article which he wrote for the *North American Review* after assuming
the editorship. In "Harvard College" he stated his cardinal principle:
"No system of education can be very successful which does not make
the scholar its chief object of interest." Granted that the principle
might seem a mere truism, it had "rarely been put into practice on
any great scale," because it was, "in the daily work of education . . .
the most difficult of all principles to act upon." The "true historical
method" would seek "to know what the student, at any given time,
thought of himself, of his studies and his instructors; what his studies
and his habits were; how much he knew and how thoroughly; with

what spirit he met his work, and with what amount of active aid and sympathy his instructors met him in dealing with his work or his amusements."

In the conduct of his courses and in his personal relations with his students Henry Adams forcefully illustrated what he conceived to be "active aid and sympathy." Edward Channing, the historian, recalls that once he encountered Adams in the library and confessed his inability to get started on his assignment. Together they spent an hour gathering books, and then Adams put a warning sign on the heap to protect it from the librarian. In this direct fashion he seems to have introduced the hitherto unheard-of practice of setting aside books on reserve for the exclusive use of his classes. After he moved to his house in the Back Bay in 1873 he regularly held his seminar in the book-walled library, where, before an open fire, following dinner, the little group of coworkers explored the monuments of German scholarship and "read and searched many times the whole collection of Anglo-Saxon laws, and ploughed through 25,000 pages of charters and capitularies in Mediaeval Latin." Adams adopted the utopian practice of buying all the important authorities in his field, and his shelves bristled with their works.

His classroom manner was a triumphant union of dignity and frankness. "There was no closing of eyes in slumber when Henry Adams was in command," Lindsay Swift recalled. "All was wholly unacademic; no formality, no rigidity, no professional pose" stood between him and his enthusiastic students. He did not allow friendliness to degenerate, however, into undue familiarity; even in the intimacy of his seminars he smoked his cigar and sipped his vintage sherry serenely aware that such privileges were not for students.

The historian Channing testifies to the resourcefulness and prodigious memory of his onetime master. After a month of investigation on an assigned subject, Channing came to class ready to make his report. "Fully primed and quaking in my shoes, I stood up to read my report, when the door opened and in walked President Eliot with a stranger, an Englishman. Adams uncoiled his legs, arose to his full length of about five foot three, greeted the Englishman warmly, gave him a seat, and President Eliot departed. Then Adams without a blush said, 'I will conclude my remarks on the career of Simon de Mountfort,' of whom he had never mentioned a word. But he proceeded with so much learning that the Englishman was amazed and so was I." Mostly his students recall his lively irreverence. Ephraim Emerton once asked, "How were the Popes elected in the eleventh century?" Adams retorted, "Pretty much as it pleased God." A remark in defense of John Adams elicited the unsettling comment, "You know, gentlemen, John Adams was a demagogue." On another occasion, when an unwary student asked for an explanation of transubstantiation, he snapped, "Good heavens! How should I know? Look it up." For mere facts he always expressed a "profound contempt." He was wont to say, with characteristic extravagance, "One fact or a thousand, that makes no difference."

If Adams was unusually sympathetic toward his more promising students, the authorities were equally considerate of him. Before his first year was out he had "managed to get into the 'inside ring' . . . the small set of men who control the university," and he could boast that he had things pretty much his own way. His work as teacher and editor brought him into close contact with many of his colleagues—with James Russell Lowell, Chauncey Wright, J. D. Whitney, Raphael Pumpelly, William Dean Howells, and many others, including Wolcott Gibbs, the famous chemist. As a member of "The Club," the equivalent, for the younger wits, of the more august Saturday Club, he dined convivially with Oliver Wendell Holmes, Jr., John Fiske, Henry James, William James, Thomas S. Perry, Moorfield Storey, John T. Morse, Jr., and other "clever, ambitious young fellows," to use Morse's characterization.

Intimacies with eminent older men, the titans of the Saturday Club, were slow to form, and Adams, whose boyhood had been enriched by daily association with Sumner, Palfrey, and Dana, felt the lack keenly. Professor Gurney's home was the one "oasis in this wilderness" for him. It was at this oasis that Henry Adams met a spirited and intellectual young woman of twenty-eight whom Gurney was tutoring in Greek. She was Marian "Clover" Hooper, the youngest daughter of Dr. Robert W. Hooper, a wealthy retired oculist. Henry James, an intimate of her Boston circle, admired her as a "Voltaire in petticoats." When Henry's mother, worried about his celibacy at thirty-three, suddenly remarked one day, "I wish you would marry Clover," Charles, taken by surprise, blurted out, "Heavens!—no!—They're all crazy as coots. She'll kill herself, just like her aunt." Charles's tasteless outburst fell on deaf ears. What prominent Boston family did not have a skeleton or two in the family closet? Hadn't their uncle George Adams taken his own life?

Henry and Clover were engaged on February 27, 1872. At the moment Henry's father was in Geneva as one of the arbitrators considering the American claims for compensation from England for the raids of the *Alabama* during the Civil War. When the news of the engagement reached him he was surprised. Word of Marian Hooper's good reputation among their friends somewhat reassured him, and he piously recorded in his diary, "I trust that the issue may be propitious."

To Brooks, Henry wrote that he had in fact pursued Clover since the previous May and found her "so far away superior to any woman I had ever met, that I did not think it worth while to resist." There had of course been flirtations with younger women, for, as he wrote Gaskell a few weeks before his engagement, "I still have a contemptible weakness for women's society." He told of entertaining "a principal beauty" of that season at an uproarious luncheon. "I assure you," he went on, "the young women in this land are lively to go, and the curious thing about it is that, so far as I know, these Boston girls are steady as you like. In this Arcadian society sexual passion seems to be abolished . . . I suspect both men and women are cold, and love only with great refinement. How they ever reconcile themselves to the brutalities of marriage, I don't know."

With marriage impending, Henry Adams now added a third term to his usual complaint of overwork: "What with teaching, editing and marrying, I am a pretty well occupied man." Restless of spirit, he had been more than commonly elusive, instinctively recoiling from the yoke which his friends persisted in accepting gracefully. Now his defensive bearishness merged into the pose of scholarly detachment as he contemplated matrimony: "Socially the match is supposed to be unexceptionable," ran his comment to Gaskell. "She is certainly not handsome; nor would she be quite called plain, I think . . . She talks garrulously, but on the whole pretty sensibly. She is very open to instruction. *We* shall improve her. She dresses badly. She decidedly has humor and will appreciate *our* wit. She has money enough to be quite independent. She rules me as only American women rule men, and I cower before her."

By coincidence, his friend William Dean Howells had just published *A Wedding Journey*. Adams gave it to Clover as an engagement present, and in reviewing it in the *North American Review* he wrote, "The book is essentially a lover's book. It deserves to be among the first of the gifts which follow or precede the marriage offer . . . If it can throw over the average bridal couple some reflection of its own refinement and taste, it will prove itself a valuable assistant to American civilization." For once, the iconoclast wrote like a cooing dove.

His stint for the April *North American* also included two other notices, one of them being of rather curious biographical interest for its reticence. This was a review of Clarence King's *Mountaineering in the Sierra Nevada*. It gave no hint of the arduous weeks he had spent in the saddle as one of King's companions in the Rocky Mountains the preceding summer, and its impersonality comes as a shock in view of Adams's dramatic recollection of their meeting in the *Education*. He had no inkling that the collection of realistic sketches of life in the high mountains would one day be valued as a minor American classic. All he saw was that the book, "though agreeable reading enough, is but a trifle . . . To be appreciated it should be read with the five huge volumes now appearing" under the direction of Mr. King, the "dignified chief" of the Fortieth Parallel Survey. Adams's intimacy with King lay years in the future.

Adams had expected to salvage a good deal of political capital from his role as editor of the *North American*. At the very beginning he proposed to make the review "a regular organ of our opinions" and thus avoid breaking "entirely from old connections." His responsibilities had begun with the January 1871 issue. Viewing the activities of his former colleagues from the editor's chair, he thought that his group might soon return to power. His correspondence with Jacob Dolson Cox during the harried weeks in which he tried to round up a corps of contributors reveals that there was no lessening of his interest in the tragicomedy that was playing itself out in Washington. Late in November 1870 he allowed his flock at Harvard to "wait for their historical fodder" while he ran down to New York with Charles to attend a political council of "revenue reformers" and to arrange with booksellers to push the *North American*. In reporting to Cox, he said that it was still premature to make plans for a political convention that would formally unite the dissident Republicans. One of the first persons whom he approached for an article was his political chief, David A. Wells, whose term in the Treasury Department had expired in July to the evident relief of President Grant. Adams good-naturedly bullied him into acquiescence. He next addressed himself to his friend Cox, proposing as a suitable companion piece to Wells's contribution an article on civil service reform. Cox, whose tussle with

Grant had ended in cold dismissal on October 30, was peculiarly well placed to present an anatomy of the degrading scuffle for offices.

He also tried to draft two other leaders: Samuel J. Tilden and Carl Schurz. His intention, he told Tilden, was to place "on record . . . an account of the Tammany frauds and their history . . . You alone know the private history of the affair." Adams's plea to Senator Schurz touched on another aspect of the whole movement, the rise of the Liberal Republican party in Missouri. "I want the public to know, if possible, how far you and your party represent principles which are of national interest; how far free-trade and reform are involved in the result; and what influences have been at work to counteract success." Wells was unable to make the December 1 deadline; Tilden, preoccupied with New York politics, had to beg off; Schurz was equally busy. Cox saved the issue with an article which Adams found "excellent in both matter and tone." His brother Charles also came to the rescue with "The Government and the Railroads"; but the editor's sanguine hopes for a sensational political issue for his debut were sadly deflated.

Fortunately, a suitable restorative already brewing was soon to justify Lowell's approving comment that Adams was out to make the old teakettle think it was a steam engine. "The New York Gold Conspiracy," which had at last been dropped into the muzzle of the *Westminster Review,* exploded against its targets so brilliantly as to satisfy all of its author's wishes for advertisement. From London came the threat of a libel suit. Eagerly sensing the value of an international row, Adams wrote that he would welcome a court test of his article.

Late in February 1871 Adams made another political visit to New York, where the "men of Erie" had discovered the authorship of the offending article and talked of reprisal. To the grandson of John Quincy Adams the prospect of "a very lively scrimmage in which some one will be hurt" called for the application of a single principle of strategy: an immediate offensive. With his brother Charles, now a veteran of the "Erie War," and Albert Stickney, the New York attorney who represented an aggrieved claimant in the Erie proceedings, Henry concocted a new attack. Not one, but two articles spread the scandal of Erie in the pages of the *North American;* Charles's lead article, "An Erie Raid," made a frontal attack upon the management, and Stickney's "Lawyer and Client" managed the flank with an impeachment of David Dudley Field's conduct as counsel for Fisk.

Adams's campaign against the Lords of Erie ended in September 1871 with the joint publication by himself and his brother of *Chapters of Erie and Other Essays*. Here were reprinted the first mature fruits of their collaboration. Henry contributed "Captain John Smith," "The Bank of England Restriction," "British Finance in 1816," "The Argument in the Legal Tender Case," and "The New York Gold Conspiracy." Charles made up his share with three of his railroad articles.

A few of the revisions in Henry's articles have more than a stylistic interest; they reflect the sobering effect of second thought on some of his more vituperative phrases. Though he did not alter the malevolent portraits of Fisk and Gould in "The Gold Conspiracy," he discreetly withdrew the lie direct against Fisk. Spaulding, whom he had pursued into the columns of the *Nation*, fared slightly better in the reprint of "The Legal Tender Act." The accusation that he had "perverted legislation into an instrument of fraud, and is proud of it," for example, was wholly deleted, and other harsh passages were softened.

BEFORE ADAMS'S FIRST YEAR of teaching was up he came to feel himself "all behindhand in the gossip of my trade," and he laid plans to "go over next year" to improve his acquaintance with John Richard Green and to consult with William Stubbs at Oxford, meanwhile "solemnly" reading their works in anticipation of his visit. The prospect of an extended wedding journey to Europe promised an opportunity for "mediaeval work in France and Germany" as well. What Adams thought of the value of his profession appears in a letter of advice which he now sent to Henry Cabot Lodge, who was one of his most promising students. "The question is whether the historico-literary line is practically worth following; not whether it will amuse or improve you. Can you make it *pay?* either in money, reputation, or any other solid value . . . No one has done better and won more in any business or pursuit, than has been acquired by men like Prescott, Motley, Frank Parkman, Bancroft, and so on in historical writing; none of them of extraordinary gifts . . . What they did, can be done by others . . . With it, comes social dignity, European reputation, and a foreign mission to close." It seemed a statement of his own expectations.

Adams's wedding took place very privately on June 27, 1872, fol-

lowing a month's stay of the engaged couple at Clover's uncle's sea-
side house at Cotuit. One of Adams's churchman book reviewers performed the ceremony. The newlyweds left for England on July 9, and
among their fellow travelers were the Lowells, Francis Parkman, and
John Holmes, brother of Dr. Oliver Wendell Holmes. As usual the
voyage made Adams very seasick: "Worse than ever," he recorded in
a joint travel letter he and Clover wrote aboard ship. "Deadly sick
and a calm sea. Wish I were too hum! Wish I were dead! Wish I'd
never been born!" Though he was to become one of the most widely
traveled of men, he never succeeded in making his peace with Ocean.

In order to delay their arrival in Berlin until September, when more
scholars would be accessible, they proceeded first to Geneva, where
Charles Francis Adams was engaged in the final deliberations over
the *Alabama* claims. After a short stay they pushed on to Berlin.
There the American minister, George Bancroft, who was a cousin of
Clover Adams, gave two dinner parties for them to which he summoned the most notable German scholars in history and public law.
Aged Leopold von Ranke, the first of modern historians, was not
among the guests on either occasion, but his chief disciple, Heinrich
von Sybel, was an adequate spokesman for the scientific method in
history. Theodor Mommsen represented the domain of Roman law
and history; Ernst Curtius, the archaeology and history of Greece;
and Heinrich Rudolph von Gneist, the history of German legal institutions. Another guest, George H. Pertz, venerable editor of the *Mon-
umenta Germaniae Historica,* whose long career of scholarship and
politics was then drawing to a close, was especially "cordial and
kind."

Among these distinguished authorities Adams felt most drawn to
von Gneist, and he "pumped" him diligently all one evening. As the
foremost European student of English constitutional and administrative law, von Gneist had most to offer him with respect to early English constitutional history, a subject which Adams had begun to
teach—and study intensively—only a little more than a year before.
In the German master he could recognize a kindred ambition, for von
Gneist in spite of his immense erudition was intensely practical in his
approach to legal studies. Tens of thousands of students flocked to
his lectures, yet he was equally celebrated as one of Prussia's greatest
liberal statesmen. En route across Europe Adams continued "reading
history in German." Fortunately his wife shared his interest, and they

enlivened their wedding journey by reading together in German Johann Schiller's *Thirty Years' War.* In Florence the versatile German scholar Dr. Ernst Gryzanowski called upon them and drenched his hosts with Hegelian metaphysics.

On November 15, 1872, Henry and Clover sailed from Brindisi to Egypt, where for three leisurely months they voyaged on the Nile in a comfortable dahabeah to the First Cataract, then transshipped for the voyage to Abu Simbel. There, gazing on the colossal figures of Ramses, which he photographed, Adams exclaimed, "Nothing I have seen in the world [is] equal to this temple." He tirelessly studied the vestiges of a civilization so ancient as to make his own field seem modern. During the six-hundred-mile journey downstream through the jumble of millennia from Karnak to Memphis he busied himself with his new photographic equipment with growing skill. Clover did not share his scholarly interest in Egyptian archaeology, being, as she confessed to her father, "painfully wanting in enthusiasm." The river voyage was marred at one point when she experienced an ominous attack of depression, an attack that elicited Adams's tender concern. Nevertheless, the winter on the Nile in the peace and quiet of the desert proved a "great success," Clover assured her father. They had enjoyed the comfort of the *Isis,* which served as their hotel on their slow progress from one temple site to another. Clover learned to make Turkish coffee so good that they felt "existence without it would be impossible."

In mid-March 1873 they returned to Italy, where Henry could show his wife the historic sights that had so stirred him fourteen years before. They had a "charming week" in Naples. At William Wetmore Story's studio in Rome Clover irreverently reported that Story spoiled "nice blocks of white marble with his classic Sybils." In Florence they were warmly welcomed by Henry's brother-in-law Kuhn, and they duly contemplated the artistic treasures of the Pitti and the Uffizi.

In April their wanderings brought them to Paris, where they were invalided for several days with colds. When Henry's brother Charles, who happened to be abroad, visited them, the extreme solicitude that the pair showed for each other roused his hostility. He poured out his disgust to his wife: "My brother," he said, "has grown to be a damned, solemn, pompous little ass, and his wife is an infernal bore;—they are the most married couple I have ever seen." He felt they had spoiled his time in Paris.

A few weeks later Henry and Clover were again back in London, enjoying as a "wedding present" the use of his friend Gaskell's town house in Park Lane. James Russell Lowell came over from Bruges in June to stay with them for a few days "until made a Doctor at Oxford." Adams had already made a professional visit to Oxford, where he "saw all the men I expected to see—Stubbs, Burrows, etc.—and a number I did not expect to see—as Sir Henry Mayne [Maine] and Laing of Corpus." To arm himself for his interview with William Stubbs he first "inspected the early English manuscripts in the Bodleian." Stubbs, the Regius Professor of History, was then at work on his *Constitutional History of England,* a project of especial interest to Adams after his interview with von Gneist. He was thoroughly familiar with Stubbs's *Documents Illustrative of the Constitutional History of England,* having made it required reading in his Harvard course on English history. The meeting with Sir Henry Maine, who was professor of historical and comparative jurisprudence, gave Adams the opportunity to exchange views with the author of the two chief staples of his undergraduate seminar in medieval institutions, *Ancient Law* and *Village Communities.* He also dined with Benjamin Jowett, Regius Professor of Greek and Master of Balliol, and lunched with Montague Bernard, the professor of international law and diplomacy. Yet amidst all these giants of his profession Adams was not tremendously impressed. "The English universities run too much into money and social distinctions," he reflected. "The spirit is better in ours."

To Lodge, who desired guidance for his graduate studies, Adams wrote, "The first step seems to me to be to familiarise one's mind with thoroughly good work; to master the scientific method, and to adopt the rigid principle of subordinating everything to perfect thoroughness of study." Later he added, "I have this year been engaged in investigating and accumulating notes upon some points of early German law . . . If you like, I will put these notes in your hands next term, and we will proceed to work the subject up together." The seminar would have its work cut out for it in "German, French, Latin, and Anglo-Saxon."

In London the former private secretary garnered a rich social harvest from his earlier residence in the city to which he now returned as a well-known editor and writer. His letters and those of his wife chronicle the renewal of old friendships and the making of new ones and crackle with the gossip of incessant entertaining. The beadroll of their pages includes Sir Charles Trevelyan, the India statesman and historian; Dean Arthur Stanley, onetime professor of ecclesiastical history at Oxford and now dean of Westminster; Frederick Locker, the poet (not yet married to Hannah Lampson, whose surname he took); Francis Palgrave, the poet and art critic, with whom he was on the friendliest terms; Thomas Woolner, the Pre-Raphaelite sculptor; Stopford Brooke, the churchman and man of letters; and Sir John Romilly, the Master of the Rolls. He paid his respects as well to the two great statesmen who had stood by his father during the darkest days of the Civil War: William E. Forster and John Bright.

He compared notes with young James Bryce, whose professorship in civil law at Oxford was as recent as his own. To the Park Lane house there also came the editor and critic Leslie Stephen and old friends of the legation circle, like Thomas Hughes. Most welcome perhaps was Gaskell's cousin, the affable young M.P. Sir Robert Cunliffe, one of Adams's dearest friends. As the time of departure drew closer Henry and Clover Adams became increasingly aware of the attractions of life in a world capital. "I like giving dinners in such a big society—one can get more variety of material than in Boston," she told her father. With far more reason than ever before Henry could repeat his old ejaculation: "How much of this sort of thing could one do in Boston!"

THE TWO TRAVELERS got back to Boston early in August 1873, "bobbing up on this side of the ocean, like a couple of enthusiastic soap bubbles," and beguiling their friends with extravagant tales of their travels. Adams needed to be gay, for he would have to call on all his resources of sardonic comedy to cope with a schedule now demanding "twelve hours a week in the lecture room." Fortunately, he would not have to reshoulder the editorship of the *North American Review* until after January 1, 1874, by which time the January issue would be safely out of the way. Moreover, the newly purchased house at 91 Marlborough Street, Boston, would provide a refuge three or four days a week at a safe distance from his hundred students.

Washington attracted him more than ever as the nearest equivalent to London, and in February he again set foot upon his "native asphalt" to enjoy surcease from the "ways of Boston" and to smile "contemptuously on men in high place." Official life as a career repelled him as always, although its workings and its society fascinated him. "To be a free lance and to have the press to work in" was his "ideal of perfect happiness, at least so far as perfect happiness is to be found in a career." Such reflections, however, were hardly more than a fond backward glance at those Washington days when he had been wound up in a coil of political conspiracy.

Immediately after reassuming the editorship of the *North American* Adams asked Henry Cabot Lodge to act as assistant editor; the young man leaped at the chance. "Nothing has ever come to me which gave me so much joy as that offer," he later wrote. Under the division of labor agreed upon, Adams retained active general direction of the magazine, and Lodge was responsible for getting out each issue once the contributions were turned over to him. By this means the editor freed himself from much time-consuming drudgery; in exchange he directed Lodge's literary apprenticeship with unexampled patience.

Despite the valiant aid which Lodge gave him, Adams continued to suffer from countless demands upon his energies, especially after he began to work his way back into the political councils of the liberal Republican remnant in Massachusetts. As time went by the "dreary waste of examination books and Division Returns" became more onerous; and the petty exactions of teaching intruded unpleasantly upon larger work. Ambitious students with "no minds" had to be reconciled to their lot; more richly endowed students had to be rescued from undue humility. If his contributors were not "all behaving like the devil," he was busy conciliating men like Parkman or Gamaliel Bradford who offered articles that could not be accommodated, or peremptorily demanding that Howells stand by with one "in case one of my men, as is probable, disappoints me." But no matter what the state of his relations with his contributors, the financial condition of the magazine was unvaryingly bad. Always hanging over his head was the danger that the *North American Review* would become hopelessly insolvent. He lived in terror that it might die disgracefully on his hands or, as he expressed it in the phrase of a fastidious Brahmin, "go to some Jew." To cap his difficulties, his overstrained eyes gave him trouble for a season.

In spite of all these recurring exasperations he never relaxed his surveillance. Brief nervous jottings directed Lodge to solicit manuscripts, check proofs, stave off the printer, pay contributors, or run errands: "I go to Newport on Friday to stay over Sunday, so keep an eye on that last sheet and get us out punctually . . . You might ask Harry, or (better, if he would) Willy James to do Bayard Taylor's Prophet . . . If Weir Mitchell refuses Clarke, don't write to Dalton or anyone else till further notice. Damn C. C. Everett. Tell him (very civilly) that the pressure for space etc., etc. we can't promise publication within any given time . . . Who is the best military critic in the United States? I want an article from him on Sherman's *Memoirs*." Sometimes the printers got out of hand and needed to be sharply rebuked. "I wish the printers to understand that my orders are to be taken notice of and obeyed."

Adams's violent criticism of the status quo in teaching was matched by his unconventionality as an editor. If he had dared he would have flown a skull and crossbones on the masthead of the quarterly. He wanted articles that would carry out his favorite intellectual maneuver of smashing things generally. "If you care to write thirty pages of abuse of people and houses in England," he cajoled Gaskell, "send the manuscript to me and if you are abusive enough you shall have £20." He promised Norton to "put more energy into the literary notices," and he undertook to do so with his customary unrestraint: "Stand on your head and spit at someone," he admonished his English friend. "Fake up a heap of old family scandals, no one will know who did it."

In Adams's eyes the editor was not a passive intermediary between author and publisher, but rather an ex officio collaborator with full powers of revision. On one occasion, receiving an article by "an eminent local historian and antiquary," he directed Henry Cabot Lodge to "go over it and strike out all superfluous words." Once, he caught a Tartar and gave considerable embarrassment to the publisher, James R. Osgood and Company. Osgood brought out Bayard Taylor's poetical translation of *Faust,* and Adams arranged to have it reviewed. The review never went beyond the page proof stage, for Adams, in cutting it down from twenty-five pages to ten and drastically altering its character, infuriated Taylor, who promptly took his case directly to Osgood. "I have worked for years in the interest of the *North American Review,*" he fumed, "but if the *North American Review* is to represent Adams with his tastes and prejudices only, it is time to take another view of the matter." On a proof sheet Adams inscribed the following obituary: "This notice, written originally by a strong admirer of Mr. Taylor, but much changed by me in tone, led to a protest from the author, and a request from Mr. Osgood that the notice should be suppressed. Which was done."

Adams took as his special province for review the writings of contemporary English historians of early law and institutions. As a convert to the German historical method, he reproached English scholars for their inferiority. "It is the misfortune of England," he said in the course of a highly commendatory review of Sohm's *Lex Salica*, "that she has never yet had a scientific historical school." And when he reviewed Professor George W. Kitchin's *History of France* he found no reason to abate his harsh view. He had hoped to see "better fruit from the new English school" represented by that Oxford don.

A newcomer in the field, Adams nonetheless chided his colleagues for their ignorance and their neglect of duty: "The early history of law has never been written." Indeed, the student of English history, after reading Mariette Bey's model study of early Egyptian institutions, could easily see "that no really thorough acquaintance with his subject matter is possible without tracing the stream of legal institutions back through the German hundred, as well as through the Roman city to its Aryan source."

Running through all his incisive and opinionated reviews was an almost obsessive interest in effectiveness of expression. No writer whose style lacked grace and vigor escaped his censure. He lectured even the great constitutional historian Bishop Stubbs: "The historian must be an artist. He must know how to develop the leading ideas of the subject he has chosen, how to keep the thread of the narrative always in hand, how to subordinate details, and how to accentuate principles." Of such an art, "of late superbly developed" in Germany, Stubbs was "altogether innocent." He was equally unable to forbear taking his friend Bancroft to task for "the inevitable peculiarities of his style," especially his tendency to fall into his "old excursive ways." Among the English historians, only John Richard Green delighted his sense of literary form.

Adams indulged his passion for stylistic criticism even in his private reading, and a burning trickle of comment would often run down the margin of the book. In Edmund Burke's *Abridgement of English History*, for example, he jotted down such editorial memoranda as: "Strange assertion for a contemporary of Gibbon"; "Surely this was always a colloquial phrase!"; "This is very droll"; "Curious want of critical capacity"; "This is bad grammar, bad style, and bad sense"; and much more of the same, as if in imagination he were revising the text before him. To incite himself to a better performance he once proposed to young Lodge that each write a review of Hermann von Holst's *History,* "and then we will take what is best out of each and roll them into one . . . I think it will give us both a spurt of emulation, so that we shall do the most perfect work we can." Rigorous towards himself, Adams was equally rigorous towards others. "He sent me to Swift," Lodge tells us, "to study simplicity of style as well as force and energy of expression . . . I rewrote [my first article] eight times before it passed muster."

Fortified by his discussions with von Gneist, Stubbs, and Maine, in 1873–74 Adams offered the course "Medieval Institutions" exclusively for "candidates for honors," and centered most of his interest upon this small group of talented young men. He prescribed for Lodge "a course of special study . . . with a view to ascertaining and fixing the share that the Germanic law had in forming the Common Law." The larger possibilities of their joint labors becoming apparent, Adams proposed to President Eliot to teach a class of doctoral candidates at his own expense. The president and fellows approved "his generous action," and he went ahead to inaugurate graduate study in history at Harvard. As soon as the new class could be established Adams disencumbered himself of one of his more elementary and more popular courses, "General History of Europe, Tenth to Sixteenth Century," and thus freed himself for a new course in colonial history in which he expected "to expose British tyranny and cruelty with a degree of patriotic fervor which, I flatter myself, has rarely been equalled."

In 1875, the five-year term of his original appointment ending, he accepted reappointment for another five years at the same rank, assistant professor, and apparently at the same salary, $2,000. The occasion inspired characteristically sardonic reflections. "I am going on to thirty-eight years old, the yawning gulf of middle age. Another, the fifth, year of professordom is expiring this week. I am balder, duller, more pedantic, and more lazy than ever. I have lost my love of travel. My fits of wrath and rebellion against the weaknesses and shortcomings of mankind are less violent than they were, though grumbling has become my favorite occupation. I have ceased to grow rapidly either in public esteem or in mental development." His correspondent, Gaskell, had no difficulty seeing through the pose. Outwardly, Adams may have begun to settle down; but ambition was in the blood.

After two years' work in colonial history he felt ready to venture into the crucial period in which his ancestors had played such important roles, the new course being "History of the United States from 1789 to 1840." Lindsay Swift, one of the students who listened to Adams's lectures in the course, later wrote: "Out of it grew, beyond a doubt, not only his largest work, *The History of the United States of America during the Administrations of Jefferson and Madison,* but also his studies of Albert Gallatin and of John Randolph."

7

In Quest of Historical Principles

WHAT HAD MADE the greatest impression upon Henry Adams in his medieval studies was the Teutonic theory of history, the now largely abandoned notion that constitutional and representative government had its origin in the folk life of the early Anglo-Saxons. In employing that theory as a touchstone in his historical reviews, he aligned himself with the so-called Germanist school of such English historians as John Kemble, Edward Freeman, William Stubbs, and John Green. Though he accepted the general theory of Teutonic origins, he relentlessly questioned the weaknesses of the supporting details. Stubbs, he contended, had been misled "by a sentiment of patriotism" to imply that Parliament was the outgrowth of the Anglo-Saxon Witan or royal council. Adams acutely observed that the old "witenagemot perished with the class it represented" and that "two whole centuries elapsed between the last genuine meeting of the Witan and the first meeting of Parliament." Sir Henry Maine's "clever theories" that the English law of primogeniture was the product of Teutonic "tribal leadership in its decay" he regarded as equally unacceptable because the break in continuity lasted for centuries. Still, whatever the shortcomings of the theory, it at least represented "a healthy reaction against the old tendency to consider everything good in civilization as due to Rome and Greece, to Cicero, to Homer, and to Justinian."

The grand problem of his research in early English history was to forge the vital link that bound the remote democratic past to the democratic present. In this enterprise he enlisted the most gifted students in his seminar in medieval institutions. The result of their collaboration, *Essays in Anglo-Saxon Law,* was studded with scholarship in the manner of the most formidable German models. Published in

1876, it included his own treatise, "Anglo-Saxon Courts of Law," and the dissertations of his first three doctoral candidates: Henry Cabot Lodge, Ernest Young, and James Lawrence Laughlin. In his essay Adams argued that the establishment of public jurisdiction in modern times was not an innovation but a restoration of the liberal elements of the old Teutonic constitution, a happy recurrence to a vital first principle after the decline of feudalism. The passing of the manorial system made way for the return of ancient principles—democratic, popular, and free.

By a piece of linguistic analysis that would have done honor to any hairsplitting German seminarist, he demonstrated that "socn" conferred fiscal jurisdiction, judicial jurisdiction being conferred by "sacu." It was an exquisitely learned tour de force, and he was pardonably delighted with his own ingenuity. At the same time he saw the humor of his having been seduced into such a parody of Dry-as-Dust in order to win reputation as a scholar. As some penance needed to be made if he were to assert his sense of proportion as a man of the world, he afterwards composed a derisive epitaph in twelfth-century Latin: "Hic Jacet / Homunculus Scriptor / Doctor Barbaricus / Henricus Adams / Adae Filius Et Evae / Primo Explicuit / Socnam." In after years he made the tag of Soc and Sac a standing jest between himself and his friends.

The eclipse of the Teutonic theory of democratic origins has invalidated the main assumptions of the *Essays,* but the light which the book casts on the survival of Anglo-Saxon laws makes it a permanent contribution to the literature of the subject. The strong partisanship for the Teutonic position was unquestionably inspired by the desire to bolster a political thesis. France, whose star had set in 1870 at Sedan, provided the example of a nation that lurched from a mongrel monarchy to an equally mongrel despotism of a third Napoleon. Across the Rhine, however, political reform proceeded not from the barricades but from the scholar's and jurist's study. What was especially admirable, no doubt, to Englishmen like Freeman, Stubbs, and Green and Americans like Henry Adams was that the German "revolution" did not overturn the social and economic order. To the conservative statesmen who shrank from claiming even institutional kinship with the turbulent French, the racist theories of the German universities supplied new strength through ties of blood.

Henry Adams, brought up on François Guizot, on Edmund Burke, and on the conservative philosophy of American Whiggism, had additional reasons for welcoming the Teutonic theory. It supplied an ancestry for American institutions that made them venerable and not merely virtuous. The account it gave of the origin of national sovereignty finally legitimated the scheme of government which his ancestors had so largely helped to establish, as it traced it beyond the speculative laws of nature and of God to the primeval polity in the forests of Germany. The American government of checks and balances was also a grand bequest of Anglo-Saxon times, for out of the conflict of interests between kings and nobles there arose "that partnership of nobility and commonalty which is the peculiar glory of the English constitution," a glory that shone all the brighter when transformed in the Massachusetts constitution and the U.S. Constitution into a system of checks and balances operating within a framework of separated powers.

Not all of Adams's zeal as a censorious "teacher of teachers" was expended on his English colleagues. On occasion the ferrule of the *North American Review* thwacked the knuckles of a compatriot scholar. In 1875 the flamboyant Hubert Howe Bancroft assembled the imposing volumes of his *Native Races of the Pacific*. Adams sensed the gross shortcomings of the work. Confirmed in his suspicions by the ethnologist Lewis Henry Morgan, he incited Morgan to make a full-dress attack. Morgan's merciless language delighted Adams, but he was even more pleased with Morgan's congenial thesis that the Aztec confederacy was not monarchical, as Bancroft romanticized, but "essentially democratical." Adams believed that the desire of European historians to exalt monarchy had led to precisely the same kind of blunder he had discovered in English history. "Our American ethnology," he assured Morgan, "is destined to change the fashionable European theories of history to no small extent."

The publication of Morgan's *Ancient Society* awakened all Adams's proselytizing zeal: "I have lost and shall lose no opportunity to impress on our scientific men and institutions the need of a careful scientific inquiry into the laws and usages of the village Indians." One of the questions which he addressed to Morgan broached a subject which had increasingly come to interest him—the place of woman in civilized society. "Can you tell me," he began, "where I can find information on the customs regulating marriage among our Indians?" At the moment his interest was distinctly practical, for five months hence he was to deliver in Boston his Lowell Institute lecture, "The Primitive Rights of Women." The subject is of peculiar importance because woman finally achieved an almost mystical significance in his philosophy. Both of his novels—*Democracy* in 1880 and *Esther* in 1884—were to present their heroines as endowed with special moral and spiritual energies. And in *Mont Saint Michel and Chartres* of 1904 he would go on to analyze the power of woman when it had achieved its highest form in the "Queen of Heaven," who, in defiance of theology, reestablished the dignity of her sex. Thus, as he was to say in the *Education*, "as he grew older, he found that Early Institutions lost their interest, but that Early Women became a passion."

Every chivalrous impulse impelled Henry Adams to revolt against the legal handicaps, as distinguished from the political ones, imposed on women; for the legal barriers implied inferiority. His lecture might well have been entitled "A Vindication of the Legal Rights of Women." He did not need Mill's essay, *The Subjection of Women*, to prove to him that the degradation of women grew out of convenient myth and not out of the nature of woman. As a descendant of Abigail Adams he knew woman's capacity for greatness within her sphere. He had a similar respect for his mother; in one of his early letters from Germany, he confessed how "like a selfish, low-minded fool" he felt after certain long talks with her. Moreover, within the family circle had sparkled the bright intellect of his elder sister, Louisa, whose death in 1870 had left him with an oppressive sense of wasted talent. In London he had also learned the importance of women in the great world of public affairs, where their brilliance and beauty had captivated him. And now in his own household the flashing wit and self-assurance of his wife made the myth of inferiority even more incredible.

If the history of institutions showed that woman was not strictly property nor a slave in the early Christian era, as was commonly asserted, how could one account for the elements of degradation that survived in Continental law and especially in the English common law? The answer which he gave in his lecture was that the church was the principal agency in degrading the status of women. "The Church established a new ideal of feminine character, thenceforward not the proud, self-confident, vindictive woman of German tradition received the admiration and commanded the service of law and society . . . The Church raised up, with the willing cooperation of men, the modern type of Griselda,—the meek and patient, the silent and tender sufferer, the pale reflection of the Mater Dolorosa ... To justify in theory the sacrifice of right surrendered by the wife and children ... men fell back on what they called the patriarchal theory, and derived the principles they required from the curious conglomeration of Old Testament history and pure hypothesis." Woman's civil rights had thus been impaired by the same fiction which obscured the originally free character of the English people. Cromwell and Luther in recurring to earlier free institutions "represented more than the protest against religious or political absolutism." They sought to restore the natural equilibrium of the family.

If there were any representatives of the New Woman in his audience, they could hardly have relished this learned disquisition on the women's rights question. True, it gave the social and legal rights of women as noble an ancestry as the political liberties of men; but its strong emphasis upon the family as paramount to the individual played into the hands of the pulpit demagogues who opposed any extension of women's rights on the ground that they threatened the purity of the American home. It happened that on December 10, 1876, the evening following Adams's address, Susan B. Anthony gave an address in Boston advocating women's suffrage in which she declared that only through the ballot could her sex hope to redress its immemorial grievances.

In his more optimistic moments Adams believed that the study of early comparative jurisprudence might train American lawyers to be historical jurists. For himself, he had mastered method. It was time to approach the nearer objects of study, which, as he pointed out to Lodge, were the historical forces at work in modern England and America. This study brought him to the threshold of American colonial history, and he began the investigation with his students of the long foreground to 1789. The thread of human liberty, which he believed he had traced back to its beginnings in the forests of Germany, was bringing him out at last to the great westward movement of democracy into the forests and prairie lands beyond the Appalachians.

The reviews which he wrote for the *North American Review* discussing current works in American history provide a cross section of the historical principles which he adopted in the course of his new researches, and they indicate what was to be the main subject matter of his future work in American history. In an article which he wrote with Lodge in 1876 reviewing Hermann von Holst's *Constitutional and Political History of the United States,* Adams revealed the drift away from the a priori conceptions which had characterized his Civil War view of the Constitution. Earlier, when he had been preoccupied with the effect upon the Constitution of the struggle over slavery, he had reasoned about it in terms of purely legal theory and idealistic preconceptions, but after Grant's inauguration he came to believe that "essential and fatal changes" had affected the organic law, and that these were the result not of the Civil War "but of deeper social causes." He was now ready to concede that the Constitution had not met the "theoretical requirements of the political situation" any more than had the great documents of the English constitutional system; but it had succeeded remarkably from the purely practical point of view. Its success deserved to be measured by the effectiveness with which it had implemented the movement towards nationalism.

On this note of the higher expediency, Adams concluded with two pages that were wholly his: "*my* Centennial oration," he called them. They vibrated with the organ tones of his deepest hopes: "If the historian will only consent to shut his eyes for a moment to the microscopic analysis of personal motives and idiosyncrasies, he cannot but become conscious of a silent pulsation that commands his respect, a steady movement that resembles in its mode of operation the mechanical action of Nature herself."

One of the most disputed points of the history of the early national period was whether the New England ultra-Federalists had planned or attempted treason against the federal government, as John Quincy Adams had charged in the campaign of 1828 in defending himself against Jackson's partisans. John Quincy Adams had not presented his evidence. Von Holst concluded that "the final decision of history must therefore be suspended" with respect to Adams's veracity. The question involved not only Henry Adams's ancestor but also George Cabot, the ancestor of Henry Cabot Lodge, who had been one of the leaders of the disaffected Federalists. Von Holst's challenge came at a fortunate moment in the work of Adams and Lodge. Henry Adams had recently unearthed in the Adams family archives the document that might have resolved von Holst's doubts. It was John Quincy Adams's devastating reply to the Federalists' "Appeal to the People." With this remarkable polemic, which some motive of prudence had caused to be suppressed, and a series of incriminating letters from the

Pickering Papers in the Massachusetts Historical Society collections, Henry Adams could prove the truth of the charge which his testy ancestor had made.

By the middle of the following year, 1877, Lodge published his *Life and Letters of George Cabot* defending his ancestor. In it he dissociated Cabot from the extremist faction headed by Pickering. Adams then moved to present the evidence in support of his grandfather's probity. This appeared in *Documents Relating to New England Federalism, 1800–1815,* which he edited. The collection of documents was the first published result of Adams's studies in American history.

FRUITFUL AS HIS WORK WAS in his role as scholar and teacher, it confined his speculations within academic limits. The editorial chair, on the other hand, was an incitement to speculations of the widest sort concerning contemporary American life. The approach of the nation's centennial suggested to him that a scientific survey of the progress of American civilization might appropriately be made in order to predict its future lines of development. For the centennial issue he recruited six experts in as many principal fields of American thought: Simon Newcomb in science; J. L. Diman in religion; William Graham Sumner in politics; C. F. Dunbar in economics; G. T. Bispham, a Philadelphia lawyer, in law; and Daniel Coit Gilman, president of Johns Hopkins University, in education. His plan, he explained to Gilman, was "to measure the progress of our country by the only standard which I know of, worth applying to mankind, its thought."

Such an investigation would round out the pattern of development of the national character, which Adams was already studying in its constitutional and political aspects. What he had in view was the method recommended by the historian Hippolyte Taine, whose philosophy had been the subject of an article Adams had accepted for the *North American Review.* "The historian," said Taine, "notes and traces the total transformation presented by a particular human molecule or group of human molecules, and, to explain these transformations, writes the psychology of the molecule or group." To achieve that task of scientific description the historian needed to adopt, according to Adams, "some theory of the progress of civilization which is outside and above all temporary questions of policy."

The centennial issue did not depict a uniformly progressive motion. In fact, upon the thoughtful reader the effect must have been decidedly sobering. Though the possibilities of progress were recognized, formidable obstacles stood in the way. Edwin Godkin, of the *Nation*, who conscientiously boosted the *North American Review* at every opportunity, published a long review praising the remarkable centennial issue. He regretted, however, that the tone of it might limit its usefulness. "The 'practical man'—or, in other words,—the Philistine—comes in for some pretty hard knocks, a fact which will probably prevent the number from having a wide circulation among members of Congress or among the aldermen and mayors of large cities. This is a pity, for what the Philistine needs to know is the depths of his own ignorance."

If Adams's "Centennial oration" in the von Holst review voiced his greatest hopes for the future of America, the centennial issue reflected his continuing fears. Those fears had kept him allied from the beginning with the reform elements in politics. On his return from his wedding journey in Europe with Clover he had reopened the pages of the *North American* to the reform group. To James Garfield he had then written, "I want a horoscope cast; a birds-eye view of the situation; a vigorous statement to our friends of what they can hope to do and what they can't, and whether their wisest policy is to organize inside the party or out of it. Tell me whom I could apply to."

Preoccupied with his own struggles in Congress, Garfield had gestured in a friendly fashion and declined. As a result reform went unserved in the April number. Then on March 12, 1874, Charles Sumner, spiritual head of the Republican party of Massachusetts, died. An unseemly clamor arose over the succession. When Sumner's mantle was finally draped about George S. Boutwell, the nonentity who as Secretary of the Treasury had epitomized administrative incompetence in Adams's eyes, he was driven to action. If ranking officers could not be found to direct the campaign, subalterns must serve. Adams had enlisted his outspoken younger brother, Brooks, and the always dependable Charles.

Brooks Adams, admitted to the Massachusetts bar only a year before, struck off an article for the July 1874 issue, "The Platform of the New Party." In a measure it was a reworking of Henry's scathing "Civil Service Reform." Brooks's statement was supplemented in the same issue by Charles's long article "The Currency Debate of 1873–

74," which forcefully asserted the conservative position against inflation of the currency. One by one he scornfully pilloried the inflation-
ists, but his best strokes he reserved for Messrs. Butler and Boutwell.

Even though the July 1874 issue may have had the air of a family
publication, Henry Adams could at least be satisfied that he had
put the *North American Review* in the van of the reform movement.
Henceforward in almost every issue he harried the Philistines. For the
rest of his term as editor Adams could count on aid from only two of
his old Washington colleagues. Francis A. Walker helped him out with
a carefully documented criticism of the classical wage fund theory
and gave academic comfort to the labor reformers who sought higher
wages. Of more practical bearing was David A. Wells's article, "The
Reform of Local Taxation." Adams had reminded Wells of the "evils
and absurdities" of the tax system, and as a starting point he had
suggested that the Massachusetts tax system should be "ripped up
without mercy." Wells followed the directive by exposing the confusion and deceptions always produced by efforts to levy personal property taxes.

Articles in the *North American Review* might help the good cause,
but much more would be needed to defeat the continuation of Grantism at the next presidential election. To do his part Adams needed
first to reconnoiter Washington. He had not lost contact with his
friends at the capital. At every opportunity during college recesses he
hurried down to Washington to draw strength like Antaeus from the
raw earth of politics. In the winter of 1875 on one of those life-giving
visits he set about to "organise a party of the centre" which might
wield the balance of power and impose a reform candidate upon one
of the major parties. It was a daring scheme, requiring strict secrecy
and "devious and underground ways," pleasurably exciting to one
bored with Boston.

One of the first requirements was a newspaper to serve as the organ
of the group. Henry Adams briskly entered upon negotiations to ac-
quire the *Boston Daily Advertiser* and commanded Lodge to join the
syndicate. For some reason the plan fell through, but the work of
organization flourished. The little nucleus formed in Washington
busied itself under Adams's energetic direction to promote a meeting
of notables in New York. In April 1875 he reported to his chief, Carl
Schurz, that "Sam Bowles, my brother Charles, Henry Cabot Lodge
and I concocted a letter and issued it . . . to such gentlemen who were

on your lists." Some sort of working organization was effected at the April meeting at Delmonico's, and Adams returned to Boston filled with new hope.

The first scheme of the new organization had been Schurz's plan to force the nomination of Henry's father for the Presidency upon the party caucuses. The elder Adams showed no enthusiasm for the project. Hence the scheme had to be abandoned, much to Henry Adams's relief. As he told Schurz, "I have no taste for political or any other kind of betting, and for us to attempt forcing one of ourselves on a party convention, necessarily entails jockeying of somebody." The attack should be centered on the caucus system, "the rottenest, most odious and most vulnerable part of our body politic." He suggested to Schurz that, lacking sufficient public support to set up their own man, they must turn to the one who came nearest their stand, Benjamin H. Bristow, the Secretary of the Treasury. Bristow had won fame for his prosecution of the distillers and revenue agents in the "Whiskey Ring" who had defrauded the government. If Bristow should receive the regular nomination, that was the most that could be hoped for in the present campaign. The cardinal need was to act as a unit and to agree upon "resistance to caucus dictation."

Meanwhile Lodge had run down to Washington, largely as Adams's emissary, and was immediately "plunged up to the ears in Washington intrigue." Adams cautioned that if it was necessary to telegraph, "Schurz and Bristow had better figure as Smith and Brown." The newspaper scheme was revived, this time looking toward the purchase of the *Boston Post*. During Lodge's absence in Washington the chief work of negotiation, including organizing a purchasing syndicate, fell upon Adams. He planned to put in $5,000 himself toward the $150,000 needed.

By the end of May 1876 it became apparent that all this labor had been wasted. The newspaper scheme evaporated. Bristow fell victim to the caucus. Speaker James G. Blaine emerged momentarily only to be eclipsed by a cloud of scandal. Only one more straw was needed, the nomination of Rutherford B. Hayes, "a third rate nonentity." Schurz, mindful of the main chance or at any rate more realistic than Adams's coterie, went over to Hayes and left his followers in the lurch.

Once more political idealism had gone down to defeat. In that defeat one piece of strategy must have afforded Adams a bit of satirical amusement. At the height of the political negotiations that spring, his group decided to procure a Harvard LL.D. for Schurz. Adams urged the proposal upon President Eliot and directed Lodge to apply a little pressure from his side. The maneuver worked, and the hero of the independents joined Adams's doctoral candidates at the commencement exercises late in June. It pleased Adams to have carried his point with Eliot, but his high estimate of Schurz tumbled. Masking his own bitterness, he consoled Lodge, "You are indeed the one who had the best right to complain for you had the most trouble in forming that rope of sand, the Independent party. I cannot help laughing to think how, after all our labor and after we had by main force created a party for Schurz to lead, he himself, without a word or a single effort to keep his party together, kicked us over in his haste to jump back to the Republicans."

There was ample cause for disappointment. Adams and Lodge had driven themselves without respite. Success in their political campaign might have emancipated Adams from the "ways of Boston" and have somehow utilized his talents for politics. We can only guess what dreams of glory and power passed through his mind. Political disappointment had come so often and so unfailingly to the members of his family since the Civil War that he did not dare confess to either hope or personal ambition. Sadly he foresaw that the corrupt party machine would very likely outlive him. "I prefer to leave this greatest of American problems to shrewder heads than mine," ran his disillusioned comment to Lodge. "When the day comes on which it will be considered as disgraceful to be seen in a caucus as to be seen in a gambling house or brothel, then my interest will wake up again and legitimate politics will get a new birth."

The contest between Republican Rutherford Hayes and Democrat Samuel Tilden seemed to offer little more than a choice between Tweedledum and Tweedledee; but Adams decided to support Tilden. As he ruefully acknowledged to Wells, "After chattering about voting for the best man without regard to party, I cannot well do otherwise."

If direct political action was now out of the question, there yet remained the rostrum of the *North American* from which to hurl Parthian epithets against all of their enemies. His spirits rose as he prepared to hold inquest over the national body politic in the October 1876 issue. The publishers got wind of one of the articles, "The Independents in the Canvass," the joint production of Henry Adams and his brother Charles, in which they advised Republicans to kick over the party traces. Such an affront to Massachusetts Republicans was too much for the publishers, and they condemned the heresy, especially as the finances of the magazine were in a precarious state. In spite of the favorable puffs from Adams's friends and his own efforts to solicit business, the magazine had not attracted an adequate number of paying advertisers.

Availing himself of the quarrel over the October issue, Adams resigned, leaving the volcanic October issue as his "monument." Helpless to do more, the publishers inserted the following disclaimer: "The editors of the 'North American Review' having retired from its management on account of a difference of opinion with the proprietors as to the political character of this number, the proprietors, rather than cause an indefinite delay in publication, have allowed the number to retain the form which had been given it, without, however, committing the Review to the opinions expressed therein."

The offending "political manifesto," "The Independents in the Canvass," restated point by point the intense convictions of the two crusading brothers as expressed in eight years of fearless public discussion. In every plainspoken line it showed that they had not deviated from their youthful ambition to "blow up sophistry and jam hard down on morality." In the impending election, the independent voter would have to decide what he must do "whichever party comes to power." The independent voter must in future constitute a third party, prepared to act with either of the other parties when it might serve his interest but resolute in adherence to the one great end: "to overcome the tendency of our political system to corruption."

The October *North American Review* was indeed "a very strong number," as assistant editor Lodge reported to historian Bancroft in Washington. The printing was immediately exhausted, an unprecedented occurrence in the history of the magazine. Here once more was advertisement beyond Adams's hopes, but once again it was unusable. The *Nation,* which had so long approved the magazine, whose reformist policies paralleled its own, reported that "a severe internal convulsion" had taken place. Thus by forcing the retirement of Adams the publishers had struck a severe blow to the liberal cause.

JUST AS THE OCTOBER *North American* stood as the "historical monument" to Adams's editing, the *Essays in Anglo-Saxon Law* was a monument to his teaching. The equivocal election of 1876, which was somehow resolved in Hayes's favor, dropped Adams into an emotional vacuum. The failure of politics left him suspended between the Stone Age of President Grant and the Brazen Age of President Hayes.

Assuredly the time had come to take stock of his career. Once, like Disraeli's Coningsby, he had thought, "I should like to be a great man," but like him he had learned that "the history of heroes is the history of youth." He was all too conscious that youth was gone. By thirty-nine his bald head gleamed like that of Chaucer's monk, and he was beginning to see himself as "Casaubon in *Middlemarch*." "Aridity grows on me," he declared to Lodge. Beneath the spirited badinage in his letters to Charles Milnes Gaskell, who was now a member of Parliament, runs a persistent note of regret, the regret of an ardent young man who had taken to heart Disraeli's and Bulwer-Lytton's heroes as models. In London, in the sophisticated company of his friend Gaskell, it had been flatteringly easy to identify himself with the irresistible Coningsby and the exquisite Pelham. Had not he and his friend Gaskell once wished to be "both men of the world, and even, to a certain degree, men of pleasure, and yet to be something wiser, nobler, better"? Nineteen bewildering years had gone by since he set sail from Queenstown aboard the *China* to seek his fortune in Washington. There was no prospect now of being either a Coningsby or a Pelham, and the names of those youthful literary enthusiasms could survive only in mocking allusions.

Already he had shifted to his doctoral students' shoulders the courses in which he was no longer interested. Henceforth even graduate seminars would only be repetition, for he had baked his first "batch of Doctors of Philosophy." The vivid pleasure that he had taken in the achievement of his three distinguished students would not come again; they were now the first of an endless file of scholars. He had spent his energies during the past year with prodigality, and he was tired. In the fall of 1872 he had returned to his chair in medieval history with relish for the work lying ahead. In the fall of 1876 he unwillingly braced himself for the new year. Eager to base his new course—"History of the United States from 1789 to 1840"—upon original documents, he buried himself beneath "avalanches of State Papers," and when he emerged he faced an unexpectedly large class. "I am just beginning my grind at the university wheel," he wrote to Gaskell, "and for my sins I am becoming popular in my old age. My classes are very large; one of them is near seventy in number. As I detest large classes, I am much disgusted at this, and have become foul and abusive in my language to them, hoping to drive them away."

His discontent was of no sudden origin, however, and it ran deeper than a distaste for large classes. A year and a half earlier he had meditated, "marriage makes a man quiet." But quiet, he discovered, did not bring content. The Boston which his brother once described in the *North American* as having lost both its influence and its past was becoming a provincial city in which intellectual life had foundered in moral earnestness. Adams's reaction to this decline was almost violently chemical. Only gross exaggeration satisfied his feelings. "For twenty-five years, more or less, I have been trying to persuade people that I don't come from Boston," he later wrote to Godkin. He had a horror of growing provincial, of becoming the "most odious" of Boston prigs, an "intellectual prig." He confided his sense of frustration as a teacher to his friend Francis A. Walker: "Between ourselves the instruction of boys is mean work. It is distinctly weakening to both parties. I have reduced my pedagogic work to the narrowest dimensions and am working more and more back into active life." Yet when he thus wrote to Walker, more than a year of "pedagogic work" still lay ahead; and by chance the drudgery was to be redoubled.

The impending election had irresistibly drawn his thoughts to Washington. There lay the best hope of escape. "If the new Secretary of State is a friend of mine," he reflected, "I shall try the experiment of passing a winter in Washington." In any case he resolved to keep his hands free and make no new commitments. President Daniel Coit Gilman of Johns Hopkins University enterprisingly used the quarrel over *North American Review* policy as the occasion to offer Adams a professorship in history in the new university. It was tempting bait, but acceptance might well tie him irrevocably to the academic life. "I feel so uncertain whether I shall stay quiet more than a short time longer, that I cannot put on harness again."

The uncertainty of the winter continued into the early spring of 1877. His contract at Harvard, however tenuous its legal hold upon him, still had three years to run, and he continued to go through the motions of hard work. He thought of a plan for stimulating the interest of students in American history. Why not introduce the principle of competition between teachers of the same subject? In a letter to President Eliot he offered to set up a rival course to his own in American history "to be given by Mr. Lodge." The Corporation assented to his bizarre plan. His resolve to quit had not yet reached the sticking-place, though he believed that his university work was "essentially done" and nothing remained but "mere railing at the idiocies of a university education."

His half-formed intentions were finally crystallized by a chance occurrence. Albert Rolaz Gallatin, the son and literary executor of Albert Gallatin, Jefferson's Secretary of the Treasury, invited Adams to edit his father's papers and prepare the biography. Adams's current researches in the period 1789–1840 peculiarly qualified him to undertake the work. He accepted the job and he went down to New York, his students left in Lodge's charge, to arrange the "great mass of papers," which he was relieved to discover would "give me some years' work and exercise a good deal of influence on my future movements." With such a tangible and important piece of work in hand, he could now resign from Harvard and establish himself in Washington as a scholar in residence.

The political situation in Washington promised to be helpful. His friend William Evarts was the new Secretary of State, and he offered Adams a private desk and free access to the archives of the State Department. Whatever the "higher" prize he sought, its shadowy outlines prefigured the intellectual and the artist. His apprenticeship to the muse of history had been protracted and arduous. As if to symbolize his emergence and to make his departure from Harvard irrevocable, he gave "all his German books on law and sources" to his friend Oliver Wendell Holmes. "Put them all to the best use in your power, and I shall then feel as though I were still teaching." Embarking at last on a career as writer and historian, fulfilling after a fashion his undergraduate ambition for a quiet literary life, he now surrendered all thought of a joint career with his brother Charles, whose single-minded devotion to railroad affairs was soon to lead him from the Massachusetts Railroad Commission to the presidency of the Union Pacific Railroad. A brief obituary to Adams's political career appeared in *"Warrington" Pen-Portraits* in 1877. The author, William S. Robinson of the *Springfield Republican*, onetime partisan of the unforgiving Charles Sumner, wrote, "Mr. Henry Adams had too much of the English, and diplomatic and supercilious character which belongs to the New York *Nation* to allow him to become a useful public man."

The decision to leave Harvard and Boston once made, Adams put the past resolutely behind him. Any allusion to it seemed an intrusion, as when President Gilman some six months after his resignation asked him to lecture on his experiences as a teacher. He replied, "I confess I would rather not talk about my own experiences as a teacher. They satisifed me so completely that teaching is and always must be experimental if not empirical, in order to be successful, that I was glad to find an excuse for abandoning any wild ideas I might have had of creating a satisfactory method of pedagogy."

In October 1877 Henry and his wife came to Quincy to spend a final few days at the Mansion House with the family. His father found their visit "very pleasant," but he somberly reflected that his favorite son was leaving for a place where "none of our name have ever prospered."

To Gaskell Adams described the change in November 1877 with a freshness and buoyancy long absent from his correspondence. "We have made a great leap in the world; cut loose at once from all that has occupied us since our return from Europe, and caught new ties and occupations here. The fact is, I gravitate to a capital by a primary law of nature. This is the only place in America where society amuses me, or where life offers variety. Here, too, I can fancy that we are of use in the world, for we distinctly occupy niches which ought to be filled ... As I belong to the class of people who have great faith in this country and who believe that in another century it will be saying in its turn the last word of civilisation, I enjoy the expectation of the coming day, and try to imagine that I am myself, with my fellow *gelehrte* here, the first faint rays of that great light which is to dazzle and set the world on fire hereafter."

8

The Return of the Native

T HE PASSIONS of the "stolen" election still eddied about the cloakrooms and flared in recriminations through the press when Henry and Clover Adams arrived in Washington on November 10, joyously self-exiled from Boston. Eight months had passed since the March morning when Rutherford B. Hayes had been shoved and hustled into the White House with the reluctant last-minute blessing of a wrangling Congress. Grantism, which had driven Adams into political opposition, was dying. The indulgent and gullible host at the Great Barbecue had taken his salute of twenty-one guns from the frigate *Constitution* at Philadelphia and set off in mid-May for a tour of the world, glad to be free of the bewildering exasperations of public office.

On the surface Adams's coming to Washington was an "experiment," merely "searching archives," in his deprecatory phrase. But when he made his farewells in Quincy, he and Clover more pleasantly relaxed than was their wont, his father sensed the truth. "I feel," wrote Charles Francis Adams in his diary, "as if he was now taking a direction which will separate us from him gradually forever." With his intimates Henry did not conceal his own relief. He and his ambitious wife could occupy the "niches which ought to be filled."

To Adams the broad, outward-thrusting avenues of Washington offered vistas unknown to the narrow lanes of Beacon Hill. The softer climate promised a wider margin of life and surcease for rheumatic bone and muscle tormented by New England winters. One of the earliest planned cities in America, Washington was a chant democratic in brick and stone, celebrating the new order for the ages. There were a few blemishes. The unfinished shaft of the Washington Monument, upon which work had been suspended since the beginning of

the Civil War, hinted the disproportion between reach and grasp. But
Governor Alexander Shepherd's remarkable transformation of the
cluttered and overgrown Civil War city reflected a Napoleonic daring—and knowledge of the power of "honest graft." Fine new paving
and spacious sidewalks met the eye; the open sewers had disappeared,
and sixty thousand new trees lined miles of streets. There was a re-
freshing hint in the air—at least to transplanted New Englanders—
of Yankee bustle and enterprise. Modern horsecars glided along Pennsylvania Avenue where a few years before omnibuses and hackney
coaches had lurched through clouds of dust and quagmires of mud.
The first telephone had begun its impertinent clamor in the White
House.

To Gaskell Adams prophesied, "One of these days this will be a
very great city if nothing happens to it. Even now it is a beautiful one,
and its situation is superb." Three weeks after his arrival the *Nation*
carried a lyrical tribute to the city which should have silenced most
criticism of his move. The city, it said, offered a remarkable union of
society and politics. There had been an extraordinary growth of libraries, museums, and art galleries, and the "opportunities for literary and scientific study [were] almost, if not quite, unsurpassed on
the continent." Only a short canter from President's Square lay the
wooded ravines of Rock Creek, still an almost primitive wilderness,
which lent the city an idyllic aspect unique among world capitals. For
the nature lover, dogwood and flowering Judas, rhododendron and
hepatica lavished their beauty upon the seasons.

The last great exodus of officeholders had taken place eight years
ago when Grant came into office. Now, on the departure of his ap-
pointees, a new generation arrived with Hayes. Change was the law
of life, and it gave Washington society something of the fevered quality of a fashionable casino with its mysterious entrances and exits, its
dazzling stakes and disappointed ambitions. Family connections were
duly honored, but no long-established families dominated the munic-
ipal life or reproduced the inbred provinciality of Boston.

Henry Adams and Clover established their comfortable ménage in
William W. Corcoran's "yellow house" at 1501 H Street, a short
block from President's Square, the elm-bordered little park occupying
two city blocks whose official name became Lafayette Square in 1878.
The Republican city administrator quietly ignored Andrew Jackson,
whose statue dominated the center of the square, and honored Lafa-

yette, whose statue graced one of the corners. After two winters there, out of sight of the White House, they moved down the street to another Corcoran property, "the little White House" at 1607 H Street, where Adams could train the quick-firing guns of his wit directly upon the front door of 1600 Pennsylvania Avenue, a scant three hundred yards away across the lawns and flower beds. At a safe distance from family counsels of prudence, Adams and his wife shopped with a touch of defiant extravagance. Fine paintings and watercolors hung from the walls. Their baggage of Oriental rugs made an impressive show. A fashionable clutter of Japanese vases and bronze lent a special emphasis. Looking about their charming parlor from which the "dreary Congressional look" had been exorcised, the two happy refugees from Boston felt pure bliss. "We strut around as if we were millionaires," said Clover. "Henry says for the first time in his life he feels like a gentleman."

The State Department, "magnificently hospitable" in its new quarters, installed Adams at a private desk with space for his personal copyist and gave him free access to the restricted archives. From the library windows there was a fine view across the Ellipse. Directly south were two small lagoons adjoining the vaguely edged tidal swamplands. The report of a fowling piece occasionally startled the reflections of statesmen—and historians, for the low ground was still favored by duck hunters. The great South Front, which had been completed in 1875, presented to an awed nation the most extensive and colossal version of a French chateau yet seen on the continent, a baroque kaleidoscope of pavilions, porticoes, porches, colonnades, and chimneys, topped with a mansard roof, the effect French neoclassical or Italian Renaissance, depending on the tourist's mood. Clover Adams, eager to be pleased with the new surroundings, considered it beautiful. After twenty-five years of irritated contemplation, Henry Adams was to call it "Mr. Mullet's architectural infant asylum."

The coadjutors who had survived Grant promptly rallied to Adams's convivial little dinners of six and eight. In spite of his resolution to "keep clear of politics" and merely listen to the "monkey show," he found himself once again helping to manage the affairs of the liberal Republican clique and becoming involved in their feuds. Carl Schurz's efforts in the cabinet to reform the civil service drew the fire of Senator James Blaine's secretary, Mary Abigail Dodge, writing under the pen name of Gail Hamilton in the *New York Tribune*.

Adams promptly tried to get Charles Nordhoff of the *New York Herald* to "sass" her. This maneuver failed.

Living so close to the political center, where the currency debate tended to obscure every deeper issue, Adams followed his bent toward finance but found the old dogmas no longer easy to apply. He was shocked to learn that one of his former allies in the civil service reform movement, onetime Secretary of the Interior Jacob Dolson Cox, had come out in support of the "silver mania." The conservative opinions aired at the Adamses' table found their way into Godkin's editorials. The *Nation* declared that "advocacy of a change in the coinage not in order to make the standard of value steadier, but in order to make the payment of debts easier . . . [is] *prima-facie* evidence of dishonesty."

Except for this obsessive interest in the currency question, Adams was singularly untouched by the social and economic disorder of the time. The intimates of his circle denounced political and commercial fraud, but they were even more hostile to the activities of labor unions. There was reason enough for conservative alarm over the violence of the labor disputes of 1877. To historians it was to be one of the blackest years in American history. Railroad rate wars had led to wage cuts; these in turn provoked an epidemic of bloody strikes throughout the nation. There was desperate fighting in Chicago, where in a single clash between the police and "a mob of the dangerous classes" ten rioters were killed and forty-five wounded. Regular army troops put down mob violence in Wilkes-Barre, Scranton, and Easton. The stories of these happenings came to Adams each day in his copy of the Washington *Evening Star,* but they touched him only as vague reverberations from some kind of half-world, if not underworld, of American experience.

There was no lack of generous impulses, warm affection, and sympathy within the Adams circle, but these were lavished upon the elect and withheld on principle as well as preference from the outsider. The anti–labor union bias of John Hay's novel, *The Bread-Winners,* a best-seller of the early 1880s, had its germ in the comfortable study of Henry Adams, where the two friends shared a passionate belief in political democracy joined to an equally passionate disapproval of economic democracy.

If the world outside Lafayette Square, with its well-tended lawns and flower beds and great sheltering elms, was disorderly and uncouth, ravaged by violent strikes or by devastating yellow fever epidemics, within its proximity lay a world pleasurably reminiscent of the Mayfair and Belgravia which had so charmed the Adamses during their wedding visit five years before. Lafayette Square offered the nearest thing in the United States to compare with the purlieus of Grosvenor Place. It needed no daring imagination to see the nation's capital as a new London, a London improved and methodized, shorn of the vast residential and business purgatories of the English capital. Having tasted the best of the Old World, Henry Adams and his resourceful wife set about to reproduce a center of culture and politics, of cosmopolitanism, of literature, art, and learning, of wit and inspired table talk.

There was but one cloud on the horizon of their new felicity. They keenly felt their childlessness. A certain philosophical resignation colored Henry's reflection. "One consequence of having no children is that husband and wife become very dependent upon each other and live very much together. This is our case, but we both like society and try to conciliate it."

Their Boston salon had had serious limitations. The admixture of academic figures had been excessive. Interests were unavoidably provincial and almost unbearably familial. The prevalence of Adamses was especially trying to Clover, and she too had been eager for emancipation. Except for Henry the Adamses all dominated their womenfolk, and Clover had not been happy at the influence that Charles Francis, Jr., had continued to exert upon Henry's career.

Clover had taken Charles's measure fairly early, and he soon learned to respect—and a little fear—her satirical wit. Not a submissive type nor given to demure self-effacement, she could be as censorious as her husband. Though Henry's family had accepted his wife into the "family concern," it was with a trace of reserve. As the last of Dr. Hooper's children to marry, Clover had been his much-indulged favorite, and her expensive tastes rather worried Henry's father. Shortly after the pair removed to Washington, he sent an admonition on the subject which he felt Henry "will not relish."

A somewhat plain person alongside Charles's wife, Clover had her own kind of distinction. Petite, no more than five feet two, she was still only an inch shorter than her scholarly-looking husband, who walked beside her with a certain emphasis of stride as if to make up for his short stature. Clover reflected in her exquisite bearing and

restrained but elegant dress a kind of perfection of Boston society. She
had a colonial lineage at least as old as the Adamses'. The Hoopers
on her father's side and the Sturgises on her mother's had helped create the aristocracy of Massachusetts.

In her regular Sunday letters to her long-widowed father, Dr. Robert Hooper, she kept up unbroken the close communion of the Boston
years. In her "hebdomadal drivel"—"my diary"—she shared the excitements of her new and emancipated life, bringing to view with extraordinary immediacy the Washington milieu. She gaily threatened
to inflict her reports unless she were "ill in bed or dead." There runs
through her letters a decorous and yet ebullient high spirit, a patter
of quick nervous characterizations, serving the week's social adventures hot on the skewer of her satire.

In passages like the following, graphic vignettes of prominent persons shared the page with Pepysian glimpses of Washington life and
culture: "The new Minister to Russia was introduced to me—he
looks like a handsome unprincipled old white buffalo . . . The Hayes
suffer much from rats in the White House who run over their bed and
nibble the President's toes . . . We went to a 'Literary Club,' a 'Washington' literary club. Pickwick pales beside it—I thought I had seen
fools—but not until I had seen & heard Judge Drake of the Court of
Claims did I know what an ass was & is—he must be self-made—it
would be blasphemy to attribute him to any other creator."

Clover took command of their social life from the beginning, and
Henry submitted with affectionate docility to her management.
Henry James once remarked, "We never knew how delightful Henry
was till he lost her; he was so proud of her that he let her shine as he
sat back and enjoyed listening to what she said and what others let
her say."

Ruefully the Adamses surrendered to the calling-card evil, distributing their social largess with extreme care, however, as it became
more coveted by the social climbers of the capital. As they did "not
hanker for a large circle of congressional friends," they found the
rules of etiquette "a delightful hedge." Still, social crises recurred.
Their friend Charles Nordhoff, "green as a gosling," sponsored one
aspirant who turned out to be a "female lobbyist of shady repute." It
was, as Clover wrote, a "process of picking off burrs, which is not
pleasant." When Congressman Fernando Wood, onetime mayor of
New York, "condescended" to call first, Clover was not to be so eas-

ily placated. "I may be squeamish but I do prefer the hospitality of gentlemen who have not forged."

In the "social vortex" of Washington they had "to steer gingerly, tack, reef, and at times scuttle one's ship." Clover's antipathies were perhaps more violent than her husband's, and her unsparing witticisms went from mouth to mouth. At times she felt a little constraint in writing to her father because he relished circulating her vivid diary among at least a dozen relatives and friends, all the while protesting his innocence. She had to caution him repeatedly that some of her choicest bits had come back "twisted and sharpened."

One of the few houses at which they became habitués during their first season was the Schurzes'. There on Sunday evenings Carl Schurz, whose political apostasy had been forgiven, would feelingly improvise at the piano. He became one of the regulars at their tea table, appearing three times a week to add his authoritative voice to the cheerful clamor. Even more devoted was General Richard Taylor, son of President Zachary Taylor, who would come every day at "the stroke of five and stay till six." He was one of their contingent of ex-Confederate admirers, a group which included the gallant Senator Lucius Q. C. Lamar of Mississippi, then beginning his service in the Senate. There was also William H. Trescott, a former slaveholder and Southern spokesman, who not long before had helped Adams out with an article titled "The Southern Question" in the *North American Review*. General Taylor usually played devil's advocate. He "disbelieves in democracy and universal suffrage as firmly as Mr. Frank Parkman," said Henry's recording angel, "but is too much a man of the world to wail over the inevitable, like our friend Trescott."

Adams became fast friends with the Japanese minister Kiyonari Yoshida, who shared his lively interest in archaic law. Yoshida converted him from whist to gobang, to the accompaniment of heroic collations of oysters and champagne. Adams promptly began teaching the game to friends like Aristarchi Bey, the Turkish minister, and set a fashion for the season. As Clover did not have her husband's sturdy constitution and tired more quickly than he, Henry accommodated himself to her pace. Besides, he was now forty and "the grave was yawning for him." In Boston he used to be "frivolous" and "flicker out to a ball," alone if need be, while Clover sat by the fire. She had long since given up waltzing, much to the disgust of Henry's mother. In Washington Henry grew more sedate, though not quite willingly, as one of Clover's latest entries in her "diary" was to hint. "Thursday to bed early and made Henry take my regrets to a young dance . . . where my frisky husband even danced."

Clover ran their household with the aid of a staff of four regular servants, including an "indoor man," a staff that later increased to six. In the spring of 1878 Henry and Clover began their habitual rides together, prowling through the woods to Georgetown, "finding about as much country life as in Beverly," and returning laden with white "bloodroot and other flowers." They were usually accompanied by their scampering Skye terriers, Boojum and Pollywog.

For a number of weeks during their first season in Washington Clover helped collate manuscripts with Henry at the State Department, the two of them looking like "Cruikshank's illustrations to *Old Curiosity Shop,* Sampson and Sally Brass on opposite stools." The household ran on with agreeable and efficient smoothness. To save time they would sometimes have a guest to breakfast to talk, for Henry was "economical of hours," and one hour was lost "anyway in eating and feeding dogs." Zealously, she protected him from unwelcome interruptions. "Henry meantime being a man works hard, eats, sleeps, has no social scruples, but divides all my pleasures and doubles my burdens."

Fond of entertaining, the Adamses had ample means to make an art of it. Their joint income had now grown to twenty or twenty-five thousand a year. The guests were always skillfully paired as for a play. Sometimes a sample of a particularly successful dish like terrapin would be expressed to Boston to delight Dr. Hooper, with the precious recipe attached in case of spoilage. Although across the way Mrs. Hayes would not serve wine, deferring to the prohibitionists, at the Adams table the members of the diplomatic corps found the ritual of fine vintages faithfully respected. Once the German minister Captain von Eisendecker, quite carried away by the cuisine, exclaimed to his wife, "Oh, Lilly! Dass wir immer so essen könnten! [Oh, Lilly! that we might always eat like this!]"

The fame of their salon spread rapidly through the social circles of Washington, New York, and Boston, and admission to it became the brevet to fame—and a certain envy—among outsiders. Society columnists, ruthlessly held at bay, were not easily placated and bided their time. The twenty wax tapers in the chandelier would "light up to great advantage" the superb Oriental Worth gown of Mrs. Bigelow

Lawrence, the New York social leader, or their glow would fall upon the peripatetic Jack Gardners of Boston, she, as their friend Nick Anderson once noted, "homelier than ever in person" but the "same generous, hospitable, cheery little body as of yore," and already a notable collector of art. John Hay, still exiled to Cleveland, where he was serving his congenial apprenticeship to his father-in-law, one of the chief financial and railway barons of the city, began his visits. Started at last on the Lincoln history, Hay would come in for a fortnight's work with his coauthor, John Nicolay. William James, visiting Washington for the first time, seemed "a wee bit hypochrondriac" but roused them agreeably with his combative talk.

For science Adams could count on another favorite, Professor Simon Newcomb, the astronomer and mathematician, now in charge of the great new telescope at the Washington Observatory. When he and Clarence King came together, only the most valiant survived the abstruse talk of "curves of heat" and "catastrophic environment." King was an intermittent houseguest. A debonair little man, no taller than his host, with "blithe blue eyes and fresh tint" and close-cropped hair that "early grew sparser and sparser," his carefully trimmed Vandyke belying the athlete, King relished the paradoxes of his career, mystifying his hosts with sudden arrivals and as sudden departures to investigate gold and silver strikes all over the continent. There was a dashing versatility in the way he played his role as their "Byron" of the sagebrush and the drawing room. He would show up with a Piute basket or send antelope horns as a New Year's greeting, each gift accompanied by an Othello-like tale.

The politicos were the most frequent visitors, coming in occasionally like Abram Hewitt, after a rough handling in the House, to be comforted by one of Senator Lamar's inexpressibly funny stories. At an impromptu caucus on the silver purchase bill, the "Bland Swindle," as Adams called it, David A. Wells dinned into their ears the distasteful jargon of the silverite. Then Horace White, former editor of the *Chicago Tribune*, would come in to counter with the gospel of the "gold-bug" and "bloated bond holder." Adams and Godkin severely lectured Congressman Jacob Dolson Cox for his wild talk of social upheaval if the silver bill were defeated. At another session they prodded Attorney General Charles Devens on the danger of the silver legislation until he assured them that President Hayes would do "the proper thing" if the bill passed. At this time also Adams began his acquaintance with Wayne MacVeagh, former minister to Turkey, who, though son-in-law of the boss Simon Cameron, rejected the "family's principles or want of principles" and made common cause with the reform wing of the Republican party. The suave and knowledgeable Aristarchi Bey had come early into their orbit, without waiting for them to call, but they at once recognized him as useful "for filling in at dinner."

President Hayes was the first of a long line of Presidents with whom Adams was to endure an intimacy of sorts. During the winter of 1878 Hayes dropped in at the Schurzes', where Lamar, Godkin, and Adams were relaxing over cigars. The trio hardly looked up. Baffled by their pose, he left after twenty minutes. Encountering Nordhoff at the White House, he grumbled, "Nordhoff, I've just met two of your reformed Democrats at Schurz's—Godkin and Henry Adams. What dull owls they are!" Nordhoff, in ecstasy, hurried across Lafayette Square to share the presidential *mot*.

As Adams looked back on the experimental first winter in Washington he was able to call it an unqualified success. He had "worked hard and with good effect." His wife "had a house always amusing and interesting." For her part, the drama of Washington life was so agreeable that she looked ahead to their continued residence with avid anticipation. When they had first moved to Marlborough Street four years before, she had exclaimed, "Life is so pleasant I wish death and old age were only myths." After a season in Washington, there was even stronger reason for such a wish.

Yet death and old age were visibly not myths. In Washington death had its picturesque side. The white and gold hearses in the frequent processions to St. John's Church looked to Clover "just like bon bons on wheels." All too often the Adamses had to endure the clichés of the Episcopal ritual that ended the chapter for friends and acquaintances. Unbidden, there would rise to the surface Clover's horror—and fear—of a lingering death, and her brief comments regularly expressed a kind of *absit omen*. "He was a pleasant courteous old man," she wrote of one of her departed friends, "and had a happy life until his wife died, and is to be envied for having laid it down so easily—I cannot understand why the Episcopalians pray to be delivered from 'sudden death.' Henry and I have made up our minds that where we die there we will be buried and not expressed to Boston like canned terrapin."

In their summer place at Beverly Farms in August 1878, when Henry Adams began to think about going to Europe to collect source materials for a major historical project to follow the Gallatin biography, he could hardly avoid stretching himself with a luxurious yawn. "Every now and then, in my bourgeois ease and uniformity, my soul rebels against it all, and I want to be on my wandering again, in the Rocky Mountains, on the Nile, the Lord knows where. But I humbly confess that it is vanity and foolishness. I really prefer comfort and repose . . . It is ludicrous to play Ulysses. There is not in this wide continent of respectable mediocrity a greasier citizen, or one more contented in his oily ooze, than myself."

ADAMS'S VISION of Washington as the future cultural and intellectual center of the nation was the common dream of the large number of scientists who had been drawn to the capital by the exigencies of the Civil War and had stayed on to man the many new bureaus and departments that had sprung into being. One of the most active spirits in that scientific renaissance was Clarence King. For several years King had been busy publishing the reports of the Geological Exploration of the Fortieth Parallel and contributing his *Systematic Geology* to them. Adams had seen part of the far-flung field work of the expedition in the summer of 1871, when he joined the Geological Survey in western Wyoming. He had spent a month with the outfit of Arnold Hague, one of the principal geologists of the group, in the Medicine Bow country, and then he rode with the party down to Estes Park in Colorado. There he chanced to run into King, who was the geologist in charge of the survey. The versatile King, as Adams was to praise him in the *Education,* "had everything to interest and delight" him, and the famous friendship of the two men took root as if predestined.

Adams was now on intimate terms with the extraordinary coterie of men surrounding King and his chief associate, John Wesley Powell, the explorer of the Colorado River. He followed with the closest interest the series of seven reports as they were brought out under King's direction. Three other lesser surveys, each independent of the others—Hayden's, Wheeler's, and Powell's—brought their own contingents of scientists to Washington. Inevitably Henry Adams became involved in the rivalries arising from the overlapping of the surveys and the differences in their methods. There were differences also over the political and economic implications of their work, especially over Powell's revolutionary proposals for conservation of the western lands. The clash of rival ambitions erupted into violent public controversy. Scientists leagued with their chiefs until the behind-the-scene activities in the clubs of Washington resembled rival conspiracies as they jockeyed for control of the proposed reorganization of the surveys.

King and his allies gravitated into a scientific and social organization of their own when it became obvious that their group would carry the day. They founded the Cosmos Club "to bind the scientific men of Washington by a social tie and thus promote that solidarity which is important to their proper work and influence." Henry Adams joined the original promoters as an "author" at the founding meeting on January 6, 1879, and was made a member of the first Committee on Admissions. Among the many notable adherents, besides King and Powell, were Spencer Baird, secretary of the Smithsonian; Daniel Coit Gilman, president of Johns Hopkins; William Harkness, the Navy mathematician; Lester Frank Ward, a professional paleontologist with Powell's survey; and Theodore F. Dwight, librarian at the State Department. The first club rooms, opposite the Treasury on Pennsylvania Avenue, were only a short walk from Adams's home.

The excitement over the impending consolidation of the surveys grew from day to day. King hurried in and out of town at frequent intervals, making his headquarters at the Adamses'. On March 3, 1879, the bill passed setting up the consolidated United States Geological Survey in Schurz's Department of the Interior. The Senate confirmed King's appointment as director of the new bureau early in April. To the Adamses it was a "Waterloo victory," for they knew King's royal tastes. The $6,000 salary would severely handicap him, as he would be barred from the private practice of his profession.

Adams's interest in the new directions of science took a great leap forward when he came to Washington. Clarence King's arresting lecture in 1877 at the Sheffield Scientific School, "Catastrophism and Evolution," had reopened for Adams the old argument between Agassiz and Lyell. He had dashed off a brief notice for the *Nation* to call favorable attention to King's dramatic theory. "In the face of the facts of our geology the uniformitarian theory breaks down and must be abandoned." Nature "did proceed by what amounted to leaps," and the leaps corresponded with the alleged "gaps" in the geological record.

When King's *Systematic Geology* appeared in 1878, Adams continued his scientific reflections in a two-column review in the *Nation*. Once the "laws" of stratigraphy could be enunciated geology would become "a science in a new sense, and many of the most serious difficulties in studying past and even future changes of the earth's history might be overcome." King's theory of catastrophic volcanic agencies rested on William Thomson's application of the Second Law of Thermodynamics and entropy to the cooling of the earth's crust. Adams's allusion in the review is his earliest mention of the law that would later engross him. King later regretted the extreme features of his hypothesis, but by that time Adams was moving on to fresher skepticisms.

Not since the great days in the London of the 1860s had Adams lived in so vital and intoxicating an atmosphere. The grand visions of the possibilities of science which had so excited his imagination fifteen years before were now being realized on the largest scale under the aegis of the federal government. His grandfather's dream of lighthouses in the sky, of a frontier transformed by science, came daily closer to fulfillment. No wonder that he exulted to his English friend that he and his "fellow *gelehrte*" might help bring in an American century which would say in its turn "the last word of civilisation." Here a science of society was at last within the grasp of mankind; here theory and practice might learn to run toward the future on both feet.

9

Literary Debut

ADAMS'S MERE "SEARCHING ARCHIVES" in Washington proved a characteristic understatement, for he kept to a rigorous schedule of work each day before yielding to the pleasures of society. He had begun collecting documents on Albert Gallatin during his last few months at Harvard, and the reams of transcripts had risen on his study table at Beverly Farms in the summer of 1877. The first volume of the projected three volumes of Gallatin's writings was already in type by the time he moved to Washington.

At the State Department he struck "rich soil" in the Jefferson Papers, and his copyist matched his industry. He interrupted the editing of the papers to begin the biography and by Christmas Eve 1877 was able to send off for approval to Gallatin's son the draft of the first three chapters. Thereafter Adams appears to have alternated work between the papers and the biography. At the end of November 1878 he reported to Gaskell that his "ponderous work is more than half done." He was able to date the preface for the three volumes of writings "January, 1879," and the preface of the biography "May, 1879."

Avid for anecdotes of Gallatin, he went to Baltimore to interview the picturesque old Madame Patterson-Bonaparte, living alone with her raffish memories of the emperor's family and of the ruthless decree which had annulled her marriage to Napoleon's youngest brother. She had once been on the closest terms with Gallatin and his wife, and Henry's vivid impressions were promptly related to his father-in-law. "She is ninety-three years old and a miser. Henry was shown into a squalid room high up in a boarding house . . . Madame Bonaparte was dressed in old calico duds, sitting in her armchair. Henry says very handsome still if she would wear lace and diamonds and black velvet . . . She told Henry her memoirs are all prepared ready to be published." The piquant reminiscences with which he had hoped to enliven the biography did not materialize.

The writing of the background story of Revolutionary Virginia inspired Adams to visit the localities where that history had been made. One focus of interest lay at Mount Vernon. Twenty-eight years had passed since as a boy of twelve he had trudged along the mazy paths of that national shrine at the side of his father. He and his wife went down by steamer and "moused" about like all other tourists, reverently pausing at the deathbed, yet not overlooking the quaint touch of the opening in the bedroom door for the use of the cat. The visit deeply impressed Adams, for now every facet of the place was drenched with historical significance. At Monticello they visited Jefferson's granddaughter Sarah Randolph. They did not head north for their annual summer at Beverly Farms until they had made a swing through western Pennsylvania, visiting the backwoods locale of Gallatin's early career and the scene of the Whiskey Rebellion. On June 7, 1878, Adams wrote from Beverly Farms to old George Bancroft, "We are at the end of our wandering for the present and I am at work again, to my great joy."

Adams called on a number of experts for help, gracefully acknowledging his chief debts in the preface. He owed most to his venerable neighbor George Bancroft, profiting especially from Bancroft's critical reading of the proof sheets. "I have adopted your amendments in every case but one," he gratefully wrote. To get the woman's point of view, besides that of his own fireside critic, he enlisted two notable Boston blues. Writing to one of them, Mrs. Samuel Parkman, a Beverly Farms intimate, he gallantly exaggerated, "My two readers are you and Mrs. George Bancroft. I shall have no more, but these two are enough to satisfy my ambition."

The biography gave Henry Adams as agreeable a problem as a philosopher-historian might wish. He could be as objective and detached as he ever was in his essays on British finance and yet point a moral for the times with even more stunning force. The issues which had stirred the country since the Civil War had all had their counterparts in Gallatin's time: currency and government financing, tariff revision, naval expansion, the spoils system, taxation, the retirement of the public debt, public improvements, relations with England, the power of the executive, and the role of the cabinet. Gallatin's career was a touchstone that might expose the political hacks who under Grant had debauched the government and whose influence still darkened national councils.

As a historian and literary artist Adams had a multiple problem—to bring Gallatin out of Jefferson's shadow, to rehabilitate his character from the Federalist calumnies that had gathered about it, and to show that if his public career ended ultimately in failure, it was the failure of a tragic hero confronted by a hostile destiny. Like the Adamses, Gallatin achieved leadership "by the sheer force of ability and character without ostentation and without the tricks of popularity," but in one vital trait he excelled them: "His temper was under most perfect control."

The artistic need—and wish—to exalt Gallatin at Jefferson's expense tempted Adams, for he nursed the family grievance that Jefferson had "turned my harmless ancestor into the street at midnight." Perhaps even more compelling was his wish to identify himself with Gallatin, seeing in Jefferson the mirror of his own weaknesses, his aversion to rough combat, his love of abstract generalizations, and his own Hamlet-like indecision.

From the dramatic contrasts of the biography there emerges Adams's ideal of the modern statesman, one able to "move with his generation" and still to lead it. The book was both testament and prophecy: it epitomized the political morality of which all the Adamses were trustees, and it warned of the dangers that lay ahead for the Hayes administration and its successors if the lessons of the past were ignored. In Gallatin's management of the Treasury Adams found the true secret of power of the ideal statesman. "There are to the present time," Adams wrote, "in all American history only two examples of practical statesmanship which can serve as perfect models . . . to persons who wish to understand what practical statesmanship has been under an American system . . . The conditions of the highest practical statesmanship require that its models should be financiers . . . Washington and Jefferson doubtless stand pre-eminent as the representatives of what is best in our national character or its aspirations, but Washington depended mainly upon Hamilton, and without Gallatin Mr. Jefferson would have been helpless."

Into the writing of the biography, his first major literary undertaking, Adams poured so much of his personal conviction and so thoroughly made himself a partisan of his hero that he always looked back upon the work with special affection. Blemishes he willingly conceded, but these sank from view before the image he had evoked. "To do justice to Gallatin," he wrote to Samuel Tilden, "was a labor of love. After long study of the prominent figures in our history, I am more than ever convinced that, for combination of ability, integrity, knowledge, unselfishness, and social fitness, Mr Gallatin has no equal." Eager for a symbol to which his political ideals might cleave, he found it in Gallatin.

Outwardly the massive one-volume *Life of Albert Gallatin* resembled the conventional and still popular life-and-letters biography, but Adams superimposed upon the form an artistic and dramatic tension that was new. The interaction of the chief actor with the secondary personages gave rise to a succession of dramatic moments. The action leading up to these tableaux he developed with a novelist's feeling for intrigue and narrative complication, as for example in the treatment of the Whiskey Rebellion, the working out of Randolph's charges against Madison, the fateful progress of the embargo of 1807, and the struggles of the Ghent negotiation. He therefore placed the emphasis upon Gallatin's "political and public career." The personal aspects of Gallatin's life, its varied interior drama, was little more than hinted at. Nevertheless Adams was aware of the biographer's responsibility, regretting at one point that for the period of greatest interest, from 1801 on, "of his social life, his private impression, and his intimate conversation with the person most in his confidence at this time, not a trace can now be recovered."

The congenial stress on politics produced a rather curious disproportion. Gallatin retired from public life in 1827 at the age of sixty-six. "Intellectually," said Adams, "the next fifteen years were the most fruitful of his life." He devoted himself to science, especially Indian ethnology, with such success that he came to be recognized as the Father of American Ethnology. Yet of the nearly seven hundred pages of the biography Adams devoted only two to these years.

The *Gallatin* and the three volumes of *Writings* were a formidable assault upon reviewers, but the indifferent and grudging reception was to put Adams lastingly on the defensive. The *North American Review,* which he had edited for six years, dismissed it with the briefest mention: "a valuable repository of information for the real student of history" but "too voluminous, and has too much of the character of a digest of material, to be attractive to a general reader."

In England the *Saturday Review* condemned him for having "monstrously . . . enlarged his work," provoking his annoyed comment that the magazine had always been "idiotic" on "everything American." The *Athenaeum* also deplored the book's excessive length, though it conceded that it offered "much instruction" if the reader had the necessary "patience and perseverance." Lodge praised it in a long and judicious article in the *International Review.* "Patient investigation is everywhere apparent," he declared, "and is supplemented by a firm historical grasp, and by vigor and originality of thought and opinion." He acknowledged that because of Gallatin's character the narrative was "too uniformly sombre—a defect which Mr. Adams does not always overcome." Gratefully, Adams told him it was "the best by far of the reviews I have seen" save that like the rest it sinned in staying too close to the book. "All are obnoxious to the complaint they mostly bring against Gallatin, that of being dull, and with no excuse, for there is ample material for a very spicy review."

The defense of his attitude gave him an opportunity to press upon Lodge the ultimate implications of the book. "To my mind the moral of his life lies a little deeper than party politics and I have tried here and there rather to suggest than assert it. The inevitable isolation and disillusionment of a really strong mind—one that combines force with elevation—is to me the romance and tragedy of statesmanship."

Adams was especially let down by Godkin's *Nation.* Its review attacked the work with a strangely personal violence. The anonymous critic charged that in make-up "this volume falls little short of being an outrage both on Albert Gallatin and on everyone who wishes to know anything about him." Its author had "sinned knowingly, and is accordingly entitled to no mercy." If Adams resented the fact that Edwin Godkin, his good friend and political ally, had published such an equivocal review of his first major writing, he did not give any sign. When Godkin tried to get his reaction, he insisted that he "never dreamed of taking offence at it."

Too full of a piquant secret to realize his tactlessness, Godkin had hurried to inquire of Mrs. Adams whether Henry had taken offence at the review. With ironic aplomb, Clover had replied, "If as you say a genial and suave notice of the Life of Gallatin was intended to 'do Henry good,' I've no doubt it will." Unable to endure the uncertainty, Godkin tried again after the lapse of a year. Adams reproached him with such forceful dignity that Godkin did not dare pursue his curiosity any further. The author of the anonymous review of the *Galla-*

tin was none other than Henry's elder brother, Charles Francis Adams, Jr.

In his review Charles took all too literally Henry's long-standing invitation to criticize him. Charles's motives had their mixture of jealousy. "You know perfectly well," ran his disingenuous justification to Godkin, "that my article was very complimentary on its substance, merely criticizing sharply certain defects in details ... If Henry and his wife can't stand that, but insist on pure and solid taffy, he'd better stop writing. My good sister-in-law don't favor me much now, and if she finds it is I who dared criticize her adored Henry, my goose will be finally cooked ... My sole object in writing the review was to induce Henry not to treat any audience at all as a thing beneath an author's consideration." There is no evidence that Henry ever learned the identity of his *Nation* critic. It is tempting to believe, however, that he hit upon the secret and decided to relish the cream of the jest by never letting on.

The biography surmounted the early detractions and ultimately established itself as a definitive work among professional historians. To the distinguished authors of *The Growth of the American Republic* it stands as "one of the best Republican biographies." Only after three-quarters of a century did it have to surrender its title of "definitive" to Raymond Walter's scholarly and comprehensive biography. But though Walters added flesh and far more of the color of life to the irreproachable Gallatin and his times, he revealed no serious flaw in Adams's scholarship and left unaltered Adams's high estimate of this ideal statesman.

WHILE THE GALLATIN VOLUMES were making their way through the press, Adams secretly turned to a more engrossing project, one far less imposing in mass but calculated to have a much more stirring effect upon reviewers and the public. It was his novel *Democracy*. To his confidante Mary Dwight Parkman, the widow of Dr. Samuel Parkman, he wrote on February 20, 1879, "The great work you are kind enough to remember is still trembling on the edge of the fire and may at any moment become ashes. That way lies safety if not immortality." He was to choose the more satisfying safety of anonymous publication. Godkin and Clarence King were also the first secret sharers, and of course the publisher of the book, Henry Holt. After

Democracy came out in 1880, John Hay, his wife, and Raphael Pumpelly joined those already in the know.

Few literary secrets have been better kept from the public. Librarians continued their conjectural attributions to Clarence King and John Hay until the fact of Adams's authorship was confirmed by Holt in 1920, two years after Adams's death. Holt, who received the manuscript in the late spring of 1879 "with the most strenuous injunctions regarding secrecy," recalled that Adams had explained that it was not that he feared unpopularity so much as that "some of the characters were carefully drawn from prominent living persons who were his friends, and some of these he had touched humorously and ironically."

In the person of the heroine, Madeleine Lee, Adams drew not only the portrait of his wife but also more tellingly the psychological portrait of himself. Mrs. Lightfoot Lee, a sophisticated, wealthy, and high-principled widow, comes to Washington "to see with her own eyes the action of primary forces; to touch with her own hand the massive machinery of society; to measure with her own mind the capacity of the motive power. She is bent upon getting to the heart of the great American mystery of democracy and government." The education of Madeleine Lee in national politics gives her a pretty grim picture, and in the end she runs away in horror and disgust to Europe, quite as her creator sought a moral bath in 1870, after a year of Grant's administration, flight being the only apparent way out of the impasse.

Late in March 1880 the *New York Tribune*'s "Literary Notes" carried a brief item which concluded: "It is intimated that many readers will imagine they see portraits in the book." The sly hint "fetched" them. Before the end of April, a second printing was called for. In all there were nine printings of the 1880 edition. Word of the novel's scandalous success winged across the ocean. The appetite whetted by such critics of American democracy as Carlyle, Dickens, Ruskin, and Matthew Arnold snapped hungrily at this domestic confession of failure. The new book, though a little critical of English snobbery and bad taste in women's clothes, allowed a cultivated Englishman to glow with pleasurable complacency. Prime Minister Gladstone recommended it highly. Mrs. Humphry Ward in her review said that everyone was talking about it in England.

The reception of the novel in England was nothing short of sensational, so much so that Adams saw to it that excerpts from the American reviews of the 1880 edition were included in the 1882 reprint in England. "I was afraid," he explained to Holt, "that the little bastard was fairly becoming British." All the British periodicals treated it as a major literary event and devoted column after column to praising the force of its satire. Critics willingly overlooked the gibes at the vulgarity and dowdiness of English duchesses where there was so much to flatter British vanity in really important matters. *Blackwoods* pronounced the definitive epitaph. "The curious separation of elegant Pharisees standing aloof and watching contemptuously and mournfully . . . is one of the most extraordinary spectacles ever presented to the world."

The spirit in which the novel was conceived was kin to the fierce idealism which had moved Adams ten years before to write the "Session" articles. Here was another hard blow at democracy. Violent as the satire was, it reflected a mind anxious to amend democracy. To the philosophic reader the tone was by no means hopeless. Adams was careful to remark that "underneath the scum floating on the surface of politics, Madeleine felt there was a sort of healthy current of honest principle, which swept the scum before it and kept the mass pure." The wife of John Richard Green wrote a keenly perceptive letter to Clover Adams. "I hope you enjoyed *Democracy* as much as we did. Mr. [Henry] James looks very severe and grave over it, but I am not sure whether it was on patriotic or artistic grounds. I don't understand the patriotic objection, for the author seemed to me profoundly convinced that America had made the only solution worth having of the problem of government."

Clarence King brooded over the novel as unhappily as James, but with the added provocation that he knew the identity of the author. To Adams he seems to have held his peace, but he unburdened himself in "moral lectures" to Hay and even made some progress on a sequel, titled *Monarchy*, which would expose the errors of *Democracy*.

Democracy did achieve a kind of symposium on democratic government. Like a symposium it sought to explore all sides of the question with intelligent skepticism rather than to answer it. To the Massachusetts aspirant to the Spanish mission, Nathan Gore, Adams assigned his most cogent affirmation of faith: "Democracy asserts the fact that the masses are now raised to a higher intelligence than formerly. All our civilization aims at this mark . . . I grant it is an exper-

iment, but it is the only direction society can take that is worth taking; the only conception of its duty large enough to satisfy its
instincts; the only result that is worth an effort or a risk."

The book provoked an angry and baffled clamor from American
reviewers, and an occasional grudging admission that it hit the mark.
Much of the annoyance spent itself in scornful attacks upon the anonymous author. One can imagine the hilarity with which some of these
press clippings went from hand to hand among the little group of
conspirators. The reviewer for the *Boston Evening Transcript* wrote
that the author had obviously not "mingled in what is really, in the
true sense, the best society of the Capital." *Appleton's* declared, "In
spite of its aristocratic air of cosmopolitanism, ease, and man-of-the-
world experience, there is more than a suspicion of callowness about
it—of that state of mind which it has become popular to characterize
as provincial."

As a *roman à clef* the novel was thoroughly searched for clues to
the identity of the originals. This seems to have been its chief attraction in American political circles. Newspapers sensitive to possible
libel suits and political repercussions generally named no names. Loving a secret that teased so many people, Adams never spoiled his private mirth by identifying the originals of his satire, and the guesses
and surmises of friends and enemies as to the identity both of the
characters and of the author eddy and swirl in a cloud of high-spirited
badinage through his letters and those of Clover and John Hay. The
portrait of the politically ambitious James G. Blaine as Silas P. Ratcliffe was most easily recognized. Blaine publicly cut Clarence King,
supposing him to be the author of the novel. For Adams the masterly
speech in which Blaine managed to extricate himself from the notorious Mulligan letters simply indicated that he could "squeal louder
than all the other pigs." Blaine's subsequent attacks upon Carl
Schurz's civil service program sealed his fate. From then on Blaine
became for the Adamses "our pet enmity," and they "refused him
even social recognition," deliberately cutting him and his wife even
after he became Secretary of State under Garfield.

As an Adams, Henry had been brought up to despise the fetish of
party loyalty. It was the sacrifice of personal honor and integrity on
that altar that most deeply shocked his heroine. In condemning Blaine
in the person of Ratcliffe with such uncompromising rigor, Adams
was preparing an untenable position for himself that could end only

in complete political cynicism. John Hay, who soon became his closest friend, not only supported Blaine but developed an affection for him. Learning of Blaine's reelection, he congratulated him, "Pass greatly on! Thou hast overcome." Adams had to close his eyes to what he saw as Hay's moral eccentricity while the moralist in him would grow more sardonic at the world—and at himself. Soon another exception would have to be made for the notorious Pennsylvania politician Senator James Donald Cameron, whose lovely young second wife, Elizabeth, was destined to transform the social life of Lafayette Square. What could Adams make of a world that divided a man against himself and compelled morality to be selective?

The literary excellence of the novel was widely appreciated despite the patriotic reservations. Some saw similarities to Henry James in the use of the technique of psychological self-examination and the rejection of elaborate and realistic setting. A few thought the idea stemmed from Alphonse Daudet's *Nabob,* one of the successes of 1877. The book was compared favorably with Trollope's political novels. Mrs. Humphry Ward in the *Fortnightly* rated it with the best of Lord Beaconsfield. The reviewer in the London *Spectator* believed that in "grafting political interests on a romance" the author surpassed Lord Beaconsfield and showed "the touch of a master hand." The undoubted power of Ratcliffe's characterization drew much praise. "Nothing in its way so good in our literature," said the *Atlantic.* The *Saturday Review* called it a "masterpiece." The *New York Tribune* gave the most judicious explanation of the success of the novel in England: "There is a certain fine workmanship, a polished style, a brightness and finish, of which Englishmen have learned to look for better examples in American fiction than in their own . . . But its chief attraction was the piquancy of its subject . . . the picture of social and political life at the American capital for which the Old World had been looking—a mob of coarse, ignorant, smart, and dishonest people, with only the British minister moving among them as a superior person."

The guessing game as to the authorship went merrily on for several years, to the vast entertainment of Adams and the elect few in the secret. In their letters Adams and his wife tossed about the names of nominees in a flood of raillery at each new flurry of public interest. "I am much amused but not surprised at your suggesting me of having written *Democracy,*" Clover wrote her father, "as I find myself on the 'black list' here with Miss Loring, Arthur Sedgwick, Manton Marble, Clarence King, and John Hay . . . All I *know* is that I did not write it. Deny it from me if anyone defames me absent." Indeed the secret *had* to be kept if the Adamses were to hold up their heads in Washington.

How the hilarious brew was doubly distilled appears in an exchange of letters which immediately followed the anonymous publication of John Hay's anti–labor union novel, *The Bread-Winners,* in the winter of 1883. Charles Francis Adams, Jr., took pen in hand again and addressed himself to the editor of the *Nation,* saying in part: "It is written by the same hand that wrote the novel 'Democracy' some years ago, which had so large a circulation in England. It has the same coarse, half-educated touch; and the Nast-like style of its portrait and painting is unmistakable . . . Could you have a short paragraph written for the 'notes' of the 'Nation' suggesting this idea?" Godkin sent the letter on to Adams and at the bottom he succinctly queried, "What shall I say to this?" Godkin, of course, did not yet know that Hay was the author of *The Bread-Winners.*

Delirious with joy, Henry dashed off a letter to "Colonel John Hay," enclosing the one from Godkin. "I want to roll on the floor; to howl, kick and sneeze; to weep silent tears of thankfulness to a beneficent providence which has permitted me to see this day; and finally I want to drown my joy in oceans of Champagne and lemonade. Never, No, never, since Cain wrote his last newspaper letter about Abel, was there anything so droll." He enjoined the strictest secrecy upon his "Dear Heart," saying that he would urge Godkin "to get the 'Note' if possible, and print it with the author's initials." He signed himself "Ever your poor, coarse and half-educated friend, Henry Adams," and added, "My coarse and half-educated wife has had a fit over her brother-in-law's Nast-like touch." The scheme succeeded. The unsuspecting Charles rose like a trout to the fly. His note to the editor duly appeared over a modest "A," dated February 8, from Boston. Both novels, he said, had "the same strong, coarse, Nast-like drawing of aspect and character."

IN THEIR SECOND AUTUMN in Washington, the Adamses had settled into the accustomed grooves with almost audible sighs of pleasure. Their "establishment" was "set afloat *à la* Noah's ark," said Clover. "Henry and I . . . 2 dogs . . . 2 horses, 2 women servants, 2 men servants." Each morning at nine, except when the ice became treacherous, they would clatter off into the countryside along the back streets to avoid the crush of horsecars and provision wagons. A favorite run took them along the laurel-margined road up the Potomac to the Chain Bridge, and they relished the "glorious glimpses of the distant city." Entranced by the autumn colors edging the country roads, they wished "the days were twice as long." Usually back at Lafayette Square by eleven, Henry had several hours at his desk at the State Department before tea. Life was inordinately full as his head buzzed with projects—the *Gallatin* rapidly finishing, a much more grandiose historical project beckoning in the distance, and his first novel burgeoning, the germ having probably been planted on the visit to Mount Vernon that spring.

Henry did not need to dissemble when with a touch of complacency he fretted, "Life is going so fast that I hardly know whether the remnant is worth exerting oneself about." The "riot of interests and individualities" almost stunned the pair, yet the ceaseless dance that began with five o'clock tea so fed his restless cravings that at the slightest letup in the round of dinners and receptions, he felt neglected and abandoned.

A typical week brought Congressman Cox and historian von Holst on a Sunday with "good talk until midnight." On Tuesday a small party at Madame Outrey's, the wife of the French minister, "mostly diplomates—counts and barons and marquises thick as blackberries." Thursday they had to miss a "game" party at the Schurzes' when an unexpected guest dropped in. As for the circle round their new Japanese tea table, all the regulars were back in attendance, reinforced by numerous birds of passage from the legations. During the doldrums of the Christmas week, Clarence King, Schurz, and Henry Cabot Lodge joined the court. King, ever their favorite guest, agog with "politics" of the Geological Survey, captivated Clover with his bright chatter, whether "raving" about the latest New York fashions in silk turbans or joking about his California escapades. "No one was so good company" in the drawing room or on a shopping trip to beguile the hours until Henry got back from his desk. Secretary Evarts came in to clot the air with his habitual oratory and to pass on a venomous tidbit from the great-grandson of Hamilton: "The Adams family grow viler in each generation." Adams could afford to smile, knowing that as a historian he would have the last word.

The liberal Republican remnant came so incessantly as to mark his as a "political house." The good-natured wrangling would leap from currency to the recent Southern outrages or to Schurz's efforts to protect the Indians. Even the ambitious Garfield put in an appearance, risking the suspicions of the orthodox Republicans. Notably absent that winter and spring was John Hay, busy with his part of the Lincoln biography and too ill to visit Washington. And in the intervals there were always "our eminent Boston constituents" to entertain and lobbying friends like their New York lawyer friend Sam Barlow. In mock anguish Clover declared, "I am going to put a sign out 'Railroad Hotel. Meals served at all hours.'" At least they were growing skillful at dodging receiving lines. Adams contrived some spare moments to begin brushing up on his French in anticipation of a research trip abroad. Clover gave up early because their tutor, a "nasty little Jesuit," too obviously shunned soap and water.

One experience of the winter made a profound impression upon Adams. Leaving King as guest in residence, he and Clover accompanied the British minister Sir Edward Thornton and his distinguished entourage for a ten-day trip to Niagara Falls. Snugly quartered at Prospect House on the Canadian side, they sang English ballads and looked out at the enormous icicles that glittered from the lip of the falls. While Clover nursed a sore throat, Henry joined the rest in a wild sleighride in a snowstorm, "shinnied" up icicles, and "lunched on mince pie and pickles in some squalid restaurant." Utterly carefree, they passed the time with whist and poker and singing the irresistible lyrics of "Give my chewing gum to sister, I shall never want it more." Thriftily Adams noted the eerie beauty of the scene and the camaraderie, storing them away for the right literary moment in a second novel.

The tuneful evenings about the fire inspired Clover to rent a piano and order all her music sent down from Marlborough Street and her German lieder from her father's home. Washington could now be home to them without reservation. In the spring Dr. Hooper made his headquarters with them for several weeks, in what had become a regular custom. The days went by, as Adams told Gaskell, "like a dream of the golden age." As usual Adams was unable to avoid continued involvement in the affairs of his friends. Lodge enlisted him to dragoon contributors for the *International Review,* a task which he went at so vigorously that it was mistakenly assumed that he was a coeditor with Lodge and John T. Morse. Adams persuaded the ever-reluctant J. D. Cox to do an article on the Indian question, and he put Simon Newcomb to work on the silver question.

As one reviews the pell-mell rush of activities of that second season in Washington, a forge full of irons kept busily glowing, one can accept Adams's defense to his friends that he had little time for letter writing. All his projects were moving better than he had dared hope; the *Gallatin* was lumbering through the press, and *Democracy* was off to Holt. He was free to begin work again on the large project in American history that had begun to take shape in his mind during his last year at Harvard. His searches among the Jefferson and Madison papers in the State Department archives revealed that the important American counterparts of the foreign diplomatic dispatches were buried in the national archives of England, France, and Spain. Further progress in his project required that those archives be attacked. Unwilling to "dawdle about Beverly Farms" any longer than necessary, he booked passage on the *Gallia* for May 28, 1879.

Though the happy pair gave up the house at 1501 H Street with its lovely wisteria and "superb rose trees" coming into bloom, there was no intention of returning to live in Boston. Boston had receded even farther into the distance since their last visit, especially because Clover's relations with Henry's family had deteriorated as a result of her "indiscreet conversations," reports of which had enlivened Boston gossip. Henry went alone to Quincy shortly before sailing and talked long with his parents in an attempt to mollify them. They did not blame him, his father assured him. Henry had always been one of his "most trusted supports," and he had no feelings "but those of an affection and love for him." However, he confided to his diary, "I pity rather than dislike his wife. But henceforth I must regard her only as a marplot and as a subject for commiseration." He nevertheless went into Boston to Dr. Hooper's home to make his peace with Clover for Henry's sake. As she was herself on the way to Quincy, he left his card "and felt relieved."

Before embarkation there was time for an act of prudence that reflected the maturing of Henry's and Clover's respect and affection for each other. Just before their marriage in 1872 they had made out reciprocal wills. Now they executed codicils changing the provisions for life estates to unlimited bequests. A week later they sailed for England.

10

European Orbit

SIX YEARS HAD PASSED since Henry Adams and his wife had last visited England and the Continent on their wedding journey. He donned his "cloak of historian" with a sardonic flourish, his soul a rebel against "bourgeois ease and conformity," and set out to enjoy the agreeable cachet that his work had inspired in scholarly circles. The small sprinkling of American and British reviews of the *Gallatin* that had begun to appear circulated usefully among his English acquaintances. James Russell Lowell wrote from Madrid to compliment his onetime student and, being a scholar, judiciously noted an error in a quotation in the biography. Adams responded with his usual stammer of self-depreciation. "No one has ever read it, or ever will, but perhaps, some centuries hence, antiquaries will use it."

His intention to go abroad had crystallized in August 1878. He needed "a winter in Spain and Paris, and a spring in London," he said, "to study the diplomatic correspondence of the three governments, in regard to America, during the time of Napoleon, from 1800 to 1812." Working in the records of the State Department, he had very quickly seen that he lacked transcripts of the reports sent home from Washington by European envoys.

In September 1879, several months after his arrival in England, he wrote to Ambassador Lowell, "The papers I want from the Spanish government belong wholly to the time of the first Napoleon. That brigand, as you know, swindled Spain out of Louisiana, and then sold us that province in violation of his contract with Spain . . . I want to tell the whole truth, in regard to England, France and Spain, in a 'History of the United States from 1801 to 1815,' which I have been for years collecting material for."

For nearly a month after their arrival on June 5, 1879, the Adamses surrendered to the long-anticipated pleasures of London. It felt good to get back, for they agreed with Dr. Johnson that "he who is tired of London is tired of life." They took lodgings in Half Moon Street in Piccadilly, but one street away from their friend Henry James. Adams's good companions, Sir Robert Cunliffe and Charles Milnes Gaskell, royally welcomed them, and they were soon embarked on a succession of dinners and receptions. They keenly relished the long-deferred holiday; but Adams did not forget his mission. At the "smart reception at the Foreign Office" he fell into talk with the foreign secretary about the rules of the record office that blocked the use of papers after 1802. Adams asked that the ban be lifted to "the year 1810, or, if it is not thought improper, even to the year 1815." Within a week the coveted permission was issued. He was soon "pegging away hard" at the bonanza of untouched documents.

"The second act of 'The Innocents Abroad' began," as Clover said, in September when they crossed to France and called on the French premier, William Waddington, who promised access to the secret papers in the Office of Foreign Affairs and the Ministry of Marine. However, permission was provokingly delayed. While waiting, Adams decided to try Madrid. He and Clover had been studiously cramming for the journey for several months. There had been Spanish lessons three times a week. "We have a blazing fire and read Spanish out loud; a thrilling romance with twenty-five murders in the first four chapters." Adams, sleepy with wading "through cords of plays and novels," begged Lowell, "Teach me to adore Spanish literature, for the more I read of it, the meaner my intelligence seems."

The Spanish archives in Madrid proved even balkier than the French, and Lowell, preoccupied with the desperate illness of his wife, could do little for him. The Duke of Tetuan, the foreign secretary, protested that there were papers of "too reserved a character to be shown." It was a painful check. The onset of the rainy season made Madrid even more of "a hole." There was one compensation: the Titians in the Prado galleries knocked "all my expectations flat." They fled southward. "Andalusia received us with open arms. The sun came out. Cordova was fascinating."

While Henry reveled in the scenery, Clover did not relax her practical vigilance. Aboard the train to Granada she "fell to prattling" with the women members of a family party sharing their compart-

ment. "I muttered to Henry that perhaps the Señor might know the
Chief of Archives in Seville, and why didn't he make a shot in the
dark and see what he could bring down. Henry, true to the characteristics of his first ancestor, wished me to 'bite first.' So, with an assumed air of casual curiosity, I bit deep into the core." As a result they
became acquainted with Don Leopoldo Equilaz, a rich lawyer, antiquarian, and professor of Arabic, who did happen to have connections with the national archivist.

Seeing Adams's interest in ethnology, Don Equilaz urged a visit to
Tetuan and supplied them with introductions to the "best Moorish
circles." To Tetuan they must go. "One suffers much in Spain," began
Adams's extended narrative of the expedition, "but in Africa one is
flayed alive . . . We escaped the next morning on two donkeys, my
wife seated in an arm-chair as a throne supported by a donkey, while
I modestly rode in a saddle. We were nine hours on the backs of these
animals, and reached Tetuan, 27 miles, in a condition resembling
martyrdom; but the ride was almost the most beautiful thing I ever
saw, along the Mediterranean all day, with a view that justified self-
destruction . . . At Tetuan we were deposited at the house of [the]
Consular Agent Isaac Nahon, an Ebrew Jew . . . Tetuan is the filthiest
hole I ever saw, and the most eastern . . . I have now seen enough of
Jews and Moors to entertain more liberal views in regard to the In-
quisition."

When they returned to Spain, a four-day public holiday in Seville
honoring the wedding of King Alphonso XII to the Austrian Haps-
burg Maria Christina nullified the magic of Don Leopoldo's letter.
Adams was again vanquished, but not so his resourceful wife. "Was
it by chance possible," she asked, "to give a present to some sub-
official who might let us in for the sake of a new gown for his señora?" It was possible. For three hours Adams hunted fruitlessly
among "the millions of bundles" in the archives, but at least he had
the consolation that "no other fellow can come here and trip him up
by later information and spoil his work." Back in Madrid Adams
found an ally in the young Marquess de Casa, grandson of the Spanish minister to the United States during Jefferson's administration.
The key turned in the lock. He was at last assured of John Quincy
Adams's dispatches.

They dropped back to Paris after two months in Spain to find that
the smoldering cabinet crisis had erupted as if Adams carried infec-

tion in his baggage, a fantasy of his that was to grow with the passing of the years. Premier Waddington's resignation, forced by the republicans, left Adams up in the air. He was providentially rescued by Professor Gabriel Monod, youthful editor of the *Revue historique* and a former contributor to the *North American Review*. Other intermediaries also helped untie "the knots in French red tape." A "celebrated French astronomer" supplied an entrée to the Ministry of Marine. The American chargé, Robert Hitt, interposed for access to the archives relating to Santo Domingo and Louisiana. The second secretary of the legation, Henry Vignaud, a former Confederate captain, agreed to supervise the work of transcription. Suffering setbacks with some archives, Adams had phenomenal success with others, so that there came times when he was "up to his eyes all day in fascinating work and very happy." He was "off at ten every morning, home to breakfast at twelve, and then off again from one until dark," after which he "read hard all the evening." Ahead of him lay a "mountain of papers and books to digest" and not "an hour to lose."

In the early fall Paris had been an agreeable place. Henry, still bent on improving his wife, had persuaded her to make the pilgrimage to the great Worth, where she commissioned a gown whose colors suggested "a serious peacock." Her ultrafastidious husband insisted on a complete wardrobe, an idea to which she demurred, but he twitted her, "People who study Greek must take pains with their dress." In any case their Calumet copper stock had just touched 200¼, and some extravagance was warranted. Henry James had also come over and they were much together. They whiled away their evenings dining about Paris and visiting the theater, sometimes joined by the Jack Gardners of Boston. Chill weather blocked a trip to Mont Saint Michel, but Adams managed to see a few Norman Gothic churches, which delighted him more than "watering places and casino life," and at his first sight of the cathedral of Amiens he exclaimed it was "a whacker," with features that "beat anything I knew."

By midwinter Paris lost its charm. Their English and American acquaintances had flown, and James had gone back to haunt his fireside in London. Except for a few friends at the American embassy and infrequent visits with scholarly associates like Auguste Laugel, Gabriel Monod, and Marcel Thévenin, they were rather much alone, for Parisians were not cordial to Americans, "in spite of their purchasing power," as the *Nation* observed. Adams's letter to Premier Waddington opened no social doors, and he and Clover were left to match each other's detestation of the great inhabited desert. For her it was nothing but "a huge shop and restaurant." Henry fretted even more violently. "At the best of times Paris is to me a fraud and a snare; I dislike it, protest against it, despise its stage, condemn its literature, and have only a temperate regard for its cooking; but in December and January Paris is frankly impossible." It was all the harder to bear because of his nostalgia for the Paris of the Second Empire, which he had known as a flaneur of twenty-two.

Dissatisfaction had much to thrive on. The unusually extreme cold of that winter was made even less bearable than usual for American tourists because of the shortage of firewood. The vagaries of the weather were more than matched by the howling political tempest. Léon Gambetta, who struggled to rescue the Third Republic from the royalists, Bonapartists, and Catholic clericals, had their sympathies, but the turbulence of the debate in the press and the disorderly reflection of the social and intellectual struggle on the stage and in the books of the naturalist school poisoned the atmosphere.

With the press still denied full freedom and a general amnesty of the Communards of 1870 still withheld, the protest against the established order found liveliest expression in the theater, where the freedom to give outrage was quixotically respected. They had tried a new play at the Gymnase with Henry James and had found it "very indecent and charmingly acted." If the police had "come in and borne actors and audience to the nearest station house," said Clover, "I should have conceded that they had a strong case." The immorality of the stage—and of all Paris, for that matter—seemed incarnated in the reigning favorite, Sarah Bernhardt. Of course she had to be seen at the Comédie Française in *Ruy Blas,* for she was "chic and the rage," but her tantrums and peccadilloes could not be forgiven. They joined with Henry James in taking the part of his friend the great Benoît Coquelin in his long-standing quarrel with her over the management of the Comédie and adopted Coquelin's angry judgment— "Elle n'est pas sérieuse, ni comme femme ni comme artiste [She is not to be taken seriously either as a woman or as an artist]." Adams shared as well James's rather prudish view of recent French literature. What the *Nation* said of James's *French Poets and Novelists* fitted Adams as well: "He cannot, however, help showing at times the puritanic instincts of a well-bred inhabitant of New England" in his dislike of "Andalusian passions, of ladies tumbling about on disordered couches."

When they crossed to England at the end of January they received a deepening impression of loss and decay, a sense of a dying order. Everywhere Henry and Clover perceived signs of a "great change," a palpable diminution. More of a sentimentalist than he cared to acknowledge, Adams seemed to feel himself a ghost in a strangely different England. Having once talked much to "liberal friends from John Bright downwards," he now considered English politics to be bankrupt and deprecated the political ambitions of his friend Robert Cunliffe. To build up a party, he said, a Liberal leader "must have the nerve to lay his hands on the pillars of the state, and to risk his neck for a distant future." He was not encouraged by the talk at the home of his old friend William Forster. On the lookout for large principles, he heard only petty chatter about the last debate. There was no "wit, humor, nor taste in it," but it "amused" him because it showed "how a political life vulgarises and narrows intelligent people."

Since Adams's last visit in 1873, however, England had made progress toward a new imperium. By threats and masterly bluff Disraeli had thwarted Russian designs on Constantinople and the Dardanelles, cheating her of the fruits of victory in the war with Turkey, and he had given the Turkish empire enough medication to restore it to chronic illness. By another shrewd stroke, without waiting for authority from Parliament, he had bought up the bankrupt khedive's shares in the Suez Canal and occupied Egypt. By still another stroke he liquidated the East India Company and made Queen Victoria Empress of India. To counteract Russian intrigue in Afghanistan, British troops again defiled through the passes to open the Second Afghan War. Meditating on the expansion of British rule, Adams speculated that "Afghanistan and India would swamp any ministry." Yet Disraeli had hung on. In far-off Zululand the last great colonial adventure had already begun. Annexation of the Transvaal led to full-scale war with the neighboring Zulus early in 1879. The hordes of ill-armed natives melted away under the fire of the British square, and the land passed to Queen Victoria.

Even as Adams grumbled that his Liberal friends were squandering their talents on politics, the signs had begun to point towards Disraeli's overthrow. Misled by his long-standing distrust of Gladstone, the Liberal party leader, Adams underrated his political energy and sagacity. When Adams relieved the gloom of Good Friday in London by "visiting the monkeys and lions at the zoo," the voters went to the polls to sweep the Liberal party into office by an overwhelming majority. Adams's friends Gaskell and James Bryce were carried in; Forster became chief secretary for Ireland in Gladstone's new ministry. But now that his prognostications had collapsed, Adams discounted the development. "We were more startled by George Eliot's marriage to John Cross," he wrote, "than by the elections themselves." Nevertheless, the pair of travelers were impressed, as Clover said, by the "springtide of Liberalism which has risen over the land this week." Especially pleasant was the fact that Disraeli, "that Jew bagman with his quack medicines," had been "ordered off the premises."

From the distant perspective of American progress, English politics and imperial adventures seemed less important to the Adamses than the state of English society which confronted them. "At this Belshazzar's feast, not only do we see the handwriting on the wall, but the givers of the feast do too; and they are scared, and say it's giving way. On all sides are wails of unlet farms, discontented tenants, no money, good servants who won't wear livery. The 39,000,000, who get no cakes and ale, think it's about time for the 1,000,000, who do, to treat." To Lodge, Henry Adams echoed his wife's sentiments. "I am you know a little of a communard myself ... In my uniformly untrustworthy opinion, this old shebang will come to grief. Europe has got to do some more heavy revoluting in the next twenty years, and America has a long start."

Still, life in England took on an even more magical and charmed quality for Adams than it had on his wedding journey, in spite of the air of menace that floated like an equivocal second thought about the drawing rooms and country houses which they visited. He wore his "cloak of historian" with graceful authority, and Clover had all the serene assurance of a successful Washington hostess. On their return from the Continent they were deluged with hospitality, resuming the ritual of three and four dinners a week with redoubled zest. Since the Tory "swells" were notoriously inhospitable, they had "no affiliation with that crowd." The one opportunity that Adams had to meet Disraeli was spoiled by two matrons who so harassed him at the Palgrave dinner table that he "came home foaming at the mouth." They drifted into a "respectable, mildly literary and political set," seasoned by the ecclesiastical society of the church historian Dean Stanley of Westminster, another one of the large circle of acquaintances dating from Adams's earlier visits. The Liberal victory at Eastertime naturally threw a pleasant social coloring over the remainder of their stay.

They made their headquarters in a house overlooking Birdcage Walk, the great trees beside their parlor window and the quiet surroundings putting them in mind of their beloved Beverly Farms. They reverted to their Washington custom of "breakfast" at 11:30, having found English luncheons destructive of "time and gastric juices." Afterwards they would often go together to the British Museum to work until closing. They rediscovered the ghostly terrors of a London fog, one as thick as "cream cheese" through which they groped their way at the heels of a pair of boys with flaming torches. As once before in London, Adams was induced to make one of his very rare afterdinner speeches, this time at the Shakespeare Club dinner. With the aid of a couple of American anecdotes he successfully did his patriotic duty.

Henry James was their most frequent companion. He would come in almost every day at dusk and sit chatting by the blazing fire or stand "on the hearthrug with his hands under his coat-tails." Sometimes the talk went on till midnight, and Clover would threaten that she would abandon them at 10:30. One of the chief conversational gambits was James's decision to settle in England. On this point the Adamses had violent convictions, and the debates regularly overflowed into Clover's "diary." "What it is that Henry James finds so entrancing year after year we cannot understand—for once it is very nice—but for life it seems to me a weary round."

When word reached Adams and his wife that they had been missed in Washington, they glowed with pleasure, reassured that "it was a wise move to go there to live." They had never flattered themselves "that the Hub missed us." As the end of their stay in England drew near, they eagerly looked forward to escaping the "discipline" of another shivering winter in Europe. "Winter in a first class American coffin" was preferable to "any home on this side." Adams was quite of his wife's "way of thinking and having passed more than eleven years of the twenty-two since leaving college on this side of the water he doesn't want to pass any more."

Adams's entrée to the art world of London was assured by his friendship with Francis Turner Palgrave, art critic and poet, and Thomas Woolner, the sculptor and Pre-Raphaelite poet, both of

whom helped him collect drawings and watercolors. The sensitive
Palgrave was especially voluble with advice, his talk "like Niagara,
rushing over one." At the new Grosvenor Gallery, "a refuge for the
Pre-Raphaelites," Adams met all sorts of "queer and pleasant folk"
at the exciting series of "tea fights" that launched the exhibitions.
Gustave Doré received homage, and William Holman Hunt, and
about them eddied "poets, good, bad, and indifferent; fat duchesses,
American beauties with diaphanous reputations; a social ollapod-
rida." The expatriate American James McNeill Whistler was a chief
curiosity of the show, having been well advertised by his libel suit
against Ruskin for describing one of his nocturnes as "flinging a paint
pot in the face of the public." The Adamses naturally took Ruskin's
part, for, on meeting Whistler, they found him "even more mad away
from his paint pots than near them." Their own tastes ran to Turner
and Bonington, Constable and Corot, though as collectors they were
obliged to fight "on the water color line."

Wherever they went, Mrs. Adams's reputation for pungent American slang preceded her like an agreeable shock wave. Her figures of
speech convulsed her husband as much as they did other auditors,
and he would often joyfully appropriate them. Dean Stanley guffawed
to hear that General Sherman had "the inside track" to the Presidency
and that a dull neighbor did not "enthuse one cent." In her letters one
tastes the ginger hot on the tongue as the characterizations race across
the scrawled pages. "A nice, sweet, good woman," she remarked of
one aspirant, "but not too deep for wading"; of another, she "has
taken to frescoing her face"; and of still another, "fat, rosy, placid,
torpid like a feather bed." At a reception the British women were "fat
fugues in pea-green; lean symphonies in chewing gum color; all in a
rusty minor key." A Boston adventuress "would have euchred Becky
Sharp." At a dinner party a baronet made sneering remarks about
America. "I laid him out stiff," Mrs. Adams bragged patriotically.

They found many occasions to feel their American superiority.
Even at Sir Francis Palgrave's "the social *savoir faire* and ease [were]
what one would expect in Pawtucket centre." As devotees of the great
Worth, Mrs. Adams and her compatriot Mrs. Jack Gardner had to
"smile pityingly on the Britons" for "their awful gowns." Their ultrafastidious glances searched out the dirty linen that was occasionally
more than a mere figure of speech. And yet British society had its
puzzling contradictions. "For all that, the men are poets and painters,

and the women are intelligent and have fine handles to their names."
The most agreeable Englishmen, they became convinced, were those
"in the 'upper middle class,' as they call it, whose brains and opinions
are not entailed."

Browning they met again as he made his sententious way around
the circle of established houses, but resuming the acquaintance did
not improve their opinion of the aging seer. He had "the intellectual
apathy in his face of a chronic diner out and talked incessantly in a
voice like steel." Matthew Arnold, whom Adams met for the first
time, made quite a different impression. Adams had long admired the
author of *Culture and Anarchy,* seeing in him the model for his own
well-bred moral idealism. For a time they encountered him weekly,
sometimes at the Forsters' or Smalleys' or at their own fireside in
Birdcage Walk. The Adamses encouraged him to plan an American
tour, and Clover asked her father to sound out the trustees of the
Lowell Institute.

Of all Adams's new English friendships, the one he most cherished
was that with John Richard Green, the brilliant author of the *Short
History of the English People.* Nearly the same age as Adams, Green
was one of the most attractive personalities of his time, erudite and
yet incapable of being dull, and, what must have specially pleased
Adams, sufficiently independent as to take issue with the great Edward Augustus Freeman, whose disciple he had once been. His ideal
of history, as a coherent development flashing with picturesque and
dramatic incidents, captivated Adams. He "bids fair to become my
most intimate guardian and teacher," Adams confessed. Green, for
his part, regarded Adams as "one of the three . . . people in the world
to whom early history has any meaning."

The only other acquaintance that added "greatly to [Adams's]
score" was William Lecky, a vigorous forty-one like Adams, who had
recently published the first two volumes of his *History of England
during the Eighteenth Century.* Lecky, a pioneer scientific historian,
had already demonstrated the value of the positivist approach to history in two notable books, *The History of Rationalism* and *The History of European Morals.* The meeting with Lecky in March of 1880
initiated an exchange of several visits at which Adams pursued his
double role of student and schoolmaster, putting down his Nilometer
into the turbid currents of English positivism. Lecky's home was a
chief intellectual center of London. There Henry met another famous

historian whom he had briefly encountered at the legation many years before, James Anthony Froude, who in his very successful *History of England* was content to exploit the sheer drama of events. There too at a notable dinner he met the reigning French intellect, Ernest Renan, then in London to give a course of lectures in French.

The affinity of Adams's ideas and attitudes with those of the skeptical French humanist must have instantly drawn him to the jovial pessimist. Even as the apostle of disenchantment Renan clung to an inextinguishable residue of moral idealism. Agnostic and seeming materialist, he could yet bend his spirit in eloquent religious homage, as in his moving "Prayer on the Acropolis." On Adams, restlessly in quest of an education, the example of such an aesthetically satisfying resolution was not to be lost.

At that memorable dinner Adams also met the great physicist John Tyndall, a pioneer in the field of thermodynamics, and once again he listened to Herbert Spencer, the pontiff of English positivist thought, then at the height of his enormous vogue. Adams had met Spencer the preceding summer one evening at John Fiske's rooms over "pipes and grog" at the same time that he took the measure of Thomas Henry Huxley.

They were all Darwinists who greeted Adams over the pipes and grog, whatever their doctrinal differences. John Fiske, the notorious "positivist" whom Adams had supplanted at Harvard in 1870, was the most wholehearted devotee of the group. He was then lecturing in London and scoring an immense personal triumph. Darwinism, he declared, had freed him from Agassiz's "pseudo-Platonic attempt to make metaphysical abstractions do the work of physical forces." Henry Holt, another ardent Spencerian and Darwinist and an intimate of Fiske's, was probably also of the company, for he was then in London and presumably in touch with Adams concerning the publication of *Democracy*.

Adams kept Lodge posted on his progress in the spring of 1880. Old newspapers occupied him for a month at the British Museum from eleven to four daily, work that seemed "pure loss of time, but inevitable." There would occur moments when he felt himself becoming a desiccated pedant like George Eliot's Casaubon. In May he reported that he had "finished with the Record Office, completed my search through newspapers, collected the greater part of my pamphlets, and sounded all the wells of private collections . . . In Paris and Madrid copyists are at work for me . . . I foresee a good history if I have health and leisure the next five years . . . My belief is that I can make something permanent of it, but, as time passes, I get into a habit of working only for the work's sake and disliking the idea of completing and publishing . . . On the other hand I enjoy immensely the investigation."

Adams and Lodge had worked closely together on the American archives for the period out of which had come Lodge's *Cabot* and Adams's *New England Federalism*. Lodge now helped fill in one gap by sending over to London transcripts of envoy Charles Pinckney's notes on the 1802 Claims Convention with Spain. They helped Adams to put some of the pieces of the historical mosaic together. The American diplomatic maneuvers during the Napoleonic period began to emerge as the materials for Olympian comedy. Pinckney and Monroe "made an awful blunder in signing that treaty; they were fairly scared to death. Now that I see the English side, they appear utterly ridiculous, and poor dear old Jefferson too, but our beloved Federalists most of all. Ye Gods, what a rum lot they were!" Two months later he made his final report of progress and a forecast of the immense task ahead of him. "I have made a careful study of English politics from 1801 to 1815, and have got my authorities in order . . . My material is enormous . . . Burr alone is good for a volume. Canning and Perceval are figures that can't be put in a nut-shell, and Napoleon is vast. I have got to contemplate six volumes for the sixteen years as inevitable."

Never far from the surface of his thought was the memory of his own ambition to be "a power in the land." He therefore read with a degree of envy of Lodge's political activity at the Chicago convention of the Republican party in 1880. Starved for political gossip, he grumbled at the failure of so many of his correspondents to reply to his copious letters. With Lodge's inside accounts before him he resumed, as in 1876, the role of political strategist. At all costs the Grant influence must be counteracted, and the present status preserved. Their friend James A. Garfield seemed to Adams "a very strong candidate" whose influence might be very valuable to Lodge. Adams counseled that "all your money and work must go" to the crucial state of New York. With Lodge's election to the Massachusetts legislature, the time had come for practical advice. "If you can make friends with the most influential members, including the Speaker, if you can occasionally bring one home to a family dinner, or to a talk in your library; if you can, in short, make yourself important or agreeable to the leaders, you will next year be in a position to claim a good committee and be a leader yourself."

The summer of 1880 wore on. After six intense months they were, as Adams quoted his wife, "pretty well dinnered out." Like sated revelers they sometimes toyed a little dully with their pleasures, and the prevalence of "octogenarians," however distinguished, dampened the first flush of enthusiasm. Even Lecky, his head nodding gently on the stalk of his neck, seemed a little preposterous to his American guests when he regretted that England and America did not have a common government. They had had a respite from the London ritual in a short stay with the Russell Sturgises at Grove Farm, Leatherhead, the country seat of the senior partner of Baring Brothers, England's leading bankers. Then James Russell Lowell arrived to brighten the remainder of the season for them. Happy with his appointment as ambassador to England which had ended his ordeal in Madrid, he plunged into London society with his old zest, an elegant personage in his silk stockings and knee breeches. His most delightful conquest came one evening when he gave a "delicious" reading of the "Blue Jay Chapter" from Mark Twain's just-published *A Tramp Abroad*. For the Adamses it was an evening of pure and patriotic delight.

Early in August the pair set out for a holiday in Scotland at Sir John Clark's estate at Tillypronie, journeying about in leisurely fashion to historic houses and castles. At one quaint inn they encountered Bret Harte, who had just been rescued from his exile in Germany by an appointment to the consulship at Glasgow. Hay, now Assistant Secretary of State, who idolized Harte, had worked hard to have him transferred. Adams spent the afternoon chatting in the garden with him and fell under his spell almost as thoroughly as had King and Hay.

Before they could sail for home, Adams had yet to wind up the Paris chapter. Crossing the channel again early in September, he found that all obstacles in the bureaus had been overcome. Gabriel Monod received them so warmly that they felt that he and a few like him "redeem this race of monkeys." Even the session with the Napoleonic Worth became an agreeable chore. The expensive new wardrobe was a triumph, and Clover had the diverting experience of seeing Mrs. Astor and Mrs. Vanderbilt cavalierly set aside while the master devoted himself to her. Her thirty-seventh birthday was indeed a success.

More than wardrobes and archives, however, required attention. Arrangements had to be made to rent a house in Washington, and there remained the question of what to do with the Marlborough Street house. Still unsold, it was "a horrid bore." Business conditions had taken a turn for the better in Boston, and the time was at last ripe to sell, but there was little chance that they could realize the $50,000 they had put into it in 1873. Negotiations with William Corcoran in Washington went smoothly. They took a six-year lease, with option to renew, on his three-story "White House" at 1607 H Street facing Lafayette Square. The six bedrooms and two baths on the second floor would give them ample facilities to entertain their Boston "constituency." For the modest rental of $200 a month Corcoran agreed, in addition, to provide a five-room annex for servants' quarters above the stable. To the two homesick wanderers the future seemed secure. "I look forward placidly," said Adams, "to recurring winters and summers in Washington and Beverly [Farms], until a cheery tomb shall provide us with a permanent abode for all seasons."

They bade a long farewell to England on September 26, 1880. Adams, facing his tenth crossing, dreaded "the horrible ocean before me," but as they stood at the rail of the *Gallia* and watched the foreland recede, they had every reason to be content with their richly varied journey. They departed, however, with "no more regret," in Clover's words, "than on finishing a pleasant story, which began well and ended happily and had agreeable characters in it."

11

The Golden Age of Lafayette Square

WILLIAM CORCORAN'S AGENTS labored with a will, but for nearly two months the Adamses languished impatiently at Wormley's Hotel, a short way down the street, rubbing elbows with itinerant diplomats and statesmen while a swarm of workmen rejuvenated the house at 1607 H Street. Henry and his wife had debarked in New York on October 4, 1880, and hurried down for a week to survey progress, before making a visit of ten days to Boston "to pull our house to pieces and get out the furniture." Henry's parents were "much pleased to find him well and active in mind." His father thought he had but one fault, a "passion for roving—a difficulty incident to a person not favored with children." Determined to receive the Washington place "in perfect order," Adams encouraged the contractor with suitable "spherical oaths." The thick brick walls allowed them to indulge their taste for capacious fireplaces and fine handmade mantelpieces. By the first of December fifteen wagonloads of furniture sent down from Boston had been finally deployed, the horses stabled, and the winter's campaign of writing and society fully launched.

The period that now opened in Adams's life had the halcyon ripeness of early autumn with nothing but bountiful harvests in prospect. For the two epicureans a vista of productive years curved beckoningly across the horizon. Whatever the chaos of the world outside, within there would be an oasis of impeccable taste and select companionship. Days were religiously devoted to research and writing, but once the tea table blossomed at five the life of the Adams salon began, and it often vibrated with off-the-record politics until midnight. The Lord's remnant of the liberal Republican leadership continued to make its social headquarters there, so that within the glow of his study fireplace Adams still exerted his influence in behalf of mild re-form. A typical entry in Clover's Sunday letter to her father reads: "Sunday, a pleasant dinner. Carl Schurz, Aristarchi Bey, and Mr. Bel-mont, and Mr. Nordhoff after dinner—all politics and public affairs." To offset Adams's preoccupation with history, Clover was driven to take up a hobby as Henry's apt pupil. "I've gone in for photography and find it very absorbing," she wrote. She felt she had much to learn, for Henry had had the advantage of Richardson's instruction. She soon became known as a skillful amateur photographer, and her por-traits of friends like Hay and Bancroft were widely admired. Some-times their parlor looked like a photographic studio as she posed her subjects.

Adams and Clover had indulged their collector's instinct abroad, and their house on Lafayette Square reflected it in its profusion of objets d'art, Oriental rugs, and vases. The major part of Adams's art collection was probably completed by this period, reflecting as much his wife's taste as his own. Visitors particularly noted the drawings by Watteau, Tiepolo, Rembrandt, Michelangelo, and Raphael. A Turner watercolor of the Rhone valley stood by the library chair; on the wall hung an oil by Constable. The prizes of the collection were two Tur-ner oils in the dining room, where nine lesser oils also graced the walls, and an imposing Cotman landscape in the reception hall. Forty-four watercolors were kept in the library, and thirty-two framed prints in the study. The visits to Egypt and Morocco had cov-ered their floors with rugs whose names read like a catalogue of the art: Shiraz, Kashmir, Kurdistan, Baluchistan, Bokhara, Yomud, and so on. Everywhere there was a profusion of Japanese and Chinese vases, bronzes, and porcelains.

When Adams got back from Europe, the political picture that greeted his critical eye had offered only dubious pleasure. The change of administration that came with the election of Garfield meant the breakup of familiar associations and the loss of political connections. Schurz would leave the Interior, but what was far more disappoint-ing, Evarts would be replaced in the State Department by Blaine. John Hay, who had served as first Assistant Secretary of State since Novem-ber 1879, returned to New York and the editorship of the *Tribune*. Adams gave up his convenient desk in the State Department, not wishing to be indebted to a man he despised. He rejoiced at the suc-cess of the "rat hunt" which their friend Charles Nordhoff had con-

ducted in the *New York Herald* to expose Blaine's unsavory intervention in the Chilean-Peruvian war then raging. When at long last
Blaine was replaced by the socially acceptable Frederick Frelinghuysen, Adams sighed with relief: "I no longer dread going out to dinner
for fear I should have to take Mrs. Blaine to table."

The political tension never relaxed for a moment. A kind of breathlessness always hung in the air. Each day during the Washington season some new disclosure, some overwhelming turn, seemed always to
lie around the corner. When Henry James visited the Adamses in
Washington he thought the place "revolting in respect to politics and
the intrigues that surround it." Adams declared that "its only objection is its over-excitement. Socially speaking, we are very near most
of the powerful people either as enemies or as friends." The stimulus
encouraged him to indulge his inclination to play the part of political
Jeremiah. Shortly before leaving the White House, Hayes encountered Adams at a dinner at the Bancrofts and afterwards noted in his
diary, "Mr. Adams said, 'Our system of government has failed utterly
in many respects. The House is not what it was intended to be, a
deliberative body. The majority can't control its action.'" The point
was one which Adams had vigorously reiterated in his letters to his
English friends. "Our legislative system broke down long ago. It is
absurd to think of doing business with a crowd." Towards Lodge,
however, he took a somewhat less pessimistic tone. Two months after
Garfield's inauguration, he declared, "Our fight is now pretty well
won. Grantism, which drove us to rebellion, is dead."

Adams had barely become reconciled to eight years of well-
intentioned bumbling under Garfield when Charles Guiteau, a disappointed office seeker, violently upset his shaky calculations by fatally
wounding the President. The trial of Guiteau became the sensation of
1881, and the Adamses eagerly accepted an invitation to attend one
of the sessions. Afterwards, Dr. Charles Folsom of the National Board
of Health took them down to the jail to see Guiteau. Adams came
away convinced that Guiteau was insane. "To say that any sane man
would do this," he argued to Wayne MacVeagh, "is a piece of, not
insanity, but of idiocy, in the District Attorney." Guiteau, however,
was adjudged sane and hanged in the following year.

The alternative to Garfield had to be faced by Adams and his reformer allies when Vice-President Chester A. Arthur, who had been
inflicted upon Garfield by Senator Roscoe Conkling's faction, took

office and the Grant "Stalwarts" trooped hungrily to Washington. Something more than paradox and pessimism was called for. If Adams did not have time to spend, at least he did have money. He put himself at the disposal of the *Nation* with reservations. "This is not my usual way of investing money," he wrote Godkin, "for I rather affect business-like principles, but in this case it is with me rather a question of keeping in with my crowd than of investing money, and I want to do precisely whatever suits best the interests of the paper and its managers . . . Put me down for $20,000 if it suits your interests to do so." Part of the deal was that Schurz would become editor-in-chief of the New York *Evening Post*, which had bought the *Nation*.

When Godkin happened to suggest a misgiving about Schurz's tendency to become "sentimental," Adams reproached him with whimsical ferocity: "If you dry one of his tears, I will denounce you at a stock-holder's meeting. Every tear he sheds is worth at least an extra dollar on the dividends." Two years later Schurz resigned from the *Post*, unable to stomach longer the doctrinaire economics of his associates, who disapproved of his pro-union stand in a telegraphers' strike.

As a silent partner in the *Evening Post*, Adams avoided direct participation, preferring to work from the sidelines. Interested chiefly in matters of policy, he stayed away from stockholders' meetings; the financial arrangements he willingly took on trust. His admonitions he saved for matters of editorial policy. The independents he believed had no choice but to support Arthur, distasteful as that chore might be, but at the same time they must carry the fight for good government directly to the people and thus put pressure upon the administration. One of his directives ran: "I want one of you to come on in order to see how and when to begin. I think Schurz had better come now, and you later. Please tell Schurz to hide with me and keep out of the newspapers, about ten days hence." President Arthur, across the way, understandably waited some time before inviting the Adamses to a White House reception.

The more Adams tinkered with political reform, the more frustrated he grew. Except on the free trade issue, none of the proposals of their group went much beyond improving the efficiency of governmental operations, hardly a program to capture the imagination of the Grangers and nascent Populists. The moments of disenchantment grew more frequent as he solaced one friend after another on losing office. When Lodge lost the election to the Massachusetts senate, he wrote: "I suppose every man who has looked on at the game has been struck by the remarkable way in which politics deteriorates the moral tone of everyone who mixes in them." Attorney General MacVeagh was another casualty. Failing to extract a bold pronouncement on civil service reform from Arthur, he resigned. Adams's condolence letter to him likewise preached the vanity of human wishes. "As for the office, as you know, I always thought political power the most barren of all forms of success; my conviction is that you are lucky in escaping."

Affairs took a disconcerting turn when Arthur astonished everyone by supporting the merit system in his first message to Congress, thus proving Adams and MacVeagh unduly pessimistic and impatient. Early in 1883 the Pendleton Civil Service Act became law, and Arthur won universal approval by appointing Dorman Eaton first chairman of the Civil Service Commission. A far more difficult cause was the free trade movement, the one great effort of the independents to solve the economic problems of the nation. Adams plied Schurz once more. "For my own part I would gladly help to organise a free trade party, and if we had the strength to contest a single State, make an independent nomination for the Presidency." Schurz was already of the same mind, for in the air were the first stirrings of the Mugwump movement of 1884. Adams did not attend the great Mugwump meeting in New York which denounced Blaine and called for support of Grover Cleveland, but he did attend a similar meeting in Boston of the Massachusetts Reform Club which repudiated the Republican ticket.

Too busy with his literary labors during the summer of that campaign to follow his political inclinations, Adams bantered Republican friends like Hay by describing himself as "a good Democrat" and announcing to all who would hear that he would vote for Cleveland along with his brothers; he was "in opposition, fairly and squarely on the free trade issue." Cleveland won by a narrow margin after one of the most bitter campaigns in American history, during which he was accused of having an illegitimate child. The inauguration was the occasion for a tremendously stirring parade of war veterans. Adams and Clover rode out on their horses to see the march past of regiments in Rebel gray and Union blue, and they listened to the bands alternately playing "Dixie" and "Union Forever." At the head of a Virginia regiment rode his old classmate "Rooney" Lee, proud on a black horse.

For all the fanfare that ushered in the new administration, Adams anticipated little change in his personal affairs. Only the State Department concerned him personally. The appointment of his friend Thomas F. Bayard assured him that his privileges would be unmolested. Loyal Democrats soon taught their leader the necessity of rewarding the famished faithful, and Cleveland was driven to exasperated fits of swearing and to removing tainted incumbents. Free trade collapsed under the enormous pressure of the high-tariff lobby, so that the tariff bill emerged a monstrosity. Inevitably Adams turned away from Cleveland as from another clay idol.

Adams made one more effort to make his political influence felt through the *Evening Post* when Cleveland announced the appointment of Daniel Manning to the Treasury. To Adams, Manning represented "the incarnate machine." Learning that the *Post* had agreed not to oppose Manning, Adams sent an angry note to Edwin Godkin. "Of course I have nothing to do with E. P.'s policy, and nothing to say in regard to it; but it is only fair that I should give notice of parting company on a point which may prove to be vital." The unterrified Godkin stood pat. Difficult as silence was to Adams, he had no alternative now but to try to hold his tongue.

One episode in the preceding administration had taught him something about the paradoxes of politics and produced the axiom that "as a rule one's opponents are more obliging than one's friends." Arthur had appointed Frederick Frelinghuysen to succeed Blaine in the State Department. The new Secretary and Adams soon became fast friends. Frelinghuysen even made a confidant of Mrs. Adams, inviting her to suggest candidates for the Spanish mission. Shortly afterwards, quite unconscious of any satire, he startled his new friends by offering Adams the mission to Central America in Guatemala City. That this out-of-the-way post should have been proposed in good faith as suitable to a man of his qualifications must have struck Adams as a priceless piece of irony. Upon Mrs. Adams fell the job of gently disabusing the Secretary of State. "I told Mr. Frelinghuysen it was an unwise appointment."

THE WORLD OF HENRY ADAMS as he shared it with his wife in that period which the historians of Lafayette Square call its golden age was a world of society as well as politics. Adams's prospectus of November 1882 could serve as model for the opening of any season from 1881 to 1884. "Here we are," he reported to Robert Cunliffe, "back again at Washington at this loveliest of earthly seasons, when we ride every afternoon into the country more wild than most parts of Wales, and as charming as anything I know. In November this place is like Bath or Nice, a sort of off-hand, sociable lounging-spot for a set of people who make no money and are generally intelligent. We are mostly poor as the world now goes. Three thousand pounds a year for Washington is still a handsome income, and the most important people here have no more . . . It would amuse you to see what a bright little place it is, and you would understand better why I am not specially anxious to leave it for Europe."

Marriage thoroughly suited him. Long ago he had said with facetious understatement, "From the start, [I] have felt as though my wife were my oldest furniture." Occasionally they might differ in an artistic judgment, Clover having a fondness for portraits, Adams preferring landscapes. But in all else their tastes were remarkably alike, and Clover habitually would write "we" when voicing opinions of persons and politics. Children were denied them, and that deprivation caused concern. For light on the problem Henry acquired a medical work dealing with "the management of sterile conditions," but to no avail. As a result Adams lavished affection upon their nieces, brother-in-law Edward Hooper's five daughters. Hooper, a noted Blake collector and treasurer of Harvard, had replaced Adams's brother Charles as a trusted counselor.

As the years went by, Adams's protective watchfulness over his wife became a settled habit. When in 1881 her brother's wife died, the news was not telegraphed to her until the day of the funeral. "Henry flatly refuses to let me go alone" to help look after the five nieces, she told her father, and she hadn't the heart to drag him off from his work. Two years later she made a short visit alone to New York to be feted by their friends. It was their first separation since their marriage in 1872. She enjoyed the week's freedom, but Adams, lost without her, in spite of "a charming ladies' dinner . . . and a party at the British Legation," announced that it was "*his* last alone." So far as the weekly and sometimes even more frequent letters to her father show, her health had ceased to give cause for concern. There were of course the occasional claims of the dentist, sessions with an aurist for a collapsed eardrum, and a recurring sick headache. "I suppose a machine is bound to get rickety after running for thirty-nine years," she philosophized. "I earnestly pray that its final fate may be that of the 'one-hoss shay.' " As in past years the pace of teas and dinners, followed by evening receptions or champagne suppers at the legations, was too much for her, and her indefatigable husband would go on alone.

In Washington Clover found a theater for her varied talents. Her passion for novelty, for fresh experience, was as insatiable as Henry's, but like his it was often frustrated by an even greater passion for propriety. Washington was a whispering gallery, and few prominent people escaped the rumor factories. Gossip writers, alert for scandal and infidelities, did not hesitate to name names. The Adamses passed through the ordeal relatively unscathed. Nevertheless, Clover's skill in adding a barb and winged words to a piece of gossip made her many enemies in the outer darkness. Envious and malicious gossip contrived to link her romantically with intimates of their circle, like Hay and King, whose extravagantly gallant attentions piqued curiosity behind the starched lace curtains of Lafayette Square.

Adams himself did not quite escape the incessant clack of tongues, for like all the male members of his circle, he paid homage to the reigning beauties. In this he obeyed the current fashion of placing a beautiful woman on a pedestal. Adams gallantly averred to Hay, "All I care for is a lovely woman," and when a new "stunner" shone in the social sky he promptly made his obeisance.

The most dazzling vision of them all in Washington was Elizabeth Cameron, the young second wife of Senator Don Cameron of Pennsylvania and niece of Senator John Sherman of Ohio. Her Titian hair, incredibly fresh complexion, and inexhaustible vitality amazed society reporters, captivated a host of middle-aged "uncles," and agitated puritanical tongues. Shortly after the Adamses returned from Europe, the Donald Camerons became regulars at their tea table. From the start it was evident that the "poor little woman" had "drawn a blank in Don." Nevertheless, they all got on famously, and it was not long before Adams, conquering all aversion, could playfully remark to Hay that Don "loves us like a father ... I am now tame cat around the house. Don and I stroll round with our arms round each other's necks. I should prefer to accompany Mrs Don in that attitude, but he insists on my loving him for his own sake." When the Camerons went to England in 1883, Adams warmly commended Mrs. Cameron to Lowell: "Both my wife and I are very fond of her ... For our sakes be kind, if you have a chance, to all the Camerons, and especially take

Mrs Don to some big entertainment and point out to her the people she wants to see or know." In a similar vein he was writing to Hay, "I adore her, and respect the way she has kept herself out of scandal and mud, and done her duty by the lump of clay she promised to love and respect."

Mrs. Adams looked indulgently upon her husband's courtly admiration of their young neighbor. She too was immensely drawn to the young "Perdita," who had been snatched away from them for a year in Europe. "We miss, miss you, miss you," she exclaimed. In May of 1884 Mrs. Don "popped in on the Adamses . . . all in white muslin and blue ribbons, looking very young and pretty, just back from a year in Europe and enchanted to get back."

The Adamses continued to bar the door to unvouched-for or dubious visitors and to sound the alarm along the wires which held their society together. Oscar Wilde's celebrated visit to America early in 1882 probably posed the most serious challenge. News of Wilde's affectations had preceded him, and when he arrived at the customs house with nothing to declare but his genius, sides had already been chosen. Clover forehandedly asked Henry James, then visiting in Washington, *not* to bring his exotic friend. Henry James privately reassured his friends that "Hosscar" Wilde is "a fatuous fool and a tenth rate cad."

The bars had also gone up when Sarah Bernhardt made her triumphal tour in America, her occasional "caprices" being whispered about in Brahmin circles with gratifying results. "Our English cousins made such asses of themselves," Mrs. Adams warned her father. "See to it that Boston snubs her off the stage." The moral quarantine provoked a wave of protest from people who saw in it an unpleasant sign of snobbery and intolerance. "It is the superb actress that people go to see," protested Gail Hamilton in the *New York Tribune,* "not the bad woman." Adams's college crony, Nicholas Anderson, now a Washington neighbor, was also distressed by the outcry. He thought Bernhardt "superb as of old" and wrote to his son, "I am almost disgusted at times with people whom I really like, but who show petty meannesses and vices alien to their real nature."

Society was soon again torn by the arrival of Adelina Patti and Dame Emma Albani in a week of opera. Madame Albani bore a letter from Minister Lowell in London testifying to her social acceptability, but Patti had no credentials but her art. Clover thought Patti a "cat in temper with a damaged reputation" and declared that a distinction ought to be made. The beauteous Lillie Langtry also had to run the Adams gauntlet, though Henry realized he was very much in the minority. "I do not dare hint a doubt of Mrs Langtry's virtue, for fear of getting myself into trouble. I expect to see her dined by the President and embraced by every staid matron in Washington. It is revolting."

A more agreeable English visitor was Matthew Arnold, who arrived for a lecture tour in the fall of 1883. He hoped to earn enough under P. T. Barnum's management to clear his son's name from the stain of a debt of honor at Oxford. Meeting Arnold again, Adams felt a certain letdown. "He is, between ourselves," he admitted to Hay, "a melancholy specimen of what England produces at her best." Clover set him down as "St. Matthew . . . Apostle of Sweetness and Anarchy." She felt his "vanity and egotism" had been "terribly developed by his keeper [Barnum]." In time the unpleasant effect wore off, and a few years after Arnold's death, Adams graciously wrote, "I am better pleased to have known Matt. Arnold a little, than any one else of the literary cusses."

Henry James visited Washington for a short time in January 1882, falling into his old pattern of easy informality at their fireside, but his pose of alienation continued to pique his friends. That he should use an alias to escape the newspapers was hardly a good omen. Washington seemed to James, at least in his "darker moments . . . too much of a village—a nigger village sprinkled with whites," to be really habitable. He studied his opinionated hosts with a keenly appraising eye and saved a delicately barbed retort for his farewell note. Clover, he wrote, seemed to him "the incarnation of my native land." She flared out, "Am I then vulgar, dreary, and impossible to live with?" Later, when he planned his story "Pandora," he hoped it would allow him to "do Washington, so far as I know it, and work in my few notes, and my very lovely memories of last winter. I might even *do* Henry Adams and his wife." The doing, as it turned out, permitted only a light stroke or two. The "Bonnycastles' [Adamses'] parties were 'the pleasantest in Washington,'" but James caught to the life the special brand of snobbery. "Hang it," said Bonnycastle, "there's only a month left; let us be vulgar and have some fun—let us invite the President . . ." If a fault were to be found with their salon, "it left out, on the whole, more people than it took in."

Adams had enjoyed *Daisy Miller,* but he "broke down on the *Portrait of a Lady,*" for a reason supplied by Mrs. Adams. "I shall suggest to Mr. James to name his next novel 'Ann Eliza.' It's not that he 'bites off more than he can chaw,' as T. G. Appleton said of Nathan [Appleton], but he chaws more than he bites off." The picture of "alienated Americans" in the opening installment of the novel sounded to the pair like "a cry from the heart." Their friends quickly recognized the portrait of Adams's wife in James's "Point of View," published in the *Century* several months after his Washington visit, for the satiric criticisms of England and the Continent read like verbatim transcripts. Adams's intimacy with James lasted through all differences of opinion. He kept a safe distance from James's later novels, only by chance being inveigled into reading *The Sacred Fount.* "I recognized at once that Harry and I had the same disease, that obsession of the *idée fixe.* Harry illustrates it by the trivial figure of an English country-house party, which could only drive one mad by boring one into it, but if he had chosen another background, his treatment would have been wonderfully keen. All the same it is insanity, and I think that Harry must soon take a vacation, with most of the rest of us, in a cheery asylum."

Nothing so epitomized the exclusiveness of the Adams salon from 1880 to 1885 as the tiny club of inner-circle intimates that called itself the "Five of Hearts" and exchanged confidences on specially printed notepaper. It came into existence during a merry dinner of the "Hearts" early in 1881 when Adams, just back from Europe, was renewing his intimacy with Clarence King and John Hay. Hay's service as Assistant Secretary of State was then drawing to a close. The two wives, Mrs. Adams and Mrs. Hay, were the other conspirators in the little game that titillated the curiosity of their neighbors in Lafayette Square. If Clover's letters to her father are any gauge, the minutes of the meetings belonged in Pope's "Rape of the Lock," where "at every word a reputation dies."

Adams prized the drollery and verve of Clarence King and his freedom from inhibition. When he once groused that Boston society existed "in a polar condition of isolated icebergs," King capped the idea: "Boston was 1387453 years under the ice, and then the Adamses came." When one of the Adamses' Skye terriers showed up with a bad eye, King diagnosed it as a "Tom-cataract." But what most delighted King's homekeeping hosts were the tall tales of his adventures.

King was a remarkable mixture of Newport culture and frontiersman. He delighted to varnish fact with fiction. He evidently was the catalyst that changed the acquaintance between Adams and Hay into an almost rapturous friendship, memorialized in letters which in the earlier years are filled with an adolescent spirit of intellectual romping and playfulness. By 1881 King had had his fill of government service as much as Hay, and, as Mrs. Adams remarked, they were "as eager to get out as most fools to get in." Hay and King had become inseparable. "I never imagined," she exclaimed, "such fanatic adoration could exist in this practical age." King soon involved himself in speculative mining promotions and then drifted off to England for a few years. A strange, brilliant, and appealing bird of passage, an exotic among tame doves, he was a fitful correspondent and an unpredictable visitant, rarely arriving when expected. In a mountain camp he sometimes startled visitors by appearing in "immaculate linen, silk stockings, low shoes and clothing without a wrinkle," as if about to be presented at court. Byronic to the end, King saved one secret, a secret of a double life, that would astonish his friends beyond any literary secrets they had kept. Though regarded by all as a confirmed bachelor, King, at the very height of his social triumphs, became the common-law husband of a Negro woman and faithfully supported their children.

King's restless quest epitomized for all of them the lure of what William James called the "bitch goddess" success. How they all hungered for her, all feeling they were contestants in some kind of desperate footrace. Great wealth was an object, if it somehow could be acquired without chicanery. The spirit of Mark Twain's Beriah Sellers did not pass them by. Friendly tips were always gratefully received from promoters and engineers like Alexander Agassiz, whose success with the Calumet copper mines runs like an agreeable grace note through the story. Adams's flier in King's Sombrerete mining scheme, on the other hand, returned little more than sardonic amusement as it became "more sombrereteer than ever." Adams was never a plunger, nor did he care to play with the "edge tool" of stock speculation like the astute Hay, who prospered "as do the wicked" in that art. He tended toward the banker's caution of his father and relied on Ned Hooper, his financially conservative brother-in-law, for financial advice. When it came to investments, he told Godkin, he was accustomed to getting "8 and 10 per cent" on his money and would "slander you all with violence" if the paper paid less.

Hay had the ambitious midwesterner's yearning for the accolade of

eastern culture. Howells had basked in it; Bret Harte had been irresistibly drawn; Sam Clemens of Hannibal had come East to be civilized and to be paid handsomely for submitting to the process. As a
young law student Hay wrote with considerable clairvoyance, "I am
not suited for a reformer. I do not like to meddle with moral ills. I
love comfortable people. I prefer, for my friends, men who can read."
In the highest degree Henry Adams met John Hay's ideal.

The Adamses helped open doors for Hay not only to Washington
society but to English society as well, and Hay was everlastingly appreciative. Significantly, Adams felt the need of explaining his friendship for Hay to his English friend Robert Cunliffe. "He [Hay] has
everything the world can give except strength. He is amiable and
clever, and the only fault I have to find with him is that in politics he
has always managed to keep in what I think precious bad company
. . . This curious obliquity makes him a particularly charming companion to me, as he knows intimately scores of men whom I would
not touch with a pole, but who are more amusing than my own
crowd." Adams clung to Hay as one more contact with the world of
large affairs. The salutations of their letters tell the story of deepening
dependence as each tried to outdo the other in affectionately facetious
epithets. The great wealth which came to Hay on the death of his
father-in-law, and his native talent for increasing it, made him the
"capitalist" of their group.

The lamps often glowed late in Henry's study when Brooks Adams
came down to beat his obstinate theories into shape with the aid of
Henry's trenchant criticism. He was the most frequent family visitor,
limping about with a gouty ailment and "much out of sorts and spirits." When he arrived, Clover was hard put to it to "leaven the family
dough" with suitable feminine guests. Given always to violent contradiction of each other's opinions, the two brothers had nonetheless
grown very close. Brooks was turning from magazine articles to history, and had begun work on his *Emancipation of Massachusetts,* in
which he attempted to apply the principles of scientific determinism
to the process by which the Puritan oligarchy had been overthrown.
More than any other of his intimates, Brooks challenged Henry to
increasingly serious thought about the science of history.

Oliver Wendell Holmes, Jr., only infrequently in Washington during this period, brought the kind of intellectual stimulus on which
Adams thrived. An intimate friend from their professorial days to-

gether, Holmes was welcome also as one of Clover's girlhood circle, his father, Dr. Holmes of the "Breakfast Table," being one of Dr. Hooper's closest friends. Of deepest interest to Adams was the fact that Holmes had greatly extended the institutional approach to legal history, paralleling the work he and his doctoral scholars had done in Anglo-Saxon law.

Brooks Adams, more susceptible to Holmes's positivistic analysis, accepted its implications with greater alacrity than his brother. In his course of lectures at the Harvard Law School in 1882–83, Brooks uncompromisingly applied the dictum of Holmes's *Common Law:* "It is of little moment whether the meaning of our great charter is slowly construed away by the ingenuity of lawyers, or whether it is roughly thrust aside by force: its fate is sealed; it must yield where it obstructs . . . In our country and our age that which the majority of the people want will be the law, and the President and the Congress, who represent the people, will see that the work is done."

Henry Adams yielded reluctantly to the logic of Holmes and Brooks. He could not gainsay the anlaysis, but he was uneasy about the direction of this force of the popular will which had been working its way upward to power since the Reformation. All social, political, and ethical values seemed ultimately at its mercy. Preoccupied during these years with his *History* and its offshoots, Henry Adams could not pursue the implications of the new sociology and psychology with the speculative rigor of his brother. Yet the revolutionary ideas coming from Harvard could not be ignored.

By 1884 Brooks had already formulated a preliminary theory of the nature of the struggle between vested economic and political minorities and the exploited majority. Freedom had come to Massachusetts only when the majority had seized control of the legal institutions by which the priestly oligarchy had maintained their despotism. Henry was not yet ready to move down this path. When in 1884 the Supreme Court finally declared that the Constitution allowed Congress to do what it pleased with the currency, he sadly agreed with George Bancroft that the "peau de chagrin" of liberty as guaranteed by the Constitution was rapidly shrinking. Behind the ordered amenities of daily existence in Lafayette Square, the thoughtful bystander could already sense the shape of a wholly alien future.

12

Portraits Past and Present

ONCE SETTLED in Lafayette Square, with owner Corcoran's minions dispersed and the plaster dry on the walls, Adams had plunged into the long campaign of writing *The History of the United States of America during the Administrations of Jefferson and Madison*. His determination to meet his own deadlines drew strength from his wife's firmness. If on rare occasions he showed signs of faltering, she would hold him to the mark by telling him how many candles their neighbor Cousin Bancroft burned at his desk *before* breakfast.

Uncertain at first as to how to open the work, he sketched in later portions while waiting for a clue. After a few months he asked the Harvard librarian to send him books on the "social and economical condition of the country in 1800." Evidently what was taking shape in his mind was the pattern for the famous first six chapters. Adams now saw his work as the study of a dynamic development from the datum line of 1800, the opening to be a kind of continental cross section of the societal, economic, and political energies of that year. In meticulously kept ledgers he set up tables of items: "Population of the United States in 1800," "Log houses," "Roads," "Diet," "drink," "cleanliness," "honesty," and the like with a brief précis of authorities. On one page under "Literature" he tabulated: "Newspapers, libraries, schools, universities, writers, belles-lettres, history."

The ordering of the facts was a fairly simple task; but the artistic problem was more difficult. He was struck by the "extreme monotony of the subject," he told Lodge, "and I have pretty much made up my mind not to attempt giving interest to the society of America in itself, but to try for it by way of contrast with the artificial society of Europe, as one might contrast a stripped prizefighter with a life-guardsman in helmet and breastplate, jack-boots and a big black horse."

The road to the *History* was not destined to be a straight one. The first interruption came only a few months after he set to work. His friend John T. Morse, editor of the American Statesmen series, approached him to do a volume on John Randolph of Roanoke. Morse must have felt a certain piquancy in inviting the descendant of a house which Randolph had traduced above all others to sit in judgment upon the assailant, but his instinct was sound if he wanted a provocative and salable book. Morse's invitation so thoroughly intrigued Adams that he could not help playing with the idea like a cat with a ball of yarn, finally sending in a facetiously coy acceptance: "If you will agree not to expect a line of it before next November, and not to ask for it ever at all, and not to get mad if I don't do it . . . and not to make any allusions or hints to me when you find me lazy in the summer as though you had your eye on me,—then perhaps—well!—I'll think about it." He added that "if I find Randolph easy, I don't know but what I will volunteer for Burr. Randolph is the type of a political charlatan who had something in him. Burr is the type of charlatan pure and simple, a very Jim Crow of a melodramatic wind-bags. I have something to say of both varieties."

The project had all the attractions of window breaking, of creating a much greater sensation than his article on Captain John Smith and Pocahontas. Here was an opportunity to debunk another favorite son of Virginia, venerated as a descendant of Pocahontas. Randolph had been a chief adversary of John Adams and John Quincy Adams. "For thirty years," as the biography was to say, "he never missed a chance to have his fling at both the Adamses, father and son."

The zest with which Adams went at fashioning the portrait of Randolph may be deduced from the speed with which he wrote; it may not have been a labor of love like the *Gallatin,* but it was if anything the more congenial labor of detraction. Morse had first sounded him out toward the end of March 1881. Three months later, just back from the Harvard commencement, he gaily wrote, "*John Randolph* is finished. Rah, rah, rah. Now for Aaron Burr. Rah, rah, '81." By July there was even greater reason to boast. "I have written two whole volumes in exactly two months," he jubilated. It had been hard work. "Ten hours a day to get myself on the shelf—my books I mean— before I am fifty and have lost my powers of work."

Prior to Adams's book, there had been only one important biography of Randolph, that of Hugh A. Garland, a Virginian and a devoted states' rights partisan. He had eulogized Randolph as the chief architect of Southern statesmanship whose "bold and masterly efforts arrested that centripetal tendency which was rapidly destroying the counterbalance of the States." Adams's book was a violent refutation of this appraisal. From his seat in the Senate Randolph had organized the opposition to the administration of John Quincy Adams and, with his genius for invective, had effectively prevented the reelection of Henry Adams's grandfather. Henry Adams's destructive analysis of the struggle between Randolph and John Quincy Adams gives the biography its peculiar animus.

The political purist in Adams rebelled violently against the kind of idolatry lavished upon Randolph's memory by a biographer like Garland. Could he permit the man whose quixoticism had reduced a whole section of the country into a sympathetic dementia to be regarded as a hero? In Adams's view the Southern cause was, from its inception, not so much wrong as wrongheaded, and as for Randolph's personality, it was twisted and diseased. What Randolph touched, he blighted, and he infected his followers with his own abnormality, appealing to the latent irrationality of the Virginia and Southern character.

The *Gallatin* had not been planned as a popular book; the *Randolph* was, and its special character derives from that fact. "I have but one prime test for a popular book," Adams remarked to Lodge. "Is it interesting?" For biography to be interesting to a popular audience, he felt, its personages must be treated dramatically. The more Adams looked at history in this light, the more he felt its attractions. The posturings of the young Randolph's friends, their bombast and rodomontade, struck him as something out of Kotzebue. As an ironist, he tended to see the figures of history diminished in stature, and almost invariably they put him in mind of satirical comedy. Only in the rarest instances did a great figure walk the stage of history and arouse pity and terror. Such a one had been his grandfather John Quincy Adams.

Adams was keenly aware that there was a destructive principle in all biography, even the most laudatory. Under the magnifying lens, all life tended to become Brobdingnagian, and beauty vanished, as Gulliver found, in pimples and worse. He read biography and autobiography with a passionate interest and always a little fearfully as if he were himself the subject. Reading Trollope's autobiography at about this time, he shuddered at the spectacle. "I mean to do mine," he promised Hay. "After seeing how coolly and neatly a man like Trollope can destroy the last vestige of heroism in his own life, I object to allowing mine to be murdered by any one except myself."

To give the interest that art lends to nature, Adams felt that biography must take its cue from the great novelists and seek the depths of character in the flaws and weaknesses of its heroes. It was not enough to portray the strengths, the highlights, of a man's career. In his gentle demurrer to Dr. Holmes on his life of Emerson he said, "As a mere student I could have wished one chapter more, to be reserved for the dissecting-room alone. After studying the scope of any mind, I want as well to study its limitations."

With the cold pages of proof before him and the vehement afflatus gone, Adams deprecated the book's shortcomings. "The fault," he told Hay, "is in the enforced obligation to take that lunatic monkey *au serieux*." He continued, "A book to me always seems a part of myself, a kind of intellectual brat or segment, and . . . this particular brat is the first I ever detested."

After its publication in October 1882, John T. Morse hastened to thank Adams for the admirable way in which he had performed his assignment. Adams replied, "If you like 'Randolph,' I am pleased, for you are the only person I was bound to satisfy. To me it is an unpleasant book, which sins against all my art-canons. The acidity is much too decided. The rule of a writer should be that of a salad-maker; let the vinegar be put in by a miser; the oil by a spendthrift. In this case however the tone was really decided by the subject, and the excess of acid is his."

IN LATER LIFE Adams liked to recall with a certain amount of cynical self-satisfaction that he had burned many offending manuscripts to save his self-respect. How far this was literally true and how far a characteristic exaggeration it is now impossible to say. But Adams's remark seems only too true so far as it applies to his biography of Aaron Burr. That it was completed and practically ready for publication is an unquestionable fact.

Once the *Randolph* was on its way through the press, Adams

glanced again at the Burr, which he had set aside in August 1881. The manuscript had safely passed his wife's scrutiny; in fact she thought the Burr "much better" than the *Randolph*. Houghton Mifflin declined to publish the book in its series "because," as Adams fumed, "Aaron wasn't a 'statesman.' Not bad, that, for a damned bookseller! He should live a while at Washington and know our *real* statesmen."

Nettled by the rebuff, and not knowing that the misgivings were really Morse's, he told him, "I want you to understand that my offer to write Burr was an offer to *you*, not to Houghton, to help you out in your editing." Harassed by the pressure of work on his major opus, he soon wrote fretfully to Hay, "Aaron Burr is not to be printed at present. He is to wait a few years. I hate publishing, and do not want reputation. There are not more than a score of people in America whose praise I want, and the number will grow with time. So Aaron will stay in his drawer and appear only as the outrider for my first two volumes of history, about a year before they appear, which may give Aaron three or four more years of privacy."

Beyond these indications there is no further trace of the manuscript nor any further allusion to it in Adams's correspondence. The manuscript was probably destroyed in one of the periodic holocausts by which Adams purged his files. Apparently, however, Adams worked the main sections of the Burr into the relevant chapters of the *History*, finding it easier to do that than to attempt a wholly fresh departure. A comparison of the structure of the published *Randolph* with the corresponding sections of the *History* suggests what may have happened. In that biography he dealt at considerable length with Randolph's career as majority leader in Jefferson's administration; but once Randolph went into opposition Adams lost interest and hurried over the remainder of his life in a rather summary way except for his struggle with John Quincy Adams and Henry Clay. Burr's significant participation in American national history clearly ended with the collapse of his treasonable conspiracy. His subsequent travels in Europe and his later career as a New York lawyer could hardly have tempted Adams's sensation-seeking pen. Substantial parts of the *History* are devoted to Aaron Burr and his conspiracy, so much space in fact that Adams afterwards felt obliged to justify it as a concession to popular curiosity about Burr.

Adams's plan to publish the Burr volume as an "outrider" was no longer feasible, the outrider having been impressed into the ranks. He would have had to turn once more from the *History* and rework the biography in order to give it an independent character, a thankless task at that point. Moreover, his annoyance with the publishers for turning down the manuscript was real enough. He was sensitive as well about the sales of the *Gallatin* and the *New England Federalism* and had already convinced himself, with a degree of wry petulance, that "there [was] a rooted opposition which amounts to conspiracy" against the reading of his books.

WITH THE TWO maleficent figures of Randolph and Burr exorcised, as if they were fetish counterparts of Blaine and Conkling, Adams resolutely turned again to his *History,* a little ashamed of his preoccupation with the two most fantastic personalities in the Jeffersonian entourage. "I have worked very steadily and have felt for the first time a sort of nervous fear of losing time," he apologized to Lodge, to explain his neglect of his friends. "I have but one off-spring, and am nearly forty-four while it is nothing but an embryo . . . Life is passing too fast for me to bother much about anything." By the end of January 1882 he had got "to Chase's impeachment and the close of my first four years, the easiest quarter of my time . . . As yet I have not even put it together so as to be read, but I keep hammering ahead, day by day, without looking backwards." Reminded of the new biographies of Cobden and Lyell, men whom he had known well, he felt a shiver of incredulity. "It is not only the *fugaces annos,* but the *fugaces continentes* that bewilder me with a sense of leading several lives."

Nonetheless he felt that he had hit his stride. Life was full to overflowing, and he hugged his satisfaction close. "Indeed, if I felt a perfect confidence that my history would be what I would like to make it, this part of life—from forty to fifty—would be all I want. There is a summer-like repose about it; a self-contained, irresponsible, devil-may-care indifference to the future as it looks to younger eyes; a feeling that one's bed is made, and one can rest on it till it becomes necessary to go to bed forever."

The summer of 1882 whirled by at Beverly Farms in a surge of unremitting labor. He had gone north again with a certain feeling of relief, for, as the Washington season closed, he had felt himself surrounded by "a hospital of broken-down family and friends," his father "an amiable and contented" wreck, his mother ill, his brother Brooks, who had languished with him for three weeks, "in pieces, used up," Hay "barely able to get home to Cleveland, with palpitations of the heart." King had nearly died in the wilderness from "the opening of an old rupture," and his third friend, Henry Hobson Richardson, had been stricken with Bright's disease. Richardson defiantly joined the other two for a jaunt to Europe. Contemplating the somber outlook in the Quincy homestead that year, he reported his musings to Charles Milnes Gaskell. "A very few years now will bring me and my generation into the fifties and start us down the home quarter. I am working very hard to get everything out of my brain that can be made useful. If my father is a test, I can count on twenty years more brain, if the physical machine holds out."

The turn of the year found him "grinding out history with more or less steadiness," occasionally fretful against the tyrannies of oncoming middle age, the recurring bouts of rheumatism, the traitorous behavior of his teeth, and the old enemy that sometimes interdicted the joys of the table. "I am very irritable," ran one note to Hay, "and several gentlemen who have been dead these fifty years, are catching singular fits in Hell on account of my dyspepsia." In this mood he looked with jaundiced eye upon Jefferson, Madison, and Monroe. He found himself "incessantly forced to devise excuses and apologies or to admit that no excuse will avail. I am at times almost sorry that I ever undertook to write their history, for they appear like mere grasshoppers, kicking and gesticulating, on the middle of the Mississippi River." He was resolved that his work should be "readable," at least as readable as Macaulay, whose Life he was then enjoying in the English Men of Letters series. His target now was to get out two trade volumes in 1885, covering the first administration of Jefferson.

Another summer came, and he secluded himself in the playhouse in the woods which Clover had built for her nieces, working "like a belated beaver," according to her, "from nine to five every day, garbling the history of his native land as run by antediluvian bosses." His version to Hay sounded a plaintive note. "I toil and moil, painfully and wearily, forward and back, over my little den of history, and am too dry-beat to read novels. I would I were on a mule in the Rockies with you and King, but at forty-five every hour is golden and will not return. I painfully coin it into printers' ink, and shall have a big volume of seven hundred pages to show *you* next winter." And in the same mood he wrote to Gaskell, "There is a kind of pleasure and triumph in proving to oneself that one does not care a nickel cent for the opinion of one's fellow-men." After all, his work amused him and seemed "worth quite as much as the work I see of other people." He saw no use "in fashing oneself about success."

Sardonically, he foresaw the fate of his own work in the "humiliating" reception of Francis Parkman's *Montcalm and Wolfe.* A first edition of only fifteen hundred copies was printed, "when," he said, "ten thousand ought to be a very moderate supply." It was patent that his chief reward would have to be "the brevet of literary aristocracy." Yet as a historian he would have to run the gauntlet of popular criticism. Under such conditions of national intellectual apathy, the presumption of the average critic seemed more intolerable than ever, all the more so perhaps because his own conscience was not clear on that score. "Every now and then, in life," he admitted, "my critics have succeeded in making me feel very sea-sick for a day or two. I am a sensitive cuss and a coward." Recalling his own career of lethal journalism, he formulated the self-denying strategy by which he would abide: "I never fight except with the intent to kill; and you can't kill a critic . . . Reply is like scratching their match for them. I have been one, and I know."

THE MOMENT that Adams came to a halting place in the seemingly interminable *History,* he turned to the writing of another novel, *Esther.* Early in November 1883 he was simultaneously correcting proof on it while reading proof on the completed first draft volume of his history. And with his left hand, so to speak, he turned out a historical article in French, "Napoléon Ier et Saint-Dominique," for his friend Gabriel Monod of the *Revue historique.*

By some miracle of domestic management all these projects raced on without interfering with an extraordinarily active social life. Henry and his wife commonly avoided large receptions as "twaddle business," even begging off once from a diplomatic gathering across the way at the White House to which the Secretary of State had personally invited them. The "nauseating society rabble" was not for them, but private receptions and dinners and theater parties were another matter. Once again Clover's letters of that season to her father read like a roll call of the eminent. More than ever Washington permitted "the kind of dinner one can have only here and the only kind that amuses us." Still there were frequent quiet evenings reading by the fire and the oft-sighed-for pleasure of an early curfew. Photography became a deepening preoccupation as Clover mastered the new platinum-type process. When the artist F. D. Millet came down to lobby for removal of the tariff on works of art and spent a few days with them, there was a great flurry of picture taking, the artist draping his pretty wife in statuesque poses.

Their friend Richard Gilder of the *Century* pressed Adams to do a sketch to accompany Mrs. Adams's fine photograph of old George Bancroft, but she declined for both of them, saying, "Mr. Adams does not fancy the prevailing literary vivisection. The way in which Howells butters Henry James and Harry James Daudet and Daudet some one else is not pleasant." For Hay's understanding eye, Adams remarked, "The mutual admiration business is not booming just now. Between ourselves, there is in it always an air of fatuous self-satisfaction fatal to the most grovelling genius."

A fresh and agreeable distraction seized them before the end of 1883. They decided to build a house. Their landlord, William Corcoran, had sold the lot next to their house to a real estate promoter, and plans were ominously afoot by the buyer for a seven-story apartment house on the whole tract to the corner. For more than a year the Adamses worried about the smoke and darkness that would be cast upon them and the likelihood that their absurdly moderate rent would soar. Hay, then living in Cleveland, decided to build next to them. Leaping into the breach, he bought the entire tract and conveyed the westernmost forty-four feet to Adams on January 14, 1884. Squarely opposite the White House, it was indeed, as Adams crowed, "a swell piece of land." Even before the deal was concluded, Adams had "drawn to scale the whole interior." Henry and Clover knew just what they wanted, "a square brick box with flat roof," and fireplaces, of course, in every room, and not subservient to steam heat as in the new Anderson mansion at the corner of Sixteenth and K, where the fireplaces were "only for show." For $30,000 they counted on getting a "squalid shanty—no stained glass—no carving—no nothing," a thoroughly functional house and small stable. One feature would be decidedly omitted, "a company parlor." They did not wish "a fine house, only an unusual one." Amazed at her own impulsiveness, Clover wrote, "I who have always been utterly opposed to building am the one who jumped first. I like to change my mind all of a sudden."

Hay and the Adamses engaged H. H. Richardson as architect, now much in demand after his triumphant—and expensive—design for the Nicholas Andersons. They planned at first for adjoining entrances with the Hays on H Street, but Richardson, insisting on a symmetrical treatment of the double mass, was inexorable. Hay must face on 16th Street. Richardson, enormous of girth and height, regal in a bright yellow waistcoat, swept his clients away with him. Busily consulting with them over sketches, he did not get the actual plans to them for six more months. There remained much negotiation, as Hay wanted more land for a rose garden, and in the middle of things he dashed off to London for two months with King, leaving Adams with a power of attorney and a free hand to get the two houses under way. Living next door to the site, husband and wife could watch "every brick and plank" and make photographs of the progress. Fascinated by the details of allocating costs, Adams sent on to Hay elaborate tables of figures, finally arriving at his share of the price of the land as approximately $28,000.

In the midst of all this delightful stir, the more serious business of Adams's career went on with extraordinary intensity and concentration. The private printing of six copies of the massive draft volume of the *History*, covering the first administration of Thomas Jefferson, was at last on his desk in the early days of February 1884, the wide margins and interleaved blank pages ready for the comments of the little group of private critics to whom he sent copies: George Bancroft, John Hay, Abram Hewitt, Carl Schurz, and his own brother Charles. He thought he would be ready to "reprint" the book in two conventional volumes in 1886. He felt sure he had made it readable, though not to Englishmen, for, as he explained to Gaskell, "I am writing for a continent of a hundred million people fifty years hence; and I can't stop to think what England will read."

But the *History*, consciously aimed at American posterity, gave little scope for the tumult of his thought as he responded to the fresh currents of ideas that were eroding familiar mental landmarks in his society. It was that other book, *Esther*, so quietly and circumspectly issued in March 1884 as to die stillborn, that came into existence out of the deeper levels of his being. In it he came to grips with the issues that were agitating social thinkers everywhere, issues that had sprung forth from the Pandora's box of modern science, overshadowing even politics and economics. Science, as Clarence King had said, was "clearing away the endless rubbish of false ideas from the human intellect"; but that clearing away had now reached the foundations of the great social institutions, the Church and the Family, and the old and the new order challenged each other in attitudes ranging from despairing hostility to hopeful reconciliation under the rival shibboleths of Religion and Science.

The circumstances of the publication of *Esther* are not the least of its interest. Adams was in a mood to experiment, to play a kind of serious hoax, to prove something to himself. Annoyed by what he thought was the parasitic nature of the book publishing business, he persuaded Henry Holt to publish the novel without the customary advertising, wanting to see whether it could make its way in the world without factitious aids and puffery. Naturally he guaranteed the costs of the experiment. To make sure that the book should be judged solely on its merits, Adams adopted the pseudonym Frances Snow Compton. Reluctantly Holt humored his friend's whimsical scheme, issuing the book as the third in his new dollar series of quality novels. This time he maintained absolute secrecy about the authorship after due warning by Adams. The few who in time were let into the secret were equally discreet, and the identity of the author did not become known until after Adams's death in 1918.

The title was left out of the publisher's regular advertising. However, *Publishers Weekly* printed the following paragraph:

> Quite unconventional in plot, characters, and denouement. Esther is a New York girl of good social position, who had been educated in an unusual manner. She had been taught no religious belief, and had been allowed perfect independence in choosing her friends and arranging her life. She is a fine artist, and her studio is the lounging place of several notable men. One of them, an Episcopal clergyman, loves her, and is after a struggle accepted by her. The story shows their mutual unfitness for each other—neither being willing to make any concession of opinion—and the final rupture of their engagement.

Adams held out against Holt's suggestion for "whooping up" the book, and by early January 1885 he was ready to concede, "My experiment has failed." He complained to Holt, "Not a man, woman or child has ever read or heard of *Esther* . . . My inference is that America reads nothing—advertised or not—except magazines." In spite of the conspiracy of silence, 500 copies of the edition of 1,000 were sold the first year. The circulating libraries acquired copies, and many nameless folk who knew nothing of Lafayette Square and its genteel vagaries presumably enjoyed the work.

Whimsy aside, Adams's reasons for anonymity in this case were probably much the same as those which applied to *Democracy*. Again it was a *roman à clef*, his wife and a number of his intimates serving as models or supplying traits of character. Moreover, the novel was a deeply felt exploration of the reflections and feelings of himself and the members of their intimate circle. After Clover's death only a year later it was inevitable that he should feel a special sacredness about its many private echoes. "Perhaps I made a mistake even to tell King about it," Adams wrote to Hay, "but having told him, I could not leave you out. Now, let it die! To admit the public to it would be almost unendurable to me . . . its value has nothing to do with the public who could never understand that such a book might be written in one's heart's blood." Five years later, when the *History* was at last a fully accomplished fact, he wrote to Mrs. Cameron, "I care more for one chapter, or any dozen pages of Esther than for the whole history, including maps and indexes; so much more, indeed, that I would not let anyone read the story for fear the reader should profane it."

Adams believed that the higher reaches of feminine character had yet to be adequately explored by a novelist. "Howells cannot deal with gentlemen or ladies," he declared; "he always slips up. James knows almost nothing of women but the mere outside; he never had a wife." In *Esther* Adams attempted a more authentic "portrait of a lady," modeling his heroine on his wife. The book must have come to seem a piece of genuine clairvoyance, as if somehow he had pierced the mask of reality. Clarence King afterwards spelled the matter out to Hay. Henry "conceived the quaint archaic project of putting forth the novel without any notices or advertisements to see if a dull world would do their own criticizing and appreciate his work. Later [there] came to his mind a second reason why he should let the novel lie where it had fallen in the silent depths of America and that was a feeling of regret at having exposed his wife's religious experiences and, as it were, made of her a chemical subject *vis à vis* religion, as in *Democracy* he had shown her in contact with politics. Later when Dr. Hooper died of heart failure, as the old man in *Esther* died, he felt that it was too personal and private a book to have brought into its due prominence so he had let it die."

The novel germinated in the highly charged intellectual atmosphere of the Adamses' salon, and it reflected the increasing public debate over the impact of the new science upon traditional religious beliefs. Hardly a season had passed without an important discussion of the controversy by a friend or acquaintance of Henry Adams. Asa Gray attempted mediation in *Natural Science and Religion* in 1880. Sir John Seeley attacked supernaturalism in his *Natural Religion* in 1882, and in the same year Leslie Stephen in *Science and Ethics* stated the agnostic position of the school of Mill and George Henry Lewes. Also in 1882 Frank Cushing of the Bureau of Ethnology, Adams's fellow member of the Cosmos Club, published *The Myths of Creation*.

Adams brings the struggle between science and religion to its sharpest focus in the courtship of Esther, the "sternest little pagan," by Stephen Hazard, an Episcopalian rector modeled on Adams's second cousin Phillips Brooks, the rector of Boston's Trinity Church. Hazard tries and ultimately fails to convert Esther. Although Esther continues to love Hazard, she runs away from her impasse like the heroine in *Democracy*, taking refuge in the mystical hope expressed by Strong, a geologist modeled on Clarence King, "We may some day catch an abstract truth by the tail, and then we shall have our religion and immortality."

William Roscoe Thayer, who obtained a copy of the novel from Henry Holt at the time of Adams's death, characterized it as "the product of a man who has *generalized* deeply and widely on life . . . but his persons talk like the embodied doctrines which we used to read in dialogues." He conceded that the novel was "amazingly clever," although the wit and irony dazzled rather than convinced one.

There is indeed a great deal more than a Platonic symposium in the novel, for Adams achieved a tour de force in making the intellectual questions central to the action of the story. The tensions between the claims of religion and those of science in the minds of the characters arise in a psychological and cultural context in which intuition is pitted against reason. "Is religion true?" Esther demands of geologist Strong. He replies, "Ask me something easier! Ask me whether science is true!" He had leagued himself with science "because I want to help in making it truer . . . There is no science which does not begin by requiring you to believe the incredible . . . The doctrine of the Trinity is not so difficult to accept for a working proposition as any one of the axioms of physics."

In this willing suspension of belief and disbelief Adams epitomized the position to which he had been driven since his immersion in Lyell's *Principles of Geology*. It was the stand recently taken by his English statesman-friend Arthur James Balfour in his *Defence of Philosophic Doubt:* "The whole of science is incapable of any rational defence. The premises of science are not yet properly determined."

13

The Forsaken Garden

B Y MAY 1884 the new house, which was still in the planning stage, had become Adams's chief interest, surpassing even the politics of the Mugwump campaign. Construction was to begin within a month. The twin houses began to rise almost simultaneously, their highly conspicuous situation opposite the White House inspiring widespread curiosity. Wiseacres promptly built a communicating door in the party wall, a door whose existence was entirely imaginary. According to a much more curious and malicious legend, a variant of the first one, Adams is supposed to have "refused his wife's request to cut a door through a partition for the convenience of spirit visitors." In view of Mrs. Adams's scorn for such credulities, one surmises that the story is a solemn echo of some hoax played by the Five of Hearts to discourage vulgar curiosity.

The intimacy of the two friends was effectively translated into the handsome dark red brick Romanesque façades that rose majestically to the steeply gabled roofs. The Adamses did not get their flat roof, but the treatment was simpler than the array of intersecting gables and pointed turrets on Hay's structure. Rows of deep windows lanced the thick walls, those of the fourth floor rounded at the top as in a medieval abbey. The cryptlike recesses of the two arched bays on the ground level accentuated the Romanesque aspect. The red brick represented a compromise, for the original elevation called for stone which would have produced a more impressive façade and a better scale. But $30,000, the first estimate of the Adamses, would never have realized Richardson's dream, nor in the end did it cover the compromise by a long way.

Progress was slow, the construction taking almost a year and a half as architect and clients debated costs and aesthetics with friendly vehemence. The building activity which was going on practically under his study windows made for considerably more distraction than Adams had bargained for. "Ten times a day I drop my work," he reported to Hay in the following autumn, "and I rush out to see the men laying bricks or stone in our house." Clover practiced her photography on the clutter of scaffoldings.

No amount of resolution could withstand their imperial and mountainous friend. Adams reported to Hay, "Richardson put back into my contract every extravagance I had struck out, and then made me sign it." Richardson's methods tended toward the bizarre. He did not allow blueprints to stifle his conception, but working from the drawings of his assistants he commonly treated his building as so much plastic material. Adams lectured him, even the affluent Hay sometimes demurred, but Richardson disarmed them both with his "ravishing designs."

The ground note of correspondence during this hectic period was always the house. Adams hunted stone for the main fireplace like the most fastidious of sculptors, going through the whole Smithsonian collection for a suitable sample of porphyry. Temptingly he described his find to his wife, "a small slab of Mexican onyx of a sea-green translucency so exquisite as to make my soul yearn." In spite of cost, the Mexican onyx went in. When Theodore Dwight, librarian at the State Department, was left in charge as a kind of general factotum, the prelude to his becoming Adams's private secretary, Adams kept firing off admonitory bulletins: "If you see the workmen carving a Christian emblem, remonstrate with them like a father . . . I wanted a peacock. The architect wanted a lion. Perhaps you could suggest a compromise;—say a figure of Mr Blaine, Conkling or Bayard."

Between architecture and politics, Adams yet managed to wind up work on the second administration of Jefferson, finishing that draft in the summer of 1884. Shortly before the end of the year he could tell Parkman, "My own labor is just half done. Two heavy volumes have been put into type, partly for safety, partly to secure the advantages of a first edition." Six copies of the second volume went out to the same loyal band of readers who had received the first.

His brother Charles proved his most exacting critic, displaying an instinct for the jugular as pitiless as his own. Henry had once written to young Judge Oliver Wendell Holmes that he had "settled down for the winter and Mr. Jefferson is feeling the knife." The surgery owed

most, however, to Charles's animus toward Jefferson. Where, for example, Henry had at some length praised Jefferson's public welfare
message of 1806, Charles scoffed, "Before this J. was a doctrinaire;
he now became a wobbling doctrinaire . . . devoid of executive ability
and had no real conviction." Henry expunged the whole passage. Of
another passage Charles wrote, "The thought is puerile." Out it went.
Again and again Henry's addiction to picturesque epithets and high-
colored figures of speech fell victim to Charles's scorn. Sometimes
Henry rebelled, as when Charles scored a passage on Monroe's diplomacy as "long, obscure, and dull . . . It will bear boiling down."
Henry protested, "Nonsense! This is the most important passage in
the book."

With so many admonitions that demanded attention from Charles
and some from the other readers, Henry felt a certain weariness of
spirit. Already he seemed aware of a kind of anticlimax in his effort.
The political revolution that he witnessed confirmed the sense of
break and transition. Chester A. Arthur's almost silent disappearance
from the scene, the epitome of political frustration, must have seemed
an artistic parallel of Jefferson's inglorious departure at the end of his
second term.

In the political slack water his personal situation, however, seemed
secure. "My history will go on," he ventured to Gaskell, "I hope, as
quietly under Mr Cleveland as under Mr Arthur." But the work was
not destined to go on quietly in 1885. The distractions of building
were about to be multiplied by far more alarming difficulties. The
personal crisis which Adams had imagined in *Esther* broke upon him
in March 1885. Clover's seventy-four-year-old father, Dr. Hooper,
had been ill for some months, suffering agonies of angina pectoris. He
now suddenly took a turn for the worse. Clover and Henry reached
his bedside in Cambridge almost as rapidly as her Sunday letter,
which bubbled with news of the "Mugwumpish tendencies" of Cleveland's appointments. She stayed on with the anxious family to help
nurse the old man whom she idolized, the person who since her early
childhood had been both father and mother to her. For a month she
endured the round-the-clock ordeal while next door her five young
nieces demanded attention.

Adams's letters to his wife during this month were the first he was
ever under the necessity of writing to her. He felt a sensation of
strangeness with the first letter, he who had written thousands to oth-

ers. "As it is now thirteen years since my last letter to you," he rallied her, "you may have forgotten my name. If so, please try and recall it. For a time we were somewhat intimate." He had inspected the new house once again and he assured her that it would be even more handsome than the Hays'. In any case the twin result was bound to "make a sensation." Poetically addressed "Dear Mistress" and "Dear Angel," the letters are filled with the surface concerns of household and society, visits to the dentist, dinners with Hay and other friends, queries about library fixtures and bells for the new house—all the small talk of a busy household. Richardson and he had called on President Cleveland. "We must admit," Henry said of their new neighbor, "that, like Abraham Lincoln, the Lord made a mighty common-looking man in him. I expected it, and I was satisfied."

There were recurring alarms, so that Adams bolted "forward and back like a brown monkey" between Washington and Cambridge, feeling thoroughly useless and unwanted. For the first time he watched the delicious overture of spring along the bridle paths without his wife's companionship, but he reported nature's progress to her with loving detail. "10 April. 9 A.M. . . . The day was fine though cool (Therm. 44°), and I took my first three-hour spring excursion round by the dog-tooth violets and Rigg's farm. A few maples show a faint flush here and there, but not a sign of leaf is to be seen, and even the blood-root and hepatica hid themselves from my eyes. A few frogs sang in the sun, and birds sang in the trees; but no sign of a peach-blossom yet, and not even the magnolias and *Pyrus Japonica* [flowering quince] have started." He carefully checked nature's performance against his journal record of other springs. "In 1878 the magnolias were in full flower and killed by frost on March 25, and in 1882 the frost killed them on April 10. I have not even seen the yellow Forsythia in flower, though it should have been out as early as March 15."

At last, on April 13, 1885, the ordeal came to an end. "Poor Dr. Hooper," as Adams tersely reported to Hay, was dead "of heart disease." Clover wrote, "He went to sleep like a tired traveler." In his will he named Adams one of the three trustees of the half-million-dollar estate, of which one third of the income was to go to Clover. Outwardly composed, Clover thanked the Hays for their sympathy, recalling how they had "gone over the same road," after the suicide of Mrs. Hay's father in 1883, but "without the comfort or even gaiety with which my father walked to his grave." The full impact of the shock was yet to be felt. For Clover it meant the end of the strongest attachment of her life, the arrest of the years-long ritual of letter writing to which father and daughter had simultaneously consecrated a portion of every Sunday of their lives.

In need of a change of scene, Henry and Clover quietly sojourned for a month at Old Sweet Springs, a spa in the mountains of West Virginia. Henry brought down their two saddle horses, and they enjoyed long rides in the mountain wilderness in country "like the most beautiful Appenines," as Adams wrote Gaskell. Arriving in mid-June, they were the first guests and picked a wooden cottage near the bathing pool. They passed their days in "swimming, reading, writing, and riding." At the end of their stay they planned a camping trip to the Yellowstone country. However, a worrisome change became apparent in Clover, and, as a result, instead of renting out the Beverly Farms place for the summer as they had planned, they took refuge there after first stopping off in Washington to view progress on the new house.

During the summer Adams, supplied with boxes of materials for his desk, thought to end the hiatus of two months in his writing. Doggedly he pushed on. "History is always with me,—and be hanged to it." "We vegetate," he wrote their old family friend, John W. Field; "I do what I still call history, which is now a mere mechanical fitting together of quotations." He also diverted himself constructing elaborate genealogical tables of the Adamses and the Hoopers, "But I lose my temper when I cannot find a missing grandmother, and the temptation to swear at her becomes irresistible." The months passed in a kind of nightmare as his wife's composure gradually gave way to nameless fears. Not since their wedding journey on the Nile, thirteen years before, had she experienced such a seizure of depression, but that episode had been short-lived. She rallied sufficiently by the end of the summer for him to put in an appearance at the second annual meeting of the American Historical Association at Saratoga Springs in September. He and his Washington friend Eugene Schuyler, the diplomat, had no academic connections but were received as "eminent specialists."

The outgoing head of the association, President Andrew D. White of Cornell, had thoughtfully distributed copies of his address, but did not forgo an oral commentary. He also read an extremely long paper, "A History of the Doctrine of Comets." Historian Charles Kendall

Adams pontificated more informally. It was all too much for Henry. "The prevalence of Andrew D. White and C. K. Adams," he remarked with acerbity, "was rather disastrous to History." The final trial to his patience was the reports on local history projects by some members of women's groups. "Unless we get more history and less flatulence into our management," he angrily commented, "we shall not get far towards omniscience except in cometary theory and female story-telling."

Clover's rally was short-lived. When they entrained for home in mid-October Henry's brother Charles, who was traveling with them, was shocked by her condition. He went to where they were sitting and "tried to talk with her. It was painful to the last degree. She sat there pale and careworn, hardly making an effort to answer me, the very picture of physical weakness and mental depression." Settled again in Washington, Adams informed Theodore Dwight, "We lead a quiet and very retired life at present as my wife goes nowhere." Preparations nevertheless went ahead for occupying the new house. By mid-November Adams was able to write to "Dear Troglodyte" Hay, "My shanty also nears completion." At this moment Henry Holt, unaware of Clover's plight, proposed actively pushing the slow-selling *Esther*. Adams wrote a nervous veto. "By-gones are pretty well bygone, and I am not so particular as I was; but, all the same, I am peculiarly anxious not to wake up the critics just now. Luckily they have not seen my little red flag. For the fellowship of the Holy Saints, do not wave it at them! I never had so many reasons for wishing to be left in peace, as now."

Disturbed as he was by his wife's mental state, he did not yet suspect its full gravity. He drove ahead with his researches in the State Department and hunted for materials on the War of 1812. Masking his disquiet, he sent off late in November one of his periodic eight-page letters to Cunliffe on politics, allowing himself to say only that his wife had "been, as it were, a good deal off her feed this summer, and shows no such fancy for mending as I could wish."

But if Adams could find surcease in the accustomed round of historical scholarship, his wife could see no light in the darkness of her despair. With gathering swiftness the depressive phase of her psychosis ran its course, accompanied by the usual sense of profound unworthiness. Once she had thoughtlessly jested about such things to her father, having heard that a noted friend of theirs had voluntarily gone to the Somerville mental hospital for treatment. "The insane asylum seems to be the goal of every good and conscientious Bostonian, babies and insanity the two leading topics. So and so has a baby. She becomes insane and goes to Somerville, baby grows up and promptly retires to Somerville." Dr. Hooper, himself active in the affairs of the Worcester Asylum, had reproached her for her "taste for horrors" when she asked him to brief her on the season's toll in Boston. Clover defended her curiosity with grim wit. She only wanted to prepare herself for her annual return: "otherwise in June I must visit Somerville and ask to see the patients' book, and then explore Mt. Auburn for new-laid graves."

Lost in an anguishing sense of guilt, Clover wrote to her sister, Ellen, on Sunday, December 6, 1885, "If I had one single point of character or goodness I would stand on that and grow back to life. Henry is more patient and loving than words can express. God might envy him—he bears and hopes and despairs hour after hour . . . Henry is beyond all words tenderer and better than all of you even." The note remained on the desk, unsent.

The next day the evening issue of the Washington *Critic* reported:

> Mr. Henry Adams of 1607 H Street, while leaving the house yesterday morning for a walk, was met at the door by a lady who called to see his wife. Mr. Adams went upstairs to learn if his wife could see the visitor, and was horrified to see her lying on a rug before the fire, where she had fallen from a chair. He hastened for assistance, after placing her on a sofa, and meeting Dr. Charles E. Hagner they returned, when the physician stated that she was dead and had probably died instantly from paralysis of the heart.

In its first account of the tragedy the *New York World* glossed over Mrs. Adams's death as "caused by heart trouble," adding that "she was a very skilful amateur photographer and was a member of the Amateur Photographers' Club. She has made a number of very artistic negatives of distinguished people among her friends and acquaintances."

The true story could not long be suppressed. On Wednesday, the ninth, the Washington *Critic* asked—and answered—the shocked surmises behind all the fashionable doors of the capital:

> The certificate of Coroner Patterson and Dr. Hagner in the case of Mrs. Henry Adams, who died suddenly in this city on Sunday last, is to the

effect that she came to her death through an overdose of potassium [cyanide], administered by herself. [The chemical was among those used by Clover in her photographic darkroom.] A New York *Sun* correspondent states further that there is no doubt Mrs. Adams intended to take her own life. She was just recovering from a long illness, and had been suffering from mental depression. Mrs. Adams was formerly Miss Marian Hooper of Boston. She was well known and highly esteemed in society in that city and in Washington, which had more recently been her home. She left no children.

There was a crushing finality in the last sentence that only those who knew the Adamses well fully appreciated.

The correspondent for the New York *Sun* added a macabre touch for its more jaded readers: "Although she was still warm they could not revive her. The fumes of the poison and the empty phial that contained it, told plainly enough the cause of death." In this sensational fashion the tragedy was trumpeted to the social and political world of Washington, New York, and Boston, where the couple and their families were widely known.

All his life Adams had lived in terror of clacking tongues. Unfavorable publicity had always made him acutely miserable. Throughout the years of their marriage he and Clover had successfully defended their privacy from the society columnists. One can imagine his humiliation and panic now, especially when he saw that there were those in the press who were not above petty revenges. Less than a week after Clover's death the Washington *Critic* repeated the retaliatory gossip of Senator Blaine's friends:

The late Mrs. Henry Adams is generally supposed to have been the author of 'Democracy,' a novel in which the society of Washington was almost savagely criticized. She had a reputation of saying bitter things of men and measures, and of her fellow women too, and although an entertaining talker, was generally distrusted and failed to become socially popular.

The *New York World* followed the *Critic*'s lead, observing that Mrs. Adams "was the possessor of that most dangerous woman's weapon, a sharp tongue, and was not at all popular in society. She was believed to be the author of the anonymous novel 'Democracy,' which created such a sensation in Washington and was regarded in England as the great American novel of the year."

The sympathetic and respectful obituary in the *Boston Evening Transcript* was to set the tone, however, of all future published references.

> In the death of Mrs. Henry Adams, Washington loses one of its most brilliant and accomplished women. Her house was the pleasantest resort of the cleverest men and women who live in and who visit the capital. She came nearer being the head of an intellectual coterie than any woman there, and to be asked to her home was a privilege which comparatively few obtained, and to which many aspired.

Adams's first impulse was to hide from his friends. He sent "a pitiful cry from the heart" to their neighbor Rebecca Dodge: "Don't let *any one* come near me." It was an unlucky impulse. Nick Anderson wrote in bafflement to his son, "I called as soon as I heard it, and offered to do all I could, but Henry refused to see anyone. I appreciate his state of mind, but I am sorry he would not let me show my sympathy by my acts. Until his family arrived he saw, as far as I can learn, no one whatever, and I can imagine nothing more ghastly than that lonely vigil in the house with his dead wife." Residents of Lafayette Square wondered also as they saw him stare fixedly out of the window.

Henry had instantly telegraphed his brother Charles, who reached Washington the following afternoon, soon after the arrival of Edward Hooper, sister Ellen, and her husband, Ephraim Gurney. At dinner, moved by a sudden impulse, he startled the family by coming down wearing a bright red tie, tearing off the mourning crepe from his arm and throwing it under the table. His wife would have understood the gesture, for she scorned such tokens of mourning. Charles laconically recorded in his diary that the next day he "drove with Henry out of town and took a walk with him." One matter that would have to be attended to was Clover's estate. Her trust interests would of course expire, but of the rest of her small fortune of $40,000 and the house at Beverly Farms, which had been owned by her, Henry was the sole legatee. Very soon afterwards he followed the Brahmin custom of putting the entire estate in trust, naming himself as beneficiary, but he afterwards treated the income and, at his death, the principal as belonging to his wife's five nieces. Their future, as he explained to one of the trustees, "is much more on my mind than is my own."

John Hay had wired at once from New York and followed the telegram with a letter. "I hoped all day yesterday and this morning to hear from you, and thought it possible that you might summon King and me to be with you at the last . . . I can neither talk to you nor remain silent. The darkness in which you walk has its shadow for me also. You and your wife were more to me than any other two. I came to Washington because you were there. Is it any consolation to re- member her as she was? That bright, intrepid spirit, that keen fine intellect, that lofty scorn of all that was mean, that social charm which made your house such a one as Washington never knew before, and made hundreds of people love her, as much as they admired her."

By the eleventh Gurney was able to assure Godkin that Adams "has in a measure recovered his tone, and is setting his face steadily towards the future. He is anxious to go into the new house,—or rather to go out of the old, as soon as possible, and settle down to his routine life and work." To the ever-solicitous Hay, Adams sent assur- ance that he was getting through the days somehow. "You will under- stand as I do that my only chance of saving whatever is left of my life can consist only in going straight ahead without looking behind. I feel like a volunteer in his first battle. If I don't run ahead at full speed, I shall run away. If I could but keep in violent action all the time, I could manage to master myself; but this wretched bundle of nerves, which we call mind, gives me no let up, and I am only grateful beyond words that it allows me to sleep." He therefore urged the Hays to come on to Washington and occupy their house. He meant to sleep in his "before New Year's."

On December 30 Clover's sister sent a further report to Godkin: "I hear from Henry constantly . . . I trust he will be in his new house tonight. The associations of the old were too intense to be safely borne . . . Henry rides—moves his books—looks out of window—is like a small child—reads Shakespeare aloud evenings—has several familiar friends of theirs, mostly Mrs. Field and women just now." His favorite, Mrs. Cameron, was one of the loyal company who min- istered to him.

Cosseted and mothered in this fashion, Adams now set out on the long career which was to be lived increasingly among an entourage of women, of nieces real and imaginary, in fact and in wish. The turning was almost a reflex action. A worshipper and idealizer of woman from his earliest days, he came to prefer "women's society," as his brother Brooks recalled, "in which he could be amused and tranquil- lized."

There also asserted itself the old family trait of "self-mortification," which, as Brooks once wrote, all of the Adamses had "inherited from Calvinism." In such an access of self-mortification Adams declared that he had "also died to the world." To Godkin's letter of sympathy, he responded, "I have had happiness enough to carry me over some years of misery: and even in my worst prostration I have found myself strengthened by two thoughts. One was that life could have no other experience so crushing. The other was that at least I had got out of life all the pleasure it had to give. I admit that fate at last has smashed the life out of me; but for twelve years I had everything I most wanted on earth."

What remained to him could only be a kind of posthumous existence. He had no more interest in life, he said, "except as a by-stander." The role came easily to him, for he had always prized his vantage point on his stool high above the crowd. Now there was a special sanction for his habitual disclaimer of responsibility. "When one cares for nothing in particular, life becomes almost entertaining. I feel as though I were at a theatre—not a first class, but a New York theatre." His life with Clover was "closed forever, locked up, and put away," as he would write, "to be kept, as a sort of open secret, between oneself and eternity." The private drama of his mourning sometimes startled an acquaintance. When the president of the American Academy of Arts and Letters much later invited him to prepare an address for a public meeting, Adams turned to him "with a quizzical look, as if [he] were the most ignorant person in the world, and said: 'Do you know, Mr. Johnson, that I have been dead for fifteen years.'"

Faithfully nurturing his own grief, Adams became a master of the condolence letter, each one falling gently upon its recipient like a sad accolade of initiation into "the Hearts that Ache," as he termed their fraternity. In 1892 when Nick Anderson died, he stoically reviewed his own plight. "He is almost the last of my college companions, and sad as I am to bid him goodbye, I have long ago looked on my own life as quite finished, and have accustomed myself to the idea of waiting only a little while, more or less, before joining him and the rest." He little dreamed that he would have to hold himself in readiness for twenty-six years more.

The new house into which he moved in the very last days of 1885 became a kind of symbolic tomb for him, and he inhabited it with a macabre gaiety. On Christmas Day he sent to Elizabeth Cameron, on the other side of Lafayette Square, "a little trinket . . . a favorite of my wife's," asking that she "sometimes wear it, to remind you of her." To the Corcoran Gallery of Art he gave as a memorial the two Joshua Reynolds portraits whose discovery had so delighted Mrs. Adams.

The mood of almost gothic sensibility in which he now luxuriated had its literary and poetic preparation in the prescient pages of *Esther*. The sonnets which he had translated out of Petrarch for the novel were now suddenly clothed with tragic personal meanings. How often he had sounded the note, unaware of waiting fate, of the lover faithful unto death who finally turns through his spiritualized love to a contempt for the world. The somber fantasy of having died with the death of the loved one was a favorite theme of Petrarch.

> In her I lived, with hers my life is sped
> The hour she died I felt in my heart death.

His mood fed also on the romantic despair of Swinburne, whose poems he had read with undiminished excitement as each volume appeared. He had mused, pencil in hand, over such ecstasies of disenchantment as "A Forsaken Garden" and "Ave Atque Vale." To Adams the lovely house and the acres of woodland by the sea at Beverly Farms became his own "forsaken garden by the sea," the dead lovers gone. He resolved never to return to it and kept the resolve until almost the last year of his life. His library held his wife's precious copy of Swinburne which she had bought in London in 1886, the volume containing the haunting "Itylus," a poem filled with the same lyrical pain as one of Petrarch's sonnets he had translated in *Esther*, "Vago augelleto che cantando vai . . .":

> Oh, little bird! singing upon your way,
> Or mourning for your pleasant summer-tide. . . .

More than thirty years afterwards, the news of Henry James's death touched a long-hidden spring, and the words of "Itylus" came again to his pen. "I have been living all day in the seventies," went his meditation to Elizabeth Cameron, "Swallow, sister! sweet sister swallow! indeed and indeed, we were really happy then." On every anniversary of Clover's death one of their young friends, the faithful Rebecca Dodge Rae, placed a bunch of white violets, one of Clover's favorite flowers, upon her grave. "I think that now," Adams wrote to Rebecca in 1892, "you and I are the only ones who remember."

14

The Season of Nirvana

WITH THE DRAFT of the first half of his history safely in print by the end of 1884 and sent off to his little corps of editors for their criticism, Henry Adams had felt the time at hand for a holiday in Japan with Clover. There had been intense interest in their circle in Japanese art and Buddhism. Adams had relished the courteous proselytizing of his friend Kiyonari Yoshida, the Japanese ambassador to the United States. Cousin William Sturgis Bigelow, happily teaching in Japan, had sent fascinating reports of his life there. Clover, too, had keenly felt the attraction, and the pair had begun to make plans for the journey.

Now, with his wife dead, the making of the trip seemed to Adams a kind of moral duty to her memory. He told Hay he would go ahead just as Clover and he had "planned it together." He soon set about to find a companion for his journey. Who was free to go with him to the ends of the earth? King was mired again in England; Hay had his wife and "babes" and his *Lincoln* on his hands. Raphael Pumpelly, the far wanderer, had his professional interests; Alexander Agassiz, back from India on one of his many quests for health, was preoccupied with the Calumet and Hecla mines in the Michigan peninsula.

Chance finally played into Adams's hands. John La Farge had reached an impasse in his design for the famous *Ascension* painting in New York City's Tenth Street Church; he was baffled how to achieve the mystical effect of levitation for the angels. Adams approached him at precisely the right moment. La Farge thought he might capture the appropriate atmospheric effect in the mountains of Japan. Adams, his purse always open to his friend, temptingly offered himself as host, for La Farge led a somewhat hand-to-mouth existence, maintaining his large family in Newport while he kept bachelor's hall in New York. His devoutly Catholic family, already long accustomed to his bohemian absences, could as usual be left to their prayers.

Tall, impressive with his black beard, a charming conversationalist, an original genius, La Farge had his depths. "My temper is frightful," he once told Adams, "and the world is stuffed with sawdust." He could hardly have supplied a more congenial view at that moment. Fifty-one to Adams's forty-eight, La Farge was the ideal complement to him. He could match Adams's chronic dyspepsia and insomnia with an impressive array of what his wife called "diplomatic illnesses." Highly intuitive, even mystical, in his approach to art and life, a poetical philosopher and an enraptured colorist in painting and stained glass, he brought an outlook that would give a fresh vitality to Adams's perceptions. For five months Adams was now to go to school to La Farge to try to absorb something of his receptivity to experience and, like him, open all of his senses to the visual world. They had agreed to "bring no books, read no books, but come as innocently as we could." The innocence was a piece of poetic license, for La Farge was already something of an expert on Japanese art.

Early and late, Japanese and Chinese art and life had attracted the Adamses; their collecting was well under way even before they settled in Washington. Henry and Clover had made allies of Oriental art dealers in Boston, Washington, and New York as they hunted eagerly for kakemonos. Adams's collector's judgment was already a byword among their friends. To check the provenance of a Chinese vase he turned with practiced eye to the authoritative works in his library. Not only had he cultivated the Japanese and Chinese envoys in Washington, but even earlier, when a Japanese visitor came along, he would "pump" him unmercifully for light on what Adams fell to calling the "Asian mystery."

The journey finally arranged itself after six rather desultory months of mourning in Washington. The great echoing new house could be left in charge of Theodore Dwight with a staff of three servants. Though Adams had gone through the motions of research, his history languished in dead water. Paul Leicester Ford copied some letters for him of William Henry Harrison, the famed Indian fighter in the War of 1812. Ford's mother sent him the manuscript of her biography of Noah Webster for criticism. Feelingly he warned her, "a great mass of material is almost as troublesome to a biography as a short allow-

ance." Her voluminous work forcibly recalled him to his own tor-
menting editorial creed: "My criticisms are always simple; they are
limited to one word:—Omit! Every syllable that can be struck out is
pure profit, and every page that can be economised is a five-per-cent
dividend."

Late in April 1886 the American Historical Association held its
annual meeting in Washington as a tribute to the president, the aged
George Bancroft. Adams enjoyed his role as one of the hosts. At one
of the sessions he fell back easily into his old role of classroom cross-
examiner when a young Harvard Law School student, John M. Mer-
riam, attacked Jefferson's use of executive patronage as a repudiation
of principle. Adams pointed out that "on both sides the game was
selfish." His remarks must have had an arresting quality. In the only
such entry in the minutes of the *Proceedings,* Secretary Herbert
Adams wrote that it was "a suggestive paper, provoking some comment by Mr. Henry Adams of Washington."

Luck was with Adams when he set out from Boston with La Farge
on June 3, 1886. The directors' private car of the Union Pacific was
being deadheaded West. Thanks to his brother Charles, president of
the railroad since 1884, he and La Farge had the palatial car to themselves. Full of high spirits, the two travelers dashed for the train, La
Farge having spent the day, as King gaily put it, "dodging creditors
and sheriffs . . . and trying to borrow a few thou' right and left where-
with to paint Japan red." Safely under way, Adams entertained Madame Modjeska and her husband at twelve o'clock breakfast aboard
the train, clear proof, as he said, that he was "a breakfasting animal."

In spite of a promise to preserve his innocence of mind, Adams
whiled away the long hours by studying Buddhism, with its Four
Noble Truths and the Noble Eightfold Path by which Nirvana was to
be attained. La Farge surrendered to the intoxication of the western
scenery and sketched. An alert newshawk at Omaha, spotting the
private car, clamored for a story. He lost the story but won the encounter; "for when in reply to his inquiry as to our purpose for visiting Japan, La Farge beamed through his spectacles the answer that
we were in search of Nirvana, the youth looked up like a meteor and
rejoined: 'It's out of season.'"

The voyage, which began on June 12, belied everything that Clarence King and Arnold Hague had told him about the repose of the
Pacific. "We have been more miserable by the linear inch than ever

two woe-begone Pagans, searching Nirvana, were before." La Farge's charm was so irresistible, however, that they managed to stay as "gay as petrels" and unrepentant in their seasick misery. They arrived on July 2, 1886, to find Japan in the grip of a cholera epidemic and broiling under a summer sun. The guidebook's elaborate cautions about Japanese cuisine and hotel accommodations away from the treaty ports turned out to be judicious understatements. Even the hotel food had "a pervasive sense of oily nastiness," and every journey was a full-fledged expedition requiring "food, sheets, flea-powder, and if possible drink." The overpowering stench of night soil in the streets and paddyfields had one compensation: it proved to him he had not wholly lost his sense of smell. Somehow they managed to escape with only the briefest attack of cholera.

Their friend Sturgis Bigelow took charge of them, acting as "courier and master of ceremonies" and interpreter. His associate, Ernest Fenollosa, who had gone out from Harvard to Japan in 1878 to teach political economy and philosophy, lectured and bullied them on what to admire and roused the picador in Adams. "My historical indifference to everything but facts, and my delight at studying what is hopefully debased and degraded, shock his moral sense," Adams informed Hay. "He has joined a Buddhist sect; I was myself a Buddhist when I left America, but he has converted me to Calvinsim with leanings towards the Methodists."

In spite of the homilies of their expatriate friend, the extraordinary discomforts of travel, the baffling barrier of language, and the utterly alien quality of their surroundings, Adams acknowledged that Nikko, which they reached on July 12 for a month's stay, was "worth coming to see." But getting there while weak from a bout of cholera, jounced about for twenty miles beyond the railroad over execrable and muddy roads, staggering up the steep rises afoot in ninety-degree heat were factors that gave a certain bite to his admiration. "Japan is not the last word of humanity, and Japanese art has a well-developed genius for annoying my prejudices; but Nikko is, after all, one of the sights of the world. I am not sure where it stands in order of rank, but after the pyramids, Rome, and Mme Tussaud's wax-works, and 800 16th Street [Hay's residence], I am sure Nikko deserves a place." The economics of this manifestation of religion staggered him. "When you reflect that the old Shoguns spent twelve or fourteen millions of dollars on this remote mountain valley, you can understand that Louis

Quatorze and Versailles are not much of a show compared with
Nikko." He busied himself making scores of photographs of the exquisite temples and mausoleums. When they passed through the long
anteroom of the vast shrine of Yeyasu with its carved and inlaid ceil-
ings, its gilded pillars and flowers and mystic birds, Adams echoed
the rhapsodies of La Farge: "The impression is that of a princess's
exquisite apartment, as if the Tartar tent had grown into greater fixity,
and had been touched by a fairy's wand." He was not to feel the same
impression again until he saw the "private apartments" of the Virgin
at Chartres cathedral.

When on an excursion to a backcountry village Henry saw the
whole town bathing "naked as the mother that bore them . . . as their
ancestors had done a thousand years ago," he "broke out into carols
of joy." Here was his archaic society. The prudery that had once led
him to argue the superiority of draped Venuses to undraped ones began to slip away. After examining the many signs of phallic worship
at one of the temples, he conceded that "one cannot quite ignore the
foundations of society." Yet the casual indifference to nakedness at
the public baths suggested to him a wholly alien social psychology.
"In spite of King," Adams protested to Hay, "I affirm that sex does
not exist in Japan, except as a scientific classification. I would not
affirm that there are no exceptions to my law; but the law itself I
affirm as the foundation of archaic society. Sex begins with the Aryan
race." The imagined absence of sexuality explained for Adams why
the beautiful wife of a Japanese marquis was simply a "successful bit
of bric-a-brac" rather than a woman.

It was a constant irritation that the women seemed not women.
They were "badly made and repulsive." The contrast with the feminine visions of Washington society struck him at every turn. The superb geisha ball on the eve of their departure seemed to him "an ex-
hibition of mechanical childishness" in which "the women's joints
clacked audibly, and their voices were metallic." His very interest in
archaic society and its presumed "laws" led him astray, for he was yet
bound by the stereotypes that passed for science at the meetings of
the Anthropological Society of Washington. It would take still another venture in education before Adams would discover sex as a
universal energy.

Contemporary Japan was too chaotic and strange for understanding. Japanese politics were as opaque as all other aspects of contem-

porary Japanese life. Adams gave no sign of responding to the new social movement or the political revolution going on before his eyes. The politics and history of the Orient still hid from his vision. However, he was on other ground when he contemplated Japanese art and architecture. Here he felt in his element, continually urging La Farge to attempt serious work. His impromptu lectures supplied a steady corrective to the Pre-Raphaelite dreaminess of La Farge's aesthetic.

Adams collected curios, porcelains, kakemonos, Hokusai drawings, and silken gowns for his friends' wives, spending at least a thousand dollars on his own account. The gowns were virtually to set a fashion at Newport. But what deeply moved him was the past, the great symbols of a once stable tradition, the monumental past of incalculably costly temples and shrines. They made Japan seem to him a kind of gilded Egypt. He saw them as symbols of a vanished order and dignity, of ideals that were passing. Democratic doctrines were hard to hold on to before the great tombs and impressively wrought relics. When silence fell on their talk, these asserted their deep authority, and Adams strove with the aid of all of La Farge's intuitions to grasp the solacing inwardness of Buddhism.

The brooding spirit of Nikko took possession of him. "One feels no impulse to exert oneself; and the Buddhist contemplation of the infinite seems the only natural mode of life. Energy is a dream of raw youth." Slowly the weeks went by with the Fenollosas and Sturgis Bigelow summering in nearby homes. They all made pilgrimages to the shrines and sacred waterfalls. Bales of merchandise arrived from Tokyo, in which they hopefully rummaged for the always elusive examples of high art. The infinite variety of their meditative talk together, the echoes of the esoteric disquisitions of Fenollosa and Bigelow, reported afterwards in La Farge's *Artist's Letters from Japan,* provided a running gloss for the mysterious objects of their daily view. History and myth, old custom and legend, fell evocatively upon their ears. The soft and misty outlines of those conversations took shape in La Farge's philosophical "vagaries," but in Adams the inner struggle still prevented his full release.

While at Nikko, Adams received a letter from John Hay praising his "melancholy little Esther" and urging him to republish it under his own name. He recoiled with a kind of horror. The suppressed anguish that began when his wife was called to her dying father's bedside rose up with a rush. "Today, and for more than a year past, I have been and am living with not a thought but from minute to minute." He was pleased that his book had found "one friend," but the desire to suppress it as an act of mourning, to celebrate a kind of spiritual suttee, had swallowed up all lesser vanities. He was now carefully tending his grief with a touching ceremonial of poetic meditations. In one of his little pocket notebooks he copied out Alfred de Musset's romantic idealizing of Beatrix Donato of the white bosom and divine figure. The poem told that the son of Titian had painted her portrait, regarding it as the immortal witness of their love. From that day he did not paint again, not wishing ever to celebrate anyone else. De Musset, too, had known the crushing loss of a loved one.

Swept by crowding impressions as he sat on the veranda of their little house near the burial place of the shoguns, Adams would often look up from the pages of Dante's *Paradiso* to contemplate the great temple of the Buddhist Mangwanjii beyond the waterfall. He jotted down little notes as if in an effort to bring into some kind of harmony the ideas of East and West, of the Nirvana of Buddhism and the heavenly paradise of Christianity. The Eternal Feminine of Kwannon had its echo in the spiritualized beauty of Beatrice. How to reconcile these two images of the eternal woman? In the pages of his notebook the pendulum of his thought swung back and forth.

They had arrived at Nikko, some ninety miles north of Tokyo, on July 12. After six weeks of leisurely exploration of the shrines in the environs of that summer resort country, whose scenery and temperature were much like those of Virginia Springs, they were ready to concede the truth of the Japanese proverb "Do not use the word magnificent till you have seen Nikko." When they got back to Yokohama on August 29, the sun was still broiling, but the pursuit of curios went on with redoubled zeal. Extremely fine things were scarce and costly, but the stuffs were "cheap and beautiful," and Adams yielded to temptation. To avoid the reputed severity of the San Francisco custom house, he planned to send most of his things by tramp steamer via Suez to New York.

The time of their stay was drawing to a close. On September 3 they made their expedition to the great Buddha of Daibutsu at Kamakura, and Adams duly photographed it. On the way back to Yokohama they tried unsuccessfully for a view of Fuji. Adams, overwhelmed by the heat, carried his clothes in his hand and waded through the surf. Finally he resigned himself to a rickshaw and hurried through the darkness past the open-walled houses, his eyes awhirl "with the wild succession of men's legs, and of women's breasts, in every stage of development and decomposition, which danced through that obscurity." They reached Kobe on the ninth after a short and seasick run in a steamer, and installed themselves royally at nearby Kyoto. Their letters of introduction performed the usual magic, and they went about "followed by a train."

Kyoto seemed to Adams as charming as Granada, scenically at least. Playing host in Japanese dress, he found his legs would not fold beneath him gracefully or comfortably. He watched his guests get thoroughly drunk on saki while the geisha troupe he had hired solemnly executed the formal dances for which he had no taste. After much search he arranged for the Butterfly Dance at a nearby temple. His notebook entry for the day also mentions a sword dance of their guardsman and the curious sight of two court nobles playing hide-and-seek. There followed another picturesque journey, thirty miles by rickshaw to Nara, the ancient capital, and other excursions about Yokohama, sometimes in the bone-breaking comfort of a *kago* or litter. Finally they caught a satisfying view of the great mountain, Fuji, near Kambara on the gulf of Suruga Bay. Adams made a tiny sketch of the peak and clouds to remind himself of the astonishingly sudden slope of the sacred mountain.

On October 2 he took his last look at the pale, watery light of the coast from the deck of the *City of Peking*. Running a genius had been a fascinating experience for him. Heat and discomfort had occasionally driven him to contradiction and perverse satire, but he had been enormously diverted. The eighteen-day return voyage across the Pacific astonished him; for once he did not suffer badly from seasickness, though he did take the precaution of religiously dosing himself with acid phosphate. He had the uncommon pleasure of being able to smoke his cigar occasionally, the severest test of sea legs. With the learned Fenollosa, who was a fellow passenger, he could thrash out at leisure the meaning of his three months' education in Japan, his first experience with a completely exotic culture. He could hardly wait to send his newest generalization to Hay, a "nugget of golden learning." As soon as he got ashore on October 20, he wrote, "Japan and its art are only a sort of antechamber to China, and . . . China is the only mystery left to penetrate."

The news that greeted him was gloomy enough to test his most sardonic resolutions. His old Harvard colleague, Professor Ephraim Gurney, had just died of pernicious anemia, a "savage blow" indeed for his childless widow, Ellen, who had lost her father, Dr. Hooper, and her sister Clover in little more than a year. Moreover, his own father's decline was now so rapid that Washington would have to wait while he hastened to Quincy to perform the familiar ritual of the "death beds one has to watch."

His brother Charles was waiting for him at the quayside to take him home by way of southern California on the Atlantic and Pacific Railroad. The route took him along the great Sierra Nevada range so often described by Clarence King, then through the Mojave Desert and across the vast wastelands of mesquite, yucca, and cactus to Albuquerque, rejoining Charles's railroad, the Union Pacific, at St. Joseph, Missouri. It was one of the increasingly rare occasions for the two former allies to be so long in each other's company. Charles had reached the pinnacle of the active life as head of the Union Pacific. What Charles could tell him of that impressive achievement was hardly the stuff to fire the ambition of middle age, but rather to make the pursuit of Nirvana doubly attractive. In *Chapters of Erie* the two brothers had studied and damned the brilliant depredations of Jay Gould. The rape of the Erie had been followed by that of the Union Pacific, which Gould then abandoned to build up his own southwestern railway empire to the Pacific with the loot. Henry and Charles rode eastward from California through that enormous rival domain with ample time for cynical reflection. At least they were keeping the memory of Gould's sins green, for they had that year republished *Chapters of Erie*. Charles's opening remarks expressed their joint thoughts in 1886 even more aptly than they had been expressed when the book was first published in 1871. "Call things by their right names, and it would be no difficult task to make the cunning civilization of the nineteenth century appear but as a hypocritical mask spread over the more honest brutality of the twelfth."

At Quincy the darkness was slowly deepening upon the deposed head of the family, the centers of memory quite gone. Quietly on November 16 Charles Francis Adams drifted into the deeper forgetfulness of death. To the four sons gathered about his bedside it was a moment for the most sobering reflection. Their father's motto had been "Work and Pray." Prayer had long been lost to them, but all of its intensity had been transformed into a capacity for work. They had inherited their father's fierce probity and ambition, but an ambition fatally compromised, as it had become in him, by a sense of the vanity of things. Late in life he had written to young Henry Cabot Lodge, "When I was entering into life I was disposed to mount a high horse and challenge the world to disputation for prizes which now I would not cross the room to secure." Lodge had shrugged off such disenchanted widsom. In two of the sons it had begun to take root.

But if Henry and Charles were disillusioned, their younger brother, Brooks, still had a certain leeway. Brooks, moody, irascible, and lonely, "a kind of exaggerated *me*" to Henry, had just finished his *Emancipation of Massachusetts,* an attempt at a scientific case study of historical progress. The lesson for him of that moment in family history could only be that there must be a revolution in their political thinking. Only he was left to undertake the revolution. Their eldest brother, John Quincy, stood somewhat apart from the others, somehow spared his portion of the irritable genius of the family. As Henry said, "He is the only one of the family who can make one laugh when one's ship is sinking."

On July 4, 1887, Henry's cousin William Everett delivered the eulogy in Quincy on the departed statesman. The choice of their cousin Everett had historical fitness. Nearly forty years before, William's father, the great Edward Everett, had in the same place delivered his eulogy of John Quincy Adams, whose unyielding austerity had kept his generation at bay. Outwardly Henry's father had been cold and reserved, but within the family circle he had tried in his fashion to drop the mask which protected him against public hostility and suspicion. For Henry he had had a special fondness. When Henry had gone to Europe as a youth of twenty, his mother had quoted his plaint, "I miss that boy terribly." His lifelong anxiety about his ambitious children inspired countless homilies. On Henry's side, what great things he had once expected for his father—and for himself! How he had urged his mother to be glad that duty and ambition came together. He had written proudly, "You know I'm ambitious; I needn't remind you of it: not on my own account, but as a family joint-stock affair." But even then he had sensed his father's fatal weakness. He was too fastidious. For himself he had discovered after painful trial that he was his father's son. Besides, there had been practical impediments. "My father and brothers block my path fatally, for all three stand before me in order of promotion."

When the estate was probated it was apparent that their father had managed his patrimony with frugality and shrewd judgment, the total inventory amounting to slightly over a million dollars. In language that now seems quaintly formal, he aimed at scrupulous justice among his four sons and daughter, his wife having been "so amply provided for" under her father's will. "I have thus far had abundant reason to thank God, that I have had no occasion to make any distinction of affection between my children." He exhorted them against "unworthy jealousies or contentions." His valuable "cabinet of coins and medals, founded by my father, but greatly enlarged by five and twenty years of collecting myself," he gave to Henry to keep as a memorial of his family.

How much Henry Adams's income was enlarged by his inheritance it is hard to estimate. He was already the beneficiary of a number of trusts. Ward Thoron appears to have begun acting as his Washington financial agent about this time while Edward Hooper looked after his interests in Boston. His income may now have reached as much as $50,000 a year, of which he habitually reinvested half.

What Henry felt about his father's passing he kept out of his letters, trusting perhaps that his friends would know how to construe his reticence; a just estimate would take time and a careful inward scrutiny. The task of preparing the epitaph for the grave at Mount Wollaston fell to him as the most literary of the four sons. Posterity, at least, could learn its obligations.

> Trained from his youth in politics and letters
> His manhood strengthened by the convictions
> Which had inspired his fathers . . .
> He failed in no task which his government imposed
> Yet won the respect and confidence of two generations.

The winding up of family affairs in Quincy depressed him almost beyond endurance. His mother got about painfully in her wheelchair. Henry knew that his summers must henceforward belong to her. But Quincy now spoke of death and decay. As he walked through the orchard and the well-kept paths of the rose garden, he realized with a pang that his dulled senses no longer caught the rush of springtime fragrances. "The worst of a childhood's haunts like this place," he said, "is that it forces on one's mind the passage of time."

BACK IN WASHINGTON with his cargo of Japanese art objects in place, Henry Adams sat down at his desk once more chastened and a little dubious of success, but determined to boil up his old interest and bring his history to a close. Through his letters there now began to run a trickle of bantering reports of progress. "Every day I pass at my desk is passed in the idea that it is so much out of my way." He saw himself setting out "after the manner of Ulysses, in search of that new world which is the old." He began to learn Chinese, spending two hours a day on it after a stint of six hours making the history "dance." He entertained Hay with his dictionary version of the First Beatitude: " 'Pure heart of man is possess blessing of, for has God kingdom approach are of kingdom.' What it means I can't say."

The draft of Madison's first administration now went swiftly on. When the winter's work was over and "China so much nearer," he paused briefly in New York on his way north to visit with La Farge and Carl Schurz. A new reader whom he had pressed into service, Samuel Gray Ward, the New York representative of Baring Brothers, returned the first two draft volumes, and these Adams left with Schurz. Hay's opinion of the draft was lyrical. "It is, in my impartial opinion, the best piece of writing this generation will see from the hand of a Yankee," he wrote their friend Sir John Clark at Tillypronie, and added admiringly, "He is up to his eyes in Chinese art, history, and geography, and proposes to leave Marco Polo out of sight in his travels and explorations."

Boston and family affairs depressed him sadly on his spring visit. Summer in Quincy fulfilled his gloomiest expectations. His ailing mother injured her foot in the elevator, and the Mansion House was overhung with anxiety. The urge to be quit of all burdens harried him. There could be no thought now of issuing his work in leisurely installments. He would finish and decamp. Anyway, long-drawn-out publication blunted the impact of a work. He would take his own advice to Parkman, "Sling the whole at the head of the public as a single work. Nothing but mass tells."

Already Hay's *Lincoln* was finished. Hay had dashed off to England for a holiday, leaving Adams chained to his documents and the intricate narrative of the War of 1812. When Hay returned to prepare his ten volumes for publication, Adams, in friendly rivalry, now projected a ten-volume set of his own, planning to eke out nine volumes with a volume of historical essays. A decade had passed since the project had begun to take shape in 1878, and the work had become an incubus. Word of its progress had got around among historians and his wide circle of friends, so that much was expected. In self-defense, he forbade his "eternal history" to be mentioned in his hearing, "the bore of my friends and myself for ten years," making it a point of his social relations not to discuss his books at all, even with close intimates, except when he sought criticism.

Settled down in the churchly quiet of the Stone Library, adjoining the Mansion House, he fell into his usual Spartan routine. Writing "history as though it were serious . . . and when my hand and head get tired, I step out into the rose-beds and watch my favorite roses," for he had "taken to learning roses" as a diversion. Seized with fits of impatience, he took savage pleasure in lengthening his stint like a conscience-stricken monk. "I work near ten hours a day, and shall soon finish the cosmos at this rate." The pressure to finish grew more intense. "I must explode into space somewhere, after this summer of galley-slave toil," he fumed. "My comfort is to think that the public shall suffer for it, and any number of defunct statesmen will howl, in the midst of their flames, at the skinning they are getting this season, owing to my feeling cross."

By the end of August 1887 he saw no alternative to employing a stenographer, as Hay had been driven to do—not without protest, however. "With this vile modern innovation I shall spoil my work," he wrote his "dear Prodigal" Hay, "but I shall either be in my pleasant grave on this day two years, or my history will be done and out. I have notified the Japanese government to begin operations in China at that date." He drove his blonde "calligraphess" through nearly a chapter a day. In three weeks the revision of Madison's first administration was ready for draft printing. "The beautiful-writer," he reported, "is dismissed." It had been "a month of dry-rot" to him, but the reward was before him, the steady flow of proof sheets from Wilson the printer. In his bantering comment to Hay he said, "I am seasick every time I see a proof, the sense of its being a baby becomes overpowering." He was ready to "start at any time, with anybody, for anywhere." He fretted in his new greenhouse, "forcing roses" and complaining of the expense. Deeply dejected, he studied his reflection in the mirror, more conscious than ever of his gray hair and bald head, and "the crows-feet that are deep as wells under my eyes."

When his wife was alive, she had always succeeded in teasing him out of his recurring mood of dust and ashes, a mood which from the earliest years of his marriage he felt was honestly his through "race and temperament." Clover used to subdue his violent tirades against the inadequacies of the human race to mere "grumbling." Now no one stood between him and his determined melancholy. He summed up his plight for Gaskell: "I am well, as far as I know; with everything in the world, except what I want; and with nothing to complain of, except the universe."

15

History and the Posthumous Life

A DAMS'S ELDEST NIECE, Mary Adams, a vivacious girl of twenty, came down to what King liked to call "Adams's expurgated tea house" in Washington for her second season as niece-in-residence, the first of a succession of blithe and faithful spirits who helped brighten Adams's celebrated breakfasts. He watched their flitting about in Washington society with a benevolent and paternal eye. There were moments, however, when the froufrou of silk about the table grew cloying. There was much affectionate fussing over Mrs. Cameron, who was soon to present her impassive husband with a daughter, a little to the embarrassment of the six grown stepchildren. Sometimes Adams longed for Hay's salty wit. "My breakfast table is crowded with suffocation and famine; Mrs Don [Cameron] is tender and is going to Beverly, and has taken me to call on Mrs Cleveland; Miss Lucy [Frelinghuysen] comes at one o'clock; Rebecca Dodge is affectionate; Sally Loring, bright; Miss Thoron, Catholic; and they are all as one family; but oh, my blessed Virgin! they feed my soul with but thin nectar."

The engaging young British diplomat Cecil Spring Rice joined the privileged circle at 1603 H Street, to begin a thirty-year friendship. He was one of the first of the young "nephews in wish" in whom Adams sought the authentic marks of the new men of the future. Twenty-eight to Adams's fifty-seven, the personable young secretary of the legation was an instant success. Adams thought him "an intelligent and agreeable fellow" with "creditable wits." "Mad, of course, but not more mad than an Englishman should be." He paid for his meals "in a certain dry humor."

Spring Rice found his host a fascinating enigma and already a legendary figure in Washington. "The Adams family are as odd as can be," he wrote home. "They are all clever, but they all make a sort of profession of eccentricity . . . I like the one here, who since his wife died has no friends and no absorbing interest and takes an amused view of life, tempered by an attachment to Japanese art." Spring Rice was very soon on the most cordial terms with Adams, but, continually amazed by his personality, he kept returning to the puzzle. After a little more study he wrote, "He is queer to the last degree; cynical, vindictive, but with a constant interest in people, faithful to his friends and passionately fond of his mother and of all little children ever born; even puppies. He lives in a Japanese house full of strange trophies from Japan and a precious idol given him by the Japanese Minister."

It was not long before Spring Rice was as hopelessly enamored of Mrs. Cameron as were Adams and Hay. He is "chanting your hymns," Adams told her. "He is certainly better worth having in your train than most of us others who are there." Spring Rice's sonnets to her beauty challenged Hay and Adams to chivalrous rivalry. It was a game of adoration such as true Pre-Raphaelites might delight in, imagining themselves Petrarchs and Dantes. The senator had little appetite for such frivolities, being busy with the guerrilla warfare of Pennsylvania politics, but, a little flattered perhaps by the distinguished persons in his wife's train, he looked on indulgently. As senior courtier, Adams's dependence on their young charmer grew, and he haunted the Cameron drawing room as a "tame cat." For a while he had a gay companion again for his horseback rides and a confidant to whom he could send a casual note across Lafayette Square for a diverting cup of tea or a ride under the winter sun. "The roses are sweet," ran one missive. "I feel very belle. How about our ride? Is it off?" The congenial group broke up early in 1886. Mrs. Cameron took the Adams house at Beverly Farms to await the birth of her daughter, Martha, which occurred on June 25.

Adams's attachment to the infant drew him even closer to her mother, so that he found himself helplessly whirled along in her train, his thoughts leaping ahead in anticipation of their meetings or sinking despondently when they missed them. He yearned to call on Elizabeth Cameron at Beverly Farms, but an indefinable dread held him back. Then one rainy Monday she visited him at Quincy, bringing more joy than he had felt "for these many moons." When he thought he could get off to Mexico with King, his only regret was that she could so easily spare him. "I am sorry," he said, "for time does not seem to clear away the wreckage of life, or to show how to climb over it."

Fate was by no means done with his sensitive nerves. Another blow fell in November 1887. His widowed sister-in-law, Ellen Gurney, ill in mind as Clover had been, wandered off from her sickroom into the railroad freight yard and was fatally injured by a Cambridge train. The shock brought on a nervous breakdown in her brother, Edward Hooper, and prostrated him for six weeks. Adams hurried north in the hope of being useful and meanwhile visited his mother, "very infirm and complaining." The cumulative tragedies were enough to try the most sardonic of stoics. This kind of *joie de vivre*, he felt, only a Zola could celebrate.

His state of mind for the ensuing year and a half can be followed in a remarkable twenty-five-page fragment of his diary that somehow escaped the periodic winnowing of his papers. The entries were usually made on Sunday, apparently summarizing the notes of a pocket journal. Most of the entries prosaically narrate his comings and goings or the progress of the *History*, but these are occasionally interspersed with passages of troubled introspection: "February 12, 1888—The winter drags along about as miserably as it began. I am still quite off my balance, and have been peculiarly depressed by an attack of what seems malaria, perhaps the growth of my greenhouse ... My little knot of friends are steady in their allegiance, and Mrs Cameron more winning than ever; but Clarence King telegraphs that he will be ready to start next Thursday [for a trip to Cuba] ... I am weary of myself and my own morbid imagination, but still more weary of the world's clack and bustle, and the dreary recurrence of small talk. History is in Chapter VI of Book II. No proofs of [draft] Vol. III this week."

King, suffering from chronic illness, was forbidden to go to Cuba. Hay, ill with a chronic throat, dropped out after two weeks in Florida. Adams resolutely pushed on with the third valetudinarian, Dwight. To Mrs. Cameron he confessed his great excitement at witnessing his first *corrida* and sent a vivid and, in spots, macabre account of it, some dozen pages long. "The show was just thrilling, but what turned my poor old addle-brain on end was the dozen or two ladies in more or less soul-moving costumes." One ravishing creature made him wish he was "a picadero or a peccadillo, or anything to her." The picturesque opening ceremony recalled the Roman arena and Heliogabalus: "I felt that life was still left in the worn-out world. My true archaic blood beat strongly in my heart." Then with sick fascination he watched the goring of the horses. When the bull was finally brought to his bloody finish and the men howled, Adams was unimpressed by the moment of truth. "On the whole I was too unwell," he said, "to watch long; and the moment the bull was dragged out of the arena, I told Dwight that I would keep company with the bull."

In Washington he recalled his month-long trip in the privacy of his diary. "If it was not happiness, it was at least variety." At Vedado, "I looked out seawards and asked myself whether honestly I wanted or not to return. As near as I could tell my real feeling, I had not one wish ever to see Washington or home again . . . If it were not for Mrs Cameron and John Hay, I should turn and run."

For a week he was poised at his desk doing "one small chapter of history," then he was off again for a jaunt to Norfolk with King and Hay. Refreshed by travel, he felt ready for the final push. "I have not suffered much from depression, and not at all, of late, from excessive and alarming turns of temper." A week later he probed inwardly: "At work again on History . . . Spirits much better, and almost no acute depression; only indifference and tedium." One sure distraction for his tedium lay across Lafayette Square at the Ogle Tayloe house, now the Washington residence of the Camerons, for there the baby Martha took full possession of his heart. "I have made love to Martha Cameron," he confided to his diary on May 6, 1888, "and by dint of incessant bribery and attentions have quite won her attachment so that she will come to me from anyone . . . Her drawer of chocolate drops and ginger-snaps; her dolls and picture-books, turn my study into a nursery." Soon he was to keep an elaborate doll's house behind a sliding panel in his library.

The sense of living on the edge of life, shadowed by death and extinction, rose often to the surface of consciousness. When he despaired most he would seize upon the vague hope of a brave new life that might lie beyond the Pacific horizon, when he should be "set free forever from my duties in life, as men call the occupations they are ashamed to quit, but are sorry to follow."

As the Washington season drew to an end once more, he saw no escape. The record took on an even darker tone. What he once wrote near the close of his life was never more appropriate than during these months when his spirits reached bottom. "Thank God, I never was cheerful. I come from the happy stock of the Mathers, who . . . passed sweet mornings reflecting on the goodness of God and the damnation of infants." Doggedly he marked his progress in his diary through the War of 1812 like a staff officer with a map before him. "May 13 [1888]. Finishing the northern campaign . . . May 20 . . . the Washington campaign . . . I see the day near when I shall at last cut this only tie that still connects me with my time . . . I am almost alone except an occasional visit from Martha or her mother, and I have been sad, sad, sad. Three years! . . . June 3. I have had a gloomy week, not quite so desperate and wild as in my worst days, but, so far as I can remember, equally hopeless and weary." The Lodges dragged him from his desk for a visit to Mount Vernon but to no avail. "The dissipation cost me three days of despondency." The black mood suited a new project, the final ordering of the vast store of family papers at Quincy. "Dwight has left the State Department and come into our family service."

The return of summer obliged him to "repeat the old desperate Quincy effort," for it was his turn to look after his mother. He found her "sensibly declined in body and mind . . . A quick and easy end would be a great blessing for her . . . I might say the same for myself. I would certainly be quite willing to go with her." The writing resumed. "June 24 . . . am at Ghent. Dwight has arranged with Burlingame of Scribner & Co for publication . . . July 22. Deep in Ghent negotiation . . . Interesting to me more than most . . . August 12. I have taken up my Chinese again and find I recover it fairly quick. I mean to make a new attempt to learn a thousand characters thoroughly . . . September 2. Contract made with Stanford White for stone-work of Buddha monument at Rock Creek. Have written to [Augustus] Saint-Gaudens to send his contract for signature."

Impatient to be free, he drove on with the second administration of James Madison and abandoned the plan to put it into type for the scrutiny of his committee of critics. The manuscript of the second administration would go directly to Scribner for publication. On September 9 he noted that he was almost at the end of "Chap. IV, Book V, which closes my narrative, March 4, 1817 . . . Four economical and literary chapters remain to be written, and I hope to have these in shape before I return to Washington. I think I never before wrote eight chapters in less than two months; but I have now nothing else to do. Life is at least simple. If I have no satisfaction, I have little interest. I am nearly Buddha."

In the next entry he tasted to the full the bitter fruit of his scholar's triumph. "Sunday, September 16 [1888]. The narrative was finished last Monday. In imitation of Gibbon I walked in the garden among the yellow and red autumn flowers, blazing in sunshine, and meditated. My meditations were too painful to last. The contrast between my beginning and end is something Gibbon never conceived. Spurred by it into long meditated action, I have brought from Boston the old volumes of this Diary, and have begun their systematic destruction. I mean to leave no record that can be obliterated." Turning to the *History* he went on: "Of the four concluding chapters, I have already written one third, and all are in my mind, outlined and partially filled in . . . Nothing yet from St Gaudens whose contract is the only serious undertaking now left." Another week of despair followed. "Sunday, September 23. No sunshine since last Sunday, and floods of rain. In the midst of gloom and depression I have come to the last page of my history. I wish I cared, but I do not care a straw except to feel the thing accomplished. At the same time I am reading my old Diaries, and have already finished and destroyed six years, to the end of my college course. It is fascinating, like living it all over again; but I am horrified to have left such a record so long in existence. My brain reels with the vividness of emotions more than thirty years old."

The macabre ritual before his study fire went on and on. "Sunday, September 30. Steadily working ahead towards my demise . . . I have read and destroyed my diary to the autumn of 1861. Nothing in it could be of value to anyone, but even to me the most interesting part was my two closing College years. Much is unpleasant and painful to recall. Sunday, 6 October . . . Continue reading old diary, but I hesitate to destroy much of the record since 1862, not that I think it valuable, but that I may want to read it again. Portions are excessively interesting to me; nothing to anyone else."

With the publication of the *History* begun, Adams got off on October 12, 1888, to join his friend Sir Robert Cunliffe on a western tour. They were indefatigable sightseers, making the grand circle from the Shoshone Falls in Idaho, to Portland, down through the length of California, across the Southwest by way of El Paso, with a stopover at New Orleans to visit the famous battlefield. They hastened back to Washington having "travelled in all about nine thousand miles with perfect success." The diary account served as a prosaic *aide-mémoire*. The color, the dust, the picturesque encounters, the sublime landscapes, the adventures and misadventures, he worked up with appro-

priate ironic gaieties and exaggerations in his letters to Gaskell and
Mrs. Cameron. But the heartiness of manner and his best travel-letter
style did not wholly cover the malaise that lay beneath. "I took my
baronet out to the Cliff House, where the Pacific was rolling in its
long surf in the light of a green and yellow sunset," he wrote Mrs.
Cameron, "and there I pointed to the Golden Gate and challenged
the baronet to go on with me. Ignominiously he turned his back on
all that glory, and set his face eastward for his dear fogs; and I, too,
for the time, submitted; but the longing was as strong as ever, and, if
I had not wanted to see Martha once more, I am not quite sure that I
would not, then and there, have run for it."

His letters to the infant Martha played a poignant and affectionate
counterpoint which only her mother could understand as she read the
palimpsest messages. Beneath the playful chatter of gumdrops and of
dogs ran a vein of pathos that must have touched Elizabeth Cameron
to tears as she read the romantic fancies to her prattling babe: "I love
you very much, and think of you a great deal, and want you all the
time. I should have run away from here, and looked for you all over
the world, long ago, only I've grown too stout for the beautiful
clothes I used to wear when I was a young prince in the fairy-stories,
and I've lost the feathers out of my hat, and the hat too, and I find
that some naughty man has stolen my gold sword and silk stockings
and silver knee-buckles. So I can't come after you, and feel very sad
about it. If you would only come and see me, as Princess Beauty came
to see Prince Beast, we would go down to the beach, and dig holes in
the sand." To Mrs. Cameron herself Adams sent a steady flow of gossip and persiflage, paying homage with graceful bagatelles or turning
to Shakespearean compliment. "I will not question in my jealous
thought where you and Martha may be, or your affairs suppose, but
like a sad slave stay."

His "haunting anniversary," December 6, turned his thoughts again
to the projected Saint-Gaudens statue. The idea for the memorial had
taken shape in his conversations with La Farge in Japan. Not long
after they returned, the two of them sought out the young Japanese
scholar Kakuzo Okakura, whom they had first met in Japan, to discuss with him the symbolisms of Buddhist art, especially of the figure
of Kwannon. The idea of timeless contemplation seemed the perfect
note, and they hurried to Saint-Gaudens at his studio on West Thirty-
sixth Street. On the spur of the moment Saint-Gaudens posed an Italian boy mixing clay in the studio, no female model being handy, and

flung a blanket about him. Adams vetoed the first pose: "No, the way you're doing that is a 'Penseroso.'" Not at all sure just what the figure should be, Adams was positive on one point: it should fuse the art and thought of East and West.

After the initial spur of interest, progress was excruciatingly slow, as always with the dilatory Saint-Gaudens. The friendship of the men made bargaining peculiarly difficult, but Adams was insistent that a businesslike contract be drawn so that there might be some probability of early completion. Saint-Gaudens, at a loss to know "what to ask" for his share of the work, tried to take refuge in Edward Hooper's remark that Adams would spend $10,000. White's share for the foundation, however, would probably run to $7,000. The mere casting of the bronze figure would come to another $3,000. Perplexed, Saint-Gaudens asked Adams to "state a limit," adding, "I have not the 'cheek' to ask any sum of a friend for a work that may not set the world afire." Stanford White, more practical, sent on his contract for the foundation and headstone "against which Saint-Gaudens' masterpiece is to rest," and urged Adams to get Saint-Gaudens to commit himself in writing. "Even with a contract and time and a price set, it is hard enough to get anything out of him." Meanwhile, Adams made his preparations: "Have sold at a sacrifice two thirds of all the railroad stock I still own, and am beginning to provide twenty thousand dollars for Saint-Gaudens and Stanford White."

In November 1888 Saint-Gaudens began the work, the contract calling for completion in May 1890. To bring the chaotic suggestions of Adams and La Farge to a focus he jotted down: "Adams. Buddha. Mental repose. Calm reflection in contrast with violence of nature." As he slowly and painfully worked free from the oppressive philosophic abstractions of Adams and La Farge, he moved with surer instinct back to the hooded figure he had designed a dozen years before, the "Silence," in which he avoided the suggestion of any particular mode, Greek, Roman, or Egyptian.

Adams managed to escape seeing the models of the final design, getting reports at second hand from La Farge, who acted as a kind of referee and agent. He passed on to La Farge Stanford White's sketches for the architectural setting with the proviso that the architecture "have nothing to say," and above all that "it should not be classic," but Stanford White resisted, and Saint-Gaudens succeeded in winning agreement to a "small classical cornice."

As the end of his labor on the *History* hove into view Adams redoubled his efforts. "To admit the truth, the frenzy of finishing the big book has seized me." He hurried off the revised chapters as if they were letters. To Theodore Dwight had fallen the responsibility of initiating the negotiations for publication with Charles Scribner, but the arrangement seems to have complicated matters more than it simplified them, since Adams constantly intervened. He took much the same patronizing tone toward Scribner as he took toward the indulgent Holt; but Scribner was less ready to humor his whims.

A month after Dwight had sounded Scribner and got a tentative acceptance in advance of seeing the work, Dwight forwarded Adams's memorandum of terms, which included the following unconventional proposal: "After the expenses of publication are repaid . . . the author ought to share equally with the publisher." Scribner counteroffered with a 15 percent royalty arrangement, to which Adams replied, "If I were offering this book for sale, I should, on publishers' estimates, capitalize twelve years of unbroken labor, at (say) $5000 a year, and $20,000 in money spent travelling, collecting materials, copying, printing, etc; in all $80,000, without charging that additional interest, insurance, or security per-centage which every business-man has to exact . . . As I am not a publisher but an author, and the most unpractical kind of an author, a historian, this business view is mere imagination. In truth the historian gives his work to the public and publisher; he means to give it . . . History has always been, for this reason, the most aristocratic of all literary pursuits, because it obliges the historian to be rich as well as educated." Pessimistic about the sales of the work, Adams submitted his detailed calculations countering those of Scribner and renewed his offer to share equally after all costs were met, but excluding "advertising, rent, salaries, putting on the market, etc."

Appalled at the accounting aspects of such a partnership, Scribner riposted with a "firm" offer of 20 percent royalty after 2,000 copies. Adams capitulated. To his diary he grumbled on September 16, 1888, "I expect no afterwards, but if my book has the large sale of five thousand copies, I shall receive twelve thousand dollars for twelve years' work, or a thousand dollars a year. I have spent more than that on it." It was difficult to resign himself to the truth of his own proposition that a historian's work was necessarily a gift to the public. He took sardonic refuge in the hope that his work would be pirated. If Adams's irony needed any buttressing, his royalty checks were to furnish it. After ten years these amounted to $5,000. The contrast between his experience and that of Gibbon and Macaulay could only confirm his impression of the swift decline of American culture. Macaulay's *History* had sold 140,000 copies.

Scribner was willing to forgive much, as he felt that he had achieved a publishing coup. "It is a great book," he told Adams, "and will create a profound impression among students of history and thinking men generally." What followed was something of an ordeal for both author and publisher. There were countless details about typography, maps, setup, paper, and binding. On every point Adams had very definite opinions, and no detail was too small for his careful consideration.

The printing was to be done from the three printed draft volumes with their corrections and insertions and directly from the manuscript of the fourth large volume on the second administration of James Madison. To Adams the text was all-important, and he wanted it to read as a continuous narrative without marginal notes. "They were never of use to me in any book, except Coleridge's 'Ancient Mariner.'" Page headings, too, seemed a waste of effort. At his own expense he ordered a deluxe edition on thin paper of twelve copies of the initial two volumes on Jefferson's first administration, for a "Ladies Edition" for himself "or family and a few special friends."

The moment the copy for the first two volumes went to Wilson, Adams's Cambridge printer, whom Scribner had consented to employ, Adams dashed off for a three months' holiday, this time "knocking about an unknown region called the North Carolina sounds" and "as far south as Savannah." He joined two lively young Washington lawyers, Tom Lee and Billy Phillips. He vainly hunted duck, fished for shad, lost at euchre and poker, and happily trudged about Raleigh's Lost Colony. He sent off for his dress suit and plunged into Savannah society for a few days' agreeable dissipation. He had to be persuaded to return to Washington in time for the inauguration of Benjamin Harrison, but the advent of his new presidential neighbor bored him, and he shut himself up in his study to rewrite the concluding chapters of his final volume.

As the proof sheets passed back and forth over his desk, his mind turned with growing anticipation to a China expedition. Raphael Pumpelly, the Asian expert, came to dine again, Hay and Mrs. Cameron sharing the enlightenment. The diary entry for Sunday, May 5,

1889, was not easy to make. "Mrs Cameron left here last Tuesday and sailed for Europe the next morning. I went to Baltimore with them." His little world was breaking up for the year. As offset, Clarence King dropped in and there was much "Central Asian talk." In spite of departures, Washington became livelier for him. He was seeing "rather more society than usual," dining at Mrs. Cabot Lodge's, whose charm did much to palliate her husband's aggressiveness, doing "Sinfony concerts," and riding the trails in Rock Creek. He called on the Russian chargé "to give information of our intent to visit Central Asia."

The final event needed to round out his practical Calvinism now broke with the rush that a long-expected catastrophe sometimes takes. His eighty-one-year-old mother, to whom life had become increasingly painful and burdensome, was to be spared no horror. In May her mind gave way. She fell into a drugged lethargy, and when he arrived in Quincy after his customary spring visit in New York with King and La Farge, she was already unconscious. His diary recorded the event with stoical restraint: "She died at half past ten o'clock, Thursday evening, June 6 [1889]. I was present. We buried her yesterday (Saturday) afternoon by my father's side at Mt. Wollaston. I shall remain here this summer with Miss Baxter and Dwight." Attached as he had been to her as a favorite son, he could not but welcome her release, as well as his own, for the outrages of time had done their worst. Another valve of feeling went shut. Her nature was so much a part of his, even to the complaints and forebodings, as he always said, that grief was irrelevant, and he never betrayed their timeworn bond by futile tributes. A gray atmosphere hung over the family house, that retreat to which his presidential ancestors had come back "to eat out their hearts in disappointment and disgust." Adams thought he would be the last to occupy it, but he was forgetting Brooks and the tenacity of even the most irksome tradition.

Toward the end of the summer he was wound up, as he would say, in a perfect coil of activity. The draft volumes circulating among his staff of readers had to be called in and gone over. Scribner kept pressing him for copy, eager to publish promptly. Certain of publication, Adams now luxuriated in fits of cynicism. Delay was indifferent to him, "the longer, the better, for my objects;—but I would much prefer to be free of the whole job as soon after January, 1890, as possible, so that I can go abroad in that year." Then he added a comment which was all too firmly based on fact: "I have only two wishes: one is to be free, and the other to escape the annoyance, which to an old author is considerable, of infuriated grandsons and patriotic women-critics crying for redress."

He had already had a foretaste of the indignation that was to pursue him from Paul Hamilton, grandson of the South Carolinian Paul Hamilton, Madison's Secretary of the Navy. Unsuited for his cabinet office, Hamilton had been obliged to resign. Adams, hoping to unearth the private reasons for his failure, had sent an inquiry to the grandson, accompanied by a patronizing little lecture. "The whole country south of Virginia is removed from the region of intellectual phenomenon, capable of study," especially because the absence of private records made it impossible for historians to "describe or understand what kind of men they were." Hamilton proudly retorted that "the private life of our great, though above reproach, has ever been considered sacred." As for the absence of records, he coldly added, "All relics of that kind, in Carolina, were destroyed by the vandal hordes of Sherman and Potter."

Scribner issued the initial pair of volumes, on the first administration of Thomas Jefferson, in October 1889 and the second pair, on the second administration, in February 1890. The third pair, on the first administration of James Madison, came out in September 1890. The fourth set—volumes VII–IX—on the second administration, appeared in January 1891. A tenth volume, *Historical Essays,* uniform with those of the *History,* followed in September 1891, thus ending the friendly "race" with Hay and Nicolay in a kind of tie. The ten volumes of their *Abraham Lincoln* were published in 1890. Adams's *Historical Essays* reprinted seven articles, revised and corrected, beginning with "Captain John Smith" and retrieving the unpublished "The Declaration of Paris, 1861" and "The Primitive Rights of Women."

THE *New York Times* noticed the first two volumes on October 27, 1889, in two and a half columns of appreciative comment that reflected the general estimate. Adams had achieved a "historical work of great importance," though rather "cold and grudging" in his treatment of Jefferson. The diplomatic sections, as was to be expected, were particularly able. Considering the importance of the archival materials, it would have been "nothing less than a public misfortune if this work should have been done by a vulgar or pretentious writer or by a dull and confused one. But it is in perfect taste. The style is admirable; combines clearness with elegance and simplicity with dignity and a gravity worthy of the greatness of the subject."

The Critic in New York assured its readers that the work fulfilled "the expectation of a brilliant narrative" and drew particular attention to the opening panorama of the United States in 1800: "No American writer has given so true a picture of American life and ideas." Abram Hewitt, one of Adams's staff of readers, who performed his stint while reform mayor of New York, told Adams that the volumes had "all the charms of romance," the chapters being like "successive scenes of a drama."

The public and private praise greatly pleased Charles Scribner, and its "exceptional success" in America led him to expect "some market abroad." Adams's idea of success did not square, however, with Scribner's modest expectations. As he commiserated with Francis Parkman, whose works had had small sales, they had come too late into the world. It was pleasant to have "solid butter laid on with a trowel" by the New York press, but it would have been pleasanter to have the public besiege the booksellers for his *History*. It was obvious that no American could hope for the acclaim and substantial fortune that had greeted Gibbon and Macaulay.

Besides, there ran beneath the columns of praise a disagreeable undertone of qualification and captiousness. The *Atlantic* begrudged the "nearly score of years . . . since it was first whispered abroad that this work was in creation," although the reviewer conceded that "the anticipation [of a great production] is very nearly fulfilled." He felt that the ambiguities in the treatment of Jefferson made the author's attitude toward him "almost a psychological study."

Perhaps least gratifying was the series of long reviews in the *Nation*, which almost parodied the judicial manner of the *History* by carefully balancing praise and censure in the manner of a critical Polonius. Edwin Godkin, it would appear, once again cast himself in the role of literary Dutch uncle, a fact which may partly explain the disappearance of his name from Adams's later correspondence. The anonymous reviewer, James Clarke Welling, president of Columbian College in Washington, thought that Adams's style and grasp of materials and the "striking" and "philosophical" introduction warranted the highest praise. On the other hand he argued that Adams had so lost himself in contradictions in Jefferson's character as to overlook the "key" to it in party history. Like others, he noted the absence of any preface or recital of obligations, but he conceded that Adams's qualifications were already plainly manifest from his earlier work. Thus he went, back and forth, cautiously turning the pages of the volumes as they came out until he left at least the impression of a great forest somehow lost among the trees.

The outcry which Adams anticipated from English readers did not develop. The *Times* did not condescend to take notice of the book or of Adams's obnoxious criticism of the Tory tradition, but the few reviews that greeted the work were disarmingly friendly. Like its American counterparts, the *Spectator* singled out the admirable opening chapters and the skill with which the fearfully complicated diplomatic skeins were unwound. With perfect good humor, it praised the fairness of the treatment of English statesmen, even suggesting that Canning was dealt with very leniently. After all, if not for the blunders of these men, America might have been an ally in the war against Napoleon. The *Athenaeum,* in one of its brief notices, remarked that "Mr. Adams has had Macaulay's ideal in view as an historian, and his success in making his pages as attractive as those of a novel deserves recognition." When the war volumes arrived, the critic added that "while patriotic, Mr. Adams is not unduly partisan."

In this benevolent climate of measured praise and qualification, one significant fact emerged. Critics obliged to read the work piecemeal did not perceive the extraordinary novelty of its approach or the grandeur of its "scientific" architecture. They contented themselves with appreciative nibbling at the overwhelming mass of details, rode their particular hobbies and historical favorites, relished the picturesque and dramatic moments, and missed the philosophical point of the work.

FOR THE SECOND TIME in a dozen years, Adams felt the keen relief of casting off harness that had begun to gall him unbearably. Six years of classroom teaching at Harvard had sent him to Washington railing at education. The incubus of the *History* had ridden him like the Old Man of the Sea for nearly twice as long and inspired a similar satiety. Once he had been "ashamed to seem restless" and thought it "ludicrous to play Ulysses"; now no other role seemed possible. Eagerly he looked westward again to distant China and the tantalizing "Asiatic mystery," to which his adventurous friends Rockhill and Pumpelly had grativated. Hay, watching the bustle of preparation, saw a cheerless vista ahead. "That pleasant gang, which made all the joy of life in easy irresponsible Washington, will fall to pieces in your absence. You were the only principle of cohesion."

Adams planned to approach the mystery by way of the South Seas and India, for he was taken with the notion of tracing out the medieval trade route explored by Marco Polo. He would see for himself the elements of the problems that were exciting ethnologists and anthropologists in Washington and elsewhere. He planned to reascend the trail of history in the South Pacific in the manner once suggested to him by Lewis Henry Morgan. He began to fit himself out for "two years in the South Seas," reserving the right to retreat the moment boredom set in. He talked facetiously of imitating Robert Louis Stevenson, whose expedition to the Marquesas and Tahiti had created a worldwide stir two years before.

A thousand details needed to be attended to and all contingencies provided for. To his family cotrustees he could conveniently leave the management of his substantial fortune. His eldest brother, John Quincy, and Edward Hooper could attend to Boston affairs. In Washington, Dwight would be left in charge of the house on Lafayette Square with a budget of $3,000 a year. Intervals came as he sat at his desk putting his house in order when he somberly brooded over the spent years. "In anticipation of a long absence," he wrote Gaskell, "I have gone through all my papers lately and destroyed everything that I should have wished an executor to destroy." He added that he had bundled up Gaskell's letters, "going back five-and-twenty years," not daring, as he said, to look at them again.

As the time for his departure began to fix itself as a fact upon the horizon, a tiny shadowing cloud rose and grew with the passing months. More and more he had fallen into the pleasant habit of taking his mint julep across the Square in the gracious oasis presided over by Elizabeth Cameron. There he had basked with his fellow courtiers in the candid, melting glance that still charms the eye in Anders Zorn's portrait. With affectionate tact she had humored Henry in his incessant Hamletizing and daily drew him closer into her confidence. Sometimes, in a mood of painful self-analysis, he had deplored to her that bitter and cynical "other self" which he hoped she might help him overcome.

He had in fact become almost wholly dependent upon her for "feminine society." Every few days, and often daily, letters had passed between them on a hundred topics of common interest, on friends and family, on grave matters and trifles, and trifles of trifles. When in the autumn of 1887 Mrs. Cameron had returned to Washington with the infant Martha, her trio of cavaliers—Adams, Hay, and Cecil Spring Rice—had resumed their sonneteering. Adams had made his playful vaunt to her: "I too was in Arcadia born—or in Hancock Place, beneath the shadow of the State House dome—much the same thing I presume."

Strolling in the Mall in moonlight he had sung his melancholy plaint to her:

> Endymion, dreaming still that on his Latmian height
> He feels Helene's breath warm on his eyes and hair.

Sometimes the note was that of a faithful Petrarch to whom love had come unbidden and unforeseen, making him an idolator at her shrine.

> As a musician who, in absent thought,
> Touching a viol that he chanced upon . . .
> Careless at first, deeming the task his sport,
> Till, as its notes grow deeper and more sure;
> Its scope more ample with each ripening year,
> He joys to touch its chords, strong, sweet, and clear,
> And strives to make its purity more pure,
> So I, who all these years, my mistress task,
> Find more and richer charm, the more I ask.

Gallantly he declared that "poetic merit must be given" his lines "by you." His Laura chided him; he was indeed a poet, "one of a very high order," she said. "I have suspected it and [the sonnets in] *Esther,* if not my own sonnets, have convinced me."

But these two romantics soon had to acknowledge to themselves that courtly love masked deeper and less tractable emotions. Formal salutations and conventional "Yours truly's" could not hide the intensity of their feelings. He discovered the truth of what he had himself written in *Esther:* "Every man who has at last succeeded, after long effort, in calling up the divinity which lies hidden in a woman's heart, is startled to find that he must obey the God he summoned." No choice now remained to him except flight, and his fair lady of the sonnets had no alternative but to send him away. For her part she resolved to find distraction in Europe. Adams bowed to her wishes though he suspected that for him flight would be useless. He diverted himself with errands for her voyage. Up to the moment of his own departure he continued to grasp at straws. From Nahant on August 15, 1890, he wrote posthaste, "The mere hope of seeing you again made me try the experiment, but it was foolish, for the disappointment is worse than the regret . . . Tomorrow evening, at six o'clock, we start for San Francisco. I feel that the devil has got me, for I have said to the passing moment 'Stay,' but the devil gave a splendid price for a very poor article."

He had angled first for the companionship of the elusive King, jesting that they would "drink our enemies' blood from their empty skulls"; but in the end he had to fall back on La Farge. La Farge had his usual unrealistic qualms about finances. Adams talked him out of his scruples against traveling once again as his guest, listening with indulgent amusement to his threats to pay his own way. On a budget of $1,000 a month they could travel in lordly fashion. La Farge lashed himself into a frenzy of work to try to finish his painting and stained-glass commissions, and finally carried his Japanese boy Awoki triumphantly off with him, leaving a trail of unfinished windows behind.

Aboard the train with the irrepressible La Farge, Adams regained his equanimity. In lieu of a diary he made a daily entry in a long travel letter to Elizabeth Cameron. The play of color on the western desert "seemed pure purple joy." La Farge fairly danced about trying to "catch the shadows and colors." He quieted down sufficiently to give Adams his first watercolor lesson, and the pupil "dabbled all day in cobalt, indigo and chrome." He beguiled some of the vacant hours across the plains with more sonnets, sending off one to the departing Elizabeth called "Eagle Head," the name of a seagirt promontory near Beverly Farms.

> Here where of old the eagles soared and screamed
>   Answering the ocean's restless, longing roar,
> While in their nest the hungry eaglets dreamed
> —Here let us lie and watch the wave-vexed shore,
>   Repeating, heart to heart, the eagle's strain,
>   The ocean's cry of passion and of pain.

In San Francisco he felt a moment of panic as his mind winged back to Elizabeth Cameron and her daughter. "A sudden spasm came over me," he said, "just at the foot of the hotel stairs, that I must see Martha." He tried to skirt that perilous shoal; "I got over it with the help of a bottle of champagne and a marvelous dinner at the Club." Yet he could not dissemble. Not willing to trust his own pen, he urged Elizabeth to look at Arthur Hugh Clough's poem, the one "beginning 'Come back. Come back,'" for, as she might see, he like the poet could only ask

> . . . and whither and for what?
> To finger idly some old Gordian knot,
> Unskilled to sunder, and too weak to cleave.

"Poor Clough was another wanderer who could not make his world run on four wheels," he sighed. The golden era that had opened with such promise in Washington nearly thirteen years before was closing with strangely unforeseen anguish. There could be no turning back. He almost visibly straightened up: "Here goes, then, for Polynesia."

16

The Paradoxes of Polynesia

IN AUGUST OF 1890 Henry Adams had at last "run for it" in earnest, after five years of whimsical and sometimes desperate talk of hunting for Nirvana. Now, at fifty-two, he found himself once more in San Francisco poised for immediate flight, hopeful that this time he would succeed in loosing the cords that tied him to a purposeless existence.

In the crowded hours before boarding ship, he had little time to brood over the deepest reason of all for embarking on a year's voyaging in the far Pacific. Life had capped his verbal paradoxes with a paradox of its own. Like Faust, the devil had got him, he had ruefully admitted to Elizabeth. Love had tempted him to say to the passing moment, "Stay!" Elizabeth had sent him away, and he had to acknowledge that her logic was unassailable. What was past remedy should be past regret. Her command had crystallized his intentions for travel and had cut through a complicated tangle of rebellious impulses, motives, and secret longings. Yet as he thought of her on the beach at Beverly Farms with Martha he wrote a despairing cry, "I would desperately like to be with you."

La Farge and he sampled again the luxuries of the Union Club, "interviewed all the leading citizens," as he embroidered matters for Elizabeth, and equipped themselves with "letters of introduction to all the nobility and gentry of Polynesia." The South Seas would be the antechamber to China, the track by which the course of civilization might be traced back to the Asiatic mainland. In his mind there floated the conjectures on primitive civilizations of Henry Maine and Lewis Henry Morgan, accompanied by the more exciting improvisations of Clarence King. To Adams's questing vision the Pacific hid as well the dawning problems of global politics. There still seemed a likelihood that Ferdinand de Lesseps' project for a transisthmian canal would be completed by the liquidators who had just taken over the bankrupt venture. And this hope gave a certain urgency to the current struggle over control of the Pacific sea-lanes. Samoa and Pago Pago were again in the news, and the talk of annexing Hawaii filled Americans with dreams of empire. There would be ample time to think of these issues on the long voyage out when the tiny dots on the charts which Adams studied would be translated into a succession of island landfalls.

On August 23 he boarded the *Zealandia,* and as the bay shore receded from view he hurriedly finished his diary letter to Elizabeth in order to put it aboard the pilot boat. He joked that the ship was "largely filled with cowboys and Indians of the Buffalo Bill persuasion, going somewhere to do something." (They were in fact a complement of pretty girls, as La Farge observantly noted.) There was the usual sprinkling of "Jews and Jewesses; the irascible old gentleman denouncing the company's officials; a few quiet young men, and the conventional big-nosed female."

Happily, Elizabeth's final budget of lighthearted gossip reached the steamer at the moment of sailing and was brought to his stateroom the evening of the first day out when the bow of the *Zealandia* was already rising and falling to the long swell of the Pacific. By then Adams had succumbed to his seasick fate. "All night I lay on my face in my clothes," he confessed, "clasping your letter between my hands, and only after twenty-four hours did I indulge in the pleasure of opening it." After three days at sea he felt a certain pride in having "got so far" without losing control of himself, though, in "the long watches of [the] nights," his thoughts paced by the rhythmical rush of the water, for the life of him he could "see no way out of it."

Above these dangerous depths, however, life began to take on a fresh zest. By day La Farge educated him in the nuances of the "butterfly blue" of the Pacific and the "lilac grey" of the cumulus clouds. At night the symphony of color ran through an infinity of modulations. In the crystalline sky overhead they could almost see the satellites of Jupiter. The iridescent spectrum of the partly veiled moon suffused the sky like a lesser sun. To Adams's less visionary eye it was such a moonlight as "set everyone to singing and spooning." His eye and ear made fresh discoveries as he followed after his friend, seeking to master the evanescence of shape and hue. Into his letters to Elizabeth there began to flood a new vocabulary of concrete shapes, of daring imagery and elusive color, as he moved back and forth from paint box to writing pad.

Disembarking at Honolulu, Adams, La Farge, and the Japanese boy Awoki came to rest with their "enormous baggage-train" at the charming house lent by Adams's classmate Judge Alfred Hartwell, set in palm trees and a rose garden. As visiting dignitaries they were entertained by Judge Sanford Dole and taken to the new Bishop museum of Polynesian artifacts by its founder. They had an audience with David Kalakaua, the king of Hawaii, a "Chester A. Arthur type" and more amusing, said Adams, than Benjamin Harrison. The king, who towered over him, delighted Adams with talk of archaeology and art, sparing his visitors the unpalatable grist of island politics. Kalakaua had traveled to Washington to negotiate the reciprocity treaty which had brought prosperity to the islands, but his dream of a Pacific empire of Polynesian peoples had floated away on seas of brandy, for the king was a valiant toper. Already the struggle between the royalists and the nonroyalists threatened to reduce him to a figurehead. Six months later he was to capitulate to death, the victim of his epic conviviality.

Adams deliberately kept aloof from the signs of the social and political revolution that was transforming the island capital. As a sentimental journeyer he resented the bustling inroads of civilization and the passing of the virile archaic culture which ethnologists like Lewis Henry Morgan had studied—and celebrated—by way of criticism of the new industrial society. How incongruously naïve had been his original idea of a tropic paradise of beach-fringed forests and frolicking natives swimming in the ocean. Honolulu would soon be just another American city, an imitation Washington or New York.

After a fortnight of luxurious laziness they sailed for Punulau on the island of Hawaii to make their strenuous pilgrimage to the crater of Mauna Loa; thence by sea again around the island of Hilo hoping to find "the waterfall of old-gold girls" with which Clarence King used to tantalize them. But the brown-skinned naiads were gone—or had tumbled down the cataract only in King's ardent imagination. "So passes the glory of Hawaii and of the old-gold girl," ran Adams's mock lament. "Woe is me!"

Not yet had the hoped-for shock of a wholly new sensation or experience swept him off his feet. In a few brief years civilization had literally covered over the living archaic world that King and Arnold Hague and the others had taught him to expect. Only once did he catch a hint of what that world had been. Instead of taking the steamer back to Kawaihae, the two pilgrims rode eighty miles through the wild coastal scenery where "the land and ocean meet like lovers, and the natives still look almost natural." Happy to be back in a saddle, Adams traversed ravines, each "a true Paul and Virginia idyll, wildly lovely in ways that made one forget life." One afternoon, especially, repaid "five thousand miles of weariness." In the hills two young women with enough "old-gold quality and blood to make them very amusing" fed them raw fish and squid and garlanded them with leis. At night they stretched out in a native hut overlooking the sea, while "Venus sank with a trail like the sun's," lulled half-asleep by plaintive Hawaiian songs.

After the ten-day excursion into the backcountry, Adams had to admit that Hawaii was indeed "fascinating." Honolulu society, however, proved inexplicably distant, though what glimpses he caught of the custom of informal festivity made him imagine "worse than Washington horrors." In the absence of society's diversions he preferred the savages, he said, and he took perverse pleasure in admiring the memory of the chiefs who were "great swells and very much gentlemen and killed Captain Cook." The occasional white men of the tropics whom they encountered impressed him as "ninth-rate samples."

To Elizabeth he poured out with deepening lyricism the discoveries of his awakened senses. La Farge taught him "subtleness and endless variety of charm in the color and light of every hour." However, he could not escape the incessant nudge of artistic and literary comparisons. Turner and Rembrandt lurked in his eyes, and in his ear the romantic lines of Charles Warren Stoddard's *South Sea Idylls*. To the "beckoning" of the palms Adams added the Arnoldian note, "the human suggestion of distress." He wrote of the "strange voluptuous charm" of the slopes of Mauna Loa, of mountainsides "absolutely velvety with the liquid softness of its lights and shadows." He hung upon the magic of La Farge's brush and joked ruefully at his own daubs. He felt a boy again going fishing: "I recognise that I am catching no fish on this particular day, but I feel always as though I might get a bite tomorrow." Intoxicated with the play of color, he fell into Proustian reveries. He was a youth of twenty again, he confided to

Elizabeth, carried away with absinthe of a summer's evening in the Palais Royal, his senses stirred to depths unknown to Boston. He felt "a sense of living, more than I had done in five years." The *Alemada,* which was to carry him twenty-three hundred miles to Samoa, had brought two of Elizabeth's weekly letters. He seized the moment for a last-minute injunction. Elizabeth must be sure to keep writing. "You are my only strong tie to what I suppose I ought to call home. If you should go back on me, I should wholly disappear."

Once more he gave himself to the sounding sea and its visceral terrors. He felt this time that he had never been so miserably seasick before. It was like having a baby; "but to endure it all, and have no baby, seems to take the fun out of life." In spite of the undulating horizon, he anchored himself in a sea chair and stoically marched his thought along the straight lines of his notepaper as precisely as though he were at his desk at home. On October 5, eight days out of Honolulu, the *Alemada* raised the coast of Tutuila, in the Samoan archipelago, where she was to rendezvous with a forty-ton coastal cutter due to pick up the twenty-nine-year-old American consul general, Harold Sewall, at Pago Pago. Manned by six native sailors, "as little fluent in English as though they had studied at Harvard," the little cutter beat to windward through tropical squalls until forced to seek shelter later in the bay off Anua. Taken to the hut of a local chieftain, Adams at last came face to face with the long-dreamed-of archaic world. First came the ritual drinking of kava, the root fortunately grated by the girls rather than chewed in the classical manner. Conversation struggled along fitfully on a few dictionary phrases, but playful gestures and smiles bridged the many hiatuses. "Communication was as hard as at a Washington party [but] it was more successful." The afternoon wore on, and as the travelers squatted on the mats engrossed with their inevitable sketching and journalizing, the girls of the village hung over them with eager curiosity. They crowded so close, Adams remarked to John Hay, that "we seemed all mixed up with naked arms, breasts, legs, yet apparently as innocently as little children."

Hay read on with rapt attention: "The sensation of seeing extremely fine women, with superb forms, perfectly unconscious of undress, and yet evidently aware of their beauty and dignity, is worth a week's sea sickness to experience." But all this proved merest prelude. What followed was recounted in Adams's voluminous diary letter to

Elizabeth. In Hawaii, said Adams, they had heard the magical word *siva,* the name of the fabled Polynesian dance, but had caught no glimpse of its exotic beauty. Now, after supper, in the eerie glow of a kerosene lamp set on the matting, they clamorously invoked it. First the elders had to be assured that the visitors were not spying missionaries, for the *siva* was forbidden by the church. Then the girls disappeared. The moment of waiting dragged on discouragingly. Then, suddenly, out of the dark five girls dramatically reappeared and sank to the floor. Sitting cross-legged the dancers sang and swayed through all the undulating figures of the sitting *siva.* "Naked to the waist, their rich skins glistened with coconut oil. Around their heads and necks they wore garlands of green leaves in strips, like seaweeds, and these too glistened with oil, as though the girls had come out of the sea. Around their waists, to the knee, they wore leaf-cloths, or *lavalavas,* also of fresh leaves, green and red. Their faces and figures varied in looks, some shading the negro too closely; but Sivà was divine, and you can imagine that we found our attention absorbed in watching her. The mysterious depths of darkness behind, against which the skins and dresses of the dancers mingled rather than contrasted; the sense of remoteness and of genuineness in the stage-management; the conviction that at last the kingdom of old-gold was ours, and that we were as good Polynesiacs as our neighbors,—the whole scene and association gave so much freshness to our fancy that no future experience, short of being eaten, will ever make us feel so new again. La Farge's spectacles quivered with emotion and [he] gasped for sheer inability to note everything at once."

The *siva* was but one of many adventures which had to be retold with varying emphasis to a dozen correspondents. With a novelist's eye he marched the native chieftains and their dependents across his pages, especially taken with the "sad and despondent" King Malietoa, recently abdicated, and "the intermediary king" Mataafa, who were both victims of the international scramble for control of Samoa. He felt a grandly archaic simplicity in the royal invitation: "To the Distinguished Chiefs of America. This is my letter to you. Will you please my wish to meet your Honours . . ." The art of Mataafa's rhetoric and his overwhelming dignity made Adams feel as though he were "the son of a camel-driver degraded to the position of stable-boy in Spokane West Centre." Adams was overawed by the mere size of the men. To one of his short stature they seemed giants, heroes out of Homer, any one of whom could "handle him like a baby." It was a relief often to escape from them and sprawl contentedly on the mats among the far less formidable young women, in an archaic version of his Washington breakfast table with its bevy of young worshippers.

Samoa swept him off his Puritan feet. "Hawaii is nowhere," he exulted to Hay. Here was the true archaic in all its barbaric voluptuousness; here Clarence King was vindicated. It was all there, including the pretty waterfall at Sliding Rock where they picnicked while six of the prettiest mermaids in Apia slid laughing and screaming over the small cliff into the forest pool. "The water," as Adams said, "took charge of the proprieties." The long-hoped-for awakening from dullness of spirit had come at last. In Japan he had tried to persuade himself that sex did not exist except as a scientific classification; Samoa demanded a readjustment of his opinions. He had caught it "all alive and find just what I did not expect. The queerest jumble of professors' books rolled into a practical system that no one would guess at."

No picturesque detail escaped his indefatigable pen: the preparation of exotic foods; the colorful and often interminable *sivas;* the barbaric splendor of the military receptions of a *malanga* or a ceremonial tour of the islands; the appearance of the notable *taupos* or official virgins ("perpetual Queen of the May," Stevenson called each of them); and all the customs of a society that exuded health and cheerful spirits. Much as he had been impressed by the lovely Sivà whose beauty La Farge had sketched at Anua, it was a certain Faauli's dancing that dazzled him most. He was the more touched since she, the daughter of a great chief, had risked excommunication by the missionaries to entertain him and La Farge with the forbidden figures of the ancient dance. Her dancing "made our ballets seem preposterous . . . Glistening with cocoa-nut oil, she stood out against the rich brown of the background like an ivory image of Benvenuto's. Her movements were large and free, full of strength; sometimes agile as a cat's, as when she imitated a rat and swung on the cross beam." Once the figure of the dance required the guest to be kissed. "Mine was a good square kiss, squarely returned by me."

Adams made a special point of explaining to Hay, as he had to Elizabeth Cameron, that in all this he saw no licentiousness, although "any European suddenly taken to such a show would assume that the girl was licentious, and if he were a Frenchman he would probably ask for her." However, the *siva,* "like the Japanese bath, is evidently connected with natural selection; the young men and women learn there to know who are the finest marriageable articles." The ultracorrect German consul had warned that visiting dignitaries like them must be scrupulously correct toward the native women. To Adams the warning was superfluous. "As elsewhere, vice follows vice. We have not sought it, and consequently have not found it . . . I might as well be living in a nursery for all the vice that is shown to me, and if I did see it, I should only be amused at its simplicity beside the elaborated viciousness of Paris or even of Naples."

Adams illustrated his impressionistic anthropology with a great many photographs taken with his new Kodak, though he cautioned that the stiffly posed "photograph takes all the color, life and charm out of the tropics." Smitten with envy, Hay read and reread Adams's tantalizing description and repented his lost opportunity. "I hang over your photographs and contemplate your old-gold girls, and interrogate the universe, asking if there ever was such a fool as I—who shall never *à grand jamais* enter that Paradise." Dubbed "Atamu" by his hosts, Adams cheerfully entered into the elaborate playacting of his role of visiting *ali* or lord, on one occasion hilariously entertaining his royal friends by performing his own version of the sitting *siva*. He boasted of harmless flirtations with the girls who always surrounded their party, but at one village "a muscular maiden," emboldened by his friendly attentions, "announced a strong desire" to elope with him. He averred that, if nothing else, the pervasive odor of their "raiment of cocoa-nut oil has proved an impassable barrier between them and me."

Baffling to all Adams's preconceptions was the fact that under circumstances in which the race ought to be "chockful of languid longings and passionate emotions . . . they are pure Greek fauns," apparently without sensuality or voluptuousness. Good-natured they certainly were; they smiled as meaninglessly as the Japanese, being like all Orientals "merely children." They had the "virtues of healthy children,—and the weaknesses of Agamemnon and Ulysses" in the sphere of lovemaking. They had no sense of indecency; it was a "European fiction." Adams expatiated on the subject at great length to Gaskell, assuring his friend that "for men of our time of life, and tastes, the danger is not terrifying . . . but even at twenty I think I should have wanted something more or less than the Polynesian women have to give."

After reading Adams's analysis of Polynesian morality, or lack of it,

Hay reminded him of King's saying, in one of his tirades against women, "Sex is such a modern affair, after all." Adams disciplined King's fervid curiosity by first sending a twenty-eight-page letter on the geology of Polynesian atolls, questioning the subsidence theory of Darwin and James D. Dana along the lines taken by their friend Alexander Agassiz. He knew, as he admitted to Hay, that the treatise would "exasperate him because it says not a word about old gold." Six weeks later, in another gargantuan letter to King, he allowed himself to touch on the "old-gold problem," but only as an aspect of the scientific question of racial origins. By that time he had also observed Tahiti, an experience which required considerable revision of his generalizations.

In wonderfully broad strokes he reviewed for King the conjectural migration of this people, the diffusion through the islands and atolls of the tools and arts of primitive civilization. He saw the Tahitians as unique among their race, refining the simple elements of Polynesian life, the wreathing of garlands, dancing, and warfare, "to a degree of depravity that implied considerable crowding." In Samoa there was ignorance of "what we call morals." In Tahiti, however, the depravity seemed to him childishly self-conscious, the voluptuousness studied and organized. Evidently sexuality was not, as he once supposed, an Aryan invention, for the Polynesians were obviously pre-Aryan. Coming at last to the "old-gold woman," he declared his belief that even in the state of unclothed nature she "was very much a woman" and more complicated in Tahiti than Samoa. Though as mindless as the Polynesian man, "the woman of Tahiti was pretty near the European standard of female faults," but without the nervous diseases. Even in Arcadia women were fickle and vain.

Finally facing up to King's unspoken challenge, he wrote, "I prefer the old ones to the young ones, except for looks; but although I have seen many, and lived intimately with some, I have not yet met one who inspired me with improper desires. Fifty-three years are a decided check to sexual passion, but I do not think the years are alone to blame. Probably I should have behaved differently thirty years ago; yet as I look back at the long list of dusky beauties I have met, I cannot pick out one who seems to me likely, even thirty years ago, to have held me much more than five minutes even in her arms. They are jolly, obliging, and quite ready to attach themselves ... My young Telemachuses and Anacharses, born and bred in these islands, tell me that one need only say—Come! I have not been tempted to say it, nor has La Farge."

The next words of his curious lecture made a quixotic and revealing shift, as if following a subterranean and divergent course. "The moral of this is whatever you please. To my mind the moral is that sex is altogether a mistake, and that no reversion to healthier conditions than ours, can remove the radical evils inherent in the division of the sexes . . . As the matter is no longer of much consequence to me, I can afford to sit still. Deadheads ought not to hiss the actresses." Thus he disposed of King's romantic dream which had beguiled them all. From every rational standpoint he must regard "the old-gold woman as a failure almost as emphatic as the New York female."

For the most part Adams averted his gaze from the troubling present by identifying it with the literary past, when feelings were somehow purer, intenser, uncorrupted. He liked to sit and look out on the long rolling surf with the *Odyssey* in his hand, annotating its pages with the vestiges of archaic life about him and sometimes rendering the sounding Greek into metrical English for his Polynesian friends. "Homer is constantly before me," he said. In fancy he saw the wine-dark sea beyond his page. "Homer's women—Penelope, Helen, Nausicaa—are modern types compared with Faauli and Leolofi. My Samoan princesses knew only the bathing-pool and the naked castaway; they never dreamed of the fortified city, the bronze-doored palace, the silver and gold drinking bowls and the rest. They were dead ages before Troy was built."

From the first day that he set foot ashore in Samoa, Adams adopted a characteristic routine, the habit of a lifetime easily asserting itself. Almost every day, for a few hours, La Farge saw Adams seat himself with his writing pad and inkstand before him just as if he were at 1603 H Street, completely heedless of his exotic surroundings. A pretty young *taupo*, Taele, assigned to "Atamu" would silently crouch on the mats beside him while he "would be absolutely immersed in his letter-writing, a feat of which he is always capable apparently." The devoted girl thought him to be ill because he seemed so troubled by thought. Even in the bow of a whaleboat at dawn while voyaging "like Robinson Crusoe" round Upolu with "my five men rowing and singing, and much disturbing my handwriting," Adams appreciatively noted "how the mountains take the morning light."

There was one dawn that no opalescent glow could brighten, that which ushered in the fateful anniversary of the death of his wife, December 6. As November waned, his spirits sank lower and lower. After one sleepless night he began a poem for Mrs. Cameron.

> The slow dawn comes at last upon my waiting;
> The palms stand clear against the growing light.

He imagined little Martha calling him by his pet name, "Dobitt"; then, in fancy, John Hay and Sister Anne (Mrs. Lodge) drew near; but it was Elizabeth toward whom he turned. He strained "To catch the whiteness of the dress you wear," but it was only "the surf upon the coral streaming." Nothing remained for him but death. At last the vigil passed. "I am not positively hilarious," he said. "I am rarely so on this day, but if five years can pass, I suppose I can stand ten."

He was touched to learn that she had visited the grave in Rock Creek cemetery on that day. With both Adams and La Farge away, Saint-Gaudens had finally ended his long irresolution and was now proceeding with the casting of the memorial figure. In the following March it would at last be in place, gaunt and stark on the bare slope. The photographs set at rest his worst fears. "If it is not exactly my ideal, it is at least not hostile," he wrote Hay. But by no stretch of fancy could he any longer call it his "Buddha" figure. "St Gaudens is not in the least oriental, and is not even familiar with oriental conceptions. Stanford White is still less so. Between them, the risk of going painfully wrong was great. Of course White was pretty sure to go most astray, and he has done so."

When Elizabeth's letters arrived he read them over and over, each a kind of talisman. Clad in sketchy native costume, he would drift in his canoe lost in meditation upon them. He was a Robinson Crusoe, he said, who could not get back to land, condemned to wander the world and tire himself out. "Perhaps you may cure me after all, and I shall come back contented and in repose of mind, to be your tame cat, after the manner of Chateaubriand, and various elderly English gentlemen, once my amusement to watch. Is it worth your while? Please say yes." A week later another fit of the blues: "The horrors of thinking are intolerable. I feel at times as though I must just run home to have an hour's conversation with you, and that without it the world would run off the trestle."

Elizabeth apologized for the prosaic chitchat with which she requited his literary outpourings. He protested that they gave him "the delight of a famished castaway." He could think of no combination of "love and angel" sufficient to praise her. Vanquished by his confidences, she withdrew her proscription and urged that he return. "How can I come back?" he replied. "Matthew Arnold asked what it boots now that Byron bore, with scorn that half concealed his smart, from Europe to the Aetolian shore, the pageant of a bleeding heart. I am not Byron, and bear no pageant, nor, for that matter, a bleeding heart,—any more than he did,—but I wish you would tell me how I can come home and be contented there."

Hay, treasuring his share of Adams's outpourings, was sure that the "writing machinery was never in better trim." He passed the letters on to Henry James in London. But to James their interest was not literary but personal. As a historian of fine consciences James saw his old friend in an arrestingly new light. "What a power of baring one's self hitherto unsuspected in H A!"

James's perception suggested the transformation taking place in Adams's sensibility. From earliest boyhood he had been taught the importance of hiding his emotions, of suppressing the emotional tempests to which as an Adams he was naturally prey. Clover, realistic and skeptical, had habitually scoffed at any sign of vaporish notions. Now, though he denied the pageant of a bleeding heart, he could not help showing it. Out of the game, without a stake in it and only posthumously alive, as he liked to think, he was free to cultivate the garden of his sensibilities. He could be Ulysses, or Faust, or a Polynesian Prince Hamlet if he pleased. In spite of the ennui that finally overcame him in Tahiti, he had to confess "the secret truth" to one of his correspondents: "I am more like a sane idiot than I have known myself to be in these six years past."

What he really yearned to do was not to write but to paint. "What fun to paint a beautiful naked figure, standing on her swimming board, with the surf around her, and one of these divine sunsets of rose and violet in the sky! I hope La Farge will do it." La Farge did do it. The painting, *Fayaway Sails Her Boat,* shows the figure of a girl, tall and almost boyishly lithe, holding a billowing cloth with outstretched arms above her head, the sensuous flesh more American than Polynesian. Adams's gentlemanly dabbling in watercolors was at first extremely diverting. He soon discovered that figure drawing was beyond him and settled for scenery. Having carried his sketching to the point where "real labor" began, he found the labor oppressive. "I can already see that my way of seeing is just the way I do not want to see . . . I spread my net with infinite labor, and catch only my own fingers in the mesh."

ADAMS HAD TRIED to keep clear of local politics in Samoa as he had avoided in Honolulu the annexationist stir and the rumors of rebellion. However, he reluctantly found himself pitched into a nest of intrigue and social rivalries, all to be graphically described in his letters home as if he were the Horace Walpole of the islands. History was being made under his nose, the tiny island recapitulating in almost comic-opera fashion the worldwide impact of colonialism on native populations. An uneasy epoch was ending in the life of the islands. In the half-century of competition among the German, British, and American traders, the Germans had achieved such a commanding position that they attempted to set up a native puppet, Tamasese, as "King" of Samoa. Civil War had broken out three years before, with the United States and British interests supporting the lawful chiefs, Malietoa and Mataafa. The Berlin Conference agreed upon a joint protectorate, under a Swedish justice, Otto Cedarkranz. Adams wrote that that young dignitary "looks honest and fairly intelligent, but has one eye that seems to be fixed, and glares perversely into space."

Determined not to take the politics of "this poultry yard" seriously, he nevertheless had to listen to all the rumors of intrigue and possible renewal of the civil war that agitated his hosts wherever he went. The chief, Mataafa, talked "with his grave, quiet smile, as though he were sorry to amuse us with his people's folly." Robert Louis Stevenson, a great partisan of Mataafa and Malietoa, told them all he knew of the tangled maze, for he was already working on his impassioned plea for justice to the Samoans, *A Footnote to History.* Samoa seemed visibly the key to the Pacific; hence, Adams felt, Mataafa's fate at the hands of Bismarck's Germany bore directly on the question of American expansion in the Pacific. In his enormous thirty- and forty-page journal-letters home he tried to keep to the picturesque and farcical aspects of the imbroglio. The great "Asian mystery" which he hoped to penetrate seemed at the moment indissolubly linked with the Pacific islands. A few months later, however, viewing them from the perspective of Australia, he wrote Lodge what may have been the germ of Hay's Far Eastern policy: "On the whole, I am satisfied that America has no future in the Pacific . . . Her best chance is Siberia. Russia will probably go to pieces . . . If it can be delayed another twenty-five years, we could Americanize Siberia, and this is the only possible work that I can see still open on a scale equal to American means."

Stevenson's impact upon Adams in Samoa was violent, disturbing, disquieting. He seemed a satire of the art of living that Adams had attained. Like most of his brilliantly etched first impressions, Adams's portrait of Stevenson is even more revealing of Adams, and shows both the unsparing clarity of his self-knowledge and the tightening hold of his social prejudices. Jealous of his own prickly individualism, Adams had to reconcile himself from the very beginning to treading in the still-warm footsteps of Stevenson, who at forty was not only a sensationally successful writer but also a romantic and bohemian legend, the defender of Father Damien of the leper colony at Molakai and the adopted spokesman for Polynesia.

Adams had reached Samoa only a short while after Stevenson had decided to settle with his wife Fanny at "Vialima" on a four-hundred-acre tract three miles from Apia, on a mountain shelf eight hundred feet above the sea. Adams and La Farge mounted horses and toiled up the forest path for an hour under lowering skies until they reached a backwoods clearing of burned stumps, in the center "a two-story Irish shanty with steps outside to the upper floor, and a galvanized iron roof." Out came a figure "so thin and emaciated he looked like a bundle of sticks in a bag, with a head and eyes morbidly intelligent and restless." Stevenson stood before him in "dirty striped cotton pajamas, the baggy legs tucked into coarse knit woolen stockings." Fanny, in a soiled "missionary nightgown," hurried inside for a moment to cover her bare feet with shoes. Adams could not tear his eyes away from Stevenson's mismatched stockings, one brown, the other purple. He looked like "a sort of cross between a Scotch Presbyterian and a French pirate," his wife looking even "more piratic" than he. Stevenson was, however, "extremely entertaining" and tremendously knowledgeable about the South Seas. But, as Adams admitted to Hay, he was not prepared for such eccentric squalor "and could see no obvious reason for it."

Adams found it a little disconcerting that he was unknown to Stevenson; "not the faintest associations with my name, but he knew all about La Farge." The artist and the novelist were quickly drawn to each other, so that Adams found himself in the unfamiliar role of listener to Stevenson's incessant talk. Stevenson's own account of that initial meeting quickly became an international anecdote which Hay, not averse to teasing his absent friend, sent right on to Tahiti: "Now I will have to tell you,—perhaps a dozen fellows have done so—of Stevenson's account of your visit to him. Your account of that historical meeting is a gem of description . . . His is no less perfect and characteristic. He writes to N____ B____ 'Two Americans called on me yesterday. One, an artist named La Farge, said he knew you. The name of the other I do not recall.' Bear up under this, like a man, in the interest of science!"

Adams saw Stevenson many times in the succeeding weeks, and falling into the gypsy spirit of the occasion he would come to dine bringing his own food with him. As it happened they had surprised the Stevensons at the most inopportune moment of a new project. The ground was just being cleared for the building of a large and comfortable manor house. The temporary home was hardly more than a construction shanty. As his first impression faded, Adams wrote in a more kindly spirit. He was amazed at Stevenson's phenomenal energy, considering how much he had been ravaged by tuberculosis. He began to see a "certain beauty, especially about the eyes," and "came round to a sort of liking" for his wife, who "seemed more human than her husband." Occasionally they met and dined on the veranda at the American consulate and talked long about art and island politics and their friends in London.

At each meeting, Adams felt himself brought to bay, and he struggled to explain the thing to his friends—and to himself. That Stevenson should abdicate the privileges—and duties—of world fame argued some kind of lunacy. But if he thought Stevenson wanting, his bad conscience suggested that Stevenson must have found him out also. "My Bostonianism, and finikin clinging to what I think best, must rub him all over . . . I dare not see him often for fear of his hating me as a Philistine and a disgrace to humanity, because I care not a copper for what interests him."

Stevenson obviously surmised nothing of Adams's elaborate struggles of taste and conscience. A little later he wrote to Henry James, "We have had enlightened society: La Farge the painter, and your friend Henry Adams: a great privilege—would it might endure. I would go oftener to see them, but the place is awkward to reach on horseback. I had to swim my horse the last time I went to dinner . . . They, I believe, would come oftener to see me but for the horrid doubt that weighs upon our commissariat department; we have often almost nothing to eat; a guest would simply break the bank."

Within a relatively few months the Stevensons moved into their new house, with Mrs. Stevenson presiding over their social functions in elegant attire, but by then Adams was back in Europe. Stevenson's letter to Adams accompanying his book *A Footnote to History* showed that Adams's diplomacy had successfully concealed his neurotic fastidiousness from his host: "I wish you would accept the expression of the great enjoyment in your society I had when you were here and of the regret I have felt since your departure."

Adams had a field day investigating archaic law and custom in Samoa, following out the lines of what he had learned about anthropology from Lewis Henry Morgan. He was constantly astonished by the healthy physical development of the natives, and he busied himself with tape measure and Kodak recording the impressive physical features of the daughters of the chief and the notable *taupos*, all of whom were much entertained by such flattering scientific attentions. One tabulation he supplied to Elizabeth ran as follows:

	Aotoa	*Aotele*
Height	66 [inches]	65½ [inches]
Round chest and arms	41¾	43½
" upper waist	33½	32
" hips	39	38
" head	23½	22½

He badgered the chiefs so persistently about "the rights of law, of property, of kinship" that at one point one of them remarked, "Years ago I would have killed a man who asked me that question." The abdicated chief Mataafa, though beset with troubles, was impressed by Adams's boundless zeal and brought him old songs.

Adams approached Tahiti with keyed-up anticipations which Stevenson had greatly helped to heighten. He somehow felt that Samoa would be a curtain raiser for a new drama of the archaic. "Tahiti! does the word mean anything to you?" he challenged Elizabeth Cameron two days after his arrival. "To me it has a perfume of its own, made up of utterly inconsequent associations, essence of the South Seas mixed with imaginations of at least forty years ago; Herman Melville and Captain Cook head and heels with the French opera and Pierre Loti."

La Farge and Adams arrived at Tahiti in the Society Islands on February 4, 1891, after an uneventful fifteen-hundred-mile voyage east by south from Samoa. After a few weeks Adams found Papeete's "eternal charm of middle-aged melancholy" getting on his nerves. He had run through all the available works on Tahiti, and in his boredom he hoped he might now see some of the alleged vices. In Samoa they had had a competent and amusing young interpreter; here, for want of a good interpreter, they were unable to talk with the villagers. The women were painfully shy and plain, for the districts no longer cele- brated the rivalry of their professional beauties as in Samoa. The na- tives had no great fun in them, and there were no picnics to waterfalls that cascaded old-gold girls. The letdown was very great. Not even "in the worst wilds of Beacon Street or at the dreariest dinner-tables of Belgravia" had he been so bored. "My mind has given way. I have horrors."

Going from the relative independence of Samoa, with its vigorous native culture, to enervated Tahiti, subdued and tamed by French co- lonial administration, Adams saw everywhere the marks of degener- ation. To the historian's eye the moral was far more marked and sad- dening than in Samoa. Stevenson had been hopeful that Samoan culture might be saved in some way; but no political pamphlet could be written for Tahiti. Here Adams saw the "wreck of what was alive in Samoa." The distinctive lineaments of the race vanished in the Mother Hubbard, and the girls no longer frolicked in the surf. There were the telltale signs of rum and private debauchery and a down-at- heel parody of French civilization. After the bustle and almost festive spirit of Samoa, the *sivas,* the delightful camaraderie of the women, the ceremonious *malangas* from village to village, the whole sense of a vital pagan life, Tahiti, for all its startling beauty of scenery, over- whelmed him with its atmosphere of stagnation. "The pervasive half- castitude that permeates everything" repelled him: "a sickly whitey brown, or dirty-white complexion that suggests weakness, disease, and a combination of the least respectable qualities, both white and red."

What one could "honestly enjoy" in Tahiti was something quite different from Stevenson's prospectus. "Tahiti is full of charm, but the charm is almost wholly one of sentiment and association. The landscape is lovelier than any well-regulated soaker of Absynthe could require to dream in; but it is the loveliness of an *âme perdue*." In the shimmering tropic light, the spirits of the two restless friends rose and fell, erratically, causelessly, each vibrating to the other's malaise. La Farge complained fitfully of fever; Adams dismissed it as imaginary. Adams fell back on the tourist resource, novel reading, dawdling over *Ivanhoe* and *Guy Mannering*. "True, this is what I came for," he admitted; "the Nirvana I wished to attain." But looking out at the narcotic horizon, he felt "empty minded as a cockroach."

THE PURSUIT of art and beauty and fresh sensation compassed the primary objects of Adams's voyage, but characteristically he heated an array of scientific irons in the fire of his skeptical curiosity. His probing eye watched suspiciously for signs of new scientific orthodoxies and shaky hypotheses. Once again he gravitated toward controversy. Many years before, in his review of Sir Charles Lyell's *Principles of Geology*, he had detected the theory of glaciation as the weak point of Lyell's demonstration that geological change was a gradual process. Now he was drawn toward another scientific controversy, the problem of accounting for the building of the coral reef atolls of the South Seas. In his baggage was Dana's new edition of *Corals and Coral Islands,* which had been called forth by the growing number of attacks on Darwin's theory that the coral reefs were formed by the upgrowth of the coral from slowly subsiding foundations. Dana temperately supported Darwin's position as the likeliest general hypothesis. The 1890 edition of his work added a long section refuting the spate of new objections, especially those of Alexander Agassiz.

Challenged by the fresh array of contradictions, Adams approached the islands with his customary appetite for an argument. He recounted to King with suspenseful irony the steps by which he, "a full blooded Darwinian," was finally "obliged to surrender my dear Darwin and my own Dana, very unwillingly too, for their view was much more entertaining than mine." He had hoped, he said, to be the one to convert Darwin's hypothesis of submergence into "scientific certainty," to make a "neat demonstration" of it. The coastline of the island of Samoa left him in perplexity; he could see no evidence of "subsided coral reefs."

He had been still hopeful for confirmation when he reached Tahiti in the Society Islands, "the peculiar property of Darwin and Dana," since they were supposed to be remnants of "a submerged continent." But his first thrilling view of the knife-edge peaks of Moorea made him incredulous of Dana's theory of prolonged subaerial erosion. Only an ice age could explain such rock sculpturing within so limited a drainage area. "I was dead-bent on ice," he went on, "and came ashore, as it were, on a cake of it." He walked along the beach and observed the same phenomenon as at Samoa and Hawaii, namely, evidence of an elevated coral reef. If Tahiti has not subsided, Adams asked, "what becomes of the Paumotu continent and Darwin's theory?" Obviously the Pacific swarmed with paradoxes.

He had diligently paddled along the Samoan reef in a canoe with the young *taupo* who had taken him in charge, geologizing by the hour, collecting specimens and jotting down pages of notes under her wondering gaze. He regularly tried out his theories upon the sympathetic La Farge, "all to the greater confusion and defeat of Mr Darwin." The upshot of his speculations was "that the theory is nothing but a theory," one still without proof, a conclusion much like the one he had reached in his review of Lyell's *Principles of Geology* twenty years earlier.

17

Between Worlds

AFTER FIVE MONTHS of restless travel which had dropped him into the very pit of boredom in Tahiti, Adams was at last able to report to Elizabeth Cameron that he "felt disposed to say to the passing moment—Stay!" That moment came at Papara when he was set down at the old French house of Tati Salmon within sight of the blue sea and the rolling surf, and had surrendered himself to the hospitality of his host. Adams already knew something of the romantic history of the Salmon family and its tribal connections. His interest had been aroused by Stevenson, who gave him a letter to Tati, the ruling head of the Tevas. Tati's father, the late Alexander Salmon, a London Jew, had married Ariitaimai, heiress of the dispossessed Teva clan, and founded a kind of island dynasty. The old widowed "chiefess" had just retired to honorary status, still maintaining among her European-educated children the old island customs. "She will not sit at the table with us," said Adams. "She sits on the floor like a lady, and takes her food when she wants it." Unlike her children, she spoke only Tahitian and with such charm that one was held by its very music.

Tati, thirty-eight, had a quiveringly jovial gaiety about him that was irresistible. He was "like a Northwest wind at home," dissipating all the chill of the hated east wind. Adams was instantly struck by his resemblance to his old friend H. H. Richardson, both in the vastness of his bulk and in the exuberance with which he swept everything before him. Although the French had initially recognized the titular sovereignty of the usurping Pomare clan, they prudently acquiesced in the traditional authority of the Tevas. Overflowing with life, the half-caste Tati exhibited the robust best of two worlds. "Hebrew and Polynesian mix rather well," Adams declared, "when the Hebrew does not get the better." The two men became fast friends. Adams found himself taken to the heart of the multitudinous Salmon clan.

At Papara Adams reclined on the mats, engrossed by the old matriarch's tales of pagan custom and legend as her children translated the musical phrases. Adopted into the household, he felt he now knew the true delight of travel. He had met greatness in Samoa in the person of Mataafa; he encountered it again in the person of Ariitaimai. She ruled with such natural dignity that he took pleasure in deferring to her. He asked her approval for exchanging names with Ori, one of the chieftains of the Teva clan, when he learned that Stevenson's adoption by the tribe had offended her.

Because he liked to dangle his legs from a canoe when watching the afterglow, he adopted the native custom of a brief *pareu*, a kind of sarong, for it saved him the trouble of changing clothes at sunset. However, he asked Hay to keep the fact quiet, as he did not want to be regarded as "a servile copyist" of Stevenson, and he made a similar injunction to King about the exchanging of names. The initiation made him an adoptive brother of Stevenson, a matter for satire at first, since Stevenson had taken the ceremony seriously, but Adams soon repented his levity when he realized that the exchange of names was indeed a solemn matter in Polynesia.

Ariitaimai summoned the two travelers to her presence and with majestic graciousness conferred family names of the Teva clan upon both of them in the presence of Tati and the family. Adams received the historically famous name of Taura-atua, "Bird Perch of God," which with his name of Ori a Ori made him a member of both the outer and inner Tevas. La Farge became Tera-aitua, "Prince of the Deep." They drove out to the little ancestral plot, the Amo, from which the Tevas were once ruled, where the first Taura-atua had presided many generations before. There Adams took investiture of his infinitesimal duchy by ceremoniously plucking an orange.

As an adoptive member of the ruling family, Adams began to feel a proprietary interest in the island and its history, becoming, as La Farge said, "more Teva than the Tevas." Listening to the family legends, Adams quickly saw their possibilities for a history. A history would also have a practical value for Tati's family. The French administration had decided to quiet the titles to land on the island by establishing written records. The question of royal pensions also needed to be settled. Since ownership followed descent, the natives were everywhere busy reconstructing the oral traditions of their family trees, and the local court sounded like a meeting of a genealogical society.

Tati's sister, Queen Marau Taaroa, loved to tell the stories of the ghostly *aitus* who haunted the island and was an authority on Tahitian "poetry, legends, and traditions." To pass the time of waiting for a ship to carry him on to the Fijis, Adams suggested that Marau write her memoirs, and he offered "to take notes and write it out, chapter by chapter." Marau took up the idea with un-Tahitian energy. After three lethargic months on the island, Adams suddenly found himself with congenial occupation. The note of boredom disappeared from his letters. He plunged into the work as if he were back in his study in Lafayette Square. He got his hosts "into a condition of wild interest in history," the household working out the family genealogy back into remotest island antiquity, ransacking their prodigious memories for legends and traditions, and comparing notes in the liveliest fashion. There was enough of a parallel between the fortunes of Tati's family and those of the Adams family to give an almost reminiscent flavor to the research. The Salmons were the elite family of that microcosm, proud of their Teva descent and accustomed and trained to rule. Civil war and foreign intervention, the coming of a new social order, had displaced them. Social distinction they still had, but political power was gone.

Three weeks after the Tahitian seminar began, Adams wrote to Elizabeth Cameron: "Positively I have worked . . . I have untangled two centuries of family history, and got it wound up nicely. I have rewritten two chapters, making a very learned disquisition of Tahitian genealogy, mixed up with legends and love-songs. The thing would be rather pretty if I only knew how to do it, or perhaps it might be better if I were writing it on my own account; but as it is for Marau in the first person, I have to leave out everything risky."

Adams left his notes with Marau, a little skeptical of Tahitian resolutions, but she promised with a "ferocious air of determination, half-Tahitian and half-Hebrew," to go on with the autobiographical memoirs and send them to him in Washington. As an addict of that literary genre he gave her a final piece of advice, "to put in all the scandal" she could. News came out, just before he left Tahiti, that put a kind of seal upon their collective enterprise. The wayward Pomare V, last of the Tahitian kings, was reported to be dying. Adams remarked, "Apparently I am fatal to kings. Kalakaua [of Hawaii] and

Pomare march to the grave as I pass. I should be employed by the anarchists." Seven months later, when the superstitious Marau wrote that her royal ex-husband had expired, she reminded him of his fateful saying.

During that winter and the spring of 1891, however, Adams was forcefully reminded that Samoa and Tahiti were only episodes on the outskirts of a vaster drama—or tragedy. The counterpointing came in telegrams, letters, and months-old newspapers from home. In December 1890, like the premonitory rumblings of a volcano before the eruption, news arrived of financial upheavals in the money centers of the West, the first symptoms of the devastating Panic of 1893. The House of Baring, the chief banking firm of the world, had in the flush of financial expansion guaranteed a very large loan to Argentina. The revolution there showed how dubious a venture it was. As a result of the bursting of that speculative bubble in London, American securities were dumped on the market, and a tide of gold flowed out of New York. Hay wrote of "a tornado of falling stocks" that had made them all poorer "by an average of ten million apiece." It had been no laughing matter for their friend King, for his affairs had grown even more luridly chaotic. In a short time he would seek temporary refuge in Bloomingdale asylum.

Off in Tahiti there was nothing for Adams to do but hope—and jest. "If things get so bad," he wrote his brother-in-law Edward Hooper, "that neither my brother John, nor you, nor Kidder, Peabody, nor the Barings, nor the Bank of England, nor the United States Treasury, nor Cabot Lodge nor the Republican Party, can pay my drafts of a thousand dollars a month, you had better beg enough money to telegraph the fact to me, via Sydney and Auckland; and I will cut La Farge down to yams and breadfruit, with an occasional banana for a treat."

The newspapers were full of his brother Charles's forced retirement from the presidency of the Union Pacific, Baring's failure having ended his hope of a loan to refinance the floating debt of the hard-pressed line. Charles had used all his influence and had drawn on his personal funds to support Cleveland's bid for reelection, but with Cleveland's defeat in 1888 he saw that all his lobbying on behalf of the funding bill to rescue the railroad had been wasted effort. The speculators became busy, and control now passed to his old adversary Jay Gould and his "pirate band," who came baying into his office like "blood-hounds." For Charles the year ended with a shrinkage in values of half a million dollars and the triumph of the Wall Street crowd. The spectacle suggested to Henry mysterious forces blindly rushing to a fatal conjunction. Had he not foreseen it all twenty years before in "The New York Gold Conspiracy," when he had shown what mischief could be done through the manipulation of the stock of a great corporation?

Adams decided to escape from the cloying lotus ease of Tahiti, with its "purple mist and soufflé," but getting away turned out to be a major enterprise. He was determined on visiting Fiji, to "see one black island before closing the chapter," and there mount the stream of archaic life to find the source of the ritual cannibalism once practiced by his honorary ancestor, Taura-atua. Steamer schedules being infrequent and erratic, he finally had to pay a charter fee of $2,500 to induce the master of the "wretched little steamer 'Richmond'" to go out of his way.

On June 5, 1891, five months after their arrival, the two white chiefs of Amo, the "Bird Perch of God" and the "Prince of the Deep," made their affectionate farewells to their family at Papeete. The old "chiefess," Ariitaimai, delivered a little exhortation in Tahitian, and though Adams understood not a word of it, the spirit was so movingly clear that he "quite broke down" with emotion. The peaks of Tahiti slowly dropped astern as the little *Richmond* headed southwestward for Rarotonga in the Cook Islands, six hundred miles away. Once more the Pacific belied her name, and Adams suffered his customary misery. Two and a half days later they made their first landfall. The stopover at Rarotonga confirmed what was now Adams's settled opinion. The tiny islands were "so like each other, that they tell nothing." In this one, too, the natives were "missionary ridden" and regimented into clothes and churchgoing. On they sailed, steadily westward through the Tonga island group, twelve hundred more miles of rolling seas to the port of Suva, capital of the Fijis, arriving there on June 16.

Their genial host, the British governor, Sir John Thurston, presided over "a scrap of England dropped into space," in which one dressed for dinner, played lawn tennis, watched cricket, talked of home, and discussed botany and politics. The contrast with Samoa and Tahiti could not have been sharper. Sir John and Adams hit if off from the start, finding a common interest in geology, ethnology, and archaeology. At the dinner table Adams especially enjoyed the sensation of being served by smiling ex-cannibals. Their recent customs, he quipped, amounted merely to a criticism of mankind. Adams, like his host, had the anthropologist's desire that native life retain as much savagery as was "consistent with a cuisine which excludes man-steaks from the *menu*." These picturesque races could thrive only if protected from the missionaries, whose well-intentioned efforts invariably depopulated the islands by discouraging the brutal but vital traditions. Nature's paradoxes outdid Voltaire's satire: "All is for the best in our best of possible worlds. The virtuous woman flourished with the help of the club at Fiji. The excessively unvirtuous woman flourished like the breadfruit at Tahiti. Both perish in the presence of our enlightenment and religion."

The five weeks in Fiji differed enormously for Adams from the Polynesian experience. Here the natives ranged in color from "African negro" to "light Polynesian." A deep social gulf separated the whites from the multihued population, and precluded any friendly intimacy. There were neither *taupo* maidens with Circe-like blandishments, nor Teva brethren to offer kinship. Adams and La Farge traveled of course as great chiefs and ceremoniously drank from the chief's bowl at Rewa, but the color line was sharply drawn. Sir John took them on a three-week tour of the remotest mountain recesses of the island of Viti Levu, first by steamer to the head of navigation of the Rewa, then by canoe poled upstream by six natives, finally afoot, sliding up and down steep muddy trails. Adams kept a sharp lookout in the canyons for telltale layers of sedimentary conglomerate to confute Darwin and Dana and was gratified to discover shells in the soft rock at considerable elevations. Their safari of six white men, sometimes accompanied by as many as two hundred bearers, strung itself out in a long picturesque line. Often the trail had to be widened with machetes for the wildly jolting litters in which La Farge and, much less often, Adams found respite during the daily four-hour stint on the boulder-strewn trail through the rain forest. The expedition worked its bone-wearying way from the headwaters of the Rewa to Nasonggo, around Mt. Victoria, the highest peak on the island, finally debouching through the coastal range to the sea at Tavua. On July 4, while they halted on a mountain peak, Sir John ordered a salute of rifles for President Benjamin Harrison and drank his health. For Adams, however, distance lent no enchantment, and he inwardly stood on his right as a Mugwump to disdain the joke.

At the various halting places, while a village of huts quickly arose about him, he doggedly went on with his journal to Elizabeth, but all was anticlimax. "We are now far from Samoa and Tahiti, and never shall wear garlands any more, or see the flaming hibiscus in the hair of our fauns and naiads." The archaic went too much to dark skins and physical ugliness for his fastidious taste in primitives. Besides, the hilly interior chilled the travelers to the marrow; the native food was neither exotic nor palatable. "They had not even songs or traditions or legends, and no satisfactory ghosts, to take the place of good food . . . They have only two ideas, eating and women, therein being quite Parisian."

Nonetheless, the Fijians gratified his love of paradox. Though the most brutal of cannibals they were "sexually very correct and respectable, and despise the immorality of my poor Samoans . . . No man can have a ghost of a dream how fantastic this world is till he lives in the different moralities of the South Seas. Every fresh island has been to me a fresh field of innocent joy in extending my museum of moral curiosities, and in enlightening me on the subject of my fellow men."

The visit to Fiji closed the exploration of the archaic world of the South Seas. Thereafter the voyaging of the two friends, to Australia, Batavia, Singapore, Ceylon, Suez, Marseilles, took on a more conventional tourist character and gave rise to a whirling succession of impressions all reported by Adams with dazzling verve and whimsical humor. On July 31 they reached Sydney after an eight-day voyage by way of the New Hebrides. Australia was "only an unavoidable bore," merely a "second-rate United States." He sent off a mammoth dispatch to Elizabeth as soon as he disembarked and then, after devouring the mail held for him at the consulate, devoted most of the next few days to letter writing. China, it now appeared, was closed to him, as the powers were about to "break up" the empire.

Lodge's "political and social" summary he requited with appropriate generalizations on the political and economic import of his travels. "As financial investments, none of the Pacific islands, except the Sandwiches, are worth touching." To Hay's "babble of green fields in London and Paris" he responded with insouciance and a veiled glimpse of inner depths. "We have done our South Seas at last, clean cooked and eaten. The dream of hot youth has become the reality of what we will call mature and sober experience. I am almost sorry—and yet rather glad—to have accomplished the queer sensation of realising so old a vision, and one so fixed that the vision and reality still manage to live peaceably together in my head—two South Seas, not in the least alike, and both in their ways charming . . . To have escaped a year of Congress and high-thinking, by bagging a year of solid Polynesian garlands and materialism, is as sweet a joy as to run away with another man's wife."

Cities and islands began to fall behind, in steady succession. Brisbane, reached by train from Sydney, dropped below the horizon on August 8. They finished the passage of the dangerous Torres Strait by the fifteenth, anchoring every night for safety. Adams took out his impatience with the slow mode of travel in a stream of irritated annotations of Walter Savage Landor's *Pentameron and Other Conversations,* scoffing at the "washy historical commonplatitudes." Landor's style grew "as monotonous as Gibbon's," an unexpectedly harsh judgment of his "dear Gibbon."

They anchored off Bali on August 21, but the sun burned too hot for him to want to accompany La Farge ashore. By way of compensation he ate his first mangosteen and thus "accomplished half my object in going round the world." Now only the durian, praised by the naturalist Alfred Wallace, remained to be experienced. Without these, he punned, "life would have been unendurianable." At Batavia, reached on the twenty-third, La Farge was "radiant with delight" at the picturesque mixture of Dutch and Javanese life, but the sight of the transplanted Dutch burgher, beer swilling and fleshy, gave Adams a fit of the blues.

His pertinacious quest of the durian did furnish some moments of comic relief. If he ever wrote a roaring farce, he said, he would call it the Chasse au Durian in the manner of Dumas. The foul-smelling fruit with reputedly delicious meat was abominated by the Dutch. Adams tried to smuggle one into a hotel in a hill town near Batavia. The landlord, catching sight of it, "burst into a fury, and became as offensively Dutch as Limburg cheese, and far more so than the durian." Not one to surrender easily, Adams persisted in his quest, and finally the travelers got all the durian they could stomach. Adams handed down judgment, his colleague generally concurring. "I regard the durian and the alligator pear as two shameful disgraces to humanity; but the durian is a vice, while the alligator pear is a slimy subterfuge,—a meanness." The mangosteen, on the other hand, was "a poem in fruit; a white sonnet of delight, shut in a lovely case of Japanese lacquer with a purple exterior like a small pomegranate."

By September 13 the still unwearied travelers reached a major destination, the remote holy city of Anuradhapura in Ceylon, eighty miles by oxcart north of Kandy. It too was the end of a chapter, one that had opened many years before when, caught up by the popular vogue of Buddhism, Adams had added the talismanic Nirvana to his vocabulary of symbols. The enormous ruins of the holy city disappointed him, for he had come, as he said, "to see the art which is older than anything in India, and belongs to the earliest and probably purest Buddhist times." In Kandy he had visited the famous temple of the Sacred Tooth, "the last remaining watchfire of our church, except for Boston where Bill Bigelow and Fenollosa fan faint embers," and thought it fell far short of the Japanese standard and was "quite modern." In Anuradhapura all the art seemed "pretty poor and cheap . . . [and] second rate." It was a relief to catch sight of the roving jackals and monkeys, for they at least gave "a moral and emotion to the empty doorways and broken thresholds." He had sensed the religious force of the cult in Japan. Here the temples struck him as shoddy and resembling the mercenary religion of the Roman Empire rather than the Buddhism of Japan.

He dutifully performed the last aesthetic ritual of his sentimental pilgrimage by going to the sacred bo tree, "now only a sickly shoot from the original trunk," and he sat under it, as he mockingly related to Elizabeth, "for a half hour, hoping to attain Nirvana . . . I left the bo-tree without attaining Buddhaship." Yet, in spite of the sobering moral of Anuradhapura and the vulgarized art of the rock temple of Dambul, which had cost him another night's jolting oxcart journey, he did not lose his vision of the mystical reality which time had so cruelly obscured. At Kandy in the little tower library of the temple of the Sacred Tooth Adams had found a volume of Max Müller on Oriental religion. He had been greatly impressed by the Socratic unworldliness of the parables of Buddha and Brahma, though his positivist leanings forbade assent to the mystical cosmology and the untidy occultism being preached with so much success by Madame Blavatsky under the name of theosophy. Nonetheless, the afflatus was hard to resist. He felt moved to put his meditations into verse. The result was the poem "Buddha and Brahma," which fused the disenchantment of Matthew Arnold with the otherworldliness of Indian thought. In it he tried to crystallize the basic alteration in his outlook on life that had taken place beneath the flux of his eddying moods, to figure forth the meaning of his "posthumous" existence.

Diffident about any public expression of feeling, Adams delayed showing the poem, even to Elizabeth Cameron, for four years. She told Hay of it, and he promptly asked for it. Adams explained to him that after his meditation beneath the sacred bo tree he and La Farge "found ourselves on the quiet bosom of the Indian Ocean. Perhaps I was a little bored by the calm of the tropical sea, or perhaps it was the greater calm of Buddha that bored me. At any rate I amused a tedious day or two by jotting down in a notebook the lines which you profess to want. They are yours. Do not let them go further."

In the contest between Buddha and Brahma Adams found a fresh touchstone for the questions he had debated in *Esther,* the meaning of the concept that thought is eternal. Why might not a bridge be built between the physical and the metaphysical? The end of the human quest would be to "catch an abstract truth by the tail," for thus, by attaining possession of the absolute, the eternal truth, the mind would itself become eternal. What had caught Adams's curiosity was the fact that the metaphysical question was almost the only one that Buddha had declined to answer explicitly, the question of the ultimate reality of matter and mind. In the jungle of the world, of selfishness and striving, the perfect life is unattainable. There the obligation is to submit to the tyranny of the world of appearances. But behind the veil of appearances there is possible the life of thought, the activity of the uncorrupted soul, in contemplating the world of abstract truth where, as the poem asserts:

> Life, Time, Space, Thought, the world, the Universe
> End where they first begin, in one sole Thought
> Of Purity in Silence.

For the disciple who has renounced the world to follow Buddha there is no need for knowledge of final things, since the acts of holiness end in Brahma, the world-soul where being and knowledge become one. It was a tenuous transcendentalism such as Emerson had epitomized in his poem "Brahma," in which the Oversoul enfolds the red slayer and the slain, "the doubter and the doubt," in a higher synthesis of opposites.

Adams enjoyed the intellectual play of the poem, with its sally into the infinite; but his wish to make that leap showed the troubling chasm in his nature between analytic reason and feeling. The world jungle is in effect the world of will and appearances. The true world is the world of "pure contemplation," as Schopenhauer said, "freed from ourselves." Though he might wish to escape, he could not fly the jungle of world or self.

Nirvana, as Max Müller taught him, signified "rest, quietness, absence of passion." This was the idea that Adams had hoped Saint-Gaudens would infuse into the memorial, the silent contemplation of absolute existence in which being and nonbeing become indistinguishable. Thus the statue and the poem would complement each other. Behind the veil of the world, the highest wisdom must be the wisdom of silence, the silence of perfected knowledge and being. Philosophy could carry him no further on this side of his "posthumous" thought; thought perfected itself in the release from thought. In that arc the pendulum of his despairing vision reached the end of its swing. As the ship steamed steadily across the Indian Ocean, through the Red Sea and into the Mediterranean, the counterswing had already begun.

THE TWO TRAVELERS left Ceylon on September 17, with a few more straws added to Adams's burden of misanthropy by the callous indifference of the ship's officers to the wants of the passengers in the stifling heat. Twelve days later, after a passage marred only by the fact that they had to rub elbows with "some Dutch swine" and "Portugese *pecora*," they put ashore briefly at Aden, where the sun hit them "like a baseball." The small steamer moved placidly in ninety-one-degree heat through the Red Sea. On October 8, after an uneventful run from Alexandria, Adams found himself at last brought up short by the thought that on the morrow he would land at Marseilles and have to face the realities of his situation. His whole world seemed to be lying in ambush for him, after having been held at bay for more than a year. He felt an unreasoning and morbid panic, tinged with self-contempt. In almost the last entry of his travel diary to Elizabeth Cameron he felt obliged to say "that all the old perplexities, with plenty of new ones, are going to revive." Most disturbing of all would be his meeting with her. She was then in England with her daughter Martha and stepdaughter Rachel. Her husband, the senator, evidently preoccupied with reelection, sent his wife abroad so that she would not have to endure another season of Pennsylvania boss politics. Though Elizabeth had bravely dismissed her scholarly courtier more than a year ago, she had called him back again when the magic of his letters exerted itself. He had brilliantly played Petrarch to her Laura when there stood between them the distances of the South Seas. But now the clock of their world began inexorably to tick again.

At Marseilles her letters from London were waiting for Adams. How silly he had been, she said, to dream that she would sail without seeing him. Late as he was, they would still have at least a month together in Paris. She had been thinking with a touch of uneasiness of one of his love sonnets and its endearing phrases. "I like to have that and other things just between you and me alone . . . The kiss must be poetic license." She hurried to Paris on October 2 with Martha and Rachel to await his arrival. "Fourteen months!" she exclaimed. "It is almost a life." Having been delayed at Suez, Adams did not reach Paris until the tenth.

The reunion turned out to be an unnerving experience. Adams made the inevitable discovery that Platonic love embraces a contradiction. His love for Elizabeth was stronger than ever and his dependence greater. She was obviously both flattered and somewhat alarmed by the romantic intensity that burned beneath his correct attentions. Now thirty-four to his fifty-three, she wore her radiant beauty with a certain authority in international society, eliciting the comment of one peeress that she was "a very dangerously fascinating woman." Nothing seemed to go right for the lovers. She had counted the days to their meeting, fearful that with so much to say she might not "be able to say anything." They hardly had a moment alone together. For Adams the scant two weeks in Paris with her was of a piece with the rest of his visit, "fragmentary, interrupted and unsatisfactory." With Hay he was noncommittal. "I had La Farge, Mrs Cameron, Miss Cameron, and the engrossing Martha to beguile my ennui at intervals. I haunted the theatres, operas and concerts."

La Farge went off to visit cousins in Brittany, sallying out to the cathedrals to study the stained glass. Then the good companion of so many adventures departed with his portfolios of South Sea paintings. Presently Elizabeth Cameron followed. Everyone was gone, said Adams, and he was "the gonest of the lot." Elizabeth's letter from shipboard prudently said little. "Goodbye. Thank you a thousand times for everything. Write me what you do—*all* that you do." It was not much, a mere straw to grasp, but he made the most of it.

Desolate in spirit, Adams took refuge with Gaskell at Wenlock Abbey, in Shropshire, where his gaze could rest again on the ivy-covered ruins beyond his windows in the old Norman wing. He brooded over the impasse which he had reached, and he poured out his feelings to the abashed cause of them in a despairing confessional that concealed the hope against hope: "A long, lowering, melancholy November day, the clouds hanging low on Wenlock Edge, and stretching off to the westward where you are streaming along the Irish coast and out to sea . . . I have passed a bad *quart d'heure* since bidding you good-bye in your Hansom cab across the darkness of Half Moon street . . . You saw and said that my Paris experiment was not so successful as you had meant it to be. Perhaps I should have done better not to have tried it, for the result of my six months desperate chase to obey your bidding has not been wholly happy . . . As a collegian I used to read Aurora Leigh and Lady Geraldine's Courtship and the Swan's Nest on the River, and two lines have stuck: 'Know you what it is when Anguish, with apocalyptic *Never* / To a Pythian height dilates you, and Despair sublimes to Power?' "

Adams applied the fable with sad irony. "The verse is charmingly preposterous and feminine, for a woman never recognizes an impossibility; but an elderly man, when hit over the head by an apocalyptic *Never,* does not sublime to Power . . . and for a time does not even squirm; then he tumbles about for a while, seeing the Apocalypse all round him; then he bolts and runs like a mad dog, anywhere,—to Samoa, to Tahiti, to Fiji; then he dashes straight round the world, hoping to get to Paris ahead of the Apocalypse; but hardly has he walked down the Rue Bassano when he sees the apocalyptic *Never* written up like a hotel sign at No. 12; and when he, at last leaves London, and his cab crosses the end of Cork St, his last glimpse of No. 5A shows the Apocalyptic *Never* over the front door . . . As I am much the older and presumably the one of us two who is responsible for whatever mischief can happen, I feel as though I had led you into the mistake of bringing me here, and am about to lead you into the worse mistake of bringing me home. Not that I take a French view of the matter, or imagine you to be in the least peril of falling into the conventional dilemmas of the French heroines; but because, no matter how much I may efface myself or how little I may ask, I must always make more demand on you than you can gratify, and you must always have the consciousness that, whatever I may profess, I want more than I can have. Sooner or later the end of such a situation

is estrangement, with more or less disappointment and bitterness."
The reasoning could hardly be gainsaid. The facts were obvious: "I
am not old enough to be a tame cat," he said; "you are too old to
accept me in any other character. You were right last year in sending
me away." Unfortunately, neither logic nor good sense could save
him. "As I have learned to follow fate with docility surprising to myself, I shall come back gaily, with a heart as sick as ever a man had
who knew that he should lose the only object he loved because he
loved too much."

As he hung anxiously over his feelings, engrossed by every fibrilla-
tion, he had the satisfaction at least of finding the granite datum of
his existence. His "long, tearing, wild jaunt," he told her, had finished
at Wenlock Abbey "in a sense of ended worlds and burnt-out coal-
and-iron universes." Musing again among the broken walls and silent
arches of the ruined abbey, his thoughts went back to an age of faith
tragically lost to him. Now he had infinitely more need for the lost
refuge. "Progress has much to answer for in depriving weary and
broken men and women of their natural end and happiness; but even
now I can fancy myself contented in the cloister, and happy in the
daily round of duties, if only I still knew a God to pray to, or better
yet, a Goddess; for as I grow older I see that all the human interest
and power that religion ever had, was in the mother and child ...
There you are again! you see how the thought always turns back
to you."

To the last moment Adams doubted the wisdom of sending the long
screed; but it could not be withheld, for it would have to serve as the
basis of their future relations. Never in the many hundreds of letters
and notes that were to pass between them during the next twenty-
seven years, until his death in 1918, was he again to bare his feelings
toward her and Martha in such unguarded fashion. But this time, as
he said, with a trace of superstitious feeling: "Kismet! Let fate have
its way."

Like Petrarch at Vaucluse he too had found his Madonna, and in
his symbol-haunted mind, she had fulfilled, as his own marriage had
tragically failed to fulfill, his vision of the highest role of woman in
the world, maternity. His imagination had thus evoked two compelling symbols to mark the limits of his life behind the veil. His buried
life had its sacred bronze witness in Rock Creek cemetery, anchoring
his thought to Nirvana, to the ideal of the self-denying intellect, of

the mind purged of passion. His worship of Elizabeth and the child Martha gave him his other anchor to the infinite, in the life-accepting symbol of the compassionate Madonna.

For a little while yet Adams vibrated to the effects of the crisis through which he had just come, going back again and again in his letters to the worn ground of debate. Abjectly, he conceded that she had played her part with proper circumspection, whereas his position was "all wrong and impossible." She was Beauty and he was the Beast. He was doomed to be a nuisance to both of them, like Hamlet or the ridiculous Prince Bulbo in Thackeray's fairy tale.

His state as a cross-gartered Malvolio was all too apparent to his Scottish host at Tillypronie, Sir John Clark, who quaintly recommended he "find a *Frou-frou* . . . a companion" whom he might marry. "The old-old wish, so familiar to me from my women friends," he commented to Elizabeth. He had been tempted, he said, to say in his own defense "that in forty years of search, I have never met but one woman who met me all round so as to be a real companion," but held his tongue. "How I pity at times that imaginary lady, my possible wife!" he exclaimed. "How quickly and comfortably I would suck the blood out of her . . . [an] innocent victim to my *ennui*." His friends seemed in league to sacrifice "some new Iphigenia to secure my safe return home."

To his dismay, his Madonna added her voice to the others: "And it is I who say it to you," and she reproached him for his low opinion of eligible women. "Women are not so cheap and worthless as you think them and fine noble characters do exist who could overcome that other self about which you used to talk . . . Perhaps I can talk of your marriage at this distance when I shouldn't look at it so comfortably from a nearer view. I am as selfish as the rest of my sex." Then with charming irrelevance she added that she had heard that his brother Brooks "affectionately calls his wife, 'idiot from hell.' "

Tame cat or not, he would have to run for haven to the house on Lafayette Square and somehow sheathe his nervous claws. The thought of beginning "merrily the old dance" filled him with foreboding. Elizabeth Cameron had not made his decision any easier by telling him that "everyone is furious at you for not coming back, and you quite deserve it." He was sure his friends were wrong in urging him home. Low in spirit, he could think only of hiding, of running off to Paris again. But first he foresightedly booked passage for home,

telling only Mrs. Cameron and repeatedly imploring her to say nothing of his intentions, as for "private and personal reasons" he did not
wish to stir up his "people in Boston." "I do not make secrets; I have
none; as far as I know, my life has never had a secret of any consequence, not even a love-affair or a political bargain for office; but I
am dead to the world;—dead as Adam and Eve, only just not yet
buried; and I have been hoping, and still try to hope I may come to
life again . . . Respect my phantasmodesty, I implore, and let me slink
back to my place like a ghost, to find out in silence and peace whether
I am still a little bit alive."

HENRY ADAMS IN BERLIN, 1859

ABIGAIL BROOKS ADAMS

CHARLES FRANCIS ADAMS

CHARLES FRANCIS
ADAMS, JR.

CHARLES MILNES GASKELL

MARIAN HOOPER, 1869

HENRY ADAMS, 1875

HENRY ADAMS AT 1607 H STREET

THE ADAMS HOUSE AT 1603 H STREET

CLARENCE KING, EARLY 1880S

JOHN HAY IN HENRY ADAMS' STUDY, 1883

BROOKS ADAMS

JOHN LA FARGE IN HENRY ADAMS' STUDY

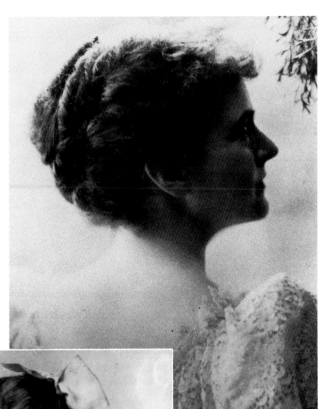

ELIZABETH
CAMERON

MARTHA CAMERON

ELIZABETH CAMERON, 1899

HENRY ADAMS, 1914

THE ADAMS MEMORIAL BY AUGUSTUS SAINT-GAUDENS

18

Journey into Chaos

IN A STATE of luxurious despair, Adams returned to Paris in December 1891 for a three-week reconnaissance to pick up "the lost pieces of broken crockery scattered over twenty neglected years of French manufacture." Paris had everything to gratify a determined pessimist. The *fin de siècle* had brought to a toxic flowering the motifs of an earlier generation and produced a nihilistic rebellion against received values and dying institutions. It defiantly flaunted the heresies of art for art's sake and cultivated the flowers of evil of Baudelaire.

Adams took for his mentor Jules Lemaître, whose series on contemporary writers already filled four volumes. Surrounded by piles of yellow paperbacks, he felt it a poor day's work when he didn't finish at least one volume, skimming a volume of the Goncourts or swallowing Maupassant with his roast. The six-volume edition of the Goncourts' *Journal* he put aside for the ocean voyage, but he searched their *Manette Salomon* for the key to French cynicism in the proper mockeries of *La blague,* the evil jesting of children, as it was said, "decayed by the old age of civilization." Maupassant's short stories engrossed him more than any other writer's. Taken together, these writers, he said, had "at least the merit of explaining to me why I dislike the French, and why the French are proper subjects for dislike."

The stage confirmed the impressions of putrescence which he got from the fiction. The indecency seemed no worse "than in old times," but somehow it was less amusing. He found the realistic portrayals of sexual violence and immorality "revolting and horrible." The fascinating Réjane, more mature and accomplished than ever, delighted him, but the comedy in which she starred, *Amoureuse,* made him "sick" and sorry that he went. "Always marriage!" he fumed. "I am deadly weary of the whole menagerie." The plays, he said, professed to show how much better virtue and marriage were than vice and adultery, but he "was quite unconvinced by the demonstration." Ibsen's *Hedda Gabler,* which was then scandalizing Paris as *A Doll's House* was London, did not raise his opinion of the stage. "Talk about our American nerves!" he exclaimed, "they are normal and healthy compared with the nerves of the French, which are more diseased than anything on earth except the simple Norwegian blondes of Mr Ibsen."

The universal clamor of world-weariness irritated him. It was superficial, commercialized, a vulgar parody of his own disgusts. All this self-pitying pessimism, he complained, began with Alfred de Musset, whose libertines like Rolla had been disenchanted by pleasure. "I am going through a regular study of the whole," he exclaimed to Elizabeth, "and feel as though the drollest experience of modern history were that all these people should—like Victor Hugo, Lamartine and Leconte de l'Isle—take themselves au serieux."

Adams wished that he and John Hay could flay the world with alternate *feuilletons* in a newspaper of their own. Better still, they might enlarge an old satirical scheme of theirs and write "a volume or two of Travels which will permit me to express my opinion of life in general." It would be "a sort of ragbag of everything; scenery, psychology, history, literature, poetry, art; anything in short, that is worth throwing in; and I want to grill a few literary and political gentlemen to serve with champagne." The lurid flash of the allusion showed like an afterimage of the six paper bags of Carlyle's Herr Teufelsdröckh, which were stuffed with the chaotic autobiography of the "pilgrim of eternity," the wandering Jew who had cast off the clothes of a dead philosophy. It was a beam of light shot forward to the *Education.* Were not "all us Puritan New Englanders," as he said, "children of the Wandering Jew"?

Held captive in Paris by his dentist, Adams exploded into measureless abuse of the town where, in his exile, he was finding that the very sound of his own voice startled him. "Oh! Lucifer son of the Morning!! If I could only express the extravagance of my intensity of hatred for this good city of Paris." He begged off dining with Hay's friend and former employer Whitelaw Reid, the American ambassador, but finally enjoyed a breakfast with him, finding him "greatly improved" now that he had "arrived." An encounter with the young Edith Wharton signaled the beginning of another enduring friendship. She looked as "fragile as a dandelion in seed," he thought; "an American product almost as sad to me as M Puvis de Chavannes," but surprisingly knowledgeable of "the literary and artistic side" of Paris.

He walked the familiar length of the rue de la Paix and along the boulevards. They were a sounding cavern to his memory. A Proustian eddy of associations lurked everywhere. The long moments of introspection, arching back and forth from past to present, made him a philosopher of time and duration as if he were already a disciple of Bergson, whose *Time and Free Will* was the talk of the Paris literati. When a sentimental "act of piety" took him to the Opéra Comique to hear André Grétry's *Richard Coeur de Lion,* he surrendered himself to reverie. His grandfather John Quincy Adams had first heard the opera when he was a young diplomat at The Hague, a hundred years before. The grandson now recalled that after he had been "turned out of the Presidency he could think of nothing for days together but a line from the play, 'Oh, Richard! oh, mon roy, l'univers t'abandonne.'" The music and words had once been *fin de siècle* to the young John Quincy, heralding the French Revolution which followed. "I tried to imagine myself as I was then," Henry Adams beguiled Elizabeth, "and you know what an awfully handsome young fellow Copley made me—with full dress and powdered hair, talking to Mme Chose in the boxes." Each experience was a remembrance of things past. He had often played Faust in imagination; now, full of anticipation, he went to hear a part of Berlioz's *The Damnation of Faust.* He felt "a little disappointed" with his diminished appreciation, for the past, as he said, had placed him on his knees before the artist.

The sense of haunting unreality pursued him across the Channel when he returned for a few weeks to England. He made another "effort of piety" and called on aged friends surviving from his earlier days in London, the economist Thomson Hankey and the artist Thomas Woolner. He felt as if he were "coming to life again in a dead world," in a kind of mesmeric state that he could not shake off. Gripped by this hallucination of a double life, he declared that "even Harry James, with whom I lunch Sundays, is only a figure in the same old wall-paper, and really pretends to belong to a world which is extinct as Queen Elizabeth."

During the weeks in London and Paris the habit of scholarship had reasserted itself, and he directed "searches in various archives to fill gaps in my collection of papers," for, as he told Theodore Dwight, "I have thought it wise to go back a few years before 1800, to make sure that I have everything which can throw light on my period." Anticipating the need of a corrected edition of the *History,* he was determined to make good his boast that no scholar would find gleanings after him.

The reviews of the *History* which awaited him left him dissatisfied; none seemed to meet the challenge of the whole work nor seriously to test its accuracy. In Samoa he had shrugged off the strictures of the long letter signed "Housatonic" which appeared in the *New York Tribune* under the title "A Case of Hereditary Bias." Shortly afterwards, when the article was reprinted as a pamphlet, Theodore Roosevelt sent Adams a copy with the inscription, "kindly, but firmly presented." The anonymous writer (afterwards identified as William Henry Smith, a well-known midwestern historian) protested the "glaring perversion of facts," especially the deprecation of the Federalists. He saw the *History* primarily as a family document and rancorously charged that it "thinly veiled the prejudices and hatreds of the elder Adams and his son."

On Adams's return to London in January the weather gave frigid impetus to a wave of hostile generalizations about the Continent. The steamer was icy cold, the footwarmer in the Dover train freezing. "I can understand that their art should be bad and their literature rotten and their tastes mean," he growled to Hay, "but why the deuce they should inflict on themselves cold and hunger and discomfort, hang me if I can understand. Actually, in Europe I see no progress—none!" They had the electric light and that was all.

London still exerted much of its old charm. England rested and amused him, for he felt at home among "the preposterous British social conventions; church and state, Prince of Wales, Mr Gladstone, the Royal Academy and Mr Ruskin, the London fog and St James's Street." He accepted them like the sun and moon, he said, because they let him alone. Unlike Paris and the French, they did not fret him with "howling for applause because they are original." One change in the London scene rather startled him, however: the unaccustomed elegance of the upper-class prostitutes. "The old simplicity of vice had given place to the strangest apeing of high society." After the stridencies of Paris he liked the quaint understatement of British life, but the brilliant society he had known a decade before seemed oddly diminished, enfeebled, autumnal. Influenza raged as if to match his mood. He had an almost superstitious feeling that pestilence accompanied him wherever he went. There had been cholera in Japan, fever in Tahiti, cholera at Batavia. Native kings had succumbed.

His social activity contrasted painfully with the festive air of his previous visits. Then "the days were hardly long enough to meet the engagements." Now he turned gratefully to the companionship of young Larz Anderson, a private secretary at the embassy as Adams once had been and son of his Washington intimate Nicholas Anderson. Rooming at the same address, 38 Clarges Street, the two spent much time together. Young Anderson found him "just as anxious 'to go' and have a good time as any young man, and infinitely more interesting." They got up a Thanksgiving Day feast, and Adams, beaming cheerfully after four patriotic helpings of turkey, reminisced of a similar feast thirty-three years before at Magdeburg when Larz's father, Adams, and three other Harvard classmates had celebrated a Thanksgiving Day rendezvous.

For politics he went to Birmingham to see Joseph Chamberlain, the leader of the radical wing of the Liberal party. Chamberlain, like Cobden and Bright of Adams's youth, attracted him as the representative of the most progressive political thought of England. Their interests met at a number of points. In 1887 when Chamberlain had come to Washington to settle the Canadian fisheries dispute, one of the matters on which John Quincy Adams had staked his diplomacy in 1814, he had sought out Henry Adams as an expert in Anglo-American diplomatic relations. Chamberlain had married the extremely pretty Mary Endicott, daughter of Cleveland's Secretary of War. Returning the visit, therefore, had all the pleasures of a reunion.

Although *fin-de-siècle* pessimism was the vogue also in London, and his old friends despaired of art and life, he felt none of the rages that had swept him in Paris. He was undisturbed by the "wild women" of society, the "social insurgents" whose libertine and provocative manners alarmed the press. The English version of the disease of the age seemed somehow more tolerable and easier to ignore. Gissing's somber realism matched the harsh fatalism of his contemporary Maupassant, but without the disturbing sexual aura. Although Adams appears to have met Thomas Hardy at this time, he made no allusion to the current outcry over *Tess of the D'Urbervilles*, which had scandalized respectable England and inspired clergymen to burn the volume. No doubt he agreed with his friend Gaskell that Hardy had "sexual intercourse on the brain."

THE RMS *Teutonic* bore Adams "wobbling" out to sea on February 3, 1892. He was dismayed to notice the social decline in first class. His two hundred fellow passengers seemed somehow all to be Jews. The ship, however, showed the first indubitable sign of mechanical progress. After thirty years science had fulfilled the exciting promise he had envisaged as a young man in London. The power, speed, size, and comfort gave him a pleasurable sensation of change. "The big Atlantic steamer is a whacker," he confessed. Thanks to an introduction from Henry James, he had the companionship of Rudyard Kipling and Kipling's new American wife for the voyage. He conceded Kipling's "undeniable vulgarity," but he respected his artistry, and the two men struck up a friendly acquaintanceship. During the voyage Adams read Walter Pater's *Marius the Epicurean*, a book whose style and disenchanted temper peculiarly chimed with his own. Its grave hero, steeping himself in the philosophy of the age of the Antonines, ended his spiritual quest on the threshold of the Christian church. As an evocative record of the struggle of a poetic sensibility to come to terms with its time, the book fell upon fertile ground.

Adams was still a public figure and his return to Washington was duly noted by an inventive gossip columnist of the *Albany Argus*. Under the caption "The Last of the Adams" he was described as "one of our most productive authors . . . the successor among historians of Bancroft . . . He has written a dozen histories, besides the history of Jefferson and Madison's administrations in nine volumes. Adams is a man of independent fortune and an extensive traveler . . . He organized a fleet of his own at Tahiti consisting of twenty or thirty boats manned by natives." Adams sent on the piece of journalistic "hogwash" to Hay with a wry chuckle: "My dozen histories besides the nine volumes, please my ear, besides my Tahiti fleet."

Shortly after landing, and while painters refurbished his house, Adams with John Hay joined the Camerons at their place at St. Helena Island, off the South Carolina coast. There they dug clams and lolled about for a fortnight. The spring and summer passed almost without incident, except for a sprained ankle got falling from a horse.

He fairly settled down to his role as "tame cat." After the emotional outburst of the preceding fall he became almost exasperatingly correct. He urged Elizabeth to spend the summer again at Beverly Farms to exorcise the "nightmare" of the empty house; no one belonged there who was not a part of the old life. He reminded her also that she must not forget her part of their "contract of keeping [him] out of mischief." Mostly, he spent his large leisure "studying French Revolution," whose centenary had produced a spate of books and revived the great debate in the magazines between the friends and enemies of the revolution. The course of reading formed the first stage of his renewed exploration of the past.

Palace politics whirled about Adams's head at the noonday breakfasts, at which the nieces-in-residence usually matronized, the "Board of Works" in domestic matters including Mrs. Cameron, Mrs. Rae, Mrs. Lodge, and Mrs. Hay. Cleveland carried the election of 1892, leaving Adams wondering, as he wrote Hay, what had become "of all that McKinley money that ought to have been on hand" from grateful "Republican manufacturers" to reelect Harrison. It was evident that "after pocketing the swag, [they] refused to disgorge."

Adams's first duty when he got back to Washington in mid-February had been to go out to Rock Creek cemetery to pass judgment on Saint-Gaudens's handiwork. The photographs had not done justice to the massive bronze figure, heavily enrobed like a seated nun, the face within the deep recess of the cowl lost as in a cave of thought. The classic perfection of features, the straight line of the nose, the firm descending curve of the cheek exhibited all the ideality of the Pre-Raphaelite. No identifying inscription of any sort compromised the universality of the symbol. Whatever second thought came to him he put aside before the severe authority of the figure. If not the greatness of his ideal, it had unquestionably the greatness of Saint-Gaudens's artistry.

He gave his formal approval early in March, bringing with him, as a kind of committee, his brother-in-law Edward Hooper and William Sturgis Bigelow. Thereafter the spot became the most familiar to him in Washington, his favorite retreat where he was often to be found. In his imagined posthumous existence he mockingly came to call the place his home. The statue became a touchstone of aesthetic and philosophical insight, his private challenge to a money-grubbing world. He refused to affix a label to it, insisting that it should pose its enigmas directly to every beholder. Eventually his elaborate precautions for privacy and anonymity backfired. People soon began to pass through in small crowds, and he ruefully fretted that he never got more than ten minutes' peace, seated on the stone exedra, from the sharp-nosed schoolteachers who came to inspect the statue. In after years he would sometimes linger in the shadows of the circumjacent shrubbery for the ironical amusement of hearing the comments of baffled tourists. There was a certain amount of clacking of tongues over the cost of the memorial, but the general admiration of it was epitomized by one of Galsworthy's characters, who thought it "the best thing he had come across in America."

Not averse to a little mystification, Adams himself helped to throw about the figure veil after veil of significance, making it the mirror for his changing moods. In a musing letter to Saint-Gaudens he declared that sometimes he saw or thought he saw a defiant expression about the lower part of the face, an expression that neither he nor the sculptor had intended. It seemed to be saying "Futile Infinite!" Whether this was real or only his fancy remained an enigma to him. Although Saint-Gaudens had to bear the brunt of most of the inquiries, Adams's distinguished friends, as puzzled as the hapless tourist, often turned directly to him. To Richard Watson Gilder he patiently explained: "The whole meaning and feeling of the figure is in its universality and anonymity. My own name for it is 'the Peace of God.' La Farge would call it 'Kwannon.' Petrarch would say 'Siccome eterna vita e veder Dio [as sight of God is the eternal life],' and a real artist would be very careful to give it no name that the public could turn into a limitation of its character." He had handed it over to Saint-Gaudens with "the understanding that there shall be no . . . attempt at making it intelligible to the average mind and no hint at ownership."

Theodore Roosevelt was another one of the baffled ones. At a dinner at the White House near the end of his administration he incautiously referred to the figure as that of a woman. The next day Adams set him straight. "If you were talking last night as President, I have nothing to say . . . But!!! After March 4, should you allude to my bronze figure, will you try to do St Gaudens the justice to remark that his expression was a little higher than sex can give. As he meant it, he wanted to exclude sex and sink it in the idea of humanity. The figure is sexless." Roosevelt protested that "there has been some question in the minds of people whether the figure was of a woman or was nonhuman." He had assumed it was female without attaching any importance to it as such. Then, with a certain firmness, he adjoined, "I think that the acceptance of sex often obviates the danger of over-insistence of it."

IN 1892 Henry's brother Charles, eager to have Henry's achievement as a historian properly recognized by Harvard, set the machinery in motion through Edward Hooper to have an honorary degree awarded. The proposal won prompt approval. President Eliot duly tendered an invitation, subject only to the customary requirement that Adams appear in person to receive the degree. To President Eliot's amazement he declined the honor. "You know that for ten years past I have not appeared in the world, even so much as in a drawing room," he reminded him with characteristic exaggeration; "and the idea of facing a crowd of friends and acquaintances in order to receive a distinction troubles me more than you, who are used to such things, will readily believe."

He was not content merely to retreat but went on to lecture Eliot—and Harvard—on the error of the proposal. "No work of mine warrants it in itself; and still less when compared with other contemporary work." Harvard should long ago have honored Nicolay and Hay for their *Life of Lincoln,* not only because it was a great work, but because it offered "the chance for once to escape from the circle of University limitations, and to take a lead in guiding popular impressions." He concluded his examination of conscience by stating that "with Hay and Nicolay beside me I could stand up before public criticism, but alone I cannot." Eliot patiently countered, "You are not conferring this degree on yourself—it is the act of the University. To decline it would require a thousand explanations—to accept it is natural and modest." But Adams remorselessly stickled for principle and for his right to depreciate his own work. Eliot had no choice but to accept his disingenuous plea that a sprained ankle would anyway make it impossible for him "to bear the inevitable fatigue of such an occasion."

The rebuff to Eliot did not sit well with Charles, and it helped widen a little the unacknowledged breach between the two brothers. Bitterly Charles noted in his diary that Henry was "showing with almost insulting aggressiveness that he had quite outgrown his own poor mundane family and that the etherealized intercourse of the Hoopers, La Farge, and Mrs. Cameron alone satisfied his lofty soul."

Almost immediately afterwards Adams impulsively agreed to accept in absentia an honorary doctor of laws degree from Western Reserve University, whose president was Charles F. Thwing, a former student. Hay, who had taken over his father-in-law's responsibilities as a trustee and principal benefactor of the new university, had proposed Adams's name, and Thwing, eager to honor his former teacher, had gladly acquiesced. In his letter of acceptance Adams repeated what he had often said before about "the idiocies of university education." Hay, having been shown Adams's quixotic letter to Thwing, reported back, "Thwing goes pondering through the town, wondering if you *really* think education is on the whole worse than infanticide. I told him it was, but doubted if you really thought so; because being a Mugwump you naturally took the wrong side of everything."

Two years later Adams's prickly modesty was to be tried again when President Seth Low of Columbia University informed him that his *History* had been awarded the Loubat Prize of $1,000 and asked him to allow that fact to appear thereafter on the title page of the work. Adams stubbornly protested that he was "no longer a candidate for honors or even a man of letters," and, what was more important, he could not accept a designation for his title page that it did not deserve. He suggested that Nicolay and Hay's *Lincoln* or Alfred Mahan's *Naval Warfare* better deserved the honor. He quieted his scruples by returning the $1,000 as a gift to the university for the purchase of books on American history and kept his title page unadorned.

For want of more serious occupation Adams began his tourist role in earnest during the summer of 1892, initiating a practice that was to become a main avocation, shepherding pretty nieces about Europe; or dashing off to Cuba, Mexico, or the Yellowstone with King or Hay or any tolerable substitute for them. His brother-in-law Edward Hooper and the five Hooper girls—now ranging in age from thirteen to twenty—made up the party for the first of such expeditions, a three months' jaunt to Scotland. Ever since the tragic death of their aunt Clover, Adams had felt a special responsibility to the girls. Landing at Liverpool on July 13, they settled down at Aboyne, ten miles from hospitable Sir John Clark at Tillypronie, and not far distant from Balmoral Castle, a summer residence of Queen Victoria. The familiar bustle of fashionable acquaintances enlivened his journal-letters home, interlarded with running comments on the muddled state of English politics.

The explosive Irish Question found most of his friends arrayed against Gladstone and Irish home rule. A Liberal Unionist, Sir Robert Cunliffe lost at Flintshire; Gaskell did not even chance the election. However, such notable Liberal acquaintances as Sir George Trevelyan, James Bryce, and their leader, Joseph Chamberlain, were successful. Surmising the "hardest kind of political impossibility" before them, Adams had "no particular wish to hear their patter" on this visit, though his sympathies were with them. To Adams the "political riot" was a spectacle in which the chief interest was what happened to one's "high-minded Liberal" friends who sought to wield power. More to his devil-may-care taste, for the moment, was playing baseball with his nieces or exploring historic castles in the Highlands. In the midst of the universal dullness, however, one controversial topic caught his ear—bimetallism, the question whether international trade could continue to be carried on with settlements in either gold or silver. His English acquaintance Moreton Frewen was preaching silver as a panacea. The idea took silent root in his mind, to grow within a year to distracting proportions.

History faintly stirred as he loitered in the hills still reading "French Revolution," and he now bestirred himself about the French transcripts. Henry Vignaud reported progress, and the bills began to come in for copying diplomatic documents at four francs per thousand words. At the same time the Far East still called to him, though he sought fruitlessly for a travel companion. Knowing that the current anxiety of the highest diplomatic circles was the bearing of India on the shifting balance of European power, he went directly to Sir Alfred Lyall, the highest authority on India. The rival designs of Germany and Russia for Asiatic expansion were already common knowledge. He came away feeling that "he and Rudyard Kipling and I are all three, in different ways, befooled by India." He saw little chance of swallowing "the great Asian mystery with any hope of really enjoying it." His last word as he sailed westward on the *Majestic* from Queenstown was one of continued frustration. "Hang me if I know where else to go, for get to Asia I must."

Life in Lafayette Square flowed on in its accustomed pattern, and a kind of lull descended upon its residents. John Hay, inwardly out-of-

sorts at the want of public employment, talked of his "languid vegetable life" and matched ennui for ennui with Adams in a Washington
that, but for Adams, was "the dry-suckedest orange you ever saw."
The irrepressible Theodore Roosevelt, then established in Washington
as a civil service commissioner, frequently dined at the twin Richardson residences opposite Lafayette Square, good-humoredly biding his
time while his sardonic hosts, Hay and Adams, twitted him for his
youthful optimism. Young diplomats, aspiring to be honorary nephews, made their way to the celebrated noon breakfasts where, as
Lloyd Griscom wrote, "Uncle Henry presided and discoursed in his
dry ironical manner on everything under the sun, from the daily
movement of gold to the evolution of furniture at the French court."
The real focus of Uncle Henry's social existence was the salon over
which Mrs. Cameron reigned. There he would make an almost daily
appearance of an afternoon, "a small man with a small gray beard
and an intellectual face . . . He would sit down, glance around sardonically, and in a tired manner begin to hold forth."

Fresh employment came to him shortly after his return from Scotland in October 1892. Tati Salmon, his Tahitian "relative," had come
to the United States filled with projects for selling Tahitian coffee and
mother-of-pearl, and Adams devoted a month to taking him about to
his clubs in New York and Washington and arranging business con-
tacts. Marau had kept up her researches for their joint project of the
Teva memoir, sending results by Jacob Doty, the American consul.
With Tati now present to aid him, the interpretation of the complex
genealogies could go much more quickly. Adams incorporated the
new materials and returned the revised manuscript with fresh queries
to Marau Taaroa. "You would laugh," wrote Tati after he got back
to Papeete, "the means she uses to get [Varii] to the old house, and
once there he has to write what Marau dictates, not daring to put in
a word of his own." Marau always carried her point by saying that
"Taura [Adams] could put it in better words for her."

Adams wrote to Marau that he was determined "to make a lively
story of it, so that our ancestors will be amusing, the more, the better
. . . We want the whole local color. Tahitian society today is frightfully proper, but in old days it was almost as improper as Europe, and
very much more frank about it. The memoirs must be *risqués* to be
amusing; so make Tati, I supplicate, translate all the legends for me
literally, so that I can select what suits our time." There followed

many queries on the minutiae of Tahitian history as detailed as the following: "My chief want now is the Pomare pedigree. Of course I have some of it, but every now and then I am puzzled. For instance, why did Tutaha of Haapape care to make young Otoo wear the Maro-ura and upset Teriirere? Tutaha's sister Tetuaraenui married Purea's brother Auri, which might give Tutaha an interest in Purea; but what interest had he in Otoo?" The arrival of the questions generally excited a spirited family conclave.

The writing went by leisurely fits and starts, for the mails took three to four weeks in each direction. Besides, the desire to travel harried Adams intermittently like a benign fever. Late in February 1893 he hurried off to Havana with "Loonatic" Phillips, who was always game for an Adamsian lark. The carefree pair roamed the markets, drank fresh coconut milk, experimented with "squashy fruits," dined at "angelic" restaurants, and "smoked frightfully the most delightful cigars after seeing them made in a manner that would disgust a pig." Even the prevailing litter seemed picturesque: "The dirt is quite glorious—more of it than ever, and the light is that of my childhood, just blue and white and dirty in floods." They ran into Alexander Agassiz, who had come in on the auxiliary yacht *Wild Duck,* which had been fitted with sounding gear for his reconnaissance of the coral reefs. Thereafter Adams was chiefly with Agassiz, "geologizing on the coral reefs" in a fruitless effort to solve the mystery of the underlying rock formations. Here were more puzzles to challenge Darwin's "Song of McGinty."

Refreshed by his taste of the exotic, Adams drifted north again in the middle of March to take his ease with the Camerons for a fortnight at the Coffin Point retreat on St. Helena Island. It was a particular consolation to him that he escaped being in Washington for Cleveland's second inauguration. His Republican friends who shared the champagne and politics of his breakfast table gloomed at the prospect of four more years of exile. Fresh Tahitian materials awaited him when he returned to Lafayette Square in April. By the close of the year the little book was finished. Printed "ultissimo-privately" in Washington in an edition of not more than ten copies, the *Memoirs of Marau Taaroa, Last Queen of Tahiti* went off on December 22, 1893, to Marau and her brother Tati.

Though called *Memoirs* both in the 1893 edition and in the revised and expanded version of 1901, it was in fact a history of the rise and fall of the ruling Teva clan. So far as they were personal memoirs at all they were those of the old "chiefess" Ariitaimai, and not of her daughter Marau Taaroa, who had been only the intermediary in translating and writing down the history and legends. Adams acknowledged this fact in the revised 1901 edition by changing the title to *Memoirs of Arii Taimai* at the earnest suggestion of Marau herself. The pretended point of view was that of the proud old matriarch, but the literary additions which are sprinkled through the book as if they are hers, the allusions to Odysseus and Helen of Troy, to Samson and Delilah, to Charlemagne and Rousseau, and the skillful manipulation of the historical sourcebooks, all indicate that the autobiographical form was more a literary convenience than a representation of fact.

Tahitian history carried Adams back into a rational world of family relationships and revived ancestral memories of Quincy in the time of its ascendance. A charming archaic primitivism hung about the murmurous Tahitian recollections for him even though they told of a society addicted to human sacrifice and civil war. He saw it all in political and military terms and invested it with a barbaric chivalry as if Tahiti were a chapter in medieval history. In fact the seven genealogical charts of the "chiefly" families curiously resemble the dynastic outlines he once made for his lectures on the French kings when he taught medieval history at Harvard, and they foreshadow those that would be interspersed in the pages of his *Chartres*. To Adams the history of Tahiti particularly reflected the mercenary nature of modern capitalistic and nominally Christian society, and the *Memoirs* closed on a denunciatory note. The bringing of the blessings of civilization and Christianity to native peoples had been, as he showed, an almost unqualified catastrophe because both French and English policy rested on naked self-interest, enforced by a ruthless tyranny.

The greatest attraction of Tahitian legend and history for Adams lay perhaps in its confirmation of his attitude towards women. Women "figured as prominently in island politics as Catherine of Russia, or Maria Theresa of Austria, or Marie Antoinette of France, or Marie Louise of Parma, in the politics of Europe." Not only did the women of early Tahiti recall Europe; they evoked for him as well the legendary women of Rome and Greece. "The fight about a woman is the starting-point of all early revolutions and poetry." Tahiti also had its Helen of Troy. The coincidences, Adams declared, ran though every island in the South Seas, so that "no traveler has been able to keep the Odyssey out of his mind whenever he approached a native village."

The many philosophical and historical interpolations of the *Memoirs of Marau Taaroa* proved a kind of offshoot of the extended philosophic "Travels" Adams had once proposed to Hay. He even spoke of them as his Tahitian "Travels," and in the 1901 edition added the halftitle "Travels—Tahiti," anticipating the halftitle "Travels/France" of his *Mont Saint Michel and Chartres*. The book had as well a more special meaning for him: it was his personal tribute to the venerable "chiefess," her adopted son's return for her affectionate trust. The enterprise gave a certain sacredness to his South Sea experience and forestalled any more public record of his long voyage. The South Seas, he said, he could not touch for fear of betraying himself.

19

Brothers in Prophecy

IN MID-MAY OF 1893 Henry Adams made a flying visit of two days to the Chicago World's Fair with the Camerons in their private railway car before embarking with them for Europe. He was stunned by the spectacle because, as he wrote the Chicago merchant prince Franklin MacVeagh, he had always despaired "of seeing his age rise to the creation of new art, or the appreciation of the old." Chicago taught a lesson in modesty, having produced something that "the Greeks might have delighted to see, and Venice would have envied, but which certainly is not business. That Chicago, of all places, should turn on us, with this sort of defiant contempt, and fling its millions into our faces, in order to demonstrate to us that we understand neither business nor art, was not to be expected; but I admit that the demonstration is complete."

The journalistic excitements of the fair preempted the front pages, but even in May ominous signs of trouble appeared in the financial columns which no amount of published reassurances about the essential soundness of business could obscure. Australia, scourged by bank failures, was already in the throes of panic. India suspended the free coinage of silver, cutting off a vital market for the enormous production of the American silver states. Bank closings in the West, Midwest, and South had already begun, and a wave of bank runs and the hoarding of gold greatly exacerbated the shortage of currency. For the moment, however, the financial East still seemed secure. In an emergency the powerful silver faction in the Senate would surely prevent the repeal of the Sherman Silver Purchase Act that banking interests were advocating in their drive to establish the single gold standard for the currency. There seemed, therefore, no urgent reason for silverites like Adams or the Camerons to change their plans.

After pausing for a few days in Washington, Adams sailed with the Camerons on June 3 in the van of the summer exodus of tourists. From England the Camerons continued on to the Continent while Adams made the round of his usual haunts: the Clarks in Scotland, the Gaskells at Wenlock Abbey, and London for a visit with Henry James. He sat a couple of hours at lunch with his friend Joseph Chamberlain, who had been leading the fight against Gladstone's Irish Home Rule Bill, and found him "in great force, swinging the tomahawk" over his opponent. He made no formal calls and avoided dining out in society. "I crawl in corners," ran his deprecating comment to Hay, "and lie in dark holes like a mangy and worn-out rabbit, and play pretend to be alive when noticed." As usual the pose was a facetious extravagance. If there was anything special to be seen he donned his topper and went. One day, when Mrs. Cameron lent him her box at Covent Garden, he dropped in at the American embassy and invited young secretary Lloyd Griscom to hear Madame Melba. Adams fondly reminisced about his own days in the London legation when he was private secretary to his father during the Civil War.

On July 11 Adams joined Senator Cameron and his daughter Rachel in their tour of Switzerland. Mrs. Cameron and Martha met them at Zermatt on the seventeenth. Word came to them there that the Senate was scheduled to convene in special session on August 7 to consider the repeal of the Sherman Silver Purchase Act. Senator Cameron, a convert to the cause of silver, was eager to return, as Adams put it, "to fight for silver with the beasts at Washington." However, the financial stringency on both sides of the Atlantic did not yet seem desperate when the party set out in their carriage to cross the Furka Pass to Lucerne. Adams lent only an idle ear to the senator's unaccustomed eloquence on the importance of supporting silver, though he was a little alarmed by the signs of abnormal "cerebral excitement" in his companion. When they emerged from the Alpine silences on the twenty-third, they learned that a hurricane of business and banking failures was sweeping America. The letters waiting for Adams said there was urgent need of him in Quincy. Charles supplied the grim details. Their eldest brother, the likable and easygoing John, to whom the direction of the family trust had been left, had suffered a nervous collapse under the stress of the panic which had placed the trust in "serious financial trouble." Within a year he would be dead. Knowing Henry's penchant for avoiding vulgar money matters, Charles warned him that their affairs were too complicated and personal to allow anyone outside the bosom of the family to meddle with them. By the time Henry reached London and read of the impending failure of General Electric, he was thoroughly scared. Brooks's cablegram "Come soon" underscored the emergency that howled in the press. There was no choice but to follow hard after the senator and take the first steamer home.

After so much haste and anxiety, the situation that greeted Henry when he arrived in Quincy on August 7 seemed an anticlimax. True, everyone was "in a blue fit of terror" at the indescribable disorder and confusion of their affairs, but, unlike his brothers, he had no notes to meet and had "plenty of money for a year ahead." As it turned out he brought to the family council a shrewd business acumen and an expert knowledge of stocks and bonds. Brooks later wrote, "We owe our safety, largely . . . to you. Your action ten years ago gave us substantial control of the estate." To Brooks fell the task of managing the salvage operation and imposing economies on the free-spending Charles. By mid-September Henry rejoiced that they had come through the crisis "with our colors flying and have defied all Hell and State Street."

After the first urgent protective measures were initiated, little remained for Henry to do but to turn his attention to the larger implications of the financial convulsion. It had taken such a heavy toll among his friends that he felt "the whole generation had had notice to quit." The most conspicuous casualty was Clarence King, who escaped from the hopeless confusion of his financial affairs by going quietly mad. He had to be packed off to the Bloomingdale asylum for a few months. Everywhere social circles chattered of suicides and sudden deaths. The moment of calm which Adams had felt when he discovered that he was personally safe did not last long, for Brooks's pessimism and the hysteria of the business community were irresistible. The more resilient Charles could hardly bear the endless stream of pessimistic talk from Brooks and Henry, and he complained that they drove him "nearly wild by talking through their hats on things in general."

Brooks had resumed work on the manuscript of his *Law of Civilization and Decay* and now put it into Henry's hands for criticism. For a month, from mid-August to mid-September, in the isolation of Quincy Henry turned over the pages of Brooks's jeremiad, an economist's latter-day version of Jonathan Edwards's "Sinners in the Hands of an Angry God." Brooks stood at Henry's elbow ready to add his violent oral annotations. Incapable of his brother's detachment or devil-take-it humor, Brooks ranted that society was "about to relapse into the middle-ages," unwilling, said Henry, "to take real enjoyment, like me, even in that prospect."

Licensed by the disastrous events about him, Henry peppered his correspondence with one derisive outburst after another, playing the role of a rhapsodical, perversely jesting prophet at home in a world whose outer chaos at last matched that within. To Hay he capered: "I was scared last November; I was scareder last May; and I have gone on getting more and more scared ever since . . . My lunacy scares me." He entertained Elizabeth Cameron with even more picturesque tall talk: "I am in a panic of terror about finance, politics, society and the solar system, with ultimate fears for the Milky Way and the Nebula of Orion. The sun-spots scare me. Ruin hangs over the Polar Star."

Recalling that memorable summer, Brooks afterwards reminisced, "Henry and I sat in the hot August evenings and talked endlessly of the panic and of our hopes and fears, and of my historical and economic theories, and so the season wore away amidst an excitement verging on revolution." Henry's elder brothers, especially the ill-fated John, had invested heavily in the future of the Far West, acquiring substantial holdings of property in Spokane. As a result of the panic the paper losses were very great. The ancestral quarrel with the financial lords of State Street grew continentwide, for the Adams brothers saw that the Eastern banking interests could suffocate the West almost at pleasure through their control of the flow of money and the manipulation of freight rates. It was also plain that the Eastern money market was dominated by the Lombard Street bankers of London. The sense that the two brothers then had of being caught in a ruthless and inhuman trap was never to be effaced.

Congress bitterly debated the repeal of the Sherman Silver Purchase Act. What had made the crisis acute was that England, to protect her gold reserves and her position as a creditor nation, had been unloading American securities, simultaneously depressing the stock market and draining away gold for which all creditors were desperately clamoring. Seeing the naked self-interest of the Bank of England and its allies, Sir William Harcourt, Chancellor of the Exchequer, and the Rothschild syndicate, revived all of Henry's anti-British feelings. He diverted himself with satisfying fantasies of hanging Rothschild and Harcourt to a lamppost. He became convinced that the panic was deliberately engineered by the "gold-bugs," the collective money power of creditor capitalists, to prevent the remonetization of silver.

When Adams returned to Washington on September 19 from his conference with Brooks in Quincy, the fight over silver had entered a decisive phase. Alone among Republicans east of the Mississippi, Senator Cameron spoke out against repeal of the Silver Purchase Act. Cameron not only attacked repeal but proposed the free coinage of domestic silver and the granting of authority to state banks to issue their own notes so as to relieve the "poorer and weaker states, especially in the South" from "their servitude to the capitalist cities."

His argument sounded very much as if it had come directly from Adams's vitriolic pen, as indeed there is evidence that it had. America's chief merit, Cameron declared, was that she had "from first to last, on all occasions and in every form . . . asserted the most emphatic negative to the policy and methods of the moneyed power of England," a power which was "selfish, cruel, and aggressive, as well as sordid, to a degree that made them dangerous to all the world and fatal to the weak. Our manufacturers might flourish on low silver and a high tariff; they must perish on gold and a low tariff."

The speech made a profound impression, as Henry reported to Hay, and drew "violent diatribes" from the sound-money press, which formed an almost solid phalanx in the East. He also added, with more than a trace of disingenuousness, "We who know him feel pretty sure that someone helped him, perhaps Wayne MacVeagh, but the speech is a good speech anyway, and it is certainly his. No other eastern man has the courage to make it." Matthew Quay, Don Cameron's fellow senator and the political boss of the state, chaffed him that Elizabeth had written the speech. Adams had at least lent a friendly polish to the senator's eloquence, for a draft of it in his hand is still extant.

Adams mistakenly felt repeal would not come to a vote. He therefore joined his brother Charles in early October for a second and longer look at the Chicago World's Fair. It was "a seductive vanity," and even the violently skeptical Charles, who at first cried "Hell! I would exactly as soon take a season ticket to a circus," insisted on staying on an additional week. Henry's second impression was even stronger than the first. For two weeks he reveled in the "fakes and frauds" of the Midway Plaisance and "labored solemnly through all the great buildings and looked like an owl at the dynamos and steam-engines," feeling quite sure that neither the wickedness nor the genuineness of the Fair was understood "by our innocent natives." The anarchic polarities insistently challenged comment. "You know the tenor of my thought," went a letter to Hay, "so I will spare you; but if we ever write those Travels of ours, I've a volume or two to put in for the Fair. I want to talk among other matters about the architecture . . . I like to look at it as an appeal to the human animal, the superstitious and ignorant savage within us, that has instincts and no reason, against the world as money has made it. I have seen a faint gleam of intelligence lighten the faces even of the ignorant rich, and almost penetrate the eyes of a mugwump and Harvard College graduate."

He descended on Washington in time to see confirmed in the Senate the victory of the hated new class, the "gold-bug" capitalists. The banking and business community closed ranks, and the Senate fell into line on September 30, the vote for repeal being forty-three to thirty-two. It was now devil take the hindmost. Said Adams, "The gold-bugs have undertaken to run things, and have already shown such incompetence, terror and greed that nothing but disaster can come of it."

If part of the credit for Henry's awakening to the perils of the gold-bug future should go to Senator Cameron, a much larger share should go to Brooks, who was far more deeply resentful of the dilemma in which they all found themselves. At forty-five he felt himself politically isolated. Though he had campaigned for Cleveland, he had not been rewarded with a post in the administration. The truth was that Cleveland did not trust Brooks's circle, doubtless having heard echoes of the breakfast-table satire of his neighbor on the other side of Lafayette Square. When sometime later Secretary of State Richard Olney suggested one of Henry's boon companions, William Hallett Phillips, for a post in the department, Cleveland demurred: "What is a settler with me [is] that his close intimates are John Hay, Henry Adams, Cabot Lodge, and such. I would feel very unhappy if anyone with such associations who wish nothing but ill for the administration were connected with the State Department."

Now for the first time the two brothers, feeling the grip of finance capitalism, discovered that their lifelong defense of sound money had turned out to be the final trap of State Street for expropriating Quincy and bankrupting its naïve moral order. They had helped dig their own pit. The highly trained members of a political dynasty found themselves in futile opposition to the new centers of power. They had failed to keep pace with their time. Brooks with Henry's help set himself to find the reason for that failure. The knowledge was vital if a new elite was to come into existence capable of overcoming the "gold-bug."

What characteristics disabled them in this race for the survival of the fittest? What was taking place in their environment to which they were unable to adapt themselves? Closely associated with Charles, Henry had learned much about the machinations of Wall Street and the new finance capitalists like Jay Gould, Russell Sage, and Commodore Cornelius Vanderbilt, who had outwitted Charles at every turn and had finally driven him from the presidency of the Union Pacific. Charles, too, was an outmoded type. Charles had discovered, and he had shared his discoveries with his brothers, that the power of these invaders was not that of a little band of unscrupulous interlopers: it was rooted in the developing financial structure and grew out of the insatiable demands of an expanding economy for fresh capital. The new breed of men were part and parcel of what Brooks Adams had called the "Plutocratic Revolution." They performed as vital a service to the great industrial corporations in hastening the revolution as Congress did in adopting the McKinley tariff. That these forces should have united to obtain repeal of the Sherman Silver Purchase Act indicated to Henry and Brooks that bankers' control of the currency was the price that would have to be paid for an adequate capital market.

To Henry the practical aspects of the movement were boring, but thanks to Brooks he could redefine his attitudes, and he set out to follow the dangerous path through the wilderness of the money question at his own pace and in his own way. He would discover the truth of the popular witticism that of the three main causes of madness— love, ambition, and the study of currency problems—the last was the worst.

The fruit of Brooks's intense study and subsequent collaboration with Henry was the revised *Law of Civilization and Decay,* in which the historical basis for the moral condemnation of the finance or usurer capitalist was stated with stunning power. Its effect upon Henry was electric, bringing to an end the period of intellectual tor-por and irresolution, and it helped launch him upon the greatest effort of his thought. It brought his anarchic disgusts into focus, gave him a scapegoat, identified the enemy, and supplied him with a scientific rationale for rejecting contemporary civilization. Here was the scientific basis for modern pessimism. Brooks had shown him the "potential book" with many misgivings about its value, even of its sanity. Henry reassured him, "It is not the dream of a maniac," but he warned, "The gold-bugs will never forgive you." Remembering the quiet menace of the humming electric generators at the Chicago Fair, he added, "You are monkeying with a dynamo."

Eager to do something more direct on behalf of silver, Brooks summarized the historical thesis of the book in a thirty-page pamphlet called *The Gold Standard,* published in April 1894, copies of which Henry distributed in strategic quarters in Washington. The ostracism that followed confirmed Henry's warning: "The silver business has brought Brooks's position in Boston to a crisis," he told Mrs. Cameron. "As I refuse even to enter the place, for fear of downright quarrel, or to talk with a Bostonian for fear of insulting him, or talk of Boston, for fear of expressing my contempt and disgust for it, and its opinions and for everything it is, or ever was, or ever will be, Brooks is left without even my little aid or countenance, and writhes like a worm under the process of being stepped on."

Brooks asserted, "Perhaps no single force has wrought so ceaselessly, and yet subtly, on man's destinies as that mysterious influence which causes variations in the value of the money with which he buys his daily bread." Tracing that influence from ancient Rome to the present, he showed how "natural selection did its resistless work," creating in the Roman Empire an insatiable moneyed class of usurers who employed the contraction of the currency as an instrument for the concentration of economic power. By steadily depressing prices they enslaved the agricultural classes and finally destroyed the military vitality of Rome. The economic prostration lasted until the "religious impulse of the Crusades opened the markets of the East and the Italian bankers invented bank credit and exchanges to increase the efficiency of the meagre coinage." The resulting monetary expansion, "all too small to keep pace with the movement of the age," ushered in the most brilliant epoch of European life, the thirteenth century.

The dynamic process repeated itself in recurring phases of equilibrium and disequilibrium. Whenever the creditor interest became dominant over the producing classes it promptly contracted the currency by establishing the primacy of the gold standard. More recently, the influx of gold from California somewhat relieved the pressure, but the "insidious and potent" money power resumed contraction of the world's currency by demonetizing silver, and thus increased the tribute laid upon the producing classes. The resulting pressure upon the standard of living was producing "Nihilism in Russia; Agrarian insurrection in Italy; Anarchism in France and Spain; Socialism in England and Germany."

This was the rationale of monetary and financial history that Brooks provided for his older brother. It came at precisely the right moment, for Henry had touched bottom again and railed against the world with hysterical vehemence. "I am myself more than ever at odds with my time. I detest it, and everything that belongs to it, and live only in the wish to see the end of it, with all its infernal Jewry. I want to put every money-lender to death, and to sink Lombard Street and Wall Street under the ocean. Then, perhaps, men of our kind might have some chance of being honorably killed in battle, and eaten by our enemies." Brooks's formulation came as the logical extension of Henry's own thinking and provided him with the great symbol of the archenemy, the usurer, a symbol which the clerical reactionaries of the period had fixed upon as the mark of the secular beast. It was inevitable for the two brothers to borrow a subsidiary symbol from the scapegoat literature of that distressed time, the figure of the International Jew, one of the most successful inventions of the anti-Semitic and clerical press of France and Germany. Thanks to Brooks's analysis it could be scientifically demonstrated that the undue love of money was the root of all evil, precisely the point which their Puritan ancestors had made. Other and higher types of men might come and go, but the usurer went on forever; he was the only permanently adaptable breed of man in the struggle for existence.

Henry's share in the venture became increasingly active during the intervals of compulsive travels in 1894 and 1895 as Brooks pressed him for editorial criticism and he in turn tried to save his brother from the morass of excessive philosophizing. Incited by Brooks's example, Henry began an intensive course of study of his own during the late spring of 1894, after returning from a two-month jaunt through Cuba and the West Indies with Clarence King, who had recovered from his nervous breakdown. In the light of his hopes of the mid-1880s, he felt cheated and baffled by what had taken place. Some incomprehensible and mysterious shock had hit society, and he wanted "to know what is wrong with the world that it should suddenly go smash without visible cause or possible advantage." He shook his head over it. "Here, in this young, rich continent, capable of supporting three times its population with ease, we have had a million men out of employment for nearly a year, and the situation growing worse rather than better." It was making him "a conservative anarchist," he said.

History seemed perversely bent on repeating itself. "As our world seems to have gone to the devil—at least in art and literature," he reported to Gaskell, "I have taken up the story of that greater world, the Roman Empire, which went so inexplicably to the devil before us." He immersed himself in "Mr. Bohn's veracious translation" of Petronius, Plutarch, Cicero, Juvenal, Suetonius, Pliny, and "other gold-bug literature of Rome." In Ammianus Marcellinus's soldierly history of the debilitating effect of luxury on the middle classes of Rome and the decay of the legions through oppressive taxation, he found his parallels to the contemporary scene. The moneylenders and their dependent allies were ranged against the money borrowers and farmers. Ovid, too, supplied ammunition; Midas, "'Ille male usurus'—that outrageous usurer—turned everything to gold, and had asses ears; two infallible signs of a banker." The reconnaissance helped him in his examination of Brooks's manuscript, which he peppered with annotations. The recent breaking of the Pullman strike with federal troops showed that Pullman, Carnegie, and Cleveland were "our Crassus and Pompey and Caesar,—our proud American triumvirate, the types of our national mind and ideals." Cleveland had won again: first, he had got the gold standard; now he "had settled the working man forever."

The conclusion of Brooks's survey of the oscillation between civilization and barbarism was sufficiently frightening, even though it left open-ended alternatives. Its implications were as uncompromising as those of Mark Twain's *Mysterious Stranger.* Brooks's wife thought he really ought to call it "The Path to Hell: A Story Book," but Brooks said even that was too optimistic, for he couldn't even promise anything "so good as a path to 'Hell.'" Houghton Mifflin turned down the incendiary manuscript. Henry undertook to make arrangements with Swan Sonnenschein in London, being once again abroad in 1895 for his annual month in Paris to preserve himself "from mental atrophy." The skeptical publisher demanded a $500 subsidy from the author. Brooks held back briefly until Henry, eager to see an English edition, generously threatened to pay the cost himself. The two read proof simultaneously, Brooks in Quincy, Henry in London. "Whatever the public may think—or not think—or say—or not say," Henry reassured him, "you may take my word for it that the book is a great book." Brooks glowed with pleasure. "To have you, who, after all, I respect more as a critic than any man alive, tell me my work deserved to stand where I should like to have it stand, is more than I ever dared to hope." Henry was immensely proud of his brother's achievement. "I think it is astonishing," he told Elizabeth. "The first time serious history has ever been written . . . I have sought all my life those truths which this mighty infant, this seer unblest, has struck with the agony and bloody sweat of genius. I stand in awe of him." Nonetheless, Henry kept to his resolve of avoiding identification with *The Law of Civilization and Decay*, by striking out Brooks's grateful dedication. "I believe silence to be now the only sensible form of expression. I have deliberately and systematically effaced myself, even in my own history."

In 1895 Henry made two sets of annotations for the New York and the Paris editions of the book, drawing upon his widening historical studies to suggest additional illustrations and confirmatory data, all of which Brooks assimilated in greater or lesser degree into the text. Of all the suggestions only one resulted in a major change. Henry declared that the ultimate and costliest disaster which befell the Western world was aesthetic, the decline of the arts through the impoverishment of the imagination. "An entire chapter," said Henry, "should be given to arts." Brooks adopted the suggestion. The chapter in the New York edition concluded: "No poetry can bloom in the arid modern soil, the drama has died, and the patrons of art are no longer even conscious of shame at profaning the most sacred of ideals."

Three years later, taking stock of himself at Quincy, Brooks reviewed their work on the book. "But for you I never should have printed it. Most of what has attracted attention has been the result of your criticism. The form is, I think, almost wholly yours." Obviously his self-mistrust made him exaggerate his debt to Henry, but the truth probably lay somewhere between their mutual disclaimers. Brooks felt too keenly the social isolation which his bristling spirit had brought upon him. In his abject loneliness he reflected, "On looking back over my life I cannot imagine to myself what my life would have been without you. From the old days in England when I was a boy, you have been my good genius."

Henry realized that their joint analysis needed buttressing with statistics in order to provide a strategic instrument of prediction. Only with the aid of tables, charts, and graphs could the dangerous velocity of economic concentration which was pitting nation against nation be properly measured. His *History* had given the preliminary formula for the relative progress of the United States compared with Britain as deduced from the movement of international exchanges up to 1816 and the relative weight of metal fired by artillerists in the War of 1812. Now there were no guns firing, but, as Brooks asserted, in the commonplace of Clausewitz, war was merely an extension of economic competition. They agreed that the current unprecedented outflow of gold specie to England precisely reproduced the situation before the War of 1812. For help with the foreign exchange statistics, Henry turned to Worthington Chauncey Ford. Ford had been in charge of the Bureau of Statistics in the State Department and after 1893 entered the Treasury. Henry began his collaboration with him in June 1895 to prepare himself for a pilgrimage to Lombard Street, where Brooks had already taken his soundings.

In a rapid interchange Ford briefed him on the world situation. His figures documented the outflow of gold but left Adams uneasy. At the outset Adams struck a snag: from 1886 to 1895 America had had an apparently favorable balance of trade, and yet the exchanges had run against her. "Will you kindly try to make clear to an extremely confused intelligence," he besought Ford, "what becomes of our favorable annual balance of one hundred millions." Back and forth the notes went with their tables and calculations of possible ratios. Ford set him to rights: the exchanges did tell the true story, for they included the invisible balance of trade in investments. Adams tried a new set of graphs. A sequence could be established for a series of ten-year intervals or again at fifteen-year intervals, all showing a "net balance left abroad" increasing by "a million a year." The figures yielded at least one crumb of comfort. The socially respectable J. P. Morgan had apparently "outjewed the Jews" by tricking Rothschild.

When Henry reached London in July 1895 he was ready to interview the leading Lombard Street bankers. Each day he pored over the financial columns of the *Times,* noting the traffic in gold. He interrogated numerous brokers; to his confusion some were bulls, some bears. He had only his usual bleak comfort: "I am no more ignorant than the most learned. No one knows. No one can answer my conundrums." Disposed to take the gloomy view of every possibility, he thought that in spite of the English bimetallists like his "pro-Silverite" friend Moreton Frewen, the "gold men must win." For a "conservative Christian anarchist" only one course remained, to become "a gold-bug *à outrance,* and bring the house down."

As he hurried restlessly from one travel expedition to another during this period he felt more and more convinced that "Faust had a sure horse on the devil in his promise about the passing hour." His mind roamed as restlessly as his body, and he seized instinctively on the books confirming his pessimism which the times flung to the surface. Two such were Karl Marx's *Capital* and Charles H. Pearson's *National Life and Character,* both studies of "morbid society," though "not as amusing as Petronius and Plutarch." Marx irritated him. "I never struck a book which taught me so much, and with which I disagreed so radically in conclusion." Marx, he once told Justice Holmes, "recognizes the inevitable but is bitter about it." Only the early sections of *Capital*—"Commodities," "Money," and "The Rate of Surplus Value"—held him. His annotations and inserted cross-references show the intensity of his effort to grasp the analysis. The sliding definition of "value" troubled him more than anything else. "This beats me," he jotted at one point. "Nothing more German was ever written than this corruption of value, values, and forms of values." Impressed by Engels's remark in the introduction that "free trade had exhausted its resources; even Manchester doubts this its quondam economic gospel," Adams transferred the idea to a letter: "When I think of the formulas of our youth,—when I look at my old set of John Stuart Mill,—and suddenly recall that I am actually a member of the Cobden Club,—I feel that somewhere there is the biggest kind of joke, if I could only see it."

Pearson's forecast of revolution was as attractively violent as Marx's. His thesis, said Adams, was that the dark races were gaining on the white races, and in another fifty years "the white races will have to reconquer the tropics by war and nomadic invasion, or be shut up, north of the fortieth parallel." Having come to share some of Clarence King's affection for dark-hued Polynesians and Latin

Americans, Adams professed to welcome the prospect. "As I rather prefer niggers to whites, and much prefer oriental art to European, I incline to make the most of the tropics while the white is still tolerated there."

So far a Marxist, he expected—and vengefully hoped—that the velocity of financial concentration would be so great that the system would break down when the great money powers were forced at last to ruthless competition among themselves. The Venezuela question in 1895, which brought England and the United States to the brink of war, demonstrated for him that "the quarrel was bound to come." The situation had its ironic aspect, for State Street, as in a parallel situation during the War of 1812, instinctively sided with England against Secretary Olney's peremptory assertion of the Monroe Doctrine. "Boston has this time managed to damn itself for another generation as it has done in every generation in past history," Henry exclaimed. On this issue he gladly placed himself in the camp of the "Jingoes," the term with which Edwin Godkin's *Nation* denounced the war party for its anti-British campaign. To Henry's horror his brother Charles aligned himself with "all the other Harvard College 'mokes,' the professors of history, by talking out loud" against Olney's interpretation of the Monroe Doctrine and signing the "State Street call" against it.

The 1894 military alliance between Russia and France considered in conjunction with Russia's territorial expansion eastward profoundly impressed Adams; and he labored to fit the movement into the scheme of mechanical centralization formulated by Brooks. He saw that the partition of the tropics at the Berlin Conference of 1884–85 had opened new imperialist rivalries of the most terrible intensity, all challenging England's monopoly of overseas trade. Possibly a new Napoleonic epoch was coming which would repeat "the diplomacy, the blunders and the disasters of 1813." "Our true point of interest is not India but Russia," he insisted to Brooks, who thought the focus lay in India with its enormous reservoir of cheap labor. With Russia's collaboration England could be checkmated everywhere. "One's mind goes far, and dreams much over such a field of vision, but in the end it loses itself in Asia. Russia is omnipotence." Viewing the developing chart of international relations, Adams could now affirm that "Russia is the great new element, which for a hundred and fifty years has caused all the chief political perturbations of the world."

There were sufficient variables to tax Adams's most imaginative

algebra. Complexity grew on complexity as he went on supplement-
ing his "ocean chart" in the currents of politics, his table of "trade
balances for England, France, Germany and the United States from
1870 to 1896." Similar tables had to be worked out for the other
industrial powers. Sometimes he invited Worthington Ford to dine, if
only to have "a notion what is the best way to say nothing." Ford's
figures proved to him that the silver controversy was part of a much
larger process. "The whole decline since 1870 would then resolve itself into an effect of the competition of the capitalist countries, which,
in lowering the profits of industry, lower the profits of capital," a
conclusion which drove him reluctantly back again to Marx. "At the
end of the vista, in any and all contingencies, stands ruin for western
Europe."

By 1897 his calculations showed that England had been steadily
running behind in her capital account since the Baring failure of
1890. Satisfied that England was on the road to insolvency, Adams
turned his attention to the Continent. "Perhaps you could ask
quietly," he suggested to Spring Rice in the embassy in Berlin, "what
amount of truth there may be in the criticisms of [Elias von] Cyon on
Witte and the Russian finances." "Springy" explained that "the sensitive point is that the expansion of Germany is barred in Europe and
that out of Europe Germany encounters England everywhere."
Adams then tried out his revised predictions on Brooks. The consen-
sus, as he saw it, was that another shock like 1893 would soon come.
"The centre of the readjustment, if readjustment is to be, lies in Germany, not in Russia or with us. For the last generation, since 1865,
Germany has been the great disturbing element of the world, and
until its expansive force is decidedly exhausted, I see neither political
nor economical equilibrium possible." Even more revisions lay ahead,
however, as the threads of Adams's quest ran farther and farther out-
ward.

While Brooks published his pessimistic polemics with furious energy, Henry kept his vow of public silence, content to make his influence felt from behind the scenes in the more congenial role of "stable-
companion" to statesmen. The only published reflection at this period
of his intense collaboration with Brooks took a very modest form, his
"communication," as president, to the annual meeting of the American Historical Association in December 1894, which was read in his
absence in lieu of a presidential address. Posthumously published as

"The Tendency of History," the essay was to stand first in his series of "letters to teachers." He thought of it at the time as a kind of unacknowledged pathmaker for Brooks's *Law of Civilization and Decay*. Without some such preparation Brooks would either be ignored or vilified. "The teaching profession," as he expressed the idea to Brooks, "is, like the church and the bankers, a vested interest. And the historians will fall on anyone who threatens their stock in trade quite as virulently as do the bankers on the silver men."

The unorthodox address climaxed his years of tenuous relation with the association and with professional historians. After the first few annual meetings he had kept himself at a safe distance and declined all invitations to read a paper. However, the executive secretary, Herbert B. Adams, was not wholly to be outwitted by his elusive quarry. At the December 1890 meeting Henry Adams had been elected a vice-president, though he was then off in Samoa and knew nothing of the involuntary honor until he saw the annual report. His absences from the speakers' table did not protect him. His teasing evasions proved irresistible to the historians, and they elected the persistently invisible vice-president to be president of the association in 1893. Adams could hardly wriggle out of the presidential address, but he was a resourceful quarry.

The convention had set the annual meeting for September 12, 1894, at Saratoga. Adams packed his kit in mid-July, soon after returning from a journey to Cuba with Clarence King, and, leaving no forwarding address, headed for the Yellowstone country with Hay to join a party of geologists in an expedition to the headwaters of the Yellowstone. Once again he felt at home in the saddle as the pack train made its way through the defiles of the Grand Tetons, traveling three or four hundred miles up and down the mountain passes and through vast forests of spruce and pine. It was a lark much like the one nearly twenty-five years earlier on which he had met Clarence King. The alpine vistas of peaks and canyons dazzled the eye, and the brandy-sharp air exhilarated the lungs, but even with Hay, "the best of companions," to cheer him, he began to find that the close camaraderie of the campfire and the recurring rigors of the trail could inspire a new variety of boredom. The wild scenery seemed to match his own restlessness: "It was a queer country up there, all striped with snow like a crazy-quilt . . . A very queer, mad, hoodoo, drunken landscape." Six weeks later he pushed on alone toward Seattle. From

Banff he reassured Elizabeth Cameron that he was enjoying the purposeless rambling, for, leading a vegetable existence, he had "succeeded in getting rid of everything but myself." He returned to Washington toward the end of September "happy in the thought that the
Historical Association had met, as announced, at Saratoga, Sept. 12,
and had by this time merrily gone its path, led by a new and, I need
not say, a less capable President." However, he found a circular waiting for him announcing the postponement of the meeting to December 27, "*at Washington,*" as Adams italicized. His "bête noire and
namesake," Herbert B. Adams, had neatly "coppered" him.

Now flight was again imperative, for the thought of addressing a
large public audience terrified him. He seized a companion in Senator
Eugene Hale's twenty-one-year-old son Chandler, and decamped late
in November 1894 for a five-month tour of Mexico and the Carib-
bean islands, leaving Hay instructions to give an evening reception
for the association on his behalf. From Guadalajara he sent off his
presidential communication, newly dated December 12, to be read in
Washington by the secretary.

It was not a cheerful lecture which Adams gave his colleagues, for
it pointed out to them the central—and disagreeable—role which
honest historians must play in view of the growing tendency of the
study of history to approach the status of a science of social prediction. Once a science of history should be achieved the historian would
be obliged to turn prophet and thus expose himself to the usual fate
of prophets, to be either ignored or liquidated. He foresaw the time
when the association would be torn by the dilemma, once confronted
by Galileo, of either asserting its truths in the face of a powerful
vested interest whose security lay in denying them, or publicly repu-
diating the science which had obliged it to make the challenge.

The great phenomenon of his generation, he said, had been the
effort to create a science of history. What professor of history had not
at some time felt himself on the verge of bringing "order to chaos,"
of dreaming himself the man "who should successfully apply Darwin's method to the facts of human history." But a science of history
could no longer expect to take "the form of cheerful optimism which
gave Darwin's conclusions the charm of a possible human perfectibil-
ity." It would have to fix "with mathematical certainty the path which
human society has got to follow."

Each of the three conceivable paths promised danger to the historian. The first was socialism, but its Marxian theory of history announced "the scientific certainty of communistic triumphs." Even if the hypothesis were scientifically sound, it could not be taught. "Would property, on which the universities depend, allow such freedom of instruction?" The second possibility would be to announce "that the present evils of the world—its huge armaments, its vast accumulations of capital, its advancing materialism, and declining arts—were to be continued, exaggerated, over a thousand years." Such teaching would "lead only to despair and attempts at anarchy in art, in thought, and in society." The third possibility, that science might "prove that society must at a given time revert to the church and recover its old foundation of absolute faith in a personal providence and a revealed religion," would entail the suicide of science. It was the "shadow of this coming event," this crisis which would confront the teacher of history, that he said had often silenced him in the past ten years "where I should once have spoken with confidence." Thus he concluded with the same embittered challenge he had addressed to Brooks: "Beyond a doubt, silence is best."

Admittedly, Adams's protestation was disingenuous. His posthumous disguise had long worn thin. The more he praised the virtues of silence, the harder it grew for him to hold his tongue, and the busier he became in his efforts to educate Brooks, Lodge, Roosevelt, Hay, and their large circle of politically potent associates. Privately, he broadcast his opinions to all who would listen and pressed his brother's book on his friends as the new evangel. And he knew his own weakness. London and Lombard Street, for example, had worn him out: "I talked too much; I thought too much . . . My temper was over-irritated and my tongue over-irritable."

In his correspondence he showed no relaxation. Wherever he turned he saw unmistakable signs of the accelerating concentration of capitalist power in rival world centers. The evils of their money-making civilization must grow increasingly worse. "Religion, art, politics, manners are either vulgarized or dead—or turned into money-making agencies." In 1895, a year after the address, he was unsure whether the world was "on the edge of a new and last great centralization, or of a first great movement of disintegration." Disintegration seemed more likely, "with Russia for the eccentric on one side and America on the other."

The parallel with Rome astonished him. Brooks, it struck him, was repeating the role of Pliny the Elder. Pliny died in 79 A.D., just as the police age of capitalist repression began. American society, however, moved more rapidly. Rome had slowly stagnated for three hundred years until the Goths successfully challenged her power at the Battle of Adrianople in 378 and crossed the Danube. "Allowing for our more rapid movement," said Henry, "we ought still to have more than two hundred years of futile and stupid stagnation." Twenty years of it would be more than he would care for. He went on, in a burst of orphic obscurity, to say that Brooks's "Bible of Anarchy" seemed to be catching on. "God knows what side in our politics it would help, for it cuts all equally, but it might help man to know himself and hark back to God . . . Only, if such is God's will, and Fate and Evolution— let there be God!"

The odd, mystical tangent of the thought gave a hint of a new stimulus that had with a certain suddenness deflected the orbit of his thought. Already he had found a source of strength with which to oppose the gold-bug. On a journey into Normandy to visit its cathedrals with the Lodges in the late summer of 1895 Adams experienced a sudden illumination like that of Pater's Marius, who discovered the beauty of the Mass "amid a deep sense of the vacuity of life." In London he had felt a "dreary, eternal sense of my own moral death," and he left for France to get away from "a sense of nightmare." Brooks had prepared him, he said: "You mapped out the lines and indicated the emotions." The ten-day tour took the party through Amiens, Rouen, Caen, Bayeux, Saint-Lô, Coutances, Mont Saint Michel, Le Mans, and Chartres and produced a cascade of letters filled with his intense response to Norman cathedral architecture. Though he had earlier visited Amiens, he had "never thoroughly *felt* it before." The austere grace of Coutances overwhelmed him. "Amiens has mercy. Coutances is above mercy itself." Mont Saint Michel was completely new to him. He climbed "up and down the walls, moats, cliffs and beaches" and emerged convinced that "in the eleventh century the majority of me was Norman."

His imagined Norman heritage colored everything he saw. He had "rarely felt New England at its highest ideal power as it appeared . . . beautified and glorified in the Cathedral of Coutances . . . Since then our ancestors have steadily declined." Into Mont Saint Michel and Coutances were built the heroic ideals of the pre-Renaissance. "When Rafael painted Saint Michael flourishing his big sword over Satan he thought no doubt he had done a good bit of religious painting, but Norman architecture makes even Rafael vulgar." Adams declared that in his "sublimated fancy, the combination of the glass and the Gothic is the highest ideal ever yet reached by man." In Washington he might thereafter immerse himself in politics and intrigue, rifle Samuel Langley's mind for what was new in science, study Ford's interminable figures on world trade, and nod his head in agreement over the spate of books heralding the decline of the West; but beneath the swirling chaos he had found a granite foothold in the past.

HARDLY HAD HENRY finished counseling with Brooks about the silver controversy and the philosophical bearings of *The Law of Civilization and Decay* when his elder brother Charles turned to him for advice on his projected life of their father for the American Statesmen series. The old intimacy between Henry and Charles had long since given way to a familial tolerance for each other's eccentricities of temperament and opinions. On the subject of their father, however, they willingly sank their differences in the deep-rooted bonds of family feeling. "Make any use of me that you like," he rallied Charles, "just as though I were real."

It was clear to him that their father's fame rested chiefly on his work in Congress during the tense months of the secession winter and on his diplomacy in England during the war years, the period when as private secretary sitting across the large worktable he had daily scrutinized the play of thought on his father's face. "For those two results [in Washington and London]," Henry advised Charles, "his character, mind and training were admirably fitted. His defects and limitations were as important, and as valuable, to him, as his qualities, within the range of those fields. Had there been a little more, or a little less of him, he would have been less perfect. As he stands, he stands alone . . . He is almost like a classical gem. From the moment he appeared anywhere—at Washington, London, Geneva—his place was never questioned, much less disputed . . . His figure, as a public man, is classic,—call it Greek, if you please.

"Of course you cannot expressly say all this, but this is really all that the public wants to know, and your business is to make them feel it. Sons are not the proper persons to do such work, but I know of no one better suited, so we may as well try." But how to do it? In his

Spartan counsel he seemed almost to be talking to himself, rebuking his own failings and temptations. "A light hand is necessary; total effacement of oneself; rigid abstention from paradox, smartness or pedagoguery; and a single purpose of painting the figure, and nothing else. Our business is to let the governor have his own say."

What especially concerned the two brothers was ascertaining the point at which their father's faculties had started to decay, and they lingered over the slowly accumulating evidence with a morbid fascination. At forty-eight their father had begun to feel himself growing old and had anxiously watched for the barely perceptible signs of aging and decay. He, too, had been cursed with an "introspective and morbid" streak which so plagued the sons. "Great Heavens!" Charles burst out impatiently, "Why wasn't I as a boy sent to boarding-school!—Why didn't I as a young man go to Hell!" To Henry the glimpses of repressed passion and thwarted feelings chimed in with his sense of a dying and mad world. What had all his father's self-denial signified? What indulgence had it purchased for the children? Was not the world a vast Lunarium after all?

The strangely macabre business was to go on for many months, a kind of filial inquest over their parent, the two sons trying to be scrupulously objective and detached as if fearful to reciprocate the suppressed tenderness of their father. Exacting to the last degree, Henry was bound to demur to the finished work when it was finally published in 1900. His advice had proved impossible to follow. Charles not only effaced himself; he came near to effacing their father in the impersonalities of politics and diplomacy. As he tried to make his way through the book, Henry could only exclaim: "Now I understand why I refused so obstinately to do it myself. These biographies are murder, and in this case, to me, would be both patricide and suicide. They belittle the victim and the assassin equally . . . I have sinned myself, and deeply, and am no more worthy to be called anything, but, thank my diseased and dyspeptic nervous wreck, I did not assassinate my father."

20

Behind the Scenes

ADAMS'S LOVE for the exotic was, for a second time, to have quite unlooked-for consequences. His visit to the South Seas had by a kind of inadvertence made him a historian of Tahiti and for years afterwards, through his friendship for the "Salmonidae," implicated him in the business development of the island. Another island, Cuba, was now about to play a more exciting role in his life and to involve him, as he said afterwards in the *Education,* in an "ocean of mischief."

It began in January 1894 when he and Clarence King fell to "corresponding wildly to arrange a meeting in the West Indies." From the Bloomingdale asylum a rejuvenated King had written, "What do you say to taking the island trip with me?" Adams leaped at the chance. In high good humor he twitted William Phillips, with whom he had visited Cuba a year before, "I expect to find a Carib woman and never reappear among civilized man." The two friends effected their rendezvous at Tampa, Adams having "torn himself," according to King's bantering report to Hay, "from the arms of—South Carolina," where he had been "condemned to 'do time' at St. Helena with the Camerons." King, having "vast geological plans in the region of Santiago," was glad to abandon Havana, where the señoritas in the plaza fell short of his dream of the "ideal negro woman." Adams, willing enough to forgo King's ideal, simply "wanted to be lazy." Havana, like Papeete, impressed him as "a wretched worn-out wreck of anemic horrors." He caught up with the archaic aboard a coasting steamer whose company was "Cuban of the commonest, in which I became wildly patriotic."

In Santiago the two middle-aged adventurers, gaily uncertain which was Don Quixote and which Sancho Panza, had hunted through the dawn for lodging, the inn being beneath discussion. The British consul proffered his country house, eight miles away in a valley among the rugged hills at Dos Bocas. The lodging for the night turned out to be a place of enchantment, and their brief stay lengthened to a month. Day by day the wild beauty of the valley grew on Adams. The habitual sardonic grumbling disappeared from the colorful pages of his travel letters. Their cook, Pepe, assaulted their palates with ever more flamboyant concoctions until Adams ruefully conceded defeat. King enjoyed him as that strange creature, "a pessimist addicted to water-colors and capable of a humorous view of the infinite." Adams dabbled happily in the blues and the yellows, mixing greens and purples and all the rainbow shades in a futile effort to capture the anarchic play of color among the orange trees, pomegranates, and palms.

King, more venturesome than Adams and not at all given to obsessive letter writing, went off nights to visit among the backcountry Cubans, swapping "views of creation" over coffee in the cabins of the red-bandannaed women for whom he had an unpatrician affinity. Winning the confidence of the natives, he suddenly discovered something more exciting than voodoo magic and legends of lost mines. He began to come back from their dances with the lurid gossip of the revolutionary underground.

The disastrous Ten-Year War for independence which had ended in 1878 plunged the Cubans into an even more terrible subjection to Spanish rule. Revolt was again astir in the fastnesses of the Sierra Maestra. The sympathetic King, possessor of a keener scent for mischief than Adams, was taken in tow by Juan Domenech Portuondo, who helped him establish contact with some of the rebel leaders lurking in the nearby hills with a price on their heads. One of them he managed to interview under the pretext of discussing Cuban mineral resources. Thereafter, Adams and King led charmed lives; they were respectable enough to escape the notice of the Spanish patrols and sufficiently trusted by the guerrillas to go entirely unmolested about the whole countryside.

The two wanderers finally tore themselves away from the sylvan paradise of Dos Bocas on March 17, 1894, and headed for the Bahamas. Three weeks later they separated at Tampa, King to see about the possibilities of phosphates in Florida, and Adams to mark time for another two months in Florida and at St. Helena with the Camerons.

Cuba remained in the background for the rest of that year until, in flight from the American Historical Association meeting, Adams drifted through Mexico and the West Indies, restless as Faust and sighing with Petrarch of "impious Babylon festering in decay." In mid-January of 1895 he briefly visited Havana again, with Chandler Hale. The situation in Cuba had greatly deteriorated. Sugar and tobacco had "gone to the dogs, along with wheat and cotton," and the country seemed "on the verge of social and political dissolution." He talked with his old Washington friend Count Maurice Sala, now French consul, and with the British and American consuls. They all feared a "general debacle, brigandage, insurrection," and he passed their warnings on to Hay.

The insurrection broke out a month after Adams left Havana, with the opening of the guerrilla campaign that was to sweep across the island before the summer was out. In Washington Adams hung back from involvement, being deep in his gold-bug calculations and his plans to reconnoiter Lombard Street and to tour the cathedrals of Normandy with the Lodges. The ever-sanguine King was already committed, however, and Byronically set out to join the insurgents and to follow the rebel General Máximo Gómez's masterly campaign across Santiago province. King's September *Forum* article, "Shall Cuba Be Free?" met Adams's eyes in London early in October 1895 on his return from Normandy. With passionate eloquence it reviewed Spanish misgovernment and atrocities in Cuba and concluded with the ringing demand that the United States "fling overboard Spain and give Cuba the aid she needs" by recognizing a state of belligerency.

The moment Adams disembarked at New York in mid-October, King enlisted him actively in the movement and, as Adams retold the matter to his fellow members of the Century Club, converted "a harmless and respectful servant of all established authority—particularly of despotisms—into the patient ally of the most uneasy and persistent conspirator your Club ever nourished in its bosom." A few weeks later he himself challenged Hay, "Come and revolute Cuba." President Cleveland's neutrality proclamation surrounded the private crusade to aid the Cubans with the apparatus of conspiracy, and greatly increased the cost and effort. American revenue cutters and naval units roamed the Florida coast to intercept the nondescript and leaky vessels carrying contraband supplies and men. As some steamers were impounded by the courts, Adams's friend Phillips found himself drawn into the movement, for his legal talents were needed to put the steamers back in service. Adams was now a principal conspirator, and Phillips frequently posted him on the progress of the libel actions.

The Cuban excitement was for a while eclipsed by the Venezuela boundary incident. President Cleveland had brusquely invoked the Monroe Doctrine against British claims in what was called a "war message" to Congress. Adams took time off from his studies of Byzantium for Brooks's *Law* to proselytize for militant isolationism: "I see no hope of safety except in severing the ties that connect [the United States] with Europe, and in fortifying ourselves as an independent centre." The budding imperialists among his intimates rejoiced in his quixotic support and quickly adopted King's idealistic program for Cuba with their own private modifications. In late January 1896 Senator Lodge was "still fussing over Venezuela and England," although Adams had been trying to persuade him that, as "he had won his stakes there," he should now go "for all his worth, for Cuba." As Adams interpreted the situation, England's gold standard policy had provoked the United States into successful defiance on the Venezuela question. Now it must be Spain's turn, and Cuba should be the instrument for driving Spain out of North America.

Adams's house was now a hotbed of Cuban intrigue. He pulled every wire within reach trying to line up congressional support, though "wholly behind the scenes," for he still had social relations with Dupuy de Lôme, the Spanish minister. He could point out that on the practical side freedom for Cuba had an economic attraction. Spanish capital would be replaced by American investments. "You had better sell all you have," Adams joked to Robert Cunliffe, "and buy with me in Cuba." In February, Navy Lieutenant Thomas Slidell Rodgers, a key figure in the Cuban propaganda campaign, effected a meeting of the cabal at the Cameron home in Lafayette Square. Senator Cameron was there, as well as Henry Adams and Henry Cabot Lodge. Rodgers brought in the "Cuban conspirators" to meet his influential friends. The visitors were two engaging and dashingly handsome young men in their early twenties, Gonzalo de Quesada and Horatio Rubens, who had set up an unofficial Cuban legation in the Hotel Raleigh.

The Senate Foreign Relations Committee had already reported out a joint resolution calling for recognition of Cuban belligerency. Pressed by his personal lobby to demand more, Senator Cameron offered a brief minority amendment proposing that the United States tender its "good offices" toward obtaining recognition of the "independence of Cuba." Lodge pleaded with his colleagues to adopt Cameron's amendment. Thanks to Adams's research, he cited damning parallels to Spain's conduct during Jefferson's administration. Not all the eloquence of Adams's allies in the Senate could bring the House to adopt the amended joint resolution, but the heavy senatorial majority in favor of recognition meant that the junta had won one diplomatic fight.

There was more to be done than lobby among senators. Money needed to be raised, the ship libels defended, the public informed. The young revolutionaries also needed briefing in internal finance. This last task Adams now assumed; he took Quesada in hand and sent him a recent copy of the *Economist* as a textbook. Quesada wrote appreciatively, "I have received some interesting papers from Madrid and should you not be busy tomorrow I will have the honor of bringing them to you. Allow me to thank you, in the name of Cuba, for your true work on our behalf."

Adams fretted at missing his regular West Indies trip, now made impossible by the fighting, but the chance to get off to Mexico again, this time with the Camerons, soon presented itself. He left Phillips behind to run his share of the Cuban show and headed for Mexico City, his presence in the senator's train taken for granted by all the members of their circle. On their social calls to President Porfirio Díaz of Mexico Adams played the congenial role of interpreter. "Cuba Libre" was still much on Adams's mind, but, as he admitted, he had "no chance for intrigue." Phillips continued to brief him on the drift of their affairs, occasionally falling into Aesopian language to protect identities or lightheartedly signing himself "Bandit Bill." The charade with the Spanish envoy, Dupuy de Lôme, came to an end. Learning of Adams's part in the Washington cabal, he let it be publicly known that he would not visit Adams's home again.

Adams paused for a brief week in Washington and gave a quick stir to the pot of intrigue before hastening off to Europe again on May 20, 1896, with Hay and his daughter Helen, but not before Brooks, just back from his researches in India, had unpacked his angry heart. Weakened by dysentery and on the verge of nervous exhaustion, Brooks did not share Henry's nihilistic joy at the march of events, and face to face he hammered home all the points he had made in his feverishly phrased letters. Thinking of the Venezuela affair, he "felt the cold hand of death upon him."

The "pure lark" in Europe which Henry had anticipated developed into a kind of intellectual circus through Holland, France, Italy, Germany, and England, the party increased from time to time by such vigorous recruits as young Adelbert Hay and Eugene Hale, Jr., Chandler Hale's brother. Adams's camera eye roved across a dizzying panorama of politics and manners. The patient's pulse beat faster, the fever rose, and he rubbed his hands in a kind of horrified glee. The young poet George Cabot (Bay) Lodge, son of the senator, then studying in Paris, guided him through the Paris bohemia and took him to see the reigning seductress of the Paris music halls, Yvette Guilbert, an artless-seeming serpent in yellow sheath and long black gloves lisping studied innuendos. It was all a manifestation of "la bêtise humaine," no matter how much he enjoyed it. In London Hay gave a dinner "to inveigle Bret Harte, Sargent and James into our company," a pleasant enough diversion, but the art salons made his brain reel "with the chaos." Venice was pretty and free of dust, but, said he, "Christ sits in a corner, much out of place, with a deeply discouraged countenance." Westward the epistolary journal to his intimates flowed in long bursts of aphorisms, oracular pronouncements, and new predictions to replace those improvised the year before, as he juggled the hegemony of Europe and Asia on the point of his pen. He darted a quizzical eye again at cathedrals and châteaux and schoolmastered his eager flock of real and honorary nieces down the halls of the Louvre. Everything his insatiable curiosity touched flickered with the St. Elmo's fire of his mockery. The new automobiles, like the new bloomer cycling costumes, were satanic inventions. "Decline is everywhere," went his dictum to Gaskell. "So spend it all." He flung his way through "a volume or two every day, trying to find some sort of clue where the devil I have got, in this astonishing chaos of a modern world."

He had the cynical pleasure of knowing that there were others who shared his intimation of universal immorality. The evangelical fervor of Max Nordau's *Degeneration,* when he picked it up in Washington the preceding summer, had made him think he was seeing himself, "but run mad and howling." He thought he must be "inventing a book in a dream." He passed the day fascinated by Edouard Drumont's "anti-semitic ravings" and the pseudo-Jacobin "antiquated democravings" of Henri Rochefort, the leading demagogue of disaffection. It did not matter greatly that the details of their indictments were wildly improbable; sufficient that they shrieked their sense of outrage against an intolerable world. Theirs was the truth of poetry, if not of fact, against "the burglar, the Jew, the Czar, the socialist, and above all, the total, irremediable, radical rottenness of our whole social, industrial, financial and political system." In the face of an incomprehensibly corrupt world, the frustrated moralist could take refuge only in a self-immolating hysteria.

Adams bent over his desk in one hotel after another drawing out to incredible length the exhaustless filament of his thought, thinking half the time, he confessed to Elizabeth, of her and Martha. Waves of neurotic revulsion swept him as he gorged himself on the filth of the anti-Semitic press. "The Jew has got into the soul. I see him—or her—now everywhere, and wherever he—or she—goes, there must remain a taint in the blood forever." Obsessed, fanatical, he poured out on paper the Gothic revenges of his uncontrolled reveries. "In all my reading in the press, in current literature and in religious discussions, I have come across no single voice that questions the approaching overthrow of the present system of society." Like "Sister Anne" in the fable of Blue Beard, he watched from the housetop for "the dust of the coming avenger," and curled up "with a delightful shiver of dread and excitement" when he thought "of the next great convulsion." Free silver was of no use to him unless it would hasten the Last Judgment. If free silver would simply prolong the debacle he "would rather keep the country on its cross of gold. Then, at least, we shall have the Passion, the Agony, the Bloody Sweat and the Resurrection."

Brooks had sent his antiphonal cry of despair. "I think we have reached the end of the republic here." He had gone to the Democratic convention in the summer of 1896 to work for a more conservative slate, hoping to head off the Populist revolt. One politico, John McLean, Adams told Hay, proposed Brooks himself as a candidate for the Vice-Presidency, but "he was shelved as a conservative." Then, into the wild and discordant wrangling William Jennings Bryan flung his evangelical challenge: "You shall not crucify mankind on a cross of gold." The party had found its John the Baptist, and Brooks accepted the miracle. Henry, largely out of a desire to please his brother, came out at first for Bryan, and at Brooks's urging contributed to the campaign fund. After all, he argued to Phillips, "Bryan is American conservatism itself, as every movement must be that rests on small landowners." As the election bore down on them, however, Henry

instinctively recoiled from the Nebraska demagogue. It would be easier to accept William McKinley as the lesser evil or—in his anarchist
logic—because McKinley was the greater evil and would hurry the
purification rites of revolution.

Phillips's Cuban dispatches tracked Adams across Europe. Their
allies, Senators Sherman, Lodge, and Gray, members of the Senate
Foreign Relations Committee, had secretly called on "His Sufficiency" Cleveland to press for action. Adams was right in his belief,
Phillips admitted, that "only some great outrage on American citizens" would force the President's hand. Meanwhile, he had managed
to persuade Lodge to put a Cuban independence plank in the Republican platform. His reports gave some encouragement, but away from
Lafayette Square Adams saw another side of the conflict. Diplomatic
informants in Europe revealed to him Spain's desperate economic
plight, and his heart bled "for the Spaniards whom I like more than
any other people in Europe." Perhaps the "present chaos and ruin" in
Cuba was better than "our exploiting it"; it might unaided bring
down the whole revolting house of cards in Europe, if "the monumental prize hog remains in the White House." But this was only
wishful thinking; more practically, he vowed to "take up the fight
again as soon as Congress meets."

What especially worried Adams was the insidious talk of independence at a price, a liberated Cuba to assume some four hundred millions of the Spanish external debt currently charged against the island. Such a scheme would mean "only one link more in our
servitude." His chief desire in the Cuban matter, he said, was "to
strike at the Paris Jews and their whole political machine." Better permanent anarchy than such a compromise. His old classmate Fitzhugh
Lee, former governor of Virginia, went to Havana as consul general
and gave comfort to the cabal with "a tremendously strong Cuban
report to the State Department." Phillips also cheered Adams with
news that the arms shipments were growing and that six expeditions
had successfully landed.

Back in his Washington study on October 5, 1896, Adams once
again turned to the Cuban question to try his practiced hand on the
lever of power. Quesada came in for "a full and deep Cuba discussion." Something needed to be done, and done quickly. The Senate
Foreign Relations Committee was the natural instrument, for there
Adams's opinion carried authority. Old Senator John Sherman, Mrs.

Cameron's uncle, was chairman, Don Cameron and Lodge were members, and the rest were known to be sympathetic. With Cameron's approval Adams set to work to write the report of the committee. Phillips, as the legal expert, hunted down the precedents in international law while Adams formulated the line of argument and garbed it in an appropriate style. King might try in the press to inflame public passion, but here the counsel of reason must prevail. Congress had only to determine the question of fact whether the conditions justifying intervention had been met. The military successes of the insurgents and their establishment of a de facto government supplied the answer.

When the report came to the committee over Cameron's name, it was unanimously adopted. Pleased but nervous at his success, Adams meditated flight "until once more forgotten" when he heard that it was being whispered in Boston that he was at the bottom of "all the Cuban mischief." The whisper had in fact been picked up by the press, as Henry's brother Charles told Lodge. Horace White expressed puzzlement in the *Nation:* "It is rather surprising that the task of embroiling this country in a war for 'Cuba Libre' should have fallen to the lot of Don Cameron." The Cuban historian Herminio Portell Vilá subsequently called the report "un documento de extraordinaria fuerzá logica," one which placed the Cuban revolution among the great movements of political redemption. He said that the actual author, Henry Adams, was "el más illustre norteamericano de la época." The report failed of its immediate object, but it did lay the juridical foundation for war with Spain.

Adams stayed on in Washington for several weeks expecting to see an early end to the Cuban excitement. With Theodore Roosevelt appointed as the new Assistant Secretary of the Navy, less interference with the flow of arms could be expected, and "Pirate" Phillips would have a freer hand. Suddenly, however, the Cuban imbroglio was pushed aside by a compelling new interest. McKinley appointed Hay ambassador to England and opened a breathtaking vista for Adams as Hay's alter ego.

Adams booked passage with the new ambassador and sailed for London to help his friend enjoy the fruits of their long collaboration in Lafayette Square. Though he could not take any credit for the appointment, he could take credit for having helped train his friend for the commanding role he was about to play in London and Washing-

ton. Their arrival at Southhampton on April 21, 1897, had its humorous aspects, as Hay described it to Lodge. There had been "an
address of welcome and flapdoodle" by the mayor of the city, from
all of which the reticent Adams had fled in terror "to the innermost
recesses of the ship—some authorities say to the coal bunkers."

Adams now addressed himself to the more pressing affairs of Hay.
Hay carried with him a special set of instructions to sound out British
government and financial leaders on the feasibility of calling a conference for the remonetization of silver. Moreton Frewen, the "Argen-
tomaniac," as Hay called him, proposed a dinner conference of British currency experts. Adams begged off: "I fear your anarchists in
dinner-dress . . . There are too many sheep in wolves' clothing. I
know only one true, thorough-going British anarchist whom I can
trust, and with whom I care to associate. He is the Jew of Lombard
Street."

Adams got together his "bimetallic and liberal friends" at a luncheon to "make Hay's acquaintance," and he also renewed relations
with Joseph Chamberlain, now Colonial Secretary, and Arthur Balfour, leader of the Commons. All confirmed what was now an old
story. Bimetallism of any sort was dead so long as England was enjoying prosperity. Adams prepared an analysis of the situation for Hay's
guidance in making his report to Secretary of State John Sherman
concerning the agenda for the commission coming to England. He
cogently pointed out that in the present temper of the government a
demand for the free coinage of silver would be "abruptly declined."
Adams could not forbear pressing his favorite measure, the establishment in the United States of some kind of central banking authority,
the nearly forgotten dream of Albert Gallatin. "In no European country is the gold reserve at the mercy of a foreign demand."

Hay and the commissioners met at the British Foreign Office on
July 15. Like its predecessors, the mission accomplished nothing.
Adams felt that there was now no going back because England's commitment to the gold standard made total wreck inevitable. Nothing
lay ahead for the great powers but "the next stage of centralisation,
which can only be the centralisation of socialism; that is, the assumption by government of those great functions which have for twenty
years past steadily drifted into government hands. We must be eco-
nomically Russianized." As he looked forward to the campaign of
1900 he gloomily predicted that Mark Hanna, the Republican king-

maker, "will drive us to Bryan—and then! Much as I loathe the ré-
gime of Manchester and Lombard Street in the nineteenth century, I
am glad to think I shall be dead before I am ruled by the Trade Unions
of the twentieth."

With Hay's displacing of the anglophile Thomas Bayard in the London embassy, Adams could retreat to the Continent secure in the
knowledge that a pro-American policy, whether on Venezuela or the
Bering fisheries, would be advanced. His friends Lodge and Roosevelt
could be counted on to continue the pressure for intervention in
Cuba. But a heavy personal blow fell early in May 1897 that cut him
off from the deepening intrigue in Washington. His righthand man in
the Cuban affair and financial adviser, William Phillips, was drowned
in a sailing accident. Lieutenant Rodgers, another of Adams's ties to
the junta, was suddenly ordered to sail with the fleet to Hawaii, for
in the midst of the negotiations for annexation—negotiations in
which Adams's friend and Hawaiian host Alfred S. Hartwell played
an important role—the Japanese sent a warship to the islands. Rodgers had to abandon their joint projects for helping to "revolute"
Cuba.

So far as practical politics and diplomacy went, behind
the scenes or otherwise, Adams for a while was whirled out to the
periphery of public affairs, still growling his comments but deliberately closing his eyes and ears for the summer "to all the subjects
which had interested me so much." As a "modern Rasselas" he had
run away from ambassadors and bimetallists. Phillips's death, he
wrote, "has shut the door to all view of what is happening, either in
Cuba or in the State Department, and I guess I am the better for it.
Yet I could dimly wish that other doors might open, as the old ones
shut."

Elizabeth Cameron rescued him from further ennui by placing her
ailing self and her daughter, Martha, in his charge, and they soon
crossed to Paris to bask in the May sunshine. For several weeks he
energetically hunted villas, having the job of settling his "dearest invalid" and the five Hooper nieces, who were once again his special
care—as he was theirs. By mid-July 1897 he and the five girls had
established themselves for the summer in an ancient house in the fashionable suburb of Saint-Germain-en-Laye, "a queer old place" called

the Pavillon d'Angoulême, with "a distant outlook towards Marly and the bend of the Seine." A few squares away Elizabeth and her daughter formed the other center of their little American colony. Health slowly returned to the restless doña, allowing her to resume the management of her courtier. "What can a man do without a woman!" he would say to her in mock despair. "I am as helpless and imbecile as a baby."

Adams's literary plans were still amorphous. He moved from the study of Byzantium to an even more intense study of the *chansons de geste,* and he doggedly battled with prepositions and subjunctives as he tried his hand at translating Old French epics. In December 1897 he was still in Paris studying and writing. Vaguely, a new work, *Mont Saint Michel and Chartres,* was beginning to take shape in his mind. He strove with all his mind to recapture the vital emotions of the dedicated Christian warriors Charlemagne and Roland, and to relate their lives to the historical problems haunting him and Brooks. Questing for the touchstones of feeling, he summoned up the "Intimations Ode" and the flood of associations which were to mark the opening pages of the *Chartres.*

The Dreyfus Affair provided the chief excitement of the winter of 1897–98. The case had been reopened after tremendous public agitation. Horrified at the miscarriage of justice, Zola published his sensational *J'accuse* in a front-page letter to *Aurore* which "kicked the boiler over," in Adams's words, and brought into the open the desperate political and religious issues which it symbolized. Committed to the theory that the military character was more noble than the commercial, Henry, like Brooks, sided with the army and the church. Such doubts as they had about the matter were resolved by Aristarchi Bey, a onetime favorite of the Five of Hearts. The former Turkish diplomat was eking out an adventurer's existence in exile in Paris as a journalist linked with the French military and the Roman Catholic anti-Semites. "I believe Aristarchi to be right," Adams affirmed to Elizabeth. "The current of opinion is running tremendously strong, now that the whole extent of the Jew scandal is realised . . . Of course all the English and the Americans are with the Jews, which makes it worse."

The long periods of secluded quiet that he managed to find in Paris would be disturbed from time to time by waves of Americans, chiefly nieces and wives of friends. He bobbed about like a cork in his role of cicerone amidst the sights of Paris. Brooks came over at the close of 1897 to get out a French edition of *The Law of Civilization and Decay* which Henry had urged upon him. He had resolved on a full revision in which he could develop Henry's provocative suggestions for reworking the first and last chapters and expanding the section on Byzantium. The two brothers resumed their inquest over Western civilization. Though Brooks vehemently differed with Henry, he needed to hammer out his ideas on the anvil of his elder brother's contradictions. The process was invariably exhausting, for Brooks gave no quarter either to his hearer or to an idea. Henry reported that he had "to go over with him the whole field of the world's doing and all the changes that would affect the ideas we had reached when we last met." The result was "of course a moment of hopeless imbecility."

The ordeal was enough to bring on another fit of depression, and Henry thought longingly of the refuge waiting for him beneath Saint-Gaudens's statue in Rock Creek cemetery. "When one has eaten one's dinner, one is bored at having to sit at the table," he sadly wrote to one of the nieces in December 1897. Filled with thoughts of his dead wife, he mused, "Do you know that I am sixty in six weeks and that I was only forty-seven when I finished my dinner?"

The Hays, after ten months of social, if not diplomatic, successes in London, rescued Adams from these melancholy reflections by taking him off to Egypt during Hay's official leave. He went gladly. Unlike Brooks, he said, he did not have a hobby to ride, and he envied Brooks his "corvée," getting out the French version of his book.

The venture up the Nile had its emotional risks for him, for it was his first return since his wedding journey in 1872 when Clover had had a frightening nervous seizure. Knowing his own morbid emotionalism, he had tried to steel himself against the inevitable associations. Boarding the steam dahabeah brought the past back with a sudden rush. Before he could catch himself, he said, he was unconsciously wringing his hands, and "the tears rolled down in the old way." The hysterical attack wore off, and after a few hours he emerged from the crisis and resumed his archaeologizing and watercolor sketching.

As always, Hay found Adams's dry and playful witticisms a constant pleasure, though the epigrams rarely survived transplantation to the written page. One subject, however, lay beyond satire—Dreyfus—and they all carefully skirted it in Adams's presence. His Jew-baiting got to such a point, Hay remarked, that "he now believes the earthquake at Krakatoa was the work of Zola and when he saw Vesuvius reddening the midnight air he searched the horizon to find a Jew stoking the fire."

One day in the midst of the Nile tour, at Aswan, Adams and Hay received the news that the *Maine* had been blown up in Havana harbor. After the first startled shock, Adams felt a sense of relief, for now there was no longer "any chance of preventing a smash. Now Spain must bust"; the necessary "outrage" had finally taken place, and he and his Cuban friends needed only stand aside. The Hays returned to London, and Adams went on to Athens, where he could view the situation with detached satisfaction. "Poor dear old McKinley stands like Olympian Zeus with his thunder-bolt ready." At last the country was taking its stand on his Cuban report. Elizabeth had also played her part, he reminded her. "After all, it was you and I who did all the real fighting against the odds when Olney went back on himself and us." They had foreseen it all for three years past and could now afford to be cool. War was, after all, "a simple old conservative business." Congress took the final plunge, a joint resolution recognizing the independence of Cuba and directing the President to use force if necessary to secure it.

As Adams sat on the platform of the Pnyx opposite the Acropolis and looked out across the Saronic Gulf, his mind wandered "terribly fast between Salamis, where Xerxes is before my eyes, and Key West where our ships are awaiting orders." The moment was a fresh "turning point in history," fixing "the lines of a new concentration." In this juxtaposition of historical perspectives Athens and Greece suddenly diminished in importance. "What a droll little amusing fraud of imagination it was, and how it has imposed its own valuation of itself on all respectable society down to this day! Fifty years of fortunate bloom at a lucky moment,—a sudden flood of wealth from a rich silver-mine, the Rand of that day,—was all that really dazzles us; a sort of unnatural, forced flower, never strong, never restful, and always half-conscious of its own superficiality." Scrambling about Greece with his friend William Rockhill, then in charge of the American legation, he found his singular impression deepening. "After seeing Egypt and Syria, Italy and Japan, Greece shrinks; and after living in French Gothic and Michael Angelo Renaissance, Greek art has less to say to the simple-minded Christian . . . Peace to the ashes of poor Palgrave! Athens leaves me cool."

Adams continued his pilgrimage through history to Constantinople, the "gloomiest spot on earth . . . only another, and perhaps the worst, face of the rotten building." From there he swung northward through the Balkans, inspecting "the President's representatives," with one ear cocked toward the war which McKinley had proclaimed on April 26. The garbled reports of Commodore Dewey's staggering success at Cavite tantalized him, but two things were clear: the Spanish fleet had been destroyed, and Manila had fallen. A wave of intoxication swept him such as he had not felt since the great victories of the Civil War. Surely, McKinley was a man of destiny. "At this distance I see none of his tricks—real or assumed," he wrote Hay from Belgrade. "I see only the steady development of a fixed intent."

In the anxious intervals between dispatches, he scrutinized economics. Hungary with its state monopolies pointed the way to the future. Its lesson, he lectured Brooks, was that in the next campaign he "must lift off from silver, and lift in to Socialism . . . Progress is economy! Socialism is merely a new application of Economy, which must go on until Competition puts an end to further Economics, or the whole world becomes one Socialistic Society and rots out . . . One need not love Socialism in order to point out the logical necessity for Society to march that way; and the wisdom of doing it intelligently."

When he reached Vienna the magnitude of the American victory dazzled him. He had hardly expected so early a realization of his South Seas dream of an American empire. "We are already an Asiatic power," he exclaimed to Elizabeth. "You and I hardly expected as much when we ran the December Report of '96." Their "political propaganda" had succeeded far beyond their hope. Like Brooks and Roosevelt and Lodge, he too felt the glow of patriotic fervor. The war was "a God-send to all the young men in America. Even the Bostonians have at last a chance to show that they have emotions." The gold-bugs had not killed the martial spirit. However, he advised Hay to get Austria to initiate a settlement which might save the Spanish dynasty and preserve diplomatic stability.

On the main points Adam and Hay saw eye to eye. Adams's plan called for independence for Cuba, autonomy for Puerto Rico, and the retention of a coaling station in the Philippines, "a settlement that abandons the idea of conquest." Hay, thinking along the same lines, remarked that his own "little project . . . was yours almost verbatim," but he was gloomy about the chances of a moderate scheme in the

Senate. "The man who makes the Treaty of Peace with Spain will be lucky if he escapes lynching." In their calculations both men reckoned without the mystical imperatives of Manifest Destiny.

By the end of June 1898 Adams was settling down to an idyllic summer in England, enjoying "a sort of Nirvana" with the Camerons at Surrenden Dering in Kent in "a house about the size of Versailles." Elizabeth, recently recovered from a nervous breakdown, serenely held court as of old. Adams kept his rooms in Clarges Street so as to be able to run up to London frequently about books and business. Since peace talk was already in the air, he resolved to stay out of Hay's way for fear of annoying him. However, when Hay came on to Surrenden Dering to make it his summer embassy, Adams could not help but honor silence as usual in the unremitting breach of it.

On July 4 the cables brought word of the annihilation of the Spanish fleet off Santiago. The victory was no more than the Q.E.D. of a mathematical demonstration to Adams, and he wasted no energy in jubilation. He quickly cautioned Brooks in Paris that "the true center of interest is now Madrid," going on from that postulate to another sweeping review of global politics. "So we can foresee a new centralisation, of which Russia is one pole, and we the other, with England between. The Anglo-American alliance is almost inevitable." Where the American imperial interest was concerned, Henry's antipathies against England would have to give way before greater antipathies elsewhere.

Of a sudden, Americans had to make up their minds as to what they were as a people and where they were going. Three days after Santiago Bay the editor of *Scribner's Magazine* begged Adams, as a "historian and publicist" whose authority was known to rest on "a larger study of history and public affairs," to contribute an article on "this whole question of 'isolation,' or an increased international responsibility, or an 'imperial policy'" and so perform "a real public service of a high order." Adams declined, as he was already too deep in the confidence of Hay to risk betraying secrets.

Developments came on with a rush such as to bewilder the Lafayette Square colony at Surrenden Dering. Spain sued for peace on July 22. On August 13, two days before the armistice protocol was signed, Henry White, the secretary of the embassy, brought in an urgent cable from McKinley tendering Hay the office of Secretary of State. The moment had all the ingredients to satisfy Adams's sense of the dramatic as the circle of intimate friends looked at each other with well-bred surmise. The sudden decision was hard to make for the valetudinarian Hay. He and Adams had often canvassed the disheartening frustrations that were the normal lot of the Secretary of State. Torn by indecision and afflicted with prostate trouble, he carefully drafted two replies: the first declined the offer—"my health will not permit it"—and the second reluctantly committed him in spite of an "indisposition, not serious but painful." The second, of necessity, went to McKinley.

Surrenden Dering was not easy to give up. Hay had waggishly written Lodge, "Don [Cameron] is the finest type of old Tory baronet you ever saw. His wife makes a lovely chatelaine, and Oom Hendrik [Adams] has assumed the congenial function of cellarer and chaplain. Mr. and Mrs. Brooks Adams are there also, and shed sweetness and light over the landscape." Something of the old intimacy of the Five of Hearts had graced the cheerful board, and Hay and Adams courted the queenly chatelaine with outrageous compliments. For Adams the time was big with opportunity. Everyone assumed that he might have the London embassy if he wanted it. Hay indeed made some sort of overture before he left. Wistfully Adams wrote to Charles Milnes Gaskell, "All my life I have lived in the closest possible personal relations with men in high office. Hay is the first one of them who has ever expressed a wish to have me for an associate in his responsibilities. Evidently something is wrong with Hay—or with me." Hay tore himself away on September 8, and Adams went up to visit Sir John Clark at Tillypronie. He sailed for America on November 5, 1898, leaving the Camerons established for the winter in the avenue du Bois de Boulogne.

When he reached 1603 H Street, Adams bumped into Hay at his "very doorstep." During the hour's talk that followed, Hay's private secretary, Spencer Eddy, dropped in and, as Adams wrote, "rather surprised me by saying that for a time they had actually some idea they might make something of me." But that corner, too, had been turned, and there was nothing left for him to do but profess his "vast relief" that the London post had been assigned to an unimpeachably loyal New York Republican and prominent corporation lawyer, Joseph H. Choate. Adams had foreseen his friend's dilemma. "Poor Hay wants help terribly," he told Gaskell, "and if he called on me I should no doubt be obliged to do whatever he wished, but he will never be given that amount of liberty." In Washington he confirmed the sorry truth that Hay's office was "pawned in advance, both in patronage and politics . . . He was not even allowed to appoint an Assistant Secretary" nor to bring into the diplomatic service "even the instruments he has at hand—meaning Rockhill and me." Adams convinced himself that he was glad of it. To refuse to help Hay "would be most disagreeable"; "but to accept office would be misery." That he had no vulgar ambition, no craving for public office like Whitelaw Reid, whose importunities embarrassed Hay, may have been true enough, but his subtler aspirations had their own gemlike intensity. Justice Holmes, who became one of his intimates, sharing his daily walks as Hay had done, once remarked to Owen Wister: "If the country had put him on a pedestal, I think Henry Adams with his gifts could have rendered distinguished public service." Wister asked, "What was the matter with Henry Adams?" Holmes replied, "He wanted it handed to him on a silver platter."

Adams's situation now as closest friend and next-door neighbor of the Secretary of State had an enormous piquancy, as he played to the hilt his role of "Hay's shadow." The two friends fell into the habit of taking a walk at four o'clock each day "to the end of 16th Street," reviewing the day's work and, as Hay put it, "discoursing of the finances of the world, and the insolent prosperity of the United States." They made "almost a common household," Adams reported to Elizabeth, with the Hays "shifting forward and back as the state-exigencies require." On the grand lines of foreign policy they had little difference of opinion. In their view the result of the American victory was that all Europe was "already arrayed with Spanish America against the British American combination." Germany was "the kerosene can" and "all Central and South America the fuel." Adams granted the justice of the fears of the anti-imperialists, but saw no way of stopping the locomotive of history. "One can't grow young again by merely refusing to walk," he continued. "The American calf is now too old to get much nourishment from sucking the dry teats of the British cow."

One result of his new eminence as Hay's confidant was that he was now sought out by the highest diplomatic figures, and his breakfast table became one of the important nerve centers of the diplomatic corps. In all Adams's bustling behind the scenes there was often, however, a curious joyless gusto. He seemed under an inner compulsion to remind himself constantly that he ought not to be enjoying himself. Always when he got ready to don his "moral sackcloth" for the anniversary of Clover's death ("my low water mark of life"), dark November moods swept over him, and his bitterly sardonic "double" took command. "It's a queer sensation," he confided to Brooks, "this secret belief that one stands on the brink of the world's great catastrophe. For it means the fall of Western Europe, as it fell in the fourth century. It recurs to me every November, and culminates every December. I have to get over it as I can, and hide, for fear of being sent to an asylum." His last slim chance to make a public career had passed. He was only sixty, and yet he was unusable. He went through the introspective ritual of burying the past, clearing his desk as he had done before going to the South Seas, "destroying all the papers, books, and other rubbish that I can lay my hands on," and "weighing and cataloguing Greek coins" to add to the collection he had inherited from his father. He wished, he said, that he could reconcile his soul to "Mammon . . . But I am homesick for Surrenden."

Such was Adams's life "behind the veil," but on the surface he never played the role of uncle more winningly. Squads of pretty young nieces petted him as the reigning sage of Lafayette Square. The malady, highly catching, as Hay's secretary said, was "avunculitis." Adams tinkered with further corrections of the *History* for reprintings, pleased to find it read so well on coming back to it. When he dined alone he would luxuriate in a volume of the memoirs of the duc de Saint-Simon and the invariable pint of champagne. "I listened to his account of the death of Mme de Montespan in 1707," he sentimentalized to Elizabeth; "so good,—so good—that I cried to think that such writing can't now be written and wouldn't be read." To show that as the Saint-Simon of Lafayette Square he was not deficient in royal anecdote, he passed on to her the latest morsel on the censorious wife of the President. " 'I don't understand these wives,' quavered poor Mrs McKinley, 'who put their husbands to bed, and then go out to dinners. When I put Mr McKinley to bed, I go to bed with him.' "

The "Cuban pepperpot" began to simmer again, now that the peace negotiations were concluded, and Adams resumed his role as chef, but unfortunately the ingredients now included the Philippines, and their disposition became the first order of business. The Hawaiian question had already been skillfully liquidated by the joint resolution of July 7, 1898, which bypassed the treaty-making machinery. Hay and Adams's modest scheme for retaining a coaling station in the Philippines, a basically anti-imperialist position, got short shrift. McKinley, with Lodge and Joseph Foraker and the Senate imperialists pressing him hard, now insisted on the whole archipelago. Hay felt obliged to acquiesce in the instructions.

Exhilarated by his success with the Philippines, Senator Lodge became an increasing trial to Secretary Hay—and to Adams—as he strove for a commanding role in the making of foreign policy and the dispensing of patronage. Adams had to use all his "professorial" authority to protect the weary and ailing Hay from Lodge's insistent demands for consulates and other favors, and he once burst out, "Does patriotism pay me to act as a buffer-state?"

Behind the scenes there soon began a desperate struggle to moderate the terms of the treaty in favor of the Philippine insurgents, a struggle into which Adams was drawn through his ties with Quesada and Rubens. A Filipino commission headed by Felipe Agoncillo came to Washington to protest ratification of the treaty. The Cuban leaders, worried about the status of Cuban independence and the liberated Puerto Ricans, made common cause with them. During the height of the debate in the Senate Rubens, acting as intermediary, came almost every afternoon to Adams's home to carry on "extra-official conversations" with Hay. At one conference Hay asked Rubens about a Puerto Rican agent who was treating with McKinley. Rubens intimated the man was a rascal. Adams dryly spoke up. "That is not the question. The question is, whether he is our rascal or the other fellow's rascal." Rubens admitted, "He is the other fellow's rascal." Whereupon Adams turned to Hay, "Then he is a damned rascal and should be dealt with accordingly."

The Filipino insurrectionists, filled with large visions of independence, had established the Visayan Republic. Through Rubens Adams sounded Agoncillo, hoping to work out a friendly arrangement, but Agoncillo alternately threatened and wheedled, insisting on possession of Manila. At this juncture a shooting affray at the sentry lines set fire to the tinderbox. The bloody fiasco that followed did not weigh heavily upon Adams—after all, the Filipinos were "the usual worthless Malay type"—but the attendant controversy between the War Department and the Senate did alarm him. The scandals about spoiled food had already broken, and General Sherman Miles and

Secretary of War Russell Alger had encouraged the newspapers to play up the matter. After talking with General Leonard Wood, Adams leaped to the conclusion that the charges could not be sustained and that Miles, Mrs. Cameron's brother-in-law, would be discredited. Adams was furious with him for the blunders and intrigues, for he had counted on Miles to back his Cuban friends in their bid for control of the new Cuban government. An anticlimactic chaos descended. Instead of independence Cuba received an American military government.

Adams fretfully contemplated his global chessboard and poured out his misgivings. "As for Cuba, we have taken a foolish responsibility and a discredited rôle, and there again the anxiety is great." The discovery of gold in the Klondike revived the Alaska-Canada boundary question so that Canada was "as vexatious though not so dangerous." Germany was "always stirring up one's senile passions by her stupid and apparently blundering interference." For all that, he had good reason to crow a little. The three great colonial powers, England, France, and Spain, had virtually been driven out of the continent and made to submit to the Monroe Doctrine, the chief legacy of his family to American foreign policy. Without undue vanity he could say that he had "won all my stakes."

Through the winter Quesada and Rubens continued to come in almost daily to consult with him about his efforts to get them into the new Cuban administration, and they made his house "more than ever a Cuban headquarters." The Secretary of War seemed sympathetic, but to Adams's annoyance he always managed to upset "tomorrow what he had we agreed upon yesterday." If not for that, went his résumé to Mrs. Cameron, "I should feel that for once I had been allowed to have absolutely my own way in the government on a policy so huge as that about Cuba since 1894, which you and I fought out to a finish." As a sop McKinley finally offered Quesada the direction of the Cuban census. Plainly the revolution was over and "the revolutionists must sell out." As a political realist Adams advised his friend to take the post. "It would give him all the wires and lead him up to control."

On balance Adams had earned the gratitude of his Cuban friends. If his grand strategy and theirs had misfired, if they failed to marshal Central and South American support for Cuban independence, at least the island had been rescued from the fiery furnace of Spanish misrule. Anxieties remained—the hostility and suspicion of the South American republics and the Philippine troubles—but these would now be material for historical calculus and not for personal intervention. Thus ended a five-year experiment in statecraft. With Clarence King he had helped make history, for King too, as Adams said, had won *his* stakes in Cuba.

With the fading out of the Cuban question into matters of patronage and administration, Adams turned with more exclusive concentration to larger questions. Seen at a sufficient distance, Cuba was only a detail in the great political and economic movement of Europe. Now that Spain was pulled down, there was the danger of the sympathetic collapse of France, where the European disease of decadence and disintegration seemed most virulent. As a doctor of calamity Adams let his mind swing toward that focus. The Treaty of Paris symbolized the immense economic revolution that had taken place. With the aid of the statistics which Ford had continued to supply him and materials in the *Economist* and the *Statist,* Adams worked hard to revise his charts of relations. The European powers continued to struggle over the division of spoils in Africa and Asia. Germany, for example, had seized Shantung; Russia took Port Arthur; and England, though approving the Open Door policy in principle, made an agreement with Russia for mutual recognition of respective spheres of influence in China. So far as he could see, the entente seemed to "settle China and close the Open Door" even before McKinley had fairly let go of the knob.

Momentous as these events were, they were overshadowed by "the greatest revolution of all . . . that astounding economic upheaval which has turned America into the great financial and industrial center of the world, from being till now a mere colonial feeder of Europe." This new development surprised him by coming far more rapidly than his figures had indicated. America must now replace England both as banker of the world and as military policeman. The Klondike gold had given an unexpected turn to the economic screw; like the California gold of 1849, it forecast a rise in general price levels. "There are the two future centres of power," Adams reminded Worthington Ford, "and, of the two, America must get there first. Some day, perhaps a century hence, Russia may swallow even her; but for my life-time I think I'm safe." To Brooks he offered more time. "We have two generations to swing in . . . Meanwhile we've got it all our own way."

With such a hypothesis formulated, there was now the need of examining the forces at first hand. Russia was the key to the equation.
It had always lurked in the background of Adams's thought ever
since, as a young man, he had read Tocqueville's prediction that
though the starting points of Russia and America were different and
their courses not the same, "yet each of them seems to be marked out
by the will of Heaven to sway the destinies of half the globe." He had
skirted the edge of the mystery in the recollections of his grandfather
and his father, had heard the incessant warnings of Spring Rice in the
British embassy in Berlin, and had canvassed the subject over and
over with Brooks. Adams wanted "much to visit Russia." Scheme
after scheme had fallen through. He had missed his "Marco Polo"
expedition to China. Missed also was a view of the "Asian mystery"
from India, as a guest of Lord Curzon, where he might have had a
"front seat on the verge of the abyss into which all governments"
were about to plunge.

The approach of the spring of 1899 found Adams hysterically impatient to get away. The winter's inactivity and incessant dinner parties had made him "a mere ball of flesh, a round puffy protuberant
mass," hardly fit for the saddle. "I want to go—go—go—anywhere—to the devil—Sicily—Russia—Siberia—China—only keep
going." This was for Elizabeth's eyes. He kept vigil over his moods
with an almost hypnotized fascination. At moments he "shivered," as
he said, "on the verge of—I won't say melancholia, but chronic
depression." John La Farge would occasionally come in, seedy in
health and nerve, to compare notes with him, and the two men traded
symptoms and "prattled about art and artists." Life was no nearer
Nirvana than under the sacred bo tree, and the more urbane his out-
ward guise, the more he secretly writhed like one of Hawthorne's
characters haunted by an inexpiable guilt. Another year of the Mc-
Kinley administration was ending, but nothing really had been accomplished, he grumbled. There had not been "a single gleam of success in any branch." Hay "had accomplished nothing." All that could
be said was that the country was "fabulously prosperous" and he was
himself "comfortably well off."

Thrashing about restlessly in his web of inner despair, Adams had
a Kafka-like vision of himself, "a little of the sense of being a sort of
ugly, bloated, purplish-blue, and highly venomous, hairy tarantula
which catches and devours presidents, senators, diplomates, congressmen and cabinet-officers, and knows the flavor of every genera-

tion and every country in the civilised world." Hay was "caught in
the trap, and, to my infinite regret, I have to make a meal of him as
of the rest." With such ample nutriment, like a spider he spun the
gossamer of his web farther and farther out to the periphery of his
hypersensitive consciousness. But if he trapped Presidents, he also felt
the terrible ennui of being trapped himself. Once again he was rescued from his indecisions by a woman. Anna Cabot Lodge invited
him to accompany the Lodge party to Europe to make a tour of Italy.
He seized eagerly upon the straw. At the very least there would be a
chance to warm himself, if only briefly, at Elizabeth's hearth in the
avenue du Bois de Boulogne. A journey to Russia and Siberia could
be improvised afterwards from Paris or London. Hay's last word to
him before he took flight to Europe again wore the color of his dark
mood. "If we should not meet again I want to say how deeply I am
in your debt for many things." On March 23, 1899, St. Ambrose light
dropped astern and Adams stood at the rail again, staring at the horizon which bounded his sea of troubles.

21

New England Gothic

T HE VOYAGE to Italy in 1899, outwardly uneventful like
the many which had preceded it, had the most unexpected
consequences, for it swept him ashore in the twelfth century, there to
serve out a long enchantment to the Virgin. William Rockhill had
been the first to drop out of his visionary travel plans, having been
obliged to give up the mysteries of Tibet for those of Washington.
Russia, China, and India beckoned for a few weeks longer. Brooks's
intervention unwittingly concluded the matter. Having just brought
out the French translation of the *Law*, Brooks too was eager to study
the calculus of Russia and China on the ground and begged Henry to
accompany him. The prospect of uninterrupted debate with his contentious brother was more of an ordeal than Henry could willingly
contemplate. He explained to Brooks that "on looking more carefully
into the matter, after coming over, I decided that, in every point of
view, it was wiser to wait." His change of plan had a deeper reason as
well, one which may be inferred from the series of provocative essay-
letters which he dispatched to Brooks and to the rest of his disciples
as he swung down through Italy and Sicily with the Lodges and Winthrop Chanler. In his role of philosopher-guide, he experienced
among the relics of past civilizations a coalescing of many divergent
lines of thought and feeling; in the process of teaching he taught himself, and he began to feel the desire to attempt his own synthesis.

He read an exquisitely allusive lesson to Elizabeth Cameron from
Agrigento in Sicily, where he had picked up another stitch as his
"time-machine" ran off the last of his Greek cities. For nearly forty
years, since he had interviewed Garibaldi at Palermo for his *Boston
Daily Courier* letters, he had been putting off a pilgrimage to this
westernmost extension of antique Greek civilization. The landscape

struck him as "Athens with improvements . . . altogether the most beautiful Greek ruin I know."

Sicily seemed more than the perfection of Greece. It was also the point of junction between Byzantium and the West, the place where Norman Gothic architecture had its birth. The Normans had driven out the Saracens and opened up the most brilliant period in the history of the island. Norman architecture soared heavenward when their builders united the freedom of the pointed arch of the Arab world with the rich symbolism of the East. When Adams gazed at last upon the splendor of the church at Monreale, with its exotic union of Italian basilica and Byzantine choir and the treasures of dazzling mosaics surpassing even those of Ravenna, he felt a sense of fulfillment. "Palermo," he exulted, "polishes off my Normans." Dazzled by the architectural record, he wished that he were his brother Brooks writing his first book. There were all the materials for "a beautiful sketch for the application of the Economical Law," an intellectual synthesis which would invest history with a true sense of form. He was sure that he himself "could now do it nicely, like an artist."

The remark was one of the first intimations that his desultory hobby of translating *chansons de geste* and turning over the literature of the twelfth century was crystallizing into the scheme of a new kind of book. The Middle Ages had in fact been playing a contrapuntal role in his thinking ever since 1893 when Brooks had pointed out to him in the manuscript of *The Law of Civilization and Decay* the significance of the year 1300 as one of the great turning points of European history. Not until the remarkable summer of 1895, however, when he confronted "the great glass Gods" at Chartres, had Henry actually begun his quest of the Norman Gothic.

For many intellectuals the age had already produced the antidote for its maladies in the revived cult of the Middle Ages. Tennyson's *Idylls of the King* had done more perhaps than any other work to fix the image of the Middle Ages as one of sanctity and heroic dedication. For Adams the idealizations of Dante Gabriel Rossetti in "The Blessed Damozel" and "Sister Helen" best expressed the special attractiveness of the medieval spirit, its veneration of women, and he began to use Rossetti's symbols with grave playfulness in his letters to his circle of women disciples.

Brooks had preceded Henry in joining the intellectual counterrevolution that had declared war upon the materialist values of the modern age, a war whose main strategy was an aggressive retreat from the present. By an invincible moralism the two brothers, like many other disenchanted idealists, joined in the escape to the Middle Ages. When on his recurring visits to Wenlock Abbey Henry Adams played with the fancy of being a twelfth-century monk, he was responding to one of the strongest aesthetic currents of his time. William Morris's reprinting of Ruskin's chapter "The Nature of the Gothic" from *The Stones of Venice* in 1892 had signaled the popularity of the movement. To Adams there must have seemed a striking appositeness in Ruskin's fifty-year-old charge: "The foundations of society were never yet shaken as they are at this day. It is not that men are ill fed, but that they have no pleasure in the work by which they make their daily bread, and therefore look to wealth as the only means of pleasure."

Esther had been Adams's first effort to translate into literary form his response to the Pre-Raphaelite doctrines of his artist friends, the effort to achieve a new truth and ideality in art, a directness of feeling and perception, and a revived reverence for Christian art. His friend Clarence King had been one of the charter members of the American Pre-Raphaelite brotherhood, the Society for the Advancement of Truth in Art, when it was founded in New York in 1863. So, too, had been Clover's cousin the architect Russell Sturgis, one of Adams's Washington familiars and an authority on medieval art. "We hold that in all times of great art," wrote Sturgis, "there has been a close connection between architecture, sculpture, and painting . . . In seeking for a system of architecture suitable for study, we shall find it only in that of the Middle Ages, of which the most perfect development is known as Gothic architecture."

There were other Pre-Raphaelites in Adams's circle, including Richard Watson Gilder and Augustus Saint-Gaudens, but John La Farge's influence went deepest. Something of a lapsed Catholic, La Farge liked nothing better than to discuss the relation of Catholic theology to the art of the church, and he was especially interested in the influence of the Virgin. The laconic inscription in La Farge's copy of *Mont Saint Michel and Chartres* has therefore a special eloquence: "His pupil, Henry Adams." "After all," Adams admitted to his former student the medievalist Henry Osborn Taylor, "it was really La Farge and his glass that led me astray; not any remembrance of my dreary Anglo-Saxon Law which was a *tour de force* possible only to youth."

When he returned to Paris in July 1899 after his tour of Italy and Sicily, Adams ensconced himself in Elizabeth Cameron's comfortable quarters under the eaves of the apartment house at 50 avenue du Bois de Boulogne. It was served, as he told Hay, by "one hundred and twenty stairs and an occasional lift." His dear *propriétaire* sailed for the States with Martha, leaving him at her desk in full possession of the Middle Ages until she should return in November. He spent four to six hours a day on the study of Old French, translating *chansons* and heartily damning the vagaries of the preposition *à,* "the basest and most servile relic of the Roman decadence." The old "Travels" project began to buzz again in his mind, but it was still a matter for jest. "I am seriously thinking of writing at last my *Travels in France with Nothing to Say,*" he ventured to Elizabeth. He continually found himself drifting "back to the eleventh and twelfth centuries by a kind of instinct" and craving his eleventh-century Norman arch. He fancied himself "a sexagenarian Hamlet with architectural fancies" whose "only luxury has been to buy photographs of eleventh-century churches and church-towers." In addition, he was "growing frightfully learned on French art of the Crusades." He thought he might "write a drama on the Second Crusade with Queen Eleanor of Guienne for heroine, and myself to act Saint Bernard and reprove her morals."

Sometimes friends would drop in from the Paris bohemia, the scholar-poet Joseph Trumbull Stickney, the sculptor Saint-Gaudens, and the eccentric Sturgis Bigelow, and they would sprawl upon the floor among the photographs of churches. Every sunny day he dashed out of town to see a twelfth-century church or to revisit Chartres as the datum mark of his new world. He let himself float in the color harmonies of the stained glass, the chanting of the holy service a counterpoint in sound. The glass window seemed to him "as emotional as music." He attempted systematic study, moving from bell towers to windows, and from windows to vaulting, and so on through the alphabet of stone. There were frequent calls to be made on Picard the bookseller, "almost within the shadow of St. Sulpice" on the rue Bonaparte, for fresh stacks of monographs, or to Welter near the venerable St. Germain-des-Prés. For all his preoccupation, Adams would sometimes feel spasms of loneliness, and his witty lectures to Elizabeth would end in a plaintive lament that he missed her and Martha terribly and was helpless without her to "run" him.

In the autumn heat of Paris he at last began to write, experiment-
ing, discarding, returning to his sources and beginning again. The
question of form baffled him. "What I do want is to write a five-act
drama, of the twelfth century, to beat Macbeth," he remarked to Gaskell. "Macbeth and Othello are about all that is worth having done
since the Greeks. The curious thing is that the literature of the twelfth
century itself, and of the thirteenth, should be rose-water, with a
childlike horror for tragedy." He bent over his desk piling up his notes
while there drummed in the background the echoes of the Transvaal
war, the Philippine pacification, the Dreyfus case, and the menace of
French socialism.

In mid-January 1900 he "tumbled back" to his unofficial diplomatic responsibilities in Lafayette Square, having loitered abroad for
nine months. His chief problem now was to persuade the perennially
ailing Hay to remain in office as Secretary of State. The daily walks
with Adams on which Hay increasingly counted began again, and all
the portentous undercurrents of Washington high politics, seasoned
with dashes of global diplomacy and scientific speculation, fulmi-
nated and sparkled in Adams's letters. "All I can see," he wrote Gaskell, as he contrasted the American movement with that of Europe,
"is that it is one of compression, concentration and consequent development of terrific energy, represented not by souls, but by coal and
iron and steam. What I cannot see is the last term of the equation. As
I figure it:—$1830:1860::1890:x$, and x always comes out, not 1920,
but infinity. Or infinity minus x." The sense of rapid change confused
him. It was the result, he thought, of "half the year burrowing in
twelfth-century art and religion; the other half, seated here in the very
centre of the web, with every whisper of the world coming instantly
to my ear." He felt too close to the Secretary of State for comfort.
Sometimes in the throes of his "acute hiding moods" he avoided
going to the theater for fear of "getting caught even in the streets."
Withal he saw the humor of his paper hysterics: "I am the drollest
little, peppery, irritable, explosive old man of sixty-two that ever
was," he told Elizabeth. "My nerves are a needle-case. The worst is
that no one believes it, and they go on, playing close to my claws, till
I scratch."

Within doors, safe in the twelfth century, he let his mocking pen
play at will with the stream of events that rushed along Pennsylvania
Avenue and reverberated at his breakfast table. Determined to avoid

public dispute, he made up for his self-restraint in the unsparing commentary of his letters. If he could play no other role, he would at least
be the Horace Walpole of his age. Yet the freedom of his private gibes
sometimes made him nervous about the figure he might cut. "No man
that ever lived can talk or write incessantly without wearying or annoying his hearers if they have to take it in a lump," he suggested to
Brooks. "Thanks entirely to our family-habit of writing, we exist in
the public mind only as a typical expression of disagreeable qualities." Stevenson's just-issued *Letters* pointed a similar moral, which
he promptly shared with Elizabeth in an unvoiced plea for indulgence: Letters "exaggerate all one's bigness, brutality and coarseness;
they perpetuate all one's mistakes, blunders and carelessnesses. No
one can talk or write letters all the time without the effect of egotism
and error." Sharp as the introspective insight was, it did not quite
reach to the heart of the matter, to the truth that he must have known
or sensed, that the secret of his own genius as a writer lay in his
irrepressible egoism.

It was mid-May again before Adams resumed his stand in Paris at
the door of the Exposition in the rue de Longchamps close to the
Trocadéro until Mrs. Cameron's apartment should again be lent to
him. His reading took another widening gyre as he laid in a fresh
supply of learned tomes from his bookseller in the rue de Rennes. He
turned to the legends of the Virgin's miracles and to scholastic philosophy in such works as William Adgar's *Marienlegenden,* Charles de
Rémusat's *Abélard,* and Charles Jourdain's *Philosophie de St. Thomas d'Aquin.*

Though immersed in the twelfth century, Adams still was not safe
from "the jimjams of politics." He had left Hay comfortably afloat in
the international chaos in which England seemed to be sinking under
the weight of the Boer War, when the Boxer uprising and the siege of
the foreigners in Peking made him take an anxious look at Hay's pre-
dicament. Hay's success in getting the nominal acquiescence of the
major powers in the Open Door policy in China had commanded
wide admiration. Unfortunately, the Chinese Boxers suddenly be-
sieged the legations in Peking in a convulsive effort to throw off foreign domination. All Adams could offer by way of comfort were several pages of mocking drollery. "How the deuce are you to get out?
. . . Your open door is already off its hinges, not six months old. What
kind of door can you rig up?" When the crisis was weathered, Hay

expressed their joint relief: "At least we are spared the infamy of an alliance with Germany."

However much Adams might gibe at the inanities and insanities of Paris and the pretensions of the Exposition for the entertainment of absent friends, he found Paris as always an excellent place to work, even when the thermometer registered ninety degrees. Week after week during that summer of 1900 he drove on through the forests of medieval philosophy, using "Thomas Aquinas like liquid air for cooling the hot blood of my youth." His medieval studies drew him sympathetically to the figures of the Catholic renaissance, the movement which had become an intellectual vogue in upper-class circles of Paris. Neo-Thomism had reached into the Sorbonne, and the attack on the philosophy of Descartes became a preoccupation of Catholic writers. The fashionable current swept over Adams at precisely the right psychological moment to provide the key to his structure. "St Thomas is frankly droll," ran his exuberant commentary to Gaskell, "but I think I like his ideas better than those of Descartes or Leibnitz or Kant or the Scotchmen, just as I like better a child of ten that tells lies, to a young man of twenty who not only lies but cheats knowingly. St Thomas was afraid of being whipped. Descartes and the rest lied for pay." Not yet ready to show his hand, he wrote deprecatingly, "All this is sideplay to my interest in twelfth-century spires and Chartres Cathedral."

To Elizabeth Cameron, however, he playfully reported an astonishing fact. "Tell Martha that my metaphysical chapter is nearly done, and I want to send it for her to read and tell me what she doesn't understand, so I can correct it." Martha at fourteen must have felt flattered at Uncle Henry's suggestion. It was of a piece with his engaging habit of reading aloud from the manuscript to her half-comprehending ears. His real audience and confidante continued to be her mother, for under his incessant tutelage and that of Hay and Spring Rice Elizabeth Cameron had ripened into a rather formidable personage, the authority of her matronly beauty allied to the *femme savante*. Challenged by her mentor to read now one book and now another as they caught his interest, she kept up in her fashion so as to provide a sympathetic or at any rate an indulgent reader. The sort of guidance he gave her is indicated in one of his many suggestions: "I want you to read Zola's *Rome* . . . The Church is going to be interesting and that is the best book to cover the situation." As his secret sharer she too would "think and think" over his mental puzzles, and she declared herself that summer as "full of metaphysic as *you* are now." She tasked him: "Did any of your Ecclesiastics decide at what moment the soul entered the body?" Her pedagogue paused considerately: "Your question in metaphysics touches a very delicate point, much disputed in the schools. Some day I will give you Voltaire's remarks on the subject."

His long communion with the Queen of Heaven and her Child had drawn him ever closer in spirit to Elizabeth and Martha. During these climactic autumn weeks he would turn from his miracles of the Virgin for a part of every day to send off a letter, however inconsequential its burden. The "Apocalyptic never" had sublimed into the enigma of their buried lives. There was no longer a doubt of his playing "tame cat" or "Chateaubriand before the shovel and tongs of Madame Récamier." Their mutual need united them in an intimacy so close as to suggest to some a conventional liaison such as was not unknown to the Anglo-American society that deplored divorce. Her Paris household, in which he came and went with utmost freedom, was indeed the center of his existence. However, their relationship had obviously become, for whatever reasons of Puritan scruple or diminishing ardor, that anomaly in nature, a Platonic one. It was true also that Adams felt himself prematurely aging, and when one of his older English friends remarried, he wrote disgustedly to Elizabeth that he never forgave a man's marrying at sixty. "The sexual period in men and women is well defined," he said. "It is even a scientific distinction like infancy and senility." It was revolting to him to see "an elderly" man flaunt a young bride in public.

Within a few more months the initial draft of *Mont Saint Michel and Chartres* was finished. Clinging to his desk, a "twelfth century monk in a nineteenth century attic in Paris . . . without seeing a saint or sinner," he confided to Martha in October that "St Thomas and the Virgin have got married." His quaint metaphor indicated that he had completed the preliminary version of the book. He paused briefly, "by way of variety" went his understatement to Hay, to finish the revision of the 1893 Tahiti volume for one of his Tahiti "sisters" who was visiting Paris. Then he plunged again into the twelfth century to fill in the clerestory bays of his work with the luminous color of medieval poetry, for the "color-theory of the glass" filled his mind as he tinkered with the rhymes of Thibaut of Champagne's ballads to Queen Blanche and the Queen of Heaven.

Ousted again from his attic in September by Mrs. Cameron's return from her incessant visiting about, he beat a gentlemanly retreat a few squares up the avenue nearer the Arc de Triomphe with his mounds of photographs and manuscript, but Elizabeth's salon remained the headquarters for their circle, as he briskly reported to "Sister Ann," Cabot Lodge's wife. "Sturgis [Bigelow] is seedy. Martha is gaudy with a Parisian accent to scorn the Comédie Française. Her mother sits on the louisquintsiest chairs, with [Anders] Zorn's portrait behind her, and talks wicked flattery to [Auguste] Rodin and [Paul César] Helleu [who had done a pastel of Martha and a sketch of Elizabeth] and [Edmond] Saglio [the venerable art critic] and any odd *arrivés* that are handy, while Martha reads Racine to me in the schoolroom and teaches me to *vibrer,* while Joe [Trumbull] Stickney is left with [the archaeologist Henri] Hubert to study in the corner." Edith Wharton also put in an appearance, and Brooks came on for another exhausting clash of predictions. It seemed almost as if "all elderly Beacon Street" waylaid him at street corners near la place de l'Etoile and the Exposition.

Social activities, however diverting or troubling, had their strict time and place in Adams's schedule of work. At his desk the counterpointing between the twelfth century and the dawning twentieth went on with furious energy as he intermittently looked up from his manuscript to send off his regular dispatches. His mind swam easily through the confusion of global diplomacy and finance, checking joint formulas of the velocity of concentration with Brooks, counseling with Hay on his favorite scheme to draw France into an Atlantic combine to rescue the hegemony of Europe from Germany, and voicing his recurring fears of England's imminent collapse. Mostly his imagination was excited by the mechanical marvels of the Exposition then closing where, for a time, alternating his daily devotions, as he said, he went every afternoon and "prayed to the dynamos."

The age of electricity had crackled into existence and, in his cosmic vision, threatened to make the scientific theories of his generation "appear as antiquated as the Ptolemaic system." Far more than the Chicago World's Fair, the Paris Exposition dramatized the silent revolution of fifty years. "The period from 1870 to 1900 is closed. I see that much in the machine-gallery of the Champ de Mars . . . [I] sit by the hour over the great dynamos, watching them run as noiselessly and as smoothly as the planets, and asking them—with infinite courtesy—where in Hell they are going." Before the new phenomenon, mere history as he had understood it "in the days of Macaulay, Mommsen, Michelet and Grote, is either quite dead or temporarily abandoned," he expounded to his brother Charles. "The history and development of mechanical energy is now more exciting and important."

With Brooks Henry could commune at far greater length. "Looking forward fifty years more," he believed "that the superiority in electric energy was going to decide the next development of competition. That superiority depends, in its turn, on geography, geology, and race-energy." The uncertainty in their calculations anguished him. America would need at least a four-to-one superiority "to clean out Euro-Asia." In such a constellation of forces his earlier observation compelled acceptance: "The new economical law brings or ought to bring us back to the same state of mind as resulted from the old religious law,—that of profound helplessness and dependence on an infinite force that is to us incomprehensible and omnipotent."

Carrying the draft of the new book, Adams returned to Washington at the end of January 1901 to experience his semiannual miracle of Lazarus dying into life again. In the pilgrimage of his awakened sensibility he had passed a significant milestone, and he marked it with another poem which he carried back with him to Lafayette Square. The state of mind that had spoken in "Buddha and Brahma" of the consolations of the Lotus and Nirvana had been replaced by that which envisioned not blank extinction but submission to the creative life force. He now sang his skeptic's alleluia to the Virgin.

In the same deprecatory formula he had used to Hay a half-dozen years earlier for "Buddha and Brahma," he told Elizabeth, "By way of relief from boredom, I have returned to verse, and have written a long prayer to the Virgin of Chartres." Naturally, she was the first to see it. "No one but you would care to see it." No one but she knew the struggle it symbolized, the mortification of the flesh that her scholarly chevalier had endured since that day ten years before when he avowed his hopeless passion for her. The "Prayer to the Virgin of Chartres" was Adams's long backward look over the landscape his imagination had explored, from the feudal masculinity of Mont Saint Michel to the deification of woman at Chartres. The state of mind which he had reached after long immersion in the ecstatic Mariolatry of his "namesake" Adam de Saint-Victor and his fellow poets he elucidated to medievalist Henry Osborn Taylor, his "Brother in the Thirteenth Century." "I think you even believe a little, or sometimes, in human reason, or intelligence; which I try to do, in vain. You respect the Church. I adore the Virgin. You find rest and peace in the Greek. I am driven to fury by the commercial side of Greek Life . . . You want to see connection. All I now care for is the break."

So in the poem as "an English scholar of a Norman name" (Was not there an Adam in the Domesday Book?) he begs the Virgin for help as his Norman ancestors had once prayed centuries before they had lost their faith to a world tyrannized by the mindless dynamo. He imagines mankind, in its desperate perplexity before the new source of energy, uttering a "Prayer to the Dynamo" demanding that it fulfill its mission no matter what the risk. Then, scorning that expedient, he humbly bows before the Virgin's throne as one who has "ceased to strive" and who remains

> Pondering the mystery of Maternity,
> Soul within Soul! Mother and Child in One!

The personal resonance of those final lines led Adams afterwards to add four more stanzas of supplication. They conclude:

> Help me to bear! not my own baby load,
> But yours; who bore the failure of the light,
> The strength, the knowledge and the thought of God,—
> The futile folly of the Infinite!

The poem marked the farthest swing of the pendulum of his thought in the direction of religious faith. The return swing was soon to begin.

DURING THE SPRING OF 1901 Adams swamped himself in "tubs of geology, working up to date after twenty years of neglect," and burrowed his way through the accumulated reports of the Geological Survey. He called on his old allies in the survey for help with his calculations of coal and mineral resources. Samuel Emmons, now in charge of the metals resources section of the Division of Economic Geology, brought his chief, Charles Walcott, and some of his expert field geologists to dinner. Samuel Langley came in to provide "science of another sort," aeronautics and astronomy, and to explain his bolometer, a device "to measure the heat of nothing," as Adams called it, which he had invented to analyze the infrared spectrum of the sun.

Brooks, Henry's fellow inquisitor-general of the universe, now working on the geopolitics of *The New Empire,* saw an intoxicating prospect for America in the figures which Henry shared with him. "Supposing the movement of the next fifty years only to equal that of the last . . . the United States will outweigh any single empire, if not all empires combined." Eager to formulate the working theories to run that empire, he turned to Henry because, as he said, "I'm all right for politics, religion, but science I funk."

Brooks's daring conjectures excited Henry's imagination, and his mind leaped to the challenge. "Hammer what ideas you like on my head," he volunteered, "provided it can stand the racket." The lectures and counterlectures during 1901 and 1902 grew longer and longer. To correct Brooks's conception of the prehistorical Euphrates basin, he referred him to "Edouard Suess, Face de la Terre, Chapter I," for a theory concerning the submergence of the Persian Gulf and with it "the cradle of civilization." "The only difficult point that worries me, after the initial Assyrian assumption," said Henry, "is the Phenician extension. I cannot resist the suspicion that the Phenicians reached Brazil, as early as the Mycenae period."

Deep as their affinity was on many points, on one they strongly disagreed: the question of America's proper role in the developing struggle for world power. Brooks stood very close to Lodge and Roosevelt and approved their imperialist schemes. The turn of international affairs, however, filled Henry with foreboding. All his and Brooks's figuring for seven years past left him "haunted by the conviction that England is bankrupt" and that "God will very soon bust up the whole circus," a prospect highly gratifying to the anarchist side of his nature. Personally, he had renounced any stake in that circus, having made his "arrangement for paradise through the Virgin Mary and the twelfth-century church."

Henry envisioned the United States as becoming a beleaguered colossus behind a "Chinese trade-wall" whose only safety from being dragged down by the fall of Europe in the economic competition with the East would lie in rigorous isolation. Brooks, on the other hand, adopted Alfred T. Mahan's gospel of an Anglo-American imperium joined by an Isthmian canal. Mahan asserted that the United States would have to abandon "the policy of isolation" and accept the fact that "to take her share of the travail of Europe is but to assume an inevitable task, an appointed lot in the work of upholding the com-

mon interests of civilization." He called for an Atlantic alliance to
bolster England and a reorganization of the economic and governmental structure of America into an efficient corporative state sufficiently armed to protect her economic supremacy in all quarters of
the globe.

Henry shrank with sensitive revulsion from such frank avowals of
the implications of their joint theories. He did not think—at this season at any rate—that England could be saved, or was worth saving.
The Panama Canal treaty struck him as premature by twenty years.
Dreading military involvement in the Far East, he implored Hay to
abandon the canal, to which Hay was perforce committed. "I incline
now to anti-imperialism, and very strongly to anti-militarism ... I
incline to abandon China, Philippines and everything else. I incline to
let England sink; to let Germany and Russia try to run the machine,
and to stand on our internal resources alone. If these are necessary to
the world, they will rule it anyhow."

Though addressed to Brooks, this counsel of desperation was no
doubt aimed at Lodge and Roosevelt, whose imperialist views on the
Philippines and China were causing trouble to Hay. Equally exasper-
ating to Henry was the Senate outcry against the nonfortification provision of Hay's canal treaty with England. Henry knew also that
Brooks was supporting Lodge's efforts to control American foreign
policy in opposition to Hay. Say what he would, he could not wean
his brother away from Lodge or from Lodge's nominee for Vice-
President, Theodore Roosevelt. Disgusted by what seemed to him the
endless badgering of Hay, Adams had to nourish in secret his "personal and political contempt for Cabot." Lodge did not help matters
with his senatorial arrogance. Not until a third try did the Hay-
Pauncefote treaty relating to the proposed canal pass the Senate. Hay
was so furious with Lodge for having lost his nerve in the face of the
anti-British jingoes that he tried vainly to resign.

Henry's discussions with Brooks commonly rose above the short-
term problems of politics or diplomacy. The level at which their minds
were most fertile of ideas was that of geopolitics. With the shift of his
research to the power nexus, Henry agreed with Brooks that conventional politics and ordinary diplomacy could not keep up with the
problems of the new industrial society. In 1893 the rivalries of finance
capitalists for control of the money market had seemed the root of
the world's evil. He now believed that money was only a secondary

agency, and he was therefore less disposed than ever to put his fingers "into the machinery."

Henry's new formulas seemed to lead to a fatalistic paralysis. Brooks, having based his program for reform on his trade-route theory of history, clung to his key. Henry stubbornly countered, "Your economical law of History is, or ought to be, an Energetic Law of History . . . Concentration is Energy, whether political or industrial." For the next several years he tried to get Brooks to shift his base: "Please give up that unscientific jabber of the newspapers about MONEY in capital letters. What I see is POWER in capitals also."

Not yet ready to immure himself again in the twelfth century, Adams joined the Lodges in mid-July of 1901 for a tour of northern Europe, prepared to put up with Cabot's political vagaries for the sake of Mrs. Lodge, who stood next to Elizabeth Cameron in his affections. Everything that Spring Rice had written him about Germany's materialism seemed confirmed at first hand. The unpleasant impressions of forty years before were heightened by "the Wagnerian beer-and-sausage" of Bayreuth. German bad taste culminated for him in the "flabby German sentimentality" of *Parsifal*. Once again Adams's time machine began to tick off the cities: Vienna, with its sinister hint of "the politics of the Euxine and the Balkans"; Warsaw, where the Polish Jew made him "creep"; and finally Moscow. To the connoisseur of civilizations, the Kremlin was "Byzantium barbarised." His chief pleasure was to observe the "wonderful tenth-century people" in the churches and shrines. He saw in them no signs of individuality but only confirmation of his analysis of a mass society of enormous potential.

From St. Petersburg came a flood of picturesque characterizations, faintly tinged with ancestral memories of John Quincy Adams, who had come there as minister to Russia in 1809. No revision of theory seemed called for. Russia was still in the first of Comte's stages: "metaphysical, religious, military, Byzantine; a sort of Mongol tribe, almost absolutely unable to think in Western lines." He tried another guess. It might come out ahead "on a hundred years' stretch . . . Its scale is so enormous that it is bound to dwarf its neighbors, and with such mass and momentum, speed is a subordinate element. Anyway it is a question of mathematics and of forces and strains; and wisdom and knowledge is useless." If the geopolitics was what might have been anticipated, so too was the art. The great palace at Peterhof was a "pretty, rather quaint, arctic sort of Versailles-Marly paradise" disfigured by furnishings in the "German taste of the fifties." The Winter Palace in St. Petersburg was "magnificently laid out, and meanly executed." Similarly, in the Hermitage gallery he encountered "nothing first-rate" except Dutch painting, which he scorned. Nowhere could he find a "touch of Michael Angelo." However, Catherine's taste delighted him when he saw the thousands of Chinese objets d'art she had collected. Here was an affinity. "Catherine was a great woman."

Adams elected to go on alone to reconnoiter Scandinavia while the Lodges made their way to Paris. At a breakfast table in Stockholm on September 7, 1901, he received a telegram reporting that President McKinley had been shot by an anarchist. The implications for his powerful triumvirate of friends—Hay, Lodge, and Roosevelt—were so breathtaking as to stifle even his passion for conjecture. The President might yet recover; but, as he hurriedly wrote to Hay, "Behind all, in my mind, in all our minds, silent and awful like the Chicago express, flies the thought of Teddy's luck." When the fateful confirmation came, he could only say, "So Teddy is President! Is not that stupendous!"

He pushed on northward through Trondheim to Hammerfest and the North Cape, his mind vivid with the image of Carlyle's Teufelsdröckh confronting the North Pole in utter bafflement. In his solitary hotel rooms he shared the pensive pleasures of his globetrotting with the absent Elizabeth. He looked out upon a landscape that seemed "like the music of the Götterdämmerung; it takes hold of an elderly person with unfair brutality and suddenness . . . These long mountains . . . lie, one after another, like corpses, with their toes up."

Back in the apartment on the avenue du Bois de Boulogne, his meditations fell into the pattern of his developing historical formulas. The news that McKinley had succumbed to his wounds left Adams unmoved. He had disliked McKinley's methods and had seen in him only "a very supple and highly paid agent of the crudest capitalism"; but McKinley, unlike his successor Roosevelt, at least had had "inexhaustible patience and good temper." Roosevelt was of a quite different stripe. From the beginning neither Adams nor Hay had been able to take Roosevelt's candidacy for the Vice-Presidency seriously. They had too complacently laughed at his sense of self-importance. Now his patronizing elders had to admit that luck had given their bumptious young friend ample reason to laugh at his scars. Adams looked

forward with dread to the inevitable debates on his hearthrug with
Hay trapped between their two ambitious friends, Lodge and Roosevelt.

Brooks, of course, felt a perfect rapport with Roosevelt, for he saw
in the forty-three-year-old President the man on horseback who
might regenerate America. "Thou hast it now: King, Cawdor,
Glamis, the world can give no more," went his extravagant congrat-
ulations. The prospect of a strong man in the White House opened
for Brooks visions of an imperial destiny. "You and I have been, as it
were, prophets, like the Baptist, crying in the desert," he reminded the
skeptical Henry; "and for a wonder of wonders, before we are actually in our graves someone has come to listen."

Brooks's warlike proposals for adventures in the Orient again
aroused Henry's opposition as they had the preceding winter. "All
our interests are for political peace to enable us to wage economical
war," he protested. "Therefore I hold our Philippine excursion to be
a false start in a wrong direction . . . Our true road leads to our support of Russia in the north—in both cases meaning our foothold in
Asia." This was the Pacific policy Henry was also urging upon Hay, a
policy directed toward the North China trade.

Henry hung on in Paris for several weeks in the fall of 1901, reluctant to go home. There were final touches to be put to the volume of
revised Tahiti memoirs before sending it off to the Paris printer. He
had hopes that the small private edition might help support the
Salmon family claim for a government pension. He doggedly settled
down to "a course of theatres and dinners" with his customary entourage of transatlantic Americans. Hay's letters constantly pleaded
for more comment—and entertainment: "Your cheery prophecies of
woe and cataclysm are full of joy and comfort to me." Adams tossed
off fresh showers of political generalizations. Overall, the situation
seemed materially changed because of the business depression. Germany seemed in a decline; England was drifting into a new phase of
imperialism inimical to the United States; and now there was all the
more need "to draw France towards us, and keep her out of a European combination." Then he ritualistically washed his hands: "The
usual total is that nobody knows anything." He made a brief excursion into Touraine to trace out in the glass of Tours, whose splendor
rivaled the Sainte-Chapelle, the favorite thirteenth-century legends of
St. James; but of the revision of the *Chartres* manuscript he let fall no
word of progress.

Shortly before the new year Adams shuttled back across the ocean to New York just in time to be met by a telegram inviting him to the funeral of Clarence King, dead of tuberculosis at fifty-nine. The end had come with miserable grace in an Arizona tavern. This was but the last of a succession of numbing personal blows that year. In June Hay's son "Del" had died in a tragic fall from a college window during a festive class reunion. Earlier in the year his brother-in-law Edward Hooper, his "most valuably essential friend and connection," had had a nervous breakdown and had taken his own life, reenacting the fatal pattern of his sisters. One can surmise the stirrings of grief as Adams recalled the suicide of Clover. Outwardly, however, his life moved almost serenely in its deep-worn grooves, protected by his "bodyguard" of Hooper nieces, which, as Hay fumed, "never relaxed its vigilance for an hour."

Adams rejoined Hay in Lafayette Square, where Brooks had confidently made himself at home, vainly waiting for the call to emerge from the shadows of kingmaking into public life. Henry quickly saw that Brooks had small chance of catching on. Brooks was "too brutal, blatant, too emphatic, and too intensely set on one line alone, at a time, to please any large number of people." Henry reassumed his own role of "stable-companion," but the effort to mask his personal and political anxieties in Hay's presence strained him to the breaking point. Hay, intermittently ailing, followed a strict regimen. At 5:30 Adams regularly presented himself for tea, the half-hour ending "invariably in a growl from the Secretary." "My own cynicism," said Adams, "takes more and more a religious tone and color. I shove it off on God the Father, and I hug close to the Virgin—only I've no Virgin handy, and my years forbid."

Long before he got back to Washington he had read his fill of Roosevelt's "cavorting," and he answered the first White House summons to dinner with more than ordinary apprehension. He went, haunted by his own and his ancestral past. It was his first White House dinner since 1878, and memory demanded that he savor fully the painful contrast with "that happiest time" of his life. The White House seemed "ghastly with bloody and dreary associations way back to my great-grandmother a hundred years ago." "As usual Theodore absorbed the conversation, and if he tired me ten years ago, he crushes me now. To say I enjoyed it would be . . . a gratuitous piece of deceit." At sixty-three it was hard to be patient with the youthful Caesar. "He lectures me on history as though he were a high-school pedagogue.

Of course I fall back instantly on my favorite protective pose of ignorance, which aggravates his assertions, and so we drift steadily
apart."

Roosevelt's physical courage and strenuosity ran counter to
Adams's instincts. When the President risked his health, Adams
thought him "one of the brainless cephalopods who is not afraid."
Every choice story of Roosevelt's naïveté came flying to Adams's
breakfast table. Few bettered one of Hay's morsels. "Teddy said the
other day, 'I am not going to be a slave of the tradition that forbids
Presidents from seeing their friends. I am going to dine with you and
Henry Adams and Cabot whenever I like. But' (here the shadow of
the crown sobered him a little) 'of course I must preserve the prerog-
ative of the initiative.'" Studying his victim at such close range and
blinded by personal feelings, Adams could see nothing good in Roosevelt's program. In private anguish he could only cry out, "Stupid,
blundering, bolting, bull-calf!" He felt sure that Lodge and Roosevelt
would never get on together. "The most dangerous rock on Theodore's coast is Cabot," he said. Yet it turned out that Lodge was far
closer in spirit to Roosevelt than Adams realized. Indeed, Lodge's influence became proverbial. The boy Quentin Roosevelt once blurted
out to a White House guard: "I'm going to see Lodge; that's what
Father tells everybody when he wants to have anything done."

Instinctively, Adams detested Roosevelt's unabashed courting of
popular favor: it signified something immoderate, vulgar, and blatant
about the man. He was wholly indifferent to what the ordinary citizen
thought of Roosevelt. He would have brusquely argued that the citizen had neither the knowledge nor the intelligence to judge. Yet Roosevelt was responding to currents and forces that Adams, in his profound detachment, seems not to have apprehended at all except
insofar as they made statistics in the *Statist,* the *Economist,* or the
election returns. Below the level of diplomacy, high politics, and
equally high finance, the world seemed to affect his introspection
hardly more than as a blur of forces.

It was a triumph of Adams's social tact that he continued on intimate terms with the President. "Actually! I am a courtier! an *intime*
at the White House! A neighbor of Respectability Row!" he mockingly exclaimed to Elizabeth as he rehearsed Roosevelt's follies. In
private he was severe, as he conferred at leisure with his "committee
of matrons" on the strain of the strenuous life upon Roosevelt's ador-

ing wife. "In correct expression, his mind is impulse," he disapprov-
ingly remarked, "and acts by the instinct of a school-boy at a second-
rate boarding school. Mind, in a technical sense, he has not." He
studied his victim with fascinated absorption. "Theodore is blind-
drunk with self-esteem. He has not a suspicion that we are all watching him as we would watch a monkey up a tree with a chronometer."
In self-defense Adams would extricate himself from the noisy collo-
quies of Roosevelt, Lodge, and Elihu Root and radiate his charm
upon the wives.

In his house, despite its constant stream of guests, political and
social, he managed to seclude himself in his study, again in his
"twelfth century." His year's additional study of philosophy and science now bore fruit as he turned to revise and expand the manuscript
of the *Chartres*. Each day, after letters were out of the way, he would
surrender himself, as he said, to six hours' communion with the Virgin. He saw the ironic humor of his situation: "Four weeks at home,
in the very heart of the world with my fingers close to the valves, and
I pass my time entirely in the twelfth century, as far away as mind can
get." Destiny was in it. "I was born a schoolmaster," ran his wry
epigram, "and I am dying a pedagogue." Having left his key books in
Paris, he enlisted his "Dear Brother in the Thirteenth Century," Henry
Osborn Taylor, to lay his hands on a few reference works. The revision went forward with astonishing rapidity. His pen, long freed from
the Spartan rigors of historical exposition, was master at last of his
medium, a style compact of metaphor and epigram, daring in its imagery as that of any symbolist, learnedly allusive and yet lightened
with pervasive irony. A vatic mood swept him upwards to creative
heights which he had never before attained. He leaned over his fool-
scap "sheets of twelfth century" to such good purpose that by April
27, 1902, he boasted he was "perfectly square with the Virgin Mary,
having finished and wholly rewritten the whole volume." He felt a
sense of exultation as he rode into the countryside. The spring seemed
"young and beautiful as ever, and absolutely shocking in its display
of reckless maternity." The white and purple-pink blossoms of the
roadside pronounced a benediction upon his spirit. "No one ever
loved the dog-wood and Judas-tree as I have done," he caroled to
Elizabeth, "and it is my one crown of life to be sure that I am going
to take them with me to Heaven to enjoy real happiness with the
Virgin and them."

Riding the crest of the creative inspiration, he began a new work which he playfully referred to as "a historical romance of the year 1200." The allusion was his ironic way of announcing that the long-deferred Carlylian ragbag of commentary had been initiated, the work that would become *The Education of Henry Adams*. A further bit of evidence pointing towards the genesis of the *Education* in the late spring of 1902 is a facetious allusion in one of his letters to his receiving imaginary telegrams from J. P. Morgan "addressed to Yacob Strauss aus Cracau." The datum image of the *Education*, on its very first page, would be the stereotype of "Israel Cohen," who rose like a medieval grotesque out of the idealized brutalities of the First Crusade.

Adams joined the spring exodus to Europe, sailing on May 7, 1902, from New York on the *Philadelphia*, "coddled all the way over," as he was pleased to tell, by his young actress friends Elsie de Wolfe and Ethel Barrymore. In Paris, as long ago for a different reason in Japan, his sense of smell revived at the new odor of the automobile exhaust, but the fumes exhilarated him as he thought of owning an automobile and living "long enough to take some pretty new nieces round to see twelfth century glass." The idea tickled his fancy. "My idea of paradise is a perfect automobile going thirty miles an hour on a smooth road to a twelfth century cathedral." Summoned to Scotland by Don Cameron, who had impulsively acquired a castle, Adams joined the ménage there for the summer, taking his familiar place in Elizabeth's retinue. The quiet enforced by a sprained ankle permitted him to return to further study of commentaries on Aquinas, so interlarded with science that he felt himself "a mixture of Lord Kelvin and St Thomas Aquinas."

Reaching Paris again early in October 1902, he resumed enthusiastic automobiling to churches off the beaten path. He went again to Bourges, where he at last "got the windows by heart." However, the philosophic controversies in the concluding chapters of the *Chartres* would not let him rest. He secluded himself in his new apartment on the avenue de Bois, his only companions "the Virgin, St Thomas and St Francis of Assisi." By early December he was "dying to know how it would look in type."

His seclusion was as always a relative matter, for the poet Joseph Trumbull Stickney had free entry and occasionally brought with him his companions from the rue d'Assas and the rue du Bac. One of these was the Irish youth Shane Leslie, then in attendance for a season at the Sorbonne, where medieval studies were the rage. Adams, warmed by the frank admiration of the young men, talked "exquisitely," as Shane Leslie recalled, "about blue china, the modern dynamo, Chartres cathedral, and the Latin medieval hymns." As the "wise and weird old man" wove his spell, the Paris of Abelard seemed more real than that of the Third Republic. One felt oneself "walking in the groves of Greece with Plato," but a Plato who talked disturbingly of the failure of democracy, who jeered that the White House was becoming "a cage for thwarted statesmen."

Again came the shock of "annual rebirth" in Washington in 1903, where in the January chill the walks with Hay began again with their budgeted hour of talk of treaties and White House gossip. To his "safety valve," Elizabeth Cameron, he continued his coruscating monologue, serving up choice bits of diplomatic or political gossip winged with mockery and exaggeration. Throughout the countless pages there continued to dance the names of Roosevelt, Root, Hay, and Holmes, politicos like Depew, Hoar, Quay, and Platt, and an endless roster of important senators and congressmen, statehouse bosses, meddlesome ambassadors. Always swarming about the men was an entourage of their ambitious and long-suffering ladies. It was all as "comic as a Palais Royal vaudeville" as he watched Hay's adroit moves amidst the jockeying of Germany, Russia, and France on the Continent while England played her deep game with Japan in the Orient. "What a pantomime it is," he exclaimed; "and of all the men who saw the dance of Europe over us in 1860–64, Hay and I are left alone here to gloat over our revenge. Standing back in the shadow, as I do, it seems as though I were Nemesis."

He was not so far back, however, as to relax the discreet pressure of his counsel, sought all the more exigently because he seemed so reluctant to offer it. Nor did he forget his own special projects. When, for example, the death of his old family friend Justice Horace Gray created a vacancy on the Supreme Court, he urged the candidacy of Wendell Holmes upon Lodge. Perverse as ever, he gritted his teeth at the good who needed murdering and the people past fifty who played at being happy when, as he said, they "ought to be as dreary as I," a train of reflection that sent him back, teased out of thought, to tinker with his chapter on the poet-scholar Abelard, so like himself in his quixoticism and romantic passion, "but a much bigger fool than I."

However, the notes for his new book competed with the old as he calculated the "potentials and logarithms when the world is going to break its blooming neck," coming out now at 1932, again at 1952.

The writing resumed on the *Chartres,* and the manuscript "swelled and swelled to the size of an ox." By mid-March he confidently reported to Elizabeth Cameron, "My great work on the Virgin is complete even to the paging, and I've no occupation." Presumably he had reorganized the manuscript. His complaint was premature, for he found that much remained to be done. At the end of the following January he was at last able to say, "I am going to put my Chartres into type; it will amuse me till May." He had placed the book with J. H. Furst and Company of Baltimore. In the following week a great fire destroyed the business district of Baltimore, and a portion of the printer's copy was consumed. The "snarl" lasted for the rest of the year. The private printing of his "Miracles de la Vierge," as he sometimes called the book, was not completely finished until mid-December 1904. Copyrighted in 1905, it was issued in one hundred wide-margined quarto copies.

After a complete literary silence of nearly fifteen years, so far as his wider acquaintanceship was concerned, Adams now addressed a carefully handpicked audience in a voice wholly different from that of the *History* of 1890–91. Recognizing, even insisting on, his alienation from the general reader, he made no gesture whatever towards the professional critics: the private printing contemptuously excluded them. If he did not care any longer for popular reputation, what he wanted was far more precious to a "teacher of teachers" upon whom the Pentecostal flame had descended: the new book required not readers but disciples. "It is my declaration of principles as head of the Conservative Christian Anarchists," he wrote Gaskell; "a party numbering one member. The Virgin and St Thomas are my vehicles of anarchism. Nobody knows enough to see what they mean, so the Judges will probably not be able to burn me according to law."

22

Thirteenth-Century Unity

BENEATH THE TITLE *Mont Saint Michel and Chartres* there appeared the simple legend "Travels/France." Adams withheld printing his name as author, playing out the fancy that he was an anonymous twelfth-century monk who in all humility had forsworn the world. It was kin to his pose of having only a posthumous existence since the death of his wife. He disliked and dreaded the crass and intrusive general public. So he had barred it by conspicuously omitting the Adams name from Saint-Gaudens's monument in Rock Creek cemetery. So, too, he would offer this book only to his circle of relatives and friends.

The volume opens with a playfully arch and disarming preface in which the author professes to be setting out in imagination as an avuncular guide to a group of "nieces," or "those who are willing, for the time, to be nieces in wish," on a verbal tour of the cathedrals of northern France. Nephews were hardly to be seduced to join the tour, for as a social class they "no longer read at all." The page turns and "The uncle talks." Time and space dissolve as our guide informs us what the true itinerary is to be. "We have set out to go from Mont Saint Michel to Chartres in three centuries, the eleventh, twelfth, thirteenth, trying to get, on the way, not technical knowledge; not accurate information; not correct views either on history, art, or religion; not anything that can be useful or instructive; but only a sense of what those centuries had to say, and a sympathy with their ways of saying it."

A disarming and paradoxical disavowal it is, and one to be matched by many another, for technical knowledge will challenge the reader on nearly every page, accompanied by a cloud of views, however unorthodox, on history, art, and religion. What is constantly to be sought is "not a fact but a feeling," and that phrase will be the *absit omen* for all his essays in scholarship. If along the way he encounters a medieval poem, he will translate it in his fashion, in spite of the risk to feeling, only because "tourists cannot stop to clear their path, or smooth away the pebbles."

In the dramatic opening pages he evokes the spirit of the first great datum point of the aesthetic journey. It is the year 1058 on the Mount of St. Michael when the great piers were rising and the masculine Norman energies were gathering for the forward surge of their race, and the pages vibrate with lyric nostalgia. It is the period of the *Chanson de Roland*, when God is a feudal seigneur who absorbs in himself the Trinity, the Virgin, and her Son. Looking out in imaginative retrospect across the Normandy landscape, one could "almost take oath that in this, or the other, or in all, one knew life once and has never so fully known it since."

Having established the datum point of energy at Mont Saint Michel on the eve of the Norman conquest of England as symbolized in the masculine architecture and poetry of the Mount, Adams moves swiftly on to the upsurge of feminine energies at Chartres, a period more important to the creative imagination than the first and requiring far more extensive treatment. The "architectural highway" takes Adams "through Coutances, Bayeux, Caen, Rouen, and Mantes," but the journey does not long detain him, it being only necessary to identify the Norman, military elements of Coutances, Bayeux, and Caen "in order to trace up our lines of artistic ancestry."

To reach the opposing pole of the dialectical travel, the genial uncle carries us "straight to Chartres," to confront the great west portal that exhibits the Transition Gothic in architecture as it symbolizes the transition in spirit from the Church Militant of the eleventh century to the Church Triumphant of the twelfth. As the spire of Mont Saint Michel symbolized aspiration, so this most perfect of portals symbolized the "Way of Eternal Life." But it is the north portal, devoted wholly to the Virgin of Majesty, which reflected the full movement of thought and art, for in that portal love and femininity held sway. The narrative conducts us through chamber after chamber of the palace of this greatest of queens, through nave and transept, choir and apse, so that we may observe the Virgin's imperial commands and taste displayed in every triumphant leap of the vaulting and every breathtaking radiance of stained glass, for the Virgin of Majesty was also "the most womanly of women." Therein lay the secret of her power and authority.

In his 1876 Lowell Institute lecture, "The Primitive Rights of Women," Adams had argued that the early Church had "dethroned the woman from her place" by elevating the masculine godhead but that nature had rebelled against the denial of its deepest instincts, and the reaction was the "irresistible spread of Mariolatry, the worship of the Virgin Mother." Now in returning to the subject Adams found elaborate evidence in the volumes of the great French architect Viollet-le-Duc of the incredible fetish power of the Virgin. During the period of her ascendancy she overshadowed the Trinity and stood as a shield for the hapless sinner against the rigors of divine justice. The enormous investment in the churches of Our Lady was "based on the power of Mary as Queen rather than on any orthodox conception of the Virgin's legitimate station."

She had small respect for well-regulated society. Like a good conservative Christian anarchist, she detested the "gold-bugs" of her age and admired the self-sacrificing soldier-knight. "Her views on the subject of money-lending or banking were so feminine as to rouse in that powerful class a vindictive enmity which helped to overthrow her throne . . . Her conduct was at times undignified," and she did some "exceedingly unconventional things." Certainly none of her votaries in the courts of the regnant queens would have been allowed to suffer the anguish of the "Apocalyptic Never." She was "by essence illogical, unreasonable, and feminine."

Beneath the veil of romantic metaphor which dramatized Adams's idealistic vision, the Virgin of popular belief stands forth as the great myth which responded to the felt realities of existence, embodying man's immemorial protest against usurpation, denial, restraint, against all stiflings and deprivations of nature. The Virgin of Majesty was a wonder-working myth which had made possible the harnessing of the economic and constructive energies of the age. Nascent bourgeois capitalism made an enormous investment in the Virgin's power, "not unlike the South Sea scheme, or the railway system of our own time," hopeful, as Adams put it, that "God would enter a business partnership with man to establish a joint-stock society for altering the operation of divine and universal laws." The partnership, however, eventually broke down; the fetish power lost its efficacy for "shortening the road to heaven." The centuries of dynastic and religious wars that followed, with all their attendant horrors, measured the extent of the bankruptcy.

One grand illusion united all the diversities of the Middle Ages. "The twelfth and thirteenth centuries were a period when men were at their strongest; never before or since have they shown equal energy in such varied directions, or such intelligence in the direction of their energy; yet these marvels of history—these Plantagenets; these scholastic philosophers; these architects of Rheims and Amiens; these Innocents, and Robin Hoods and Marco Polos; these crusaders, who planted their enormous fortresses all over the Levant; these monks who made the wastes and barrens yield harvests;—all, without apparent exception, bowed down before the woman. Explain it who will! We are not particularly interested in the explanation; it is the art we have chased through this French forest; like Aucassins hunting for Nicolette; and the art leads always to the woman."

The student who tries to follow Adams's scintillating track in more prosaic histories and monographs for a closer view of the life of the time must rub his eyes in astonishment at the world that lies behind Adams's colorful and benevolent vision. The apparent unity of the world of art and religious imagination is belied at every turn by the fact of discord and tension. The politics of the time were a trackless jungle in which feudal monarchs and nobles stalked each other in a ceaseless contest for territory and power, a contest in which the rival ambitions of great priests and prelates were inextricably confounded. Serfs and peasants were hustled off to fight and die in a thousand nameless quarrels or stayed at home to be plundered with savage ferocity by lawless marauders. Whole populations were decimated in the hysterical frenzies of the Crusades, the surviving remnants looting and massacring as they made their way to the Holy Sepulcher. It was a society in which barbarous superstitions were maintained by a penal system whose tortures confront us in graphic paintings. It was also a world undergoing an immense transformation as commerce rapidly expanded, dotting the landscape with thriving towns, developing manufactures, and encouraging science.

In place of Adams's imaginative and quasi-occult explanations of the energy of the Virgin of Majesty, the sober historian indicates that churchbuilding was not quite the spontaneous expression of simple faith, but much more often the work of masterful and determined clerics whose ambition marvelously energized their piety. They shamelessly vied with one another in the magnificence of their edifices and skillfully used the earthly and supernatural sanctions of the Church to produce needed revenues and work. For example, the great Suger, abbot of St. Denis, a "political prelate," in Adams's restrained phrase, was notorious for his vainglorious boasting and his love of worldly pomp. Nevertheless, he was an enlightened patron of the arts, and his reconstruction of St. Denis pointed to the Gothic marvels to come. St. Bernard cried out against the luxury of the new abbey churches, "Alas, if there be no shame for this foolishness, why at least is there no shame for the cost."

No doubt there was great force in Adams's argument that the rise of science ultimately destroyed faith in the fetish power of the Virgin and that this skepticism became peculiarly congenial to the commercial world of the Renaissance. Besides, by 1250 the supremacy of Louis IX of France was well established, and the tyrannical powers of the ecclesiastical courts were curbed. There was no further need of the bourgeoisie or the peasants to support the urban bishops against the feudal barons and powerful abbots. As society grew more secular and the king's writ and the king's equity provided surer sanctuary than the Virgin of Majesty, the great levies for churchbuilding and decoration imposed by the bishops encountered more and more resistance. The revolution inspired by the Virgin of Majesty had in effect cleared the way for the future.

The secret of the twelfth-century renaissance, Adams asserted in the *Chartres*, was bound to shock "tourists of English blood and American training . . . The scientific mind is atrophied, and suffers under inherited cerebral weakness, when it comes in contact with the eternal woman—Astarte, Isis, Demeter, Aphrodite, and the last and greatest deity of all, the Virgin." Perhaps only the artist, "owing to some revival of archaic instincts," can rediscover the woman. "The rest of us cannot feel; we can only study. The proper study of mankind is woman and, by common agreement since the time of Adam, it is the most complex and arduous. The study of Our Lady, as shown by the art of Chartres, leads directly back to Eve, and lays bare the whole subject of sex."

What the Pre-Raphaelite idealizing of women had taught Adams was given fresh emphasis in the pages of Maurice Maeterlinck's recent book *The Life of the Bee*, a rhapsodic parable of the power of instinct. Inspired by that book, Adams wrote: "Perhaps the best starting-point for the study of the Virgin would be a practical acquaintance with bees, and especially queen bees." If the analogy seemed a satire on his own sex, based as it was on the fact that "Nature regards the female as the essential, the male as the superfluity of her world," it reflected his wry acceptance of a truth with which he often chaffed young men. Shane Leslie recalls Adams's fixing him with a piercing eye one day. " 'You must come to a conclusion sooner or later,' he said to me in awe-inspiring tones, 'whether the center of the universe is masculine or feminine.' " For himself Adams had no doubts, and he paid his homage accordingly. The modern society woman might be a failure, but that failure did not invalidate the principle. The instinct remained, however much it was betrayed.

In one of his perennial jeremiads of reminiscence to Mrs. Cameron Adams wrote, "But all one has really cared for has been a few women, and they have worried one more than falling worlds." Woman and not man was a social animal. "Socially," he declared, "man is a mere rooting grunting hog." He continually insisted that "only women are worth cultivating." Only women could be trusted: "Lord! how often I have said that, in the course of a life, at times accidented, I never knew a woman to go back on me, and I never knew a man who didn't." When he read Mark Twain's *Diary of Adam*, he said, "It is me myself; a portrait by Boldoni." The principle was immemorially true. "Is it not curious," he mused, "that the man should always have instinctively represented himself as a tool and a fool in contact with the woman?" As Adams's contemporary Lafcadio Hearn epitomized the matter for his Japanese students, "In western countries woman is a cult, a religion, of if you like still plainer language, I shall say that in western countries woman is a god."

If the study of the Virgin ultimately carried one back to sex and sex was to be identified with the archetype symbolized by Eve and Isis, the corollary of this universal worship of the woman principle was the fact of her natural superiority. "The superiority of the woman was not a fancy, but a fact," the *Chartres* declared, and in the Middle Ages strong-willed women placed their stamp on the manners, politics, and literature of the time. Adams's demonstration of the medieval gynecocracy proceeds through legend and poetry to show "that while the Virgin was miraculously using the power of spiritual love to elevate and purify the people, [Queen] Eleanor and her daughters were using the power of earthly love to discipline and refine the courts." As the

Virgin of Majesty eclipsed the Trinity, so the medieval queens eclipsed the kings, and so also did the merest woman eclipse the merest man.

Nearly fifty years had gone by since the days when Mill and Tocqueville were "the two high priests" of Adams's faith. Mill in *The Subjection of Women* had given him a rationale for his devotion to the cause of women. Tocqueville had offered him a noble vision to which he had been faithful in his fashion. Wrote Tocqueville in *Democracy in America*: "If I were asked, now that I am drawing to the close of this work . . . to what the singular prosperity and growing strength of that people ought mainly to be attributed, I should reply—to the superiority of their women." Desperate as the case now seemed to Adams, the *Chartres* made clear that if in the eleventh hour the world was to be saved from apaches and trade unions, the woman must regain her sovereign authority through maternity.

The final triad chapters of *Mont Saint Michel and Chartres* make explicit the great parable of "Travels in France." They stand clear of the rest of the structure and complete it like one of Adams's favorite Norman towers. They were his "anchor in history," he remarked to William James. In their triple movement they parallel the fortunes of the Church Architectural with those of the Church Intellectual. The doctrinal struggles of the schools opened with the victory of Abelard over William of Champeaux not long after the building of the great piers at Mont Saint Michel and closed with the death of Aquinas in 1274.

The evolution of the Church Architectural in Adams's highly simplified scheme is concentrated at three points. The initial point is the original Romanesque fabric of Mont Saint Michel; the second is the Transition Gothic of Chartres; the third is exemplified by the sculptured splendors of the High Gothic of Amiens, the "Parthenon of Gothic," as it has been called, and the tragically unfinished Beauvais, in which the medieval architects outreached themselves in attempting to build the loftiest vaulted tower in all Christendom. The architect of Beauvais was as daring an artist as Aquinas. However, "both the 'Summa Theologiae' and the Beauvais Cathedral were excessively modern, scientific, and technical, marking the extreme points reached by Europe on the lines of scholastic science."

As Adams conceived the parallel movements, the period of the Transition Gothic, 1140–1200, whose finest flowering occurred at Chartres, coincided with the crisis in scholastic philosophy. The early

scholastics had "tried realism and found that it led to pantheism.
They tried nominalism and found it ended in materialism. They attempted a compromise in conceptualism which begged the whole
question. Then they lay down exhausted." Not until the coming of
Aquinas was the crisis resolved. The first epoch of scholasticism
ended thus in the discrediting of reason and logic, the position to
which Pascal would be driven in the seventeenth century. The alternatives to reason and logic were skepticism, love, ecstasy, and mysticism. "In the bankruptcy of reason," the Virgin, the goddess of instinct and emotion, "alone was real." During this interregnum of the
schools the great mystics of the Church flourished and the Virgin's
inspiration reached its greatest intensity.

The was the moment that Adams admired most, the moment toward which every motive of the symbolist aesthetic drove his sensibility. He turned toward the mystics, especially to St. Francis of Assisi,
with a deep sense of fellow feeling. Who better than St. Francis exemplified those epiphanies of ineffable feeling that he and his fellow
Pre-Raphaelites sought? In the mystery of St. Francis he could pursue
his reason, like Sir Thomas Browne, to "an O altitudo!" His own
skepticism toward both religious and scientific dogma, he felt, resembled that of St. Francis and Pascal. His *Chartres* was his "Prome-
theus lyric" of doubt, and he thought it belonged in the twelfth century, the period when the mystics "touched God behind the veil of
scepticism." Adams could admire Aquinas for his philosophy as he
did Newton for his scientific achievement; but toward St. Francis he
felt a warmth of affection approaching his feeling for the Virgin of
Chartres. St. Francis was the earthly counterpart of the Virgin, "the
ideal mystic saint of Western Europe." In the pattern of historical
parallels St. Francis went with Chartres, Thomas Aquinas with
Amiens and Beauvais.

The Platonizing metaphysics of scholastic philosophy supplied the
perfect vehicle for Adams's criticism of contemporary scientific
thought. The real destination of the "Travels in France" was his own
age. All the raptures of the uncle, the fervors of scholarship, the bra-
vura flourishes of drama with which he evoked the spirit of the bygone age were an elaborate rhetoric of condemnation of his own age.
If modern science was far ahead of the science of that earlier time,
philosophically it was no better off, for while professing to deny the
value of theology and metaphysics for the discovery of "universal

truths," wrote Adams, "it strives for nothing else, and disputes the problem, within its own limits, almost as earnestly as in the twelfth century."

The question—or dilemma—of unity and multiplicity became the touchstone of every inquiry, whether involving the nature of consciousness or the nature of society. For one who had once looked askance at Concord, the metaphysical leap has its irony, for Adams was now as impatient as Emerson to solve the problem of the one and the many. He was unwilling, to use Emerson's phrase, "to wander without end" in the "splendid labyrinth" of his perceptions. Yet in spite of his mystical yearnings Adams could not take the final step toward pure idealism. His lingering skepticism kept him ever at the threshold of unity, where he enviously contemplated the anarchic pantheism of a St. Francis—or a Spinoza—who could achieve "mystical union with God, and its necessary consequences of contempt and hatred for human intellectual processes."

Of all the writers over whose works Adams pored, Pascal's influence was greatest. Spinoza clarified the nature of the great debate and offered the pantheist solution in its purest form, but Pascal saved Adams from final commitment by uniting skepticism with mysticism. Yet the problem of subject and object, of the true relation of the mind to the cosmos, would not down. There were, Adams insisted to Elizabeth Cameron, but two schools of thought: "One turns the world onto me; the other turns me onto the world." The Middle Ages as Adams read them explored every possible resolution of this stubborn dualism, from the realism of William of Champeaux to the disguised nominalism of Abelard, ending at last in the so-called moderate realism of St. Thomas Aquinas. "The attempt to bridge the chasm between multiplicity and unity is the oldest problem of philosophy, religion, and science," Adams wrote. On each side of that chasm he saw a whole array of energies, each with its opposite or contradictory on the other side and all polarized within an unimaginably subtle field of force.

The doctrine of universals, which, as Adams said, "convulsed the schools of the twelfth century," was but an earlier expression of a modern problem. "Science hesitates more visibly than the Church ever did, to decide once for all whether unity or diversity is ultimate law; whether order or chaos is the governing rule of the universe, if universe there is." In Adams's dramatic re-creation of the famous de-

bate of 1100 between William of Champeaux, the realist, and Abelard, the nominalist, the relevance to contemporary thought required
but a turn of phrase. " 'I start from the universe,' said William. 'I start
from the atom,' said Abelard." Had Abelard truly joined issue it
would have been clear that nominalism ended in the heresy of materialism as surely as William's realism ended in heretical pantheism.
The abyss between subject and object could not be bridged by pure
thought alone. "The most impossible task of the mind," said Adams,
"is to reject in practice the reflex action of itself . . . The schools—
ancient, mediaeval, or modern—have almost equally failed." The figure that seemed most apt to him was that of a complicated mirror in
which the mind tried to absorb itself in its own reflection. The "irregularities of the mental mirror" haunted science as ineradicably as they
had haunted the medieval Church.

The final chapter of the *Chartres* describes the synthesis which St.
Thomas attempted to impose on the wilderness of antinomies that
perplexed the official Church. It was the longest-meditated and admittedly the most difficult chapter to bring within the frame of the
Chartres. For more than a year Adams had tinkered with it while
counterpointing his ideas in the latest books on science and the philosophy of science, so that it was inevitable that he should feel it more
and more a parable of contemporary dilemmas of thought.

How, then, must uncle and niece, so close to the end of their tour,
approach the work of Aquinas? The solution is a bewildering piece
of virtuosity. The tour began in the pursuit of art and feeling; so it
must end. Adams's problem as a literary artist was to establish the
equilibrium of the parts of his own work at the very moment that he
demonstrated the equilibrium of Aquinas's theology. The soaring
spire of St. Michael, which marked the point of departure of the
"Travels," is balanced by the intellectual spire of Aquinas. The
Church Architectural of the Virgin, which gave the key to the treasures of the imagination of the Middle Ages, is balanced by the
Church Intellectual, which displays the beauty of abstract thought
and the final unity of beauty and truth.

In the chapter on Aquinas the masculine-feminine dichotomy drops
out altogether. Aquinas's solution not only dethroned the Virgin; it
ignored her. It went even further; it attenuated the persons of the
Trinity. Adams makes this of Aquinas's doctrine: "God, as a double
consciousness, loves Himself, and realizes Himself in the Holy Ghost.

The third side of the triangle is love or grace." The "architecture" of the intellectual church of Aquinas reflected this transformation of the Trinity. God, the Aristotelian prime motor, formed the foundation and walls. "Then came his great tour-de-force, the vaulting of his broad nave; and if ignorance is allowed an opinion, even a lost soul may admire the grand simplicity of Thomas's scheme. He swept away the horizontal lines altogether, leaving them barely as a part of decoration. The whole weight of his arches fell, as in the latest Gothic, where the eye sees nothing to break the sheer spring of the nervures, from the rosette on the keystone a hundred feet above down to the church floor. In Thomas's creation nothing intervened between God and his world ... only two forces, God and man, stood in the Church."

Adams saw in Aquinas that remarkable balance of theory and practice which he had found so admirable in Albert Gallatin. But just as Gallatin had not been able to bend the bow of Ulysses, so in the profounder universe of Aquinas the bow could not really be bent, and the ultimate problems still remained unsolved as the forces of history swept even the greatest philosophers as well as statesmen helplessly downstream. Thirteenth-century religion had finally to meet the challenge of Aristotelian science, to harmonize faith and reason, or, more strictly, to support revelation by philosophy. Aquinas went as far as intellect alone could go, and the subsequent history of philosophy and science showed that his sublime failure was the great archetype of intellectual failure. The unsurpassable art of Chartres rested ultimately on rebellion and heresy; the incomparable architecture of Aquinas's thought rested on equally dubious foundations. The marriage of faith and reason had in fact taken place outside of the official church as had the nuptials of the archaic warrior and the woman which opened the road from Mont Saint Michel to Chartres.

At the beginning of the tour Adams had written, "No architecture that ever grew on earth, except the Gothic, gave this effect of flinging its passion against the sky." His concluding words asserted its tragic instability: "The equilibrium is visibly delicate beyond the line of safety; danger lurks in every stone. The peril of the heavy tower, of the restless vault, of the vagrant buttress; the uncertainty of logic, the inequalities of the syllogism, the irregularities of the mental mirror— all these haunting nightmares of the Church are expressed as strongly by the Gothic cathedral as though it had been the cry of human suf-

fering, and as no emotion had ever been expressed before or is likely
to find expression again. The delight of its aspirations is flung up to
the sky. The pathos of its self-distrust and anguish of doubt is buried
in the earth as its last secret. You can read out of it whatever else
pleases your youth and confidence; to me, this is all."

Much of the special animus of the Aquinas chapter undoubtedly
flowed from the explosive second thoughts inspired by Adams's in-
dustrious reading of the commentaries of the new science. The work
of the laboratory was a closed book to him. The nearest he came to
it was in his musing play with iron filings and a magnet, suggested
perhaps by James Clerk Maxwell's remark about Faraday: "In his
mind's eye, [he] saw lines of force traversing space where the mathematicians saw centres of force attracting at a distance." The more
Adams played with the magnet the more he felt the presence of occult
forces. Nothing more forcefully symbolized for him the apparent
helplessness of contemporary science than Clerk Maxwell's whimsical
suggestion that "a sorting demon" might conceivably reverse the operation of the Second Law of Thermodynamics in a gas and make
more energy available despite entropy. The playful fancy gave Adams
just the ammunition he needed for the last pages of the *Chartres*. No
wonder modern art had been divorced from philosophy and science.
"The highest scientific authority, in order to attain any unity at all,
had to resort to the Middle Ages for an imaginary demon to sort his
atoms!" With all of science to choose from, it was the satirist's instinct for the jugular to single out that picturesque image with which
to discredit the adversary.

DROPPED INTO the palpitant center of his Washington circle, *Mont
Saint Michel and Chartres* stirred a wave of delighted response, and
the fortunate possessors of the precious copies could only tantalize
those who were not on Adams's list. To his embarrassment the large
bevy of nieces fluttered as if his "talk . . . were divine revelation."
Appreciative letters flowed in—from his beloved Martha; from Elizabeth Cameron, her mother; from the brilliant and *spirituelle* Mrs.
Winthrop Chanler, who as a Catholic convert had read much in scholastic philosophy and was alert to the nuances about the Trinity and
the Holy Ghost. When someone interceded on behalf of a prominent
educator, Adams flatly refused: "No, the book was not written for

college presidents." Another Catholic convert, the poet-professor Charles Warren Stoddard, cheerful in spite of wretched health, scoffed at Adams's talk of "falling off." "You are a brilliant ornament of the Church and ought to be canonised." Saint-Gaudens was lyrically rowdy: "You dear old Porcupinus Poeticus, you old poeticus under a Bushelibus . . . You know (damn you), I never read, but last night I got as far in your work as the Virgin, Eve, and the Bees, and I cannot wait to acknowledge it until I am through. Thanks you dear old stick in the mud. Your brother in idiocy. ASt.G."

Henry James wrote his avowals with his customary mannered grace: "I have of late, after much frustration, been reading you with bated breath of wonder, sympathy, and applause. May I say, all unworthy and incompetent, what honour I think the beautiful volume does you, of how exquisite and distinguished an interest I have found it, with its easy lucidity, its saturation with its subject, its charmingly taken and kept tone. Even more than I congratulate you on the book I envy your relation to the subject." William James responded with forthright delight, for Adams was obviously now one with him in his detestation of vulgar positivism and all arrogant intellectualism. "I can't help sending you a paean of praise," he wrote. "From beginning to end it reads as from a man in the fresh morning of life, with a frolic power unusual to historic literature . . . Where you stole all that St. Thomas, I should like to know! . . . Moreover why this shyness and anonymity in such a work. Are you afraid of German professors noting the jokes and irony?"

The judgment that counted most came from his fellow Vulcan, Brooks, and it came with a generous uprush of feeling that drew the two brothers closer together. "Mixed with my delight in the intellectual effort and the great art," said Brooks, "is gratified pride and ambition . . . I perhaps alone of living men can appreciate fully all that you have done, for I have lived with the crusaders and the schoolmen . . . I think I have a right to insist that you should put this work of yours, this crowning effort of our race, into a form where it can be read and preserved. I want you to publish an edition and let it be sold, or at least distributed to the libraries. You have no right to let the best thing we have ever done die."

Henry had already distributed some fifty copies to friends and a few university libraries and thus regarded the book as "strictly published." Feeling as he did about popular taste, he scorned an audience of lecture-goers and Browning Clubs and similar dilettantes. "I imagine that neither you nor I care much to be admired by these," he rallied Brooks; "but in any case they will admire us the more at second hand." For the time being there the matter of further publication rested. He did take the precaution of copyrighting the book, though he insisted to Brooks that he would welcome the compliment of its being pirated. The "single real triumph" of his life, he added with a characteristic flourish of exaggeration, was "the wholesale piracy of *Democracy*." To his jaundiced eye his greatest failure had been the publication of his *History*, whose relatively small sale still rankled. He grumbled that he had "never heard of ten men who had ever read my history."

The crotchet made him all the more appreciative of Brooks's generous enthusiasm. "You are, as far as we know, the only man in America," Henry wrote, "whose opinion on this subject has any value; that is, whose opinion is decisive because it's all the opinion there is. No one else, to our knowledge, has been over the ground, or has tried to approach it from the same side . . . This is a singularly suggestive fact. You are alone, because it was you who shoved us into it. You started me ten years ago into this amusement. You mapped out the lines and indicated the emotions. In fact I should find it difficult to pick out of the volume what was yours from what was mine. The family mind approaches unity more nearly than is given to most of the works of God. You and I think so nearly on the same lines that, even when not directly interacting, the two minds run parallel, and you can hardly tell whether they are one or several."

23

The Shield of Protection

F AR FEWER TRACES remain of the writing of *The Education of Henry Adams* than of the *Chartres*. No reference to it occurs in the letters that streamed from Lafayette Square or from the avenue du Bois de Boulogne. Adams's intimates may have conjectured from certain hints and allusions that he was up to some literary experiment, but if they knew or suspected that it was an experiment in autobiography, they all preserved a discreet silence. In any case it was not the sort of book that he dared advertise before the fact, for to do so would have clouded his social relations with those who might have reason to fear the witty bite of his pen. Far better for the literary artist would be the *fait accompli,* the stage completely set, the portraits hung on the wall, and the curtain raised with a single dramatic gesture.

What led Adams to begin an autobiography in the midst of his work on *Mont Saint Michel and Chartres* can only be guessed. The time was ripe at the turn of the century for a retrospective look at his own career in it. Everywhere the press in 1900 was celebrating the remarkable progress of the world in the century just ending. For Adams, an old man at sixty-two, the century had its ambiguities. His ambivalent feelings may well have been stirred when in the spring of that year he enjoyed seeing the exquisite Jeanne Granier in Maurice Donnay's comedy *Education de prince.* As queen-in-exile she wished to complete the education of her youthful nephew so that he would be fit to reclaim the ancestral throne. He had already been instructed in Latin, Greek, modern languages, mathematics, fencing, equitation, military science, economics, and politics. The practical queen arranged to have him tutored in one more subject—women. The elaborate scheme of education comes to naught when it is discovered that the young man is not the legitimate heir to the throne. The piquancy of this ironic miscarriage of education must have more than amused Adams.

In the opening pages of his *Education* Adams was soon to write, "Probably no child born" in the year when he was born "held better cards than he." Why, then, had he failed in the race for riches and political power? What was it in the nature of his ancestry and education that had caused him to be pushed aside? The disenchantment that engulfed Adams at the turn of the century, the sense of a "descent from glory" that came to him as he helped his brothers with their biographies of their ancestors, demanded explanation. His own last chance to add luster to the family name had passed with the appointment of Joseph Choate as ambassador to England.

Having shared so many famous lives, known so many great ones of the earth, Adams read the increasing stream of memoirs and biographies with an almost morbid fascination. So many lives of his contemporaries were drawing to a close in the long troubled evening of his life: there were so many summings-up, so many apologias that he grew a connoisseur of their flaws as each broken cup was put upon the shelf. As one whose family's lives had been lived so much in the public eye, he knew he was fair game. The gossip mills had not spared him, especially after his wife's suicide.

When he read Charles's life of their father he could hardly contain his revulsion. Reading a biography of Hippolyte Taine, he thought it a "piece of evisceration," and it made him "cold to think of what would be the result of the same process applied to me." His dictum ran that even the greatest biographies "destroy their heroes." Hence, when he sent Henry James a copy of the *Education* he explained, "The volume is a mere shield of protection in the grave. I advise you to take your own life in the same way, in order to prevent biographers from taking it in theirs."

His sixty-fifth birthday, February 16, 1903, had found him in the mood to close up shop. "Only, I wish it was over!" he grumbled to Elizabeth. "Nothing annoys me more than the sense of preparing to start on a journey, especially paying my bills and catching the train." Here and there his letters began to throw off a shower of intimations. Ideas and themes which would dominate the *Education* appeared in provisional forms: coal and iron formulas; equivalences of social and physical phenomena; acceleration theories; the relative success of his generation; the ignorance of his social class; the Russian problem; the status of women; and always the recurring predictions of when civilization would collapse. The break of continuity between the world of his youth and the chaotic present called for definition. The contrast seemed to him as violent as that between the present day and the twelfth century.

Raphael Pumpelly's visit to Washington in March 1903 gave a fresh impetus to his historical and economic calculations, for Pumpelly was going to explore the "Asian mystery" that had so tantalized Adams. Anticipatory generalizations became increasingly frequent by the middle of 1903. Seizing on the admissions of repentant idealists like Lord Kelvin and Arthur Balfour for authority, Adams leaped to a conclusion with his usual alacrity. "Forty years ago," he wrote Gaskell, "our friends always explained things and had the cosmos down to a point, *teste* Darwin and Charles Lyell. Now they say they don't believe there is any explanation, or that you can choose between half-a-dozen, all correct. The Germans are all balled up. Every generalisation that we settled forty years ago, is abandoned. The one most completely thrown over is our gentle Darwin's Survival which has no longer a leg to stand on. I interpret even Kelvin as throwing it over."

His next remark to Gaskell showed the drift of his developing "chart of relations": "You have not answered my question about our breakfast at Sir Henry's [Henry Holland] and William Everett's dinner, if it was a dinner, at Cambridge. What year was it, '62 or '63; and what year did you come up to read law? I want to make some calculations of figures on it. What will be the next term of an equation or series like this:—$1823:1863::1903:x$? Figure it out in coal production; horsepower; thermo-dynamics; or, if you like, just simply in fields—space, energy, time, thought, or mere multiplicity and complexity. My whole interest is to get at a value for that x before I break up, which is an x more easily calculated . . . Science has given up the whole fabric of cause and effect. Even time-sequence is beginning to be threatened. I should not at all wonder if some one should not upset time. As for space, it is upset already. We did that sixty years ago, with electricity." That breakfast, he felt, had marked a turning point in his personal life, while it strikingly juxtaposed two English generations for the study of the transformation of society.

Other elements and themes left traces in his letters. The question needed to be settled, for example, of the relative success of the leaders of his generation in the race for prizes which the century had offered. He was surprised, he remarked to his brother Charles, "how few of our college mates, with all their immense advantages, seem to have got or kept their proportional share in the astounding creation of power since 1850. I should say that ten out of a thousand would cover them. We ought all to have rolled in millions, but nearly every one of my friends in College is now dead, and none was powerful or rich, except Lewis Cabot who married it. Yet we started ahead of everybody."

For a devotee of the Virgin it was a strange avowal to make; he seemed to feel no inconsistency in despising the "gold-bugs" and yet envying their power and riches. If he had failed, he hastened to add, as always when he stood himself back to back to his contemporaries, he had a consolation that was denied them. "The curious thing is that on the whole, I come out rather better than my neighbors, and at least have an enormous advantage of not caring." The crux of their difficulty—and this would be the ground note of the *Education*—was that they had all been "educated politically." They had tied their fortunes to reform, and "reform proved a total loss." They had banked on "abstract morality," and that "went into bankruptcy with the Church."

The complex pattern slowly coalesced, Adams's sensibility heightened with each new stimulus. Two recently published biographies powerfully agitated other clusters of reminiscence: John Morley's *Life of Gladstone* and Henry James's *William Wetmore Story and His Friends*. The *Gladstone* revived for Adams the diplomatic enigmas of forty years before. The life of Story struck closer to home. "The painful truth," he told James in November 1903, "is that all of my New England generation, counting the half-century, 1820–1870, were in actual fact only one mind and nature; the individual was a facet of Boston . . . We knew nothing—no! but really nothing! of the world. One cannot exaggerate the profundity of ignorance of Story in becoming a sculptor, or Sumner in becoming a statesman, or Emerson in becoming a philosopher. Story and Sumner, Emerson and Alcott, Lowell and Longfellow, Hillard, Winthrop, Motley, Prescott, and all the rest, were the same mind,—and so, poor worm!—was I! Type bourgeois-bostonien! . . . God knows that we knew our want of knowledge! the self-distrust became introspection—nervous self-consciousness—irritable dislike of America, and antipathy to Boston

. . . So you have written not Story's life, but your own and mine,—
pure autobiography . . . Improvised Europeans, we were, and—Lord
God!—how thin!"

The anniversary of Henry's wedding day on June 27, 1904, opened
the door upon still another train of reminiscence, the language of
which hinted at the literary frame in which the new "Travels" would
be cast. "If I could live to the end of my century—1938—I am sure I
should see the silly bubble explode," he confided to one of the matrons of his breakfast table. "A world so different from that of my
childhood or middle-life can't belong to the same scheme. It shifts
from one motive to another, without sequence. Any mathematician
will say that the chances against such rupture of continuity were a
million to one;—that it has been impossible. Out of a mediaeval,
primitive, crawling infant of 1838, to find oneself a howling, steam-
ing, exploding, Marconing, radiumating automobiling maniac of
1904 exceeds belief."

Adams's sixty-sixth birthday tolled insistently for an end to uncertainty. As he looked down on the turmoil of the world, he announced
to Mrs. Cameron, "It is time to quit, and I shall be glad to take leave."
His morbid expectation of his own imminent mental decay drove him
from one neurotic anxiety to another. The outbreak of the Russo-
Japanese War in February 1904 threatened universal cataclysm just
as he saw himself "on the brink of my own precipice of anarchy." To
his "coward fancy" France must be swept under as an ally of Russia
and Germany must become more than ever the arbiter of Europe.
Shuttling back and forth between Washington and Paris, he was "now
only a fluttering and venerable white moth, exceedingly irritable and
ridiculously explosive, who [does] nothing but flicker from perch to
perch, and damn the universe in general." The global inventory of
gloom and wreck and bankruptcy was as usual paralleled on the domestic front. Theodore Roosevelt's trust-busting tactics struck him as
utterly wrongheaded, redeemed only by the chance that enforcement
of the Sherman Act might hurry a general collapse. He saw chaos
reflected in his social circle as he ironically recorded the breakdowns
and diseases that were overtaking his acquaintances. "Oh, but it's
gay," he wrote Mrs. Cameron, who was off touring Italy, "and I was
never in so cheery a temper!"

The disastrous collapse of the Russian war effort brought Adams
hurrying to Secretary of State Hay with prophecies of the breakup of

that empire and financial catastrophe in Europe and America. Whenever Adams was slow to write from Paris Hay would beseech him for another installment of cheerful gloom. So for Hay's benefit he played Kaiser Wilhelm in imagination to make his point that while Germany must be appeased Russia must somehow be rescued. He argued for an "Atlantic system" including Germany, from the Rocky Mountains to the Elbe, since this was the energy center of the world. If Russia was to be saved from revolution and detached from Germany, equally important was the maintenance of Japan as an effective counterpoise in the Orient. But the task of diplomacy would have to be to deprive Japan of the more dangerous spoils of victory, control of the Asiatic mainland. This, Adams felt, must be Hay's final task, and he hoped against hope that the ailing Hay would live to finish it. Hay did not last out the negotiations, and Roosevelt alone reaped the diplomatic triumph of the Treaty of Portsmouth.

As Adams drew together the multiple strands of thought and reminiscence, he had reason to feel, when each winter he took up his station across from the White House and its strenuous occupant, that he was approaching the end of an epoch. He had continued to act as a buffer state to protect Hay from Lodge and Roosevelt, but the struggle grew increasingly useless. His constant effort had been to discourage Hay's recurring attempts to resign as Secretary of State, for Hay could at least temper the diplomatic excesses of their imperialist friends. However, as Roosevelt more and more seized the diplomatic initiative, Hay's cheerful cynicism deepened. The Isthmian canal project, which had become a fixed idea with Roosevelt, had dragged Hay as a loyal instrument of policy into lurid negotiations "trying to steal Panama," as he quipped to Adams. When Hay had tried again in 1903 to resign, Roosevelt countered with the irresistible plea, "I could not spare you." Since Hay's serious illness in 1900, his physical stamina had declined alarmingly, and there being then no safe treatment for prostate disorders, he visibly aged before the eyes of his devoted friend.

In the spring of 1904 Adams accompanied the Hays to the St. Louis Exposition, where Hay gave the opening address. It was to be Adams's last world's fair, and he enjoyed it as if already aware of the fact. With his usual chaffing satire he voiced his amazement. "Really, I think it astonishing for the beer-swilling dutchmen." The architecture might come "straight from the Beaux Arts," but it was "interesting," and the layout was "superb." He was sure, he told Gaskell, that "neither London, Paris, or New York would dare attempt what this half-baked city of St. Louis has done."

He went on to Paris shortly afterwards, bought himself an eighteen-horse-power Mercedes, and pounded up hill and down dale in quest of sixteenth-century windows, determined to die, as he said, at the "head of the menagerie." It was a summer of blown tires, endless repairs, and frequent mirings, but the writing of the *Education* went on. It was better than reading, he averred, because it compelled attention. By the end of November habit asserted itself again and he got back to Lafayette Square to contemplate Roosevelt's "ghoulish joy" at his "immense personal triumph" at carrying the election.

Hay clung loyally to his post in spite of an attack of angina pectoris that presaged worse things to come. On one of their regular walks he remarked to Adams that by the time he "got out of the office" he would "have lost the faculty of enjoyment." Adams retorted dryly, "Make your mind easy on that score, sonny; you've lost it now." An agreeable distraction during that anxious winter was provided by Adams's election to the newly formed Academy of Arts and Letters. The initial group—William Dean Howells, John La Farge, Augustus Saint-Gaudens, Samuel Clemens, John Hay, and Edward MacDowell—named Adams, Henry James, Charles Eliot Norton, Charles F. McKim, John Q. A. Ward, Thomas R. Lounsbury, Thomas Bailey Aldrich, and Theodore Roosevelt to the second group of electors. In the waning winter months Adams helped evaluate the claims of additional candidates for immortality. He carried out his task with high seriousness, for the new Academy promised to provide a "rank list" of American achievement to match those of France and England.

After long absence Henry James returned to the United States for an affectionate visit, and when he came to Washington he was "full of excitement," as Hay observed, "over his discovery of America." As Adams's houseguest he once more leaned against the mantel, descanting on his impressions in the hesitant and subtle dialect that was second nature to him. After his departure James found that he had "committed the grave inadvertence" of carrying off the latchkey, and he returned it with blessing and contrition. "I pine a little," he wrote from Philadelphia, "for the larger issues of your wonderful talk centre."

Adams kept his main job steadily before him as his "formula of anarchism" approached its final form. "I have done it scientifically," he assured Henry Osborn Taylor in January 1905, "by formulating the ratio of development in energy, as in explosives, or chemical energies. I can see it in the development of steam-power, and in the various economies of conveyance. Radium thus far is the term for these mechanical ratios. The ratio for thought is not so easy to fix. I can get a time-ratio only in philosophy. The assumption of unity which was the mark of human thought in the middle-ages has yielded very slowly to the proofs of complexity. The stupor of science before radium is a proof of it ... From the relative unity of twelfth-century conceptions of the Prime Motor, I can work down pretty safely to Karl Pearson's Grammar of Science or Wallace's Man's Place in Nature, or to Mach and Ostwald and the other Germans of today. By intercalating Descartes, Newton, Dalton and a few others, I can even make almost a time-ratio. This is where my middle-ages will work out."

HAY'S CONDITION continued to worsen, and the famed Sir William Osler was called in, but nothing could arrest the slow poisoning of his system. Two weeks after Roosevelt's inauguration Adams had his old friend in charge aboard the *Cretic,* carrying him off to the Mediterranean for a rest. Hay seemed to improve in Italy, and the two men parted late in April at Nauheim, where Hay had gone for the baths. In Hay's journal we catch a rare echo of their talk: "Adams in a high philosophical mood. He had been reading on causation and was full of his subject. He used one very good phrase. He said the man who in critical times appears to be guiding events is merely the medium for the direction of Energy." They needed to look no farther than the Kaiser and Roosevelt for apparent illustration. Hay was loathe to part with "porcupinus Angelicus," lamenting to Saint-Gaudens, in a parody of the lines from Scott's *Marmion,*

> Oh, Adams! in our hours of ease
> Rather inclined to growl and teaze,
> When pain and anguish wring the brow
> A ministering angel thou.

In Paris the anxious Adams beguiled himself with playgoing. One of his nieces of the theater, Elizabeth Marbury, was interested in a new play, *Vidocq,* by Emile Bergerat, which Benoît Coquelin was to produce the following winter. She persuaded him to make a translation for her, the apprehensive author swearing him to secrecy. Doing ten pages a day, Adams completed the work in about six weeks. It was "just a Gaboriau spectacle of the Conan Doyle type," he said, "and naïf for babes," that was to say "rot," but he consoled himself that it had taught him some French. Miss Marbury appears to have lost interest in the play, and the translation disappeared from sight.

In the last week of May, Hay, racked with cardiac pains, rejoined Adams in Paris, having begged off from his visit to Kaiser Wilhelm and King Leopold. Adams whirled his friend on repeated jaunts through the Bois in the Mercedes at what seemed to Hay "an incredible rate of speed," but the gay abandon suited the reckless mood of their last reunion. There was ample matter for sardonic reflection. The Senate had so dismembered Hay's arbitration treaties that Roosevelt was obliged to withdraw them. However, the proposed treaty negotiations at Portsmouth, New Hampshire, to end the Russo-Japanese War would at least be free from senatorial interference. "You must hold out for the peace negotiations," Adams entreated Hay. "I've not time!" he parried, with a shake of the head. "You'll need little time!" said Adams. Not that it mattered, Adams afterwards reflected, for the peace would "make itself without bothering; but it would have been a nice climax for Hay's career."

The news of Hay's death at his summer place in New Hampshire on July 1, 1905, brought no surprise. As Adams wrote Elizabeth Cameron, "Both of us knew when we parted, that his life was ended . . . We had been discussing it for at least two years." Hay's passing closed the most intimate chapter of all. Feelingly, he wrote to Mrs. Hay, "As for me, it is time to bid good-bye. I am tired. My last hold on the world is lost with him . . . I can no longer look a month ahead, or be sure of my hand or mind . . . He and I began life together. We will stop together." Richard Watson Gilder sounded him for a memorial article for the *Century,* but Adams put him off with an ambiguous and capering sort of reply. No one seemed to understand his profound scruples against writing a biography of his closest friend, of committing "murder," as he would say, in print. He had expressed his animus to Hay himself with Rabelaisian violence shortly after reading Morley's *Gladstone:* "When I read,—standing behind the curtain— these repetitions of life, flabby and foolish as I am;—when I try to glug-glug down my snuffling mucous membrane these lumps of cold calves'-head and boiled pork-fat, then I know what you will suffer for your sins . . . On the whole, I foresee plainly, that the biographer's work on you will be strychnine."

Seated at his desk that summer at 23 avenue du Bois de Boulogne, he wrote with furious speed, for his days were often interrupted by hundred-mile motor sallies to his favorite churches, "much to the delight of a lot of pretty women" who went with him. The mask of his gaiety dropped, however, as soon as he took up his pen. "I'm bored, I'm mouldy, I'm breaking fast," he wailed to Elizabeth. "At this rate I've barely a year before me . . . In my opinion I've made a muddle of my universe, and it's time I dropped out." The antic pose was of course second nature; but how much was flourish and how much genuine anguish no one, least of all himself, could say. Not long before, Brooks had taken him to task for his hypochondria and depression: "Seriously the trouble with you is that you are so uniformly well and active that you do not know what it is to be hurt . . . you can write longer, remember better, and read double the number of hours that I can." Whatever his imagined state, the manuscript marched and the letters flowed, as usual laden with gossip, *Realpolitik,* and the obsessive central theme of the *Education.* "I do not know what is going to happen in the world," he wrote Mrs. Chanler, "because the sequence of centuries has now brought us far beyond the elements of our old curve, and the acceleration of speed is incalculable; but all my figures lead me to conclude that the present society must succumb to the task within one generation more."

He brought back from Paris in December 1905 a manuscript sufficiently near completion to make arrangements for printing it with Furst and Company, the same firm which had done the *Chartres*. The winter slipped away with unaccustomed quiet in the void left by Hay's death, though life in Lafayette Square was brightened by the return of Mrs. Cameron as a Washington hostess with her daughter, Martha. His "hotel for nieces" flourished, and the rustle of their coming and going calmed him as he put behind him his sixty-eighth year. He did not see Roosevelt anymore and had no desire to be lectured by him. He effaced himself from public notice so successfully that he had the macabre amusement of seeing himself referred to in a book review in the *New York Times* as "the late Henry Adams." His house was now "mostly frequented by women, children and anarchists who make no noise and are not in politics." For the first time in nearly twenty years he broke his rigid rule of avoiding weddings and journeyed to Boston to give away his niece Dorothy Quincy at a ceremony in Boston's Trinity Church. The visit revived all his antipathies to his native city. It was "green with mental mould." One exotic thrived there, however, Mrs. Jack Gardner, and when Adams made his way to Fenway Court to see the baroque marvels of her art collection in her reconstituted Venetian palace he burst into superlatives: "Your work must be classed as a *tour-de-force,*—no Evolution at all,—but pure Special Creation in an adverse environment."

He sailed again for Paris early in May with Mrs. Cameron to resume his role as neighbor and aging cavalier. The final didactic chapters of the *Education* on his "Dynamic Theory of History" still needed to be fleshed out, as may be inferred from the intense course of reading into which he plunged. Now, in the light of his researches on the Virgin as a force in history, he followed his Catholic guides to the great Church fathers of the period, when the fetish power of the old religion had been transformed into that of the new. He began to browse, as he said, on St. Ambrose and St. Augustine "to see what the devil they were driving at," reading "nothing but third and fourth century,—fascinating and lurid,—full of Saint Augustine, Saint Jerome, Saint Chrysostom and the Alexandrines." The historical enigma which had challenged Gibbon, the fall of Rome, needed to be reexamined in the light cast by St. Augustine's *City of God* and his *Confessions.* For the most part he pursued the subject in French historical studies like those of Amédée Thierry and Gaston Boissier.

The main part of the *Education* was probably in proof when Adams took up his stand again in Lafayette Square early in November 1906. Three months later the original forty copies of the privately printed edition—later augmented to one hundred—began to go out to his intimates, only a week after the date appended to the preface, February 16, 1907, his sixty-ninth birthday. It was a comfortable quarto volume printed on heavy paper with wide margins on which he asked his readers to supply their corrections. The moment called for a gesture of conciliation. He devised a formula that almost none of the recipients would be bold enough—or careless enough of their prize—to adopt. In the variant of it that he used to Gaskell he said, "In case you object to any phrase or expression, will you please draw your pen through it, and, at the end, return me the volume." The book contained merely "certain reminiscences which are taking shape in my mind," ran his deprecatory addition, "which are meant as my closing lectures to undergraduates in the instruction abandoned and broken off in 1877." Down the index he went, asking the imprimatur of "every friend drawn by name into the narrative." From first to last he diffidently insisted that the book was "in the nature of proof sheets."

The "permissions" came in with gratifying speed—and submissiveness. He had of course written with considerable restraint and self-censorship. One need only compare the violently scornful epithets which he rains upon Theodore Roosevelt in his private letters with the relative moderation of the estimate in the *Education*. Adams knew his victims so surely that they dared not show a sign of offense at the irony that lurked in the shadows of some of his portraits. After all, ought one to complain of immortality at such a deftly exacted price? Donald Cameron, whom he described as the type of the "Pennsylvania mind" that "reasoned little and never talked" though "in practical matters it was the steadiest of all American types," temperately replied that "if what you said suits you I am content, feeling sure that you have written what you believe and one has no right to ask any more." In the case of Senator Lodge, with whom his relations had been much closer, the measure of praise was just sufficient to be damning: "Lodge had the singular merit of interesting," more than Roosevelt. The career of both men in politics, however, illustrated the inescapable law of politics: "Power is poison." Like himself, Lodge suffered from "Bostonitis," restlessness, and uncertainty, a tendency toward a double standard of conduct. "Double standards are an inspiration to men of letters," Adams declared, "but they are apt to be fatal to politicians." There was no visible flame in the gracefully turned epigrams, but one saw the marks of the grill which he and Hay had heated so long in helpless frustration.

Lodge suffered for a while in silence but finally swallowed his senatorial pride and called on Adams. Adams waited expectantly through dinner and a long evening to see what effect his instruction had had. At last as Lodge took his departure he managed to blurt out, "I have read your *Education*. I didn't know I was as British as you make me out." Mrs. Lodge, the "Sister Anne" of the letters, afterwards protested: "Brother, why are you so hard on poor Pinky? You didn't mean all you said, did you? And of course you are going to change it and leave all those remarks out?" Adams answered, "If Cabot objects, I will take out what he objects to. No wives are allowed to complain of what I've written about their husbands." Lodge failed to object, and the estimate stood. Perhaps the shade of John Hay would rest easier.

Of almost everyone Adams felt reasonably sure; but, as he told Roosevelt, there was one censorship he feared above all others, that of Charles W. Eliot, and with reason, for though he had been personally respectful towards Eliot he was scathing toward Harvard. "In spite of Eliot's reforms and his steady, generous, liberal support, the system remained costly, clumsy and futile." Henry had added insult to injury, for he had refused an honorary degree in 1892 in set terms of reproach. Perhaps a guilty conscience spoke when he exclaimed that "Eliot's sentence will be damnation forever." Eliot, taking Adams at his word, returned his copy of the *Education,* one of only three who are known to have done so. Long afterwards, Professor Bliss Perry overheard Eliot remark, "An overrated man and a much overrated book."

The reaction of his brothers was curiously divergent. Charles read the opening chapter on the Quincy childhood with pure delight: "I couldn't help thinking that it was written for me alone of the whole living world . . . Curious! that old Boston and Quincy and Medford atmosphere of the 40's; and you brought it all back out of the remote past! But you're not a bit of a Rousseau . . . Lord! how you do bring it all back! How we did hate Boston! How we loved Quincy! The aroma of the Spring,—'Henry greedy, cherry-eater'—and you and I alone of all living, recalling it all! . . . Oh dear! Oh dear! I'm a boy again." For him the vivid evocation was enough; the philosophy of history was irrelevant. Brooks, who had so rapturously welcomed the *Chartres,* was disappointed. Though he too read the account of Henry's childhood "with great amusement and sympathy," he recorded long afterward that "Henry, after 'Mont Saint Michel,' drifted off into his 'Education,' in which, as I warned him to weariness, I feared that he had attempted too much. I told him that he had tried to mix science with society and that the public would never understand his scientific theory."

Justice Oliver Wendell Holmes, who had to bully him to get a copy, protested, "I note in your Education you talk very absurdly as if your work has been futile. I for one have owed you more than you in the least suspect. And I have no doubt that there are many others not to be neglected who do the same. Of course you may reply that it is also futile—but that is the dogmatism that often is disguised under scepticism." Holmes, youthful in spirit, increasingly deplored Adams's pessimism. "When I happened to fall in with him on the street," Holmes recalled, "he could be delightful, but when I called at his house and he was posing to himself as the old cardinal he would turn everything to dust and ashes. After a tiresome day's work one didn't care to have one's powers of resistance taxed by discourse of that sort, so I called rarely."

Hay's widow, understandably baffled by Adams's esoteric tribute to her husband, gave him a gentle lecture about his quest for "Force": "Why, instead of all those other books you have gone to, to find it, did you not go back to your Bible?" Saint-Gaudens, with the honest vanity of an artist, enjoyed the book "immensely . . . trotting out pages referring to himself," according to his son, "asking everybody around here if they don't think that he seems like that." What Henry Osborn Taylor wrote to his onetime teacher is lost; but in his copy he noted, "In this book the mind of Henry Adams rattles around the universe to little purpose." John Jay Chapman teased the adoring Mrs. Chanler, after looking into Taylor's copy: "You are a sort of pupil—and castaway, drowning, clutcher at the piping Adams as he sits on his raft in the sunset and combs his golden hair with a gold toothpick . . . How amusing and delightful the book is. Why it's quite a social fan and Horace Walpole sort of book." Henry James surrendered to the ambience of the book. "I lost myself in your ample pages as in a sea of memories and visions and associations. I dived deep, and I think I felt your extraordinary element, every inch of its suggestion and recall and terrible thick evocation so much that I remained below, as it were, sticking fast in it, even as an indiscreet fly in amber." The widening circles of pleasure and bafflement that radiated out from each copy warranted his friend Moreton Frewen's remark that the *Education* was "a very stone of Sisyphus" which "defies all analysis."

Adams himself could not quite make up his mind about the book and from the first found himself on the defensive, throwing off explanations with every degree of paradox and humility, now serious, now grimly facetious, and almost always deepening its puzzles in spite of himself. Unless his readers helped him revise it, he theatrically declared to former Secretary of State Richard Olney, he would "throw it into the fire like half a dozen of its predecessors. It has at least served one purpose—that of educating me." "Take your old book!" he wrote to President Charles Thwing of Western Reserve, who had asked for it; "it's a rotten one anyway." He would permit Pumpelly to read his "drivel," he told him, for it did have "one or two ideas . . . which are fairly anarchical and sound," but he wanted it borne in mind that they were "just open air sketches." It was meant "as an experiment and not as a conclusion," he told another suppliant. He was sending the book "out into the world only to be whipped."

No amount of fanciful chaff could obscure the fact that he was very serious about what he had attempted to do. He adjured one of his circle of married women, "Please try,—though in vain,—to think of it as what it was written for—a serious effort to reform American education by showing what it ought to be. The Ego is purely imaginary fiction." Much in the same vein, he explained to Professor John W. Burgess of Columbia, "What would gratify my ambition would be to help our teachers to move towards common ground and definite agreement of view." To another historian he wrote, "My object was to suggest a reform of the whole university system, grouping all knowledge as a historical stream to be treated by historical methods, and drawing a line between the University and technology." In fact he entertained the idea, not long afterwards, of sending out copies of the book to some of his fellow historians to pave the way for his essay "The Rule of Phase Applied to History." He went so far as to draft a kind of follow-up letter in which he explained that "the volume starts, as usual, with the commonplace that the subject of it, the lay-figure, the manikin, had no education, since the Universities of his time were a hundred years behind the level of his needs, and the technical schools at least fifty; but that the technical schools had the advantage of unity and energy of purpose. After illustrating this statement in a great variety of ways, through some four hundred pages, the book closes by a belabored effort to state the problem for its special domain of history, in a scientific formula, which affects the terms of astronomy merely because every child is supposed to know the so-called law, as well as the fact, of gravitation. In order not to exasperate the reader too much, the volume stopped there."

Again and again he returned to the charge, each time with a somewhat different preface. Thus to Whitelaw Reid: "But pray do not for-

get that it is what it avows:—a story of how an average American
education, in spite of the most favorable conditions, ran down hill,
for twenty years, into the bog labelled Failure; and how it had to be
started again, under every disadvantage, and the blindest fumblings,
to crawl uphill a little way in order at last to get a little view ahead of
the field it should have begun by occupying. Of course the path is
sugar-coated in order to induce anyone to follow it. The nearer we
can come to romance, the more chance that somebody will read—
and misunderstand. But not one reader in a thousand ever under-
stands." The most arresting image of his intent he invented for James
Ford Rhodes: "If you can imagine a centipede running along in
twenty little sections (each with a little mathematical formula carefully concealed in its stomach) to the bottom of a hill; and then la-
boriously climbing in fifteen sections more, (each with a new mathematical problem carefully concealed in its stomach), till it can get up
on a hill an inch or two high, so as to see ahead a half an inch or so—
you will understand in advance all that the 'Education' has to say."

The clamor for copies was understandably far greater than that for
the *Chartres,* and whether Adams granted or denied the request he
felt obliged in either case to justify and extenuate himself. The pressure for publication especially embarrassed him. He would not publish, he told Charles, because his notion of work was consultative, by
"comparison, correspondence and conversation. Ideas once settled
so,—as you see in Darwin's Life,—anyone can explain them to the
public." It was a hazardous experiment, not as history but as art, he
told Ambassador Reid. "To write a heavy dissertation on modern
education, and fill up the back-ground with moving figures that will
carry the load, is a literary tour-de-force that cannot wholly succeed
even in the hands of St Augustine or Rousseau."

One young and ambitious editor, Ferris Greenslet of Houghton
Mifflin Company, dipped into Richard Watson Gilder's copy one day
in 1907 and read through the night, blithely unaware of Adams's extreme scruples. Greenslet immediately dashed down to Washington to
offer a contract. He recalled how the "aged colored butler" let him
into the drawing room "where all the chairs were of nursery altitude."
Adams entered, "small, scraggly-bearded, coolly polite." Greenslet's
anecdote continues: " 'Mr. Adams,' I said, struggling with an untimely
return of my adolescent stammer, brought on by excitement, 'I have
just finished reading your *Education*. It is one of the great books of

the new century. Houghton Mifflin Company want to publish it.' 'I only printed a hundred copies of that book for my friends,' said Mr. Adams. 'I don't know how you got hold of it!' " The porcupine quills subsided a little while the dream of an editor's coup vanished. Greenslet did not give up the chase, however, and bided his time until Adams's death for what eventually became one of his firm's greatest successes.

BOUND IN DARK BLUE COVERS, the handsome quarto volume of *The Education of Henry Adams* with its wide-margined pages duplicated the appearance of *Mont Saint Michel and Chartres.* What lay between the covers was a work whose form had posed a far more difficult challenge. The question of form had haunted Adams during the writing of the book, and he now, in retrospect, realized he had not really solved it. Sometimes he asserted that he had written both books simply to educate himself "in the possibilities of literary form." Between artists "the arrangement, the construction, the composition, the art of climax are our only serious study." His scheme, he insisted, had proved "impossible."

William James's response particularly stirred his misgivings. "The boyhood part," James wrote, "is really superlative. It and the London part should become classic historic documents." He then went on to speak presciently for many a subsequent reader: "There is a hodgepodge of world-fact, private fact, philosophy, irony, (with the word 'education' stirred in too much for my appreciation!) which gives a unique cachet to the thing, and gives a very pleasant *Gesammteindruck* of H. A.'s *Self.* A great deal of the later diplomatic history is dealt with so much by hint and implication, that to an ignoramus like W. J. it reads obscurely. Above all I should like to understand more precisely just what Hay's significance really was. You speak of the perfection of his work but it is all esoteric." He went on to object also to Adams's historical thesis, perhaps the only one of his initial readers to do so. "I don't follow or share your way of conceiving the historical problem as the determination of a curve by points. I think that that applies only to what is done and over . . . But unless the future contains genuine novelties, unless the present is really creative of them, *I don't see the use of time at all.*"

Quick to take refuge in self-depreciation, Adams responded that his book was really "rotten." "Did you ever read the Confessions of St Augustine, or of Cardinal de Retz, or of Rousseau, or of Benvenuto Cellini, or even of my dear Gibbon. Of them all, I think St Augustine alone has an idea of literary form,—a notion of writing a story with an end and object, not for the sake of the object, but for the form, like a romance." What St. Augustine did could no longer be done: "The world does not furnish the contrasts or the emotion." Coming back to the problem in a letter to Barrett Wendell, Adams volunteered "that our failures are really not due to ourselves alone. Society has a great share in it." The literary faults of St. Augustine and Rousseau were really worse than his. "We have all three undertaken to do what cannot be successfully done—mix narrative and didactic purpose and style . . . St Augustine's narrative subsides at last into the dry sands of metaphysical theology. Rousseau's narrative fails wholly in didactic result; it subsides into still less artistic egoism."

Adams had felt a kinship with the great Church father who also had had cravings for worldly success and who learned at last to despise it. The Puritan self-contempt and the low regard for "insect" man, as Adams liked to write, found confirmation in Augustine's horror at the depravity of humankind. Adams had read Augustine's self-denunciations with an appreciative pencil in hand. Again and again a poignant recollection demanded a recognitory mark. Ancient Hippo on the African shore might have been Quincy or Boston in the way it tamed a boy's spirit. "But elder folks' idleness is called 'business'; that of boys, being really the same, is punished by those elders." Augustine had loved the stage plays of Carthage, had given himself to warm friendships and learned the terrible "mourning if one die, and darkenings of sorrows, that steeping of the heart in tears, all sweetness turned to bitterness." He, too, had "panted after honours, gains, marriage." For him, too, all had turned to dust and ashes. He had embraced the Manichaean heresy with all the enthusiasm that Adams seemed to see in his own interest in science, and it left the telltale vestiges of skepticism and ambivalence. Augustine had also been a schoolteacher, and he, too, had welcomed the day when he was "freed" from his "Rhetoric Professorship" so that he could devote himself to writing. Living in a time of great crisis in the Roman world, feeling the shock of Alaric's sack of Rome, Augustine dramatized his disenchantment and revulsion in the very spirit of Adams's own *fin de siècle*. Augustine's *Confessions* may at the end have run off into the "dry sands of metaphysical theology," but it was the metaphysical question that led Adams to conclude his book with his own didactic chapters on a "scientific" theory of history.

In the ripeness of age Adams had returned to his "favorite prophet of disenchantment." He had again read Thomas Carlyle, and he carefully inscribed in his boyhood copy of *Heroes and Hero Worship*, beneath the notation "Cambridge, March 8, 1855," the legend "Washington, June 28, 1894." His idealist criticisms of science, never completely quieted by Herbert Spencer and Thomas Huxley, rose again to the surface after his immersion in medieval metaphysics. He became more and more preoccupied with that science of mind for which Carlyle had clamored.

Adams had often toyed with the notion of creating a literary "double" whom he could freely criticize. The trick had never been turned before except by Carlyle's eccentric philosopher Herr Diogenes Teufelsdröckh, the visionary prophet of a new social order in *Sartor Resartus* who sometimes spoke of himself in his pseudo-autobiography as "The Wanderer." Wanderer Adams had certainly been, and when he visited the North Cape it was Carlyle's baffled persona that had sprung to his mind. He was a "newer Teufelsdröckh," perplexed by the spectacle of the vast Atlantic empire of coal and iron pressed upon by the "icecap of Russian inertia."

There are many suggestive parallels between *Sartor* and the *Education*. Adams's Latin epitaph satirizing his professorial essay on Anglo-Saxon law—"Hic Jacet/Homunculus Scriptor . . ."—recalls the "Hic Jacet" of *Sartor* memorializing the noble knight who spent his life building a heap of manure. The preface to the *Education*, with its play on the tailor's manikin and its clothes symbolism, is equally Carlylian. Carlyle's bewildered Teufelsdröckh through long years had swept downwards into the abyss of alienation. At last, in the *rue d'Enfer*, he experienced his "Baphometic Fire-baptism," freed himself from the spirit that denied and was spiritually reborn. In roughly similar fashion Adams plotted the spiritual orbit of the *Education*. His spiritual rebirth came on the architectural highway from Mont Saint Michel to Chartres, where, in a moment of transcendent vision, he recovered his ancestral Norman soul.

His pilgrimage in search of education had been beset by will-o'-the-wisps which led him into the bog he ironically called "Failure," the period 1870–1877 when he taught history at Harvard, edited the

North American Review, and got married. Marriage, like the teaching and writing of history, was, in his dialectic, merely the trying out in experience of what one had presumably learned. It did not count towards a philosophy of history. For the purposes of instruction in the mastery of power, the richly productive middle period of his life, the period of marriage and literary achievement, vanished from his pages in the deceptive crosslights of paradox.

The manikin-persona marches on his foredoomed way where all values and terms are reversed as old knowledge is discovered to be new ignorance and the whole garment of education hangs in tatters about him. Out of his intellectual storm and stress comes at last Adams's formula for salvation, his own version of the "Everlasting Yea," a dynamic theory of history.

A final illumination is offered by *Sartor,* and this is upon the style of the *Education,* which is far removed from the almost classical cadences of Adams's early writing. The exuberant and vatic allusiveness of *Sartor* seems to have inspired Adams to give the loose to his poetic faculty and to fill his pages with allusions and analogies, paradoxes and epigrams. The play of symbol and metaphor that rises to the images of the Virgin and the dynamo and culminates in the comet analogy and a meteoric shower of scientific metaphors reads like an illustration of Carlyle's chapter "Symbols."

The psychological theory that controls the work and gives it its partially fictive character appears in one of the earliest chapters, "Washington," in which Adams recounts the journey he took in May 1850. In retrospect it fixed "the stage of a boy's thought in 1850 . . . This was the journey he remembered. The actual journey may have been quite different, but the actual journey has no interest for education. The memory was all that mattered." Adams's acknowledgment helps account for the characteristic transformations of the autobiographical record in the volume. No note is more insistently struck than that of November melancholy, the fears and forebodings that always preceded December 6, the anniversary of his wife's suicide in 1885, the dread event of which no mention occurs in the *Education.* Adams's return to New York in November 1904 marks the virtual conclusion of the book, and the note is distinctly that of November despair. New York had "the air and movement of hysteria, and the citizens were crying, in every accent of anger and alarm, that the new forces must at any cost be brought under control . . . The two-thousand-years failure of Christianity roared upward from Broad-way, and no Constantine the Great was in sight."

The contrast between the centuries is made on the very first page of the *Education* with all the shock which Adams's rhetoric was capable of inflicting. "Had he been born in Jerusalem under the shadow of the Temple and circumcised in the Synagogue by his uncle the high priest, under the name of Israel Cohen, he would scarcely have been more distinctly branded, and not much more heavily handicapped in the races of the coming century, in running for such stakes as the century was to offer." Midway through the *Education* he invoked a similar image for his return to America in 1868, when he found that "his world was dead," a moment in his career that seemed in retrospect a rebirth in an alien world. "Not a Polish Jew fresh from Warsaw or Cracow—not a furtive Yacoob or Ysaac still reeking of the Ghetto, snarling a weird Yiddish to the officers of the customs—but had a keener instinct, an intenser energy, and a freer hand than he— American of Americans, with Heaven knew how many Puritans and Patriots behind him, and an education that had cost a civil war . . . He had been unfairly forced out of the track, and must get back into it as best he could." Imagination and memory coalesced about the symbol which had become the focus of Brahmin alarm. Carlyle's pathetic "Wandering Jew" of Victorian Christian prejudice had now grown to satanic stature as the universal scapegoat of the turn of the century.

In the *Education* Adams answered for himself the questions he had asked at the conclusion of his *History*. The American "democratic experiment" had shown its efficiency in achieving material progress. Would the experiment be crowned by a corresponding moral progress? By 1906 he was prepared to answer no, and that nothing could be hoped for until the gold-bugs were swept away along with the political institutions they had captured. Starting from premises very close to those of Carlyle, he arrived by a similar idealistic absolutism at Carlyle's repudiation of democracy. Charles W. Eliot could not avoid sensing the drift of the book. "I should like to be saved from loss of faith in democracy as I grow old and foolish," he wrote Grace Norton. "I should be very sorry to wind up as the three Adamses did. I shall not unless I lose my mind."

The "air of reality" with which Adams invested the tragic hero of his autobiographical-philosophical romance is the product of a masterfully sustained illusion. Not that the author really undervalued his "manikin"; no theme is more often reiterated than that if he was wrong his fellows were even more mistaken. From the naïve young man with whom one imaginatively identifies oneself, the *ingénu* who had but dimly felt the dilemmas of existence, the doll figure is transformed into the type of all the great symbolic questers, whose images are ironically invoked as conjure forms: Faust, Teufelsdröckh, and Ulysses. He becomes a "weary Titan of Unity," a "wrinkled Tannhäuser," a Seneca to Theodore Roosevelt's Nero, a Rasselas and a Candide, a Candide most of all perhaps, for the spirit of Voltairean raillery hovers over the book with its suggestion of the eternal ludicrous. Voltaire's gibe against Leibnitz in *Candide* ("all that is is for the best" in "this best of all worlds") reechoes in a dozen variations through the *Education* as it does in Adams's correspondence.

The philosophical undercurrent of the early chapters emerges in the later chapters as the principal subject of inquiry. In the opening chapter Adams suggested that these autobiographical experiences raised metaphysical questions: "From cradle to grave this problem of running order through chaos, direction through space, discipline through freedom, unity through multiplicity, has always been, and must always be, the task of education, as it is the moral of religion, philosophy, science, art, politics, and economy." What Adams began with as his tool of analysis was the philosophical apparatus which the reeducation of the turn of the century had finally given him, the apparatus of the concluding philosophical chapters of the *Chartres*. As he said in the *Chartres,* "The attempt to bridge the chasm between multiplicity and unity is the oldest problem of philosophy, religion, and science." The *Education* exhibited the operation of this dichotomy in the life of the young Henry Adams, in the world in which he found himself, and ultimately in the very constitution of cosmological reality. What weighed heavily on his mind in the later 1890s, he said, was the need for "a historical formula that should satisfy the conditions of the stellar universe," a formula that would allow the philosopher-historian to achieve for human society a science of prediction.

As the intellectual and aesthetic synthesis spreads out in ever-widening gyres, Adams's inability to hold the centrifugal elements of science, metaphysics, politics, and autobiography in suspension becomes increasingly apparent. To no part of the *Education* is his own caveat more applicable than to the final chapters on his theory of history: "No one means all he says, and yet very few say all they mean, for words are slippery and thought is viscous." The scientific outlook at which he aims is, as he freely acknowledges, one of unimaginable difficulty, for the chaos of external forces is inevitably duplicated in the chaos of thought. The new education thus ends in intellectual ironies even more disillusioning than the personal ironies of his quest of a career. The search for unity, for running order through chaos, which had been proposed as the object of all education, ends in the discovery that this search too is an illusion and a self-deception. In an expanding multiverse of thought, unity becomes an expanding synthesis coextensive with chaos. As Adams put the matter in one of his orphic metaphors, "The mind must merge in its supersensual multiverse, or succumb to it." Such is the dilemma which the new science posed to the historian.

The famous thirty-third and thirty-fourth chapters, "A Dynamic Theory of History" and "A Theory of Acceleration," stand either as a monument to intellectual ambition, or as the most prodigious tale of a tub by which a supreme ironist defies reason to pursue him. Who is not lost in wild surmise at the crux? What unit of mind power, what psychic erg, ohm, or volt, would give the Laplace of the future a common denominator for Newton, Shakespeare, and Michelangelo? For the riddle of the higher energetics Adams does not even venture an analogy. Here indeed was the task for a greater Newton, to postulate the universal psychic atom and to plot the orbit of the psycho-physical cosmos. The closer Adams approached the ultimate object of his speculations, the more remote any solution became. The impasse of his own mind seemed to foreshadow the impasse of the human race itself. This, then, was the staggering challenge that he offered the young "men of the world" whom he had addressed in the preface. They would indeed "need to jump."

Man's comet-mind seemed to Adams to be racing to some unimaginably terrible and imminent rendezvous. Cotton Mather, Michael Wigglesworth, and Jonathan Edwards had summoned sinners to repent in much the same spirit. The rough beast of the apocalypse was about to spring upon the human race, and it had more faces than Siva. It was incarnated in the "Trusts and Corporations" whose "unscrupulous energy . . . tore society to pieces." The baffled teacher, absorbed at last by the moralist, can do little more than teach his pupils to meet the end with stoical resignation, for the final economy of energy was in Adams's view the contemplation of Nirvana. Part of his nature clung desperately to the hope that the mind of the race, redeemed by a "new man" of prodigious mental power, should like a comet be able to defy dissolution at its nearest approach to the sun of ultimate forces. The other side of his prophetic soul, that which had always taken a gloomy pleasure in the imagination of disaster, spoke through the image of the meteor whose end was an incandescent trail of light against the dark sky. The contradictions were unresolvable.

After such apocalyptic visions there remained only the formality of departure; the manikin figure had served its purpose. "Nunc Age [Now Act]" is the title of the concluding chapter, dated 1905. It was his leave-taking to the young men who must now confront the seemingly impossible. If there was artistic symmetry in human affairs, it was also time for him to go. Hay's death had ended Adams's career as "stable companion to statesmen." For the weary "pilgrim of power" on the "darkening prairie" of the mind, the wish would have to stand for the deed.

24

Schoolboy at Seventy

INISHED with the proof sheets of the *Education* by Christmas of 1906, Adams looked forward bleakly again, as after the *Chartres,* to "another winter of vanishing interests." His elegiac "last will and testament," as he called the *Education,* went the rounds of the elect on both sides of the Atlantic. His involvement in unofficial diplomacy and palace politics for half a dozen years as Hay's "shadow" had ended abruptly with Hay's death. The moment, as he had poignantly foreseen, gave a painful check to his life. The succeeding interval had brought him no closer to the court of the Rough Rider; rather, the last excuse for "sitting" on President Roosevelt was now gone, and the frail social relation that continued to subsist encouraged few forays across Lafayette Square. Hay's successor, Elihu Root, may have been the "best man" for the job, as Adams freely acknowledged, but Root, with his background as secretary of war under President McKinley, moved in an alien social and political orbit. Root had no need of a "buffer state" against Roosevelt and Lodge, being wiser in the ways of the Senate.

Adams had thought to escape the troubling chore of "biographising" John Hay, hoping that the *Education* would serve as sufficient tribute. He explained to Elizabeth Cameron that he was driven to print the *Education* "only as a defence against the pressure to write a memoir of Hay, which I will not do, not on my account but his. All memoirs lower the man in estimation. Such a sidelight is alone artistic." Clara Hay, however, felt that in spite of the scruples of Hay's closest friend some literary tribute was due her husband's memory. In her direct and artless way she decided to undertake a publication that would present Hay to posterity as she thought he should be presented, and thus initiated one of the oddest memorials ever printed,

Letters of John Hay and Extracts from Diary. Adams was drawn into
the scheme during the closing months of 1906 while seeing the *Edu-*
cation through the press.

After getting his agreement to act as a kind of subeditor, Mrs. Hay
circulated a request among friends like Roosevelt, Whitelaw Reid,
Henry White, John Nicolay, and others that they turn over their collections of Hay letters to Adams. One source left discreetly unsought
was the collection of merry and boyishly adoring letters to "Dearest
Lizzie Cameron," letters sometimes impishly written to while away
the tedium of a cabinet meeting.

In March 1907 a package of Hay letters came to Lafayette Square
from Henry White in London to swell the mass accumulating in
Adams's study. Their journalistic frankness told Adams little that he
did not already know, but the picturesque epithets with which Hay
embellished his remarks on troublesome governments and statesmen
tantalized him. "Naturally as sub-editor I am greatly tempted to print
everything," he told White, "but am worse bound to advise Mrs Hay
against it . . . And yet—! What do you really think?" Ambassador
Reid, whose intimacy with Hay dated from 1870 when Hay went to
work for him as a reporter of the *New York Tribune,* had perhaps the
most uninhibited collection. Confronted with the recurring injunction
"Burn when read," Reid asked Adams's advice. The command posed
no great obstacle, Adams rejoined. It meant no more than "personal"
and "private" and served simply as a protection during Hay's life. "As
editor," he declared, "I have always strained liberality of assent." His
own family had lived by that principle. "No editor," he went on,
"ever spared any one of my family that I know of, and, in return, we
have commonly printed all that concerned other people."

Adams used his newfound leisure to transcribe in hundreds of
pages of impeccable script the engrossing excerpts from Hay's Civil
War diaries, full of candid sketches of the great and near-great who
beleaguered Hay's beloved "Tycoon" in the White House in those far-
off days when Adams had watched the war from the London sidelines. As he patiently copied out the lines he felt the long waste of
years, for working "over one's friends' dead bones [was] not cheery."
The current unmarried niece in residence, Louisa Hooper, the favorite
"Looly" of his letters, now an accomplished young woman of thirty-
three, devotedly bore the brunt of his avuncular chaff during what he
called his "rest cure." The cold and snow brought on his "pulls of

rheumatism" and kept him indoors most of the time. Favorite card games like Metternich, Napoleon at St. Helena, and Patience helped while away the recurringly restless hours. Occasionally "Dr. Dobbitt's Celebrated Academy for Youth and Age" welcomed a new crowing granddaughter of one of his friends to the delights of the dollhouse that was brought out from behind its secret panel in his study. James Bryce, just appointed British ambassador to Washington, came to see him, and the two contemporaries tried to bridge a decades-long hiatus. To Adams Bryce seemed singularly naïve in his liberalism. Afterwards he reflected, "I find Trades-Union-philosophy a farce. Nothing but blood suits me."

Advancing years threw about Adams's short and still plump figure the cloak of sage, and his court of ladies sought his wisdom with flattering deference. Nieces required his blessing for their marriages and he would give it, a little grudgingly as befitted a benevolent pessimist, though he conceded that, on the whole, marriage was the most successful step in life. In a long life one might be more or less bored and unhappy, but "the first ten years of marriage, if what they ought to be, make it worth while." More nieces came down to hover solicitously about him in the warm Washington spring. Sometimes the carefully ordered repose would be shattered, as when Brooks stormed in to jangle his nerves more painfully than ever, wildly impatient with his friend Roosevelt's momentary slackening of executive zeal.

In Paris during June and July of 1907 Adams added more hundreds of pages of faultless transcript as he worked through Reid's collection of Hay letters, occasionally including morsels which he hoped would survive Mrs. Hay's censorship. Her blue pencil canceled all such passages wholesale. Thus were lost all references to his early poverty, the inside struggles of boss politics in Ohio, the sordid schemings and ribaldry of his political associates, the ludicrous social climbing of acquaintances, the moments of self-doubt and self-mistrust, and the occasional slighting references to the clergy.

Only rarely did Adams use his own veto. Having on occasion himself voted the Democratic ticket, he was disinclined to pass Hay's scurrilous thrust: "The Democratic Party is down below the standard of Jackson. Take out the Ku Klux and the Irish and there is hardly a crust left to the pie." Another revealing veto was his dropping a passage praising Bayard Taylor's *Faust*, the translation which he had denigrated when editor of the *North American Review*. Nor would he

permit a slighting reference to Bret Harte to stand. In the main, however, the voluminous transcription shows that Adams did indeed
strain liberality of assent. As his pen covered the long pages, he found
the record even more interesting than his own *Education*. "He did
what I set out to do," Adams wrote to Elizabeth Cameron, "only I
could never have done it."

Adams crossed the Channel in August to spend a few days going
over the mass of transcripts with Whitelaw Reid and debating the
numerous "questions of delicacy." Adams sent back to Mrs. Hay
nearly a thousand pages of transcription, after getting Reid to add a
few annotations to the anecdotes. Mrs. Hay now took principal
charge of the project, drastically censoring those letters that Adams
had passed and swelling the collection with long runs of innocuous
travel letters. Adams's last chore was to write an introduction to the
proposed memorial. The twenty pages of that coolly detached essay
were all that he was ever to write about Hay, beyond what he had
already said in the studied sidelights of the *Education*.

As the months went by without any word about publication, Reid
became understandably anxious about the project in which he and
Adams had invested so much effort. He had every right to hope that
the collection would be, in a way, a memorial to himself as well, for
he had played a large role in advancing Hay's career. A year after the
meeting at Wrest he asked Adams, "What has become of the book of
Hay's letters? I hope it is not abandoned, and equally that it was not
eviscerated by Mrs. Hay's fear of living people." Adams informed him
that Mrs. Hay had decided to bring out a privately printed edition in
three volumes. He already had an inkling what was in store for them,
as earlier in the year, when Mrs. Hay sent over some material for
inclusion, she had attached a note: "You see I have suppressed all
names. I thought it best, as it seems to be personal." The handsomely
printed work on handlaid paper with uncut edges, "printed but not
published," descended upon Adams in November 1908. Looking
upon the monumental miscarriage of his plan, he could do nothing
but laugh at his own gullibility. With relentless impartiality Mrs. Hay
had reduced practically every one of the hundreds of names of persons and places to initials. There was no indication of the authorship
of the introduction. The effect was indescribably grotesque. Every letter became a maddening puzzle. A letter to Nicolay, for example, ran:
"I saw today in the G—— a paragraph by T——, on the authority of

F——— M——— of C——— that I alone had finished the first volume of our History."

To the disgusted Reid, Adams offered what extenuation he could. "I was in no way responsible for the omissions or insertions in the Hay volumes." He explained that for his own pleasure he had since "rescued all the names that came within my reach" and had made a "key" to the volumes. Not long afterwards, he regaled Reid with the choicest irony of the whole venture. "My copy of Hay's letters is lent to Mrs Hay for her to fill the blanks in her own copy!"

THE ANNUAL HEGIRA to Paris in the late spring of 1907 gave Adams a parallax on the disintegrative movement of Western society unlike any that he had had since 1893. The barometers of business heralded the approach of another economic hurricane, and waves of selling shook the stock exchanges of the world centers. The disastrous pattern of business failures, falling prices, and unemployment suggested the presence of uncontrollable cyclic forces. The first hint of trouble had come in June with the failure of an American steel company. There was strong criticism of Theodore Roosevelt's deflationary fiscal policy as the stringency steadily grew worse. Early in September Adams felt the vibration in Paris. "Already copper had gone to the devil and my own little dividends are cut off one fourth. Steel must follow." There was a certain compensatory satisfaction in seeing his predictions of the breakdown of a worthless society bearing fruit only a few months after the jeremiad eloquence of his *Education.* "I am going to comfort and encourage my fellow-countrymen," he wrote Gaskell, "by assuring them that total ruin is at hand."

The grim financial process, once started, proved irreversible. Hostile critics called it the "Roosevelt Panic" and the "Republican and high tariff panic." The acute phase of the crisis passed when J. P. Morgan seized the initiative from Roosevelt, efficiently mobilized his Wall Street satellites, and rescued the securities markets, giving Adams arresting evidence of the accelerating concentration of economic power. Nearly all of Adams's wealthy friends appeared to have been "caught and skinned." He declared himself "a little surprised that so few people have killed themselves." The financial troubles touched off a disturbance in myriad directions, heightening the clamor for work-

men's compensation, a minimum wage, factory inspection laws, child
labor laws, and a ten-hour day in industry.

Adams, with his quixotic allegiance to McKinleyism as the more
beneficent evil, had no sympathy for such palliatives, for he had long
since said his farewell to reform. Tinkering was no substitute for root-
and-branch measures. Having seen no escape from the Marxian analysis, he could only take a savage pleasure in the impending *Götterdämmerung* of the gold-bug capitalists, though it meant the ultimate
arrival of the "socialistic hemiptera called lice." Too keenly aware of
his own impotence to alter the course of events, Adams took refuge
in a furious contempt for social reform and reformers. His attacks of
irritable nervousness became more frequent until the constant effort
of his household of women was to keep out the unendurable noise of
the world. "Domestic reform drivels," he jeered. "Reformers are always bores." He grew violent against the "goo-goos," the good-
government men, whose little projects only illuminated the universal
corruption. He figuratively retched at the thought of meeting reformers, male or female, and vehemently closed his doors to them.

In Paris the social and economic troubles of America, bad as they
were, showed as but a pale reflection of the disorder of Europe, where
the diseases of the capitalistic system had reached an acute phase.
Wherever Adams looked he saw vistas of frightening disequilibrium.
The vindication of Dreyfus brought the Radical Socialists to leadership in 1906 under the power of Georges Clemenceau, who had led
the fight for separation of church and state. The disestablishment of
the Roman Catholic church brought to Adams a deep sense of loss.
He lamented to his niece Mabel La Farge, who was a Catholic, "As
you know, I regret it, for all the thought or imagination that ever
existed, and all the art, had its source there, and the world is left to
trade unions and Apaches without it."

Adams wrote in a growl that "Paris seems to me stupider in ideas
than I ever knew it before . . . Not a book or a play or a picture or an
opera or a building have I heard of." For all its intemperance his indictment had its core of truth. The influential magazine *Nineteenth
Century* reported the French novel in a state of crisis, with the great
nineteenth-century figures gone and the new ones, including Anatole
France, turned into polemicists. As for art, the autumn salon offered
a retrospective show of Cézanne in which, it was reported, the few
great works were swamped by the many failures. Only Rodin's bold

and rugged sculptures commanded general respect. Adams had been on friendly terms with Rodin ever since his first visit to the sculptor's studio in 1895, where he shuddered agreeably at the "too, too utter and decadent" Venus and Adonis. He had thought of buying one of Rodin's small bronze figures, but lifelong prejudices made him hesitate. "They are mostly so sensually suggestive that I shall have to lock them up when any girls are about, which is awkward; but Rodin is the only degenerated artist I know of, whose work is original."

The world of art may have been calm, but it was the illusory quiet of the eye of the hurricane. The turmoil of politics and diplomacy whirled furiously around it. From his lofty perch in Paris, Adams figured and refigured the ratios of foreign exchange and coal resources, the military estimates of the rival powers, and the guessed values of the countless imponderables. He was obsessed by the incompleteness of his dynamic theory of history. In the early winter of 1907, hibernating once more in his active fashion at 1603 H Street, he bent to the task of revising his law of acceleration to make it serve as the basis of a revolution in the teaching of history. Reading about the disintegration speeds of radium in Gustave Le Bon's *Evolution de la matière,* he tried extrapolating his figures for the movement of society into a logarithmic curve analogous to the orbit of the comet of 1843. While ministering nieces came and went and the little dinners of the select rang with wide-ranging talk, Adams began to dabble in the mysteries of higher mathematics. He spoke of "trying to study curves and functions." He was particularly stirred by reading a popular lecture on the wonders of mathematics by Professor Cassius J. Keyser of Columbia University.

To Mrs. Winthrop Chanler, the "Dear Professorin" of many letters, who had lent him the little book, he wailed, "I now see that we can do nothing without mathematics and that my babblings are quite vain. All that we have said must have been said by Mach and Poincaré, but we can never read it. It lies there, as in the bosom of hyperspace, inaccessible to other space or mind." Nevertheless, acting on Keyser's dictum that the most "etherealized" concepts of science could be expressed in ordinary language, he tendered to Mrs. Chanler the draft of a new essay that he planned to send out to professors of history as "a sort of circular" to accompany the *Education.*

The first version of the essay evidently made its way into the fire, but one may surmise from the care with which Adams began to study

Oliver Lodge's *Electrons, or the Nature and Properties of Negative Electricity,* Despeaux's *Cause des energies attractives,* John Trowbridge's *What Is Electricity?* and Heinrich Hertz's *Electric Waves* that he was now concentrating on electromagnetic analogies for his dynamic theory and that a second version was under way. He was especially taken with Lodge's calculations of the speed of cathode ray emanations and Trowbridge's formulation that electromagnetic forces vary inversely in their attraction as the square of the distance (the "usual electric law of squares," as Adams finally put it). The crux of his problem was the mathematical representation of immaterial and psychic "energies."

When he saw, however, that mathematics seemed to have "lost itself in the multiplicities of pure abstraction," he put aside the puzzles of n-dimensional space. He resumed his quest in Paris, in the summer of 1908, reading physical science "eight hours a day . . . more of a schoolboy at seventy than I was at seven." He was determined to wring some kind of answer from the endless pages of asymptotes and abscissas with which he paced his progress and which he tossed in the fire as they failed him. The margins of the books on the philosophy of science in his Paris apartment recorded his steadfast progress in self-education. Ceaselessly he asked what really was the atom, the electron, the electric current, and tartly challenged definitions that did not define or that led him in a circle of words. In his baffled search for the nature of matter, energy, force, and radiation, he took grim comfort in Lord Kelvin's final admission "that he totally failed to understand anything." "I, who refuse to face that admission," he told Margaret Chanler, "am delighted to have somebody do it for me by proxy." But failure was only a challenge to press on, to play with magnets and iron filings at his desk, pondering the mysteriously shifting whorls, the thumbprints of an unimaginable visitant. "The solution of mind," they seemed to say to him, was "certainly in the magnet," if one but knew what magnetism really was.

Each new batch of statistics called for a recalculation of his unorthodox projections. Each spectacular advance in applied science challenged extrapolation. Henri Farman's flight that year from Bony to Reims, which won him the Grand Prix d'Aviation, seemed to indicate the next-to-last step on his "acceleration law." Guesses and predictions were now a confirmed obsession. He confidently declared to historian Rhodes that "whether the calculation is based on popula-

tion or exhaustion of cheap minerals or on mind, etc., all the speculations come out where I did in my ratio of unity to multiplicity—
about twenty years hence."

The scientific currents which successively polarized Adams's mind
always brought him back to the overwhelming question with which
he began. Was the world one or many? Could the seeming multiplicity
of the twentieth century be resolved into a higher unity? Only the
French, he thought, were really grappling with the "question of Unity
for they had a sense of it which the English and the Germans never
had." Since the French physicists stated the problem in literary form,
they were intelligible to him in a way that Sir Oliver Lodge was not.
The brilliant amateur sociologist Gustave Le Bon particularly attracted him for his way of treating social classes and races as distinct
entities. But even Le Bon's impressionistic journalism did not go far
enough. "He can't tell me," he complained, "whether our society is
now a solid, a fluid or a gas."

In spite of the sense of overwhelming muddle, Adams had already
begun to grope his way to a new hypothesis for his law of acceleration, thanks to such textbooks as Lucien Poincaré's *La physique mo-
derne*, Sir William Ramsay's Textbooks of Physical Chemistry series,
and J. Livingston Morgan's *Elements of Physical Chemistry*. Poincaré
wrote knowledgeably of the paradoxes of Willard Gibbs's "Rule of
Phase" and discussed the work of the Dutch physical chemists in the
field of chemical equilibria pioneered by Gibbs. Adams summarized
the new direction of his thinking in a letter to Gaskell of September
27, 1908, just one month before he sailed for home: "On the physico-
chemical law of development and dynamics, our society has reached
what is called the critical point where it is near a new phase or equilibrium." The transformation of society struck him as so rapid that
the spectacle resembled that "of swarms of insects changing from
worms to wings." The Wright brothers had provided the wings; a
"new insect" must arise to use them. But the new hypothesis dragged
him once again into pathless thickets. "I have run my head hard up
against a form of mathematics that grinds my brains out," he reported
from Paris. "I flounder about like a sculpin in the mud. It is called the
Law of Phases, and was invented at Yale. No one shall persuade me
that I am not a phase." The catalyst that finally crystallized the seeth-
ing solution of "rays and phases and forces and fads" was Alexander
Findlay's *The Phase Rule and Its Applications*. Findlay, a pupil of

Wilhelm Ostwald, attempted a simplified exposition of the varieties of chemical equilibria which Josiah Willard Gibbs of Yale University had defined by his famous Rule of Phase. Though the complex equations of Findlay's text bristled with difficulties, the lucid preface and the accompanying historical "Introduction to the Study of Physical Chemistry" by Sir William Ramsay cut a straight path through the mathematical jungle. Adams inscribed his copy "Washington, December, 1908."

THE LONG SESSIONS of study in Paris were often intermitted by agreeable irruptions of old comrades and new recruits, generally of nieces and other bright young women eager to be nieces. He was an "aged Pierrot," he would say. "Nieces by scores flatter and pet me till I blush and shrink." The pattern of days in France had long since fallen into a familiar routine which he would continue to follow at a slowly diminishing tempo until the lights should go down in Europe in August 1914. Each new covey of nieces meant a gay lecture-tour of the cathedral country or even an expedition to Mont Saint Michel. Once when he ran down to the Mount and found its pristine luster smudged by tourists who overran the little island, he exclaimed that it had become a "fatiguing pigsty." Besides, the quaint charm of Madame Poulard's inn and its fabled *déjeuner* of *omelette avec jambon* seemed tarnished now that she had entrusted the amiable tradition to a joint stock company. This, too, was a symptom of the general decline.

Adams found himself the beneficiary of a striking American phenomenon as more and more business and political leaders took to sending their wives and children abroad instead of to the New England mountains or the seashore of Newport and Bar Harbor. To the role of "benevolent sage," as he called it, he added increasingly that of guide and companion to husbandless matrons. " 'There are no men in Paris,' he would say to the well-dressed good-looking women," one of them later recalled. The chore, he quipped, would be more desirable if they paid the bills. There were also times, however, when he would drink his "solitary pint of wine on the boulevard among a score of strangers" and meditate on the condolence letters he would write on the morrow. Still a notable gourmet, he regularly made the rounds of his favorite restaurants—all starred by Baedeker as of "the highest class"—Paillard, Voisin, Larue, Café Anglais, the Pavillon in the Bois. Only when obliged by his exigent ladies did he submit to the fashionable din of the Ritz. Sometimes on his frequent forays about Paris in the labyrinth of the Métro he caught glimpses of the Paris that neither laughed nor sang as the popular revue depicted it, for the backwash of the Panic of 1907 soon engulfed the Continent. "Many hundreds of thousands have no bread," he wrote, but their despairing apathy made him wonder. "Fifty years ago we should have had riots and fury."

There was a touch of the superannuated *boulevardier* in the small, jaunty, gray-bearded figure, his distinguished profile marked by a piercingly inquisitive glance, his form always clad in an immaculate white suit, in his hand a walking stick. He was a familiar figure in the shops, his ability as a connoisseur of objets d'art already legendary. "Your brother has an *eye*," an art dealer remarked admiringly to Brooks Adams. His relations with the Left Bank and its strident bohemia had sharply dwindled with the disappearance of his young poet-companions. Bay Lodge had returned to the philistine darkness of America, like his friend and fellow poet William Vaughn Moody. Joseph Stickney, armed with a Sorbonne degree in classics, went back to Harvard to teach, hoping to sustain the muse in the genteel backwaters of Beacon Hill. Adams "sought with microscopes and megaphones for another" to take Stickney's place, "but the Latin Quarter," as he said, "swarms without use for my fishing."

For Henry Adams Paris chiefly meant cultural emancipation and a kind of anonymity unknown to Lafayette Square. Washington, in spite of all the hopes of the 1880s, had not become a great cosmopolitan center of culture but had grown more political and more bureaucratic. Paris was decadent, but it was a lovely, phosphorescent, utterly sophisticated decadence, a magnet for every expatriate of the world. It was a country of the spirit, with enclaves from every nation, American colonies, British colonies, Russian colonies. Here the Edwardians flocked in the wake of their elegant and pleasure-loving ruler. Here in the shadow of the embassies Americans like Adams and his intimates of the Anglo-American set, Henry James, Edith Wharton, Walter Berry, and Walter Gay, created an unmatched world of refined elegance. Berry, now a distinguished international lawyer, had been a Washington acquaintance of Henry Adams. He had become a great friend and literary counselor of Edith Wharton. Gay, a middle-aged genre painter, was another prominent expatriate at whose Château Le Breau at Dammarie-les-Lys Adams was already a welcome guest.

Another focus of the close-knit group was the picturesque Villa Trianon at Versailles, which the masculine Elizabeth Marbury, a noted authors' and playwrights' agent, had acquired in 1906 jointly with Elsie de Wolfe, her inseparable companion. Miss de Wolfe had by this time given up the stage and her role as "Charles Frohman's clothes horse" and embarked upon her career as an interior decorator for the ultrarich. One summer when Adams lent her his house in Lafayette Square she redid one of the upper rooms with an incongruously florid femininity. Like her companion Miss Marbury, she had a genius for attracting big names. Late in life as the fabled Lady Mendl of Hollywood she wrote affectionately of the "brilliant coterie who gathered at our hearth now and then," among whom were Henry Adams and Elizabeth Cameron. They would "sit spell-bound as Henry Adams told of his travels in the cathedrals of Europe, pursuing his hobby of stained glass." It was from his house that she got the idea for extremely low-slung chairs, which were often "nothing more than a cushion on the floor." Adams playfully acknowledged Elizabeth Marbury's dominating manner by insisting that, whereas all the other young women were his "nieces," she was his only "aunt."

It was an era of incessant art collecting for this opulent circle, and one of the most astounding members of the group was another Bostonian, Adams's old friend Mrs. Jack Gardner. Her Napoleonic art acquisitions and uninhibited extravagances were the talk of all society. Bernard Berenson of Lithuanian Jewish origin had become her field marshal, and he lavishly deployed her millions to help fill her exotic palace in the Back Bay. He, too, commanded a central position in their coterie on his frequent sorties from his Villa I Tatti on a hillside above Florence. Berenson, then in his early forties, was one of the most singularly gifted of Adams's new acquisitions. His succession of volumes on the Italian painters of the Renaissance and on the criticism of art had spread his ideas of "space composition" and "tactile values" through the art world like a new gospel, taking up the cult of beauty where Ruskin and Pater had left off. Adams hardly knew what to make of this darkly handsome young aesthete, whose sensibility was as delicate as his own. Short of stature, exquisite in manner, and as aggressive a conversationalist as Adams himself, Berenson, who as a Harvard student had been baptized by Phillips Brooks, could not help giving the impression of an exotic imitation of Boston's highest culture.

Berenson's financial, as well as literary, success was enough to give Adams painful pause during this period when he and his brother Charles were inventorying the failures of their patrician generation. At the beginning of their acquaintance it had taken all Adams's self-control to play the courteous host to his self-possessed visitor. After Berenson and his wife left his house in Washington one day in 1904, Adams burst out to Elizabeth Cameron, "I *can't* bear it. There is, in the Jew deprecation, something that no weary sinner ought to stand. I rarely murder. By nature I am humane . . . Yet I did murder Berenson . . . I tried to do it gently, without apparent temper or violence of manner." Fortunately for the friendship that developed between the two men, Berenson turned the other cheek. Adams seemed to him "like a fine dry sherry," and he was determined to relish the whole bottle. "We had much in common," Berenson later recalled; "but he could not forget that he was an Adams and was always more embarrassed than I was that I happened to be a Jew." Within a few years of their first cautious meeting Adams wrote to Henry James, "As usual, I got more information from Berenson than from all the rest," though he added defensively "and yet Berenson,—well! Berenson belongs to the primitives."

Berenson never forgot the moment of their first meeting at the Villa Trianon in 1903. "There suddenly appeared one summer afternoon a shortish old man, all bald head, with malicious eyes and a quizzical smile, who, when we were introduced to each other, spoke with a warm husky voice. He stayed but a few minutes and, in connection with I remember not what, remarked that in the Middle Ages people were more amused than in our own time . . . this observation was like a spark on tinder." Berenson shared Adams's passion for the Gothic cathedrals, as he too was a belated Pre-Raphaelite. The affinity ran deep, and the tie endured almost to the end of Adams's life. Adams acknowledged that in a world of "dismal flatirons" Berenson was the only one of his acquaintances "who bites hard enough to smart."

One of the chief Paris centers for all of their group was the "saloon," as Adams irreverently called it, kept by Edith Wharton. The paths of Adams and Edith Wharton had occasionally crossed in the upper reaches of Anglo-American society from the time of their first acquaintance in the early 1890s. In 1907 Mrs. Wharton established

herself in a stately Louis XIV *hôtel* in the rue de Varenne of the old
aristocratic Faubourg St. Germain. Her richly furnished apartment
became the favorite meeting ground of the older generation of alienated Americans and the representatives of the intellectual ancien ré-
gime of Paris. She formed, as Adams said, the center of his Paris
world. Her friendship with Catholic novelist Paul Bourget and with
former companions of her schooldays at Cannes gave her entry to the
"old and aloof society of the Faubourg." She became a familiar figure
at the noted salon of Rosa de Fitz-James, a cosmopolitan Austrian
who knew almost every important statesman and literary personage
in Europe. Edith Wharton once introduced her to her admired Uncle
Henry. She was a "charming Jewess," Adams remarked of Madame
Fitz-James, but he was unable to forbear the facetious addition in his
note to the poet Lodge that "all French ladies are Jewesses." The
many inconsequential letters, scraps of persiflage, and *petits bleus*
that floated between Adams's luxurious garret on the avenue du Bois
de Boulogne and Edith's *hôtel* record a long succession of luncheons
with the "dearest of uncles" at fashionable restaurants, interspersed
with many "bric-a-bracking" expeditions in quest of bibelots. He,
too, partook "en famille" of the "succulent and corrupting meals"
that Henry James found so irresistible, and enjoyed being one of "the
dear great sarabandistes" of the rue de Varenne. Mrs. Cameron, per-
petually escorted by Adams, shone at these gatherings, her regal
beauty as formidable as Edith Wharton's elegant presence.

In Edith Wharton he found a match for his world-weary raillery,
and he relished her irreverence, as when she teased him about his
various "wives." He riposted with his own brand of badinage, as one
gathers from a whimsical note to Elizabeth Cameron: "Luckily Pussy
Wharton—as a few contemporaries still call her—sailed yesterday,
after spoiling me by planting me in her *salon*. I told her what fate
waited her, and how she was floating into the fauteuil of Mme Récamier before the fire, with Chateaubriand on one side and Barante
on the other, both drivelling: only Chateaubriand would be Henry
James and Barante would be Henry Adams. She has her little suite,
but they are not passionate. The Bourgets and so on; Blanche, the
young painter, who has perpetrated a rather brutal, Sargentry portrait
of Henry James; Fullerton, the young *Times* correspondent; in short,
a whole train of us small literary harlequins who are not even funny."

Once his confidence was earned, Adams brought Berenson into
Edith Wharton's circle of *sarabandistes*. Berenson, the acknowledged

first connoisseur of Italian art in Europe, had just become the chief consultant for Joseph Duveen. Edith Wharton took possession of Adams's prize and soon found in him a gracious mentor when he took her on extended tours of the European art galleries. Thereafter she became a favorite annual visitor at I Tatti. Though often urged, Adams never made the journey to the fabled villa whose hospitality was as sought after as Adams's own "breakfasts" in Lafayette Square. Perhaps at seventy it was too late to risk the ennui of that sort of pilgrimage. In Paris Berenson was the most welcome sort of social solvent. Adams especially admired the way he was able to "eviscerate the world with a Satanic sneer."

Unlike James, Wharton, and Berenson, Adams never learned to effervesce easily in the demanding patois of the French salon. His French professional associates of other days fell away, and he developed few new ones. Gabriel Monod, with whom Adams's professional alliance went back a good thirty years, now stood at the head of French historical scholarship, but he had put himself beyond Adams's pale by espousing the cause of Dreyfus, eliciting the angry epithet "my idiot friend." However, Adams's acquaintance with the young aristocratic "swell" Henri Hubert, a prominent ethnologist, prospered with the years. The main intellectual interest that was to unite the two men was the search for Cro-Magnon man in the Dordogne caves near Les Eyzies. After Hubert became assistant director of the ethnological museum at Saint-Germain-en-Laye in 1910, Adams began to finance some of the excavation work.

Chiefly Adams preferred his own little group of Americans in Paris, who gave him the solicitude that his needle-case nerves required and who enjoyed his elaborate old-fashioned gallantry. The rootless character of his existence, broken off and resumed season after season, deepened his sense of alienation, which no immersion in books of science or medieval poetry could dispel. The "double" that had always haunted him, that made him a detached onlooker of his own existence, kept watch within his brain. "I have no life," he mused in Paris. "This does not prevent my seeing a good many people, and writing a good many letters, or even in being interested in a certain number of things and doings, or having influenza and rheumatism, or being depressed by gloom, and almost cheered by sunshine." So, too, in Lafayette Square he would write that he was "deadly solitary though never more surrounded."

The notices to quit which he read in the passing from the stage of one friend after another into the limbo of paralysis, insanity, or the more merciful oblivion of death suddenly became intensely personal one July day in 1908, and brought into mind with a sudden rush the humiliating memory of his father's mental decline. He had dropped into a Paris antique shop to ask a question. To his consternation his "French tumbled out all in a heap," without connection or coherence. The paralysis lasted but a few minutes, but Adams recognized the symptom: the Broca convolution of the brain, "the shelves of memory," had given the first sign of hardening. He afterwards tried to calculate his chances, coolly reviewing the records of family and friends. He hoped for two years without a breakdown; meanwhile, he determined to capture "all the quiet beauty I can." Like so many of his other prophecies, this one, too, darkly discounted the future. Ten more years of vigorous intellectual interests yet remained, and his prodigious memory, briefly impaired by a stroke four years later, would end only with life itself. The shock of discovery lingered, however, and he detailed his fears of an imminent mental breakdown to his brother Brooks. Brooks retorted with fraternal impatience: "The only trouble with you is . . . an increase of mental powers as the bodily power declines."

‹ 25 ›

Teacher of Teachers

O N HIS RETURN to Washington late in 1908, Henry grap-
pled once more with the formulas of his law of acceleration.
The time was also ripe for summing up and for last words. The last
winter of Theodore Roosevelt's administration must inevitably mark
the end of his career as statesman-in-waiting. As Adams put it, he was
coming home this time "to attend the funeral services of another long
bit of history—the career of my youthful friend Theodore Roosevelt."
Lafayette Square would become "as archaic as the Roman Forum,"
and he and Andrew Jackson's statue would be left "to sit alone."

The mood carried over into his personal affairs as well. They, too,
called for winding up. Elizabeth Cameron's daughter, Martha, who
had been the apple of his avuncular eye, the Madonna child of his
fancy, was about to be engaged to Ronald Lindsay, then serving as
secretary in the British embassy. The marriage would mean the final
breaking up of the Cameron salon at Number 21 on Lafayette
Square, foreshadowing as it did Elizabeth's expatriation to England.
On November 27, 1908, Adams executed his last will and testament,
still identifying himself as "Henry Adams of Boston, in the Common-
wealth of Massachusetts." He wished to be buried by the side of his
wife, enjoining that "no inscription, date, letters or other memorial,
except the monument I have already constructed, shall be placed over
or near our grave."

Soon after settling down at 1603 H Street with the new essay before him, Adams sent a note to John Franklin Jameson, director of
the historical research department of the Carnegie Institution, asking
help in getting "a young and innocent physico-chemist who wants to
earn a few dollars by teaching an idiot what is the first element of
theory and expression in physics." At the same time he offered to be

a host for the forthcoming Washington meeting of the American Historical Association. The upshot of the offer was his attendance at a luncheon on December 29 for a group of distinguished historians, headed by Professor George B. Adams of Yale, the president of the association. Adams appears to have been in uncommonly fine form at the meeting of the association, being full of the scientific historicism of his new essay. It was an apt conjunction of minds, for Professor George Adams's presidential address, "History and Philosophy of History," returned to the very question which Henry Adams had so cogently opened in *his* presidential address of 1894. The president spoke of "a new flaring up of interest in a philosophy or science of history."

Adams's remarks at the luncheon had been so brilliantly suggestive that Max Farrand, another Yale historian, tried afterwards, in a warmly appreciative letter, to persuade him to put them into a paper for the next meeting of the association. Another guest was Frederick Jackson Turner, then at Wisconsin, whose "frontier thesis," enunciated in 1892, was one of the early landmarks of the new school of scientific history. Turner found Adams a "loveable personality" in spite of the "prickly, hedgehoggy outside" and thought that his attitude, though "intellectually dyspeptic," helped save "history teaching from being pedagogic, uninspiring, unrelated to the criticism of life."

The new year ushered in the centennial observance of Darwin's birth and the fiftieth anniversary of *On the Origin of Species by Means of Natural Selection*. Was not the time ripe now to show the possibility of a science of history, as Adams had proposed to the association in "The Tendency of History," a possibility "if some new Darwin were to demonstrate the laws of historical evolution"? Stirred to action by his meeting with fellow historians, Adams dated a long prefatory letter to "The Rule of Phase Applied to History" January 1, 1909. The letter contemplated the reprinting and distribution of the *Education* to professional historians. The impulse passed, however, and the letter remained unpublished until long after the posthumous publication of "The Rule of Phase" itself.

In the letter he proposed that his readers should now proceed to apply his dynamic theory of history to "other branches of study than astronomy," the science which he had happened to draw on in the *Education*. He suggested, for example, that "astronomical mass" might be translated by physicists into "electric mass." He proposed for numerical convenience the round figure of 1,000 to represent the velocity of the "mental ions" of human society in 1800. From this figure the movement could be extrapolated backwards and forwards according to a suitable formula, such as that of terrestrial gravitation, in which the distance which the body falls is proportional to the square of the time.

In 1909 he carefully wrote out in longhand two copies of "The Rule of Phase" and sent one, together with the prefatory letter, to the poet George Cabot Lodge and the other to his brother Brooks. He described the essay to Brooks as "a mere intellectual plaything, like a puzzle." He offered the essay to Jameson for publication in the *American Historical Review,* still insisting that he was primarily interested in getting it into the hands of a "scientific, physico-chemical proof-reader" whom he would be willing to pay "liberally for the job." Jameson turned it down for the *Review* but resumed the search for a reader. A typescript of the manuscript came to rest at last in the hands of Professor Henry A. Bumstead of Yale, who, as it happened, had been a pupil of Josiah Willard Gibbs and had coedited the posthumous edition of Gibbs's scientific papers in 1906. Bumstead agreed to do the job. His meticulously detailed critique was not completed, however, until January 1910, by which time Adams had put aside any further tinkering with "The Rule of Phase" and had gone on to make a fresh approach to the problem of the teaching of a science of history.

Though the essay took its point of departure from Willard Gibbs's Rule of Phase, it did not go much beyond the scientific speculation of the *Education.* What Adams did was provide for his theory a scheme of development on a higher level of abstraction. He anticipated the psychology of the mid-twentieth century, which was to be epitomized by Lewis Mumford's warning that technology "multiplied at a geometric ratio" whereas "social skills and moral controls have increased at an arithmetic ratio" to produce "the major crisis of our time." Man must jump, as Adams liked to say, if he would save himself; a moral and intellectual elite must be recruited. If nothing else would serve to make moral philosophers out of historians, the fear of imminent annihilation might. University education must be revolutionized by the physicist-historian.

Adams wrestled long and hard to try to understand Gibbs's celebrated Rule of Phase. However, he found only one short section of the monumental paper "On the Equilibrium of Heterogeneous Substances" useful for his analogizing, the four pages headed "On Coexistent Phases of Matter." He put aside the key element of Gibbs's theory—the simultaneous coexistence of several phases when a chemical equilibrium was established. It was not the *coexistence* of phases that interested Adams, but the progressive change from phase to phase. As a result his analogy had only a superficial resemblance to Gibbs's Rule, though he adopted Gibbs's term and one of his chief illustrations, the three phases of water. In the opening paragraph of the essay Adams acknowledged that Gibbs's "Phase was not the Phase of History." He briefly illustrated the progression of phases in these words: "Ice, water, and water-vapor were three different phases of one chemical substance." On the basis of this model Adams made the analogical leap: "The historical or literary idea of phase is rather that of any slow-changing equilibrium." Hence, by extension, "differences in direction . . . transformations of shape, as in the egg and the insect, or possibly rates of speed in accelerated movement," as in human society, might all be treated as changes in phase.

Adams had also welcomed the suggestion of Sir William Crookes that it was not premature to "ask in what way are vibrations connected with thought or its transmissions." Most significant for Adams was Crookes's assertion that there was a real possibility of "intelligence, thought, and will existing without form or matter and untrammeled by gravitation or space," and that this dematerialization of matter did not violate physical laws or require the intervention of the supernatural. Against this background of widespread interest in telepathy and other psychic manifestations at the turn of the century must be placed Adams's fanciful extrapolations in "The Rule of Phase." He was irresistibly drawn to this beguiling fringe of scientific guesswork; the more extravagant it was, the more it charmed him.

Adams completed his framework of cosmic evolution in terms of an energy system apprehensible as a hierarchy of phases. Its direction in the lower ranges of vibration, that of physical chemistry, was subject to the Rule of Phase, behind which lurked the majestic authority of the First and Second Laws of Thermodynamics. In its highest vibrations it was the immaterial creature of thought which provided "the source of Direction, or of what in scholastic science was called Form, without which the mechanical universe must have remained forever as chaotic as it shows itself in a thousand nebulae."

Upon this highly speculative estimate of the phases of psychological evolution, Adams sought to fix an image suitable to represent the rapidity of the acceleration of the mental movement of society. Not even the spectacular comet of 1843 which had done service in the *Education* seemed adequate as a metaphor. The image of an electric current seemed better to suggest that "acceleration increases in geometrical progression." There remained the task of translating this image into a numerical curve of mind, if his exhortation to historians was to be made sufficiently emphatic. The scheme would show that the clock of history stood at the eleventh hour. With the introduction of the dynamo in the 1870s, the accelerating curve of "scientific and social thought" changed direction under the attraction of incalculably powerful new forces, an even greater deflection than at the beginning with Galileo. "The new philosophy of radiation and electricity required higher powers of mind and more elasticity of thought than had been imagined in any previous phase." If man's intellectual power, that is, the administrative wisdom and capacity of the governing elites, was to keep pace with the development of the new energies, some such development of mind must take place; if it did not, the race between education and catastrophe, to use Herbert Wells's phrase, would be lost.

Considered as a possible program of university education, the essay had rather paralyzing implications. The alternatives open to society seemed to cancel each other out. Given the current sluggishness of social thought, it would not be equal to controlling the enormous acceleration of physical energies. Since by Adams's own calculation the time was manifestly too short to reform the universities and create the needed elite to meet the emergency, he implied that it was possible only to ameliorate in some way the effects of the imminent smashup. Even more ambiguous was his notion of a possible descent into an ocean of mathematical thought. Would this be an ultimate refinement of mind capable of hyperthought and the mastery of nature in hyperspace, or would it be an ocean of diffused thought, a kind of paralysis of further progress, the socialization of mind at a dead level of mediocrity? The more one turns the generalizations, the more puzzling are their bearings, and what at first seems a broad highway becomes a labyrinth. It is not a question of whether they are true or not, or even convenient as images, but whether they are fundamentally intelligible.

In spite of the prodigious effort of thought Adams still could not, as he had said in the *Education,* either state his problem or wholly know what he himself meant.

IN 1909 Henry began a last collaboration with his brother Brooks. Just as his discussions several years before with his elder brother Charles over the biography of their father had opened up a vein of somber reflections on the ironies of fate, so now Brooks's effort to complete a biography of their grandfather John Quincy Adams initiated an even darker inquest.

Brooks had been asked some years earlier by historian Ellis Oberholtzer to write a biography of John Quincy Adams in a projected American Crisis series. Henry received sections of the draft manuscript on February 3, 1909. From then until mid-March, shortly before his departure for France on the thirtieth, he gave himself up to a searching line-by-line criticism of the ill-fated manuscript and supplemented that with voluminous letters defending his appraisal. Brooks saw their grandfather as an epic hero in an age of crisis; Henry, as he read on, going over again much of the field he had treated in his *History,* felt a violent revulsion. American history, he said, made him "physically sick, so that only by self-compulsion can I read its dreary details." He saw no inspiring heroism in the old man nor in the age in which he had been condemned to live. He read back into the story all his current discontents: "The psychological or pathological curiosity of the study takes possession of me. The unhealthy atmosphere of the whole age, and its rampant meanness even in violence; the one-sided flabbiness of America; the want of self-respect, of education, of purpose; the intellectual feebleness, and the material greed,—I loathe it all." The blighted manuscript disappeared quietly into the cavernous family archives, to be lost to view for more than forty years.

The prolonged colloquy exploring the baffling question of history and biography seems to have stirred Henry to thought in a way reminiscent of the days of the silver fight. What was fundamentally wrong with the study and teaching of history, of the science which should be the supreme tool of the statesman? What "gold-bug" spirit had debased it? American history seemed permeated with a foolish optimism about the unique destiny of the American people, as if they were exempt from the laws of historical development. Burdened in mind, Adams hastened back to Paris with Elizabeth Cameron after only a four months' absence. He dropped his plan to reprint the *Education* and to circulate with it "The Rule of Phase." Preoccupied with the mathematics of thought, he had almost lost sight of his mission as a Conservative Christian Anarchist. Current events brought him sharply back to his responsibilities.

He found Paris in the throes of near anarchy. He had scarcely got settled in his apartment when the postal and telegraph workers went out on strike to protest their many grievances. In the emergency the distracted government requisitioned all the carrier pigeons of France to maintain official communication. May Day came, and Paris took on the aspect of an occupied city as troops moved in to avert rioting. Clemenceau thundered in the Chamber of Deputies that the alternatives were progressive evolution or chaos, and the session broke up in a scene of dangerous Gallic farce as the extreme Left suddenly began singing the "Internationale" and all the other deputies rallied to drown them out with strains of the "Marseillaise." The royalist Charles Maurras boldly called for a Cromwellian *coup de force* to sweep out rotten parliamentarism, Jewish influence, and, most dangerous of all, socialism.

The disorders in Paris during that spring and early summer reflected the general deterioration of the European political situation. The world seemed to be teetering on the edge of war and socialism. The naval armament race between Germany and England had intensified, for no one could mistake the implications of Germany's rejection of a "naval holiday." France, like England, watched the rise of the German "menace" with extreme disquiet. A race of people, said the Germans, was either a hammer or an anvil, and Kaiser Wilhelm left no doubt as to who would be the hammer and who the anvil.

The troubles of the larger world had their counterpart in the smaller world of Adams's personal affairs. A sense of malaise belied the surface animation of his gadding about Paris playing "tame cat about the Embassy, and a little dog about Mrs Wharton." A troublesome iritis which no spectacles could correct hampered his incessant reading. His nervous irritability brought back the old terrors of insomnia. While his doctor experimented he predicted it would end as usual with his being sent "to some ridiculous bath," whereas, he said, "the only successful bath for me is that of Odysseus, of the western stars until I die." For another *memento mori* there was the bedside of cousin Sturgis Bigelow, who looked like "Don Quixote on his pillow" in Paris, dieting, as Adams put it, on morphine.

His youthful nieces were growing up, marrying, shouldering responsibilities which vexed him as well as them. Increasingly, he had to pay the price of having bound himself to a wide circle of friends and acquaintances, of being the "benevolent sage" to a family circle so broad that he must have felt like the patriarch of some primitive gens. Through his letters flowed the incessant rumors of illness, mental troubles, marital misadventures, and financial disappointments, as time took its growing toll. Elizabeth Cameron showed the strain of her unhappy marriage. Her daughter, Adams's beloved Martha, went abroad with her distinguished-looking young husband, Ronald Lindsay, who had been transferred to the Foreign Office in London. Elizabeth fluttered about in her company like a stricken bird of passage. Her relations with her husband were now purely formal, and in their infrequent reunions he displayed the blandest indifference. Adams looked on dismayed at Elizabeth's efforts to help Martha keep up the pace of London living. He declared she "gets your usual bitter mamma's pleasure out of playing the pelican, and denudes herself of one feather after another until she must inevitably freeze to death on the nest." He saw no pleasure in it for himself as "the uncle Pelican." Low in spirits, he broke out: "I am a coward about you all. I go to imaginary funerals every day when I don't go to real ones."

There was special reason for his desperate humor. George Cabot Lodge, whose zest for life and air of boundless promise had made him Adams's favorite, died suddenly in August 1909 at the age of thirty-six. Adams wrote to Sister Anne, the dead poet's mother, that Bay was his "last tie to active sympathy with men." The blow had struck hard, for young Lodge had been his one disciple, confiding in his critical judgment, sharing with him his innermost feelings.

THE IMMEDIATE CATALYST for a new compendium of Adams's outraged and outrageous reflections came from his happening on Andrew Gray's recently published study of Lord Kelvin. With Gray's discussion before him, Adams now concluded that the theory of entropy which underlay Willard Gibbs's work was directly relevant to his own philosophy of history. In a short section labeled "Dissipation of Energy," Gray vividly spelled out some of the implications of Kelvin's "great generalisation." Although the total energy might remain constant, he explained, "this energy to residents on the system becomes unavailable . . . and the inevitable death of all things will approach with headlong rapidity." Adams was soon to incorporate this dire prediction almost verbatim in *A Letter to American Teachers of History.*

No longer thinking of the "ethereal" formula of "Phase," Adams was off on a new tack. "In my desperate search for amusement," he wrote to Gaskell, "I have struck on your friend Lord Kelvin who began his career in 1849 by proving that the universe, including our corner of it, was flattening steadily, and would, in the end, flatten out to a dead level where nothing could live." The quest for Kelvin became the ground note of the summer's meditation in Paris, for Adams was now convinced that the physical and mental degeneration of mankind was part of the cosmic process subsumed under entropy and the Second Law of Thermodynamics. He had so far written of thought as a form of energy but had been unable to particularize what kind of energy it was, except as possibly analogous to electricity. What the peculiarly human form of energy was that was undergoing entropy now became the chief subject of his search. Henri Bergson's recently published *L'évolution créatrice* helped Adams towards a solution of the riddle, for Bergson postulated a special nonphysical human energy which he called *l'élan vital.* With the aid of Bergson and other neovitalistic writers like Hans Driesch, whom Bergson approvingly cited, Adams armed himself for a new assault upon Darwinian optimism.

What most suited Adams's thesis was the sort of view expressed in a current article in the *Fortnightly Review,* "Suggestions for a Physical Theory of Evolution." "Organisms," wrote the anonymous author, "like inorganic matter are subject to the law of equilibrium, which is a consequence of the dissipation of energy . . . There is no escape from the dead level of monotony." This was the kind of corroboration that Adams needed to support a theory of evolution that would match in speed the "headlong rapidity" of Kelvin's heat death of the world. The time was clearly ripe, as a reviewer in the authoritative *Mercure de France* reported, for philosophers to place civilization in the framework of cosmic phenomena.

Thus admonished, Adams, by the end of the summer of 1909, had completed a draft of *A Letter to American Teachers of History* in which he tried to "plaster other people's standard textbooks together, so as to see where we are." The result was an extended dialogue between the "degradationists" and the "elevationists" (that is, Darwinian evolutionists). Adams began to enjoy in imagination the effect that his Socratic missile would produce. "The only service I can do my profession is to serve as a flea." Amidst the lively rattle of conversation in the Paris restaurants there were often moments for serious talk with the encyclopedic Berenson, who seemed to know everyone of consequence in Europe. Adams deputized him to ask his "Cambridge connections" for help. "I want terribly to find an Englishman capable of explaining Lord Kelvin." Berenson assured him, "Bertie Russell might explain Kelvin to you." Adams was by this time on such a good footing with Berenson that he admitted him to the elect by giving him copies of the *Chartres* and the *Education*. Now he lent Berenson the draft manuscript of the new book.

The "incubation period," as Adams called his long Parisian summers, was over, the manuscript hatched. It now remained to make it fly. He sounded his printer in Baltimore, J. H. Furst and Company, preferring, as he said, the fun of being his own publisher. He asked his friend Jameson, the managing editor of the *American Historical Review,* for a list of all the university professors and tutors of history in the United States and of all the university presidents. By February 3 he was putting the last corrections to the proofs and squeezing in last-minute documentation. He dated the preface February 16, 1910, his seventy-second birthday, treating the essay, as he had the *Education,* as a kind of birthday message. He personally signed the preface in each of some two hundred fifty copies and dispatched them to the four corners of the academic world.

At the moment that Adams was distributing his *Letter* the lines were being drawn for the bitter fight that erupted in Congress in March 1910 as a result of the effort to break Speaker Joseph Cannon's despotic rule. The attempt, which failed, fatally split the Republican party. The administrative fiasco provided another Q.E.D. for Adams's geometry. "We cannot satisfactorily run this huge machine which bumps and jumps all over the place," he deprecated to Gaskell. "We all feel helpless. Whether our energy is really declining, I do not know; but I send you herewith my small volume discussing the subject concisely as I can state it ... As I understand the idea of the physicists, they are bound to hold that the socialist society of the immediate future is the end of possible evolution or forward movement on any lines now known to us ... The universities can settle their doctrine on this subject, if they are not afraid of it; but I thought myself warranted, as the Doyen of the historical school, to ask a settlement. So I have printed this volume, and sent it round to every University in the country ... hoping to prove that the Universities are already extinct, and incapable of facing the socialist phase of mind which we are already floundering in,—old-age pensions,—universal education,—trades-unionism,—and the rest."

Adams loved paradox and he loved contradiction; the older he grew, the more he relished the dialectics of the dilemma, the successive tossing of ideas from one horn to the other to test their vitality. Nowhere did he carry the method to such extremes as in this final philosophical essay. His imaginary confrontation between the contestants is reminiscent of his masterly reconstruction in the *Chartres* of the debate between Abelard and William of Champeaux. Though Adams neatly divided the *Letter* into two sections, the first "The Problem" and the second "The Solutions," what coherence it has comes from the recurring oppositions between the arguments of the evolutionary elevationists and those of the degradationists in the alternating patchwork of quotations. But the artistic inspiration that produced the *Chartres* had spent its force, and without that afflatus which gave the *Chartres* its matchless verve, the *Letter* foundered in its own intellectual virtuosity.

Unlike the suppressed "Phase," the essay assumed no reading of the *Education* or any knowledge of his dynamic theory of history. Privately, however, he spoke of it as "a connecting link between the *Chartres* and the *Education*" as well as "a bitter satire against socialism." Setting all his earlier calculations aside, Adams turned to the idea of entropy to dramatize his destructive critique of contemporary society. Assuming that the inanimate universe as a whole could be treated as a closed cosmic heat machine irreversibly heading downwards on the heat gradient, what part did life play in the process? Kelvin had suggested that living matter was probably not exempt from the law, but had not been explicit about the way entropy operated on living matter.

Historians, Adams asserted, were necessarily vitalists, since they were concerned with the history of "social energy." They had up to now assumed that that energy acted according to laws of its own which were little affected by physics. If, however, social or vital energy was really subject to physical laws, the approach to history must be revolutionized. If a living organism utilizes a species of nonmechanical energy which is subject to entropy, it followed that human evolution, whatever its mechanism of selection and survival, had been a process of continuously degraded vital energy.

To Adams the dilemma of the modern historical school was that the physical sciences, which had come to dominate higher education, now taught the universality of the fateful Second Law of Thermodynamics with complete freedom, whereas a social science like history feared to apply it to human society. Adams heaped up a miscellany of evidence and speculation to prove the degradation of energy in civilized society and the resultant evolutionary regression. The human teeth showed arrested evolution; the sense of smell was less acute than that of other animals or of primitive savages; the weight of the brain gave no evidence of evolution from lower to higher. Man as the most specialized of living creatures stood helplessly at the end of the evolutionary road.

To complete the rout of optimistic evolutionists, he marshaled a motley array of sensational "evidence" from the newspapers, all indicative of the loss of vital energy: the declining birthrates in the Western world; the shrinking of the rural population; the lowering of physical standards in the army; the increase in suicides, insanity, cancer, tuberculosis, alcoholism, drug addiction; and the failing eyesight among the young. He harvested the woe and misery of his accumulated newspaper clippings no matter how crackpot the source or superficial the evidence in order to pound home his theme of social decrepitude. The picture was even darker, he declared, than that already suggested, for not only was physical evolution downwards, but the mind itself had undergone degradation of vital energy.

To the historian the moral should be clear: "If the teacher of history cares to contest the ground with the physicist, he must become a physicist himself, and learn to use laboratory methods. He needs technical tools . . . large formulas like Willard Gibbs's Rule of Phase; generalizations, no matter how temporary or hypothetical." The historian needs such laborsaving devices because "man, as a form of energy, is in most need of getting a firm footing on the law of thermodynamics." With these tools the historian and sociologist will be able to demonstrate scientifically the process described so vividly by Le Bon's dissection of crowd psychology, whereby "the race ends by entirely losing its soul." Adams concluded that in a universe that has been "terribly narrowed by thermodynamics . . . the department of history needs to concert with the departments of biology, sociology and psychology some common formula or figure to serve their students as a working model for their study of the vital energies," one that would correspond to the thermodynamic model of the physicists. Such a collaboration would require, as he had so often said before, "the aid of another Newton."

The startling effect of the book upon Adams's Boston acquaintances may be gauged by Brooks's report: "I have never known anything produce so deep and almost tragic impression." Acknowledgments and demurrers came fairly rapidly; however, the score or more of responses added up to a singularly unsatisfactory reaction. Adams discovered he had not disturbed the equanimity of his colleagues nor made any converts. No one marked the imminent danger of entropic socialism; no one seconded his neovitalist critique of Darwinism; no one shared his sense of moral urgency. If he was doyen of the historical school, the school did not accept his authority. Beneath their polite phrases it was evident that they looked rather askance at his presumption.

One of the first comments came from President Arthur T. Hadley of Yale, a leading political economist. He counseled that historians should avoid "doubtful physical analogies" drawn from the complexities of physics and deal with their problems directly. With chilling frankness he remarked that the younger men cared little for "a certain kind of scientific romancing of twenty years ago." Professor Albert Bushnell Hart of Harvard observed that the book did not really call for analysis, "for you visibly do not know what to think about the universe yourself," and he good-naturedly suggested that Adams obviously enjoyed chewing the pessimistic quotations "to feel the impression of bitterness."

Barrett Wendell ruefully admitted, "After two careful readings of this little book I cannot feel that I have quite grasped it." Adams fired off an impatient rejoinder to his former student. The book "is a scientific demonstration that Socialism, Collectivism, Humanitarianism, Universalism, Philanthropism, and every other ism, has come, and is the End, and there is nothing possible beyond, and they can all go play, and, on the whole, base-ball is best."

Only William James gratified Adams's love of "bite." The stubborn
pragmatist, wasting away at Nauheim, cheerfully mocked his old adversary: "To tell the truth, it doesn't impress me at all, save by its wit
and erudition . . . To begin with, the *amount* of cosmic energy it costs
to buy a certain distribution of fact which humanly we regard as precious, seems to me to be an altogether secondary matter as regards
the question of history and progress." A dinosaur's brain may have
been as good an exchanger of physical energy as man's but it could
not "issue proclamations, write books, describe Chartres Cathedral,
etc. . . . The 'second law' is wholly irrelevant to 'history'—save that
it sets its terminus."

The tide of historical scholarship had already swept Adams's kind
of philosophical speculation into a back eddy of American thought.
Soon afterwards the philosopher Arthur O. Lovejoy would speak of
the aberrant tendency of some to give the Second Law of Thermodynamics a historical character, to make it "an epitome of the entire
history of nature, a sort of 'Rake's Progress' of an energy-squandering
universe." The reviews which greeted the *Letter* when it was reprinted
by Brooks Adams in 1919 were largely adverse, though it fared far
better than the accompanying "Rule of Phase Applied to History,"
whose fanciful mathematics seemed even more dated. A rare sympathetic comment appeared in the *Yale Review.* The reviewer called the
Letter "an authentic document of twentieth century eschatology," a
brilliant modern version of the apocalypse, "single and swift and passionate as an exclamation or a command. Nervous and mordant in
style, it rises often to eloquence and is illuminated by flashes of ironical humor."

Literary critics have continued to be fascinated by the wit with
which Adams presented the familiar dilemmas of philosophy and aesthetics. As a result entropy and the Second Law of Thermodynamics
have achieved a metaphoric character approaching that of the Virgin
and the dynamo. For the literary critic, even when all the "science"
of Adams's speculation has been expertly discredited, there remain
the poetry and virile paradox of his speculation, the science and philosophy serving at last as an elaborate kind of parable by which he
expressed the timeless quest of man for self-knowledge, a quest which
Adams himself so often figured in his own mind as that of Odysseus
and of Faust, of a man against the sky of the darkening prairie, lonely,
diminished, appalled by the intimations of darkness, and yet with sti-
fled breath still murmuring, "Seek!"

26

The Benevolent Sage

IN THE EARLY SPRING OF 1910, with *A Letter to American Teachers of History* launched on its quixotic assault against the bastions of professional inertia, Adams found himself once again without a literary project to engross him. Then, before he could make more than a few satiric allusions to his bereft state, rescue came from an unlooked-for quarter. After the death of Bay Lodge in the summer of 1909, Adams had assumed that Senator Lodge would insist on attending personally to the literary part of the memorial to his son and provide one more book for the "sort of mortuary chapel" where "nearly every friend I ever had" looked down from his library shelves. When, however, the Lodge family decided to bring out a collected edition of Lodge's poems, the young widow turned to "Uncle Henry" for an introductory volume on their beloved Bay. Senator Lodge joined his importunities to those of his daughter-in-law. Adams gave in with what grace he could.

The young poet had been a familiar visitor in Lafayette Square since 1893 when his father first came to Washington as a senator from Massachusetts. Bay, then a lad of twenty, found the heterodox opinions of Adams's breakfast table a bracing change from Harvard and Boston. A rebel in spirit, he later enjoyed leaguing himself with Adams and Hay against his father's senatorial authority. Adams loved to tramp about with the exuberant poet and to savor the violence of his impressions of the Paris bohemia and the wonderfully exciting decadence of its music halls and art salons. Much to Adams's delight Bay had turned his back on a career of being "a money lender," as he scornfully called the opportunities of Boston.

When Adams sailed for France on April 16, 1910, he carried with him the letters and memorabilia that had been assembled for him. After a few weeks of hard work he reported to Elizabeth Cameron that he had arranged Bay's letters "down as far as the Spanish War," in which Bay had served as a gunnery officer, "with a thread of narrative and explanation." He added, "I can make nothing very good out of it." Three weeks later the initial draft was ready for review by the family. He admitted that "the task of writing it had . . . very considerably raised my estimate of the poems, both as poetry and as art," though he thought the letters were "even better than the poetry." During the brief winter months in Washington Senator Lodge returned to consult with Adams on final details. "I was beautiful and approved everything," he recorded. Put in mind of his experience with Mrs. Hay, he ruefully added, "Bay's will be another case of the same sort, but not so lurid." By mid-April of 1911 *The Life of George Cabot Lodge* was in type relatively unscathed and safely out of his hands, though publication was delayed until October.

In his memoir of Lodge Adams suppressed completely the significant role he himself played in the poet's life. He quoted from none of Lodge's many letters to him touching on the problems of poetry and art nor, of course, did he cite any of his own. As with his own life story, Adams stressed the frustrations of the poet's career. For Bay Lodge, too, had never made good his expatriation from Boston. He, too, had served as secretary to a politically important father and had expected for a time to follow *his* family's "go-cart" as young Henry Adams had. There had been an effort to obtain a suitable Foreign Service appointment for him, but this proved no more fruitful than the belated effort in Adams's behalf thirty years before. In the many letters that Adams included Lodge seems at times almost a mirror image of his biographer. Lodge is devoured with ambition "to do something that will last,—some man's work in the world."

Adams could do little more for the purely poetic side of Lodge's talent than judiciously turn over a few of the poet's early poems and quote some of the lines that illustrated his love of nature and the strong influence of the pessimism of Giacomo Leopardi and Schopenhauer. It was on the other side of Lodge's achievement—his blank-verse dramas—that Adams wrote with more conviction. Adams saw the underlying theme of the *Cain* and that of the far more ambitious *Herakles* as symbolic reenactments of the process of self-knowledge and self-mastery. Lodge's greatest strength, and that which most solicited Adams, was his sheer intellectuality, his "instinctive love of logic." The reasoning in *Cain* and *Herakles* seemed to him "as close and continuous as it might be in Plato or Schopenhauer," a dialectic of sharp oppositions that reduced all questions to their metaphysical essence. Adams's analysis suggested the strong philosophical affinity that existed between the younger man and himself. "Lodge's dramatic motive was always the same, whether in *Cain*, or in *Herakles*, or in the minor poems. It was that of Schopenhauer, of Buddhism, of oriental thought everywhere."

Adams did his young friend the justice of taking his work seriously. In spite of his habitual cynicism, Adams's sympathies were deeply engaged. Beneath the tone of judicial impersonality there runs a thread of fellow feeling, for Adams, too, was a poet in his sensibility. This sensibility rose to the surface in a striking passage on the ordeal of the creative artist: "But the insidious weakness of literary workmen lies chiefly in their inability to realize that quiet work like theirs, which calls for no physical effort, may be a stimulant more exhausting than alcohol, and as morbid as morphine. The fascination of the silent midnight, the veiled lamp, the smoldering fire, the white paper asking to be covered with elusive words; the thoughts grouping themselves into architectural forms, and slowly rising into dreamy structures, constantly changing, shifting, beautifying their outlines,—this is the subtlest of solitary temptations, and the loftiest of the intoxications of genius."

The poems and dramas, collected in two volumes, were sent out for review, but in some cases without the first-volume memoir, if one may judge from the absence of allusions to it in the few reviews and critiques of the poetry. James Herbert Morse in the *Independent* adopted Adams's view of Lodge as a rebel in the great tradition of Swinburne, Verlaine, and Whitman but centered his critical observations on Lodge's poetry. The reviewer in the *Boston Evening Transcript* declared that Adams had "attempted the gratuitous task of interpreting" Lodge's poetry for the reader.

IN THE QUIET INTERVAL that followed the completion of the draft of *The Life of George Cabot Lodge*, a communication from an assistant professor at Yale redirected Adams's thoughts to the poetic landscape of his treasured *Chartres*. Frederick Bliss Luquiens, an expert in Romance scholarship who had been working on the *Chanson de Roland*, had just come upon the copy of the *Chartres* in the Yale library, one of the dozen or so university libraries to which copies had originally been sent. The chapters on medieval French literature struck him as an incomparable essay, especially on the literary qualities of the *Chanson de Roland*. The technical virtuosity of these sections impressed the young scholar as all the more remarkable because Adams occupied no university chair. Delighted to discover a fellow devotee of the *Roland*, Luquiens proposed to review the *Chartres*. Touched more than he might willingly admit, Adams welcomed this new accession to the cult. The exchange thus opened was to run on for several years exploring the difficult problems of translation and of the sources of the *chansons de geste*.

On the heels of Professor Luquiens's letter came one from an older colleague, Professor Albert S. Cook, the longtime editor of *Yale Studies in English*. Cook too had chanced upon the *Chartres* and petitioned for a copy for more leisurely study. As a propitiatory offering he sent on translations from Old English poetry, for he knew of Adams's pioneer studies in Anglo-Saxon law. Adams had to confess that the sole remaining copy had been given to the Gothic enthusiast Ralph Adams Cram. The only recourse would therefore be to reprint the whole book, a "rather arduous and expensive job." Cook pressed Adams to publish the volume or at least the long section on Chartres for use as a guide. Adams temporized by offering to reprint privately as many copies of the *Chartres* as Professor Cook might want. There the matter stood while the letters went on to relish the esoteric pleasures of Anglo-Saxon poetry and the disputed symbolism of the portrait figures of the Chartres porches.

For some months there was no visible effect of this double stimulus. In fact Adams acquired still another hobby during the Paris summer of 1910 in the intervals of work on the Lodge biography: reading up on Cro-Magnon man. His interest had been challenged by the work of his aristocratic friend Henri Hubert, who early in August was installed as director of the ethnological museum at Saint-Germain-en-Laye. Adams began to talk familiarly of Neanderthal skulls and paleolithic culture. Impatient with the niggardliness of French scientific societies and the lethargy of the government, he also advanced funds himself to Hubert to probe the mysteries of the Dordogne caves near Les Eyzies, making but one facetious condition—he was to receive a prehistoric baby in good condition.

Adams's annual hegira had begun rather badly. He had left Washington "a sepulchre without much whitening" to find London and Paris equally irritating to his nerves, the political clamor and indecision equally stupefying, the blunders of his own Republican party in Washington matched by the clumsy expedients of European governments to allay the growing social unrest. His temper was worse than ever, and at times Paris seemed uninhabitable. Brief as his periods of solitude were, they seemed endless, and he sometimes brooded glumly over his solitary chicken and pint of champagne at Paillard's in the Bois or under the frivolously gay paper lanterns of the Pavillon Royal, where the music softly ministered to his melancholy. Brooks broke in upon him briefly for an exchange of views, impatient as always with Henry's efforts to screen himself from harsh reality. Brooks's ranting tirades left him low and dispirited, lost in the muddled incoherence of existence. His life seemed "that of a black beetle," he told Berenson, "and I move from my desk to my dinner and back again without sight or sound of anything but other beetles, whom I prefer to kill."

But as always Paris had its compensations, as he grudgingly admitted. Besides, even in his worst moods he never quite lost sight of the slightly comic aspect of his crotchety faultfinding. His intimates had long learned to discount the old cardinal's pose of mockery, and he in turn grew more extravagant and sardonically facetious to keep up his credit. For the American women who spent their summer exile in the luxurious apartments in the vicinity of la place de l'Etoile, he would often shed the role of grim prophet and let the poetic side of his nature speak. No contradiction troubled the inspired flow of his talk as he descanted to his rapt little audiences on the treasures of the long-dead past. They were all devoted amateurs of the *recherche du temps perdu,* and Adams played his role of benevolent uncle with unflagging grace, sauntering out from his comfortable eyrie under the roof of 23 avenue du Bois de Boulogne for frequent dinners with Elizabeth Cameron, a pleasant walk down the broad tree-lined parkway to 88, where her salon drew the lions of the American set. Here Adams came and went with the freest intimacy. Where Elizabeth was, was a second home for him, and he quietly ignored the persistent eddy of gossip that swirled on the outskirts of their little society. If Elizabeth depended upon him for understanding companionship and steady counsel in her rootless existence, he could count on her to help him keep at bay the neurotic black-browed double who continually waylaid his thoughts.

In the autumn of that year his Paris lease was not renewed, as the building was to be torn down to make way for a handsomer structure. He thankfully surrendered to Elizabeth's natural talent for management the job of moving his books, Ming *potiches,* watercolors, and exquisite china to an apartment at Number 88, a short way from her own apartment. For the most part life centered upon the intimate dinner parties at Paillard's, which was now Adams's favorite restaurant, or a rendezvous with Berenson at Mrs. Wharton's in the rue de Varenne or at Mrs. Cameron's, for she, too, had gingerly capitulated to Berenson's worldly charm.

Berenson was omnipresent that season, sporting his "bag" of artists (for the moment it was Pierre Bonnard) or notable clients like the affluent Mrs. Potter Palmer. Berenson's recurring bouts of ill health gave a world-weary cast to his meditations. "Shocking so young as I am," he sighed, "and already so out of sorts with the house of life I smuggled into so expectantly at twenty." It was grist that Adams readily matched among his other friends ailing physically or mentally. He could cite Edith Wharton, who was troubled by the derangement of her husband. He had also just learned of John La Farge's "utterly sordid death in a Providence asylum, which reminds me," he told Berenson, "of my friend Clarence King's death in an Arizona tavern." As he ticked off the state of their mutual friends, he added, "Personally I think it is my duty to make more complaint than anyone else." His duty became more urgent when the first signs of serious trouble with his eyes appeared. The condition grew steadily worse during 1911, and he was forced to wear dark glasses. Finally he was obliged to stay within doors during the day with the blinds drawn and to venture forth only after dusk.

Settled in his new apartment shortly after the first of December, Adams put aside Cro-Magnon man and plunged once again into the mysteries of the Chartres sculpture, his interest now fully reawakened. He had a new ally in his friend Ward Thoron, whose scholarly interests had long been at war with his career as a Washington banker. Thoron pored over the Chartres archives for him, hunting out materials to set at rest some of the doubts awakened by Luquiens and Cook. As the new year opened Adams decided "to print surreptitiously a few more copies of the *Chartres*" in order to correct the text. He was still adamant against turning it into "a text-book and guidebook." "I'll burn Chartres itself," he told Thoron, "before I degrade it to such a fate. Our cult is esoteric." He completed negotiations with his Baltimore printer immediately after reaching Washington on January 15, 1911. Five days later he had already sent forty-five pages to the printer for the resetting of the volume.

Back in Washington that winter Adams continued to sound the political waters, briskly moving among a half-dozen notable houses where his raillery did little to lighten the gloom of friendly Republican statesmen. The Democrats, as he said, had the "Republicans on the run." Weakened by the defection of insurgents like Robert La Follette, Albert Beveridge, and George Norris, discredited by the crudities of Taft's Latin American policy and the tariff scandals, the Grand Old Party slid downwards, while such friends as Elihu Root and Henry Cabot Lodge grumbled helplessly over Taft's "big-fat-boyishness." Adams relieved his feelings with hyperbolical tirades to Berenson, who had asked for further symptoms of "the running down of the cosmic clock." The symptoms as Henry and Brooks saw them made Henry look "forward with consternation to the possibilities of a pessimistic America. Pessimism without ideas,—a sort of bankrupt trust,—will be the most harrowing form of ennui the world has ever known."

Not all, however, was backstairs political gossip or angry inquests over Western civilization. Late in January Adams met another candidate for his court of nieces in wish, an elfin girl whose monologues were captivating Washington society. "I love Ruth Draper," he exclaimed. "She is a little genius and quite fascinates me." They soon became fast friends. For scholarly statesmanship he could count on calls by fellow historians Lord Bryce, the British ambassador, and Jean Jusserand, the French ambassador. Nonetheless, the political anxieties of his Republican friends oppressed intellectual activity like a swamp gas and made him relish all the more the sanctuary of his library, where he could lose himself in the minutiae of translations from Old French and cultivate his garden of *chansons*.

The dead still rode fast, as he was wont to say, but he rode faster still, rather pleased that he continued to head his procession. La Farge had gone and so had William James, James, in Adams's opinion, wrongheadedly optimistic to the end. To Henry James, who had returned to Washington Square, where he hovered as a bird of passage, Adams sent stoical admonition. Silence was best now that "about the only unity that American society in our time had to show" was gone—"Richardson and Saint Gaudens, La Farge, Alex Agassiz, Clarence King, John Hay, and at last, your brother William." It was beyond condolence. Henry James responded that he, too, felt "like a lone watcher of the dead."

Outliving one's contemporaries levied a progressive tax of obituary appraisal. Royal Cortissoz asked for memorabilia for a biography of La Farge and got in reply a luminous vignette in which all that La Farge had taught of nuance and color played over the remembered image of the dead artist. What Adams had said in the *Education* of the living artist he deepened and subtilized for the dead man. He was in essence remote, "unAmerican . . . unintelligible to himself as well as to me." He advised Cortissoz, "In the portrait of La Farge you must get not only color, but also constant change and shifting of light, as in opals and moonstones and star-sapphires, where the light is in the object."

The dark tenor of Adams's repeated soundings into politics and society at his own table or at friendly houses varied little as he turned from one correspondent to another. He looked across at the White House one March morning in 1911 to reflect that it was just fifty years ago that he had "set out on that career of failure which took its start in the first great collapse of society I ever witnessed." The succession of collapses had now prostrated all societies. In the wreckage of careers and worlds there was the comfort, however, that he had "always managed to have all the money I've wanted."

He carried over to Paris with him that spring a set of proofs of the new *Chartres,* and shortly after his arrival he talked of being reduced to "indexing as a literary pursuit." The lull proved temporary, as Thoron's researches began to bear further fruit. By midsummer he was in full cry again after a half-dozen intellectual rabbits: "St Augustine's views on Grace; St Thomas Aquinas' view of Free Will; Darwin's ideas on Sexual Selection; Mâle's view of the Charlemagne window at Chartres and the Pseudo-Turpin of Reims; the relative merits of a score of MSS. of the Pseudo-Turpin in the Bibliothèque Nationale and the Arsenal; the extinction of the Tertiary Vertebrates and the action of the Glaciers; the meaning of the paintings in the Cro Magnon caverns, and of the carvings on ivory and stone of the same period." Each of these matters, he noted, had given him at least a week's reading.

The new apartment at Number 88 was more spacious than the comfortable "garret" which he had quitted at Number 23; the long and narrow library with its eighteenth-century lacquered cabinets and Louis XV table did the office of chief living room. As Adams's physical pace slowed, his cerebral activity seemed by contrast to gather intensity, and from behind the massive table he darted his penetrating glance at his visitors to mark the effect of his iconoclastic pronouncements. One visitor, the historian Waldo Leland, remembered the animation of Adams's talk that summer, his undiminished curiosity about the nature of history and its relation to physics and biology, and his skepticism of historical continuity. Energy could still flare up as of old, so that after climbing four flights of stairs to return Leland's call he entered jauntily, without a sign of breathlessness. Recalling a ride on a roller coaster at the St. Louis Exposition as "the finest thing" he had ever done in his life, he slapped his knee and proposed that they should plan at once to try the Paris variety. His chaffing irony was as astringent and elliptical as ever. Told of the catastrophic destruction of manuscripts in the burning of the Albany capitol, he remarked that it was "one of the greatest steps in the advance ever taken by historical studies in America."

As another year drew to a close, Adams could not hide from himself nor from his intimates that the physical machine was sadly amiss. It had been a hot summer in Paris, "hot as hell or Washington," as he put it with Twainian vehemence, and he joked grimly of his fear of "suddenly sitting down on the floor, before the tea party, and babbling of my dolls," for he knew the savage tricks of hardening arteries. "All my senses are gone," he humorously complained, "and I can't move, because of rheumatics, lumbago, neurosis, and several fatal internal diseases." Most disquieting was the weakening of the center of vision in his eyes that kept him within doors until evening. He finally set up a kitchen, cook, china, and Louis XV sideboard, all to avoid, as he said, parading his white hairs in restaurants. He saw himself becoming a "benevolent, Franklinian, retiring, sage-colored paralytic." In spite of infirmity Adams kept himself to the mark. His correspondence seemed scarcely to diminish in quantity or peppery vigor. Only the marvelous precision of the handwriting betrayed the effort as the words grew larger on the familiar notepaper.

Slowly he worried through the last pages of the revised *Chartres* as autumn gave way to winter and the windswept Bois grew cheerless. Henry's brother Charles sent over a copy of his *Studies, Military and Diplomatic, 1775–1865,* leading Henry to look back elegiacally once more upon their generation: "I have always considered that Grant wrecked my own life, and the last hope or chance of lifting society back to a reasonably high plane." Early in January 1912, a few weeks after getting back to Washington, Adams sent off the corrected proof sheets of the *Chartres*. He could now "clear out at five minutes notice, and everyone will be the better," he chaffed Elizabeth.

In all of the long process of collating texts, correcting errors, and tinkering with occasional passages, Adams was not inclined to make any serious concessions, even as he made room for authorities like Emile Mâle whom he had overlooked. A particular sore point to Adams was the bland assurance with which recent Catholic writers had altered the facts about the medieval worship of Mary to make them accord with official dogma. Of one work, which breathed "its Jesuit genius in every line," Adams protested that the author "does not once—so far as I can discover—speak of the Virgin of Majesty, or touch upon our Virgin of Chartres. He speaks of her only as the Mother of God, who is at last translated to Heaven with a rank of Queen, very ill-defined, and chiefly nominal over the Apostles. When I get to Heaven and stand judgment before the Virgin, I am going to charge that damned Jesuit with this piece of cowardice, and insist that either he or I ought to go to hell."

The revised *Chartres* considerably extended the circle of appreciative readers. "Think!" he exclaimed to Gaskell, "I've given away 150 copies! There's triumph!" He found that he would have to redouble his largess to dispose of the remaining 350 copies which overflowed his study. Protesting that he "would rather put a few babies on sale" than let a commercial publisher market the book, he pressed John Franklin Jameson into service again, sending off the new volume to nearly a score of additional libraries which Jameson nominated. There was "special amusement," of course, in sending copies to the principal women's colleges to unsettle the young Protestant women. He hoped also to distribute a half-dozen copies "judiciously" to some Catholic libraries "to irritate a priest or two by teaching his parishioners some dogma."

The total number of changes, apart from punctuation and typography, was surprisingly small, and they were confined almost entirely to the series of chapters on Chartres, for only there, in the great nave of his book, did he find himself vulnerable. The most significant addition was his translation of all seven stanzas of Richard the Lion-

Hearted's prison song, which seemed now to sound the leitmotif of his own existence. He had attempted only the short concluding stanza in 1904, and had then characterized the Old French song as "one of the monuments of English literature."

The impish pleasantry was in keeping with his fanciful re-creation of a Norman ancestry for himself and all English worthies and his making the *Chanson de Roland* a Norman poem. Would a niece cavil at such romantic liberties? Richard's "Prison Song" still floated in a sea of scholarly conjecture, but the view it gave of that "splendid savage" seemed more attractive to him than ever. The poem sang not of the imperious Richard who massacred Jews and Saracens and humbled Saladin, but of the piteous suppliant held for ransom in an Austrian prison. It was the gallant Richard of Grétry's opera tragically lamenting "The universe has abandoned me," a lament that had roused chilling echoes of ancestral failures when Adams first heard it in Paris long ago.

The added perspective gained from going over the ground again opened up for Adams a side of the Middle Ages that he had almost completely ignored in his book, the immense social and economic transformation of Western Europe that took place in spite of the enormous expense in lives and treasure of the disastrous and unending warfare with the Mohammedan world. Now he was struck with the book's "inadequacy. When I think that it leaves out the Crusades and the whole of politics," he exclaimed, "I wonder how I made it stand up . . . The time was boiling with energy." But stand up it had, for he had by the power of his art given reality to one of the grand illusions of the time.

The winter of 1911–12 in Washington had been as usual a phantasmagoria of palace politics that swirled about Adams at the dinner tables where, with the relish of a latter-day Juvenal, he noted the signs of the Republican collapse that would bring down so many of his circle of acquaintances. Being jovially encountered in Lafayette Square one day by President Taft, Adams winced at the sight of the "hippopotamus" figure who seemed the vast compendium of party blunders. His other bête noire, Theodore Roosevelt, had, as he noted, "set off his fireworks and is busted" as a result of his breaking with Taft and announcing his own candidacy for the Republican nomination. The likelihood grew that the fracas among the Republicans would bring in a Democrat, possibly Governor Woodrow Wilson of

New Jersey. Having made his diagnosis, it was time for Adams once more to abandon the moribund patient. His own health seemed as unsatisfactory as that of his disorganized party. With gallows gaiety he wrote, early in April, that he was now living "in a sort of medicated cotton, carefully protected from pin-pricks and aches. Doctors stick things into my eyes, and rub me down like a training horse." Following his usual frugal practice, he had booked off-season passage for the annual crossing to France. He would sail April 20 on the first return voyage of the *Titanic*. The great liner had already left Southampton on her maiden voyage when he wrote, and the new engines were being confidently pushed toward full speed.

In the midnight darkness of Sunday, April 15, off the Grand Banks of Newfoundland, there was a slight jar as an iceberg brushed past the side of the swiftly moving ship. Two and a half hours later the "unsinkable lifeboat," as it had been called, went down in a perfectly quiet sea with more than fifteen hundred persons. Not until Tuesday morning did the full horror of the disaster reach the newspaper "extras," and for days thereafter the eyewitness accounts, the obituaries of the lost notables, the lists of survivors in first and second class crowded all other news from the front pages. Inured as he was to cataclysms, Adams took the news in his pessimistic stride; it was only another symptom of the decline of the West. "The foundering of the *Titanic* is serious, and strikes at confidence in our mechanical success," he confided to Elizabeth Cameron. "But the foundering of the Republican Party destroys confidence in our political system." He shifted his passage to the *Olympic* for May 4.

There was no escaping the incessant horrified gossip of his friends as the details of the bungled rescue efforts came to light at the hearings, stories of tragically garbled radio messages, of half-empty lifeboats and the haunting cries of abandoned swimmers. The loss of Archie Butt, the close friend of Lodge and Roosevelt, touched him only through them, but the death of the artist Francis Millet struck home, for that acquaintanceship went back to the golden years of Lafayette Square. In spite of his stoicism he felt low in spirit. It gave him dyspepsia, he said, to keep from taunting them all with "I told you so!" Had not he predicted it all in his *Education,* he burst out with emotionally satisfying illogic. "The sum and triumph of civilisation, guaranteed to be safe and perfect, our greatest achievement, sinks at a touch, and drowns us, while nature jeers at us for our folly

... and nature has beaten me by fifteen years on my mathematics." The gloom cast by the shipwreck and the pervasive political anxieties soon linked itself to worry about his sailing date and the condition of his Paris apartment.

Then for the first time the flesh rebelled against the incorrigibly restless will. The blow came lightly, not much more than the premonitory shudder that had run along the hull of the *Titanic*. Dining alone on April 24, he ate with his usual hearty appetite, though his man William noticed that he used his left hand to help himself. Out of the room for a moment, William heard a fall. Adams had slipped from his chair. "I can't get up," he said. "You will have to help me." The alarm was quickly sounded; doctors summoned; and his brother Charles took command. It was apparently a slight stroke, later diagnosed as a cerebral thrombosis, and the paralysis was not severe. For a time he seemed to be rapidly recovering, and the almost daily lengthy reports by his brother and by Cabot Lodge went radiating out to anxious relatives and friends. He himself took the misadventure philosophically, as Lodge wrote to Mrs. Cameron, who, after the first cable, was hovering distractedly in Paris. Within the week it became clear he would survive the stroke, for the physical improvement was marked. Then the brain suddenly faltered, and for several weeks he swung disquietingly from rationality to periods of delirium and coma. He would talk quite lucidly of having given up his plans to go to Europe and of wanting to go to Quincy. Then, after a bit, he would ask to send a message to his long-dead friend Willie Phillips and on another occasion to his mother, who he somehow imagined had been lost on the *Titanic*. He would talk compulsively in an unintelligible murmur and then, as Charles scrupulously noted, he would break out quite lucidly in his characteristic strain of half-humorous faultfinding and bantering seriousness. The one thing which he most dreaded and feared, mindless senility, seemed inevitable. Apparently realizing this mortal danger, he once tried desperately to throw himself from a window.

In Paris Elizabeth Cameron set about with a heavy heart to close up his affairs. It had been almost his last rational request before his relapse. The lease had to be terminated, customs regulations satisfied, and the valuable furnishings shipped. There were, she reported to Charles, "a number of books, but very few papers, and no manuscripts at all." While the cables flashed back and forth, she hoped from day to day for her stricken "Dordy" to summon her, but his physician dashed her fond imaginings of nursing him back to health. Then, miraculously, Adams began to mend. In mid-June he was moved, through Lodge's intercession, in a private railroad car to a quiet cottage on his brother Charles's estate, Birnam Wood in South Lincoln, which was to serve as a kind of annex to the Waltham hospital. There he enjoyed "listening to the silences," as he said, free from the torturing clatter of the streetcars passing Lafayette Square. An elaborate program of massage and exercise began to produce results.

The time finally came when Charles could no longer conscientiously "protect" Henry from Mrs. Cameron's ministrations. Fearful of the effect of a reunion of the stricken "Chateaubriand" and his faithful "Madame Récamier," Charles had done all he diplomatically could to stem the barrage of pitiful letters and cables. Toward the end of June Henry was able to dictate his gratitude to Elizabeth for looking after his affairs in Paris. From Brooks, visiting in London, she learned of Henry's vast improvement and immediately booked passage to New York. The competition to look after the invalid soon developed a humorous side. The doctor, fascinated by the conversation of his distinguished patient, whiled away time by the hour in Adams's company. Adams found him equally diverting. Meanwhile Brooks and Mrs. Lodge schemed to find more luxurious and congenial quarters than the isolated cottage. All of this further dismayed Charles and inspired him to unaccustomed flights of satire as he saw that the management of Henry's recovery might be hustled out of his capable hands precisely because his Spartan regime had been successful. Charles foresaw "a series of teas, afternoon receptions, and other summer gaieties" if Henry accepted the Lodges' hospitality at Nahant. The only question, he said, was "whether the unconscious Henry will survive the course of treatment. This, however, I regard as of secondary consequence. If it is to be a short life, at least it will be a merry one!"

Henry's devotion to "Mrs Don" and her proprietary affection for him obviously made Charles uncomfortable. "Perhaps it would fill the bill to overflowing," he rallied Anna Lodge, "if Mrs. Cameron took advantage of your kind invitation, and carried Henry off in triumph and our motor to your castle by the far-sounding sea, there to enjoy a somewhat superannuated honeymoon. But all this time where is Don?—Where?—oh, where?—Henry Adams of Washington, D.C. as 'co-respondant,' and your house as the *locum in quo* will sound good!" Thus chided, the friendly conspirators promptly relented. What troubled Henry, however, was not the imagined proprieties but, as he admitted to Elizabeth, simply his vanity: he could not bear the thought of exhibiting himself to her or any other friend while still a paralytic.

Mrs. Cameron swept into the cottage on July 26 all grace and complaisance, and Charles had to admit that as a woman of the world she was suavity itself and her society very agreeable. Henry, who by this time was able to walk about, was overjoyed to see his matronly Madonna. The humor of the situation, as it appeared to Charles, was that, expecting to find Henry a valetudinarian, she had decided while in England "to devote her life to him" as nurse, secretary, and companion. She arrived and discovered that he had need of neither company nor assistance. She made her daily journey from Boston increasingly aware of the awkwardness of her position. Though she did not wish for the society of her aged husband nor he for hers, she was nonetheless financially dependent on him. Rather enjoying the stir he caused, Adams trudged about the countryside, after her departure, geologizing his way "over the hills and through the woods around Walden Pond," doing more walking than he had for twenty years. His friends in America and abroad had meanwhile circulated the reports of his condition from week to week. The sympathetic and diverting inquiries must have more than satisfied his appetite for letters. As soon as he was again able to put pen to paper he resumed his correspondence, "mainly female," as Charles succinctly put it. There were large arrears of rumor and friendly gossip to be made up, marriages and divorces, sickness and death, transatlantic comings and goings, all the epistolary small talk of their numerous circle.

Characteristic missives flowed in from old allies. Henry James expatiated with much diffident circumlocution on the resources of their friendship. Mrs. Cameron had "in a manner given me leave to tap on your more or less guarded door," and he had ventured to "stand by the fondness of my desire that some echo of my voice of inquiry and fidelity shall somehow reach you." Edith Wharton in her first letter to Adams told of "the anxious confabulations that have gone on in your little group, and the telephoning for news and the comparing reports, and 'Who's heard about him last?' whenever any of us met." Later she cheered him with praise of his life of George Cabot Lodge, which she was rereading.

Adams had early dictated a plea to Berenson, his "staff and hope," that it would not only "confer an enormous grace" but might also "cure me of the terrible habit that I am falling into of taking for granted that the world is coming to an end" if he would bring him up to date. So challenged, Berenson replied with sixteen pages of his own brand of chaff. In one letter he gently admonished Adams that he didn't believe the world "is coming to an end because *my* world is." One ought not to despair "when twenty life-times would not suffice to let one drain the cup of beauty and interest distilled for us by the Past."

Such trustful innocence was just the red rag that Adams needed to lunge for the carotid artery, and he promptly dashed off a retort to his "dear Prophet" calculated to singe his angelic wings. Cheerfulness was just what Unitarianism had ignorantly tried to introduce to Boston so that "we walked about, slapping each other in the stomach saying, 'Let's be gay,'" with the result that serious thought had died out. "No one now goes to Hell. Dante and others were good for a stage-scene, but to believe in Tragedy is the mark of a humbug, a liar, and a busted delusion." To Edith Wharton, who was shown the sulphurous creed, it seemed "like the last act of Lear."

The worst had not happened after all. Adams had received his notice to quit and for a wonder remained in possession. A shadow of change came over him, a perceptible mellowing as he savored the narrowness of his escape. All the old intransigence remained, the mad flings against reformers and politicians, would-be statesmen, and pretenders of all stripes, even of his own, but underneath the satirical tirades there were signs of thawing. Perhaps it was also the mild influence of the secretary-companion who now took charge of him in Washington, Aileen Tone. She kept him alive, he declared, and made him "glad to be an imbecile and paralytic." An old friend of his niece Loolie Hooper, Miss Tone was an attractive and cultivated young woman, a Roman Catholic with "a vivacious manner and a fine Irish wit" who had already been welcomed into the circle of nieces. A capable musician, she played and charmingly sang the old French songs in a collection of transcriptions and piano arrangements. She thus opened up to Adams the exciting possibility of recovering the music of his beloved twelfth-century poems. The atonalities of the sentimental monodies delighted him, and their form met his taste for the unexpected. The songs, he would say, "end with their tails in the air."

Begun as an experiment, the relationship with Aileen Tone endured until Adams's death five years later. "Tell your mother you're not going home," was how he sealed their alliance. He bought a Steinway piano for her to use and placed it in the library. Another "pretty niece" came every afternoon to read Italian to him "by way of keeping up the fiction" that he was going to Italy. He mocked the "mushy rot" of current Italian writing, the "Italianismus" which was as repulsive as the German variety. "Honestly I would like to sauce my remaining days with a strong flavor,—not the harrowing sentimental, but the flavor of action," he lectured the Italianate Berenson. He resumed the learned exchange with his medievalist professors just as if nothing had happened, picking up his translation of the "Song of Willame" and stepping back to his place at the head of the procession with indomitable verve. He was particularly ambitious to find the music of Richard the Lion-Hearted's elegiac "Prison Song," and he launched new assaults on the printed and archival sources. He found himself almost a joyful invalid, a little slow in movement, with "busted eyes and shaky legs," and occasionally troubled by aphasia, but otherwise rather remarkably well.

At this juncture, Ralph Adams Cram, whose *Gothic Quest* had made him the leader of the Gothic revival among architects, asked for an opportunity "to argue for the publication" of the *Chartres,* as he planned to be in Washington for the annual meeting of the American Institute of Architects. Recently Adams had sent him a copy of the revised *Chartres.* Cram now tempted Adams with the offer to have the American Institute of Architects officially sponsor its publication by Houghton Mifflin. Coupled with the prayerful urgings of Luquiens and Cook and the supplications of Berenson, the proposal compelled a fresh look at his finicking scruples. "No one wants to read the book," Adams protested; "don't be foolish." Then, with characteristic impulsiveness, he gave in. "Oh, very well, be it on your own head; *I give you the book.* You may do what you like with it, but don't bother me about any details." He asked one favor, that royalties be set aside to provide copies for impecunious architects.

Adams's carte blanche left Cram almost breathless over his good fortune. It was an extraordinary windfall, as Ferris Greenslet agreed. The advance sales broke all the publisher's records and belied all of Adams's pessimism about American taste. When the handsome edition appeared in November 1913 with "a flaming preface" by Cram, the resulting éclat severely tried Adams's pose of cynicism. All that he could find to complain about in the face of the appreciative tributes and the excellent sale of copies was that none of the reviewers "has yet been aware that I ever wrote anything else."

"Here am I," he exclaimed to Gaskell, "telling everyone that I am quite dotty and bed-ridden, and the papers reviewing me as a youthful beginner." In spite of his grumbling *blague* he carefully looked out for the reviews. There were ample royalties to carry out the modest benefaction suggested by Adams, and even to go far beyond it. One project was singularly appropriate, the commissioning of a stained-glass window off one of the side aisles of Chartres cathedral. The window depicts the life of the medieval churchbuilder Bishop Fulbert of Chartres. In the bottom triad of pictures his church is balanced by American skyscrapers, the iconography attempting, like the book itself, to bridge the centuries.

The comments of reviewers, though usually highly appreciative, tended to remark the surface beauties and made no effort to unravel the intertwined themes. The professional medievalists seemed to be put off by the poetic sentiment and by the imaginative freedom of Adams's grand design; the ordinary book reviewer could only stand amazed before a baffling tour de force. The *Boston Evening Transcript* approved the book as "an admirably balanced and intensely interesting monograph," a characterization peculiarly Bostonian in its reservations. The *Booklist* extolled it as "a careful and loving study," but with a certain lapse of perception recommended it as "a work of a scholar primarily for scholars." The reviewer for the *Literary Digest* placed the work near Ruskin's *Seven Lamps of Architecture* and Ernest Renan's essay "The Art of the Middle Ages." The London *Spectator* spoke respectfully of the "considerable insight of the philosophy and religion of the Middle Ages" in a work which was a "treatise on architecture plus much else." The two most interesting commentaries were written by Henry Osborn Taylor and by Luquiens. Much as Taylor was captivated by Adams's artistry and amused by his pervasive humor, he could not conceal his uneasiness with Adams's dramatic heightening of his narrative. The book offered "great delight, if not instruction," but at the end we "are left in doubt whether we have gone the round of the twelfth and thirteenth centuries, or round the mind of Henry Adams." Luquiens, with sensitive insight, called attention to the thematic structure of the work and its systematic use of sexual symbolism to mark the transformation of medieval sensibility.

There were, he carefully noted, regrettable lapses of detail in the handling of medieval texts, but these were "few and insignificant," not exceeding fifteen errors in a thousand lines of quotations. "In essentials, indeed," Adams's "knowledge or else his instinct [was] infallible."

27

The Abandoning Universe

WITH THE INAUGURATION of the President on March 4, 1913, Adams once again had a new neighbor across the way at 1600 Pennsylvania Avenue. He was relieved to be rid of the egregious Taft, whose blunders had in his eyes been compounded by the dollar diplomacy of Secretary of State Philander Knox. The outlook for President Woodrow Wilson seemed unpromising, however, for he was "loathed in advance by everyone within my circuit, Democrat or Republican." The growing evidence of political instability confirmed for Adams all his predictions of imminent disaster, and he fell more and more into the habit of telling his correspondents that he had foretold it all in his *Education* and *A Letter*. In Latin America there was little likelihood that the American government could reverse the policy of military intervention and occupation inaugurated by Roosevelt and Taft. In fact the occupation of Nicaragua by the marines was soon followed by that of Haiti. The domestic scene was no more reassuring. Crippling strikes engulfed railroads, textile mills, and shoe factories.

To Adams's global vision the situation in Europe was even more alarming. The First Balkan War, in which Bulgaria, Serbia, Greece, and Montenegro were pitted against their historic oppressor, Turkey, had broken out in the autumn of 1912 and raged bloodily until a peace treaty was signed in London on May 30, 1913, partitioning the greater part of European Turkey among the victors. Within a few months Bulgaria attacked her former allies Serbia and Greece. Adams no longer tried to particularize his disgusts. He was in "a dead funk about Europe" because there was no possibility of a general political settlement.

With the aid of the solicitous nieces Adams had what he confessed was "an uncommonly bright, pleasant winter" in Lafayette Square. It was all on borrowed time, as he constantly reminded himself and his friends, and he felt a distinct shortening of the leash. His "best new niece" beguiled him with the music of the thirteenth century, and the Alsatian musicologist Jean Beck, who was then visiting the United States, came in to tutor him in the mysteries of modal rhythms. To Ward Thoron in France Adams sent several thousand francs to make photographs of whatever musical rarities he could find in the old archives. Once more he was full of the twelfth century, and he talked and thought of little else, straining his eyes to read the old musical notation, belatedly teaching himself to read music, and exploring the theories of how to sing the old *chansons*. Richard the Lion-Hearted was his joy, he said, and "music master Tibault of Navarre a mine of melody." As he listened he thought of the machine guns and artillery at work in the Balkans and felt a longing for the eleventh century and the crusades. They had the merit at least of being "handwork," he remarked to Berenson. "I do not care for religion and machinery."

When he reached Paris again on April 2, 1913, he camped about for several weeks from one friend's apartment to another in the vicinity of the Bois until Elizabeth Cameron's apartment could be got into on May 1. The study of medieval music had given him a new lease on life, and he put his "three slaveys" happily to work. They spent days at the Conservatoire, where they persuaded the librarian, noted musicologist Henri Expert, to explain the twelve modes. All the while the nieces diligently copied and Adams worked away on the historical puzzles of the provenance of the *chansons* or made translations of them.

Ruth Draper joined their circle again, and the proud "uncle" busied himself at Worth's to provide two handsome dresses for her performance before Queen Mary. The vivacious *diseuse* presently visited Henry James in London and enlivened his sitting for John Singer Sargent with news of Adams's recovery. James, himself ailing, wrote admiringly of Adams's feat in reestablishing himself in Paris, which made "me grovel before you even as pale compromise before flushed triumph."

The great question for Adams was how to sing the old songs that they disinterred from long-forgotten archives, tunes which had not been heard for perhaps six hundred years. Since the authorities were doubtful, Adams improvised with his usual freedom of theory, adopting the Gregorian mode as most suited to the meter of the lyrics. The learned Amédée Gastoué protested, "We know too little about the rhythmic notation, and there are too many conflicting theories. Perhaps in thirty years scholars may approach this subject." Adams retorted, "But we're singing for pleasure, and we're singing as artists. Besides, I can't wait thirty years!"

Adams escaped the summer heat of Paris by renting the Château de Marivault, a substantial French country house situated above the village of St. Crépin on the northern edge of the forest of Compiègne beyond the Aisne. Here his "boarding house" flourished as actively as ever with the nieces in residence to manage him. Almost daily he carried on his reconnaissance of twelfth-century architecture, "automobiling *d'outre tombe* like Chateaubriand." His antiquarian researches in the lore of twelfth- and thirteenth-century music made time stand still in a perpetual autumn, and he looked out upon the fevered bustle of his own era with all the indulgence—and contempt—of one who had found aesthetic salvation.

When September came he was at home again in Elizabeth Cameron's apartment in the avenue du Bois de Boulogne, adding to his bag of *chansons* those being copied for him by Gastoué. In the midst of his erudite musicologizing Brooks Adams's new book arrived, *The Theory of Social Revolution*, which sounded their common theme of the hopeless inadequacy of present leadership. It advocated a managerial revolution and the creation of a kind of authoritarian corporate state. Henry approved the volume, but he could not share Brooks's limited hopefulness. "The only decision I see is between those who prefer to perish with society, and those who are willing to help the destruction." For himself he chose pure nihilism and fifty thousand a year to enjoy it. "Set me down as Rip!" he wound up. "I wish I had a dog Snyder."

Henry Cabot Lodge's *Early Memories* came a short time later, and the kindly allusions to Adams evoked an even more distressing sense of the failure of his career. Lodge was too generous, he said: "I could rarely see which way to go, and was fantastically conscious that others knew less than I, and were doing heaps of harm. I did not want to do harm. To this moment I am at a loss to know how I could have done good . . . This attitude of mine I hold to be imbecile, and in effect I said so in my *Education*."

More the absolute idealist than ever, like Molière's misanthropic

Alceste, he scorned all compromise and half measures. No wager was worth taking, whether Pascal's or Marx's. The memory of his ardors as a civil service reformer aroused in retrospect only revulsion, for now he avowed an "insane antipathy to reform, and to virtue of every social variety." Nothing roused his ire quite so much as the female suffragists. He also detested the amateur social workers of his acquaintance: "The young women inspect things, and find fault with them."

ADAMS SAILED for home again on November 4, 1913. The confused political outlook deepened his impression of great predatory forces at work beneath the surface and made him inveigh against the oppressive "Jew atmosphere." A trace of paralysis still lingered on. He had, he informed Brooks, "only one hand, one foot, one eye, and half a brain, but I see no one else who has more than half that." The carefully ordered days passed quietly enough, and he clung tenaciously to his hobbies. His circle of correspondents narrowed as old friends dropped out one by one. With the death of his old classmate Louis Cabot that winter, there remained few asterisks for him to insert in the necrology of his classbook of 1858. His letters remained his strongest passion, and he performed the daily ritual with his pen as if life depended upon it. The precise calligraphy wavered and the words grew taller and broader, as he strained to shape his irrepressible comments. The interchange in French with Henri Hubert rapidly increased when new skeletal fragments were unearthed at Les Eyzies. Professor Wilbur Cross at Yale asked him for a contribution to the *Yale Review*. Deprecating it as "an old plaything," Adams sent him his poem "Buddha and Brahma," written twenty years before. Mrs. Hay also came in to talk with him about the biography of John Hay that William Roscoe Thayer had agreed to write for the American Statesmen series, and she paved Thayer's way for an interview with Adams. Adams was "very communicative" and offered all his Hay letters. Still adamant against being photographed, no pictures having been taken of him since Clover's death, he agreed to sit for a portrait sketch by his nephew John Potter. The result was an impressive leonine profile of the head, "evanescent in crayon."

His seventy-sixth birthday reminded him to settle one more earthly detail, the final review of his will. Charles prudently advised him to declare himself "Henry Adams, of Washington"; this he did in adding a new codicil leaving a legacy of $25,000 to Aileen Tone. With her help he was able to keep the demonic darkest thoughts reasonably at bay. The demon, however, was always ready to spring. One day Henry James unchained it. Forgetting Adams's mordant response to his biography of William Wetmore Story, James sent him his autobiographical *Notes of a Son and Brother*, the sequel to *A Small Boy and Others*. The reminiscences, Adams burst out to Elizabeth Cameron, reduced him to a pulp. Such idealizing of their common past revolted him. "Why did we live? Was that all? Why was I not born in Central Africa and died young. Poor Henry James thinks it all real, I believe, and actually still lives in that dreamy, stuffy Newport and Cambridge, with papa James and Charles Norton—and me! Yet, why!" To James he sent a "melancholy outpouring" of "unmitigated blackness," evoking James's protest, "I still find my consciousness interesting . . . Cultivate it *with* me, dear Henry—that's what I hoped to make you do."

Among the visitors at the end of winter was Berenson, who had come over to the United States to confer with American art collectors. He came in every day to lunch during his stay in Washington and listened raptly to the twelfth-century songs. Adams could not avoid wincing a bit for Elizabeth's benefit. "Is it genuine; is it a Jew? how can I tell!" Like a good twelfth-century Christian he grumbled, "Such a glory it is to be a Hebrew! That glorified people take possession of us as though *we* were Satan and he Eve." The malice was mostly visceral, however, for shortly afterwards he was to write, "There are just two people who really understand and feel these songs; one is Mrs. Jack Gardner, the other is Berenson, and I call them my '*publique d'élite.*'"

Adams escaped to Paris from Woodrow Wilson's Washington in mid-April of 1914, thoroughly confused by the American imbroglio with Mexico that had just erupted over the refusal of dictator Victoriano Huerta to fire a salute to the American flag. William Jennings Bryan's statecraft had seemed dubious before; now Adams saw it as a kind of Machiavellian farce. It had been manifest to him that everyone expected to be drowned, "so they dance and play ball . . . No one anywhere, socialist, capitalist, or religionist, takes it seriously or expects a future." As for himself, calculating on only a year or so leeway, he had set aside $50,000 "to carry me through."

Before going off to Marienbad, Elizabeth Cameron helped to settle him and the nieces temporarily in an apartment near the Eiffel Tower until they could move to the Château Courbertin, which Adams had rented for the summer of 1914. From Washington Mrs. Lodge wrote for advice in finishing the landscaping at the memorial in Rock Creek cemetery. This time they would experiment with crushed stone. "As I am to lie under it," he said, "I suppose it is not unreasonable that you should tell me whether it is becoming." Henri Hubert delighted him with news that a whole "family" had been unearthed at Les Eyzies. The much-talked-of "30,000 year-old baby" at last had become a reality, and Adams could go out to the museum at Saint-Germain-en-Laye to divert himself with archaeological surmises.

Swarms of friends eddied as usual through the apartment where Adams held forth like an aged Cassandra. Into the charged atmosphere of that summer there suddenly came the news of the assassination on June 28 at Sarajevo of the Archduke Francis Ferdinand, heir to the thrones of Austria and Hungary. After the first sense of violent shock, nearly a month of uneasy calm followed, everyone assuming that the trouble between Austria and Serbia would be negotiated. Life in Paris went on as usual, and nieces busily shopped for dresses. On July 23 the peremptory Austro-Hungarian ultimatum suddenly made the "unthinkable" a reality. There was panic on the Bourse, and surprised crowds poured into the streets, for Paris had been so preoccupied with the sensational murder trial of Madame Caillaux, the wife of a cabinet minister, who had shot the editor of *Le Figaro*, that few were prepared for the imminence of a general European war. The first declaration of war, by Austria against Serbia, came on the twenty-eighth. It immediately touched off a wave of general mobilizations by the European powers. With Germany's declaration of war against Russia on Monday, August 3, the final catastrophe could not be averted. That night, after his speech to Parliament announcing that England would honor her commitment to Belgium and France, Sir Edward Grey looked out over St. James's Park and uttered his memorable prophecy: "The lamps are going out all over Europe; we shall not see them lit again in our lifetime." The next day the German armies swept into Belgium.

While out driving near the Château Courbertin, Adams heard the ringing of the bells near and far summoning the reservists. To his ear they were sounding the end of the world, the final Q.E.D. of all his demonstrations. As all automobiles were requisitioned, he was cut off from the world for two weeks longer. The nieces wore themselves out singing medieval songs to calm his nervous anxiety for news. Brooks, exhilarated by the war fever, wrote from Paris that the sight of the regiments of quietly determined conscripts marching past his hotel window on their way to the Gare du Nord made him take back everything he had said about French degeneracy. As a foreigner in a threatened region fifty miles north of Paris, Henry was suspect, and he and his party were evacuated to Paris on the first train for foreign residents. There he found Brooks and his wife and waited for the "refugees" from Switzerland. A few, like Edith Wharton and Elizabeth Cameron, were to stay on to help in war-relief activities. At first Adams hoped to remain in Paris, believing he would be better off there than elsewhere, for with sheltering friends at the American embassy to keep him informed he once more had a ringside seat to enjoy "the crumbling of worlds."

By the end of August, however, he found his position in Paris untenable, as he felt responsible for the safety of his nieces. The party made their way to Dieppe, where trainloads of wounded had already begun to pour in, and reached England on August 26. Adams found a comfortable refuge at Stepleton near Blandford, Dorset, the country house of Mrs. Cameron's daughter, Martha. "It was an escape from what verged on Hell," he wrote thankfully, "and no slouch of a bad one." Berenson motored down from London, and they both drove in to Blandford on September 10, anxious for word about the first Battle of the Marne, which had begun on September 6. The two friends arrived just as the news of the great French counterattack was posted. A little later, while Adams lingered at Stepleton, Henry James came on for a visit. They talked far into the night. For James the posture of American neutrality was unbearable, and in the middle of the following year, while his native country clung to neutrality, he became a naturalized British citizen, performing the geste, as he wrote, that "will best express my devotion."

Washington, in the first week of November when Adams arrived, was distinctly "pro-Allied" in spite of the administration's official neutrality. "Apparently we are working day and night for the Allies," he noted, "but also for money." America's tacit acquiescence in the British blockade of Germany resulted in a stupendous increase of Allied war orders, so that from the beginning the United States became a great military warehouse for the hard-pressed British and French. Everyone Adams saw was "rabidly English, and anybody who turned away was suspect." His onetime friends in the German embassy were "half-mad with solitude and desolation." Newspapers were forbidden him for a time by his doctor and war talk declared taboo, but nothing could halt his corrosive commentary. He often thought of the parallel with St. Augustine in the fourth century when the Roman Empire was crumbling under the attack of the Vandals; "the Germans got him too," he said, with a degree of historical license.

As the winter came on, all hope of an early end to the bloodshed disappeared. The sanguinary first Battle of Ypres, which ended on November 22, led to a significant change in the character of the fighting. The British lines under Sir Douglas Haig's command had withstood the terrible assault, and the Allies were able to finish the barrier of trenches on the western front. The deadlock meant henceforward a war of attrition stretching indefinitely into the future. Adams's almost weekly letters to Elizabeth Cameron in Paris cheered her with astringent comment on the Washington life that was now so remote from beleaguered Paris. He stayed faithful to his rule to treat serious things lightly and light things seriously. When the German-born Jewish financier Oscar Straus denounced the kaiser, he quipped, "What shall I do? I had thought at least to get to Heaven without Strausses." A few weeks later, in the wake of a gushing visitor, he let fly at Christian Science: "Generally it goes with other fads, like feminism, and makes women just insupportable, but it is all a part of the general nervous collapse which marks society." From his window above Lafayette Square he sometimes beheld oddly Olympian sights, as when President Woodrow Wilson and his fiancée, Mrs. Edith Galt, strolled by. "You've no idea how sweet it is when they kiss each other out walking," went his comment to Martha Lindsay, Elizabeth Cameron's daughter.

The dinners resumed at 1603 H Street, smaller and more subdued, but still precious as a source for the inside news and court gossip on which he lived, and he thus managed to outwit the kindly censorship of his womenfolk. Now that Cecil Spring Rice had become the British ambassador Adams was drawn back more actively into the stream of world politics. Another highly knowledgeable friend was Ambassador Jusserand, whose conversation brilliantly mixed diplomacy and history. Senator Lodge was an almost daily intimate of Spring Rice, so that Adams could very fairly say that he was drenched with anti-German feeling. Pressed by his close friends to share their views, Adams listened, probed, and retreated into cautious silence, which, as he said, "infuriates all parties." Lodge kept him to the political mark when he would drop in to fulminate against Wilson's indecisiveness. A less trying visitor was Father Sigourney Fay, a professor at Catholic University, who, like Father John La Farge, the son of the artist, came in for the little recitals, for Aileen Tone was "having a *succès fou* with her twelfth century songs." Father Fay was no bore, he assured Elizabeth, but he "has an idea that I want conversion, for he directs his talk much to me, and instructs me. Bless the genial sinner! He had best look out that I don't convert him, for his rotton old church is really too childish for a hell like this year of grace."

The tenor of Adams's own religious philosophy at this time comes out in his comment on Henry Osborn Taylor's just-published *Deliverance: The Freeing of the Spirit in the Ancient World*. He read the book, he told the author, in the only light which he found at least theoretically sufficient, that of the Stoic. "Logically, the religious solution is inadmissible,—pure hypothesis. It discards reason. I do not object to it on that account: as a working energy I prefer instinct to reason; but as you put it, the Augustinian adjustment seems to be only the Stoic, with a supernatural or hypothetical supplement nailed to it by violence." His analysis ended as always in a tangle of abstractions and the tropes of intuition. For him there was no easy way out of the dilemmas of thought. If his own provisional theory must bear a label, the one that came closest to his state, he said, was "Unitarian mystic."

Debarred by the war from his annual sojourn in France, Adams whiled away the summer of 1915 in the mountains at Dublin, New Hampshire, not far from the summer place of his confidant-in-diplomacy, former ambassador Henry White. Fewer and fewer letters came from his shaky pen, but the mind behind the faltering pen still gave and asked no quarter. Whenever he could he sent his "solitary and distant maunderings" to Elizabeth, who was occupied with the Foyer for Refugees, distributing food from the "grocer's shop" which she was running. He felt hopelessly out of things. "If I am not Chateaubriand," ran his rueful plaint, "you are not exactly Mme Recamier, and the world is not in 1815." There was no escaping the depressing war news, and he trembled at the anxieties of his British friends. The German gas attack at the second Battle of Ypres in the spring of the year had added a new dimension of horror. In the summer the immense British effort at the Dardanelles bogged down in the ghastly trenches of the Gallipoli peninsula. During that campaign Elizabeth was stationed in Egypt, and her long letters vividly brought home to him the gloom and the horror inspired by the endless procession of the wounded. On the eastern front one catastrophe followed another as Poland was lost and the key fortresses of Przemyśl and Lemberg fell, and with them 750,000 prisoners. The *cénacle* piped its plaintive melodies, trying, as Adams put it, to drown out the twenty-four-inch guns. However, it was the personal losses that were hardest to take, like the death of Senator Lodge's wife, the "Sister Anne" of so many confidences. Still another letter of condolence to write, perhaps the hardest of all that long catalogue, and it stirred thoughts of his own long-dead Clover. "I have gone on talking, all that while," he wrote to Lodge, "but it has been to myself—and to her. The world has no part in it. One learns to lead two lives, without education."

Death was increasingly an intruder even among his middle-aged contemporaries. The corteges that so frequently set out from nearby St. John's gave a bitter relish to his staying alive. As he looked out he would sometimes "wonder how many more younger men's graves I shall dance on." The death of his elder brother Charles in March closed still another valve of feeling. His thoughts ran deep into the past. "As you know, I loved Charles," he told Lodge, "and in early life our paths lay together, but he was a man of action, with strong love of power, while I, for that reason, was almost compelled to become a man of contemplation, a critic and a writer."

Shortly before his death Charles urged Henry to make his *Education* available to the public. Henry replied that "any idea of publication" had ended with his illness three years earlier. The volume was "an incomplete experiment that I shall never finish." Charles's advice, however, was soon emphasized by his example. He had given a sealed package to the Massachusetts Historical Society in April 1913 containing his own "autobiographical sketch" for publication after his death. When Henry Cabot Lodge became president of the society in April 1915 he arranged with Ferris Greenslet of Houghton Mifflin Company to publish it the following year with an introduction. The introduction turned out to be the extremely lengthy memorial address that Lodge had delivered in the First Church of Quincy.

Other influences were pressing Henry to come to a decision. Long before his stroke in 1912 he had himself thought that someday his *Education* ought to be published, and he had carefully edited a copy, writing in more than a hundred corrections and small revisions. He lent that copy—probably in January 1915—to the historian William Roscoe Thayer, who desired to use it while completing his biography of John Hay. Thayer had lunched with Henry and Charles and had afterwards written to his wife of Henry, "That arch-egoist was interesting, and very expansive, compared with last year." In July Thayer hopefully—and vainly—asked Henry to describe the Five of Hearts that had flourished in the 1880s and to identify the author of *Democracy.* He told him that the *Education* had helped him "greatly" and pressed him to publish the book in his lifetime.

But that Henry Adams was determined not to do, and now that Charles's autobiography was being readied for the press he called in Lodge to discuss the possible posthumous publication of the *Education.* Lodge evidently reported this development to Greenslet, who had never given up hope of repeating his triumph with the *Chartres* by an even greater publishing coup. Meanwhile Thayer, delighted with the success of his *Hay*—10,000 copies issued in the first few weeks—and greatly pleased by Adams's praise of the book, again pleaded with him to publish the *Education.* To advance the cause Thayer turned over to Greenslet the corrected copy which Adams had lent him. Greenslet also learned from Lodge of Adams's talk of posthumous publication. He promptly wrote to Adams, "The rumor has reached the writer's ear that you are seriously considering the question of finally publishing *The Education of Henry Adams.* As I think you know, the honor of issuing this book has long been desired by this house . . . May we not, following our publication of *Mont Saint Michel and Chartres,* now have the privilege of issuing your autobiographic book? It would be a special pleasure to us if, following the publication by us next spring of the *Autobiography of Charles Francis Adams . . .* we could announce the publication in the autumn of *The Education of Henry Adams.*"

Unwilling to have his hand forced, Adams took refuge in self-depreciation. His book was in an "incomplete, uncorrected, tentative form." It would be best to "wait a few months till I am gone, and then do what you like, much as Cram did with the Chartres." Baffled by Adams's modesty, Greenslet made another deferential try. Adams fired back a clarification: "What I meant to say was that, during my life I should not publish the Education . . . That after my death I should leave my corrected copy to the Massachusetts Historical Society to do what they pleased with."

While this unsuccessful negotiation was going on, Adams, deeply moved by Thayer's *Hay,* sent a long reminiscent letter to Elizabeth Cameron suggesting that she help put his generation to bed by publishing her collection of letters. With Mrs. Lodge gone she was the only one left to help "build up the legend of our Square." He reminded her that he had kept all of her letters for thirty years and that she might draw on them as well as on her own collections. "I do want you and Nanny [Mrs. Lodge] to stand by the side of John Hay and Clover and me forever—at Rock Creek, if you like,—but only to round out the picture . . . It is all that I have left."

In the solitude and anxiety of her Paris apartment, Adams's letter unloosed a wave of tenderness. The bittersweet memories of their long intimacy, now so painfully interdicted, overwhelmed her musings. "A letter from you, in your own inimitable handwriting! I could not read it at first for the tears which would well up . . . I have no knowledge of *métier,* no literary training, no starting point even . . . But such records as I possess of you—such wonderful records cannot be lost . . . I think of my reckless wasted life with you as the only redeeming thing running through it, always giving the sustaining power to keep going, always keeping me from withering up. Whatever I have or am is due to you . . . I wish I were more credit to you."

Feeling her own inadequacy, she offered her collection of letters to Thayer. He said he would be glad to edit them, but the work could not be done while Adams was still alive, and "who knows who will be his literary executor?" He suggested that Adams ought to edit the letters himself under the title "Henry Adams and His Friends," and he urged her to propose the idea to Adams and also to press him to consent to the publication of the *Education* as a companion volume to Charles's autobiography. Both tentatives failed.

Adams prepared his sealed package for the Massachusetts Historical Society early in 1916 after making a number of corrections in another copy of the *Education,* having apparently forgotten that he had lent his original corrected copy to Thayer, who still held it. Adams dated his letter to Lodge March 1, 1916, and included an "Editor's Preface" initialed "H. C. L.," perhaps to make sure that his book would not be burdened with the sort of exhaustive eulogy with which Henry Cabot Lodge had prefaced Charles's autobiography. Lodge acquiesced in the subterfuge.

The Thayer copy of the *Education* did not turn up until after Adams's death, and Lodge and his associates at the Massachusetts Historical Society used it with considerable editorial freedom in preparing the posthumous edition for publication in September 1918. Greenslet added the subtitle "An Autobiography." Within six months the book had sold 12,000 copies. It was awarded the Pulitzer Prize posthumously. It has ever since retained its popularity as a classic of American literature.

FAITHFUL to the dogwood and the Judas tree, Adams resumed his carriage drives to the Rock Creek woods in the spring of 1916. The hopeless impasse of his thoughts impelled him to write in parables: "Yesterday I walked in the spring woods, and met a fly. To that fly I said:—'Fly! do you want me to tell you the truth about yourself?' And that fly looked at me—carefully—and said:—'You be damned.' They have told me that, now, just seventyeight times. They are not tired, but I am." From Yale there came a "sacredly confidential" letter offering him an honorary degree, no doubt inspired by his fellow medievalists there, but Adams, much too daunted by the prospect of a public appearance, availed himself of the excuse that he could not be physically present.

The annual summer displacement now took him to the palatial Robert de Peyster Tytus House at Tyringham, high in the Berkshires. In the Versailles-like splendor he reigned contentedly like a patriarchal medieval lord and remained almost constantly surrounded by guests until November. He would drive over to Harry White's retreat to meet old Joe Choate, now eighty-three, and in their sunset leisure the "three old people," as he wryly admitted, "could abuse all our juniors."

Brooks came up from Quincy, and the two discussed "the total failure of the universe, as usual, and especially of our own country, which seems to afford even more satisfaction." If not war, he averred to Gaskell, then the whole brainless mediocrity of the Middle West— all "stomach, but no nervous center,—no brains"—would overwhelm America like a "huge polypus." As always in Brooks's somber company, his own misanthropy seemed to him the height of good humor.

He regaled Elizabeth with the small beer of his domestic life and satiric echoes of the rancorous world outside. She, long reconciled to his sense of outrage, replied that his "dear old grumblings [were] more cheerful than anyone else's gayety." When word came to him of the death in London of Henry James, he felt it like a final bereavement, for James, he wrote, had "belonged to the circle of my wife's set long before I knew him or her, and you know how I have clung to all that belonged to my wife. I have been living all day in the seventies." As he read the discouraging war news, seated before the fire in his study, the weight of years sometimes seemed almost to crush him. "Farewell!" he concluded a letter to Gaskell. "Every letter I write, I consider,—for convenience—my last, and it is far more likely to be so than if I were in the trenches."

As the summer and autumn ran on, the presidential campaign proved sufficiently bizarre to please his most sardonic tastes. For a brief moment Senator Lodge hoped for the Republican nomination, but neither the Progressive Republicans nor the G.O.P. made any of the hoped-for overtures. Theodore Roosevelt, though unanimously nominated by the Progressives, quickly deferred to the regular candidate, Charles Evans Hughes, hoping to avoid the disaster that had split the party in 1912. The sacrifice was futile. Wilson's "false and sordid cry," as Lodge called the slogan "He kept us out of war," provided the narrow margin of victory, and Adams's Republican friends resumed their impotent cavils.

Wilson still expected, as Ambassador Spring Rice said, that he might play a decisive role in ending the war, but his phrase "a peace without victory" profoundly discouraged the friends of England and France. The Germans, jubilant over the collapse of the Russian armies, scoffed at the peace feelers and answered them by announcing the resumption of unrestricted submarine warfare. The stream of futile notes to Germany ended, and Wilson broke off diplomatic relations.

On April 2, 1917, Wilson delivered his war message to Congress. "The war to make the world safe for democracy" had begun. The long uncertain wavering was ended, and Adams could now greet his friends Jusserand and Spring Rice as one of their avowed allies. Senator Lodge was not to be appeased, for Wilson's increasing assumption of power infuriated him. One day at Adams's table in the presence of Spring Rice and his wife, Lodge launched out on a particularly violent denunciation of his adversary in the White House. As the story has it, Adams finally struck the board with his whitened and trembling fist. "Cabot! I've never allowed treasonable conversation at this table and I don't propose to allow it now." The two men were, of course, soon reconciled, but it was clear that Adams felt that the time of irresponsible partisanship had passed.

The house at 1603 H Street once again echoed to the tread of visiting notables. Spring Rice brought the head of the British mission, Foreign Secretary Arthur Balfour, to see Adams, but the visit turned into "a purely domestic affair" and they exchanged reminiscences of Lord Robert Cecil in Mansfield Street "about fifty years ago." He missed seeing "the great Joffre," hero of the first Battle of the Marne, but did spend ten minutes with old friend Pierre de Chambrun, who had once been counselor to the French ambassador in Washington. Another visitor was Henri Bergson, the renowned author of *L'évolution créatrice,* one of the works which Adams had mined for his *Letter to American Teachers of History.* "The great Bergson came in the other day," said Adams in one of the first letters to Elizabeth that he was obliged to dictate, "and for an hour with infinite ingenuity I fought him off and made him talk philosophy. But at last he broke through all my entrenchments and gave me an hour's disquisition on the war, about which I honestly think I knew more than he did . . . Bergson is a funny little man, taking himself terribly seriously and treated so by all society."

The procession of war visitors and women Red Cross workers increased so much that it seemed "as though the entire civilized world had been using this house for a playground." Evenings after dinner had long settled to a graceful ritual such as recorded by Mrs. J. Borden Harriman, who was then a colonel in the District of Columbia Red Cross Motor Corps: "How I love those evenings there. Aileen Tone sits down at the piano after dinner and says, '*Do,* dear Uncle Henry, tell Daisy Harriman how this little twelfth century ballad happened to be written, and then I will sing it to her.' So under lowered lights, looking like a lovely eighteenth century French picture, Aileen with her sweet voice goes from one ballad to another. In between times, Uncle Henry pretending not to know there is a war and not having any use for Democrats, whispers, 'Well, tell me, what are they up to?' "

America's entry into the war as an ally gave Adams a certain satisfaction, for it suggested that at last the country had come round to his way of thinking. "To my bewilderment," he explained to Gaskell, "I find the great object of my life thus accomplished in the building up of the great Community of Atlantic Powers which I hope will at least make a precedent that can never be forgotten ... It is really a joy to feel that we have established one great idea even though we have pulled all the stars out of their courses in order to do it." He dictated these lines at Beverly Farms, where he had come to ground for the summer of 1917, drawn by an overpowering impulse to revisit the house which he and Clover had so joyously built in 1876 when all the world seemed to lie before them.

Now the large comfortable house echoed with the plaintive strains of twelfth-century music. He dictated letters to one or another of the nieces, facetious as usual about his imaginary isolation, and took walks along the familiar paths bordered with lichened rocks. Ruth Draper was persuaded to come up and give her "most frivolous" monologues, as chosen by Adams, at the nearby home of the aged Annie Lothrop, and Adams chuckled to see his own decrepitude mirrored in "the queer old crowd" all about him. He listened to the women in the house read George Santayana's recent and "very clever essay" *Egotism in German Philosophy,* going on from that to Santayana's earlier work and to William James. Santayana's analysis of the evil consequences of German subjectivism impressed him very strongly. "Santayana is always amusing," was his characteristic way of admitting it.

At this time Brooks, who had been elected to the Massachusetts constitutional convention, was astonishing the delegates with his totalitarian proposals to save society. An extreme social Darwinist ("We men are pure automata. I doubt if even we have more than a partial consciousness"), Brooks expounded his program of salvaging a decadent capitalism through a kind of Spartan statism modeled on wartime Germany. His antipathy to Wilson grew more violent even than Lodge's, for not long afterwards in an agony of frustration he wildly exhorted Lodge, "Kill Wilson!"

Henry humorously discounted the neurotic aberrations which so terribly agitated his brother. "*He* considers the world to be going to the devil with the greatest rapidity quite apart from war, and I endeavor as you know," he told Elizabeth, "to console him by the assurance that it went there at least ten years ago ... I really think his agony of mind chiefly due to the approaching destruction of all values in the stock market." Adams's scornful witticisms could not conceal his desire to be near the center of things, though the levers of power were far out of reach of his enfeebled grasp. In Washington, when he got back in November from Beverly Farms, he welcomed the younger generation in their smart military uniforms. The war excitement and the patriotic hope of victory gave a new zest to life, and he enjoyed what was to be his last winter more than he had the winters of many years past. His house, he mock-angrily exaggerated, was "crammed and crowded . . . with soldiers or Red Cross people or with suffragettes which are worse than all, and I can hardly find a corner in it where I can escape for a moment from their chatter."

He felt "buffetted from morning till night" by the talk of war, official incompetence, and "the quarrels and suspicions and treasons which are supposed to be the result of our corrupt nature." He took to advising the bright young men from the embassies in the hope of training them up "in paths of official virtue." All the young women talked familiarly about "Uncle Henry," he remarked in pretended dismay, and even the young men in khaki were becoming self-breveted nephews. His niece-in-residence Elizabeth Adams, who was active in the Red Cross, felt that he took "a queer comfort to have even that remote connection with the government under his roof." Generally the talk was hostile to the President's rapid assumption of war powers. One day when Charles William Eliot was taking his leave after an interview, Adams leaned over the baluster to give him a parting thought: "Brooks was right. We have lived to see the end of a republican form of government. It is, after all, merely an intermediate stage between monarchy and anarchy, between the Czar and the Bolsheviki."

In spite of his incessant hypochondriac complaints of failing faculties and senses, of having nearly reached that seventh age of man "sans teeth, sans eyes, sans taste, sans everything," his mind ranged lucidly over the universe. Dictating his opinions gave him an even wider sweep and freedom of vision. His memory was still capable of prodigies of historical generalization, as became evident in a small piece of literary work that he carried out in collaboration with the Reverend Sigourney Fay. Father Fay, evidently disturbed by the crisis of conscience that troubled Irish Catholics as a result of the execution of Roger Casement by the British government, projected an article for the *Dublin Review* supporting the Allied cause on religious and philosophical grounds. He was a frequent visitor that autumn and winter, and the article, "The Genesis of the Super-German," evidently grew out of discussions with Adams of the Irish Catholic's dilemma, torn as he was between his hatred of the Germans for the violation of Belgium and his hatred of the British for their suppression of the Sinn Fein. There was urgent need to influence Irish opinion, which was hostile to England. Father Fay declared that Adams wrote all but the very last portion of the article, obviously meaning that he had placed a Boswellian reliance upon Adams's talk, for writing was now out of the question.

The article invoked Adams's favorite parallel, the likeness of the current crisis to the times of St. Augustine. "Indeed, all that St Augustine says with regard to the Teutons of his day is applicable to our present enemies, except in one point . . . In taking Rome they did spare the churches."

On Adams's eightieth birthday, "of all birthdays the most momentous," as he termed it to Gaskell, "I am, for the first time in fifty years, surrounded by talk of war and weapons which I cannot escape and which have less meaning to me now than they had then, although your British aeroplanes are sailing up and down under my windows at all hours as though I were myself a master of Aeroplane Horse in a new universe of winged bipeds. It is only twenty years since my friend Professor Langley, at my table, talked about all these things as dreams of the future, and we're already wishing to heaven they had remained dreams of the past. I am in a new society and a new world which is more wild and madder by far than the old one and yet I seem to myself to be a part of it—and even, almost to take share in it. I speculate on what is to happen as actively as I did at your table fifty years ago, and the only difference is that I terribly miss your father's conversation and his dry champagne."

If the bustle in the house went on undiminished and the ritual of the daily walk and drive were outwardly reassuring, Adams's intimates saw clear signs that he was growing feebler. He could not conceal his dread of another stroke which might leave him in mindless imbecility. Nevertheless, hardly a day passed without someone coming in to lunch or dinner, the number of guests severely restricted to shield Adams from the crosstalk that unsettled conversation. It pleased him to be dealing once more with men who were doing things. His normally cantankerous opinions took on an even more sable hue, as if the will to live were fatally afflicted.

William Roscoe Thayer wrote begging for a copy of *A Letter to American Teachers of History*. Adams's long, railing, dictated reply on March 15, 1918, may be taken as his final letter to his fellow historians, the savage farewell of an Empedocles on the edge of the legendary crater: "In those far distant days, before the war, I had a mad idea that someone endowed with energy could effect some sort of open alliance or still opener antagonism between our historical school, or part of it, and the biologists of the Jacques Loeb type who were also feeble enough to teach in universities, but such an alliance or hostility would have needed fifty years of youth and vast reservoirs of energy—to say nothing of a considerable amount of education and intelligence. I had none of these things, and my start was bound to stop short. Within a year or two I was knocked as flat as a flatiron, and within another year or two the world was knocked as flat as I, and never lifted its head so far as to draw free breath again. Personally you can imagine how, after dragging myself through the mud, I climbed up onto the stile, in a disheveled condition, where I have continued to smile, ever since. I am one of the lucky ones who have got through with the game and care nothing, any more, for my stakes in it . . . You are therefore that wonderful object in creation, my last reader, and I give you herewith my final blessing, with the prayer that when you reach the same point long hence, you may also have a last reader as sympathetic as yourself, and a Harvard College which you shall not have treated with disrespect . . . Universities are our American equivalent for a church; they will give you peace."

In the next few days the news from Europe grew blacker than ever. Haig's great offensive in the latter part of 1917 had bogged down in the mud of the Ypres salient with a toll of 400,000 casualties. Now the British Fifth Army was dangerously stretched out south to the Oise in the pleasant region where Adams had once summered. On March 21 General Ludendorff launched his desperate offensive to destroy the British army and drive it to the sea before the Americans could intervene in decisive force. The furious assault of the German corps in its first tactical successes swept almost to Amiens and engulfed the British. The news cast a pall over Washington. No one realized that the invincible Ludendorff had overreached himself.

The shelling of Paris by the new German secret weapon, the enormous "Big Bertha" cannon, roused all of Adams's gallows humor. Worried about Elizabeth and her daughter, Martha, who was gravely ill, he sent off urgent cables for them to seek refuge. It seemed that his hope of an Atlantic community was foundering in blood. "Life," he remarked to Aileen Tone, "has become intolerable. This is no world for an old man to live in when the Germans can shoot to the moon." Yet that evening, Tuesday, March 26, he appeared "unusually bright and cheerful and laughed a good deal," according to Elizabeth Adams; and she left very cheery. Aileen saw him to his room and wound the clock. As she left he called out, "Good night, my dear." They were his last words.

In the morning, when he did not come down, Aileen went up to his room. He lay perfectly relaxed, his body still warm, as if he had quietly willed his going from one sleep to an infinitely longer one. Death had come with the merciful swiftness he had hoped for, at last ending his fears of helpless paralysis. As Elizabeth Adams recalled, "He was glad to go, anxious to go." Being devoutly religious, Miss Tone took a sad pleasure in arranging his room like a "chapelle ardente" with two candles burning. If there was any incongruity in the ecclesiastic ritual whose spell was lovingly woven about him, the only one who might have smiled at it lay inert and unresisting.

There was a simple service at the house on the afternoon of March 28 read by the rector of St. John's, the Episcopal church across the way from the Hay house. Then at long last Adams took possession of that other home in Rock Creek cemetery to lie beside Clover beneath Saint-Gaudens's sculpture in the grave unmarked, as he had directed, by any inscription. His young Irish friend Shane Leslie described the last hours to Moreton Frewen: "(Easter, 1918) The dear old man was kindly, courteous and sarcastic to the last. With him passes the last link of the old-time Washington. He remembered what it was before the Civil War, and he had watched it all the days since. But never had he noted such changes as those of the last two years, and was devoutly awaiting a comet to engulf it! . . . He lay in the midst of all the books, pictures and *objets d'art* you remember, and in the room where Hay, Roosevelt, Cabot Lodge, John La Farge, Clarence King, St. Gaudens, had so often met. I noticed only Harry White, Alice Roosevelt and Jusserand . . . Tonight there is a full paschal moon, and its light falls on the St. Gaudens in Rock Creek Cemetery. There is Peace because there is Oblivion. Our lady of Nirvana, the Enigma, the perfection of Néant is there, and our dear friend will be remembered as long as the Republic, because he lies there under her protection."

NOTES

INDEX

Notes

The many quotations from Henry Adams's letters may now be found in their corresponding places in *The Letters of Henry Adams*, vols. I–III, 1858–1892 (Cambridge, Mass., 1982), and vols. IV–VI, 1892–1918 (Cambridge, Mass., 1988). In a few cases they can be located in the Calendar of Omitted Letters in vol. VI, pp. 793–809. The chief source of unpublished diaries, letters, and other manuscript materials is the Adams Papers at the Massachusetts Historical Society (hereafter cited as MHS). Reference to that collection is regularly intended whenever no other location is given. The following abbreviations are used in citing the authors of diaries and letters to and from frequently named correspondents: BA for Brooks Adams (younger brother of Henry); CFA for Charles Francis Adams (their father); CFA Jr. for Charles Francis Adams, Jr. (Henry's older brother); JA for John Adams; JQA for John Quincy Adams (John Adams's son); MA for Marian (Clover) Adams; EC for Elizabeth Cameron; RWH for Robert William Hooper (Marian's father); and *NAR* for the *North American Review*.

Adams's spelling and punctuation have usually been preserved in quotations from his letters.

1. Brahmin Pattern

Page

1   "the thundering cannon," "awful day": Abigail Adams to John Adams, June 18, 1775.

"Slave Monger," "Slave Drivers": JQA, Diary, June 14, 1843.

1f   "desecrate" to "rout": JQA to Louisa C. Adams, May 30, 1843.

2   "fourth descendant . . . line": Louisa C. Adams to CFA, July 4, 1843.

Page

2 "Papa . . . class": Abigail Brooks Adams to HA, Aug. 4, 1843.
"live . . . descends": JQA, Diary, Sept. 22, 1842.
"Family . . . passion": JQA, Diary, July 20, 1829.

2f "The continuation" to "purchased": JQA, Diary, July 29, 1834.

3 "the species . . . down": JQA, Diary, Jan. 22, 1847.
"Shall I . . . fly?": quoted in *The John Adams Papers*, ed. Frank Donovan (New York, 1965), pp. 11, 55–56.

4 "bruiser" to "tea": Ralph Waldo Emerson, *Journals and Miscellaneous Notebooks*, VI, ed. Ralph H. Orth (Cambridge, Mass., 1966), 349.
"little house": HA, *The Education of Henry Adams*, ed. Ernest Samuels (Boston, 1974), p. 6.
"gloomy fancies" to "this day": CFA, Diary, Feb. 16, 1838.

4f "a disagreeable . . . another": CFA, Diary, Aug. 6, 1841.

5 "good . . . enough": CFA, Diary, Nov. 20, 1841.
"Oh! . . . trial": CFA, Diary, Dec. 1837.
"than any . . . sermon": CFA, Diary, Jan. 9, 1842.
"on . . . scholars": CFA, Diary, June 25, 1844.

6 "Her children" to "for her": CFA, Diary, April 25, 1837. "very disorderly": Wilhelmina Harris, *The Adamses at Home, 1788–1886* (Boston, 1970), p. 46.
"looked . . . peculiar way": Louisa C. Adams to CFA, Dec. 8, 1844.
"delighted . . . dancing": Abigail Brooks Adams to CFA, Feb. 13, 1847.
"The Glory . . . departed": CFA, Diary, Feb. 24, 1848.
"A funeral" to "heart": CFA, Diary, March 11, 1848.

7 "Mr. Adams . . . dollars": *New York Herald*, March 14, 1848.
"a tolerably ample fortune": CFA, Diary, Jan. 5, 1849.
"rolls in wealth": Boston *Atlas*, March 4, 1850.
"with approbation," "absurd exclusive rule": CFA, Diary, July 17, 1850.
"the Boston . . . Harvard": *Memoirs of John Quincy Adams*, ed. CFA (Philadelphia, 1874–1877), XII.

8 "front ranks," "powerful monied interests": CFA, Diary, Jan. 8, 1847.

10 "I am . . . justice?": *The Letters and Journals of General Nicholas Longworth Anderson*, ed. Isabel Anderson (New York, 1942), p. 107.
"somewhat noisy": Harvard College Class Records, Harvard University Archives.
"calling up . . . circumstances": "Faculty Minutes," 1854–1858, passim, Harvard University Archives.

11 "Beyond" to "altogether": HA, *Education*, p. 60.
"The resources . . . man": Louis Agassiz, *Principles of Zoology* (Boston, 1848), pt. 1, p. 206.

Page
11 "befogged": HA, *Education*, p. 60.
12 "an idealizing" to "suspense": Asa Gray, ed., *Darwiniana: Essays and Reviews Pertaining to Darwinism* (New York, 1876), p. 133.
"Darwinist" to "triflers": HA, *Education*, pp. 224, 225.
"the licentious . . . flood": Francis Bowen, *Principles of Metaphysical and Ethical Science Applied to the Evidences of Religion*, I (Boston, 1855), preface.
"the facts" to "science": Theodore Jouffroy, *Introduction to Ethics*, I (Boston, 1940), 83.
"those who live" to "gradual": ibid., pp. 261, 272.
12f "one of the Moral sciences" to "save": Francis Bowen, *Principles of Political Economy* (Boston, 1856), pp. 544, 356.
13 "the able" to "great truths": ibid., pp. 17, 19.
14 "everyone . . . our age": George Henry Lewes, *Biographical History of Philosophy*, I (London, 1845), preface.
"unity" to "society": François Guizot, *History of the Origin of Representative Government in Europe* (London, 1852), p. 11.
15 "Jackson guards," "Peirce's Reliques": Anderson, *Letters and Journals*, p. 78.
16 "ancient languages": HA, *Education*, p. 60.
"ten years . . . dyes": HA, "Class Day Oration," Harvard University Archives.
"very retired" to "monotony": Secretary's Records, Sept. 28, 1858; quoted in George Elsey, "The First Education of Henry Adams," *New England Quarterly*, Dec. 1941, p. 681.
17 "a chartered . . . renown": Anderson, *Letters and Journals*, p. 44.
"three pieces" to "forcible": Elsey, "The First Education," p. 681.
"incited . . . exertions": Anderson, *Letters and Journals*, p. 116.
"Herculean job": ibid.
18 "to regenerate . . . years": HA, "The Fool's Cap and Bells," *Harvard Magazine*, April 1858, p. 125.
"a general . . . drunk": Benjamin Crowninshield, *A Private Journal, 1856–1858* (Cambridge, privately printed, 1941), passim.
"in its full" to "magnificent!": Anderson, *Letters and Journals*, pp. 82, 112.
"thrilled" to "itself": ibid., p. 105.
19 "There was . . . remarks": Crowninshield, *A Private Journal*, Jan. 6, 1857. "other wealthy men" to "politicians": Anderson, *Letters and Journals*, p. 123.
"beat . . . cane": Samuel E. Morison and Henry S. Commager, *The Growth of the American Republic*, I (New York, 1937), 624.
20 "One . . . pride": HA to CFA Jr., Nov. 3, 1858.
"A man . . . Conscience": *Diary of Charles Francis Adams* (Cambridge, Mass., 1964), I, xv.
21 "God Almighty . . . got in": HA to CFA Jr., Nov. 23, 1859.

2. The Grand Tour

3. Witness to History

Page

44 "withdrawal" to "opposition": CFA, Diary, March 18, 1861.

"in silent abstraction" to "post-office appointment": CFA, Diary, March 28, 1861.

"never . . . mind": CFA Jr., *Charles Francis Adams*, p. 146.

"For my part . . . hour": CFA, Diary, March 30, 1861.

45 "gold lace and silk stockings": CFA, Diary, May 15, 1861.

"all communications" to "injunctions": Paul Frothingham, *Edward Everett* (Boston, 1925), p. 430.

45f "The two . . . things": *The Journal of Benjamin Moran*, II (Chicago, 1948), 970, 1148.

48 series of dispatches: The letters began June 7, 1861, and ended Jan. 21, 1862.

51 "Look into . . . eminently useful": CFA Jr. to HA, Aug. 23, 1861.

52 "A Visit . . . Diary": *Boston Daily Courier*, Dec. 16, 1861; reprinted in *American Historical Review*, 51 (Oct. 1945), 74–89.

53 "Let him . . . metropolis": *Times*, Jan. 10, 1862.

"frightful risk" to "reports of us": London *Examiner*, Jan. 11, 1862.

4. A Golden Time

55 "with an English . . . jib": Henry Watterson, *"Marse Henry"; An Autobiography*, II (New York, 1919), 33.

"by a primary law of nature": HA to Gaskell, Nov. 25, 1877.

58 "We tore . . . a little": quoted in William Roscoe Thayer, *The Life of John Hay*, 2 vols. (Boston, 1915), I, 280.

60 "Darwin's hypothesis" to "surprise us": Gray, *Darwiniana*, pp. 109, 169.

62 "That essay" to "attitude": CFA Jr., *An Autobiography*, p. 179.

"all the . . . organizations": HA, "The Tendency of History," in *Annual Report*, American Historical Association (Washington, D.C., 1894), p. 17.

"Foresight . . . inmost nature": John Stuart Mill, *Auguste Comte and Positivism* (London, 1865); reprinted in *Collected Works of John Stuart Mill*, X (Toronto, 1969), 266.

"he became . . . evolution": HA, *Education*, p. 225.

"the general . . . forces": Herbert Spencer, *First Principles*, 6th ed. (London, 1908), p. 178.

"it is certain . . . laws": Henry Buckle, *Introduction to the History of Civilization in England*, ed. John M. Robertson (New York, 1925), p. 19.

63 "the most important . . . people themselves": John Stuart Mill, *Considerations on Representative Government* (London, 1861), pp. 37, 39.

63f "A representative" to "only interests": ibid., pp. 23–24, 42, 159, 160.

Page

64 "The Montesquieu" to "Democracy": John Stuart Mill, *Dissertations and Discussions* (London, 1861), p. 260.

"into . . . insignificance": ibid., p. 407.

65 a formal report: reprinted in *New England Quarterly*, Dec. 1942.

66 "a profound . . . transaction": Seward to CFA, April 13, 1863, Records of the Foreign Service, National Archives.

67 "All my . . . I must": CFA Jr. to HA, March 22, 1863.

68 "I do not . . . traveling": Abigail Brooks Adams, quoted in HA to CFA Jr., March 2, 1865.

70 The article: reprinted and revised in CFA Jr. and HA, *Chapters of Erie and Other Essays* (Boston, 1871), and further revised in HA, *Historical Essays* (New York, 1891).

"The name . . . than ever": *Nation*, Jan. 17, 1867.

"historians" to "soil of New England": *Southern Review*, n.s., 1868.

"British Finance in 1816": reprinted and revised in *Chapters of Erie* and *Historical Essays*.

73 "a very handsome letter" to "new in it": HA to CFA Jr., Nov. 23, 1868.

"talks learnedly . . . sensibly": *Nation*, Oct. 22, 1868.

5. A Young Reformer of Thirty

77 "the hall . . . full": *Diary of Gideon Welles*, III (Boston, 1911), 488.

"Sumner . . . rumor": ibid.

"It is among . . . set aside": *New York Times*, April 24, 1869.

"try his future" to "as he": CFA, Diary, Oct. 11, 1868.

79 "Calling there" to "conversation": quoted in M. A. De Wolfe Howe, *Portrait of an Independent: Moorfield Storey* (Boston, 1932), pp. 129, 124.

"a dangerous example of frivolity": HA, *Education*, p. 256.

81f "Among . . . Congress": *Springfield Republican*, May 1, 1869.

83 "rapidly rising . . . writer": Theodore Smith, ed., *Life and Letters of James Abram Garfield*, II (New Haven, 1925), 758–759.

"Civil Service Reform": published as a pamphlet by Henry Brooks Adams (Boston, 1869), 35 pp.

85 "Men and Things in Washington": *Nation*, Nov. 25, 1869.

"A Peep into Cabinet Windows": *Nation*, Dec. 12, 1869.

"cabal" to "Attorney-General": "Senate and the Executive," *Nation*, Jan. 6, 1870.

"A Political Nuisance": *Nation*, Jan. 27, 1870.

"with malicious intent": *Congressional Globe*, 41st Cong., 2d sess., pt. 2, p. 1113.

86 "What the *North*" to "animal": *Nation*, May 12, 1870.

88 "led . . . President": quoted in Smith, *Life and Letters of Garfield*, p. 449.

Page
88   "Caesarism . . . life": CFA Jr., "A Chapter of Erie," reprinted in
     Frederick Hicks, ed., *High Finance in the Sixties* (New Haven,
     1929).
89   "the most widely attractive" to "critical": *Nation*, Aug. 11, 1870.
     "The author . . . historian": *Wisconsin State Journal*, Oct. 7, 1870.

6. Harvard College Once More

93   "Harvard College": *NAR*, Jan. 1872.
94   "read . . . Latin": James Laurence Laughlin, "Some Recollections of
     Henry Adams," *Scribner's Magazine*, May 1921.
     "There was no closing" to "pose": Lindsay Swift, "A Course in His-
     tory at Harvard College in the Seventies," *Proceedings*, MHS, 52
     (1918–19), 70.
     "Fully primed . . . so was I": Samuel E. Morison, "Edward Chan-
     ning," *Proceedings*, MHS, 64 (1930–1932).
95   "You know . . . demagogue": quoted in Henry Osborn Taylor, *Hu-
     man Values and Verities* (privately printed, 1929), pt. 1, p. 40.
     "Good heavens! . . . Look it up": quoted in Henry Osborn Taylor,
     "The Education," *Atlantic Monthly*, Oct. 1918, p. 490.
     "profound contempt" to "difference": Charles F. Thwing, *Guides,
     Philosophers, and Friends* (New York, 1927), p. 231.
     "clever, ambitious young fellows": John T. Morse, *Thomas Sergeant
     Perry* (Boston, 1929), p. 63.
     "Voltaire in petticoats": *Letters of Henry James*, ed. Percy Lubbock
     (New York, 1920), p. 307.
     "I wish" to "aunt": CFA Jr., Memorabilia, pp. 283, 284, MHS.
96   "I trust . . . propitious": CFA, Diary, March 2, 1872.
96f "The book . . . civilization": HA, "Howells, Their Wedding Jour-
     ney," *NAR*, April 1872.
101 "Nothing . . . temple": *Letters of Mrs. Henry Adams*, ed. Ward Tho-
     ron (Boston, 1936), p. 70 (cited hereafter as Thoron).
     "painfully wanting in enthusiasm": ibid., p. 65.
     "great success": ibid., p. 80.
     "existence . . . impossible": ibid., p. 84.
     "nice blocks . . . Sybils": ibid., p. 94.
     "My brother" to "seen": CFA Jr. to Fanny Crowninshield Adams,
     May 27, 1873.
103 "I like . . . material than in Boston": Thoron, p. 131.
104 "Nothing . . . offer": Henry Cabot Lodge, *Early Memories* (New
     York, 1912), p. 240.
105 "I have worked" to "matter": *Unpublished Letters of Bayard Taylor*
     (San Marino, Calif., 1937), p. 153.
105f "This notice . . . done": Proof sheets of review, Harvard University
     Archives.

Page

106 "It is the misfortune" to "historical school": HA, "Sohm's Procédure de la Lex Salica," *NAR*, April 1874, pp. 416–425.

"better fruit . . . school": HA, "Kitchin's History of France," *NAR*, Oct. 1874, pp. 442–443.

"The historian" to "innocent": HA, "Stubbs's Constitutional History of England," *NAR*, July 1874, pp. 233–234.

"the inevitable" to "excursive ways": HA, "Bancroft's History of the United States," *NAR*, April 1875, pp. 424–425.

107 "He sent" to "muster": Lodge, *Early Memories*, pp. 244–245.

108 "Out of it . . . Randolph": Swift, "A Course in History," p. 70.

7. In Quest of Historical Principles

109 "by a sentiment" to "Parliament": HA, "Stubbs's Constitutional History." "clever theories" to "Justinian": HA, "Maine's Early History of Institutions," *NAR*, April 1875, pp. 432–433.

110 "Hic . . . Socnam": HA, *Education*, p. 368.

112 "The Primitive Rights of Women": delivered Dec. 9, 1876; published in revised form in HA, *Historical Essays* (1891).

"as he grew . . . passion": HA, *Education*, p. 442.

113 article: HA, "Von Holst's Constitutional and Political History of the United States," *NAR*, Oct. 1876, pp. 328–329.

114 "the final . . . suspended": Hermann von Holst, *Constitutional and Political History of the United States*, I (Chicago, 1876), 224.

115 "The historian" to "group": quoted in James T. Bixby's review of Taine's *On Intelligence*, *NAR*, Oct. 1873, p. 402.

"some theory . . . policy": HA to Henry Cabot Lodge, Feb. 1, 1878.

116 "The 'practical man' . . . ignorance": *Nation*, Feb. 17, 1876, p. 118.

118 "plunged . . . intrigue": James P. Walker, *Life of Francis Amasa Walker* (New York, 1932), p. 159.

120 "a very strong number": Lodge to Bancroft, Oct. 10, 1876, MHS.

"a severe internal convulsion": *Nation*, Oct. 12, 1876.

123 "Mr. Henry Adams . . . man": William S. Robinson, *"Warrington" Pen-Portraits* (Boston, 1877).

8. The Return of the Native

125 "I feel" to "filled": CFA Jr., Diary, Oct. 17, 1877.

127 "We strut" to "gentleman": MA to RWH, Nov. 18, 1877.

"Mr. Mullet's . . . asylum": HA, *Education*, p. 253.

128 "advocacy . . . dishonesty": *Nation*, May 2, 1878, p. 291.

129 "One consequence . . . conciliate it": HA to Gaskell, Nov. 25, 1877.

"will not relish": CFA Jr., Diary, Jan. 19, 1878.

130 "hebdomadal drivel" to "dead": MA to RWH, Jan. 13, March 24, 1878; Nov. 25, Dec. 9, 1877.

Page

130 "The new Minister . . . creator": MA to RWH, Nov. 18, 25, Dec. 2, 1877.

"We never . . . say": quoted in Mrs. Winthrop Chanler, *Roman Spring* (Boston, 1934), p. 303.

130f "not hanker" to "forged": MA to RWH, Dec. 30, 1877; Jan. 13, 1878; Dec. 2, 1877; Feb. 10, 1878.

131 "social vortex" to "sharpened": MA to RWH, Nov. 8, 1877; March 9, 1878.

"the stroke" to "Trescott": MA to RWH, March 3, Jan. 6, 1878.

131f "the grave" to "danced": MA to RWH, Jan. 6, 1878; Thoron, p. 443.

132 "indoor man" to "flowers": Thoron, p. 399; MA to RWH, March 24, 1878.

"Cruikshank's illustrations" to "burdens": MA to RWH, Dec. 23, 1877; Feb. 10, Jan. 27, Feb. 3, 1878.

"Oh . . . konnten!": Thoron, p. 427.

"light . . . advantage": MA to RWH, March 3, 1878.

133 "homelier" to "yore": Anderson, *Letters and Journals*, p. 195.

"curves" to "Byron": MA to RWH, Jan. 6, Feb. 17, 1878.

133f "gold–bug" to "dinner": MA to RWH, Feb. 17, 24, March 3, 1878; Jan. 13, March 13, Dec. 30, 1877.

134 "Nordhoff . . . are!": MA to RWH, Feb. 2, 1879.

"Life . . . myths": MA to Gaskell, March 29, 1875.

"just like bon bons" to "terrapin": MA to RWH, March 24, April 28, 1878; March 30, 1879; April 28, 1884.

135 "had everything . . . delight": HA, *Education*, p. 311.

136 "to bind . . . influence": Minutes, Cosmos Club, club archives, Washington, D.C.; Thomas M. Spaulding, *The Cosmos Club in Lafayette Square* (Washington, D.C., 1949).

136f "In the face" to "gaps": *Nation*, Aug. 30, 1877.

137 "laws" to "overcome": *Nation*, Jan. 23, 1879, pp. 73–74.

9. Literary Debut

138f "She is . . . published": MA to RWH, Jan. 27, 1878.

140 "by the sheer force" to "control": HA, *The Life of Albert Gallatin* (Philadelphia, 1879), p. 154.

"There are" to "helpless": ibid., p. 267.

141 "a valuable repository" to "general reader": A. K. Fiske, review in *NAR*, Oct. 1879, pp. 410–411.

141f "monstrously . . . work": *Saturday Review*, July 26, 1879, p. 123.

142 "much instruction" to "perseverance": *Athenaeum*, Sept. 6, 1879, p. 205.

"Patient investigation" to "overcome": *International Review*, 7 (1879), 250–266.

Page

142   "this volume" to "no mercy": *Nation*, Aug. 21, 28, 1879, pp. 128, 144.

"If as you say . . . will": MA to E. L. Godkin, Dec. 25, 1879, Godkin Papers, Houghton Library, Harvard University.

143   "You know" to "consideration": CFA Jr. to E. L. Godkin, Oct. 30, 1880, ibid.

"one . . . biographies": Morison and Commager, *Growth of the American Republic*, I, 770.

144   "with the most" to "ironically": Henry Holt, Foreword to HA, *Democracy* (New York, 1925).

145   "The curious . . . world": *Blackwoods*, June 1882.

"I hope . . . government": Thoron, p. 375n.

"moral lectures": King to Hay, from Paris (1882), Cater Transcripts, MHS.

146   "mingled . . . Capital": *Boston Evening Transcript*, April 4, 1880. For reviews see Mrs. E. T. Gough (Agnes Mary Hyde), "Henry Adams's *Democracy*"(Master's thesis, University of Chicago, 1938).

"In spite . . . provincial": *Appleton's*, June 1880.

"our pet enmity" to "recognition": Thoron, p. 252, n. 2.

147   "Pass . . . overcome": Tyler Dennett, *John Hay* (New York, 1933), p. 130.

"grafting" to "master hand": *Spectator*, Nov. 19, 1881.

"Nothing . . . literature": *Atlantic Monthly*, Sept. 1880, p. 421.

"masterpiece": *Saturday Review*, July 8, 1882.

"There is . . . superior person": *New York Semi-Weekly Tribune*, June 14, 1882.

147f "I am much amused" to "absent": Thoron, pp. 247, 284, 285.

148   "It is written . . . idea?": CFA Jr. to Godkin, Jan. 31, 1884, Godkin Papers, Houghton Library.

"the same . . . character": *Nation*, Feb. 21, 1884.

148f "establishment" to "twice as long": MA to RWH, Nov. 10, 19, 24, 1878.

149   "riot . . . individualities": MA to RWH, Dec. 29, 1878.

"good talk" to "generation": MA to RWH, Dec. 22, 1878; Jan. 5, 1879; Dec. 29, 1878.

150   "our eminent" to "Jesuit": MA to RWH, Jan. 26, 1879; Dec. 10, 29, 1878.

151   "most trusted" to "relieved": CFA Jr., Diary, May 20, 22, 23, 1879.

10. European Orbit

153   "he who . . . life": Thoron, p. 216.

"The second act" to "four chapters": ibid., pp. 171, 177, 187, 163.

"too reserved . . . shown": ibid., p. 198.

153f "fell to prattling" to "the core": ibid., p. 200.

Page

154   "Was it" to "señora": ibid., p. 216.

155   "the knots" to "very happy": MA to RWH, Jan. 4, 1880; Thoron, pp. 185, 220.

"a serious peacock" to "dress": On Worth see Thoron, pp. 183, 224.

"in spite . . . power": *Nation*, April 25, 1878.

156   "a huge . . . restaurant": Thoron, p. 221.

"very indecent" to "rage": ibid., pp. 185, 224.

156f "He cannot" to "couches": *Nation*, April 25, 1878.

158   "visiting . . . zoo": MA to RWH, March 28, April 4, 1880.

"At this Belshazzar's . . . to treat": Thoron, p. 145.

"swells" to "political set": MA to RWH, April 4, May 2, Feb. 15, 1880.

159   "time" to "cream cheese": MA to RWH, March 21, May 2, June 27, 1880.

"on the hearthrug" to "weary round": MA to RWH, Jan. 21, March 14, April 4, 1880.

"it was a wise move" to "any more": MA to RWH, April 18, Aug. 27, July 4, 1880.

160   "like Niagara" to "water color line": MA to RWH, June 27, 1880; Thoron, pp. 141, 156, 159.

"the inside track" to "stiff": Thoron, pp. 151, 154; MA to RWH, Feb. 15, 1880.

160f "the social" to "entailed": Thoron, pp. 147, 159, 148, 416.

161   "the intellectual . . . like steel": MA to RWH, April 11, 1880.

"one of the three . . . meaning": quoted in Thoron, p. 360n.

"greatly . . . score": HA to Lodge, July 9, 1880.

162   "pipes and grog": Thoron, p. 157.

"pseudo-Platonic . . . forces": Fiske to Darwin, Oct. 23, 1871, Houghton Library, Harvard University.

164   Lecky: On Lecky and Lowell, see MA to RWH, July 4, 18, 25, May 24, 1880.

"redeem . . . monkeys": MA to RWH, Sept. 12, Aug. 29, 1880.

165   "a horrid bore" to "constituency": On the sale of the house, see MA to RWH, May 30, 1880; Thoron, pp. 203, 219, 220.

"no more regret" to "characters in it": MA to RWH, July 25, 1880.

11. *The Golden Age of Lafayette Square*

166   "much pleased" to "favored with children": CFA, Diary, Oct. 14, 16, 1880.

167   "Sunday . . . affairs": Thoron, p. 358.

"I've gone in . . . absorbing": MA to RWH, Sept. 7, 1883.

168   "Mr. Adams said . . . action": Feb. 11, 1881; quoted in Charles R. Williams, *Life of Rutherford Birchard Hayes* (Boston, 1914), p. 643.

Page
172   a medical work: J. Marion Sims, *Clinical Notes on Uterine Surgery with Special Reference to the Management of Sterile Conditions* (New York, 1873).

172f   "Henry" to "one-hoss shay": Thoron, pp. 272, 441, 418.

173   "poor little woman," "drawn . . . Don": ibid., p. 352.

174   "We miss . . . you": MA to EC, Jan. 11, 1884.

    "popped in . . . to get back": MA to RWH, May 25, 1884.

    "Hosscar" to "cad": Thoron, p. 338.

    "caprices" to "off the stage": ibid., pp. 239, 282.

    "It is the superb actress" to "bad woman": Nov. 11, 1881; Mary Abigail Dodge, *Gail Hamilton* (Boston, 1901), p. 818.

    "superb" to "real nature": Anderson, *Letters and Journals*, p. 265.

174f   "cat . . . reputation": Thoron, p. 425.

175   "St. Matthew" to "keeper": MA to RWH, Nov. 4, Dec. 23, 1883.

    "darker moments . . . whites": Henry James to Thomas S. Perry, Jan. 23, 1882; quoted in Virginia Harlow, *Thomas Sergeant Perry* (Durham, N.C., 1950).

    "the incarnation . . . live with?": Thoron, p. 384.

    "do Washington . . . his wife": *The Notebooks of Henry James*, ed. F. O. Matthiessen and Kenneth B. Murdock (New York, 1947), p. 56.

    "Bonnycastles" to "took in": Henry James, "Pandora," in *Novels and Tales of Henry James*, XVIII (New York, 1909), 128.

176   "I shall suggest . . . bites off": Thoron, p. 306; MA to RWH, Nov. 29, 1880.

177   "as eager" to "practical age": Thoron, p. 286; MA to RWH, March 30, 1884.

    "immaculate . . . wrinkle": *Clarence King Memoirs* (New York, 1904), p. 345.

    "bitch goddess": quoted in Aldous Huxley, *Proper Studies* (London, 1927), p. 318.

178   "I am not suited . . . read": Hay to Miss Perry, Jan. 2, 1859, in John Hay, *A Poet in Exile: Early Letters of John Hay* (Boston, 1910).

    "leaven the family dough": Thoron, p. 368.

179   "It is . . . work is done": Oliver Wendell Holmes, *The Common Law* (Boston, 1881), p. 1.

12. *Portraits Past and Present*

180   "Population" to "history": Ledgers, Henry Adams Library, MHS.

181   "For thirty years" to "son": HA, *John Randolph* (Boston, 1882), p. 26.

182   "bold . . . States": Hugh A. Garland, *John Randolph* (New York, 1851), p. 128.

184   "much better": Thoron, p. 405.

Page
186   "like a belated" to "bosses": MA to EC, July 26, 1883, MHS.
188   "Mr. Adams . . . pleasant": MA to RWH, Jan. 6, 1884.
      "a swell piece" to "sudden": MA to RWH, Dec. 2, 16, 26, 1883;
      March 23, April 2, May 5, 1884; MA to EC, Jan. 11, 1884.
189f "clearing away . . . intellect": Clarence King, *Catastrophism and the
      Evolution of Environment* (New Haven, 1877), p. 4.
190   "Quite unconventional . . . engagement": *Publishers Weekly*, May
      10, 1884.
191   "conceived . . . let it die": King to Hay, June 20, 1886, Cater Tran-
      scripts, MHS.
192   "the product" to "clever": *The Letters of William Roscoe Thayer*,
      ed. Charles D. Hazen (Boston, 1926), p. 353.
193   "The whole . . . determined": Arthur James Balfour, *Defence of Phil-
      osophic Doubt* (London, 1879), p. 325.

13. The Forsaken Garden

194   "refused . . . visitors": Robert Shackleton, *Book of Washington*
      (Philadelphia, 1922), p. 124.
196   "Before this" to "in the book": Draft, vol. II, pp. 227, 15, MHS.
197   "He went . . . traveler": MA to Hay, April 24, 1885.
197f "gone over" to "grave": MA to Clara Hay, May 1885.
199   "tried . . . depression": CFA Jr., Memorabilia, pp. 283–284, MHS.
200   "The insane" to "taste for horrors": MA to RWH, Jan. 26, 1879.
      "otherwise . . . graves": MA to RWH, Christmas 1881, MHS.
      "If . . . even": quoted in Ellen Gurney to Godkin, Dec. 30, 1885,
      Godkin Papers, Houghton Library, Harvard University.
      "Mr. Henry Adams . . . heart": Washington *Critic*, Dec. 7, 1885.
      "caused" to "acquaintances": *New York World*, Dec. 10, 1885.
201   "Although . . . death": New York *Sun*, Dec. 9, 1885.
      "The late . . . popular": Washington *Critic*, Dec. 9, 1885.
      "was . . . year": *New York World*, Dec. 10, 1885.
202   "In . . . aspired": *Boston Evening Transcript*, Dec. 8, 1885.
      "I called . . . dead wife": Anderson, *Letters and Journals*, p. 252.
      "drove . . . him": CFA Jr., Diary, Dec. 8, 1885.
202f "I hoped . . . her": Hay to HA, Dec. 1885, MHS.
203   "has . . . work": Gurney to Godkin, Dec. 11, 1885, Godkin Papers,
      Houghton Library.
      "I hear . . . now": Ellen Gurney to Godkin, Dec. 30, 1885, ibid.
      "women's society" to "tranquillized": BA, "The Heritage of Henry
      Adams," in HA, *The Degradation of the Democratic Dogma*,
      comp. BA (New York, 1919), p. 102.
204   "also died to the world": On HA's death to the world, see ibid., pp.
      2, 12.
      "with . . . fifteen years": Robert Johnson, *Remembered Yesterdays*
      (Boston, 1923), p. 447.

Page

205 "In her . . . death": *Sonnets and Poems of Petrarch*, trans. Joseph Auslander (New York, 1932), p. 309.

14. *The Season of Nirvana*

207 "My temper" to "sawdust": La Farge to HA, in John La Farge, S.J., *The Manner Is Ordinary* (New York, 1954), p. 4.
"bring . . . could": John La Farge, *An Artist's Letters from Japan* (New York, 1897), p. 17.

208 "a suggestive . . . Washington": *Papers of the American Historical Association*, II (New York, 1887), 47.
"dodging . . . red": King to Hay, Jan. 10, 1886, Cater Transcripts, MHS.
"for . . . season": quoted in La Farge, *An Artist's Letters*, p. 81.

214 "Call . . . twelfth": CFA Jr. and HA, *Chapters of Erie*, p. 1.

215 "When . . . secure": quoted in Lodge, *Early Memories*, p. 301.
"I miss . . . terribly": Abigail Brooks Adams to HA, Oct. 4, 1858.

216 "so amply" to "myself": Last Will of CFA, Sept. 12, 1871, Probate Office, Norfolk County, Mass.

217 "It is" to "explorations": Hay to Clark, May 14, 1887; *Letters of John Hay and Extracts from Diary*, ed. HA, 3 vols. (Washington, D.C., 1908), II, 113.

15. *History and the Posthumous Life*

220f "The Adams family" to "Minister": Stephen Gwynn, ed., *Letters and Friendships of Cecil Spring Rice*, 2 vols. (Boston, 1929), I, 68, 78, 102.

227 "what to ask" to "afire": Saint-Gaudens to HA, July 8, 1888, Saint-Gaudens Papers, Library of Congress.
"against which" to "out of him": Stanford White to HA, Aug. 9, 13, 1888.
"Adams . . . nature": Homer Saint-Gaudens to HA, Jan. 27, 1908.

229 "It is" to "generally": Scribner to HA, Dec. 13, 1888.

231 "the private life" to "Potter": Paul Hamilton to HA, April 9, 1887.

232 "the expectation" to "ideas": *Critic*, Dec. 7, 1889.
"all the charms" to "drama": Hewitt to HA, Dec. 27, 1889.
"exceptional success," "some market abroad": Scribner to Bangs, Feb. 28, 1890, Charles Scribner's Sons archives, New York City.
"nearly score" to "study": *Atlantic Monthly*, Feb. 1890, pp. 274–278.

232f "striking" to "key": *Nation*, Dec. 12, 1889.

233 "Mr. Adams" to "partisan": *Athenaeum*, vol. 64, p. 253; vol. 66, p. 669.

Page

234   "That . . . cohesion": Hay to HA, July 12, 1890.

235   "Endymion . . . hair" to "As . . . ask": Unpublished poems of HA.
"one of a very high order" to "me": EC to HA, Sept. 2, 1888.

16. The Paradoxes of Polynesia

244   "perpetual . . . May": Joseph Ellison, *Tusitala of the South Seas*
(New York, 1953), p. 119.

245   "I hang . . . Paradise": Hay to HA, Dec. 12, 1890, Hay Papers,
Brown University.

246   "Sex . . . all": Hay to HA, Dec. 30, 1890, ibid.

247   "would be absolutely . . . apparently": La Farge, *Reminiscences of
the South Seas* (New York, 1912), p. 234.

249   "writing . . . trim": Hay to HA, Dec. 12, 1890, Hay Papers, Brown
University.
"What . . . H A!": Henry James to Hay, Sunday [1891], ibid.

252   "Now . . . science!": Hay to HA, Dec. 30, 1890, ibid.

252f   "We have had . . . bank": Stevenson to Henry James, quoted in HA,
The Letters of Henry Adams, ed. J. C. Levenson, Ernest Samuels,
Charles Vandersee, and Viola H. Winner, III (Cambridge, Mass.,
1982), 380 n.

253   "I wish . . . departure": Stevenson to HA, inserted in copy of *A
Footnote to History*, MHS.

17. Between Worlds

260   "a tornado" to "apiece": Hay to HA, Dec. 12, 1890, Hay Papers,
Brown University.

260f   "pirate band," "blood-hounds": CFA Jr., Diary, July 11, 1888, Nov.
15, 1899, MHS.

264   "Walter . . . *Conversations*": copy at MHS.

265   "Buddha and Brahma": reprinted in HA, *Adams*, Library of America
(New York, 1983), p. 1195.

266f   "pure contemplation" to "ourselves": Arthur Schopenhauer, *Philosophy* (New York, 1928), p. 318.

267   "rest . . . passion": F. Max Müller, *Natural Religion* (London,
1889), p. 106.

268   "a very . . . woman": Gwynn, *Letters and Friendships of Spring
Rice*, I, 115.

271   "And it is I" to "hell": EC to HA, Dec. 6, 1891, MHS.
"everyone . . . deserve it": ibid.

18. Journey into Chaos

276   "kindly . . . presented": inscribed by Theodore Roosevelt, April
1893, MHS.

Page

276 "glaring" to "son": "A Case of Hereditary Bias," *New York Tribune*, Sept. 10, 1890.

277 "just as anxious . . . interesting": Larz Anderson, *Letters and Journals of a Diplomat* (New York, 1940), p. 84.

278 "The Last" to "natives": *Albany Argus*, June 16, 1892.

280 "the best . . . America": John Galsworthy, *Two Forsyte Interludes* (London, 1927), pp. 41–42.

280f "there has been" to "over-insistence of it": Theodore Roosevelt to HA, Dec. 17, 1908, Roosevelt Papers, Library of Congress, box 49.

281 "You are . . . modest": Charles W. Eliot to HA, June 1892; *Letters of Henry Adams (1892–1918)*, ed. Worthington Ford (Boston, 1938), p. 8n.

281f "showing . . . soul": CFA Jr., Diary, June 10, 1892, MHS.

282 "Thwing goes . . . everything": Hay to HA, Aug. 26, 1892, Hay Papers, Brown University.

284 "languid" to "saw": quoted in Dennett, *John Hay*, p. 153.

"Uncle Henry" to "hold forth": Lloyd Griscom, *Diplomatically Speaking* (Boston, 1940), p. 11.

"You would laugh" to "for her": Tati Salmon to HA, Feb. 11, 1892.

285 *Memoirs . . . Tahiti*: HA, *Memoirs of Marau Taaroa* (Washington, D.C., privately printed, 1893), p. 10.

19. Brothers in Prophecy

289 "serious financial trouble": CFA Jr., Diary, July–August 1893.

290 "We owe . . . estate": BA to HA, June 7, July 5, 1903, Houghton Library, Harvard University.

"nearly wild . . . general": CFA Jr., Diary, Aug. 13, Oct. 3, 1893.

291 "Henry . . . revolution": BA, "The Heritage of Henry Adams," p. 94.

292 "poorer" to "tariff": Donald Cameron, *Congressional Record*, Senate, Sept. 25, 1893, p. 1739.

"Hell! . . . circus": CFA Jr. to HA, June 1, 1893.

293 "What . . . Department": *Letters of Grover Cleveland*, ed. Allan Nevins (Boston, 1933), p. 407.

294 "Plutocratic Revolution": BA, *The Plutocratic Revolution*, New England Tariff Reform League pamphlet (1892); reprinted in *Springfield Republican*, Aug. 13, 1892.

295f "Perhaps" to "Germany": BA, "The Gold Standard," *Fortnightly Review*, Aug. 1894.

297 "Mr. Bohn's": Henry George Bohn (1796–1884), popular series of literary classics.

"The Path" to "Hell": BA to HA, June 2, 1895, Houghton Library; Arthur Beringause, *Brooks Adams* (New York, 1955), p. 116.

Page

298 "To have . . . hope": BA to HA, Oct. 13, 1895, Houghton Library.

298f "But for you" to "good genius": BA to HA, July 5, 1899, Houghton Library.

300 "recognizes . . . it": *Holmes-Laski Letters*, ed. M. A. De Wolfe Howe (Cambridge, Mass., 1953), p. 618.

annotations: in HA's copy of Karl Marx, *Capital* (London, 1887), p. 34 and passim, MHS.

302 "the sensitive . . . everywhere": Cecil Spring Rice to HA, June 1897.

303 "The teaching profession" to "silver men": HA, "The Tendency of History," quoted in HA, *Degradation of the Democratic Dogma*, p. 97.

308 "Great Heavens!" to "Hell!": CFA Jr. to HA, Nov. 20, 1895.

published in 1900: CFA Jr., *Charles Francis Adams* (Cambridge, 1900).

20. Behind the Scenes

309 "What . . . me?": Clarence King to HA, quoted in Harry Crosby, "So Deep a Trail" (Ph.D. diss., Stanford University, 1953), p. 373.

"from the arms" to "negro woman": King to HA, ibid.

310 "a pessimist . . . infinite": HA, quoted in *Clarence King Memoirs*, p. 174.

312f "good offices" to "Cuba": Donald Cameron and Henry Cabot Lodge, *Congressional Record*, Senate, Jan. 29, Feb. 10, 20, 28, 1896.

313 "I have . . . behalf": Gonzalo de Quesada to HA, Feb. 21, 1896.

315 "I think . . . here": BA to HA, July 26, 1896, Houghton Library, Harvard University.

316 "His Sufficiency" to "citizens": William Phillips to HA, May 25, 1896.

"a tremendously . . . Department": Phillips to HA, Sept. 8, 1896.

317 "all . . . mischief": CFA Jr. to Lodge, Dec. 24, 1896.

"It is . . . Cameron": *Nation*, Dec. 24, 1896.

"un documento" to "época": Herminio Vilá, *Historia de Cuba*, III (Havana, 1939), 191.

318 "an address" to "bunkers": Hay to Lodge, in Thayer, *Life of John Hay*, II, 159.

319 "revolute": Thomas Slidell Rodgers to HA, July 27, 1897.

321f "he now . . . fire": Hay to EC, March 10, 1898, MHS.

323f "little project" to "lynching": Hay to HA, May 27, 1898; *Letters of John Hay*, III, 126, and Hay Papers, Brown University.

324 "historian" to "order": Edward Burlingame to HA, July 7, 1898.

325 "my health" to "painful": quoted in Thayer, *Life of John Hay*, II, 173.

"Don . . . landscape": Hay to Lodge, ibid., p. 178.

Page

366 "a sorting demon": On "sorting demon" see William Jordy, *Henry Adams, Scientific Historian* (New York, 1952), p. 166n.

367 "You are . . . canonised": Charles W. Stoddard to HA, Dec. 20, 1904.

"You dear . . . ASt.G.": Saint-Gaudens to HA, April 6, 1905.

"I have . . . subject": Henry James to HA, 1905.

"I can't help" to "irony?": William James to HA, April 28, 1910, Houghton Library, Harvard University.

"Mixed" to "die": BA to HA, May 12, 1905, ibid.

23. *The Shield of Protection*

374 "trying to steal Panama": Hay to HA, July 11, 1902.

"I could not spare you": Roosevelt to Hay, quoted in Dennett, *John Hay*, p. 431.

375 "got out" to "enjoyment": Hay to HA, ibid., p. 436.

"full of excitement" to "America": Hay, MS diary, Jan. 16, 1905, Library of Congress.

"committed" to "centre": Henry James to HA, Feb. 1, 1905.

376 "Adams" to "Angelicus": Hay, MS diary, April 3, 1904, Library of Congress.

"Oh, Adams! . . . angel thou": Hay to Saint-Gaudens, April 12, 1905; *Letters of John Hay*, III, 330.

377 "an incredible rate of speed": Hay, MS diary, May 1905, Library of Congress.

"You must" to "little time!": Dennett, *John Hay*, p. 438.

380 "if what . . . any more": Donald Cameron to HA, March 19, 1907.

380f "I have read" to "remarks out?": quoted in Harold Dean Cater, *Henry Adams and His Friends* (Boston, 1947), p. xc.

381 "An overrated . . . book": quoted in Bliss Perry, *Yale Review*, 20 (Winter 1931), 382.

"with great amusement and sympathy": BA to HA, Feb. 24, 1907, Houghton Library, Harvard University.

"Henry . . . scientific theory": BA, "The Heritage of Henry Adams," p. 103.

381f "I note . . . scepticism": Holmes to HA, Dec. 31, 1907.

382 "When I happened" to "rarely": Howe, *Holmes-Pollock Letters*, II, 18.

"Why . . . Bible?": Clara Hay to HA, May 6, 1907.

"immensely" to "seems like that": Homer Saint-Gaudens to HA, May 6, 1907.

"In this . . . purpose": Henry Osborn Taylor's copy, Houghton Library.

"You are . . . sort of book": Nov. 25, 1911; M. A. De Wolfe Howe, ed., *John Jay Chapman and His Letters* (Boston, 1937).

382 "I lost . . . amber": Henry James to HA, Aug. 31, 1909.

"a very stone" to "analysis": Moreton Frewen, *Nineteenth Century,* May 1919, p. 982.

384f "aged colored butler" to "hold of it!": Ferris Greenslet, *Under the Bridge* (Boston, 1943), chap. 15.

385 "The boyhood part" to *"time at all"*: William James to HA, Feb. 9, 1908.

389 "I should like" to "lose my mind": Eliot to Grace Norton, April 10, 1920; quoted in Barbara Solomon, *Ancestors and Immigrants* (Cambridge, Mass., 1956), p. 177.

390 "all that" to "worlds": Voltaire, *Candide,* chap. 3.

24. Schoolboy at Seventy

395 "The Democratic . . . pie": Hay to Howells, Oct. 14, 1880, Hay Papers, Brown University.

396 "What has become . . . living people": Whitelaw Reid to HA, Sept. 7, 1908.

"You see . . . personal": Clara Hay to HA, Feb. 1908.

403 "Your brother has an *eye*": quoted in BA to HA, ca. 1906, Houghton Library, Harvard University.

404 "brilliant coterie" to "floor": Elsie de Wolfe, *After All* (New York, 1935), pp. 31, 107.

"nieces," "aunt": quoted in Elisabeth Marbury, *My Crystal Ball* (New York, 1923), p. 183.

405 "like a fine dry sherry": Bernard Berenson, *Sketch for a Self-Portrait* (New York, 1949), p. 134.

"We had much" to "a Jew": Bernard Berenson, *Rumour and Reflection* (New York, 1952), p. 301.

"There suddenly . . . tinder": ibid., p. 214.

406 "old . . . Faubourg": Edith Wharton, *A Backward Glance* (New York, 1934), p. 265.

"succulent and corrupting meals": Henry James to Walter Berry, Oct. 5, 1907, Bibliothèque Nationale, Paris.

25. Teacher of Teachers

409 "Henry Adams . . . Massachusetts": Register of Wills, Washington, D.C.

410 "a new flaring . . . history": George Adams, "History and Philosophy of History," *American Historical Review,* 14 (1908–09), 229, 231, 236.

"loveable personality" to "criticism of life": Frederick Jackson Turner to Edmond S. Meany, Jan. 11, 1919, Turner Correspondence, Huntington Library, San Marino, Calif.

Page

410 "if some new Darwin . . . historical evolution": HA, "The Tendency of History," in *Annual Report*, American Historical Association (Washington, D.C., 1894), p. 17.

"The Rule of Phase Applied to History": in HA, *Degradation of the Democratic Dogma*.

411 "multiplied" to "our time": Lewis Mumford, *Values of Survival* (New York, 1946), p. 103.

412 "ask in what way" to "gravitation or space": Sir William Crookes, "Sir William Crookes on Physical Research," in *Smithsonian Institution Annual Report* (Washington, D.C., 1899), p. 201.

417 "great generalisation" to "rapidity": Andrew Gray, *Lord Kelvin* (London, 1908), pp. 141–142.

A Letter . . . History: HA, *A Letter to American Teachers of History* (Baltimore, privately printed, 1910).

"Suggestions . . . Evolution": *Fortnightly Review*, April 1909.

418 "Bertie . . . to you": Berenson to HA, Oct. 17, 1909.

421 "I have never . . . impression": BA to HA, March 10, 24, 1910, Houghton Library, Harvard University.

"doubtful physical analogies" to "twenty years ago": Arthur Hadley to HA, March 14, 1910.

"for you" to "bitterness": Albert B. Hart to HA, May 2, 1910.

"After two . . . grasped it": Barrett Wendell to HA, May 1, 1910.

422 "To tell" to "terminus": William James to HA, June 17, 1910.

"an epitome . . . universe": Arthur Lovejoy, "Bergson and Romantic Evolutionism," *Chronicle* (University of California), 15 (Oct. 1913).

"an authentic" to "humor": Charles Bennett, *Yale Review*, n.s., 9 (July 1920), 890–891.

26. The Benevolent Sage

425 "attempted . . . interpreting": *Boston Evening Transcript*, Nov. 1, 1911.

428 "Shocking" to "twenty": Berenson to HA, July 27, 1910.

429 "the running . . . clock": Berenson to HA, July 27, 1911.

430 "like a lone . . . dead": Henry James to HA, Jan. 26, 1911; *Letters of Henry James*, ed. Leon Edel (New York, 1955).

431 "the finest thing": Waldo Leland to Harold D. Cater; quoted in Cater, *Henry Adams and His Friends*, p. xciv.

"one of the greatest . . . America": John Franklin Jameson to HA, Dec. 17, 1912.

435 "I can't" to "help me": CFA Jr. to EC, May 2, 1912.

"a number . . . at all": EC to CFA Jr., June 3, 1912.

436 "a series" to "merry one!": CFA Jr. to Anna Cabot Lodge, July 3, 1912.

Page

436f "Perhaps" to "sound good!": CFA Jr. to Anna Cabot Lodge, July 5, 1912, Lodge Papers, MHS.

437 "to devote . . . to him": CFA Jr. to Anna Cabot Lodge, Aug. 24, 1912, Lodge Papers, MHS.

    "mainly female": CFA Jr. to Anna Cabot Lodge, Aug. 7, 1912.

    "in a manner" to "reach you": Henry James to HA, July 15, 1912.

    "the anxious . . . met": Edith Wharton to HA, June 24, 1912.

438 "is coming" to "the Past": Berenson to HA, July 12, Aug. 15, 1912.

    "like . . . King Lear": Edith Wharton to Berenson, Sept. 18, 1912.

439 "to argue for the publication": Ralph Adams Cram to HA, Nov. 29, 1912.

    "No one wants" to "any details": Ralph Adams Cram, *My Life in Architecture* (Boston, 1936), p. 227.

440 "an admirably balanced . . . monograph": *Boston Evening Transcript*, Jan. 7, 1914.

    "a careful" to "scholars": *A. L. A. Booklist*, 10 (1913–14), 215.

    "considerable insight" to "much else": *Spectator*, April 18, 1914, p. 652.

    "great delight" to "Henry Adams": Henry Osborn Taylor, *American Historical Review*, April 1914, pp. 592–594.

441 "few and insignificant" to "infallible": Frederick B. Luquiens, *Yale Review*, n.s., 3 (July 1914), 830.

27. The Abandoning Universe

443 "me grovel . . . triumph": Henry James to HA, May 26, 1913.

445 "very communicative": Thayer, *Letters*, p. 343.

    "Henry Adams, of Washington": CFA Jr. to HA, Feb. 1914.

446 "I still find . . . make you do": Henry James to HA, March 21, 1914.

447 "The lamps . . . lifetime": quoted in Edward Gray, *Twenty-five Years*, I (London, 1925), 20.

448 "will best express my devotion": Lubbock, *Letters of Henry James*, p. 477.

452 "That arch-egoist" to "greatly": Hazen, *Letters of Thayer*, pp. 242, 251.

    "The rumor . . . Henry Adams": Ferris Greenslet to HA, Dec. 22, 1915.

453 "A letter . . . credit to you": EC to HA, Dec. 17, 1915.

455 "dear . . . gayety": EC to HA, 1916.

    "a peace without victory": quoted in Gwynn, *Letters and Friendships of Spring Rice*, II, 374.

456 "Cabot! . . . now": quoted in Cater, *Henry Adams and His Friends*, p. cv.

    "How I love . . . up to?": Florence J. Harriman, *From Pinafores to Politics* (New York, 1923), p. 217.

Page

457 "We men" to "Kill Wilson!": Beringause, *Brooks Adams*, pp. 373, 383.

458 "a queer comfort . . . roof": Elizabeth Adams to EC, April 1, 1918.
"Brooks . . . Bolsheviki": W. S. Bigelow to Lodge, May 17, 1918, Lodge Papers, MHS.

459 "The Genesis of the Super-German": *Dublin Review*, April 1918, pp. 224–233.

461 "Life" to "the moon": quoted in Cater, *Henry Adams and His Friends*, p. cvi.
"unusually bright . . . a good deal": Elizabeth Adams to Henry O. Taylor, May 5, 1918; in copy of the *Education* at Houghton Library, Harvard University.
"Good night, my dear": Aileen Tone to Mabel La Farge, March 29, 1918; quoted in Cater, *Henry Adams and His Friends*, p. 780.
"chapelle ardente": ibid., p. 779.

461f "(Easter, 1918) . . . her protection": Leslie, *American Wonderland*, pp. 54–55.

Index